Strategic Planning for Public Relations

Fifth Edition

Ronald D. Smith

Routledge
Taylor & Francis Group
NEW YORK AND LONDON

Please visit the companion website for this book at
www.routledge.com/cw/smith

Fifth edition published 2017
by Routledge
711 Third Avenue, New York, NY 10017

and by Routledge
2 Park Square, Milton Park, Abingdon, Oxon, OX14 4RN

Routledge is an imprint of the Taylor & Francis Group, an informa business

Second edition published by Lawrence Erlbaum 2005
Fourth edition published by Routledge 2013

Library of Congress Cataloging in Publication Data
Names: Smith, Ronald D., 1948– author.
Title: Strategic planning for public relations / Ronald D. Smith.
Description: 5th edition. | New York, NY : Routledge, 2017. |
Includes bibliographical references and index.
Identifiers: LCCN 2016035216 (print) | LCCN 2016048687 (ebook) |
ISBN 9781138282056 (hardback) | ISBN 9781138282063 (pbk.) |
ISBN 9781315270876 (ebook)
Subjects: LCSH: Public relations. | Strategic planning.
Classification: LCC HM1221 .S77 2017 (print) |
LCC HM1221 (ebook) | DDC 659.2—dc23
LC record available at https://lccn.loc.gov/2016035216

ISBN: 978-1-138-28205-6 (hbk)
ISBN: 978-1-138-28206-3 (pbk)
ISBN: 978-1-315-27087-6 (ebk)

Typeset in Times New Roman and Helvetica Neue
by Florence Production Ltd, Stoodleigh, Devon, UK

MIX
Paper from
responsible sources
FSC® C014174
www.fsc.org

Printed and bound in the United States of America by Sheridan

Brief Contents

Contents

STEP 6 Developing the Message Strategy   197

APPENDIXES   395

APPENDIX A **Applied Research**   397

APPENDIX B **Applied Research: Focus Group**   415

APPENDIX C **Applied Research: Survey**   422

Preface

Strategic Planning for Public Relations offers college and university students a new way to deepen their understanding of public relations and other kinds of strategic communication.

It is intended for people serious about entering a profession that is rapidly changing—a profession that is shedding a past that often involved merely performing tasks managed by others and taking on a newer, more mature role in the management of organizations based on research-driven strategic planning, ethical principles, and programmatic evaluation.

This book provides an in-depth approach to public relations planning, more comprehensive than can be found anywhere else. It is built on a step-by-step unfolding of the planning process most often used in public relations, with explanations, examples, and exercises that combine to guide students toward a contemporary understanding of the profession. This book is written in a reader-friendly style designed to appeal both to students and practitioners.

The approach used in *Strategic Planning for Public Relations* is rooted in my belief and observation—from more than 27 years of teaching—that students learn best through a threefold pattern of being exposed to an idea, seeing it in use and then applying it themselves. This is the rhythm of this book—its cadence, if you will. This is the design that takes a complex problem-solving and decision-making process and turns it into a series of easy-to-follow steps. These nine steps provide enough flexibility to make the process applicable to all kinds of situations and to organizations with different missions, diverse sizes, varying resources, and differing skill levels among the staff.

New to This Fifth Edition

Textbooks are kept current by regular updating of information, accomplished by adding new material and publishing new editions.

This fifth edition of *Strategic Planning for Public Relations* follows the same format as previous editions. It is studded with real-world examples of new cases and current events in the practice of public relations, along with some classic cases that stand the test of time. In particular, this updating includes many examples involving social media and other developments in digital technology.

It also highlights the results of many new research studies on opinions and practices within the discipline. Additionally, this edition updates overviews of several award-winning public relations campaigns.

This edition also updates and expands a series of appendixes.

- Appendix A, Applied Research provides an overview of research in professional settings, with a comparison to academic research, a discussion of ethical aspects, an explanation of sampling techniques, and information on secondary research and interviewing skills.

- Appendix B, Focus Group deals specifically with ways to plan, implement, and report using this methodology.
- Appendix C, Survey similarly outlines various ways to design, administer, and report surveys, with a particular focus on developing question and response content of questionnaires.
- Appendix D, Content Analysis considers the role of content analysis as well as the mechanics of using this methodology.
- Appendix E, Media Engagement offers both a rationale and practical suggestions for effectively engaging media of all kinds. It builds from a focus on reputation and credibility and offers practical tips for engaging with reporters.
- Appendix F, Crisis Communication builds on the previous appendix with a specific focus on engaging the media in crisis situations. It includes background on types of crises, strategy, and messaging for crisis situations, and organizational preparation for dealing with crises.
- Appendix G, PR 200 offers terms, concepts, how-tos, and cases that all public relations graduates and practitioners should be familiar with.

Note to Students

If you are using this book in a public relations class, it is because your instructor finds it valuable for you.

Thank you for allowing me to share my ideas and insights into a profession that I have found to be both challenging and rewarding. I wish you much success as you proceed toward a career that I hope you, too, will discover to be exhilarating.

I stumbled into public relations somewhat by accident, at least not by my own conscious design. I began my career as a newspaper reporter, and later as an editor, with some side trips into television writing and producing, freelance magazine writing, and newsletter editing. I then made the transition into public relations—at first building on a familiar base of media relations and publicity, and only later navigating into issues management, crisis response, integrated communication, and a host of related areas.

Along the way I incorporated the new technological developments (particularly email, the Internet, and social media) and now wonder how we once managed without these tools.

Frankly, I wish there had been a book like this to guide me toward doing the work of public relations, especially the research and planning parts. So I'm pleased to be able to share with you some of the insights I've picked up along the way.

With this book and the practical exercises that go with it, you are proceeding along the road to professional success. I wish you the best of luck. You should be aware that this book is intended for group development and class activities. While you certainly can use it alone, you will find that it comes more fully alive as a text to guide group projects. Even if you are not a student in a traditional classroom, try to use this book in the context of your own project task force or professional work team.

Note to Public Relations Practitioners

I am proud to note that the Public Relations Society of America has found *Strategic Planning for Public Relations* to be relevant for practitioners. PRSA selected the book for its short list of endorsed readings for candidates of the APR professional accrediting exam.

I've heard from many public relations practitioners who have used this book and are looking forward to this new edition. Some find it useful in their day-to-day work, particularly those who are working in public relations without benefit of an educational background in the discipline. I myself entered the profession with a background in journalism, so I understand the pros and cons of learning public relations on the job. I'm pleased that this book has been helpful to many of my professional colleagues.

The book also has spurred others who have written to me with issues and comments from their vantage as leaders within the field of public relations. It has been particularly rewarding to hear not only from the PRSA and various U.S. chapters, but also from our Canadian counterpart, the Canadian Public Relations Society, as well as public relations groups around the world, including the Azerbaijan Public Relations Association. I also hear regularly from practitioners, students, and teachers around the world, in places as disparate as Hong Kong, India, Japan, Kenya, Nigeria, Romania, Russia, Turkey, the United Kingdom, and other countries.

Note to Instructors

Thank you for choosing this textbook for your students. Thanks especially for the opportunity to share with them some of my thoughts and observations on an exciting profession. I trust that you will find the information contained in this book to be well within the framework of contemporary professional practice and academic principles.

Strategic Planning for Public Relations grew out of my observation that students seem to learn best when they understand concepts, have patterns to follow and adapt, and have the opportunity to work both individually and in groups on tasks that gradually unfold to reveal the bigger picture. This is my intention with this book—to provide a structure, yet to give you much flexibility in leading your students through the planning process.

I also can share with you that your colleagues have found this book useful in introductory courses as well as in courses focusing on campaigns and case studies. Personally, I use the book for an intensive introductory course, supplemented with some online information on history and other foundational elements such as my academic and professional website—ron-smith.com—which you are free to use if you find it helpful. We also use the book in our senior-level campaign course as the basis for students developing their own campaign proposals. Additionally, the book serves as a basis for the campaigns that are developed by our graduate students.

Who Uses This Book?

I am pleased by the international acceptance of this book since it was first published in 2002 and subsequently updated in 2005, 2009, and 2013.

As the author, I am humbled by the confidence that so many educators have placed in this book, and I am quite aware of my responsibility to their students to provide the best teaching resource that I can.

To date, at least 279 colleges and universities in the U.S. and Canada, Europe, Asia, and the Middle East, have adopted this text for public relations classes at both the undergraduate and graduate levels. These courses include principles or foundations of public relations, advanced practice, campaigns, strategy, planning, research, advocacy, public relations administration/management, case studies, corporate communications, integrated communication, and issues/problems in public relations. Nearly half of schools associated with the Accrediting Council on Education in Journalism and Mass Communications use this text.

More than 1,220 academic libraries in North America, Asia, Africa, Australia, Latin America, the Middle East, and both Western and Eastern Europe have acquired it for their collections.

I also am pleased with the acceptance of this book by my professional colleagues. The Public Relations Society of America includes this book on a short list of texts recommended for people preparing for the Universal Accreditation Exam. It has been similarly endorsed by the Canadian Public Relations Society, the Public Relations Council of India, and several other national groups affiliated with the International Public Relations Association.

The book is listed by the professional resource centers of several PRSA chapters and by practitioner groups in the U.S. and around the world from Iran to Sweden. It is a recommended reading by Six Sigma Strategy Training of Sussex, England. It also has been recommended by several bloggers in the U.S. and around the world who specialize in public relations and marketing communication.

Likewise, many of my fellow educators have shown confidence in this book by citing it in their own writing, more than 375 academic citations to date.

Strategic Planning for Public Relations has been cited in several recent books, including *Corporate Blogging and Microblogging* (King, 2015), *International Political Economy of Communication* (Vivares & Martens, 2014), *Cases in Public Relations Management* (Swann, 2014), *The Strategic Context for Political Communication* (Kiousis and Strömbäck, 2014), *Business Essentials for Strategic Communicators* (Ragas & Culp, 2014), *Political Reputation Management* (Schnee, 2014), *The AMA Handbook of Public Relations* (Boynton, 2014), *Digital Disconnect: How Capitalism Is Turning the Internet Against Democracy* (McChesney, 2013), *Farewell to Journalism* (McChesney, 2012), *Relentless Pursuit of Excellence: Lessons from a Transformational Leader* (Sagor & Rickey, 2012), *Handbook of Communication and Corporate Social Responsibility* (Bartlett, May & Bronn, 2011), *Corporate Reputation* (Burke, Cooper & Martin, 2011), *Strategies and Communications for Innovation* (Hulsmann & Pfefferman, 2011), *PR Evaluation* (Siewert, 2011), *Public Relations Writing: Form & Style* (Newsom and Haynes, 2008), *Strategic Response: An Introduction to Non-Profit Communications* (Dimitrov, 2008), *Strategic Sport Communication* (Pedersen, Miloch & Laucella, 2007), *Evaluating Public Relations* (Watson & Noble, 2007), *Function of Media and Function of Public Relations at International Crisis Situations* (Gorpe & Celik, 2007), *The Future of Excellence in Public Relations and Communication Management* (Grunig, Grunig & Toth, 2007), *Managing Consumers' Online Complaints* (Lee, 2006), *Strategic Sport Marketing* (Shilbury, Quick & Westerbeek, 2003).

It also has been referenced in articles published in numerous academic and professional periodicals, including *Public Relations Journal, Romanian Journal of Marketing, Global Media Journal, International Journal of Marketing/Communication/New Media, Journal of Agricultural Education, Journal of Relationship Marketing, Journal of Vacation Marketing, Journal of Public Administration Research and Theory, Communication Theory, Comunicación y Sociedad, International Journal of Communication, Journal of Communication Management, International Journal of Strategic Communication, Strategies and Communications for Innovations, Journal of Hospitality and Leisure Marketing, Journal of Hospitality Marketing and Management, Public Relations Review, Journal of Business Ethics, Review of Journalism and Mass Communication, Baltic Journal of Management, Journal of Professional Communication, PRism Online PR Journal, Journal of Advertising, Engineering Economics, Public Relations Tactics, Journal of Media and Religion, Journal of Health Communication, Journal of Administrative Research, Journal of Health and Human Services Administration, Journal of Public Administration Research, Journal of Asian and African Studies, International Journal of Business, International Journal of Sport Communication, Portuguese Journal of Social Science, Tourism Management, Engineering Economics, Social Science Journal, Public Relations Inquiry, Journal of Agricultural Education, Middle East Journal of Management.*

In all, Google Scholar lists 324 citations for *Strategic Planning for Public Relations.*

Acknowledgments

John Donne was right that no one is an island. Neither does an author write alone, instead reflecting in some way the insight of others in the field who write, teach, critique, and engage in the practice.

Strategic Planning for Public Relations enjoys the input of many people. As the author of this textbook, I'll take personal responsibility for any errors or omissions, but I'm confident these are fewer because of the advice and assistance of many knowledgeable people who helped along the way.

Collectively, my students have been major contributors to this book. It is in the classroom that I have tested and refined the ideas contained herein. My students have prodded me to articulate my ideas and to bolster them with plenty of real-world examples.

My academic colleagues at SUNY Buffalo State (with its flagship communication department in the State University of New York) emphasize practical, applied communication, and I have benefited from ongoing professional conversations with them. My professional colleagues within the Public Relations Society of America consistently have helped me with their insight and constructive criticism.

The publishing team at Routledge/Taylor and Francis is superb. Linda Bathgate and her staff have guided me through the conceptual development of this edition, steering it to its final form.

Authors appreciate the comments and criticism of their peers, and I am particularly grateful to the faculty across the country who have taken time from their busy teaching schedules to offer comments and suggestions. Likewise, I have appreciated the comments and suggestions I have received not only from my PRSA colleagues but also from people associated with the Canadian Public Relations Society and with public relations and strategic communication professionals around the world.

I also appreciate the comments of students who use this book. You are the ultimate experts on whether this is an effective aid to your professional education. Whether I've taught you directly, or only indirectly through this book, I'm grateful for your questions and suggestions.

Personal Dedication

Like the entirety of my life, *Strategic Planning for Public Relations* is dedicated to my family. Though they don't realize it, my three sons have been an inspiration as I worked on this book.

As he progressed through college in Buffalo and eventually earned a doctorate at Osaka University, my son Josh has challenged me to explain public relations every time I suggested that he consider the insights of the discipline on his own multifaceted work as a sociologist and ethnomusicologist, as a concert performer on the shakuhachi (Japanese bamboo flute), an iaido black belt, as a restaurateur and certified sake expert, and as a university professor teaching communication research and intercultural communication.

My son Aaron graduated with a degree in public relations, having had the dubious experience of having me as instructor for two undergraduate courses. After starting his own career in the field of public relations and marketing, Aaron took his communication and strategic planning talents to the Army, where he has proudly served in Qatar, South Korea, Okinawa, Texas, and currently Oklahoma.

My youngest son, Matt, is advancing in his career in horticulture, while pursuing an active vocation in music. His writing talent and artistic sense have served him well in his career in landscape design.

Whether by their presence or Skype-facilitated association with me, my daughters-in-law Satomi, Jen, and Jessica provide me with the love and encouragement any writer needs to be successful. My granddaughters Miana, Mariella and Emalyn and my grandsons Kazutaka and Leif provide excellent reasons to step away from my writing from time to time and dream of the wonders their lives will bring.

My greatest appreciation goes to my wife, Dawn Minier Smith. During the evolution of this book from conception to this new edition, Dawn has been my sounding board. A writing teacher herself, she has lent her ear as I tested ideas, tried out new ways to present lessons, and attempted to make sense of theories, cases, and observations. She reminds me when to use "whom," and we agree to disagree on using the Oxford comma (alas, I acquiesced to use it for this textbook).

Since she doesn't see any domestic value in a wife fawning over her husband, Dawn's constructive criticism has been always trustworthy and thus most valuable. I always take her suggestions seriously. Sometimes I've even had the good sense to follow them.

An Invitation

This book is the result of much dialogue with others, particularly feedback from my students. But reader reaction inevitably is useful. I invite all readers—students, teachers, and practitioners—to share your thoughts with me. Give me comments and suggestions for future editions. Share your success stories and your frustrations with this book. I also invite you to use my website, where I have included an expanding number of pages and links related to public relations and other aspects of strategic communication.

Ron Smith
smithrd@buffalostate.edu
ron-smith.com

Additionally, I invite you to take advantage of the excellent online resources that my publisher has created for instructors and students using this book. You can access this at www. routledge/cw/smith.

About the Author

Top 5 Values: Intellectual honesty. Diversity. Body-mind-spirit balance. Kindness. Creativity.

Top 5 Likes: Sashimi. Ambiguity. Nuns. Italian reds. Liberal politics.

Top 5 Dislikes: Traffic. Crowds. Unexplored certitude. Intolerance masking as virtue. Country music.

Top 5 Aspirations: Challenging/caring/creative professor. Non-pedantic writer. Safe haven for young people in crisis. Faithful colleague. Pragmatic public relations practitioner/consultant.

Top 5 Interesting Facts: Wife of 40 years with incredible tolerance, three sons, five grandchildren. Navy journalist in Vietnam war, with conscientious objector discharge. Zen-leaning Catholic who has meditated with Buddhist monks in Japan. Amateur singer who once sang solo at St. Peter's in Rome. Among ancestors, a Scottish POW banished to England's penal colony of Massachusetts, the last woman in Connecticut hanged as a witch, American Indians, and colonial immigrants from France, Germany, Ireland, and Britain.

Ronald D. Smith APR is Professor Emeritus of public communication at SUNY Buffalo State, the largest college within the State University of New York and the first public institution in New York State accredited by the Accrediting Council on Education in Journalism and Mass Communications.

He has taught public relations planning, writing, research, and related courses to undergraduate and graduate students. For eight years, he served as chair of the 850-student Communication Department at Buffalo State, during which time his department gained ACEJMC accreditation. He served more than two years as associate dean of the School of Arts and Humanities before returning to teaching and working with students in the Communication Department.

As time permits, he also is active as a consultant in public relations and strategic communication, assisting businesses and nonprofit organizations with planning, research, communication management, crisis communication, and media training.

In this book, Smith draws on considerable professional experience. In addition to more than 27 years as an educator, he worked for 10 years as a public relations director and eight years as a newspaper reporter and editor. He also was a Navy journalist aboard the aircraft carrier USS Ranger, twice deployed to Vietnam, after which the Pentagon granted him a discharge as a conscientious objector.

Smith holds a bachelor's degree in English education from Lock Haven (Pa.) University and a master's degree in public relations from Syracuse (N.Y.) University. He has presented numerous workshops and seminars and has published research on public relations and persuasive communication.

He is the author of *Becoming a Public Relations Writer* (5th edition, 2017) and *Public Relations: The Basics* (2014) and coauthor with W. Richard Whitaker and Janet E. Ramsey of *MediaWriting* (4th edition, 2012), all published by Routledge/Taylor and Francis.

Smith has written two chapters—"Objectives" and "Strategic Inaction"—in *The Sage Encyclopedia of Corporate Reputation*, edited by Craig Carroll (Sage, 2016) and the chapter "Campaign Design and Management" in *21st Century Communication: A Reference Handbook*, edited by William F. Eadie (Sage, 2009). He also wrote *Introduction to Language and Communication: A Primer on Human and Media Communication* (United Arab Emirates University, 2004).

Smith is the founding director of the American Indian Policy and Media Initiative at Buffalo State. He is coeditor of *Shoot the Indian: Media, Misperception and Native Truth* (AIPMI, 2007). He has conducted and published research on topics such as the media coverage of the Cherokee citizenship vote and media coverage in New York State on Indian treaty, sovereignty, and taxation issues. He has assisted in strategic planning with the Smithsonian's National Museum of the American Indian and the National Congress of American Indians and has worked with research and strategic planning with several individual tribes. He has presented original research on Native Americans and media at the Association for Education in Journalism and Mass Communications.

Smith is an accredited member of the Public Relations Society of America and has served as president of the PRSA's Buffalo/Niagara chapter and as chair of PRSA's Northeast District. He was named Practitioner of the Year in 1998 and received the chapter's first distinguished service medal in 2010, in addition to numerous other awards and citations. He also has twice been nominated as PRSA Educator of the Year.

In 2015, Smith was named to the editorial board of the *Romanian Journal of Marketing*.

Cases and Examples

Following is an index of actual cases, persons, organizations, and events cited in *Strategic Planning for Public Relations* as examples of various principles, strategies, tactics, and techniques.

Introduction

Why write a book on strategic planning for public relations? For one thing, effective and creative planning is at the heart of all public relations and related activity. And because public relations is crucial to all organizations, as reflected in a comment often attributed to Bill Gates: "If I was down to my last dollar, I'd spend it on public relations."

So what is this thing called "public relations"? Understanding it is a bit like considering the parable from ancient India of the blind men and the elephant. Six men each felt a different part of the elephant. One touched the tusk and proclaimed that it was a spear. Another felt the trunk and thought it was a snake. And so on: the tail a rope, the ear a fan, the knee a tree trunk, the side a wall. They failed to understand the bigger whole.

That's often the problem when people think about public relations. They see only one part of it: special events, speeches, lobbying, media relations, promotions, crisis communication. Because they don't see the big picture, sometimes what people think they know about public relations isn't accurate. Consider the reality behind these common fallacies.

- Public relations is not about hype or exaggeration, much less about lying. Instead, it requires truth as its foundation, along with verifiable performance, accuracy, information in context.
- Public relations isn't secretive. It works best transparently in the light of day, often working with journalists and others to present its messages.
- Public relations doesn't manipulate people. It flourishes in a democracy, helping organizations and clients join the debate of many voices in the marketplace of ideas.
- Public relations isn't about spin or deception. You can put perfume on a skunk, but it's still going to stink. Public relations helps people see the good things about an organization, which is possible only when the organization actually is doing good things. Often public relations drives an organization's decisions to adapt and operate more for the public benefit.
- Public relations isn't only about publicity shoring up sagging newspaper readership. Publicity is only a small part of public relations, and today it often is achieved through social media.

- Public relations isn't the cartoon character with a shovel following the elephants in a circus parade. While it sometimes is asked to clean up a mess, effective public relations helps management avoid the mess in the first place.
- Public relations isn't only a tool of big business. It is used by every kind of organization: schools, hospitals, churches, government, unions, sports, the military, charities, the arts, and every kind of business from large multinationals to local start-ups. Even newspapers and TV stations have their own public relations people.
- Public relations isn't simply a feel-good endeavor. Rather, it is a strategic process relying on research, rooted in goals, implemented through a variety of tactics, and evaluated on its outcomes.

This takes us back to the opening question: Why write a book on strategic planning for public relations? Public relations is changing. No longer is it enough merely to know *how* to do things. Now the effective communicator needs to know *what* to do, *why* to do it, and *how to evaluate* the effectiveness of the chosen approach. The call is now for strategic communicators, and this is the heart of *Strategic Planning for Public Relations*.

Let's look at two categories of public relations practitioners: technicians and **managers**.

COMMUNICATION TECHNICIAN

Public relations professionals used to be called upon mainly for such tasks—always important—as writing news releases, drafting speeches, producing videos, editing newsletters, organizing displays, and so on. These are roles of a **communication technician**, who is a specialist in public relations and marketing communication and typically performs these tasks at the direction of others. Often these tasks are associated with entry-level jobs.

COMMUNICATION MANAGER

Beyond the work of a communication technician, the profession increasingly demands competency in directing research, making decisions, planning projects and campaigns, and solving problems. This is the work of a **communication manager**. Two types of communication managers have complementary roles within organizations. Consider the work of both of these types of communication managers, tactical and strategic.

A **tactical manager** makes day-to-day decisions on many practical and specific issues. Should they post a news release or hold a news conference? Are they better off with a brochure or a web page? Should they develop a mall exhibit, or would it be more effective to create a computer presentation? Do they need another advocacy ad, and if so, for which publication or station, and with what message using which strategy?

A **strategic manager**, on the other hand, is concerned with management, trends, issues, policies, and corporate structure. What problems are likely to face the organization over the next several years and how might they be addressed? What is the crisis readiness of the organization? Should senior personnel be offered an advanced level of media training? What should the policies be for tweeting by employees?

In the workplace, public relations practitioners often find themselves functioning in both the technician and the managerial roles, but the balance is shifting. Today's environment —and more important, tomorrow's—calls for greater skill on the management side of communication.

The manager's job of strategic communication planning calls for four particular skills:

1. Understanding research and planning
2. Knowing how to make strategic choices
3. Making selections from an expanding inventory of tactical choices
4. Completing the process by evaluating program effectiveness

A premise underlying this book is that public relations and marketing communication are becoming more strategic, more scientific—and thus, more managerial. It is this strategic perspective that will differentiate the effective practitioner from the one who simply performs tasks and provides basic services.

Strategic Planning for Public Relations is about making such decisions—not by hunches or instinct, but by solid and informed reasoning that draws on the science of communication as well as its various art forms. This book tries to make the complex process of strategic communication easily understandable by taking you through the process step by step. You'll find nine steps, each presented with the following three basic elements:

1. Explanations that are clear and understandable, drawn from contemporary theory
2. Examples that help you see the concept in action, drawn from both nonprofit and for-profit organizations
3. Hands-on exercises in both short form and expanded versions that help you apply the process in your own situation

Note also that key terms, printed in boldface, are collected into a glossary at the end of the book.

Experience shows that this hybrid format—part textbook, part workbook—can make it easier to learn about the planning process because it helps you think, see, and do. *Strategic Planning for Public Relations* gives you a solid, proven process that works. It doesn't offer any secrets of the trade, because there really are no secrets. Effective managers in public relations and marketing communication use these kinds of processes every day, and that's not much of a secret. What this book does is make field-tested procedures available to you in an understandable way so you can apply them yourself.

Organizational Process

Through contemporary eyes, public relations is seen as a central and essential aspect of organizational management.

In their influential book *Managing Public Relations,* James Grunig and Todd Hunt (1984) identified four now-famous evolutionary models of public relations. The first two—exemplified by press agentry and public information—rely on one-way dissemination of information. The latter models—an asymmetrical approach associated with persuasion and advocacy, and a symmetrical model dealing with dialogue and relationship-building—feature two-way communication for both dissemination and research/feedback.

A close look at this evolution shows a practice becoming a profession. It reveals a useful skill becoming an essential element of organizational management and the process of nurturing relationships between organizations and their publics.

The Public Relations Society of America (PRSA—prsa.org) has long used an official statement positioning public relations as a process within organizations that encompasses activities such as opinion tracking and analysis, relationship building, research, planning, objective setting and evaluation. For three decades, PRSA called this role a "management function," though a newer definition finds that term misleading because it connotes top-down control using one-way communication. Instead, PRSA's new definition focuses on "process," which implies a more open two-way model.

In *Excellence in Public Relations and Communication Management*, Grunig (1992) used the earlier definition by Grunig and Hunt (1984), defining public relations as "management of communication between an organization and its publics" (p. 6). Meanwhile, for the last 30 years or so, textbooks have identified public relations as a management function. For example, Scott Cutlip, Allen Center and Glen Broom's *Effective Public Relations* (2012) define public relations as "the management function that identifies, establishes and maintains mutually beneficial relationships between an organization and the various publics on whom its success or failure depends." All serious textbooks in the field have followed suit with an emphasis on public relations as an element of organizational management.

At the same time, scholarly research has helped pave the way for seating public relations at the management table. Stephen Bruning is a leading researcher in the role of a relationship-management approach to public relations. He has identified relationship management as "a paradigm for public relations scholarship and practice" (Ledingham and Bruning, 2000, p. xiii). The model is rooted in the relationship between organizational and public interests, and it builds in both theory and practice on a foundation that includes research and evaluation.

Benefits of Public Relations

We've seen too many corruptions of ethical public relations: anonymously funded politicians who lie about their opponents; corporations that misrepresent environmental, consumer safety, and financial information; schools, churches, hospitals, and youth organizations that hide information about abuse.

All of these are problems for society. The fault is not in public relations but rather in its corruption by organizational voices more interested in privacy than transparency and focusing on expediency instead of ethical service.

The tools of public relations can be used for good by organizations and advocates for social justice, education, minority rights, environmental safety, and so on. Government, nonprofit organizations, and businesses all can use public relations for the betterment of society. Here are some ways that organizations as well as society at large benefit from public relations.

- *Financial Health*. Companies and nonprofit organizations can shore up their financial base with programs that increase productivity, retain customers, enhance support by donors and stockholders, and influence legislation. They can generate new customers and attract interest in products and services.
- *Safety*. Public relations helps save lives by advocating behaviors related to seat-belt use, organ donations, child abduction, and many other causes.
- *Health*. Public relations can encourage healthy lifestyles through education and advocacy programs dealing with nutrition, obesity, fitness, and detection and prevention of diseases.

- *Recreation.* Sports and entertainment public relations help people enjoy their leisure time. Recreational facilities, travel destinations, athletic teams, and entertainment venues use public relations to engage fans, publicize events, and promote offerings.
- *Civic Awareness.* Government agencies and lawmakers promote programs and services to their constituents. Military units use public relations to recruit, foster public support, and report their progress to members, families, and legislators.
- *Community Service.* Nonprofit organizations such as charities, schools, and religious groups share their expertise and promote their services. Medical organizations promote health literacy and help people make healthful choices.
- *Reputation.* Public relations helps organizations minimize opposition and gain support by generating favorable publicity, encouraging alliances with like-minded organizations, and developing programs that serve the public good.
- *Survival.* Public relations helps organizations reverse negative opinions, weather crises, and survive lawsuits.

DEFINITION OF PUBLIC RELATIONS

The formal practice of what is now called "public relations" dates to the early twentieth century. Since then, the definition of public relations has been evolving as the practice of public relations has changed. The early definitions emphasized press agentry and publicity, while newer definitions focus on engagement and relationship building.

Through an international and grassroots project culminating in a vote by members, the Public Relations Society of America developed this definition:

> *Public relations is a strategic communication process that builds mutually beneficial relationships between organizations and their publics.*

PRSA explains that this definition emphasizes the key characteristics of public relations as a process of communication, strategic in nature, with a focus on mutually beneficial relationships. Meanwhile, public relations organizations around the world have articulated similar definitions of the practice. Here are a few such organizational statements.

> Canadian Public Relations Society: *Public relations is the strategic management of relationships between an organization and its diverse publics, through the use of communication, to achieve mutual understanding, realize organizational goals and serve the public interest.*
>
> Public Relations Institute of Australia: *Public relations is the deliberate, planned and sustained effort to establish and maintain mutual understanding between an organisation (or individual) and its (or their) publics. It's the key to effective communication in all sectors of business, government, academic and not-for-profit.*
>
> Public Relations Institute of South Africa: *Public relations is the management, through communication, of perceptions and strategic relationships between an organization and its internal and external stakeholders.*

Chartered Institute of Public Relations, United Kingdom: *Public relations is the discipline that looks after reputation, with the aim of earning understanding and support and influencing opinion and behaviour. It is the planned and sustained effort to establish and maintain goodwill and understanding between an organization and its publics.*

Public Relations Institute of Ireland: *The dissemination of purposefully planned and executed messages to selected media and publics to enable an organisation (or person) to establish and build relationships founded on trust, and to enhance and safeguard its reputation.*

Middle East Public Relations Association: *Public relations practice is the planned and sustained effort to establish and maintain goodwill and mutual understanding between an organization and its publics.*

International Public Relations Association: *Public relations is defined as the planned and sustained effort to establish and maintain goodwill and mutual understanding between an organisation and its public, such development being for the benefit of the practice of public relations in commerce, industry, central and local government, nationalised undertakings, professional, trade and voluntary organisations and all practitioners and others concerned in or with public relations.*

World Assembly of Public Relations Associations: *Public relations is the art and social science of analysing trends, predicting their consequences, counseling organizations' leaders, and implementing planning programmes of action which will serve both the organization and the public interest.*

Strategic Communication

Ask executives in business and nonprofit organizations what kind of employee they value, and they'll probably tell you it's someone who can effectively and creatively solve problems and make the most of opportunities.

An effective practitioner understands a problem and manages it to its successful conclusion. How do we manage problems? Sometimes by making them go away. Sometimes just by helping them run their course with the least harm to the organization.

Public relations practitioners face all kinds of problems: low visibility, lack of public understanding, opposition from critics, and insufficient support from funding sources. Marketing communicators face similar problems: unfamiliarity of companies or products, apathy among consumers, and product recalls and other liabilities. Both may deal with indifference among workers and misunderstanding by regulators. Practitioners also deal with opportunities, such as promoting new products and services or enhancing already effective programs. In most organizations, it is this positive communication that accounts for most of the time practitioners spend on the job.

Meanwhile, forward-looking practitioners try to transform obstacles into opportunities for their organizations and clients.

Such planned communication campaigns embody the discipline of **strategic communication**. Specifically, this is the intentional communication undertaken by a business or nonprofit organization, sometimes by a less-structured group. It has a purpose and a plan, in which alternatives are considered and decisions are justified. Invariably, strategic communication is based on research and is subject to eventual evaluation. It operates within a particular environment, which involves both the organization and groups of people who affect it in some way.

Strategic communication is either informational or persuasive. Its common purpose is to build understanding and support for ideas and causes, services, and products.

Where do we find examples of strategic communication? They're all around us. Public relations is the most common embodiment of strategic communication, so much so that this book uses the two terms interchangeably. Actually, however, strategic communication is the concept and public relations is its primary example. In earlier days, much public relations activity was haphazard and reactive. But the more contemporary approach to public relations is strategic, and most practitioners see themselves as strategic communicators.

However, not all strategic communicators practice public relations in a narrow sense. Marketing communication also embodies the concept of strategic communication. Still other examples are public health and social marketing campaigns, diplomacy and international relations, constituent relations, political campaigns, ecumenical or interreligious affairs, and many types of lobbying and negotiation.

International relations deals with relationships among governments, and diplomacy involves the management of these relationships. Some analysts would note a difference between diplomacy (which is discrete, formal, and official) and public diplomacy (which

OLD, YET EVER NEW

The ancient and enduring wisdom that nothing is new under the sun applies even to contemporary communication.

Building credibility, maintaining trust, repairing misunderstandings, and promoting ideas are part of the natural human impulse. Today's public relations practitioner deals with the same kind of problems that faced our predecessors last year, last decade, last century, last millennium.

Nothing is new but the timing, the tools, and perhaps our developing insight into the problem-solving process.

The roots of public relations trace back nearly 40 centuries to ancient Mesopotamia and later to the classical Egyptian, Greek, and Roman emphasis on rhetoric and aspects of persuasive communication. Governments in Europe, Africa, and Asia throughout recorded history have practiced rudiments of public relations.

It developed through the Middle Ages and the Renaissance, often employed for religious purposes—Christian, Jewish, Islamic, and Buddhist. Public relations played a major role in the European age of discovery and exploration and in the French, American, Russian, and Communist revolutions. It has been used as an instrument of both war and peacemaking.

Looking back, it is evident that public relations is a natural, essential, and enduring element of human social interaction.

For a more detailed overview of the role of public relations throughout history, you are invited to the author's website: ron-smith.com in the "About PR" section.

Introduction

involves direct and open communication among governments and foreign publics). The latter is more akin to the practice of public relations.

Moreover, public relations itself is sometimes known by alternative names, often linked to subsidiary areas such as media relations or employee communication. Nevertheless, a research-based strategic planning process is necessary for effective management of all the various aspects of public relations regardless of their names, including community relations, special events planning and promotion, membership development, political campaigns, nonprofit events, and fundraising and development (Austin and Pinkleton, 2006). To that list we can add other elements of strategic public relations: issues management, crisis communication, risk management, public information, public affairs, consumer and customer relations, lobbying, investor relations, and so on. Additionally, there are some new players on the field: litigation public relations, risk communication, and reputation management.

Regardless of the label, we look to public relations for leadership and insight in the practice of strategic communication, because most of the related fields and specialties have adopted the set of skills and approaches that public relations has developed over the last 75 years or so (Botan, 1997; Botan and Soto, 1998). Meanwhile, public relations is beginning to more consciously borrow some of the techniques and approaches developed by other fields, particularly marketing and its primary communication tool, advertising.

At the same time, the emerging field of social media is offering new tools that can be used to support the public relations missions of all kinds of organizations.

Integrated Communication

Public relations and marketing are distinct yet overlapping fields. Each has its own focus and its own particular tools, and each discipline fulfills different purposes within an organization. Yet more and more, it is becoming evident that the coordination of public relations and marketing communication can increase an organization's efficiency and effectiveness.

Let's look first at the common distinctions between public relations and marketing communication and then at how they complement each other.

- **Public relations** is a management function that classically focuses on long-term patterns of interaction between an organization and all of its various publics, both supportive and nonsupportive. In contemporary understanding and application, public relations seeks to enhance these relationships, thus generating mutual understanding, goodwill, and support.
- **Marketing communication** also is a management function. Whereas public relations generally takes a long-range approach, marketing communication focuses more immediately on products and services that respond to the wants and needs of consumers. It seeks to foster an economic exchange between an organization and its consumers. Additionally, since marketing relies heavily on advertising, it is significantly more expensive than public relations.

Both public relations and marketing communication deserve a seat at the management table. Both disciplines identify wants, interests, needs, and expectations of key groups of people, and both structure ways to interact and communicate with them.

Both of these disciplines rely on research, and they are rooted in the organization's mission and directed toward its bottom line. Finally, public relations and marketing communication share a concern about both the short-term and long-term interests of the organization.

The lines between marketing and public relations have never been neat and clean. Laypersons and the media use the terms more or less interchangeably, and distinctions have been built more on stereotypes than on a reality.

Consider, for example, the stale notions that advertising is solely a marketing tool or that public relations is only about publicity. In truth, public relations traditionally has engaged in public service advertising, and it is a public relations perspective that drives image, branding, advocacy, and political advertising. Marketing, meanwhile, has used media relations, publicity and special events while launching new or modified products, and many marketing concepts and techniques have proven useful to public relations practitioners in nonprofit organizations attempting to recruit volunteers or participants, lobby regulators, and raise funds.

Integrated communication is the name for this blending of communication functions within an organization designed to make all aspects of communication work together toward common goals, increasing impact at minimal cost.

Some organizations combine the concepts and the tools of public relations and marketing communication, though not always smoothly.

Purists argue against diluting the disciplines, often fearing that integration will demote public relations to just another piece of the marketing mix or subsume public relations under the advertising tent. Others accept integration in principle but dread lopsided implementation, such as the "full-service" advertising agency that claims to offer integrated communication while allocating most of the client's budget to advertising.

In its 2011 State of the Society presentation, PRSA pointed to increased credibility for public relations, including a finding that 9 in 10 business leaders think executives need more training in reputation management and strategic communication (PRSA, 2011a). PRSA's Business Leaders Survey found that 97 percent of business leaders think CEOs should understand reputation management and 98 percent believe that senior managers should have a working knowledge of building and protecting a company's credibility (PRSA, 2011b).

The State of the PR Profession Opinion Survey by the PRSA and Bacon's Information (PRSA, 2006) reported that top organizational managers and CEOs overwhelmingly believe that public relations enhances an organization's reputation (4.51 on a 5-point scale) and only slightly less that it furthers financial success and sales (3.94) and market share (3.90).

Guaranteed to make public relations practitioners take notice are articles such as the one about the "Future of Public Relations" study by Countrywide Porter Novelli—one of the United Kingdom's top five public relations agencies. It reported that public relations is "no longer a peripheral activity when it comes to marketing communication" but rather "an integral part of the marketing ethos" and "one of the most important aspects of the marketing mix" (Gray, 1998). Such language can incite turf battles by portraying public relations as merely an element of marketing, yet this same study reported some positive trends. Among marketing and corporate affairs directors, 92 percent said public relations is integral to business objectives, and 58 percent said public relations is of equal importance with advertising.

Whereas corporate and nonprofit practitioners have been comfortable about integrating various aspects of strategic communication, conflicting advice sometimes has come from the academic community.

When the Association for Education in Journalism and Mass Communication suggested integrating public relations and advertising into a shared curriculum to reflect new practices in the field, the PRSA Educational Affairs Committee reacted quickly to oppose such a blending. Yet in the past dozen or so years, many educators have taken a second look at the benefits of integration, as practitioners seem to be embracing the opportunities that such blending can bring.

Controversy exists even on naming rights. Some people want to call the blending "integrated marketing communication." Others dub it "integrated communication," "marketing public relations" or "total communication." Some bulky new terms being kicked around are "marketing-based public relations" and "integrated communications (advertising and public relations)."

In this textbook, we'll stick with the terms "integrated communication" and "strategic communication" to designate the comprehensive environment in which public relations practitioners and educators find themselves.

Whatever the label, the key is to respect the complementary roles of marketing and public relations while maximizing the potential of cooperation and coordination. Leaders in the area of integrated communication include CEOs who direct their marketing and public relations teams to collaborate in new-product campaigns, and university presidents who enjoin their media relations people to be attentive to recruiting and fundraising needs.

Their ranks also involve professors and other educators who blend public relations and marketing/advertising within a single academic program. The survey *Where Shall I Go to Study Advertising and Public Relations?* (Ross and Richards, 2008) identifies 128 freestanding public relations programs, 92 advertising programs and 45 combined advertising/public relations programs.

Communication integration seems to be happening globally. The concept is gaining momentum not only in the U.S. but also in the United Kingdom, New Zealand, Australia, and India.

In North America, the integrated model has been adopted by corporations such as Xerox, Motorola, HP (formerly Hewlett-Packard), and Federal Express, among many others. Such companies use integrated communication on three levels: externally with a focus on customers; internally for vertical communication between senior management and front-line workers; and internally with horizontal communication across departments and other boundaries. Red Bull, Coca-Cola, American Express, and Snickers also have been cited as companies that do integrated communication well.

Some folks say the concept of integrated communication is wrapped in the history of public relations itself. After all, public relations founding father Edward Bernays engineered the debutante march in New York City's Easter parade in 1929 to make smoking fashionable among women, enabling Lucky Strike to sell more cigarettes. Contemporary medical and ethical implications aside, it was a brilliant and cost-free strategy.

Thomas L. Harris is a leading proponent of integrated communication, which he calls an outside-in process that begins with understanding consumer publics, particularly their wants, interests, needs, and lifestyles. Harris (2000) points out that public relations is particularly effective in building brand equity, which is based on the organization's reputation. The practical benefit of reputation was seen in the 1992 Los Angeles riots, when the 30 McDonald's restaurants in the riot area were untouched while more than 2,000 other buildings were destroyed. Harris argues that is because McDonald's had long been involved and visible in the community.

A recent parallel was seen in 2015, when black-owned businesses in Baltimore generally escaped the wrath of rioters protesting the death of a black man while in police custody.

Each of the four models that Grunig and Hunt observed in the evolution of public relations—press agentry, public information, persuasion/advocacy, and dialogue/relationship-building—is evident today, often used by the same organization. While the latter two models that build from two-way communication generally find more favor among theorists, none of the approaches is necessarily "the best." Each model has its purpose, and each can be effective in achieving particular organizational objectives.

An interesting tug-of-war exists between the persuasion and relationship models. In subsequent research, Grunig (1992) himself noted that many organizations still primarily practice the persuasion model. With only anecdotal evidence, it seems safe to suggest that

---

CASE IN POINT *Kasky v. Nike*

The integrated link between public relations and marketing is a fact of life, often assumed by people and forces outside the profession more readily than it may be recognized from within.

Outsiders often link public relations and marketing, or publicity and advertising. Laypersons may ask, for example, how much it costs to get a news release published, or they may talk about sending an ad to a newspaper when they actually mean a news release.

Here's an example that is more ominous, because some external entities are forcing an unwanted link between public relations and marketing. This was the problem in play in the legal case of *Kasky v. Nike*. Consumer activist Marc Kasky sued Nike under false advertising provisions over its public defense against charges of using child sweatshop labor.

A local court sided with Nike, but a chill was caused when the California Supreme Court upheld Kasky's claim that Nike had engaged in **commercial speech**, a legal term denoting advertising messages. But Nike had done no advertising. Rather, it had defended itself against the charges by communicating through traditional public relations venues: news releases, its website, speeches, and letters to the editor.

The court based its ruling on the premise that a commercial speaker (the Nike corporation) was communicating with a commercial audience (customers) and therefore any such communication was commercial speech. Never mind that previous rulings by the federal Supreme Court had anchored the concept of commercial speech to an advertising format, explicit reference to a product, and economic motivation (*Bolger v. Youngs Drug Products Corp.*, 1983), and specifically "expression related solely to the economic interests of the speaker and its audience" (*Central Hudson Gas & Electric Co. v. Public Service Commission*, 1980).

Kasky v. Nike posed a legal question that remains unanswered. An out-of-court settlement in 2003 ended the five-year legal battle, but it didn't settle the legal question of where public relations ends and marketing begins.

most of today's public relations agencies are hired to engage in persuasion on behalf of their clients, who believe their problems can be solved if only they can gain the support of their publics.

Persuasion isn't necessarily bad. The same principles and techniques that persuade people to buy this CD or that perfume can be deployed on behalf of responsible sexual behavior, nutritional literacy, volunteerism, or other social virtues. Public relations students are exposed to this persuasion-based model through case studies and campaigns courses, through practicums and senior seminars, and especially through professional internships.

Perhaps we need to envision public relations anew, seeing it as serving the persuasive needs of client organizations as well as fostering more productive and beneficial relationships between organizations and their various publics. Public relations practitioners should be prepared to help organizations engage their publics in both word and deed.

This is the vision that guides *Strategic Planning for Public Relations*. The planning process this book presents can be used for persuasion or dialogue, because each is a strategic activity and each helps practitioners influence behavior and generate consensus. The planning process also can help organizations both overcome obstacles and capitalize on opportunities. Additionally, the process works equally well for businesses and nonprofits, whether they be large or local or international, grassroots or well organized, richly endowed or impoverished.

Advertising

From the perspective of integrated communication, advertising can be seen as a tool for both public relations and marketing. Broadly defined, **advertising** is persuasive communication through purchased media to promote a product, service, or idea on behalf of an identified organization or sponsor. As organizations set out to create such a cooperative environment, the political task can be dicey, but the potential rewards are huge. Often it is enlightened organizational leaders who see the big picture, recognizing the value of a coordinated and strategic approach to communication.

Some of the most successful corporations integrate their communication, blending the traditional disciplines of public relations, publicity, and advertising to creatively present a clear and consistent message to their various publics. Here are some examples in which advertising came after the buzz created by public relations.

- Walmart became the world's largest retailer with little initial advertising.
- Starbucks spent less than $10 million in advertising during its first 10 years.
- The Harry Potter book series soared to previously unheard of sales without any appreciable advertising, making British author J. K. Rowling literally richer than the queen of England.
- Using only media relations, special events, and social media—but no advertising—Hyundai launched its zero-emissions hydrogen fuel-cell automobile that sold out before it hit dealer showrooms. Advertising came later, much of it focused on social media.
- When McDonald's introduced its McLean sandwich, it used publicity and other public relations tactics to create awareness through the media, followed by advertising messages to reinforce the publicity and promotion.

OWNED, EARNED, AND PAID MEDIA

In public relations and marketing communications, we often categorize three types of media: owned, earned, and paid.

Owned Media

Those communication venues that are controlled by an organization are called **owned media**. These include brochures, newsletters, websites, and online newsrooms, as well as blogs, email, and social media produced by an organization. This category also includes promotional elements such as logos on company vehicles and employee uniforms. Company-owned television studios and other audio/video equipment also fits into this category.

> Advantage of owned media: Allows organization to skirt media gatekeepers.

> Disadvantages: Initial and continuing costs can be high.

Earned Media

Messages presented through communication channels that involve journalists fit into the category of **earned media**. The term comes from the idea that news coverage—and through it, positive public opinion—must be earned. We earn this through solid and accessible information. Because earned media cannot be owned or purchased, it's sometimes called **free media**.

Practitioners earn publicity by providing reporters, bloggers, columnists, and other journalists with newsworthy information or access to information sources. Tactically, earned media is gained through news releases and interviews, citations in reviews and ratings, references by columnists and online commentators, and by word-of-mouth mention by various publics.

Earned media is considered the best type of media. A 2013 Nielsen study found that consumers trust earned media more than other forms of media. The study reported a 90 percent trust level for word-of-mouth recommendations from friends, 70 percent from online consumer opinion postings, and 69 percent from newspaper articles, with lower trust levels for various kinds of advertising.

> Advantages of earned media: Higher credibility, low-to-no cost.

> Disavantage: Determined not by organization but by media gatekeepers.

Paid Media

The most expensive type of media is **paid media**, because it is purchased by the organization. This category includes print and broadcast advertising, banner and display advertising, and advertising in social media. Also in this category are direct mail and search engine optimization.

> Advantage of paid media: Allows organization to present messages without the approval of media gatekeepers.

> Disadvantages: High cost, lower credibility.

- It was publicity that enabled Goodyear to sell 150,000 new Aquatred tires before the first advertisements ran.
- Pfizer used publicity alone to sell $250 million worth of Viagra and gain a 90 percent market share before any consumer advertising began.
- In several cities, when Krispy Kreme Doughnuts announced plans to open a store in a new area, the publicity created such a huge expectation among prospective customers that extra police had to be hired for opening day to handle the traffic jams.

The integrated approach also has been used by nonprofit organizations such as the American Cancer Society in its campaign for sun block, and has been adopted by more loosely organized social campaigns dealing with bicycle safety, teen smoking, animal rights, birth control, utility deregulation, and AIDS research. One study suggested that nonprofit organizations are particularly open to the coordinated use of public relations and marketing communication techniques (Nemec, 1999).

As a practical matter, an integrated approach to strategic communication often begins with publicity, followed by advertising. Al Ries and Laura Ries note this in *The Fall of Advertising and the Rise of PR*:

> The purpose of advertising is not to build a brand, but to defend a brand once the brand has been built by other means, primarily public relations or third-party endorsements . . . Advertising cannot start a fire. It can only fan a fire after it has been started.
>
> (2004, p. xx)

Ries and Ries also note some of the differences between public relations (or publicity) and advertising: advertising uses a "big bang," while public relations uses a slow buildup. Advertising is visual; public relations is verbal. Advertising reaches a mass audience; public relations reaches a targeted audience. Advertising favors new lines and extensions; public relations favors new brands. Advertising likes old names; public relations likes new names.

The father–daughter writers also present both an opinion (public relations is more creative than advertising) and a fact (public relations is more credible).

Public Relations in the Public Interest

Public relations is known as an ally of marketing and an organizational function focused on the corporate bottom line. For some organizations, the bottom line is about more than selling products, raising money, winning votes, increasing membership, or building a customer base.

Sometimes public relations is about things that matter in more personal and societal ways, such as finding an abducted child or freeing a political prisoner. There is a long history of public relations involvement (often in a leadership role) in reform movements: suffrage for the right of women to vote, safety standards for food, immigration reform, gay rights, education reform, gun control, education for girls, animal rights, humane treatment of the mentally ill, prisoner rights, elimination of child labor, racial reconciliation, and the issues of pro-peace/anti-war and pro-choice/anti-abortion, as well as awareness campaigns focusing on smoking, drugs, alcohol, pornography, gambling, and other social vices.

Here are several cases that had just those results, from the archives of Silver Anvil awards of the Public Relations Society of America (prsa.org/awards/silveranvil/search).

HUMAN TRAFFICKING

It is estimated that 17,000 people are brought into the United States each year against their will. Some are kidnapped, some tricked or coerced, others beaten or blackmailed. All end up in prostitution or other slave-like working conditions.

When the federal Health and Human Services agency created "Restore and Rescue" to minimize this, the Ketchum public relations agency conducted research into the program. It learned that programs directed toward victims didn't work because they had little access to the outside world.

So strategic planners built a coalition of many groups, including law enforcement, social workers, religious personnel, medical staff, women's organizations, and labor groups. They launched an information website, set up a multi-language hotline, and distributed 625,000 pieces of print materials.

After the first year, the pilot project was credited with identifying more than 1,000 victims and referring them to social workers. It created more than 70 million media impressions, attracting 60,000 visitors to its trafficking website. Based on this initial success, the program has been expanded in cities across the country.

PANDA EXPRESS

The U.S. and China have an ongoing program to save endangered species, which both governments want to continue. When it was time for American zoos to return two giant pandas to China, they turned to FedEx to deliver the "packages" and to generate public support for the international conservation program.

It was a logical choice because FedEx had moved penguins from the New Orleans zoo to safekeeping after Hurricane Katrina. FedEx had learned that such projects generate much public interest. When they returned the penguins to New Orleans, it was amid fanfare that included a parade led by an emperor penguin.

FedEx wanted the panda return to be celebratory. It held news conferences in Atlanta and Washington, where the pandas had been housed. Farewell events included police escorts from the zoos to the airports for departure celebrations.

FedEx produced a video about the transportation project it dubbed the "Panda Express." It promoted the events on its website, blog, online newsroom, Twitter feeds, and employee intranet.

GUIDE DOGS

When the U.K.-based Guide Dogs for the Blind needed a low-cost, high-impact introduction to a major fundraising project, it turned to photographer Adrian Houston, who took photos of 21 British celebrities with their own dogs. The group included athletes, actors, government officials, and members of the nobility.

The celebrities posed with their pooches, gave media interviews, participated in talk shows and used social media. Their photos were used to gain publicity for the Guide Dog organization and then were auctioned to raise money for the charity.

The goal was to attract 50 donors to a fundraising event, but more than 300 contributors and celebrities attended.

FINDING BRITTANY

In 2010, Trina Smith was murdered in Virginia, and her 12-year-old daughter Brittany was abducted. Police suspected the mother's boyfriend and issued an Amber Alert. The police public information office managed a communication plan toward finding Brittany.

Strategies included developing strong internal communication with law-enforcement agencies, engaging news media to make this a national story, ensuring that information was available daily to the media, and keeping the child's family informed.

Tactics included daily news conferences, a special website with up-to-date information, distribution of fliers and photos, news releases, YouTube videos, and Twitter and Facebook social media sites. Four days after her abduction, Brittany was found safe in San Francisco. From a report on CNN, a woman recognized Brittany begging for food outside a supermarket. She alerted police, who rescued Brittany and arrested her kidnapper.

A month later, Facebook announced plans for 51 dedicated Amber Alert pages (one for each state, and another for the National Center for Missing and Exploited Children), putting local Amber Alerts on the computers and smart phones of an estimated 57 percent of the adult U.S. population.

FREE SILVA

In 2008, Silva Harotonian was arrested in Iran for plotting a "soft revolution." An Iranian-American of Armenian ancestry, Silva worked for the International Research and Exchanges Board, a nonprofit organization providing education and training for grassroots social workers. Her work focused on public health professionals working with mother-and-child projects.

Seven months after her arrest, Silva was convicted of attempting to overthrow the government of Iran. She was sentenced to three years in prison. Within a week of sentencing, her employer hired Edelman public relations firm to help secure her release.

Edelman prepared an international public-awareness campaign that required a delicate balance. Outside influence would be needed, but Iran would take a hard line if too much pressure became evident. Understanding Iran's suspicion toward Americans in particular, the campaign sought to engage people who might influence Iran's president and top religious leader. It tried to maintain a respectful tone toward Iran as it reached out to human rights organizations and to Armenians in the U.S. and Europe. Ironically for a public relations agency, much of Edelman's strategy generated behind-the-scenes private activity rather than public communication.

The campaign developed an advocacy website to leverage international support, provided interviews with Silva's family, targeted international media, and arranged for French and Armenian governments to appeal for Silva's release. After 11 months of detention, Silva was released from prison. A condition of her release was elimination of the advocacy website, so successful had it been.

Strategic Public Relations

Most textbooks dealing with public relations encourage a four-phase process. Some use the RACE acronym (research, action, communication, evaluation) articulated by John Marston (1963) in *The Nature of Public Relations*. In *Public Relations Cases*, Jerry Hendrix and Darrell Hayes (2012) use the acronym ROPE (research, objectives, programming, evaluation). In *Public Relations Campaign Strategies*, Robert Kendall (1997) offers the RAISE formula (research, adaptation, implementation strategy, evaluation). Kathleen Kelly (2001) posits ROPES (research, objectives, program, evaluation, stewardship). Sheila Crifasi (2000) has come up with ROSIE (research, objectives, strategy, implementation, evaluation).

ATTRIBUTES OF STRATEGIC COMMUNICATION

An effective communication program includes the following attributes, which apply equally to corporations and nonprofit organizations, as well as to large and small endeavors.

Spurred both by regulation and customer demand, organizations must be *accountable* to their publics. Most publics increasingly expect *quality performance* and *open communication.* Long-term success comes to organizations with high performance, delivering quality products and services. All organizations operate in a *competitive environment.* Publics besought by rivals will remain loyal to organizations that earn loyalty consistently and continuously.

Effective communication involves *cooperation* and *integration* between public relations and marketing. Just as each knight was an equal participant at the round table in King Arthur's court, so too should both disciplines have effective and equal voices.

The consumer philosophy has taken hold of all aspects of society, and organizations must answer with a *customer-driven response*, focusing on benefits for their publics. People support organizations that serve their interests and needs. Organizations, in turn, must be open to *adaptation* to new environments and changing needs of their publics and markets.

Organizational communication adheres to high *ethical standards* of honesty, accuracy, decency, truth, public interest, and mutual good. Growing numbers of organizations have developed clear credos or codes of ethics.

Mergers, downsizing, and restructuring have led both businesses and nonprofits to seek ways to operate with *lean resources,* and the duplication and counterproductive actions that exist amid the isolation of marketing from public relations often is too great a price for organizations to pay.

Strategic communication is part of an organization's *management role* and *decision-making process*. It is rooted in the organization's mission as lived out through its bottom line. This bottom line goes beyond money earned or raised; it focuses on the organization's fundamental purpose or mission. Strategists plot courses, set objectives, and measure results.

Many *media changes* are affecting the way organizations communicate. The "mass media" have fragmented to the point that none rules supreme any more. Lines have blurred between news and entertainment. Meanwhile, increasing advertising costs and tighter promotional budgets have led organizations to look at the more cost-effective communication and promotional tools from the public relations side of the house.

Strategic communication uses *multiple tools,* drawing from all communication-related disciplines to talk with various groups of people. New technologies make it easier to supplement general media with more personal and interactive targeted communication vehicles.

The strategy of choice in a competitive environment is *proactive, two-way communication*, in which organizations plan for and initiate relationships with the people important to their success. This approach emphasizes dialogue over monologue.

Organizations are successful to the extent they enjoy a strong *reputation*, which results from neither luck nor accident. Strategic planning can identify and evaluate an organization's visibility and reputation. No organization can afford to be a best-kept secret among a relatively small number of supporters.

All kinds of organizations are realizing more keenly the need for long-term, mutually beneficial *relationships* between the organization and its various publics and market segments. Public relations practitioners long have recognized this, and marketing more recently has been discussing the need for relationship marketing.

Most comprehensive public relations textbooks, including this one, simply refer to a four-stage process without constraining it to an acronym. While acronyms can be useful mnemonic devices, they sometimes are too confining.

Marketing communication books also present a step-by-step process, but with less consistency about the number of steps involved. In their crossover text on social marketing, Philip Kotler, Ned Roberto, and Nancy Lee (2002) identify eight steps in four general stages that focus on analysis of the environment, identification of audiences and objectives, development of a strategic approach and development of the implementation plan.

Strategic Planning for Public Relations offers a model that is meant to be both logical and easy to follow. The steps are grouped into four phases that are both descriptive and accurate, but their names don't lend themselves to an acronym. So without a great deal of fanfare, this model is called, simply, the Nine Steps of Strategic Public Relations.

The process of these steps is deliberate, and they must be taken in sequence. After identifying a problem, our tendency too often is to skip ahead to seeking solutions, leaping over research and analysis. This can result in unwarranted assumptions that later prove to be costly, counterproductive, and embarrassing. Careful planning leads to programs that are proactive and preventive rather than to activities that are reactive and remedial. At the same time, the steps in this process are flexible enough to allow for constant monitoring, testing, and adjusting as needed.

If you ask experienced communication managers you may find that they don't necessarily articulate their planning specifically along the lines of these nine steps. But talk with them about their work and you are likely to find that they go through a process pretty much like the one being presented here, whether they identify "steps" or not.

A few practitioners may admit (somewhat guiltily) that they don't do much planning. If they are being honest, they'll tell you they know they've been lucky so far with their hunches. Perhaps they don't do formal planning because they don't have the time or because the environment is so unstable that all they can do is react. Some practitioners may tell you their bosses and clients want action rather than planning (though such shortsighted bosses and clients often don't remain in business very long).

If you could observe how professionals work, however, you'd probably find that effective communication managers do plan, and plan well. The good ones have learned how to build the research and planning components into their work, imbedding them in their service to clients and bosses. Increasingly, public relations organizations are using their websites to set the stage for such a four-stage planning process.

Phase One: Formative Research

During the first of the four phases, the focus is on the preliminary work of communication planning, which is the need to gather information and analyze the situation. In three steps, the planner draws on existing information available to the organization and, at the same time, creates a research program for gaining additional information needed to drive the decisions that will come later in the planning process.

STEP 1: ANALYZING THE SITUATION

Your analysis of the situation is the crucial beginning to the process. It is imperative that all involved—planner, clients, supervisors, key colleagues, and the ultimate decision makers are

EXHIBIT INTRO.1 Four phases of strategic planning

> PHASE ONE
> **FORMATIVE RESEARCH**
> 1. Analyzing the Situation
> 2. Analyzing the Organization
> 3. Analyzing the Publics

> PHASE TWO
> **STRATEGY**
> 4. Establishing Goals and Objectives
> 5. Formulating Action and Response Strategies
> 6. Developing the Message Strategy

> PHASE THREE
> **TACTICS**
> 7. Selecting Communication Tactics
> 8. Implementing the Strategic Plan

> PHASE FOUR
> **EVALUATIVE RESEARCH**
> 9. Evaluating the Strategic Plan

in solid agreement about the nature of the opportunity or obstacle to be addressed in this program. It's also important to learn what researchers have discovered about the relevant issue and to note pertinent case studies.

STEP 2: ANALYZING THE ORGANIZATION

This step involves a careful and candid look at three aspects of the organization: (1) its internal environment (mission, performance, and resources); (2) its public perception (reputation); and (3) its external environment (competitors and opponents, as well as supporters).

STEP 3: ANALYZING THE PUBLICS

In this step you identify and analyze your key publics—the various groups of people who interact with your organization on the issue at hand. *Strategic Planning for Public Relations* provides an objective technique for setting priorities among the various publics, helping you select those most important on the particular issue being dealt with. This step includes an analysis of each public in terms of its wants, needs, interests, and expectations about the issue; its relationship to the organization; its involvement in communication and with various media; and a variety of social, economic, political, cultural, and technological trends that may affect it.

Phase Two: Strategy

The second phase of the planning process deals with the heart of planning—making decisions dealing with the expected impact of the communication, as well as the nature of the communication itself.

STEP 4: ESTABLISHING GOALS AND OBJECTIVES

Step 4 focuses on the ultimate position sought for the organization and for the product or service. This step helps you develop clear, specific, and measurable objectives that identify the organization's hoped-for impact on the awareness, acceptance, and action of each key public. A good deal of attention is given to objectives dealing with acceptance of the message, because this is the most crucial area for public relations and marketing communication strategists.

STEP 5: FORMULATING ACTION AND RESPONSE STRATEGIES

A range of possible actions is available to the organization, and in this step you consider what you might do in various situations. This section includes typologies of public relations initiatives and responses. No strategic campaign would include every possible option, but a well-planned campaign would consider each in light of its goals and objectives.

STEP 6: DEVELOPING THE MESSAGE STRATEGY

This step deals with the various decisions about the message, such as the person or entity who will present the message to the key publics, the content of the message, its tone and style, verbal and nonverbal cues, and related issues. Lessons from research about persuasive communication and dialogue will be applied for the ultimate purpose of designing a message that reflects the information gained through Step 3 focusing on key publics.

Phase Three: Tactics

During the third phase, various communication tools are considered and the visible elements of the communication plan are created.

STEP 7: SELECTING COMMUNICATION TACTICS

This inventory deals with the various communication options. Specifically, the planner considers four categories: (1) face-to-face communication and opportunities for personal involvement; (2) organizational media (sometimes called controlled media); (3) news media (uncontrolled media); and (4) advertising and promotional media (another form of controlled media). While all of these tools can be used by any organization, not every tool is appropriate for each issue.

STEP 8: IMPLEMENTING THE STRATEGIC PLAN

This step turns the raw ingredients identified in the previous step into a recipe for successful public relations and marketing communication. In Step 8, planners package the tactics identified in the menu review of the previous step into a cohesive communication program. Here planners also develop budgets and schedules, and otherwise prepare to implement the communication program.

Phase Four: Evaluative Research

The final phase of strategic planning deals with evaluation and assessment. It enables you to determine the degree to which the stated objectives have been met and thus to modify or continue the communication activities.

STEP 9: EVALUATING THE STRATEGIC PLAN

This is the final planning element, indicating specific methods for measuring the effectiveness of each recommended tactic in meeting the stated objectives.

JARGON OF STRATEGIC PUBLIC RELATIONS

Consider the following terms that distinguish among various types of public relations activities:

- A **project** is a single and usually short-lived public relations activity designed to meet an objective. Examples: a news release, a Facebook page, or a few related tactics for an open house.
- A **program** is an ongoing public relations activity dealing with several objectives associated with a goal. Programs have a continuing commission within the organization and focus on its relationship with a particular public. Examples: an organization's program in community relations or employee relations, or its social media program involving coordinated tools and venues.
- A **campaign** is a systematic set of public relations activities, each with a specific and finite purpose, sustained over a length of time and dealing with objectives associated with a particular issue. Examples: a campaign to reduce accidents associated with drunk driving, or a campaign to improve employee morale and productivity.

Effective Creativity

Before we begin putting a plan together, a word about creativity. Most communications professionals are creative people. They are visual or verbal artists who bring imaginative ideas to the task at hand.

But mere novelty doesn't guarantee success. We all have seen people whose creative ideas seem to flop around without any sense of direction, artists who can't seem to apply their artistic concept.

Creativity might best be described as the use of original or imaginative ideas, going beyond traditional ideas and patterns to produce new forms or interpretations and relevant alternatives. Creativity often is associated with the arts and entertainment, though increasingly it is seen as a problem-solving tool. Creativity goes hand in hand with **innovation**, and often the two terms are used interchangeably. However, creativity should be seen as the ability to imagine new ideas, whereas innovation is the ability to apply such thinking.

For creativity to be effective, it must have relevance. Groundbreaking ideas need to serve a purpose. Too many campaigns never get off the ground because they are built more on novelty than on effectiveness. Some are just too cute for words; others are downright bizarre. An inside joke in the advertising industry is that sometimes agencies win creative awards but lose the account, because their innovative advertising programs didn't sell the product or their imaginative approach didn't achieve the desired results for the client. Not a very funny joke, is it?

For example, TV commercials featuring puppies and horses are popular with Super Bowl fans, but Budweiser has to be concerned with more than popularity. "We've done the puppy commercials on the Super Bowl for the last three years and everybody loves them," said Jorn Socquet, vice president of U.S. marketing for Anhauser-Busch, in 2015. "They have zero impact on beer sales. Those ads I wouldn't air again because they don't sell beer."

In the not-so-distant past, some practitioners worried that strategic planning might interfere with their creativity. That's changing. In a crowded field of competitors all courting the same audiences, communication professionals have turned to greater use of research as a complement to the creative approach. Practitioners who once flew by the seat of their pants have found that careful planning can raise an organization's messages above the commotion of everyday life.

One thing has become clear: It really is counterproductive to separate creative and research people, because each can help the other. They share the common purpose of helping their client or their organization solve a problem.

Research nurtures creative inspiration, helps develop ideas, keeps things on target, and evaluates the effectiveness of the creative endeavors. Creativity can take the facts and data generated through research and imbue them with pizzazz to produce a Wow! factor that can make a public relations campaign soar.

Strategic Planning for Public Relations is built on two notions that can help make you creatively effective.

- A step-by-step system of planning is essential to learning how to develop an effective communication program.
- Effective creativity is more likely to result from careful and insightful planning than from a lightning bolt of inspiration.

This book is for people who appreciate road maps. A map doesn't tell you where you must go; rather, it helps you explore possibilities. You consider options, make choices, select alternatives, and develop contingencies. In short, you plan. Then you implement the plan by getting behind the wheel and beginning the road trip.

So it is with *Strategic Planning for Public Relations.* This book won't tell you what has to be done in developing your communication program, but it will lead you through the various decision points and options. The resulting program will be as unique as each individual student or practitioner and as tailored as each organization needs it to be. It will be a comprehensive, carefully thought-out program that is both deliberate and creative.

Every person can be both deliberate and creative, each to a greater or lesser degree. *Strategic Planning for Public Relations* tries to help you cultivate both qualities. It helps creative people become more organized in their planning, and it helps methodical people bring more creative energy to their work.

This book gives you a model—one to be considered, adapted to fit your particular circumstances and used to the extent that it helps you be both effective and creative in your communication planning. Use *Strategic Planning for Public Relations* to nurture your creativity and channel it to make your work more effective.

CREATIVITY AND STRUCTURE

Most people consider themselves at either side of a coin. Some are creative people. Some are analytical types. *Strategic Planning for Public Relations* is geared to both.

Are you easily creative? This book will help transform your artistry, insight, and spontaneity into something more than mere novelty. It will lead you to consider every aspect of a strategic communication plan, helping you be creative within an effective framework.

Are you analytical and well organized? This book will enhance your innate sense of organization and structure, freeing your creativity to enhance your program effectiveness.

The reality is that we are seldom one or the other, creative or structured. Don't use the either–or visual metaphor of a coin with two sides. Rather, think of a pole with two ends. Then focus not on the ends but on the continuum in between. Regardless of where you place yourself on this continuum, *Strategic Planning for Public Relations* can help you work through your strengths and at the same time shore up less dominant aspects of your work style.

PHASE ONE

FORMATIVE RESEARCH

The phrase "shooting in the dark" refers to trying to hit a target without being able to see it. In the context of strategic communication planning, designing a program without the necessary research is shooting in the dark. In any context, it's not a good idea!

Research is the strategic planner's foundation of every effective campaign for public relations and marketing communication. Your communication tactics might be innovative, but without adequate research they risk being ineffective. Without research, you will probably end up sending messages of little value to your organization and little interest to your publics, who most likely won't be listening anyway.

How common is research in public relations and marketing communication? Various studies show that formative research for planning campaigns and projects is the most common type of public relations research, with lesser use of research to monitor progress and measure outcomes. Even during crises, when reaction time is minimal, many practitioners insist on making time to do research to get a quick read on public opinion.

Anecdotal evidence suggests that research is becoming even more common. Most practitioners report that they are doing more research than ever before.

The first of the four phases of the strategic planning process deals specifically with gathering and analyzing **formative research**, which is data on which you will build your communication program. There are two types of such research.

- **Strategic research** is the systematic gathering of information about issues and publics that affect an organization, particularly one engaged in the two-way models of public relations outlined in the introduction to this book.
- **Tactical research** is information obtained to guide the production and dissemination of messages.

Whereas tactical research helps public relations practitioners do tasks effectively, strategic research more directly impacts on the organization's overall mission.

During this formative research phase, focused as it is on strategy, you will conduct a comprehensive **situation analysis** to gather the information needed to make wise decisions. To accomplish this, you will gather information in three key areas: (1) the situation you are facing; (2) your organization or client; and (3) your intended publics. More specifically, you will obtain background information on the issue, assess the organization's performance and reputation, catalog its resources, and identify and analyze key publics.

Don't let the idea of research scare you. Research begins with informal and often simple methods of gathering relevant information. Often you can look to a three-prong research program for most public relations projects:

- **Casual research** collects what is already known. It can be quite informal as you think about the situation. "Pick the brains" of clients, colleagues, and other helpful individuals. Interview other people with experience and expertise. Brainstorm alone or with other planners.
- **Secondary research** more systematically looks for existing information. Using this approach, you will investigate organizational files to learn what already exists on the issue. Search the library for information from books, periodicals, and special reports. Check for similar material on the Internet (but be wary about the validity of what you find there). Review and analyze how other organizations handled similar situations.
- **Primary research** involves gathering original information by conducting your own research. Several appendixes in this book will help with the basic primary research techniques such as surveys, focus groups, and content analysis, as well as the issue of research ethics.

As you conduct formative research, keep one thing in mind: The information you obtain through research will help in planning, but research does not offset the need for common sense. Your professional judgment remains the strongest resource you bring to the planning process. Use research to inform your professional judgment, but make decisions on relevant information as well as on your own reliable experience and professional insight.

This section looks at the three areas in which you will conduct your research, starting with an analysis of the situation.

STEP 1

Analyzing
the Situation

The first step in any effective public relations plan or marketing communication program is to carefully and accurately identify the situation facing your organization. This seems simple enough. Common sense, right? But good sense isn't all that common, and people sometimes have different ideas about what the public relations situation is.

Public Relations Situation

Put simply, a **situation** is a set of circumstances facing an organization. Without an early and clear statement of the situation to be addressed, you will not be able to conduct efficient research or define the goal of your communication program later in the planning process.

Situations vary. An auto manufacturer's situation might be the availability of side airbags (rather than just front airbags) in its new model-year cars. For a small nonprofit organization dealing with drug rehabilitation among teens and young adults, a situation might be the misunderstanding and fear that some people have of youthful addicts. For a National Football League (NFL) team, the situation may be loyalty of fans.

Note that situations are stated as nouns—*availability* of airbags, *fear* of addicts, *loyalty* of fans. Later when we talk about organizational goals, we will add the verbs to indicate how we want to impact on these situations—*promoting* consumer acceptance of the airbags, *dispelling* the notion that youthful addicts are necessarily dangerous, *nurturing* fan loyalty. For now, simply identify the situation without commenting on it.

A situation is similar in meaning to a problem, if you use the classic notion of a question needing to be addressed. The word "problem" comes from parallel Greek and Latin words meaning "a task proposed" or "a thing put forward." Based on that understanding, a public relations situation is a possible course of action that can be either a positive or negative:

- **Opportunity**. The public relations situation may be identified as an opening, something to be embraced. An opportunity offers a potential advantage to the organization or its publics (such as side airbags or fan loyalty).

- **Obstacle**. On the other hand, the public relations situation may be a roadblock, something to be overcome. Obstacles limit the organization in realizing its mission (such as fear of at-risk youth, or fan loyalty if the team is losing).

Two planners may look differently at the same situation, depending on how they assess the situation and its potential impact on the organization. One may call it an obstacle, the other an opportunity. It's important to make sure that everyone involved in planning a public relations activity should approach it from the same perspective.

Note that even in crisis situations, obstacles can be approached as opportunities, if the problem has not been self-inflicted. Organizations under attack may use the public attention generated by a crisis to explain their values and demonstrate their quality.

Learning from Research

Researching what others think about the situation and what they have done in related areas can both save valuable time and provide considerable insight into solving the problem at hand. This takes two forms: (1) reviewing academic and professional literature and analyzing relevant studies and articles; and (2) identifying other organizations that have successfully navigated the same waters that you find yourself in.

To the first point, when you are addressing the public relations situation, don't think too narrowly. If you were addressing the scenarios noted above, it would be to your advantage to take a broad view.

For example, the situation of car airbags suggests looking at the broad concept of passenger safety. A review of studies concerning consumer expectations, trends within the automotive world, parental worries about children and young drivers, even medical information about auto injuries all could shed light on the situation.

The situation involving young addicts likewise would benefit from a thorough literature review. Identify and analyze studies, reports, and articles dealing not only with addiction among young people but also about various related areas. These might include alternative rehabilitation approaches, community safety concerns, the impact on youthful addiction within the community, and the effect of rehab facilities on real estate and local businesses.

If you are dealing with the scenario about football fans, it's logical to start with a keyword search about "fan loyalty." Then expand your search to find information dealing with issues such as sports marketing, competitive sports activities within the geographic area, and economic predictions related to leisure spending. Look also to the NFL for information, including statistics, on issues such as game attendance, strategies for season ticket holders, and game-related activities such as halftime, tailgate parties, and so on.

The second area involves looking to colleagues and competitors. Organizations often use a **best practices** approach as they weigh their options. This is a method of documenting and analyzing the behavior of an acknowledged leader in the field.

The best practices approach to organizational problem solving tries to identify a **benchmark**, which is a specific and measurable standard against which an organization can compare its own products and services, with an eye toward improvement. A benchmark might be an organization, or it could be a standard of performance that you aspire to achieve.

The best-practice approach involves research into how other organizations have handled similar situations, identifying those that handle them well. It might even identify organizations that performed poorly, giving a lesson in what not to do when dealing with this situation.

Benchmarking is a continuous and systematic process of measuring an organization and its products and services against the best practices of strong competitors and recognized industry leaders, in order to improve the organization's performance. Put more simply, benchmarking is the search for better ways of doing the things you do.

Peter Schwartz and Blair Gibb (1999) note three benefits of benchmarking: (1) organizational initiatives that prevent internal inertia from taking over; (2) continual awareness of innovations coming from competitors; and (3) introduction of fresh air from outside the organization.

Obstacles into Opportunities

In what is still a classic example of good public relations, Pepsi faced an accusation in 1993 that medical syringes had been found in cans of the company's product. Pepsi fought back by issuing video news releases showing how its production process made it impossible to contaminate the product before it left the plant.

Another classic illustration of good professional practice comes from Johnson & Johnson. The company used satellite news conferences when it reintroduced Tylenol after several people were killed in 1983 after someone tampered with the over-the-counter medicine. In doing so, the company, which already enjoyed a good reputation, emerged from the crisis with even more consumer respect and confidence.

There are more contemporary examples of taking what might at first appear to be an obstacle and turning it into an opportunity.

When Taco Bell was sued in 2011 for false advertising that its tacos contain only 35 percent beef, the company countersued, then launched a media campaign, largely digital: "Thank you for suing us. Here's the truth about our seasoned beef." The media blitz explained that it serves tacos that are 88 percent beef and 12 percent seasoning to enhance the flavor.

JetBlue had to cancel 1,000 flights when an ice storm hit the East Coast of the U.S. in 2007, and some passengers were stuck in airports for nearly a week. Instead of blaming the weather, the CEO wrote a public letter of apology, detailing what the company would do to help and/or compensate all the affected passengers. The CEO followed up with an apology tour that took him to YouTube, *The Today Show*, *The Late Show with David Letterman*, and *Anderson Cooper 360*. The result was that JetBlue regained most of its reputation for customer service.

Several companies have taken up the challenge to turn negative stereotyping into consumer-friendly advocacy, especially those that draw on the many psychological studies that document the link between young women's body confidence and media images portraying female beauty. Examples of this are the classic Dove Campaign for Real Beauty, the "sexy weight" theme of Fitness First for Women (outlined in the Chapter 4 discussion of acceptance objectives), and the ad campaign by American Eagle's "Aerie" lingerie line that the company says "challenges supermodel standards by featuring unretouched photos."

Finding Consensus

Whether the issue is viewed as an opportunity, an obstacle, or simply an unrealized potential, the communication team and the organization's or client's leadership must come to a common understanding of the issue before it can be adequately addressed.

Phase One

STEP
1

CASE IN POINT Campaign for Real Beauty

Unilever is a company that created an opportunity out of a problem. Two problems, actually. One was that sale of one of its products, Dove soap, was sagging. A parallel problem was that traditional marketing of beauty products relied on idealized portrayals of women. The opportunity—to redefine the situation.

Unilever, the parent company for Dove beauty products, commissioned an international study on women's attitudes toward beauty. What resulted was a new approach called the Campaign for Real Beauty, launched in 2004 and continuing today. Dove advertising featured images of ordinary women, not supermodels.

When the campaign was first launched, it propelled Unilever and Dove to international prominence. The campaign caught the attention of news media, talk shows, and women's magazines, generating exposure that Unilever estimated as worth more than 30 times its paid-for media placements. More than a million visitors logged on to its website (dove.com) in the first year alone. Workshops and sleepovers for girls further fueled what had become an international and years-long discussion of beauty and self-esteem.

The campaign focused on social media through venues such as YouTube and Google+ Hangout, with plenty of discussion through Twitter, Instagram, and Facebook.

Results? Several campaign videos went viral. "Real Beauty Sketches" in one month after its launch in 2013 became the most-watched video ad of all time (114 million views in 25 languages). The video won the top honor at the Cannes Lions International Festival of Creativity. The campaign itself earned 4.6 billion impressions on blogger media. Sales of Dove soap jumped two-thirds.

But the campaign did more than simply sell beauty products. It sparked an international discussion about women and beauty, drawing praise for Dove from psychologists, teachers, parents, media analysts, and real women with curves. The campaign also partnered with Girl Scouts and similar organizations to involve girls in the discussion.

The Dove campaign is an example of a communication strategy that caught the public interest. But no good deed is above reproach, and even social responsibility is not without a downside. Unilever took some criticism because the corporation uses overt female sexuality to market its AXE deodorants. Additionally, Greenpeace took advantage of the visibility surrounding the campaign to accuse Unilever of buying palm oil from companies that destroy rain forests.

Consider the following example of mixed signals. The executive director of a drug abuse-prevention agency wanted a public relations consultant to focus on communication between the agency and external publics such as the courts, police, and probation personnel. The board of directors, on the other hand, wanted a plan for better communication among the board, staff, and executive director. Significantly different expectations! How might you handle this?

In this case, the consultant asked both the director and the board to reach consensus about the central issue and to rethink what they wanted. They asked themselves what the basic issues were and concluded that the focus should be on the agency's visibility and reputation with its external publics. Once this was clarified, the consultant developed a strategic plan and helped the agency implement it. The strategic planning checklist at the end of this chapter will help you clarify the issue at hand for your organization.

Ongoing communication with the research client is imperative. In their book *Applied Research Design*, Terry Hedrick, Leonard Bickman, and Debra Rog (1993) recommend at least four research touch points:

1. An initial meeting with the client to develop a common understanding of the client's research needs, resources, and expected uses
2. A meeting to agree on the scope of the project, particularly its costs and other resources
3. Following an initial review of literature and other secondary sources, a meeting to refine the research questions and discuss potential approaches and limitations
4. A meeting for agreement on the proposed study approach

Your job in this first step of the strategic planning process is to carefully identify the situation at hand. Come to consensus about whether it is seen as an opportunity or an obstacle, and if the latter, how it might be turned into an opportunity.

ZEN OF PUBLIC RELATIONS

Sometimes a new paradigm—a different perspective—can enhance our understanding. And what could be further from the practicality of public relations than spirituality?

To better understand an important public relations concept, consider the principle of interconnectedness—the duality in which everything is related. What appears to be opposite is not separate. It is only the other end of the one pole, the other side of the same lake.

When we think of public relations issues, our tendency often is to identify them as either obstacles or opportunities. But such words mask an important relationship.

The spirituality associated with Zen values harmony. A problem is not necessarily something negative but instead something lacking harmony, a point of yet-unrealized potential. An obstacle puts us at a crossroads, allowing us to go this way or that, with consequences based on the choice we make.

The ultimate public relations problem is a **crisis**. Yet even that word gives us philosophical pause. First, a definition. The dictionary defines crisis as "a turning point for better or worse; a decisive moment." It is interesting to note that the Chinese/ Japanese character for "crisis" combines two concepts: "danger" and "opportunity" (shown here in the version used in both traditional Chinese and in Japanese; it is pronounced "wei ji" in Chinese, and "kiki" in Japanese). 危機

A crisis is a decision point where choices point to consequences. This is particularly fitting for public relations professionals seeking to guide their organization through times of crisis. The job of public relations, then, is to restore harmony and to re-establish equilibrium.

It is important to take the broad view in this. Most of the major fast food-chains—Arby's, Burger King, Dunkin' Donuts, KFC, McDonald's, Subway, Taco Bell, and Wendy's—have been criticized for contributing to obesity. In response, each chain introduced more nutritional and diet-friendly items such as salads, wraps, whole grains, veggie burgers, and more grilled items.

Maybe it's a matter of seeing the writing on the wall. Maybe it's a conversion. Maybe not. After all, these are the companies that gave us supersized fried meals in the first place, so perhaps the health talk is simply part of the ongoing profit lust. Regardless of motivation, it's clear that fast-food companies are practicing good public relations by changing their ways in the face of mounting public concern over the issue of obesity.

Issues Management

An **issue** is a situation that presents matters of concern to organizations. It is what Abe Bakhsheshy (2003) of the University of Utah defines as a trend, an event, a development, or a matter in dispute that may affect an organization. Issues exist within a changing environment and often are the result of conflicting values (either different values held by the organization and one of its publics, or a different balance among similar values). In their book *Agenda Setting*, John Dearing and Everett Rogers define an issue as "a social problem, often conflictual, that has received media coverage" (1996, p. 4).

Bakhsheshy notes that early anticipation permits an organization to study the issue, to orient itself to deal with the issue, and to better identify and potentially involve itself with its publics. He asks several questions in analyzing issues: Which stakeholders does the issue affect? Who has an interest? Who is in a position to exert influence? Who ought to care? Who started the ball rolling? Who is now involved?

Issues management is the process by which an organization tries to anticipate emerging issues and respond to them before they get out of hand, perhaps even before they break onto the scene. It is a process of monitoring and evaluating information. Like many other aspects of public relations, issues management involves potential change. For example, insurance companies, hospitals, pharmaceuticals, health-advocacy groups, and health-maintenance organizations are all trying to predict trends—both within the health-care industry and in the political environment—that may have some kind of impact on the future.

Despite its name, issues management does not try to control; neither does it involve one-way communication nor manipulation of a public.

Rather, it helps the organization interact with its publics. It may help an organization settle the issue early or divert it, or perhaps even prevent its emergence. More likely, however, the organization will have to adjust itself to the issue in some way, trying to maximize the benefits or at least minimize the negative impact. Public relations often drives this early-warning system within an organization.

Background of Issues Management

F.J. Aguilar (1967) explained **environmental scanning** as a process of seeking "information about events and relationships in a company's outside environment, the knowledge of which would assist top management in its task of charting the company's future course of action" (p. 1).

W. Howard Chase (1977) coined the term "issues management," though the concept has been around since the days when Ivy Lee first did the work of what has become known as public relations. But Chase pushed the concept forward, away from a catch-as-catch-can approach and toward a more systematic technique. He outlined this in five steps (Jones and Chase, 1979). Here is an even newer six-stage synthesis of the process of issues management:

1. Identify future issues that are likely to affect an organization. Develop an early-warning scanning system that considers where the organization wants to go and looks at potential roadblocks and other outside economic, political, technological, social, and other kinds of pressures on the organization. Look for forces that could help move the organization along its path.
2. Research and analyze each issue. Carefully gather as many facts as possible about these. Consult specialists who are particularly familiar with the issues.
3. Consider options in responding to each issue. Use creative problem-solving techniques to discover as many alternatives as possible to deal with the issue at hand. Establish your standards for success and the criteria that your organization should use to make choices among the various alternatives.
4. Develop an action plan. Select the most appropriate option, usually in terms of cost-effectiveness, practicality, and organizational fit. Then develop a specific plan to address the issue.
5. Implement this plan, giving as much energy and as many resources as it warrants.
6. Evaluate the effectiveness of the response, both during its implementation when there is still time to make appropriate adjustments and when the program is completed.

After interviewing 248 public relations managers, Martha Lauzen (1997) found a link between two-way public relations and both the early detection and accurate diagnosis of issues: "The answer lies in the confluence of public relations and issues management as they become true boundary-spanning functions, acting as the eyes and ears of organizations, serving as parts of an early warning system" (p. 79).

The conclusion is that two-way public relations, which inherently involves issues management, leads to more effective outcomes and ultimately will move the practitioner into the **dominant coalition**, which is that grouping of managers and executives who together wield power and make decisions within organizations. The expectation is that senior public relations managers should be part of their organization's dominant coalition.

Risk Management

Strategic communicators often give the name **risk management** to the process of identifying, controlling, and minimizing the impact of uncertain events on an organization. The term is used in many disciplines—from politics to engineering, business to biology.

Public relations people sometimes need to prod their organizations and clients to listen to criticism. Many public relations disasters are rooted in the myopic failure to learn from others' mistakes or in the shortsightedness of not addressing internal flaws.

One reason for this is what Michael Regester and Judy Larkin (2005) call "believing your own PR." The risk-management specialists give as an example Nestlé International, which, Regester said, saw itself as a nurturing company and thus failed to recognize the intensity of

Phase One

STEP
1

criticism over its marketing of infant formula, an international protest and boycott that lasted more than 35 years and cost the corporation much in bad publicity, lost customers, legal fees, and a weakened reputation.

Similarly, Dow Corning saw itself as a conscientious company and believed that science was on its side, so it aggressively stood by its science and resisted criticism and public concern about the safety of its silicone breast implants. When class-action lawsuits were filed, the company failed to take quick action because it didn't think any response was needed. It followed common (and bad) legal advice to say nothing sympathetic about women who claimed they were harmed by the company's project, prepping the case for legal courts while ignoring the court of public opinion where reputations are made and broken.

The case yielded record settlements against the company: $5.4 million to one woman, $7.3 to another, $27.9 million to three women, $7 million to another victim. Dow Corning ended up in bankruptcy for nine years, emerging only two decades after the problem began.

Ironically, science did vindicate Dow Corning. Repeated studies show no connection between the implants and breast cancer. Nevertheless, the Dow Corning fiasco is a textbook case of how to mismanage a crisis, and over the years many other organizations have learned from its mistakes.

STEP 1

CASE IN POINT   Exxon versus BP Oil Spills

The two most famous oil disasters in North America involve Exxon and BP. Here's an overview of each case, followed by a discussion of the public relations lessons learned.

Exxon Valdez 1989 Oil Spill off Alaska

Exxon is a company that refused to take the critics seriously, apparently having little interest in risk management. As a result, the company suffered in the long run for mishandling the situation after its freighter *Exxon Valdez* spilled nearly 37 million gallons of oil in the Gulf of Alaska.

A court ordered the company to pay $2.5 billion mainly in punitive damages. Two decades later, after a series of legal appeals by Exxon, the Supreme Court cut the fine to $500 million. Exxon claimed it already had spent $3.5 billion in clean-up costs and civil or criminal charges (though much of that was covered by insurance).

The case remains a classic example of how not to do public relations. The negative effects continue far beyond the Alaskan waters.

Showing the ramifications of continuing anti-Exxon sentiment, a jury in 2000 ordered the oil company (now called ExxonMobil) to pay $3.5 billion for defrauding Alabama on royalties involving oil wells in the Gulf of Mexico. That verdict was set aside, and in a new trial in 2003 the jury upped the damages to $11.9 billion. Jurors said one reason for the high penalties was that the Alaska situation showed them that Exxon was a company that could not be trusted and deserved to be punished.

A state appeals court later reduced the award to $3.5 billion, and in late 2007 the Alabama Supreme Court split on partisan lines (Republicans for ExxonMobil, the lone Democrat siding with the state) to eliminate the punitive damages, assessing the company a mere $52 million—the amount it had failed to pay Alabama in the first place. In 2008, the state came back with another lawsuit seeking $143 million in interest. Meanwhile, the company went to court because it said the state charged it too much in tax.

The case revived public distrust of the corporate giant and underscored the long-term consequences of public opinion turned sour against a company.

While ExxonMobil in 2013 posted near-record profits of almost $45 billion, it also has been probed for its political contributions and faced other lawsuits on human rights violation in Venezuela and pollution at a Texas refinery. Meanwhile, critics also saw the whole Exxon–Alabama affair as another example of the stench of corruption in state politics, calling for ethics charges against the eight Republican justices who, according to media reports, had accepted a total of $5.5 million in political contributions from ExxonMobil over the previous five years. Legal cases being what they are, the situation could drag on for years, with continuing negative attention to ExxonMobil's reputation.

In another case involving a gasoline leak, a Maryland jury in 2011 ordered ExxonMobil to pay more than $1.5 billion (more than two-thirds of that in punitive damages), on top of a previous $150 million judgment for another case related to the same spill. Clearly the company's reputation makes it easy for juries to exact a price.

Meanwhile other lawsuits are pending: pipeline spills in Arkansas, Montana, and Wyoming; pollution in Texas; gay discrimination in Illinois and Texas; and a human rights case in Indonesia.

BP Deepwater Horizon 2010 Oil Leak in Gulf of Mexico

The 2010 Deepwater Horizon oil spill in the Gulf of Mexico was called the worst environmental disaster in U.S. history. It also was a public relations debacle for the once-named British Petroleum, raising questions about the capabilities of international corporations in crisis management.

The events are well known: A deep-sea explosion off the coast of Louisiana killed 11 oil-rig workers and led to the release of nearly 210 million gallons of oil, polluting an area of 3,900 square miles. The out-of-control spill, and efforts to cap the well, led the news for weeks. The economic impact was severe: $2.5 billion in damages to the fishing industry and $24 billion to tourism, with predictions of decades-long effects.

BP, once considered the greenest oil company in America, was blamed for the disaster and criticized for the way it handled it. CEO Tony Hayward was the face of BP. He had a reputation in Britain as being a knowledgeable, trusted, and seasoned corporate leader. But the confusion surrounding the facts in the crisis wore on him. Then he took his eye off the ball and was photographed sailing in a yacht race at the height of the crisis, followed by an outburst about "wanting his life back." All of this became a major liability and Hayward resigned several weeks after the explosion.

Early news releases tried to blame others, including drillers BP had hired, owners of the rig, and government regulators. This violated one of the tenets of good crisis communication: Accept responsibility for fixing the problem, and don't get caught up in laying blame.

Rather quickly, BP's public relations strategy backed away from shifting blame, instead turning its messaging toward the future—how to contain the spill and compensate the victims. Toward that end, BP set up a $20 billion fund to reimburse victims for their economic loss. It was a good move, though one later threatened by charges that BP mismanaged the fund.

On the point of explaining how it would contain the spill, critics observed that BP lost public confidence by ceding to the media the task (and opportunity) of providing public education about deep water drilling. It let others tell its story, never a good step. BP eventually created an educational component to its website, but the details were too technical and confusing for average visitors to the site.

Phase One

STEP
1

continued

BP said its costs totaled nearly $54 billion. Other estimates range higher. The *Wall Street Journal* estimated that BP spent $26 billion for legal and court fees (including $5.5 billion in environmental fines), $13 billion (later extended to $19 billion) to settle 300,000 lawsuits, the $20 billion trust fund for future costs, and $14 billion for actual clean-up costs. In 2014, a federal court found BP guilty of "gross negligence," prompting BP's final agreement in 2015 to settle all federal and state claims with an additional penalty payment of $19 billion.

A year and a half after the spill, BP engaged in some heavy-duty image repair. It launched a series of advertisements, including an estimated $50 million in TV commercials that were criticized by the media, environmentalists, and the White House. Three years after the spill, Louisiana Gov. Bobby Jindal complained that BP was spending more on TV ads to rebuild its corporate image than on the clean-up.

In its advertising, BP apologized, but then negated the impact of the apology by touting its clean-up activity and reporting "evidence" that the gulf ecology was not severely damaged and that the fishing industry was showing signs of economic recovery. In some highly visible special events, BP hired chefs Emeril Lagasse and John Besh to promote gulf seafood, and it gave away fish tacos and seafood jambalaya at Sugar Bowl parties in New Orleans.

Some of BP's responses raised ethical questions. For example, the company paid to place its sponsored links above relevant news stories and other sites for search terms such as "oil spill" and "leak." Search Engine Watch estimated the cost at $1 million a month. BP also donated $5 million to the Dauphin Island Sea Lab shortly before that lab announced that dolphin deaths in the gulf had been caused by cold water, not the oil.

Public Relations Lessons to Be Learned from Exxon and BP

Inevitably, the Deepwater Horizon spill draws parallels with the rupture of the *Exxon Valdez* 21 years earlier, which had reigned as the classic example of bad crisis communications. Both companies made public relations blunders in appearing to emphasize technology over people. Both seemed to minimize the environmental consequences and the emotional reaction to oil-slicked birds and oil-drenched shorelines. But BP was much quicker to begin paying compensation to fishermen and other victims. It also cooperated with government regulators more than Exxon did.

Another difference was a factual one about where the fault belonged. The *Valdez* spill was caused because the ship's captain was not at the helm, and the clean-up was delayed because the company had removed clean-up equipment from the area prior to the accident as part of a corporate strategy to de-emphasize the risk of such a spill. In a poorly thought-out message strategy, Exxon's CEO suggested that everyone who drives a car was responsible for the *Valdez* spill. The gulf explosion, meanwhile, resulted from the failure of safety equipment on a rig owned and operated by another company.

Both companies were accused of minimizing the extent of the spill and the environmental consequences. But BP's fault was more that it tried to remain optimistic that things were moving faster toward containing the spill without extensive or long-term pollution. It low-balled estimates of how much oil was being discharged, though some of this was based on what BP itself knew at the time.

Neither company appears to have had a workable crisis communications plan to address a worst-case scenario. Not only were the disasters unanticipated, but the companies seemed not to know

continued

how to act once they occurred. This violates another cardinal rule of crisis management: Imagine the worst thing that could happen, then prepare for it.

But there are some significant differences that led to the conclusion that BP handled the situation better than Exxon did. BP's corporate leaders were seen as part of the potential solution, rather than as avoiding responsibility and ducking public exposure as was the case in the *Valdez* spill. Also, BP produced fewer contradictory statements.

The question remains: Can BP rebuild its reputation after the spill and regain credibility as a green company? Good public relations emerges from good corporate performance. Not a game of deception and misdirection, public relations is a very clear reflection of the organization, less what it says and more what it does. If BP values the environment and is willing and able to stand by promises to manage the environmental recovery, BP may once again be perceived as a green organization with ethical public relations, an outcome that has eluded ExxonMobil.

When the worst nuclear accident in U.S. history occurred at Three Mile Island three and a half decades ago, it not only affected the corporation that ran the nuclear plant, it also resulted in new laws and regulatory oversight of the entire nuclear industry, a moratorium on building new plants, new requirements for emergency response planning, new rules for training and for preventative measures, and new clean-up procedures.

The Deepwater Horizon explosion is likely to fuel significant and continued public debate about the future of offshore drilling and how it can be made safer. A major player in this debate will be public relations, not only by the oil industry but also by government, environmental concerns, and political interests.

Crisis Management

The purpose of issues management, as previously noted, is to deal with issues before they get out of hand. When that happens, the issue becomes a crisis.

Crisis management is the name given to the process by which an organization deals with out-of-control issues. But "management" is a bit of a misnomer. It's more about coping with crises.

Consider this analogy: Issues management is like steering a sailboat. You run with the wind when it happens to be blowing in the direction you want to go, and you tack to make some progress against the wind. Sometimes you stall when there is no wind. But always, you adapt to an ever-changing environment. In a crisis situation, the analogy is more like trying to ride out a storm. Often the best you can do is drop sail, hang on, and hope the vessel is strong enough to survive without too much damage. A bit of luck helps, too.

Issues management prepares for potential events, risk management is about implied threats, and crisis management involves reaction to actual occurrences.

An organization committed to the concept of strategic communication is probably engaged in an ongoing issues management program that identifies crises in their early stages. Less nimble organizations that always seem to be in reactive mode are the ones likely to be caught off guard by a crisis.

Reality sometimes slaps you in the face and forces you to think the unthinkable. It happened at Sandy Hook Elementary School and the Boston Marathon, the Canadian Parliament and a Sikh temple in Wisconsin, a magazine office and a theater in Paris, and a church in Charleston, SC. It happened in police headquarters in New York City and Ferguson, Missouri.

Other incidents that seemed to burst onto the scene include data breaches at SONY and Target; privacy issues with Google; domestic violence issues with the NFL; and shootings at an Amish school in Pennsylvania, an Indian reservation high school in Minnesota, and universities in Virginia, Florida, and California.

Consider these two related crises with very different public relations outcomes. When a Malaysia Airlines flight from Malaysia to China mysteriously disappeared from the skies in 2014, generating suspicions of sabotage, the company seemed to have no crisis plan. The airline was faulted for a lack of urgency in addressing the disaster, along with an apparent corporate inability to show sympathy to the families of the 239 passengers and crew. Families were left in the dark for days, with little and often-conflicting information about search efforts.

Nine months later, an AirAsia flight from Indonesia to Singapore crashed during a storm, with 162 passengers and crew dead. AirAsia earned high marks for keeping the families informed about the search, with the CEO visibly leading with several news conferences and frequent tweets, often to correct misinformation, always showing a respectful tone toward the grieving families. It was a textbook case in good public relations in a crisis situation.

Sometimes, companies royally fumble their crisis management. That's what happened when Chevron offered pizza discounts in its "apology" to residents of a small town in Pennsylvania after a gas-well explosion burned for five days and left one worker dead.

Amid online calls for a boycott of SeaWorld because of how it treats its animals, the theme park refused to address criticism and even deleted critical posts on its website. The company later rigged an online newspaper poll by sending hundreds of "votes" using its own IP address, a misguided effort that was quickly exposed, adding to the park's descending reputation.

What happened in Chicago in 1983 remains an example of how companies can be unshakable in facing the unthinkable. Johnson & Johnson woke up in crisis when somebody laced its Tylenol medicine with poisonous cyanide. Seven Chicago-area residents died. That is an unthinkable tragedy for a pharmaceutical company. As the country worried about the safety of its medicines (not only Tylenol, but all packaged medicine), Johnson & Johnson quickly issued a nationwide warning. It pulled 31 million bottles of Tylenol from store shelves. It then reintroduced the medicine with a triple-seal tamper-resistant package that soon became the industry standard, and it offered customer incentives such as free replacements and discount coupons. The incident led insurance companies to introduce malicious-product-tampering coverage for the cost of a recall, interruption of business, and public relations/marketing costs associated with rehabilitating the product and its brand. Amid predictions that the Tylenol brand was doomed, the company saw a quick recovery of its 35 percent market share and in the process fostered ongoing customer loyalty.

Thirty years later, the legacy of Johnson & Johnson is a case study in good crisis communication and solid public relations, a morality tale that shows the value of a corporate conscientiousness that places customers first and keeps its promise of safety.

Considering subsequent corporate scandals, obviously some companies didn't get the point. But those that did take note learned the value of proactive management and quick communication in crisis situations.

Such forward-looking companies and organizations realize that preparedness is the key to effective issues management, particularly in crisis situations. James Lukaszewski (1997) focuses on a six-step program of preparedness: (1) early and competent leadership; (2) a prioritized approach; (3) strategies to preserve and/or recover the organization's reputation; (4) implementation of effective plans; (5) pre-authorization for the organization to act quickly on its own; and (6) a response based on openness, truthfulness, and empathy.

STRATEGIC PRINCIPLES FOR CRISIS MANAGEMENT

The strategic approach to crisis management can be encompassed in the following six principles:

Existing Relationships. During a crisis, communicate with employees, volunteers, stockholders, donors, community leaders, customers, government and professional authorities, and other constituent groups, as well as with colleagues. Minimally, the principle of existing relationships means keep everyone informed, because their continued support will be important in rebuilding reputation following the crisis.

Media-as-Ally. Crises invite scrutiny because they have a potential impact on a large number of people. The media-as-ally principle calls for treating the news media as allies that provide opportunities to communicate with key publics. If the media become intrusive or hostile, it may be because the organization has not been forthcoming in providing legitimate information to the media and its other publics. A good pre-existing program of media relations can minimize antagonism.

Reputational Priorities. Your top priority after safety issues is to your organization's reputation. Remembering this can help focus attention on doing what's best for customers, employees, and other key publics. Set objectives that deal with maintaining (or if necessary, restoring) credibility. Use the crisis as an opportunity to enhance your reputation for social responsibility with various publics.

Quick Response. Be accessible to your publics as quickly as possible. A standard guideline for crises that capture the immediate attention of the news media is the one-hour rule. Within an hour of learning about a crisis, the organization should have its first message available to its publics, particularly the media (which generally is the most compelling public in the early stages of an active crisis).

Full Disclosure. Silence is not an acceptable response during a crisis. Without admitting fault and without speculating about facts not yet known, the organization should provide as much information as possible. Start from the premise that everything the organization knows should be made available. Any decision not to release certain information should be based on careful deliberation with specific justification for the silence. Use of misleading or false information is never an ethical option.

One Voice. The principle of one voice calls for a single, trained spokesperson to represent the organization. If multiple spokespersons are needed, each should be aware of what the others are saying, and all should work together from the same set of facts and the same coordinated message.

Some experts have banded together as a kind of self-help group to guide each other in risk and crisis situations. One such coalition is the British-based Crisis Communications Network (CCN), a register of business and communication people with experience in managing crises that is associated with the Institute for Public Relations. CCN focuses on both external and internal communications. It offers strong encouragement for engaging in employee communication to prevent potentially hurtful rumors from developing in the first place. Writing about the network, Morag Cuddeford-Jones (2002) lists several tips for issues management.

1. Develop active dialogue with various stakeholders.
2. Make sure an issue is worth trying to manage.
3. Nurture expert contacts who can provide third-party research and endorsement when necessary.
4. Form a coalition with organizations similar to yours.
5. Create a risk-management plan and review it regularly, updating and modifying it as necessary.
6. Include senior management on this team.

Unpredicted, but Not Unpredictable

One thing to remember about crises: They may be sudden and unpredicted, but they seldom are unpredictable. Most crises are like volcanoes that smolder for a while before they erupt. Warning signs abound, at least to the trained eye.

A study by the Institute for Crisis Management (crisisexperts.com) reported in 2015 that only 26 percent of companies' crises burst suddenly onto the scene, while 74 percent had been smoldering situations that eventually ignited. That balance is on par with each of the previous 20 years of the group's analysis.

The biggest crisis categories were mismanagement (33 percent), white-collar crime (14 percent), whistleblowers (7 percent), casualty accidents (6 percent), environmental damage (6 percent), executive dismissal (5 percent), consumer activism (4 percent), cybercrime (4 percent), discrimination (4 percent), with lesser amounts for hostile takeovers, labor disputes, defects and recalls, class action lawsuits, and workplace violence.

All of these represent areas in which organizations should be paying attention to the quality of their performance and its impact on their reputation. A few crises are triggered by natural disasters such as floods, earthquakes, and so on. But many more crises are linked with human and organizational error: incompetent or unprepared management, repairs or readiness steps that were undone, warning signs that were unheeded.

Overall, the institute reported that only 22 percent of corporate crises were caused by outside influences such as natural disasters, activist opposition, hostile takeovers, and the fast-increasing crisis category of cybercriminals (aka "activists"). Most came from within, largely on the shoulders of management.

The institute has offered its observations on lessons learned from such crises.

• When executives take responsibility, say they're sorry, and then fix the problem, the organization recovers more quickly.
• In today's cyber environment, companies should plan for cyber breaches.

- While companies cannot predict when a crisis will strike, they can be prepared with three crisis plans: an operational plan to deal with the problem, a communication plan, and a recovery plan. Yet only half of organizations around the world have a crisis plan in place.
- It is less costly to face mistakes and deal with them as quickly as possible.
- Crises are more likely to break through social media. Organizations should have a program to monitor social media and prepare to respond amid negative attention.

The institute concludes that two-thirds of the crises never need to reach crisis stage and could be prevented by effective risk-management programs that involve an appropriate communication plan and that put a premium on organization reputation—two issues paramount in public relations.

Public Relations and Ethics

Part of your research into the situation should involve an examination of ethical aspects, particularly the basis on which practitioners and their organizations or clients make ethical decisions. You might begin by considering three classic approaches to making such determinations: deontological ethics, teleological ethics, and situational ethics. Most organizations —like most individuals—slip back and forth among the three styles of ethical decision making.

DEONTOLOGICAL ETHICS

The approach to decision making rooted in a standard or moral code is called **deontological ethics** (from the Greek for "obligation" or "duty"). In essence, the deontological approach says that certain actions are, in and of themselves, good; others, bad.

An example of deontological ethics is professional codes, such as the Public Relations Member Code of Ethics, which proclaims the intrinsic and unquestioned value of honesty, integrity, fairness, accuracy, and so on.

On the positive side, this is a humanitarian approach in which actions are judged on basic principles of human rights and dignity. On the negative side, it can give way to a fundamentalist application of rules without regard to consequence.

TELEOLOGICAL ETHICS

On the other hand, **teleological ethics** (from the Greek for "goal" or "result") is an approach focused more on the impact that actions have on people. It is more results-oriented. The teleological approach is rooted in the notion that good actions produce good results. Thus something is judged to be ethical because it generates good consequences.

An example of the teleological approach also is implied in the Public Relations Society of America code, which connects the need for ethical behavior and conduct with the public interest.

Teleological ethics asks the question: What will produce the greater good for the most people? A positive aspect of this approach is that it requires practitioners to consider the consequences of their actions. A negative aspect is that it creates a scenario in which the greater good, always difficult to calculate, sometimes is allowed to reign without account for the harm inflicted on the minority.

SITUATIONAL ETHICS

A third approach to ethical decision making is **situational ethics** (otherwise called **ethical relativism**), which suggests that actions are ethical to the extent they reflect particular social norms. The situational approach is considered on a case-by-case basis. While an advantage of this approach is respect for cultural diversity and conflicting values, it has the mirrored disadvantage both of dominance of mainstream culture as well as an inability to judge the basic rightness or wrongness of actions.

ETHICS BY COMMITTEE

Hospitals have their ethics committees, so why not public relations agencies? One such panel is found at the international public relations firm of Ruder-Finn. The company's ethics committee brings together account executives with outside ethical experts such as rabbis, ministers, priests, theologians, and philosophers. Their goal: to struggle with the ethical dimension of issues and then to advise management.

David Finn of the New York City–based agency has observed that ethical decision making is not a choice between good and bad but rather a choice between two conflicting goods. The challenge is first to discern the difference and then to make an appropriate choice.

Ruder-Finn's chief ethics officer, Emmanuel Tchividjian, coordinates the committee and edits the firm's ethics blog linked from the company website (ruderfinn.com). He says the ethics team has reviewed issues such as whether the agency should continue a lucrative account with a national tourism office after a military coup in that country. After the committee (including an ethics professor at a theological seminary) went to the country to investigate, Ruder-Finn resigned from the account because it did not want to assist a military dictatorship.

The agency also considered whether to accept a book-promotion account involving the Church of Scientology. That account was rejected because the firm did not want to be involved with what it considered a religious cult.

But Ruder-Finn did accept an account with the Swiss government over the issue of money and gold that the Nazis took from Jews during the Holocaust—a particularly sensitive issue for an agency where most of the managers and staff are Jewish. That account, notes Tchividjian, was accepted on the belief that much could be gained by open communication. The committee serves to remind employees that "the bottom line is not the most important thing," he explains. "We do have to make money, but there are values that have a higher priority" (Tchividjian, interview with the author).

Another ethical innovation by Ruder-Finn was borrowed from the legal profession. When a potential client approaches the company with an issue that raises ethical concerns, the agency conducts discovery research at the client's expense, soliciting information from industry insiders and ethicists about the moral dimension of the issue. Based on the findings, Ruder-Finn may reject the client or, conversely, it may use the information to help frame the client's position on the sensitive issue.

Communication strategists help themselves and their organizations when they anticipate how they will approach ethical decisions. Without advance thinking, the planner often is left either with no guidelines on determining whether something is ethical or simply with an unexamined personal feeling. Neither of those choices is particularly useful. The value of advance thinking is that you can recognize the different foundations for determining ethical actions and responses and you can consider each approach as you make your decisions.

Ethical Shortcomings

It is important for public relations practitioners and educators alike to acknowledge the occasional shortcomings of colleagues. There have been several spectacular ethical errors in recent years by public relations professionals, even more by nonprofessionals posing as practitioners. Some are well known and frequently discussed: *Exxon Valdez* and the somewhat comparable BP Deepwater Horizon oil spills.

Other examples may be a bit less well known: Vogue magazine's use of a white model in blackface; American Girl's marketing of a "homeless girl" doll; Abercrombie and Fitch's promotion of thong underwear for 10-year-old girls; automaker executives who took private jets to Washington to beg for a congressional bailout; and sluggish corporate responses to a Domino's Pizza guy doing disgusting things to a customer's food and similar videos of a FedEx employee smashing a computer monitor he was delivering to a customer.

The world of electoral politics abounds with examples of false or misleading public relations activity and deliberatively deceptive sponsorships, generally run not by real public relations professionals but rather by partisan operatives who usurp the tools of the profession.

Sometimes, however, the source of unethical practice is found within the profession itself. Here are a few more instances of public relations ethically run amok.

Hill and Knowlton public relations firm created Citizens for a Free Kuwait as a front group to promote U.S. involvement in the first Persian Gulf war. Similarly, Burson-Marsteller agency created the National Smokers Alliance pretending to be grassroots support for smokers' rights.

The Edelman agency admitted its error and accepted "100 percent responsibility" for misleading practice after the agency hired two bloggers to comment positively about happy Walmart employees during a cross-country tour it arranged for a client, Working Families for Walmart. The incident became one of the most notorious examples of a "flog" (fake blog).

Wikipedia reported that the Bell Pottinger public relations firm in London used fake accounts to make more than a thousand clandestine edits to the Wikipedia pages of their clients. Days later, journalists reported that the agency offered to create fake blogs for a would-be client.

What's Next?

This concludes Step 1 of the planning process for strategic communication. Now that you have a good foundation on the situation facing an organization, next it's time to look at the organization itself.

PLANNING EXAMPLE 1 **Analyzing the Situation**

UPSTATE COLLEGE

Because it has received permission to expand from a two-year to a four-year program, Upstate College wants to develop a strategic communication plan to deal with student enrollment and retention, financial contributions, and community support.

Situational research will focus on academic and applied articles on enrollment management, fundraising, and community support for higher education. Special attention will be given to lessons to be learned from other institutions that expanded into four-year programs within the last six years.

TINY
TYKES
TOYS

In the wake of the highly publicized recall of a defective crib toy, Tiny Tykes Toys needs a strategic communication plan focusing on consumer confidence and the eventual expansion of its customer base.

Research will identify both academic and applied articles dealing with product recalls, particularly those dealing with products affecting safety of children. The research will develop case studies of actual organizations that have faced product recalls, with particular attention to those that successfully emerged from the recall phase with a strong customer base.

☑ *Checklist 1* **The Public Relations Situation**

To participate in this exercise, use a class or group project assigned by your instructor, or select an organization that has both your personal interest and of which you have some firsthand knowledge. For example, you might select your current business, nonprofit organization, or client; a volunteer project; or an enterprise in which you were once involved. If you are a student, you might select an issue related to the college or university you attend.

Start with the basic planning questions. Careful consideration of these may satisfy your informational needs. You also may find it useful to address the more complete set of expanded planning questions. Use this checklist to the extent that the items can help you get a better understanding of the situation facing your organization. If some of these questions don't seem to address your specific planning needs, skip over them.

Basic Questions

1. What is the central issue of the situation facing the organization?
2. What is the background of the situation?
3. What is the significance or importance of the situation?

Expanded Questions

A. EXISTING INFORMATION

Answer the following questions based on what you know directly or what you can learn from your client or from colleagues within your organization.

Background on the Issue

1. Is this the first time your organization has dealt with this situation, or are you setting out to modify an existing communication program?
   - If the latter, is this a minor modification or a major one?
2. What is the cause of this situation?
3. Is there any dispute that this is the cause?
4. What is the history of this situation?
5. What are the important facts related to this situation?
6. Does this situation involve the organization's relationship with another group?
   - If yes, what group(s)?

Consequences of the Situation

1. How important is this situation to the organization's mission?
2. How consistent is this situation with the mission statement or vision statement?
3. How serious a response is warranted to this situation?
4. What is the likely duration of this situation: one time, limited/short term, or ongoing/ long term?
5. Who or what is affected by this situation?
6. What predictions or trends are associated with this situation? (These can be organizational, industry-related, community relations, nation-related, etc.)
7. What potential impact can this situation make on the organization's mission or bottom line?
8. Do you consider this situation to be an opportunity (positive) or an obstacle (negative) for your organization? Why? If you consider this an obstacle, how might you turn it into an opportunity?

Resolution of the Situation

1. Might information (quality or quantity) affect how this situation is resolved?
2. How can this situation be resolved to the mutual benefit of everyone involved?
3. What priority does this situation hold for the public relations/communications staff and for the organization's top management?
4. How strong is the organization's commitment to resolving this situation?

Best Practices

1. What topics, themes, or keywords can you research to learn more about the situation being addressed?
2. What do you learn about this situation from a literature review of scholarly and/or professional publications?
3. What organizations have faced a similar situation and resolved it successfully?
4. What organizations have faced a similar situation and failed to resolve it successfully?
5. What lessons can be learned from such cases?

B. RESEARCH PROGRAM

If there are any significant gaps in the existing information, you may have to conduct research to learn more about the issue. This section will guide you through consideration of that option.

What is the basis for the existing information noted above: previous formal research, informal or anecdotal feedback, organizational experience, personal observation, presumption/supposition by planner(s) and/or something else?

1. How accurate is this existing information?
2. How appropriate is it to conduct additional research?
3. What information remains to be obtained?
4. If the existing information is not highly reliable, consider additional research, such as the following:
    - Interviews with key people within the organization
    - Review of organizational literature/information
    - Additional personal observation
    - Interviews with external experts or opinion leaders
    - Surveys with representative publics
5. What research methods will you use to obtain the needed information?

C. RESEARCH FINDINGS

After you have conducted formal research, indicate here your findings as they shed light on the issue facing your organization, and write a brief summary of the issue facing your organization.

CONSENSUS CHECK

Does agreement exist within your organization and your planning team about the observations and findings about the public relations situation?

☐ Yes. Proceed to Step 2, Analyzing the Organization.

☐ No. Consider the value and/or possibility of achieving consensus before proceeding.

Analyzing
the Organization

The basis of effective communication is self-awareness. Before a successful strategic communication plan can be created, strategists must have a thorough and factual understanding of their organization: its performance, its reputation, and its structure. They must also seek to understand any factors that might limit the plan's success.

Analyzing the organization begins with a clear focus on what the organization is, does, and aspires to be. In broad categories, all organizations are either businesses or nonprofits. But within each of these categories are some important distinctions.

Businesses are for-profit commercial organizations of various types. Some are small enterprises, others have millions of employees. Some businesses have local, regional, or national bases; others are multinational corporations, also called transnational or global corporations. Within these fields are businesses that can be further classified as green, women-owned, minority-owned, start-up, home-based, and online.

Noncommercial enterprises, sometimes called social benefit organizations, fit roughly into several groupings: nonprofit organizations (hospitals, museums, charities, and so on) that provide services and social enrichment; government (agencies, military units, and public schools) that often involve regulatory oversight; membership associations (unions, consumer-interest groups); and nongovernmental organizations (NGOs) that focus their activities on advocacy and social change. Sometimes such groups are defined by their focus: environmental, political, charitable, religious, cultural, service, and so on. Like corporations, nonprofit groups may be community-based, national, or international.

Regardless of the answer, it is important that any public relations plan raises the questions: What kind of organization are we? What kind of organization do we want to be? What kind of organization do people think we are?

Often the response to that question is found in the organization's mission statement, a brief strategic description of the purpose of a company or nonprofit organization, indicating its major publics and guiding its decisions. The mission statement focuses on the organization's present circumstances.

A vision statement, meanwhile, looks to the future. It is a brief strategic description of what the organization aspires to become. A vision statement serves as a starting point for positioning, which is part of Step 4 of the strategic planning process.

Some organizations also articulate a values statement, which is a set of beliefs that drive the organization and provide a framework for its decisions. A values statement generally has a significant ethical dimension.

The second step of the strategic planning process involves a **public relations audit**, an analysis of the strengths and weaknesses of your organization or client. Writing in *Public Relations Tactics*, Rebecca Hart (2006) of the strategic communications/research firm of Hart and Partners, advises that an audit should be performed prior to developing an important new campaign, before rolling out a new product or service or after management changes within an organization. On the company website (hartandpartners.com), she further suggests that audits should be conducted every five to seven years, as well as following a crisis situation.

Hart also notes the value of audits for individual public relations practitioners:

First, you will gain a better understanding of how communications fits into your organization's big picture and how you can help the organization succeed. Senior managers will appreciate your numbers-oriented approach to communications and will be more likely to turn to you for advice on measuring results in the future. Finally, you'll have demonstrated strategic thinking, initiative and business-savvy through your interactions with upper management, which will give you increased credibility for future situations.
(Hart, 2006, p. 9)

A traditional method drawn from marketing is called a **SWOT analysis** because it considers the organization's strengths, weaknesses, opportunities, and threats. Typically, a SWOT analysis would consider both internal factors and external forces when focusing on each element. The analysis should not allow an illusion that the organization itself is strong but that all weaknesses come from outside.

Recall the information in the previous chapter from the Institute for Crisis Management, which found that corporate and organizational crises usually begin on the inside, most of them because of mismanagement. An effective SWOT analysis can identify potential problems before they occur.

What follows here is a more elaborate analysis focusing on three aspects of the organization: internal environment, public perception, and external environment. Exhibit 2.1 shows the relationship among the various elements of a public relations audit.

Before moving on to the details of the analysis, it's important to note that candor is the key to this step. To create an effective communication program, it is necessary to take an honest look at your organization, identifying its weaknesses and limitations as well as its strengths. If your organization is second best, admit it and proceed from that basis. Don't delude yourself by pretending that your organization is something that it's not.

No successful public relations program has ever been built on fiction, and it doesn't serve your purpose to overlook flaws or shortcomings within your organization. However, temper your candor with tact. Brutal or indiscriminate honesty may turn off a client or a boss.

Internal Environment

Because public relations involves more than words, begin the audit by looking at the organization's performance and structure, and any internal impediments to success. Here is an overview of each.

MISSION, VISION, AND VALUES STATEMENTS

Examples of Mission Statements

Aflac: To combine aggressive strategic marketing with quality products and services at competitive prices to provide the best insurance value for consumers.

Bristol-Myers Squibb: To discover, develop and deliver innovative medicines that help patients prevail over serious diseases.

Dow Chemical: To constantly improve what is essential to human progress by mastering science and technology.

Ford: We are a global family with a proud heritage passionately committed to providing personal mobility for people around the world.

Google: Google's mission is to organize the world's information and make it universally accessible and useful.

Nike: To bring inspiration and innovation to every athlete* in the world. (*If you have a body, you are an athlete.)

Examples of Vision Statements

Amazon: Our vision is to be earth's most customer-centric company; to build a place where people can come to find and discover anything they might want to buy online.

Avon: To be the company that best understands and satisfies the product, service and self-fulfillment needs of women—globally.

Disney: To make people happy.

HSBC: To be the world's local bank.

Toys 'R' Us: Our vision is to put joy in kids' hearts and a smile on parents' faces.

Examples of Value Statements

Coca-Cola: Our values serve as a compass for our actions and describe how we behave in the world. Leadership: the courage to shape a better future. Collaboration: Leverage collective genius. Integrity: Be real. Accountability: If it is to be, it's up to me. Passion: Committed in heart and mind. Diversity: As inclusive as our brands. Quality: What we do, we do well.

Marriott: Our core values make us who we are. As we change and grow, the beliefs that are most important to us stay the same—putting people first, pursuing excellence, embracing change, acting with integrity, and serving our world. Being part of Marriott International means being part of a proud history and a thriving culture.

Microsoft: As a company, and as individuals, we value integrity, honesty, openness, personal excellence, constructive self-criticism, continual self-improvement and mutual respect. We are committed to our customers and partners, and have a passion for technology. We take on big challenges and pride ourselves on seeing them through. We hold ourselves accountable to our customers, shareholders, partners and employees by honoring our commitments, providing results and striving for the highest quality.

Phase One

STEP 2

EXHIBIT 2.1 The Public Relations Audit

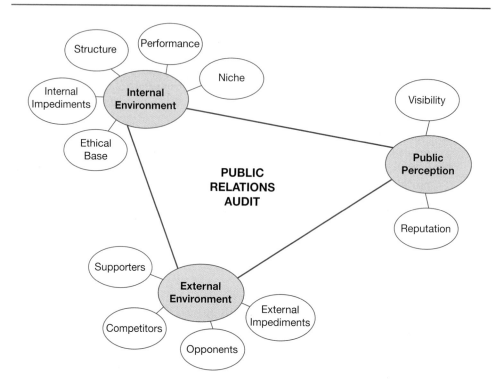

PERFORMANCE

The most important aspect of the internal environment is **performance**. This involves the quality of the goods and services provided by the organization as well as the viability of the causes and ideas it espouses. The audit looks at this quality both as it is now and as it was in the past. It also considers the level of satisfaction that the organizational leadership has with this quality. Review the discussion of benchmarking in Step 1, since one of the purposes of benchmarking is to help an organization improve its performance by reviewing related cases that were successful.

NICHE

Within the topic of performance, the internal audit also looks at the organization's **niche**. This is its specialty, the function or role that makes it different from other organizations.

The word "niche" refers to a wall recess or alcove for displaying a vase of flowers, a statue, or some other accent piece. In the context of public relations and marketing, a niche retains some of that original notion. It is a viewing point, the nook that an organization occupies in a position for all to see.

STRUCTURE

The audit considers the **structure** of the public relations operation within the organization. Specifically, it reviews the purpose or mission of the organization as it relates to the situation at hand, as well as the role public relations plays within the organization's administration.

One particularly important consideration is whether public relations sits at the management table as part of the organization's decision-making process or whether it merely receives orders after the decisions are made by others.

The audit also inventories organizational resources that can be marshaled for the communication program, such as personnel, equipment, time, and budgets. No decisions or commitments are being made at this point as to what resources to use. During the audit stage, you merely are identifying the organization's available resources as they relate to the situation to be addressed.

ETHICAL BASE

Public relations has been called the conscience of an organization, serving as its **ethical base** and moral grounding. In analyzing the internal environment of an organization, give thought to this ethical base. Consider whether the organization has a stated ethical ideal, and note if such an ideal is structural to the organization or personal to certain individuals. Is an ethical perspective based on how the organization sees itself, or is it merely the concern of an individual currently on the scene? If structural, the ethical base is likely to continue beyond the personal tenure of any individual manager or executive.

INTERNAL IMPEDIMENTS

The final part of this internal audit is a look at **internal impediments**. Here you consider any impediments or obstacles within the organization that might limit the effectiveness of the public relations program. For example, many practitioners have expressed that their college education did not prepare them for the lack of organizational support, the need for continuing vigilance, and the amount of personal intrigue and political infighting that goes on within some organizations. Wounded egos, shortsighted executives, company favorites, and other barriers must be considered as you develop the program.

The term "impediment" is chosen with care. An impediment is not an insurmountable barrier, such as a road blocked off for repaving. Rather, it is a hindrance, more like a slow-moving truck on a country road. You can allow the truck to set the pace and remain behind it, or you can carefully and safely pass the truck and continue on your way. Or you can take another road.

Public Perception

The second focus for a public relations audit is public perception. What people think about the organization is the key focus for the public relations audit. This perception is based on both visibility and reputation.

VISIBILITY

The extent to which an organization is known is its **visibility**. More subtly, this includes whether people know about an organization, what they know about it, and how accurate this information is. Public relations practitioners can do a great deal to affect the visibility of their organization or client.

REPUTATION

Flowing from an organization's visibility is its **reputation**, which deals with how people evaluate the information they have. It is the general, overall, and long-term impression that people have of an organization. Reputation is based on both word and deed—that is, on the verbal, visual, and behavioral messages, both planned and unplanned, that come from an organization.

Reputation is part of the social capital of an organization, arguably its most important public relations asset. Though we speak of reputation as a single perception, that may be too limiting. An organization's reputation can be inconsistent, varying from one public to another and from one time to another. Reputation generally lags behind an organization's conscious attempt to affect the way people perceive it. (For a fuller discussion of reputation, see the author's website: ron-smith.com.)

Promoting Perception

Generally, the stronger the organization's visibility and the more positive its reputation, the greater the ability it has to build on this positive base. On the other hand, low visibility suggests the need to create more awareness, and a poor reputation calls for efforts to reform the organization and/or to rehabilitate its public perception. First, make sure the organization is offering quality performance. Then, try to bring awareness into harmony with that performance.

Writing in *CW/Communication World Magazine*, Pamela Klein (1999) notes that psychologically, a company with a solid reputation earns the benefit of the doubt in times of crisis. Supporting her claim, she points to an Ernst and Young study, Measures That Matter, which found that 40 percent of a company's market value is based on nonfinancial assets, including reputation. Klein also cites a Burson–Marsteller study, Maximizing Corporate Reputations, reporting that a CEO's reputation accounts for 40 percent of how a company is viewed by stakeholders and other publics.

A 2006 survey of health-care executives in collaboration with the Public Relations Society of America's Health Academy showed that 64 percent of CEOs rate reputation as critical or very important to their organization's success. Two-thirds (66 percent) say a positive shift in reputation can significantly or dramatically impact the bottom line, while 86 percent said a negative shift would hurt the organization. All self-reported that their corporations have good or excellent reputations. Aside from perhaps a bit of self-deception or wishful thinking about their own reputations, the CEOs clearly see the importance of a good reputation as a real business asset.

This chapter's strategic planning checklist on analyzing public perception contains an Image Index, a tool developed to help determine the public perception of an organization. The index is a series of contrasting characteristics or attributes—fun or tedious, expensive or inexpensive, risky or safe—that can be applied to any organization. Obviously there is no right or wrong response to any of these characteristics, and the index does not lead to a numerical answer. Rather, it is meant to stimulate your insight.

By considering your organization in relation to these terms, you may come to a conclusion that perhaps you didn't have before. In the planning process, you can use the index twice, first based on what the organization thinks of itself and later based on what its publics think of it.

The related concepts of visibility and reputation play a significant role in crisis communication. Appendix E, Media Engagement is rooted in the premise that, particularly in crisis situations when an organization's visibility is high, an important public relations objective should be to focus on reputation.

SOURCES OF INFORMATION FOR A PUBLIC RELATIONS AUDIT

You can get information for a public relations audit from several different sources. Consider the following steps in gathering the information you will need.

1. See if past research has addressed some of the relevant issues and obtain that information.
2. Check the public information about your organization, such as your annual reports, past news releases, and files of published stories about your organization.
3. Ask people close to your organization if they can provide some of the necessary information from their own experience. Talk with managers and long-time employees. Talk especially with your front-line staff, such as clerks and sales representatives, and with the key service providers, such as nurses in a hospital or teachers in a school. Ask all of these sources what customers and other people outside the organization are asking and saying.
4. Conduct your own research, beginning with free or low-cost technology for online polling. SurveyMonkey, Qualtrics, Zoomerang, SurveyGizmo, and Google Forms are probably the best known, but dozens of companies offer similar products.
5. Check out your organization with an Internet search engine. In particular, see what bloggers may be saying about you and what others are posting on social media.

If additional information still is needed, conduct more research. Begin by broadening your resources for informal research. Eventually you may find that you require more formal research techniques. (See Appendix A, Applied Research for more information on secondary and primary research.)

External Environment

The analysis of the organization concludes with an examination of its external environment. In particular, this analysis looks at supporters, competitors, opponents, and other external impediments. Here is an overview of each.

SUPPORTERS

Every organization has **supporters**, the people and groups who currently or at least potentially are likely to help the organization achieve its objectives. Identify groups that share similar interests and values.

COMPETITORS

Likewise, most organizations have **competitors**, people or groups doing the same thing as you in the same arena. In a highly competitive environment, public relations activities often include messages and communication tactics to highlight differences with competitors, while lower levels of competition may lend themselves less to advocacy and more to relationship building. An organization's environment also may be uneven; it may be competitive with one public while cooperative with another.

Additionally, the mere fact that an organization is doing essentially the same thing as yours does not make it an opponent. Proximity is important. For example, a candidate for mayor in Seattle may have several competitors, but the candidate for mayor in Baltimore is not one of them.

Indeed, organizations doing similar things in different areas might better be considered as colleagues and, as such, valuable resources for sharing information and perhaps assistance.

OPPONENTS

Another important aspect of the external analysis is to consider the nature of any rivalry that may exist. **Opponents** are groups or people who are against an organization, perhaps because of something it says or does, perhaps because of its very existence. They have the potential to damage the organization by limiting its ability to pursue its mission and achieve its goals.

Note that there can be a big difference between a competitor, who provides a similar product or service, and an opponent, who is fighting your organization. Consider a store selling fur coats: a competitor might be the other fur store across town, while an opponent might be an animal-rights group. The other store just wants to sell its products, while the activists want to see you go out of business.

Even opponents come in different shapes and sizes, and planners have some important questions to ask about the nature of opposition. In some situations—political campaigns come to mind—opponents are competitors. Opposing candidates, along with their political organizations and supporters, have a primary strategy of besting the opposition candidates.

Consider the various types of opponents and the potential impact of communication when you are analyzing this aspect of your external environment.

- One type of opponent, an **advocate**, may oppose you because they support something else, and you appear to stand in the way of their goal. Their tactics are mainly vocal. Through public communication, you may be able to find common ground for discussion and perhaps even the creation of an alliance between your organization and the advocates.

- A **dissident** is another type of opponent, one that may oppose you primarily because of the position you hold or the actions you have undertaken. Their opposition is not irrational, and communication that addresses their interests and concerns might soften their opposition.

- A dissident on a global scale is called an **anti**. Antis are people or groups who seem to oppose everything. Often such opposition is generic toward any kind of change or toward any established institution, so public communication probably would have little impact on them unless it were able to show that the presumed change is only an illusion. Realize that the antis are suspicious of your organization in the first place, so they probably won't trust your messages.

- Similar to an advocate, an **activist** seeks change. But the activist has a range of tactics beyond discussion. For activists, opposition to your organization may be a by-product of their goal. Communication might reveal and promote a common basis for at least limited cooperation. Realize that activists, by definition, seek something specific and tangible, so talk alone won't move them.

- A **missionary** is a self-righteous activist in support of a cause, often operating under the presumption of moral imperative. Communication would have only limited potential for moderating the opposition of missionaries, though it could help the organization avoid being an obvious target.

- One type of opponent is particularly difficult to deal with. A **zealot** is a single-issue activist with a missionary fervor, so public communication is unlikely to coax zealots out of their opposition. These are the folks willing to engage in civil disobedience and risk jail to advance their cause.

- Another type of opponent is outright dangerous. A **fanatic** is a zealot without the social stabilizers. These are the suicide bombers and terrorist snipers ready to go to any lengths in their opposition. Because of their willingness to undertake a no-holds-barred fight and to both inflict and suffer personal injury, public communication can have little impact on them, though it may impact the less fanatical supporters in the cause.

EXTERNAL IMPEDIMENTS

Additionally, consider any **external impediments** such as social, political, or economic factors outside an organization that might limit the effectiveness of a public relations program.

What's Next?

This concludes Step 2 of the planning process for strategic communication. You now should have information and insight into your organization's strengths and limitations, providing a strong foundation on which to build. Next you will focus attention on the various publics of the organization.

PLANNING EXAMPLE 2 **Analyzing the Organization**

Here is the analysis for Upstate College.

Internal Environment

Upstate College is a private liberal-arts college with 2,000 students, primarily commuters and residents from within a 100-mile radius. Most of the students had average grades in high school. They selected Upstate because of its reputation for small classes, reasonable tuition, and practical programs. In the past, about half the graduates went into the workforce and half transferred to four-year colleges and universities.

The college has a news bureau and marketing office with a one-person staff assisted by freelancers and alumni volunteers. The office has a range of digital equipment for self-publishing, and the college publishes a weekly student newspaper and a quarterly alumni newsletter. It oversees a website and has recently ventured into a social media presence. It has only a token advertising budget.

Public Perception

Upstate College sees its reputation as being beneficial, relatively inexpensive, practical, and an essential ingredient within the educational mix of this part of the state.

Phase One

STEP
2

External Environment

Higher education in this area has been a relatively noncompetitive environment until recent years, when fewer students, less funding, and more alternatives for students have combined to create a climate that is somewhat competitive, though not unfriendly. Competition includes a private four-year college with very high entrance standards and even higher tuition, a large state university with entrance standards similar to Upstate's at about half the tuition, and a community college with only token costs, minimal entrance requirements, and a background (and continuing reputation) as a trade school.

Upstate City recently has lost several major employers, and weakening family finances have begun to affect the ability of some Upstate College students to remain full-time students. Research reveals declining numbers of students in most area high schools, indicating a shrinking pool of traditional-age candidates for college. Additionally, general research reveals growing educational opportunities for web-based distance learning available through non-local schools.

TINY TYKES TOYS

Here is the analysis for Tiny Tykes Toys.

Internal Environment

Tiny Tykes Toys manufactures toys for infants and toddlers. It recently voluntarily recalled one of its crib toys, a plush animal doll with a shiny nose. When babies chewed on the nose, it secreted an indelible green dye into their mouths and on their faces that lasted for several weeks. The dye was harmless, but the consumer lawsuits (minor) and resulting publicity (major and sensationalized) have caused a decrease in sales of other Tiny Tykes toys.

The company has 130 union workers and 27 management staff. It also has a two-person public relations/marketing staff. Unrelated to the recall, but happening around the same time, a small but vocal group of employees began agitating for increased pay and shorter working hours.

Public Perception

The recall endangered the company's reputation for quality among stockholders, consumers, pediatricians, and other interest groups. The defect has been eliminated in new versions of the toy. The company perceives its image as fun, low-tech, inexpensive, beneficial, and safe.

External Environment

The business environment for children's toys is highly competitive, and it has become more so due to increasing international rivals and the expansion into the toy market of domestic companies once associated primarily with children's clothing. Tiny Tykes has several competitors, some of them nationally known companies with huge promotional budgets. Several of these companies have products of similar quality and cost to Tiny Tykes; they currently enjoy a more favorable reputation because of the recall.

The overall business environment for toys is a growing and highly competitive market. The dissident employee faction has the potential for contributing to a wider consumer backlash against the company.

☑ *Checklist 2A* **Internal Environment**

Basic Questions

1. What is the quality of your organization's performance?
2. What communication resources, including budget, are available?
3. How supportive is the organization of public relations activity?

Expanded Questions

A. EXISTING INFORMATION

Answer the following questions based on what you know directly or what you can learn from your client or colleagues within your organization.

Performance

1. What service/product do you provide related to the situation identified in the Strategic Planning Exercise in Step 1?
2. What are the criteria for determining its quality?
3. What actually is its quality?
4. Within the last three years, has the quality improved, remained unchanged, or deteriorated?
5. How satisfied is organizational leadership with this quality?
6. What benefit or advantage does the product/service offer?
7. What problems or disadvantages are associated with this product/service?
8. What is the niche or specialty that sets you apart from competitors?
9. How has the service/product changed within the last three years?
10. How is the service/product likely to change within the next two years?
11. Should changes be introduced to improve the service/product?
12. Are organizational leaders willing to make such changes?

Structure

1. What is the purpose/mission of your organization related to this issue?
2. How does this issue fit into the organizational vision?
3. Is this expressed in a strategic business plan for your organization?
4. What communication resources are available for potential public relations/marketing communication activity: personnel, equipment, time, money, and/or something else?
5. Within the next three years, are these resources likely to increase, remain unchanged, or decrease?
6. How strong is the public relations/communication staff's role in the organization's decision-making process?

Internal Impediments

1. How supportive is the internal environment for public relations activities?
2. Are there any impediments or obstacles to success that come from within your organization:

    <u>Among top management?</u>
    *   Are these impediments caused by policy/procedure?
    *   Are these impediments deliberate?

    <u>Among public relations/marketing staff?</u>
    *   Are these impediments caused by policy/procedure?
    *   Are these impediments deliberate?

    <u>Among other internal publics?</u>
    *   Are these impediments caused by policy/procedure?
    *   Are these impediments deliberate?

3. If you have identified impediments, how can you overcome them?

B. RESEARCH PROGRAM

If there are any significant gaps in the existing information, you may have to conduct research to learn more about the internal environment. This section will guide you through consideration of that option.

1. What is the basis for the existing information noted above: previous formal research, informal or anecdotal feedback, organizational experience, personal observation, presumption/supposition by planner(s), and/or something else?
2. How accurate is this existing information?
3. How appropriate would it be to conduct additional research?
4. What information remains to be obtained?
5. If the existing information is not highly reliable, consider additional research, such as the following:

    *   Interviews with key people within the organization
    *   Review of organizational literature/information
    *   Additional personal observation
    *   Interviews with external experts or opinion leaders
    *   Surveys with representative publics

6. What research methods will you use to obtain the needed information?

C. RESEARCH FINDINGS

After you have conducted formal research, indicate your findings as they shed light on the internal environment of your organization and write a brief summary of the internal environment.

☑ Checklist 2B **Public Perception**

Basic Questions

1. How well known is your organization?
2. What is the reputation of your organization?
3. How do you want to affect this reputation?

Expanded Questions

A. EXISTING INFORMATION

Answer the following questions based on what you know directly or what you can learn from your client or colleagues within your organization.

Reputation

1. How visible is your service/product?
2. How widely used is your service/product?
3. How is the product/service generally perceived?
4. How is your organization generally perceived?
5. Is the public perception about your organization correct?
6. What communication already has been done about this situation?
7. Within the last three years, has your organization's reputation improved, remained unchanged, or deteriorated?
8. How satisfied is organizational leadership with this reputation?

Image Index

Place an "X" at the appropriate location on the continuum of what this key public thinks of your organization's product(s) or service(s):

Contemporary	_ _ _ _ _	Traditional
Fun	_ _ _ _ _	Tedious
High-Tech	_ _ _ _ _	Low-Tech
Ordinary	_ _ _ _ _	Distinguished
Expensive	_ _ _ _ _	Inexpensive
Idealistic	_ _ _ _ _	Practical
Modest	_ _ _ _ _	Pretentious
Scarce	_ _ _ _ _	Abundant
Worthless	_ _ _ _ _	Beneficial
Efficient	_ _ _ _ _	Inefficient
Ordinary	_ _ _ _ _	Innovative
Essential	_ _ _ _ _	Luxury
Risky	_ _ _ _ _	Safe
High-Quality	_ _ _ _ _	Low-Quality

Phase One

STEP
2

B. RESEARCH PROGRAM

If there are any significant gaps in the existing information, you may have to conduct research to learn more about the public perception of your organization. This section will guide you through consideration of that option.

1. What is the basis for the existing information noted above: previous formal research, informal or anecdotal feedback, organizational experience, personal observation, presumption/supposition by planner(s), and/or something else?
2. How reliable is this existing information?
3. How appropriate would it be to conduct additional research?
4. If the existing information is not highly reliable, consider additional research, such as the following:

    - Interviews with key people within the organization
    - Review of organizational literature/information
    - Additional personal observation
    - Interviews with external experts or opinion leaders
    - Surveys with representative publics

C. RESEARCH FINDINGS

After you have conducted formal research, indicate your findings as they shed light on the public perception of your organization and write a brief summary of the public perception.

 Checklist 2C **External Environment**

Basic Questions

1. What is the major competition for your organization?
2. What significant opposition exists?
3. Is anything happening in the environment that can impact the effectiveness of the public relations program?

Expanded Questions

A. EXISTING INFORMATION

Answer the following questions based on what you know directly or what you can learn from your client or colleagues within your organization.

Competition

1. How competitive is the external environment of your organization?
2. What other organizations compete on this issue?

3. What are their performance levels?
4. What are their reputations?
5. What are their resources?
6. What does the competition offer that you don't?
7. How has the competition changed within the last three years?
8. Within the next three years, is the competition likely to increase, remain unchanged, or decrease?

Opposition

1. What groups exist with a mission to resist or hinder your organization?
2. How effective have these groups been in the past?
3. What is their reputation?
4. What are their resources?
5. How have these groups changed within the last three years?
6. How have their tactics changed?
7. Within the next three years, is the opposition likely to increase, remain unchanged, or decrease?

External Impediments

1. Is the environment in which you are operating currently growing, stable, declining, or unpredictable?
2. What changes, if any, are projected for this environment?
3. What impediments deal with customers?
4. What impediments deal with regulators?
5. What impediments have financial or economic origins?
6. What impediments have political origins?
7. What impediments originate in society at large?

B. RESEARCH PROGRAM

If there are any significant gaps in the existing information, you may have to conduct research to learn more about the external environment of your organization. This section will guide you through consideration of that option.

1. What is the basis for the existing information noted above: previous formal research, informal or anecdotal feedback, organizational experience, personal observation, presumption/supposition by planner(s), and/or something else?
2. How reliable is this existing information?
3. How appropriate would it be to conduct additional research?
4. What information remains to be obtained?
5. If the existing information is not highly reliable, consider additional research, such as the following:

    *   Review of organizational literature/information
    *   Review of other published information (books, periodicals, etc.)
    *   Review of electronic information (Internet, CD-ROMs, etc.)
    *   Interviews with key people within the organization

Phase One

STEP
2

- Interviews with external experts or opinion leaders
- Focus groups with representative publics
- Surveys with representative publics
- Content analysis of materials

6. What research methods will you use to obtain the needed information?

C. RESEARCH FINDINGS

After you have conducted formal research, indicate your findings as they shed light on the external environment of your organization and write a brief summary of the external environment.

CONSENSUS CHECK

Does agreement exist within your organization and your planning team about the observations and findings about the public relations situation?

☐ Yes. Proceed to Step 3, Analyzing the Publics.

☐ No. Consider the value and/or possibility of achieving consensus before proceeding.

STEP 3

Analyzing the Publics

T he planner's ability to identify and analyze publics is the cornerstone of an effective integrated communication campaign. Both elements of this step—identification and analysis—are equally important. First, we need to address the right group of people, so as not to squander organizational resources or miss opportunities to interact with important publics. Second, we must carefully examine each public in order to develop a strategy to communicate effectively.

Public

What do we mean by the term "public"? One definition that still holds true is the classic definition given by social philosopher John Dewey in *The Public and Its Problems* (1927): A **public** is a group of people that shares a common interest vis-à-vis an organization, recognizes its significance and sets out to do something about it. Publics are homogeneous in that they are similar in their interests and characteristics. They usually are aware of the situation and their relationship with the organization. They think the issue is relevant, and they are at least potentially organized or energized to act on the issue.

Public, Market, Audience, Stakeholder

There are several different strategic groupings of people associated with an organization. The terms can be confusing, and sometimes they are used differently. Here's is an overview of these strategic groupings: publics, markets, audiences, and stakeholders:

PUBLIC

Publics exist because of their interaction and interdependency with an organization or because both they and the organization face a common issue. Don't confuse publics with other labels for groups of people who may interact with your organization. A public is like your family. You don't pick them; they just are—like generous Cousin Ezekiel and crazy Aunt Bertie. A public may be helpful or annoying, friendly or not, but an organization must deal with each regardless.

MARKET

A **market** (sometimes called a **market segment**) is more like your friends (real friends, not the Facebook kind). You pick them; they pick you. Most people select friends on the basis of shared interests and common values. Markets are particular types of publics, and organizations develop marketing efforts among those publics with whom they intend to conduct business or generate support and participation. As segments of a particular population, markets include people with characteristics (age, income, lifestyle, and so on) that can help the organization achieve its bottom line. For public relations purposes, **bottom line** is a term that identifies an organization's mission or fundamental goal (selling cars, educating students, serving patients, and so on). It has less to do with finance and more with organizational success on the broader scale.

AUDIENCE

Don't confuse publics with **audiences**, which are merely people who pay attention to a particular medium of communication and receive messages through it. Both public relations and marketing will deal with audiences. An organization's relationship with an audience is usually brief, such as the length of time it takes to read an article or listen to a speech—much more fleeting than its relationship with a public. Continuing the friends-and-family analogy, an audience is more like fellow passengers on the bus. They are not necessarily friends or family (although they could be), but they simply share a common conveyance.

STAKEHOLDER

A final category is a **stakeholder**, which some people identify as different from a public. The concept is that a stakeholder relates to an organization through its potential impact on the organization's mission and objectives, whereas a public relates to an organization through its messages (Rawlins, 2006). Others take the position that publics are people who don't necessarily care about an organization, whereas stakeholders are people who are conscious of a mutual relationship with an organization (Sandman, 2003). Still others use the term as a synonym for shareholder, someone with a vested interest in the organization and its well-being.

In unveiling its new definition of public relations, PRSA explained its preference for the term "publics," which relates to the very public and all-encompassing nature of the profession, whereas stakeholders are associated with publicly traded companies.

Because the concept of stakeholder is variously defined and inconsistently used, this text generally will use the term "publics" in referring to groups of people who have a mutual relationship with an organization.

Interrelationships

Let's consider the various ways of grouping people through the example of a presidential candidate.

The audience includes people using a particular medium, such as those who hear a speech live or watch a television commercial. Some members of these audiences may be part of one of the candidate's wider publics, such as registered party members. Other registered members may not be found within a particular media audience, though they remain part of an important public for the candidate. Additionally, other members of the audiences may be members of a different public, such as voters registered with the opposing political party.

Usually audiences are not homogeneous but more often are **aggregates**, mere assortments of individuals with perhaps nothing in common other than their use of a particular communication medium. However, the more specialized the communication medium is, the more likely its audiences are to have in common both demographic characteristics (such as age and income) and psychographic characteristics (such as lifestyles and values). So the audiences of very specialized media may coincide with your public.

Audiences as such are relatively unimportant to your planning for strategic communication. Most organizations want to develop mutually beneficial relationships with their various

GENERATION Y AS A PUBLIC

The so-called Generation Y (teens to 30-somethings born roughly between 1980 and 2000) is of interest from both public relations and marketing perspectives. Consider the following facts and observations about Gen Y-ers. Linda P. Morton (2002b) has drawn some of this information from a variety of sources for her series on segmenting publics for *Public Relations Quarterly*.

Generation Y is the largest teen/young adult population in recent American history. At 60 or 65 million, this group is larger than the celebrated Generation X (about 50 million people born in the 1960s and 1970s). It is the largest cohort group since the 75 million baby boomers born in the 1940s and 1950s.

Gen Y-ers' values and attitudes have been shaped by such formative public events as the 1999 shootings at Columbine High School in Littleton, Colorado; the contested 2000 election and extreme partisan politics ever since; the September 2001 terrorist attacks on the U.S. and the resultant accusations of government secrecy, torture, and violation of human rights; the subsequent U.S. wars in Afghanistan and Iraq, as well as the international distrust associated with them; and topping off with the elections of Barack Obama and Donald Trump and extreme partisan political divisions.

More than one in three U.S. teens are not white, the largest percentage ever. Additionally, teens and young adults today have greater experience than previous generations with nontraditional family structures, which has fostered an appreciation for diversity, equality, and tolerance. A concern for privacy and a distrust of both government and mass media also are characteristics of this generation.

Meanwhile, teens have more money to spend than in previous years. They are brand conscious but not necessarily brand loyal. Huge image campaigns mean little when brands simply go out of style. Teens don't like a hard sell, but they trust each other and respond to word-of-mouth endorsements. Celebrity endorsements, not so much. For example, Nike may be losing its grip on Gen Y-ers, who don't find it particularly persuasive that a 50-year-old former athlete (basketball, was it?) named Michael Jordan endorses the brand.

Gen Y people don't read newspapers often. They do listen to a lot of radio, but only to a narrow range of stations. They are more likely to listen to individually tailored music sources such as an iPod or their own Pandora stations. They watch TV and have access to an average of 62 channels.

They use the Internet a lot, but don't necessarily visit websites of even the organizations and brands that they like, and they don't necessarily purchase products or services associated with their favorite websites. And the high-speed action of the Internet also means that trends and fashions can change overnight.

Does this sound like anybody you know?

publics, for example, a company that hopes to create satisfactory business relationships with its customers. Strategic communicators try to understand their publics and markets to identify the media through which to reach those publics.

Much overlap exists among publics, markets, audiences, and stakeholders. While differences among these are important, sometimes it is their similarities that shed more light.

Characteristics of Publics

When you begin to identify publics, how do you know what to look for? Here are five important characteristics of a public: distinguishable, homogeneous, important, large enough, and accessible.

DISTINGUISHABLE

A public is a recognizable grouping of individuals, though not necessarily a recognized organization or formal group. For example, a jewelry company might want to promote itself to everyone who wants to buy expensive jewelry. But that isn't a public, because it does not identify a particular group of people. Rather, the jeweler might identify its public as people with incomes above $50,000 who are marking life events such as birthdays, anniversaries, graduations, and so on.

HOMOGENEOUS

A public's members share common traits and features. They may not know each other, but they have enough in common for you to treat them as a group. For example, all college professors who teach criminal justice courses do not know each other and may not even agree on specific issues within the discipline. But their collective interest in and knowledge of criminal justice warrant their identification as a public by an organization such as the National Association of Chiefs of Police. Consumer publics labeled as market segments traditionally have been identified by common traits, such as baby boomers, ethnics, seniors, Generation X-ers, and so on.

IMPORTANT

Not every identifiable group and certainly not every isolated individual is important to your organization's success. Some can prudently be overlooked or deferred. Strategists for public relations and marketing communication are most interested in those publics that can significantly impact on an organization's bottom line and affect its progress toward achieving its mission.

LARGE ENOUGH

Make sure your public is large enough to warrant strategic attention and the possible use of public media. The question sometimes comes up: How big does a group of people need to be in order to consider it a public? That's hard to answer definitively.

Don't confuse publics with the actors or relevant participants in the situation. If you are dealing with only a few people, they generally don't constitute a public, and your programming tactics would probably be limited to personal communication tools. For example, a company with five employees wouldn't need an employee newsletter; any information that needed to be shared could be done face-to-face or through personalized written information. Or the family of a motorist hurt in an accident with a company truck wouldn't be a public; it more likely would be a relevant player in what might be a wider public relations situation of the company's record on highway safety.

But good public relations suggests the need to consciously develop message strategies for interacting with these groups. With the employee scenario above, let's say the small company wants to train these employees toward a new plan for enhancing customer satisfaction. Should the owner unveil the program, or might that better come from the day-to-day manager? Or maybe from an expert from a local university or professional association? The next phase in this textbook offers information on messaging, credibility, and other strategic issues that might help you come to a decision on this point.

However, sometimes a small group will be treated as a public, and you may generate a sophisticated public relations effort toward such a small-but-important group. Your lobbying efforts may focus on only a handful of members of a senate committee, for example, but a public relations campaign might be directed toward them.

Objectives might deal with increasing their awareness of potential benefits and ultimately securing their vote, or perhaps simply minimizing the opposition that some senators might mount.

The campaign could include face-to-face lobbying meetings, engagement of their colleagues as potential intercessors, and encouragement of constituent letters and background information for their staffs, as well as print and electronic backgrounders, fact sheets, PowerPoint presentations, and such. The effort might also involve the news media, such as with issue coverage in the senators' home district, orchestration of editorials and columns, placement of guests on talk radio/TV and generation of letters to the editor—all in an effort to create a supportive environment for the organization's position, making it easier for the senators to vote in the organization's interests.

ACCESSIBLE

A public is a group with which you are able to interact and communicate. It must be accessible to your organization. For example, it is easy for a community college to reach potential students, because most are concentrated within a small geographic area, often in narrow demographics such as high school students or underemployed 20-somethings. It is more difficult for a university of world renown to reach potential students because they are thinly scattered throughout the world and have many and varied interests.

Categories of Publics

Good communication planning calls for the identification of an organization's various publics. As pointed out at the beginning of this section, there is no such thing as a general public. Rather, each public is linked with the organization in a unique relationship.

Over the years, sociologists studying organizations have developed the useful concept of **linkage**, which is the patterns of relationships that exist between an organization and its various publics (Grunig and Hunt, 1984). While various categories of linkages have been suggested, this book presents four useful categories of linkages: customers, producers, enablers, and limiters. If you consider these linkages, you are likely to identify each relevant public for your program. Exhibit 3.1 shows the relationship among the various public relations linkages.

Phase One

STEP 3

CUSTOMER

The most obvious type of public may be **customers**. These are the people who receive the products or services of an organization, such as current, potential or former consumers, as well as purchasers, clients, students, patients, fans, patrons, shoppers, parishioners, members, and so on.

This category also includes **secondary customers**. These are the customers of your customers, such as the companies and graduate schools to which a university's graduating seniors apply.

The category of customers also includes what has been called **shadow constituencies** (Mau and Dennis, 1994). These are people who may not have a direct link with the organization's products or services but who can affect the perception of an organization. For example, if hard times force a high-tech company known for its philanthropy to cut back on charitable contributions to the arts, members of the arts community (a shadow constituency) may vocally criticize the company, adding to its problems.

Consider this example of a charity seeking to raise funds for research into amyotrophic lateral sclerosis (ALS), Lou Gehrig's disease. An obvious public is people suffering from the fatal disease, but they are not likely to have the resources to support the organization financially. A better strategy might be to expand the range of publics to other groups: extended families

EXHIBIT 3.1 Categories of Publics

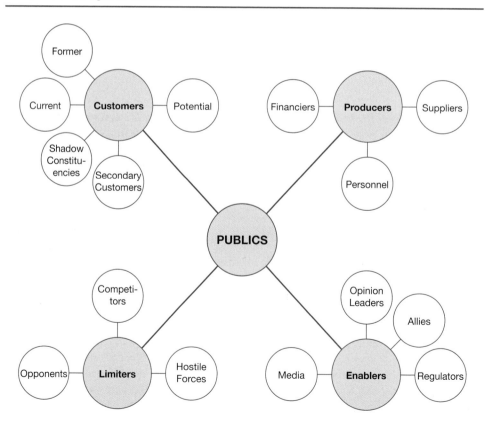

of ALS patients who look on with frustration as their loved ones become paralyzed and die; medical people who treat ALS patients; and the insurance companies responsible for many of the costs associated with treatment.

PRODUCER

Those publics that provide input to the organization are called **producers**. These include personnel such as employees, volunteers, and unions; producers of needed materials (such as vendors); and producers of the financial resources (such as investors, donors, and stockholders).

ENABLER

Another type of public are **enablers**, groups that serve as regulators by setting the norms or standards for the organization (such as professional associations or governmental agencies), opinion leaders with influence over potential customers (such as stockbrokers and analysts), and groups that otherwise help make the organization successful (such as the media). Another type of enabler involves allies with which the organization may be able to nurture parallel interests to work on cooperative projects.

LIMITER

Those publics that in some way reduce or undermine the success of an organization (such as competitors, opponents, and hostile forces) are known as **limiters**. The same activist groups that were cited above as potential enablers can become limiting publics when the organization is unable to walk in step with them. Likewise, an unfriendly blogger or television station can become a limiting public.

Alternative Typologies

The above four categories are not the only typology for identifying publics. Some practitioners distinguish between internal and external publics (often shorthand for producer and consumer publics). Another approach identifies primary, secondary, and marginal publics, which seems to be rather a listing in order of importance to the task at hand. Another categorization looks at current versus future publics. Still another identifies proponents, opponents, and uncommitted publics.

Some practitioners identify a category of special publics, groups usually outside the organization who are labeled according to age, race, ethnicity, gender, lifestyle, or some other dominant demographic criterion. In the typology of publics presented in this book, we look at each public in its relationship to the organization (customers, producers, enablers, and limiters). Thus, the concept of special publics has little practical value for a student or newcomer to the field of public relations and little to offer beyond the more comprehensive fourfold typology used here.

Additionally, some planners refer to primary publics as the key groups interacting with an organization, secondary publics as the intercessory groups who can influence the primary publics and tertiary publics as those special publics identified according to a relevant demographic.

Amid the confusing verbiage of different categorization styles, the aim remains the same: to identify all the possible publics interacting with an organization, and then to move on to analyzing their relationship(s) with the organization.

Phase One

STEP
3

Having identified major categories of publics, the next step is to look at each of them in more detail. By more narrowly identifying our publics we can understand them better.

For example, a university embarking on a recruiting campaign can't identify simply potential students as a public. That is too broad a category, because there are so many different kinds of potential students. Rather, it might classify its publics as high school students, junior college transfers, returning adult learners, employed people seeking retraining and professional development, underserved minorities, and perhaps even recreational learners. Each of these publics might have very different characteristics, and if the university is to be effective it must deal with each public individually.

We also want to eliminate from consideration groups that are not publics, having no present or impending relationship with an organization and thus no mutual consequences. For example, young people getting married and planning a honeymoon would not be a public for a travel agency specializing in senior-citizen bus tours. The best advice in dealing with groups that are not publics is *don't*. Don't waste time. Don't spend money. Don't try to communicate with people who have no reasonable or relevant relationship with your organization or no interest in your products or services.

Intercessory Public

In everyday situations, it is not uncommon to ask a friend to put in a good word with someone we want to impress. We do this to get dates, jobs, and good deals on stereos. This practice is often called **networking**. But the more appropriate term is **intercession**, which basically means using an influential go-between. Accordingly, an intercessor is a person who presents your case to another, someone who uses her influence to intercede on your behalf to obtain a favor, mediate a dispute, or to speak for you.

What's common in everyday life is also found in public relations activity. An organization often will address itself not only to its key publics but also to groups who already are in contact with that public. Such an **intercessory public** can serve as an influential bridge between an organization and its publics. In many planning situations, some of the publics listed as enablers can function as intercessory publics, because they already have the attention and respect of the ultimate public.

Take the news media, for example. In most public relations activities, the media are not the public you are finally trying to reach. Rather, they are a first point of contact, providing a means to reach another public, such as music lovers whom an opera company might identify as one of its key publics. In this case the media, particularly music critics, already have the attention of the music lovers, who presumably read and appreciate the reviews. So the public relations practitioner sets out to inform, interest, and impress the critic.

As another example, consider an organization providing job training to high school dropouts in an inner-city area. The organization might find through research that coaches in community centers and ministers in urban churches can serve as intercessory publics. These people share the organization's interest in helping the young adults who left school early, and they often hold the confidence of the young people. The job-training agency could direct some attention toward coaches and ministers, increasing their knowledge of the program and the benefits it offers the community and the participants. With proper orchestration, coaches and ministers could become vocal supporters and even unofficial recruiters for the job-training program.

TYPOLOGY OF PUBLICS

Here are some examples of the common families of publics appropriate to various public relations or marketing communication situations. Let this list spark your creative thinking about identifying publics relevant to your organization.

Customer
Occasional/regular
Current/potential/former
Competitive/loyal
Age/ethnicity/spending potential/other variables
Members/casual customers
Geographic: local/regional/national/
    international
Online/in-person customers
Secondary customers
Shadow constituencies
Stakeholders
Voters/constituents

Producer
Employees/volunteers
Veteran/novice
Volunteers: leadership/grassroots
Line/staff
Management/nonmanagement
    Management: upper/middle
    Nonmanagement: supervisory/staff/
    maintenance/production/uniformed
Management/union
Families/retirees
Investors/shareholders
Donors/foundations/grantors
    Consistent/occasional
    Current/potential/former

Enabler
Community leaders: government/professional/
    business/union/educational/religious/ethnic
Community organizations: service/professional/
    religious/social/ethnic/cultural/political/
    environmental/activist

Industry association/regulatory agencies
Academic: Faculty, alumni, trustees,
    administrators
Think tanks
Accreditation/licensing bodies and agencies
Professional experts/consultants/analysts
Government bodies: town/city/county/
    state/federal; elective/appointive;
    legislative/executive/judicial staff/
    advisory/committee/department
Diplomatic bodies: embassy/consulate
Military/civilian
Media: local/state/regional; national/
    international
Specialized media: professional/financial/
    consumer/trade; religious/ethnic/advocacy/
    academic
Media availability: general/limited/restricted
Print media: newspaper/magazine/newsletter
Newspapers:
    Daily/nondaily
    Online/in-print
Electronic media: television/radio/Internet
Television: broadcast/cable/online
Radio: AM/FM; commercial/public; satellite
Internet: newsgroups/websites/blogs/social
    media
Opinion leaders

Limiter
Competitors
Opponents
Activists
Unfriendly media
Negative opinion leaders
Watchdog organizations

Opinion Leader

In addition to intercessory publics, we sometimes deal with intercessory individuals. Usually we call these people **opinion leaders**, men and women who have a particular influence over an organization's publics. Research provides some guidance into working with people who will carry an organization's messages to others.

Paul Lazarsfeld's **two-step flow of communication theory** (Lazarsfeld, Berelson, and Gaudet, 1944) and the multi-step flow theory that evolved from it observe that the media influence opinion leaders, who in turn influence other people. Everett Rogers' **diffusion of innovations theory** (2003) notes that people who are quick to try new ideas or products are influential with latecomers to the innovation.

An opinion leader is an influential role model who has the respect and confidence of the public. Members of publics look to opinion leaders as they obtain information, form attitudes and opinions, and determine action. Opinion leaders are particularly useful because they generate **word-of-mouth** support, perhaps the most effective type of communication precisely because opinion leaders are independent. That is, they do not speak under the auspices of the organization, nor do they directly benefit from it. Because of this independence they are often quite believable. Consider the two types of opinion leaders.

Formal opinion leaders have structured roles, such as elected or appointed officials or people who hold a recognized position of authority.

Informal opinion leaders exert influence simply because they are informed, articulate, and recognized leaders on a particular issue.

For both, their influence is based on existing relationships, real or perceived. Such relationships might involve family, neighborhoods, political parties, or ethnicity, or they might be rooted in shared lifestyle, social, or professional interests. Opinion leaders may be global or local.

For example, informal opinion leaders might include talk-show hosts or other media personalities; CNN commentator Nancy Grace played a key role in the media outreach of the "Find Brittany" campaign noted in the introductory chapter of this book. Such opinion leaders might also be local people, such as an opinionated clerk at the corner store or a well-read neighbor. Increasingly, bloggers fit this category. The common thread is that audiences heed and often seek out the advice of such information sources.

Some opinion leaders can be considered **vocal activists**, people who are linked to particular issues and who are known as advocates for their cause. While some activists can be dismissed as single-issue zealots, most are perceived as both independent and critical, and their support can add credibility to an organization's message. Opinion leaders may have some characteristics different from your publics.

A 2006 international study by researchers at Shih Tsin University in Taiwan looked at media habits of more than 2,000 people interested in issues of energy and technology (Tsai et al., 2006).

The study found that 68 percent of people obtained information about technology development from the Internet, 11 percent from magazines, 6 percent from television, 6 percent from newspapers, 2 percent from radio, and the remaining 7 percent from other sources.

An earlier study by the Roper Organization found that people who are identified as opinion leaders prefer reading over television as a source of their information (Opinion Leaders, 1992). Opinion leaders also initiate action on topics of interest by writing letters to the editor, attending public meetings and rallies, working with activist groups, and the like.

CASE IN POINT Coca-Cola in Egypt

Opinion leaders can be especially important when practicing public relations in an international context.

Pepsi has always been the soft-drink standard in Egypt and in most other Arab countries. To its cultural detriment, Coca-Cola has been linked with non-Arab Western interests and with American consumerism. An old saying in Egypt, laden with cultural implications, is that Pepsi is for Arabs and Coke is for Jews. The company was the target of a 23-year boycott by the Arab League because of its business interests with Israel.

A rumor circulated in 2000 that Coca-Cola was anti-Islam, "proof" of which was that when the Coke logo was viewed upside-down in a mirror, it read as "No Mohamed. No Mecca." Coke sales plummeted 20 percent. Protests erupted. Some areas banned Coke advertising and signage.

Coca-Cola Egypt decided to move quickly, with a particular emphasis on the concept of opinion leader. The company requested a meeting with the grand mufti, the country's top religious leader, asking his advice. It also asked a panel of Islamic scholars to consider the matter. Both the grand mufti and the scholarly panel ruled that the rumor was unsubstantiated.

In a public statement, the religious leader scolded those who disseminated the false rumor for risking the jobs of thousands of fellow Muslims employed by Coca-Cola. He also later said in interviews that he himself enjoyed a daily Coke.

Besides relying on news coverage of the intervention, the company highly advertised the grand mufti's statement and gave copies to its drivers, distributors, and sales people. Within weeks, sales returned to pre-crisis levels, and Coke, though still a distant second in the cola wars, was playing more aggressively in a more balanced cultural environment.

Opinion leaders not only draw attention to an issue, but they also signal how others might respond or act. Matthew Nisbet of American University and John Kotcher of the National Academies in Washington, DC (2009) investigated the role of opinion leaders on climate change. They recounted George W. Bush's 2004 re-election campaign that sent an email questionnaire to seven million volunteers and, based on responses, identified two million willing to write letters, talk with others, attend public meetings, call into radio talk shows, and otherwise promote the candidate. Each week, the campaign team then sent email talking points to these volunteer opinion leaders.

Their research points to a multi-prong outreach to opinion leaders: identification, recruiting, and training; message coordination; and expansion of the role of online communication for digital opinion leaders; as well as the need for evaluation, transparency, and ethical norms in future research on the role of opinion leaders and social media.

Key Public

Sometimes the task of selecting publics for a strategic communication program is an easy one. In many situations, the appropriate public is quite evident: a manufacturing plant seeking to increase productivity looks to its employees; a church wanting to increase contributions looks to its congregation; a politician seeking re-election targets voters in her district.

A major element of an effective communication campaign is the identification of appropriate specific publics, called **key publics** or **strategic publics**.

Note that this book uses the term "key publics" for those specific publics that the planner identifies as being most important to the public relations activity. Other books sometimes use the term "**target public**." However, this seems to suggest that the public is merely a bull's-eye for the organization's darts rather than part of a reciprocal relationship.

Key publics are the people you want to engage in a communication process. Don't allow yourself to generalize here. The manufacturing plant may not need to address all of its employees. Some already are very productive; others are new and still learning their responsibilities, so an accent on productivity could hinder their progress. Instead, the company may focus on a particular work shift to increase productivity.

Likewise, the church may raise funds primarily among its affluent parishioners and the politician may aim the re-election campaign particularly toward senior citizens who vote proportionately more often than younger residents.

If key publics are not readily obvious to your planning team, the examples and exercises that follow can help you identify them systematically and objectively. After you have identified your various publics, select those that are particularly important for the situation you are working on. These key publics often number from two to five, though this could increase considerably with complex issues.

Readers coming from a background in marketing should be forewarned: The tendency in marketing has been to identify objectives before selecting key publics. However, this book uses the publics-before-objectives order for three reasons.

1. The first two steps in the planning process have already helped you identify the focus for your planning.
2. Publics exist in a relationship with an organization even prior to any objectives for impacting that relationship.
3. Objectives are relevant only when they link an organization's broader goals with a particular public.

Based on the issue you identified in Step 1: Analyzing the Situation, as well as the above information and insights about your various publics, select several publics that warrant particular attention. These become your key publics as you address this issue.

While all your publics may be important in various situations, not all warrant attention as you deal with the situation at hand. For example, the university's recruiting program may not choose to focus on its graduates, and the toy company's competitors may not be a significant public in a campaign to regain consumer confidence.

This is the point in your planning process where you weed out the less important publics, concentrating instead on those few that have particular relevance and the most potential for the issue with which you are dealing.

PRIORITIES WORKSHEET

Each public is not equally important, but how can strategic planners be objective in setting priorities among the various publics identified in Step 3?

Here is a worksheet that can be applied any time there is a need to set priorities among various options. Let's use it here to carefully rank publics—specifically to consider each public, evaluate it in relationship to the other publics, and arrive rather dispassionately at a priority ordering among the publics that you have identified.

Based on choices you make in one-on-one comparisons among the identified publics, this worksheet will yield a score that reflects your priorities. Generally, you will select those publics with the highest score.

To illustrate how the priorities worksheet works, we'll use the publics identified in Planning Example 3A for the toy manufacturer.

1. Create a grid, and assign a letter for each public you want to compare. In the following example for Tiny Tykes Toys, the lettering is from A to I, though the worksheet can accommodate any number of publics. The order of listing these publics is of no consequence. List each public in the spaces marked A, B, C . . . H along the right column and in spaces B, C, D . . . I across the top row. Note that the first and last spaces (A and I) are not duplicated in the listings.

2. Compare each possible combination of items: AB, AC, AD, . . . BC, BD, BE, . . . through HI. In the corresponding block, mark the letter of the item you think is the more important of the two publics in the public relations situation to be addressed.

3. In each box, also mark a number indicating the intensity of your preference for the public you selected as being more important. Use 1 for a slightly stronger preference, 2 for a moderately stronger preference, and 3 for a much stronger preference.

4. After all possible pairs are compared and your preference is marked for each on the worksheet, add up the rating numbers for each letter. Enter this number as the prioritized score. If just one person is setting the priorities, enter that number as the prioritized score. If several people are working together to set the priority, enter the average of their individual scores. The resulting score provides a sense of the priority being given to each individual public identified for this project or campaign.

5. From this prioritized score, indicate the priority ranking. You may feel a need to adjust the ranking rather than merely base it on the scores provided through this worksheet. However, carefully consider how appropriate it would be to change the priority order if you have gone through the process of comparing each public against the others. If possible, trust the process to reflect your careful analysis of the relative importance of each public.

PLANNING EXAMPLE 3A   **Identifying Publics**

UPSTATE COLLEGE

Here is a listing of publics for Upstate College.

- *Customers* include students and, in most cases, parents. Potential customers are academically average high school students or employed people seeking an education. Secondary customers include eventual employers and (with the program expansion) graduate schools.
- *Producers* include the faculty and administration, alumni and other donors, and banks and other financial aid programs
- *Enablers* include the state education department and the media (both state and local). Opinion leaders include school counselors and others who offer career and educational advice.
- *Limiters* include other area colleges and universities as well as banks cutting back on student loans.

STEP 3

After due consideration, three key publics for this campaign are identified:

- High school students
- Guidance counselors
- UC Alumni

Here is a listing of publics for Tiny Tykes Toys.

- *Customers* include parents, grandparents, and other purchasers of baby toys.
- *Producers* include employees (both union and management), stockholders, and perhaps suppliers.
- *Enablers* include other members of the American Toy Institute and media (both financial media and family- and child-oriented media). This category also includes outside consumer groups that can exert some influence as well as consumer protection agencies that can regulate toy manufacturers. Opinion leaders include child-care professionals, pediatricians, early childhood educators, and child psychologists.
- *Limiters* include other toy companies (especially importers of cheap toys), a consumer activist group threatening a boycott, and a faction of disgruntled employees challenging the union and encouraging a walkout. Limiters might also include the same consumer groups, regulators, and media also identified as enablers, depending on how the situation unfolds.

After completion of the priorities worksheet, five key publics for this campaign are identified:

- Opinion leaders
- Parents and other purchasers

Phase One

EXHIBIT 3.2 Worksheet

I	H	G	F	E	D	C	B		
A2	A3	G1	A2	A3	A2	C1	A2	A	Parents/Purchasers
B2	B3	G1	B3	B3	B3	B1	x	B	Opinion Leaders
C2	C3	G1	C2	C3	D1	x	x	C	Consumer Groups
D2	D3	D1	D2	D1	x	x	x	D	Employees
E1	E2	G1	E2	x	x	x	x	E	Stockholders
F1	F3	G2	x	x	x	x	x	F	Am Toy Inst & Regulators
G2	G3	x	x	x	x	x	x	G	Media
I2	x	x	x	x	x	x	x	H	Competitors

Column headers (top, diagonal): Activist Groups, Competitors, Media, Am Toy Inst & Regulators, Stockholders, Employees, Consumer Groups, Opinion Leaders

Priority Publics

Prioritized Score   **Priority Ranking**

		Prioritized Score	Priority Ranking
A	Parents/Purchasers	14	**2**
B	Opinion Leaders	15	**1**
C	Consumer Groups	11	**Tie 3**
D	Employees	10	**5**
E	Stockholders	5	
F	Am Toy Inst & Regulators	4	
G	Media	11	**Tie 3**
H	Competitors	0	
I	Activist Groups	2	

Phase One

STEP 3

- Consumer groups
- Media
- Employees

Other publics not selected as being strategic on this issue include stockholders, who could be addressed in part through the media or in combination with employees; competitors, which do not need to be addressed specifically except through the media; the American Toy Institute and other regulators, who would be addressed directly rather than through public relations, though they also would have access to media coverage; and activist groups, who also would have access to media coverage.

Checklist 3A **Publics**

Basic Questions

1. Who are the major publics for your organization?
2. Who are the key publics for this situation?
3. Who are the intercessory publics or major opinion leaders?

Expanded Questions

A. EXISTING INFORMATION

Answer the following questions based on what you know directly or what you can learn from your client or colleagues within your organization.

Customers

1. Who are your primary customers?
2. Who are your secondary customers who use the products or services of your primary customers?
3. How have your customers changed within the last three years?
4. How are your customers likely to change within the next three years?

Producers

1. Who produces your service/product?
2. Who provides your organization with services and materials?
3. Who provides money?
4. How have your producers changed within the last three years?
5. How are your producers likely to change within the next three years?

Enablers

1. Who are opinion leaders among your customers?
2. Who are your colleagues?

3. Who are your regulators?
4. How have regulators helped you within the last three years?
5. With whom do you have contracts or agreements?
6. What media are available to you?
7. How have the media helped you in the last three years?
8. How have your enablers changed within the last three years?
9. How are your enablers likely to change within the next three years?

Limiters

1. Who are your competitors?
2. Who are your opponents?
3. What type of opponents are they: advocates, dissidents, activists, or zealots?
4. Who can stop you or slow you down?
5. How have your limiters changed within the last three years?
6. How are your limiters likely to change within the next three years?
7. Who are intercessory publics and opinion leaders?
8. What publics are in a position of influence with your key publics?
9. How likely is it that they will speak for your organization's position?
10. Who are formal opinion leaders for this audience: elected government officials, appointed government officials or someone else?
11. How likely is it that they will speak for your organization's position?
12. Who are informal opinion leaders for this audience: family leaders, neighborhood leaders, occupational leaders, religious leaders, ethnic leaders and/or community leaders?
13. How likely is it that they will speak for your organization's position?
14. Who are vocal activists on this issue?
15. How close is their position on this issue vis-à-vis the organization's?
16. How likely is it that they will speak for your organization's position?

B. RESEARCH PROGRAM

If there are any significant gaps in the existing information, you may have to conduct research to learn more about your organization's various publics. This section will guide you through consideration of that option.

1. What is the basis for the existing information noted above: previous formal research, informal or anecdotal feedback, organizational experience, personal observation, presumption/supposition by planner(s) and/or something else?
2. How reliable is this existing information?
3. How appropriate would it be to conduct additional research?
4. What information remains to be obtained?
5. If the existing information is not highly reliable, consider additional research, such as the following:

   - Review of organizational literature/information
   - Review of other published information (books, periodicals, etc.)
   - Interviews with key people within the organization

Phase One

STEP
3

- Interviews with external experts or opinion leaders
- Focus groups with representative publics
- Surveys with representative publics

6.   What research methods will you use to obtain the needed information?

C. RESEARCH FINDINGS

After you have conducted formal research, indicate your findings as they shed light on the organization's publics.

Analyzing Key Publics

Here's a maxim that organizational communications can live by: Know your audience. The newspaper advice columnist Miss Manners demonstrates this effectively in some of her columns. Miss Manners is witty, if a bit stodgy, as she writes about protocol (which dinner fork to use), politeness (how to say thanks for a gift you don't like), relationships (how to introduce your lesbian lover to your father's former mistress), and other elements of etiquette (how to apologize for getting snockered at your best friend's wedding).

Clearly the know-your-audience counsel was unheeded by this letter writer—a 14-year-old girl whose mother wouldn't let her wear thong underwear and whose friends made fun of her because of it. Miss Manner's response: "Of all the advice columnists in the world, you chose Miss Manners as the most likely one to support the cause of thong underwear? And you wonder why your mother questions your judgment?" (Martin, 2008).

It is most important to understand the publics with which we seek to interact. Careful analysis of each key public is the cornerstone of the research phase. The more information and insight planners can bring to this step, the more effective the overall program.

The idea behind this step is to allow the planner to "get inside the mind" of the organization's key publics. Much of this information can be obtained through informal research such as interviews and brainstorming; some of it may require more formal research techniques such as focus groups and surveys. Through formal and informal research, as well as good sense, the planner carefully examines each public.

One of the most important ways of analyzing a public is to consider the consequences it has on the organization and, conversely, the consequences the organization has on the public—actively or at least potentially. In a very real way, consequences create publics, and our public relations involvement with publics often is guided by an analysis of how real and obvious those consequences are.

In this section you will reconsider the general information uncovered in Step 2: Analyzing the Organization and apply it to each key public. You'll want to note the public's stage of development and its key characteristics. Each of these topics is discussed below.

Stage of Development

Publics are not fixed in concrete; rather, they are fluid and evolving. Grunig and Hunt (1984) have identified four stages of publics: nonpublics, latent publics, aware publics, and active

EXHIBIT 3.3 Stages of Publics

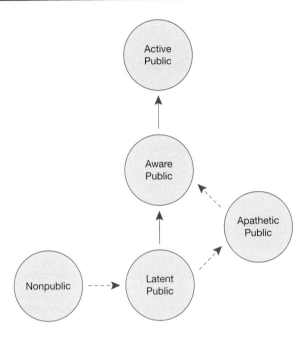

publics. To this list, this textbook adds a fifth type: apathetic publics. The relationship of each stage can be seen in Exhibit 3.3, where the solid arrow points to the changes that can be encouraged by effective public relations activity and the dotted arrow shows changes that may evolve with or without public relations input. Let's look at each type of public.

NONPUBLIC

A **nonpublic** is a group that does not share any issues with the organization with no real consequences vis-à-vis the organization. At this level and this time, this group simply is of no significance to the organization and vice versa. For example, a nonpublic for an animal adoption shelter would be people who are allergic to animals or those who live in apartments where pets are not allowed. The logical public relations response for this public is observation, periodically monitoring the situation to see if it changes; for example, if the restrictions are eased or if people move to a new building with different rules.

LATENT PUBLIC

A **latent public** (sometimes called an **inactive public**) shares an issue with the organization but does not yet recognize this situation or its potential. You might also call it an embryonic public, because it has potential but as yet no self-awareness.

Based on variables of knowledge and involvement as ways to identify various types of publics, a latent public has low levels of both—little information about a situation and little motivation regarding potential consequences. For the animal adoption shelter, senior citizens who might appreciate companionship would be a latent public.

A latent public is unlikely to seek information related to the situation. Thus an organization's public relations response is to plan communication to enhance its relationship with this public, perhaps by helping the shelter adapt itself to the interests of this group. For example, it may invite apartment dwellers to volunteer a couple of hours each week to interact with the animals awaiting adoption from the shelter, giving companionship and exercise to both the animals and the volunteers, creating knowledgeable people who might serve as opinion leaders for others who could adopt a pet, and perhaps fostering future adoptions when the volunteers are in a pet-friendly environment.

APATHETIC PUBLIC

A public that faces an issue, knows it, and simply doesn't care is an **apathetic public**. To this public, the issue is not significant enough to warrant its attention and/or the consequences are not perceived as being important. This can be frustrating for an organization, but properly identifying an apathetic public may help the organization reframe its message to overcome the apathy.

An apathetic public for the animal adoption shelter might be people who don't particularly like pets. The public relations response to such a public is to monitor the situation carefully, for it could change quickly if the issue begins to capture the public imagination. Meanwhile, the organization also should develop plans to communicate with the apathetic public, trying to transform its apathy into interest.

But realize that changing negative attitudes and opinions is a difficult task. Public relations is unlikely to be effective in transforming someone who doesn't like animals into a pet lover.

AWARE PUBLIC

An **aware public** recognizes that it shares an issue and perceives the consequences as being relevant, but it is not organized or energized to discuss and act on the issue. An aware public for the animal adoption agency may be people who have learned that psychologists believe the companionship of pets improves the quality of life for senior citizens. The public relations response is to initiate proactive communication, providing information about the issue, stressing its significance to the public, and presenting the organization's opinion or intended action. At this stage, the organization can control the tone and themes of the message.

ACTIVE PUBLIC

In the final stage of its development, an **active public** has reached the fullness of what we identify as a public. It is discussing and acting on the shared issue. For the animal shelter, an active public might be the local chapter of a senior citizen organization that is actively encouraging senior citizens to adopt pets.

In friendly circumstances such as the one described in this scenario, this can be an opportunity for building coalitions. In confrontational situations, on the other hand, an organization's response to an active public generally is reactive communication, responding to questions and often to accusations or even active opposition. In such a reactive setting, the tone or message themes are no longer controlled by the organization but instead by the active public.

Sometimes, active publics split in their relationship to an organization and issues associated with it. A **single-issue public** may be active on all of the issues important to the organization, active only on some popular issues, or active on single and often controversial issues. One animal rights group, for example, may confine its activism to local issues involving impounding of stray animals, neutering, credentialing of pet owners, and other issues related to a particular shelter. Another group may be active on a wider range of issues, including testing of medicines and cosmetics on animals, fur and leather fashion, hunting and fishing, and vegetarianism.

MASLOW'S HIERARCHY OF NEEDS

Psychologist Abraham Maslow (1987) developed the **drive-motive theory** or the theory of **human motivation**, commonly known as the **hierarchy of needs**. This theory offers an understanding not only of what people need but also of what Maslow called **prepotency**, the ordered internal relationship among needs by which more basic needs must be addressed first. His theory is presented visually as a two-part pyramid of five levels, with the stronger needs at the base. The base of the pyramid includes four levels of needs:

1. *Basic physiological needs* deal with oxygen, food and water, and sleep, as well as basic sexual urges.
2. *Safety needs* include shelter, employment, economic stability, and other kinds of security.
3. *Love needs* focus on belonging, family, friends, and group identity.
4. *Esteem needs* deal with respect and appreciation.
5. *Self-actualization needs* deal with achieving potential and with pursuing ideals such as spirituality and perfection, beauty and art, and peace and understanding.

Note that the self-actualization needs are in a category by themselves, separated from the others. Whereas a deficiency in any of the four levels in the base of the pyramid can create tension within a person, the fifth level adds to the person's freedom to explore and achieve greater ambitions.

Needs at each level of Maslow's pyramid are interrelated and can be fulfilled in different ways.

Recent research suggests that Maslow's categories of motivation are more important than their particular order. For example, while the sex urge is a basic psychological impulse, it is an urge that can be controlled and, at least temporarily, set aside. This is unlike the need for oxygen, food, or sleep, which are required and ongoing.

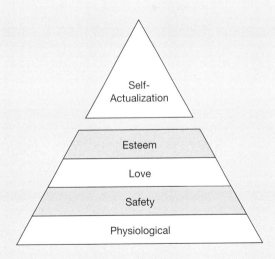

For some people, sex also can have application to a feeling of security. For others, it may be less associated with basic physiological needs and more with a sense of love and belonging, self-esteem, even spirituality.

Key Characteristics

After noting the stages of development, look at each public in reference to the following six key characteristics: the public relations situation, the organization, the public's communication behavior, and its readability level, demographics, and personality.

- *Public Relations Situation.* Assess the public's wants, interests, needs, and expectations related to the issue, as well as what it does not want or need. Consider relevant attitudes of the public. The hierarchy of needs (Maslow, 1987) outlined in this chapter can be a useful aid in considering the interests and needs of publics.
- *Organization.* Consider each key public's relationship with the organization—how your organization impacts the public and vice versa. Also consider the visibility and reputation of your organization with this public.
- *Communication Behavior.* Study the public's communication habits, such as the media or communication channels it uses. Identify people who might be credible message sources for this public and who are its opinion leaders. Also indicate whether the public is seeking information on the issue. This assessment will have major impact later when you choose your communication tools, because information seekers are likely to initiate communication or make use of tactics that require their direct involvement.
- *Readability Level.* Try to identify the educational level of each key public. Knowing that, you can use a formula to ensure that any written messages that you direct toward each public are written at an appropriate level. This is known as **readability**.
- *Demographics.* Identify **demographic** traits such as age, income, gender, socio-economic status, or other relevant information about this public.
- *Personality Preferences.* Consider the psychological and temperamental preferences of this key public. Appraise the relative merits of logical versus emotional appeals.

Knowing something about the personality of the key public and then tailoring messages to fit such psychological preferences can make communication more persuasive and more effective. During this step of the planning process, use the Personality Preferences checklist to look more closely at each of your key publics. Later in the process you will consider ways to craft messages that complement these preferences.

Like other aspects of this research phase, your answers to the questions posed in the planning checklist may be tentative and based on presumptions or common sense. However, insight from the organization's experience can prove useful as you begin to understand the communication preferences of your key publics. Eventually you may decide that formal research is needed.

Stereotype

A **stereotype** is a shortcut in describing groups of people. Stereotypes are based on common and repeated perceptions of who people are, how they act, and what they think and value. Stereotypes are what Walter Lippman (1922) called "pictures in our heads," and they are helpful precisely because they can whittle down the complexity of the real world.

AMERICAN INDIANS: STEREOTYPE VS. REALITY

Of the many populations within American society, few are more assaulted by stereotypes than are Native Americans. Consider the following facts in light of common stereotypes.

The 2010 U.S. Census reported 5.2 million American Indians, less than half of them of mixed ancestry. With nearly 2 percent of the total U.S. population, the collective Native population is the smallest minority group based on race. The largest Native nations are Cherokee, Navajo, Choctaw, Chippewa, and Sioux.

A comprehensive designation for American Indians, Alaska Natives, and Native Hawaiians sometimes is used. Half told the Census Bureau that they preferred the term "American Indian" and 38 percent preferred "Native American."

There are 565 federally recognized tribes in the U.S., plus another 250 or so seeking federal recognition. Each tribe is an autonomous and self-governing entity whose sovereignty is recognized by the federal government and whose lands are legally distinct from state lands that encircle them. Thus, in significant ways, tribal laws replace state law. Because tribes are autonomous, it is not appropriate to consider American Indians a single political entity. Official membership and citizenship eligibility varies by tribe.

Here are some facts that put stereotypes in a different light:

- *Growth*. The Native population is growing fast. While the total U.S. population grew less than 10 percent between 2000 and 2010, the American Indian/Alaska Native population increased by more than 39 percent, putting them among the fastest-growing populations.
- *Multiethnic/Multiracial*. Many of these are multiethnic and multiracial people with some Native heritage. Additionally, seven million Americans claim some Indian ancestry but are not officially counted within the Native population.
- *Language*. Native peoples of North America are richly diverse. About 200 languages are spoken by half a million people in the U.S. and Canada, many with very different linguistic roots and sophisticated grammar. About 28 percent of the Indian population speaks a language other than English at home.
- *Reservations*. More than three-fourths of American Indians live outside traditional tribal areas. Only 22 percent of Indians live on 334 reservations.
- *Population Areas*. Native populations are concentrated in ten states (led by Oklahoma, Arizona, California, Texas, and New Mexico). Only three Eastern states (New York, North Carolina, and Michigan) have sizable Native populations.
- *Age*. As a group, American Indians are younger than the general population. Their median age is 29, compared with 37 for the population as a whole.
- *Poverty*. Prosperity is increasing among American Indians. While 25 percent live below the poverty level, this is the same as most other ethnic and racial groups in America. Economically, Native Americans are second only to Asian Americans for income through minority-owned businesses. They also show an 84 percent growth in business ownership, particularly in service, construction, and retail businesses.
- *Casinos*. Two-thirds of tribes do not run casinos. For those that do operate reservation-owned casinos, it is a $5 billion industry.

- *Education*. School dropout rates are higher among Indians than any other population group. Nevertheless, 77 percent of adult Indians have a high school degree (compared with 86 percent of the total U.S. population). More than half of high school graduates attend college and 13 percent hold a bachelor's degree.
- *Mainstream Society*. Contemporary Indians are part of mainstream American life. They operate radio and television stations, run public relations agencies, sponsor colleges, and work in every occupation. New York City and Los Angeles are the two biggest cities for Native-owned businesses.
- *Health*. Though life expectancy among Native Americans is ten years less than the national average, health is steadily improving. Suicide rates are decreasing. Alcoholism remains high, and many deaths are accidental and alcohol related.
- *Taxation*. Indians pay federal income tax, state income tax except on income earned on reservations, sales tax on off-reservation purchases, and off-reservation property tax. Federal and tribal laws, but not state laws, generally apply on reservations.
- *Governance*. Some tribes and nations are led not by chiefs but by presidents, governors, or chairmen/chairwomen. Some are governed by councils.
- *Religion*. Many American Indians participate in what is loosely called Native American religion, often a spiritual rooting in life rather than a formal religious structure. Others are members of mainstream Christian denominations: Catholic, Protestant, and Eastern Orthodox; a few are Muslim. Additionally, many people combine Christianity with Native religious practices and beliefs.
- *Media*. American Indians have national newspapers and radio programs. They are increasingly exercising a presence in public relations and the media. Most tribes have their own public relations department or functions, as do many Native-related organizations, such as the National Native American Law Students Association, the American Indian Science and Engineering Society, the (Canadian) Assembly of First Nations, and the (Catholic) Tekakwitha Conference.
- *Famous American Indians*. Actors Graham Greene, Adam Beach, Benjamin Bratt, Lou Diamond Phillips, Angelina Jolie; singers Cher, Miley Cyrus; dancer Maria Tallchief; astronaut John Herrington; Congressman Ben Nighthorse Campbell; Philadelphia Archbishop Charles Caput.

Public relations strategists will be mindful of such diversity among the Native communities. In particular, communicators should be careful not to adopt icons and images of one Indian group and project it upon all.

Many Indians come from the Northeast and Southeast where buffalo never roamed. The stereotype of the Plains Indian with feathered headdresses and teepees simply does not apply to the Navajo and Apache of the Southwest, the Salish and Yakama of the Northwest, nor the Mohegan, Seminole, or Haudenoshaunee (Iroquois) of the Eastern states. Additionally, not all Indians hold powwows; some instead have fiestas or festivals.

The Public Relations Society of America includes Native Americans in its Multicultural Affairs committee, and several Native-owned public relations agencies exist within the profession.

Treaty, taxation, and casino-related issues are leading some Native Americans to get involved with government. Lobbying and the use of news media are increasing, as is activism in some areas.

In New York, for example, the six nations of the Haudenoshaunee fight the state's sporadic attempts to collect sales taxes on tribal lands, which they see as a clear violation of federal treaties and law.

What's the value of all this information? It can serve as a reminder that stereotypes are inaccurate. Are there differences between Native Americans and others? Certainly. Some are positive: close families, respect for the environment, appreciation of heritage. Some are negative: higher school dropout rates, higher rates of alcoholism. But the stereotypes often perpetuated through movies, advertising, and other forms of media are outdated at best, and often demeaning and hurtful—and thus of little value to an ethical and accurate strategic communicator.

Stereotyping has some value use for social interaction. We can identify threatening situations based on our ability to read other people. We are told to anticipate danger, drive defensively, and otherwise use what we know (or presume) about others to our advantage. Parents tell their children not to associate with "a bad crowd" or "the wrong kind of people." Despite the obvious social concerns associated with profiling, law enforcement agencies know how to look at people's behaviors and conclude when they are acting suspiciously.

The problem with stereotyping is not that it is a generalization, though it is. The problem is rather that it is an overgeneralization.

Good and appropriate stereotyping reflects judgments about people based on things about them over which they have some choice: their actions and behaviors, their choices in occupation, fashion, speech, grooming, and the like. It makes less sense to judge people based on aspects over which they have little or no control: race, ethnicity, age, skin tone, religious or cultural background, language accent, and so on.

Decisions about who is or is not part of a bad crowd may be made on the basis of both types of stereotypes—that is, (a) ethnic background or family structure over which the person has little control, and (b) grooming and fashion choices that the person has made.

Stereotype-based decisions also can be dead wrong. For years, stereotyping has led many people to associate drug use with inner-city youth, yet studies show that drug abuse, as well as underage drinking and drunk driving, is higher in the suburbs than in inner cities. The stereotype simply is wrong, and as public relations planners, we rely on such stereotypes to our own detriment.

Consider the following facts about various ethnic communities. These facts may challenge some of your own stereotypes about certain groups of people.

A 2003 poll by Zogby International found that 78 percent of teens associate Italian Americans with mobsters, gang members, or restaurant workers. The U.S. Census Bureau reports that two-thirds of Italian Americans in the workforce are in professional jobs such as teachers, attorneys, executives, and physicians.

Another poll found that 74 percent of adults think most Italian Americans are connected to organized crime, though the U.S. Justice Department reports less than .0025 percent of Italian Americans (that's one in 40,000) as being involved in organized crime. Nevertheless, the entertainment and advertising industries continue to draw heavily on the unreal mob-focused stereotype of America's fifth-largest ethnic group (*Italian American Stereotypes in US Advertising*, 2003).

ARAB AMERICANS AND MUSLIMS

What little most Americans know about Arabs and Muslims they learn through the media, which—whether news or entertainment—tends to continue negative and misleading stereotypes. Islamic and Arab publics are oversimplified by outsiders, but a good public relations strategist will work contacts within the Arab and Islamic communities to help understand the sometimes-subtle differences.

First off, note the double focus of this section. The public generally confuses Arab (member of an ethnic group originating in the Middle East) and Muslim (member of a religious group known as Islam). The two are not the same. Most Arab Americans are not Muslims, and most Muslims are not Arab.

Arab Americans

Here are some facts about Arab Americans (much of the information is taken from the Arab American Institute and Zogby Polling):

- *Population*. Though statistics are a bit unreliable, most reports indicate that the U.S. is home to about 3.5 million Arab Americans. About 94 percent live in metropolitan areas.
- *Ancestry*. Nearly half of all Arab Americans (47 percent) trace their ancestry to Lebanon; most of their families came to the U.S. a century ago. Other Arab Americans are from Arabia (14 percent), Syria (11 percent), and Egypt and Palestine (both 6 percent), with smaller numbers from Jordan, Morocco, Sudan, Algeria, Libya, Yemen, and other countries in the Middle East and northern Africa. About a quarter of all Arab Americans claim mixed ancestry.
- *Immigration*. Most Arab Americans were born in the U.S. Only about 40 percent are immigrants or children of immigrants. The largest wave of immigration began in the late 1800s.
- *Growth*. Arab Americans are one of the fastest-growing minorities in the U.S., with a 30 percent growth between 1990 and 2000 according to the federal census.
- *Politics*. Politically they tend toward the Democratic party. A Zogby poll indicated that 62 percent generally vote Democratic, 25 percent Republican. This is a shift from previous voting patterns that favored the Republican party, a change observers say reflects Arab American dissatisfaction with the Iraq War and policies of the Trump White House.
- *Education*. About 85 percent of adult Arab-Americans have a high school degree. More than 40 percent have a bachelor's degree (compared to about 30 percent for Americans in general).
- *Economics*. Arab Americans generally have a higher household income than the U.S. average. They are more likely to run their own businesses.
- *Religion*. Two-thirds of Arab Americans are Christian. About 35 percent are Catholic (mainly Latin-rite, Maronite, or Chaldean), 18 percent Orthodox, and 10 percent Protestant. About a third are Muslim (according to a Zogby International Survey of 2007). Some Christian religious groups are historically rooted in the Arab community, such as the Catholic Maronites of Lebanon, the Coptic Orthodox Christians in Egypt, and the Chaldean Catholics in Iraq.
- *Famous Arab Americans*. Singer Frank Zappa; actors Natalie Portman, Vince Vaughn, Jamie Farr, Kathy Najimy; athletes Andre Agassi, Doug Flutie; Apple founder Steve Jobs; politicians Darrell Issa, John Sununu.

American Muslims

Here are some related facts about Americans who are Muslims, adherents to the religion of Islam, making it the third-largest religious group in the U.S. after Christianity and Judaism. The following data is drawn from the Census Bureau, the State Department, and the Hartford Institute on Religious Practice.

- *Population*. Most reports indicate that the U.S. is home to about four million Muslims, though some internal sources estimate twice that number. Most live in cities, with highest concentrations in California (where 20 percent of American Muslims reside), New York State (16 percent), Illinois (8 percent), and Indiana and New Jersey (4 percent each). The annual growth rate is about 6 percent, compared to less than 1 percent for the total U.S. population. Muslim populations are growing faster than the general population, and Muslims have a younger population than the country overall.
- *Immigration*. About 70 percent of American Muslims are immigrants or children of immigrants.
- *Ancestry*. In general, the Islamic community subdivides into four nearly equal segments: Southeast Asians; African Americans; Arabs; and others (Turks, Kurds, Iranian/Persians, Berber/Moroccans, and so on).
- *Education*. Muslims lead national averages in education. About 67 percent of adults have at least a bachelor's degree (compared to 30 percent of the general population); 32 percent have a master's degree or doctorate (compared to 9 percent of the general population).
- *Income*. American Muslims have higher incomes than the general population, and often are found in engineering, computing, and medicine; they are underrepresented in journalism and law and are less likely than others to own their own businesses.
- *Religious Diversity*. There is much religious diversity within Islamic America. Only about half the Muslim population—about two million people—are affiliated with more than 1,250 Islamic centers, mosques, and other prayer locations. These are represented in every state, with the largest numbers in California, New York, Texas, Pennsylvania, and Ohio. About 30 percent of mosque members are converts. The largest groups in mosque membership are South Asian Americans (33 percent), African Americans (30 percent), and Arab Americans (25 percent). Most U.S. mosques are intercultural, with members of various ethnic backgrounds. In general, political and social divisions in the Middle East among Sunni, Shi'ite, Sufi, and Wahabi Muslims and homegrown American sects such as the Nation of Islam have had only minimal effect on most American mosques.
- *Religious Practice*. Mosques operate about 200 day schools and 500 Sunday schools, and there are six schools of higher learning. But 97 percent of Islamic children acquire religious education in their homes, where most religious practice is based. Only about 4 percent of American Muslims participate in weekly religious services, compared with 15 percent of American Jews and 40 percent of Christians.
- *Politics*. Two Muslims are in Congress: Keith Ellison (D.-Minnesota) and Andre Carson (D.-Indiana). In recent elections, American Muslims have voted for the Democratic candidate (89 percent for Barack Obama in 2008 and 85 percent in 2012, and 74 percent for Hillary Clinton in 2012)—a significant change from the 2000 election when 72 percent voted

Phase One

STEP
3

Republican. Muslims are becoming more politically active. Nearly 80 percent are registered to vote, and 91 percent of those registered say that they vote.

- *Famous American Muslims.* Comic Dave Chappelle, Aasif Mandvi; musicians Ice Cube, Mos Def, Snoop Dogg; model Iman; athletes Mike Tyson, Kareem Abdul-Jabbar, Shaquille O'Neal; writers Fareed Zakaria, Reza Aslan.

Asian Americans are stereotypically thought of as well educated. The organization Asian Nation, drawing on Census Bureau data, reported in 2011 that 50 percent of Asian Americans over the age of 25 have a bachelor's degree, twice the rate for all Americans. That supports the stereotype.

On the other hand, a 2010 study by the University of California (Chang, 2010) reported that, while only 15 percent of the general American adult population lacks a high school education, 45 percent of Hmongs and 40 percent of Laotians and Cambodians did not complete high school. Those facts go against the stereotype. Maybe the stereotype needs revision.

In analyzing publics, it is important to drill down in data to reveal the level of diversity within. Often, research and close observation show that a public is more diverse than it might appear from only a cursory glance. In particular, two groups within American society are subjected to all kinds of inaccurate stereotyping that masks a diversity that is much richer than may first appear. Consider the facts about Arab Americans and Native Americans in light of what you know to be the common stereotypes in the boxed insets.

Why are these issues important for us? Because public relations practitioners develop campaigns, craft speeches, prepare scripts, populate blogs, write newsletters, send tweets, and in so many other ways research and write about people and issues that are affected by stereotyping. Our role is not to change the social structure of our environment but to be accurate with facts and fair to people.

Cultural Context

Publics do not exist in a vacuum. Understanding their cultural context is crucial in this research phase of the strategic planning process. Public relations practitioners who give a priority to learning the nuances of the culture in which the publics exist are likely to develop campaigns that can be successful.

This is particularly important in the international arena. What works for one culture may not be appropriate for another.

Even basic communication can be hampered in international contexts. Language itself can be a barrier to communication. This is particularly true in Africa. Nigeria, for example, has more than 390 dialects. South Africa has 11 different national languages.

Technological differences can add to the problem. Social media and mobile media so common in Western societies are not present in some parts of Africa to make them useful tools for public relations, though this is changing rapidly as many countries are experiencing sustained growth in cellular technology.

Outsiders do themselves and their public relations interests a disservice when they fail to understand the diversity that exists within a culture. In the U.S., for example, we should understand that there are major differences within the Hispanic community. Mistaking cultural perspectives among Puerto Ricans, Cuban Americans, and other Hispanics from the Dominican Republic, say, can create embarrassment for organizations, and counterproductive responses from publics. Likewise Mexican, Panamanian, Columbian, and other Latin American cultures may share a common language base, but from a public relations perspective they may have more differences than similarities.

Situations get even more complicated when applied to other countries. Some nations such as Mexico, Canada, Australia, and Japan have historic tensions between indigenous peoples and the dominant culture. Others experience significant differences, even hostility based on language (such as Canada), religion (Uganda and India), race (South Africa) or tribal background (Rwanda). Gender roles and socially acceptable relations among men and women also vary greatly, as do social attitudes toward people who are gay, aged, disabled, or otherwise different from the social norm.

Often, knowing and accommodating such cultural norms impact public relations. For example, in 2015 when Michelle Obama traveled with the President to pay respects on the death of Saudi Arabia's King Abdullah and to greet the new King Salman, the first lady chose not to wear the socially expected and often mandated head covering. There was no apparent criticism from Saudi officials, who often encountered un-veiled women in diplomatic situations. Additionally, when the new king extended his hand, she shook it, against the taboo of men touching unrelated women. Some pundits suggested that—rather than a social or diplomatic breach—it may have been a subtly orchestrated signal that Saudi Arabia was or should be willing to rethink its gender policies.

Face Saving

Sometimes we want to see people squirm, especially people who have opposed us in some way. Most especially if they have been arrogant about things. Public relations strategies some-times can create conditions for a win–lose result, with the expectation that we win and they lose.

But there's another way to approach this, one that may fit well with the notion of cultural context. "Don't make your opponent look bad" isn't typical public relations advice. Yet in many cultures, face saving is important, and public relations in those cultures might well consider strategies that allow opponents to save face in public, resolving a situation while maintaining dignity and respect. Providing such an out can make it easier for an opponent to resolve the situation in your favor.

Face saving is particularly important in Eastern and Middle Eastern cultures. The Chinese call it *mianzi*. It's *kao-o-tateru* in Japanese, *hifz ma'a wajh* in Arabic. Saving face is a universal concept, though one taken much more seriously in Asia and the Middle East.

Asian business people seldom say "no" directly. A more polite euphemism for a negative decision is "Perhaps" or "The timing may not be right."

Public relations practitioners who do business in South Korea, for example, note that companies are unlikely to directly criticize their competitors. They may help circulate negative information, but it's done behind the scenes. Direct criticism likely would cause them to be outcasts within their own profession or industry. Thus doing public relations in South Korea might involve developing strategies that allow opponents to save face in public.

Face saving is behind the practice in Japan of not asking questions at a news conference. Say what? In America and Europe, news conferences can erupt into a cacophony of competing questions shouted out by journalists. But in Japan, the presumption is that the corporate or governmental leader making a news announcement would be embarrassed if reporters had to ask follow-up questions, indicating that the spokesperson had not anticipated their information needs. So rather than embarrass the spokesperson by asking questions in public,

---

CASE IN POINT Palestinian Public Relations

Sometimes the cultural context affects public relations in a significant way. Consider, for example, the role of public relations within the Palestinian community, both in the contested geography of the Middle East (Israel, the West Bank, and the Gaza Strip) and in the Palestinian diaspora (mostly in Jordan and neighboring states in the Middle East, but with large Palestinian communities in Chile, Brazil, Honduras, Canada, the U.S., and various European countries).

A study by Ahmed Ibrahim Hammad of Aristotle University in Thessaloniki, Greece, looked at the Palestinian Authority. This administrative organization that governs the Palestinian Territories had five different government agencies dealing with the media, plus public relations departments in many other agencies. Hammad found that the public relations as practiced by the long-ruling Fatah party was focused on a one-way communication method, using the communication-technician model to project a favorable image of the Palestinian Authority.

Hammad and fellow researchers later assessed the broader role of public relations within Palestinian society, where they observed that public relations of international Palestinian activism is more sophisticated than internal commercial public relations.

Because of the weak governmental structure and the lack of independent media in Palestine, "Palestinian public relations was seen as a political necessity," they said, "for communicating internally among the Palestinians inside the territories and throughout the Palestinian diaspora as well as externally with foreign publics" (Zaharna, Hammad, and Masri, 2009, p. 236).

Rather than media-focused campaigns, as might be found in many parts of the world, public relations in Palestine is more likely to center on interpersonal relationships. The research team noted that Palestine is a small territory with a close-knit social structure building around interconnected families. Mosques often are the center of social interaction. Taxi drivers are conveyers of news to many. Throughout society, the emphasis is less on disseminating information through the media but rather on circulating information among interwoven social structures.

The researchers looked at the 2006 election victory of the Hamas party, which took outsiders by surprise. They argued that the vote outcome would not have been such a surprise if observers had understood that Palestinian-style public relations is based in an interconnected social structure and focusing on relationship-building rather than public information. The media attention and support for the Fatah party that had long been in command had much less impact than Hamas' relationship-building approach within the Palestinian community.

a follow-up interview would be seen as less humiliating. It's just another example of the need for public relations practitioners to understand the cultural context in which they may find themselves.

A classic example shows the role of face saving in international business relationships. In the 1980s, Mitsubishi Electric was using a product that an American manufacturer, Fusion, claimed violated patent laws. Mitsubishi rejected the claim, and for ten years Fusion mounted a negative publicity campaign in both the American and Japanese press. The public embarrassment failed to bring Mitsubishi to the bargaining table.

Eventually the two companies were able to resolve the differences in private, issuing a joint news release announcing an agreement that, in an important face-saving gesture, gave no details and no concession statements by either side.

Rethinking Your Publics

Occasionally, this part of the process may point out a problem in previous identification of key publics. If you find it difficult to identify traits common to a public, perhaps you have defined the public in terms that are too general.

Consider the plight of a group of planners—students in a university public relations class—developing a program to raise awareness, generate interest, and obtain funds to help save the African elephant from human predators. The planners misidentified as one of their key publics "people with incomes above $50,000." As they analyzed their publics, they were having difficulty because they could not identify the mindset of this public, which was too broad and had no common traits other than income. That's because income wasn't really a public component at all but rather a demographic description, and not a very comprehensive one at that.

So the planners redefined their public more specifically as "people with incomes above $50,000 who have a pre-existing interest in issues of conservation and endangered animals." With those criteria, the planning team then could develop a profile of its public: people who want to help animals, expect a workable plan for doing so, want an organization with a proven track record, have an altruistic spirit to make the world a better place, and have the financial ability to contribute to this cause. This redefinition also helped the planners avoid wasting resources by trying to convert people to a cause in which they had no interest.

Sometimes an analysis of the publics will reveal that you simply need more information to take you beyond the insufficient common knowledge. For example, you may have identified African Americans as a key public for your campaign. Yet in your analysis you are likely to discover that, other than the physical characteristic of race itself, there may be few common elements within this public. For example, there are significant differences between American-born and foreign-born blacks; and in some cities, the foreign-born population is quite large—about a third in New York City and nearly half in Miami. Likewise, Southern blacks are culturally Southern, which may give them more in common with Southern whites than with Northern blacks.

Meanwhile, just as within Hispanic, Asian American, and Native American communities, there is much diversity among black people. Significant cultural differences are to be found among blacks from Haiti, Senegal, Nigeria, and Ethiopia (not to mention Newark, Baltimore, St. Louis, and Anchorage, Alaska). A closer look will reveal a population divided by language as well. Additionally, one might suspect that the half-million black Mormons or the 200 million black Catholics worldwide might, at least on some issues, have more in common with their coreligionists than with members of their race with other religious perspectives.

Once you are satisfied that you have identified your publics appropriately, review the analysis of each and consider whether the information you have generated should lead you to make any changes in the lineup. For example, a public that earlier seemed to be key may now be shown to be too apathetic to justify your action at this time.

Remember: Planning is a flexible process. The conclusion of Step 3 is one point along the way where you should rethink your plans so far, adjusting them based on the information becoming available to you through continuing research.

Benefit Statement

Conclude your analysis of the publics with a **benefit statement**, which is an articulation of the benefit or advantage your product, service, or idea can offer this public, or the way you can help satisfy its need or solve its problems.

For example, the benefit a community foundation might offer its donors could be stated as follows: "The Equity Foundation offers donors the opportunity to pool their money with the donations of others, thereby compounding small donations into larger, more effective grants."

In more of a marketing vein, the benefit an online bookstore might offer college and university students could be written as this: "Cyber Booksellers can assure university students that it can provide class textbooks at discount prices with immediate delivery."

What's Next?

This concludes Step 3, in which you now have a good look at the key publics associated with the public relations situation that you have been addressing in this planning process.

Step 3 also closes out Formative Research, the first phase of the strategic planning process. Having completed steps associated with Phase One, you now should have some clear insights about the issue, the status of your organization as it relates to this issue, and your various publics and their relationship to your organization.

You are probably already beginning to get ideas about how to communicate with these publics. Jot down whatever may come to mind, but it's not yet the time to develop specific program tactics. That will come later.

The next phase of the planning process addresses strategic questions such as the outcomes you want to accomplish, the approach you will take, and the message you will use to communicate with your key publics.

PLANNING EXAMPLE 3B **Analyzing Key Publics**

Upstate College alumni and other donors are a latent public on the issue of the college's program expansion. As circumstances change, it can be transformed into an active UPSTATE COLLEGE **public.**

Analysis of Key Characteristics
- *Issue*: The alumni/donor public will appreciate this program expansion. This public needs only basic information to instill appreciation.
- *Organization*: This key public provides continued support for the college, while the college provides this public with a sense of pride and value of the academic degree. This public has high knowledge of the college and thinks favorably about it. It can be called upon for action. It shares the college's self-image as a high-quality institution.
- *Communication*: This public occasionally participates in on-campus activities and has access to general news media as well as the college newsletter. The college has a mailing list of alumni and donors. This public is not actively seeking information because an announcement has not yet been made, but it could be expected to be attentive to information. Credible sources include famous alumni and respected donors.
- *Personality Preferences*: This is a diverse group, with some members having a preference for messages that are factual, logical, and reality based, while others prefer messages focused on ideas, sentiment, and vision.
- *Demographics*: Wide range. Higher than average in education. No particular significance in demographics other than geographic proximity to college.

Benefit Statement
Upstate College can provide information to alumni about the college's successes and strengths, giving alumni a sense of pride in their alma mater and an opportunity to help build on those strengths.
(Note: Similar analyses would be made for each individual key public you have identified.)

Tiny Tykes Toy Company employees are an active public.

Analysis of Key Characteristics
- *Issue*: The employee public wants to see the company reputation improved and wants to see the employer regarded as a leader in the industry. Morale has been affected negatively by the recall: employee public does not want to feel bad about making an inferior infant product, needs information on quality and safety, and cautiously expects leadership from the company in improving quality and reputation.
- *Organization*: This employee public ultimately affects the quality and productivity of the company, knows the company intimately, and has organized for action through

unions and through work teams. The company affects this public through continuing employment. Employees do not necessarily share management's self-image of being beneficial and safe.

- *Communication*: The employee public gets its information in an interpersonal setting with management and supervisors, can be reached through direct mailings and newsletters, and also receives information from local news media. This public is actively seeking info on this issue. Credible sources include management officials, veteran employees, and union leaders.
- *Personality Preferences*: Rank-and-file employees are accustomed to receiving messages based on fact, certainty, and logical analysis. Managers may be more disposed to messages that also deal with vision.
- *Demographics*: The employee public spans age groups but has in common lower-middle-class socioeconomic/educational background; there are many ethnic workers. Most members of this public do not personally use company products, but often in the past they have given the products as gifts to family and friends.

Benefit Statement

Tiny Tykes can provide information that will give employees renewed purpose and pride about the quality and safety of its products.

(Note: Similar analyses would be made for each individual key public you have identified.)

 *Checklist 3B* **Key Publics**

Basic Questions

1. What is the nature and type of each key public?
2. What are the major wants, interests, needs, and expectations of each public?
3. What benefits can you offer this public?

Expanded Questions

A. EXISTING INFORMATION

Answer the following questions based on what you know directly or what you can learn from your client or colleagues within your organization.

1. Who is your key public?
2. Indicate the category below that best describes that key public at this time and consider the public relations response indicated.

Category	Public Relations Response
Latent public. Faces an obstacle or opportunity vis-à-vis the organization. Does not yet recognize this situation or its potential.	Monitor the situation, anticipating change toward awareness. Meanwhile, begin to plan a communication process to provide information about the issue, explain its significance to the public and present your organization's opinion or intended action.
Apathetic public. Recognizes an obstacle or opportunity vis-à-vis the organization. Does not perceive this issue as important or interesting.	Monitor the situation, looking for any change toward perceiving the relevance of the issue. Meanwhile, begin to plan a communication process to provide information about the issue, explain its significance to the public and present your organization's opinion or intended action.
Aware public. Recognizes an obstacle or opportunity vis-à-vis the organization. Not yet organized for action.	Initiate a communication process to present the issue, explain its significance to the public and present your organization's opinion or intended action.
Active public. Recognizes an obstacle or opportunity vis-à-vis the organization. Preparing to organize or already organized for action.	Because you did not communicate sooner, you must now engage in reactive communication, responding to questions and perhaps to criticism and accusations without being able to control the tone or themes of the messages.

Phase One

STEP
3

Analysis of Key Characteristics

Issue

1. What does this key public know about this issue?
2. What does this public think about this issue?
3. What does this public want on this issue?
4. What does this public not want on this issue?
5. What does this public need on this issue?
6. What problem(s) does this public have related to this issue?
7. What does this public expect from the organization vis-à-vis this issue?
8. How free does this public see itself to act on this issue?

Organization (including product/service)

1. How does or how might the key public affect your organization?
2. How does or how might your organization affect this public?
3. What does this public know about your organization?
4. How accurate is this information (compared to information in Step 2)?
5. What does this public think about your organization?

6. How satisfied are you with this attitude?
7. What does this public expect from your organization?
8. How much loyalty does this public have for your organization?
9. How organized or ready for action on this issue is this public?
10. How influential does this public see itself as being within the organization?
11. How influential does the organization see this public as being?
12. Place an "X" at the appropriate location on the continuum of what this key public thinks of your organization's product(s) or service(s):

Contemporary	_ _ _ _ _	Traditional
Fun	_ _ _ _ _	Tedious
High-Tech	_ _ _ _ _	Low-Tech
Ordinary	_ _ _ _ _	Distinguished
Expensive	_ _ _ _ _	Inexpensive
Idealistic	_ _ _ _ _	Practical
Modest	_ _ _ _ _	Pretentious
Scarce	_ _ _ _ _	Abundant
Worthless	_ _ _ _ _	Beneficial
Efficient	_ _ _ _ _	Inefficient
Ordinary	_ _ _ _ _	Innovative
Essential	_ _ _ _ _	Luxury
Risky	_ _ _ _ _	Safe
High-Quality	_ _ _ _ _	Low-Quality

13. What are the similarities and the differences between your organization's self-image in the exercise from Step 2 and the image of it held by this public?

Communication

1. What media does this public use among each of the following: personal communication channels, organizational media, news media, and advertising/promotional media?
2. Is this public actively seeking information on this issue?
3. How likely is this public to act on information it receives?
4. Who are credible sources and opinion leaders for this public?

Demographics/Psychographics

1. What is the average age of members of your key public?
2. Where is your key public located geographically?
3. What is the socioeconomic status of your key public?
4. What products or services does your key public commonly use?
5. What are the cultural/ethnic/religious traits of your key public?
6. What is the education level of your key public?
7. What lifestyle traits does your key public have?
8. Is this public likely to be persuaded more by facts, more by emotion or by a combination?

9. Is this public likely to be motivated more by appeals to the past (experience, success, track record) or by appeals to the future (motivation, inspiration, vision)?
10. Are there other relevant characteristics about your key public?

Benefits

1. What benefit or advantage does your organization offer each public?
2. How does this benefit differ from the benefits available from other organizations?

B. RESEARCH PROGRAM

If there are any significant gaps in the existing information, you may have to conduct research to learn more about your organization's various publics. This section will guide you through consideration of that option.

1. What is the basis for existing information noted above—previous formal research, informal or anecdotal feedback, organizational experience, personal observation, presumption/supposition by planner(s), and/or something else?
2. How reliable is this existing information?
3. How appropriate would it be to conduct additional research?
4. What information remains to be obtained?
5. If the existing information is not highly reliable, consider additional research, such as the following:

   - Review of organizational literature/information
   - Review of other published information (books, periodicals, etc.)
   - Interviews with key people within the organization
   - Interviews with external experts or opinion leaders
   - Focus groups with representative publics
   - Surveys with representative publics

6. What research methods will you use to obtain the needed information?

C. RESEARCH FINDINGS

After you have conducted formal research, indicate your findings as they shed light on the organization's publics. Also, write a benefit statement about how the organization can satisfy the wants and needs, address the interests, and solve the problems of this particular key public.

Phase One

STEP 3

CONSENSUS CHECK

Does agreement exist within your organization and your planning team about the selection and analysis of these key publics?

☐ Yes. Proceed to Step 4, Establishing Goals and Objectives.

☐ No. Consider the value and/or possibility of achieving consensus before proceeding.

STRATEGY

Strategy is the heart of planning for public relations, marketing communication, and related areas. All the embodiments of strategic communication are rooted in the research already undertaken in the previous phase and growing toward the eventual choice of communication tactics.

Just as rushing through the research phase would have jeopardized the foundation on which to build your public relations or marketing communication plan, so will failing to give adequate attention to strategy result in weak messages and pointless activity.

Simply stated, **strategy** is the organization's overall plan. It is the determination of how the organization decides what it wants to achieve and how it wants to achieve it. Strategy has a dual focus: the action of the organization (both proactive and responsive) and the content and presentation of its messages (theme, source, content, and tone). Refer to strategy in the singular, because each program should have a single, unifying strategy.

Phase Two deals with mapping the course toward your overall destination, deciding both where to go and how to get there. By building on research from Phase One of the planning process, you will anchor your program in the mission or vision of the organization.

Specifically, this phase of the planning process leads you to a closer look at your organization: its vision of itself, as well as its hopes for the various publics important to it. These hopes will be fleshed out as goals, positioning statements, and objectives.

Then the strategy phase will focus your attention on two key aspects of your planning: what you will do, and what you will say about what you will do. The first of these delves into both action and response, following the premise that actions speak louder than words. First you focus on the things you do; then you turn your attention to how you communicate about those actions.

The entire strategic process is interrelated and interdependent: Goals guide the development of objectives, which in turn help drive decisions about what persuasive strategies to use and what tactics to employ to address the problem or opportunity.

Admittedly, there are different approaches to strategic planning and various practitioners may use different terminology. For example, some planners set goals before they identify and analyze publics. This often is true when the planner comes from a marketing perspective, where the organization starts with its sales or promotional goals, then identifies potential customers who might be or become interested in the organization's products or services.

Public relations starts with publics. We generally build our strategic plans from an understanding of the ongoing relationship between our organization and its various publics. Then we look at how the organization's goals and objectives potentially impact on these publics.

Establishing Goals and Objectives

This step is about looking inward and deciding what you want to achieve. To better understand this step, you need to understand the twin concepts of goals and objectives. It should be noted that public relations and marketing strategists generally make the distinction that goals are general and global while objectives are specific.

However, some advertisers and other specialists rooted in business disciplines either reverse the meanings of the terms or use them interchangeably. In your actual practice, you may find people applying different definitions to these terms, so make sure you understand what the words mean and how colleagues use them. In *Strategic Planning for Public Relations*, we use the terms as they are outlined below.

Here are short definitions of key concepts used in this step. They will be fleshed out in the subsequent pages.

- A positioning statement is a general expression of how an organization wants its publics to distinguish it vis-à-vis its competition.
- A goal is a global indication of how an issue should be resolved.
- An objective is a statement of specific outcomes expected for a public, indicating a way to more precisely conceptualize the goal.

Positioning

As you set out to articulate the desired interaction you can have with your publics, first focus on positioning. Having previously identified the relevant public relations situation in Step 1, ask these simple questions: What do we want people to think about us? What position do we seek with our publics?

A successful approach to strategic communication in a competitive environment is to position the organization according to its own particular niche.

Positioning is the process of managing how an organization distinguishes itself with a unique meaning in the mind of its publics. That is, how it wants to be seen and known by its publics, especially as distinct from its competitors. A **position statement** is the articulation of how an organization wants to be seen and known, especially vis-à-vis its competition.

The concept of distinctiveness is an important one for all organizations: large and small businesses, educational and charitable organizations, political and human service groups, hospitals, churches, government agencies, and sports teams.

In most settings, organizations are known more by their distinctiveness than by their similarities. For example, in the field of higher education, a dozen or more schools might be located in a particular metropolitan area. Each is likely to be identified by its unique characteristics: the large public university, the small church-affiliated college, the high-priced two-year private school, the community college with open admissions, the midsized public institution that used to be a teachers' college, and so on.

Problems can occur when the niche is not unique. For example, if your school is one of two small church-affiliated colleges in the area, you will emphasize what distinguishes it from the other, such as lower costs, a suburban campus, graduate degrees, evening/weekend programs, or sponsorship by a particular denomination or religious community.

The concept of positioning is fluid, and some organizations have made successful attempts to reposition themselves to keep pace with a changing environment.

Cadillac went from stodgy to trendy, with ads featuring sporty red cars rather than black luxury models. Competitor Ford Lincoln hired actor Matthew McConaughey as its spokesman for a repositioning campaign to appeal to a new generation for luxury autos. Old Spice updated its 75-year-old brand—and significantly increased its sales—with a new slogan and new social-media tactics centered on new spokesmen such as rapper LL Cool J, former NFL player Isaiah Mustafa, and NASCAR driver Tony Stewart.

On the other hand, some reworking attempts have failed miserably. Pizza Hut had to issue a news release that it really wasn't changing it name to The Hut, right after it had done just that. Because "radio" is considered an old-fashioned word, Radio Shack changed its name to simply The Shack, then quickly changed it back. Overstock.com flirted for three months with a new name, O.com, before returning to its original gimmick-free name.

Consider also the "This is not your father's Oldsmobile" campaign, which tried to reposition Oldsmobile from a line of cars popular with middle-aged and senior drivers to one fashionable for a younger generation. The campaign had a lot going for it: catchy slogan, upbeat music, and sporty new designs for its new models. And it achieved high levels of awareness. Unfortunately, sales declined. In terms of average age, the typical Olds owners became . . . well, older. So much for the value of awareness alone.

How does an organization position itself? First it conducts and analyzes research to determine just how various publics perceive the organization. It also considers the position held by its major competitors. The organization then identifies the position it would like to hold, seeking to capitalize on its uniqueness and to distinguish itself from its competition. Having done all this, the organization develops a strategy to modify its current position or perhaps simply to maintain the niche it already holds.

Make sure that your desired position is realistic. Who wouldn't want to be known as "industry leader" or "first name in (whatever)"? But there can be only one leader, one first name. A good strategic planner will be wary of pretense and of stretching beyond possibility. At best, it would be an exercise in futility. At worst, chasing an impossible dream wastes valuable organizational resources, invites ridicule, and exposes the organization to risk.

Don't confuse the public relations concept of positioning with its use in marketing, where the term refers to the competitive approach for a persuasive message (that is, positioning

EXAMPLES OF POSITIONAL STATEMENTS

Here are some examples of how various organizations might try to position themselves. Note how each statement highlights a desired attribute of the organization by implying a distinction from competitors:

- Leader that sets industry standards
- Best value, reflecting low cost and high quality
- Most economical
- Most expensive and most prestigious
- Hospital preferred by women
- Family-friendly restaurant
- "Green" brand

according to features such as customer focus, competitive advantage, social responsibility, lifestyle, or product attribute).

When we talk about positioning in public relations, we refer less to the presentation of the products or services and the messages about these, and more to perception on a wider scale—how we want our organization to be seen by our publics. As Al Ries and Jack Trout explain in *Positioning: The Battle for Your Mind*, "Positioning is not what you do to a product. Positioning is what you do to the mind of the prospect" (2001, p. 2).

Positioning Ethics

Carefully think through the ethical implications in creating a positioning statement for your organization.

Don't state your desired position merely to brag, particularly if the bragging is based on an inflated view of reality. Wanting to be the first, biggest, cleanest, or fastest is not the same as actually being the first, fastest, or whatever. Your publics will easily see through boasting and swaggering.

More important, don't use the positioning statement as a putdown for another organization. For example, a candidate for political office might seek to position herself as "a soccer mom who cares about her community." There could be a lot of potential to such an appeal.

But it raises an ethical question if she were to aim at being seen as "a better parent than the other candidate." While that might be true, it's far better for individual voters to conclude this rather than for the candidate's political organization to explicitly state such a positioning theme and carry it out in subsequent message strategy.

Goal

With the positioning statement hinting of what we want people to think about us, we turn our attention to a more direct assertion of what we want to accomplish. This is called the **goal**. It is a short, simple statement rooted in the organization's mission or vision. Using everyday

CASE IN POINT BYU Comes to Israel

Sometimes public relations goals are stated in negative terms: to reduce opposition or minimize hostility, perhaps even to prevent a situation from developing into a public issue. Such was the intent when Brigham Young University attempted to build a student center in Jerusalem. Initial opposition emerged from conservative Jewish organizations, fearful that the U.S.-based Mormon university would use the proposed student center to try to convert Jews to its brand of Christianity.

Gitam, an Israeli public relations and advertising agency, signed on for a campaign aimed at reducing opposition. The agency focused on key publics such as conservative Jewish organizations, liberal secular groups, and lawmakers who ultimately would decide the case.

Research identified causes of public opposition and the potential basis for public support. It also identified opinion leaders on both sides of the issue.

Campaign messages focused on Israel's self-identity as a Jewish state that valued freedom for all religious organizations, on efforts to show Mormons as ordinary people doing ordinary things in Israel, and on portraying Mormons as threatened underdogs by publicizing curses and threats received by BYU's office in Jerusalem from hostile opponents.

The campaign also sought to allay fears that Mormons would try to convert Jews. To this end, it featured a testimonial by the chief rabbi of Salt Lake City, home of the Mormon religion, pointing out that more Mormons converted to Judaism than Jews to Mormonism.

The result was permission for the student center, along with assurances that BYU would not enroll Jews and would require both students and faculty to sign a non-proselytizing pledge.

language, a goal acknowledges the issue and sketches out how the organization hopes to see it settled. A goal is stated in general terms and lacks measures; these will come later, as objectives.

In their classic book *Public Relations Management by Objectives*, Norman Nager and T. Harrell Allen (1984) use the analogy of transportation: Goals provide the direction while objectives pinpoint the destination.

Various explanations have been given for how to understand public relations objectives. This textbook presents a concept of three types of goals, an explanation that has been adopted by many public relations strategists, as well as by other textbooks such as Patricia Swann's *Cases in Public Relations Management* (2010). The concept presented here is that communication goals are of three types. These can be categorized as relating to a trinity of public relations situations that are part of the management function within every organization.

- **Reputation management goals** deal with the identity and perception of the organization.
- **Relationship management goals** focus on how the organization connects with its publics.
- **Task management goals** are concerned with getting certain things done.

The three types of goals together offer a way of laying out the various aims associated with public relations and integrated communication campaigns. It is unnecessary, even unlikely, that every campaign will have each type of goal. Planners mix and match these as they consider appropriate to their specific campaign.

Who sets an organization's communication goals? Generally, public relations managers do, usually as an implementation of the organization's strategic plans, which ideally the public relations people have had a hand in developing.

There are two sources for these overall organizational plans that give rise to goals. They may be global documents such as a strategic business plan. Or they may be embedded in implementation guidelines such as an annual strategic plan or a statement of priorities or directions.

Either way, public relations goals should map out a vision of success for achievements and consequences that are important to the organization as a whole. In doing so, strategic communication planners should note how the organization defines what it means to be successful and then develop goals that grow out of this understanding.

Objective

A public relations **objective** is a statement consistent with an organization's positioning and emerging from the organization's goals.

An objective is a clear and measurable statement, written to point the way toward particular levels of awareness, acceptance, or action. Communication managers responding to broader organizational goals often establish objectives. Like goals, objectives deal with intended outcomes rather than procedures for reaching them.

Phase Two

STEP
4

EXAMPLES OF PUBLIC RELATIONS GOALS

Here are several examples for each of the three different types of public relations goals.

Reputation Management Goals

- Improve the company's reputation within the industry.
- Enhance the hospital's prestige as the leading center for sports medicine.
- Reinforce the organization's image with potential donors or investors.
- Strengthen the agency's standing within the environmental movement.

Relationship Management Goals

- Promote better appreciation of the firm among potential clients.
- Enhance the relationship between the company and its customers.
- Maintain a favorable relationship amid social or organizational changes.

Task Management Goals

- Increase public support for organizational goals.
- Advance social change on a particular issue.
- Impact public behavior on matters associated with the organization's mission.
- Create a favorable climate for our client among regulatory agencies.
- Attract a sell-out crowd to a fundraising concert.

CASE IN POINT   Toyota's Reputation

Toyota has shown the importance of reputation goals, which are particularly significant in crisis situations. As billionaire investor Warren Buffett pointed out: "It takes 20 years to build a reputation and five minutes to ruin it."

Auto recalls for a faulty this or that are pretty common. But with three back-to-back recalls in 2009 and 2010, Toyota endured what was initially called the worst handled auto recall in history. Pundits predicted that the reputation of the Toyota brand would be damaged for years.

In the most challenging recall, faulty accelerators were linked to 19 deaths. Reports in both established and emerging social media whipped consumer anxiety to near-panic levels. The company that had built its reputation on quality and safety recalled nine million vehicles worldwide to fix floor mats and faulty gas pedals that caused unintended acceleration.

Toyota's confidence in its own reputation caused the company to fumble its public relations in the early stage of the recall crisis. It didn't rebut critics who accused the company of corporate arrogance. The accusations included withholding internal test reports, hiding the problem from unsuspecting customers, and paying off lawsuits behind closed doors without remedying the problems.

The allegations sparked congressional hearings in Washington, though some accused the government of overreaching as a political response to the simultaneous bailout of Toyota's U.S. competitors, General Motors and Chrysler. But there is no question that the incidents that surrounded the recalls stoked customer fears, causing Toyota's stock prices to fall by 15 percent.

Toyota and its supporters countered that the company acted as quickly as possible when credible information became available. It took full-page ads in major Sunday newspapers alerting consumers of the recall. It temporarily halted sales and shut down production until the problem could be corrected. American and Japanese officials gave interviews presenting messages of reassurance.

Within a year, Toyota stock prices rebounded, going even higher than before the recall. Toyota's reputation was once again an asset to the international corporation.

Most customers stayed with the company, maintaining trust that the technical problems were correctable and negligible. Toyota continued as the No. 1 automaker in the world, with its Camry the best-selling car in America.

Edmunds.com reported that, even after the recall, Toyota ranked a low 17 among the top 20 carmakers for customer complaints, with fewer complaints than American and most other imported automakers. It was another testimony to the importance of keeping reputation as a top goal of any organization.

A Rasmussen poll reported that 81 percent of Americans viewed Toyota favorably or very favorably. Another poll indicated that a quarter of Americans thought the government had criticized Toyota mainly to help General Motors after the bailout.

Media coverage seems to have made the crisis appear worse than it was. For example, most reports failed to note other contributing factors in the accelerator-related accidents: reckless driving, DUI, and texting while driving.

Analyses published in *Car and Driver* magazine said the risk of an unintended acceleration was 1 in 10,000 for Toyota, compared with a more-frequent 1 in 8,000 for American-made cars.

Was there a silver lining to the recall? Perhaps. In the aftermath of the crisis, Toyota renewed its priority on customer responsiveness.

A single goal may be the basis for several objectives. In fact, every goal should generate at least three objectives, one focusing specifically on each category: awareness, acceptance, and action.

Management by objectives is the process by which effective and efficient organizations plan their activities. While the acronym **MBO** has somewhat gone out of favor, the approach remains useful. From this perspective, organizations don't merely do something because they can; rather, they act because managers have determined that doing this particular something will further the work of the organization in some strategic and measurable way.

For instance, a reactive and nonstrategic public relations or marketing communication department may decide that because the company has just purchased new publishing software, a scanner and a color printer, the department should prepare new promotional brochures and fliers. But a proactive and strategic department first determines what needs to be done, say, to promote more understanding among potential customers. Then it might conclude that it should produce new brochures and buy the equipment with which to do so, or not. This is managing by objectives, not by whim.

As you can see by this example, objectives help direct the organization to act in ways that make sense.

Objectives also serve another purpose. They serve as a reference point to evaluate the effectiveness of the strategic communication program. Specifically, in Step 9, you will refer to each objective to determine whether messages and actions have been successful. The other benefit is that, by getting client agreement on the objectives, you have leverage and a point for negotiation if later the client cannot marshal the resources needed to achieve a goal.

Elements of Objectives

An objective is a threefold subset of a goal, an articulation of the various elements that are necessary to achieve the goal. Eleven specific elements can be identified for public relations objectives. These will become the elements of effective and practical objectives.

GOAL ROOTED

Objectives grow from the organization's goal statements, which themselves emerge from the mission or vision that the organization has defined for itself. Thus, objectives are responsive to a particular issue that the organization has recognized as important to its effectiveness. Public relations objectives often reflect organizational strategic plans and they may parallel financial projections, marketing ambitions, advertising or promotional expectations, and objectives associated with other aspects of the organization.

PUBLIC FOCUSED

Objectives are linked firmly to a particular public. They are based on the wants, interests, and needs of that public. Objectives for one public may be similar to those for another public, but each must be distinct.

IMPACT ORIENTED

Objectives are oriented toward the impact they can achieve. They define the effect you hope to make on your public, focusing not on the tools but on intended accomplishments. In writing objectives, avoid statements about writing and disseminating news releases, producing brochures, holding open houses, and engaging in other activities that belong with an eventual tactical response to the objectives. Such nonobjective language is dangerous. It confuses activity with achievement, and it can lull you into a false belief that because you are doing something you are also accomplishing something.

RESEARCH BASED

Objectives are linked to the research that you gathered in Phase One of the planning process. Good objectives aren't just pulled out of the air; they are tied to research. For example, if research shows that 40 percent of your key public is familiar with your organization's products or services, your objective might be to increase that to 55 percent—not because 55 percent is a magic number, but because it represents a reasonable ambition based on the current situation, as revealed through research.

EXPLICIT

Objectives are specific and precise. There is no room for varying interpretations; everyone involved in the public relations activity must share a common understanding of where the objective is leading. Don't use ambiguous verbs such as "educate," "inform," "promote," or "encourage." Instead, use strong action verbs to state your objective specifically. For example, instead of saying you want "to enhance knowledge of recycling," say your objective is "to increase residents' understanding of the benefits of recycling."

MEASURABLE

Objectives are defined and quantifiable, with clear measures that state the degree of change being sought. These **key performance indicators** (KPIs) are known more commonly as **metrics**. Simply stated, metrics are performance indicators that can be quantified and compared to other data. Avoid adjectives such as "appropriate" or "reasonable." Instead, for example, state that you want "to effect a 20 percent increase in recycling of paper products." Metrics for public relations objectives can be milestones achieved, or they can be data showing how the performance compares with a benchmarked standard or with baseline performance.

TIME DEFINITE

Objectives are time definite. Avoid ambiguous phrases such as "in the near future" or "as soon as possible." Objectives should include a clear indication of a time frame— "by December 31," "within six months," "during the spring semester," and so on. Some objectives may indicate a graduated or multistage approach to the time frame. For example, you might indicate that a certain effect is expected in two stages: a 50 percent increase within six months, a 75 percent increase after the first year.

SINGULAR

Objectives focus on one desired response from one public. Don't state in an objective that you want "to increase awareness and generate positive attitudes." You may be successful in the first effort but unsuccessful in the latter, making it difficult to evaluate your effectiveness. Most strategic communication programs will have multiple objectives, but each objective should be stated separately.

CHALLENGING

Objectives are challenging. They should stretch the organization a bit and inspire people to action. Don't aim at too safe a level of achievement or you might find that you haven't really achieved anything worthwhile. Instead, set your sights high.

ATTAINABLE

Though challenging, objectives need to be attainable and doable according to the organization's needs and resources, so don't set your sights too high. Seldom is it realistic to aim for 100 percent of anything, whether you are trying to expand your customer base or reduce

EXAMPLES OF PUBLIC RELATIONS OBJECTIVES

Here are two examples of well-written objectives in each category.

Awareness Objectives

- To have an effect on the *awareness* of senior citizens in Lake County; specifically *to increase their understanding* of the advantages that Upstate Health Program offers senior patients (60 percent of senior residents within six months).
- To have an effect on the *awareness* of legislators from the Southern Tier; specifically to *increase their understanding* of the environmental impact that House Bill 311 will have on their constituents (all 15 Republican and seven Democratic members of the House Committee on Environmental Affairs within two months).

Acceptance Objectives

- To have an effect on the *acceptance* of senior citizens in Lake County; specifically to *increase their positive attitudes* toward membership in Upstate Health Program (30 percent within six months).
- To have an effect on the *acceptance* of legislators from the Southern Tier; specifically *to gain their interest* in the environmental issues addressed by House Bill 311 (10 of the 15 Republican members and six of the seven Democratic members of the House committee within two months).

Action Objectives

- To have an effect on the *action* of senior citizens in Lake County; specifically *to obtain an increase in their membership* in the Upstate Health Program (10 percent within six months, and an additional 10 percent within a year).
- To have an effect on the *action* of legislators from the Southern Tier; specifically for them *to vote in favor* of House Bill 311 (six of the 15 Republican members of the House and six of the seven Democratic members of the House committee when the bill comes to a vote next spring).

Phase Two

**STEP
4**

opposition. Don't create a recipe for failure by setting objectives that are unattainable. For example, if you are lobbying for passage of a bill by the city council, you don't need 100 percent approval. Probably you need just a simple majority of the council voting members, 50 percent plus one.

ACCEPTABLE

Objectives enjoy the understanding and support of the entire organizational team: public relations or communication staff, managers, right up to the CEO. The value of objectives is not that they are written but that they are used. They need the strength of consensus if they are to be useful to both your organization's planners and its decision makers.

Hierarchy of Objectives

An ordered hierarchy exists among communication objectives, growing out of a logical progression through three stages of persuasion: awareness, acceptance, and action.

- Awareness begins the process, increasing gradually. This aspect of persuasion is based on what we want people to know about our organization.
- Interest then builds in stages and attitudes bloom into an acceptable choice. This acceptance stage of the persuasion process deals with what we want our publics to think or feel about what they know.
- Verbal and physical actions are modified in steps. This culmination of the persuasion process focuses on how we want our publics to act, based on what they think or feel about what they know.

Note how this model parallels the AIDA pattern (attention, interest, desire, and action), the hierarchy of effects associated with advertising since the 1920s (Lipstein, 1985). It also echoes the standard communication effects of cognitive, affective, and conative changes (Ray, 1973). Similarly, Philip Kotler, Ned Roberto and Nancy Lee (2007) focused on objectives for social-marketing campaigns, identifying these as knowledge objectives (information or facts), belief objectives (values or attitudes), and behavior objectives (specific actions).

Whatever formula you use, remember: In your enthusiasm to resolve the issue, don't let your expectations get ahead of themselves. Develop a plan that will take your communication with each of your publics through each of the necessary steps. Make sure your message first will reach your target publics, who will then agree with this message and finally will act on it. Here's a closer look at the three levels of objectives:

Awareness objectives deal with information and knowledge.

- Attention
- Comprehension
- Retention

Acceptance objectives focus on how people react to information.

- Interest
- Attitude

Action objectives address a hoped-for response to information and feelings.

– Opinion
– Behavior

AWARENESS OBJECTIVE

The first level, **awareness objectives**, focuses on information, providing the **cognitive** (thinking) **component** of the message. These objectives specify what information you want your publics first to be exposed to and then to know, understand, and remember. Awareness objectives particularly deal with dissemination and message exposure, comprehension, and retention.

How can you use awareness objectives? They are appropriate for transmitting purely functional information, for communicating on noncontroversial issues, and for the early stages of any communication campaign. Awareness objectives are particularly useful for publicity and public information models of public relations. In general, awareness objectives impact on what people know about an organization and its products, services, and ideas.

ACCEPTANCE OBJECTIVE

The next level, **acceptance objectives**, deals with the **affective** (feeling) **component** of the message—how people respond emotionally to information they have received. These objectives indicate the level of interest or the kind of attitude an organization hopes to generate among its publics. Acceptance objectives are useful in several situations: forming interests and attitudes where none existed before, increasing those that do exist, reinforcing positive interests and attitudes, and lessening negative attitudes.

Acceptance objectives are particularly important amid controversy and in persuasive situations using the advocacy (asymmetrical) model of public relations. They impact on *how* people feel about the organization and its products, services, and ideas. Notice how the examples of acceptance objectives above differ from the earlier examples of awareness objectives.

Acceptance is the key to effective strategic communication, and its importance has been obvious since 1947 when Edward Bernays, one of the acknowledged "fathers" of public relations, wrote about "the engineering of consent." This implies more than merely disseminating information. It involves connecting with people's inner desires. We must take time to foster the public's acceptance of both our organization and its messages, through means that are both practical and ethical. For example, in a political campaign, news releases and debates may be useful tools for achieving awareness. But awareness doesn't guarantee acceptance, and through the release or the debate voters may actually learn that they disagree with the candidate on important issues. Thus, successful awareness efforts could actually hinder acceptance of your client—just one of life's little ironies.

ACTION OBJECTIVE

The final level of objectives, **action objectives**, takes aim at expression and conduct, providing the **conative** (behavioral) **component** of the message. These objectives offer two types of action: opinion (verbal action) and behavior (physical action). Action objectives may attempt to create new behaviors or change existing ones, positively or negatively. They should be

---

CASE IN POINT   'Sexy Weight' for Women's Fitness

Sometimes the affective element is the most direct way to realize a goal. Take, for example, Fitness First for Women.

This women-owned, women-focused network of 13 gyms in the United Kingdom had a goal of increasing membership. Its objectives and subsequent strategy were focused on the emotional issue of how women feel about themselves and their bodies.

The campaign identified a theme of "sexy weight." This was described as an alternative to the often unrealistic and frequently unhealthy weight-loss target that some women set for themselves, usually based on what they thought would please their romantic partners (present or potential). Instead, the campaign set about to help women re-imagine themselves, with an attitude that curves could be desirable.

The specific task was to help women set an achievable weight goal at which they would feel more energized, their clothes would fit better and they would begin to feel good about themselves. Hence, their "sexy weight" (a term that became a registered trademark of the company).

The concept was researched through a nationwide survey. Psychologists were engaged as both advisers and spokespersons.

Eventually the campaign achieved measurable results: an increase in brand awareness nationwide, a positive attitude change associated with the presentation strategy, and—bottom line— a rise in actual numbers of new members for the fitness centers.

---

focused on the organization's bottom line, such as customer buying, student enrollment, donor giving, fan attendance, and so on.

Action objectives can serve not only as persuasive objectives that encourage audiences to act according to the wishes of the organization but also as objectives for building consensus and enhancing the relationship between the organization and its publics.

Developing Objectives

Just as most issues will have more than one goal, so too will each goal have a full set of objectives—at least one in each of the above categories for each identified public. Too often, efforts in public relations and marketing communication fail because they pursue the awareness objectives and then jump quickly to action, forgetting the important bridge step of generating acceptance.

Note how the action objectives shown in the box Examples of Public Relations Objectives differ from the earlier examples of awareness and acceptance objectives. As this hierarchy moves along the awareness–acceptance–action path from least important to most important objectives, the impact on the public will inevitably decrease. You might achieve an 80 percent awareness level among the public, for example, but perhaps only 40 percent will accept the message favorably, and only 15 or 20 percent may act on it.

Students often ask, "Where do you get the numbers from?" Good question. Here's an example that might shed some light, based on a real campaign being developed by a student group for a local Alzheimer's association. The goal was task-oriented: increasing volunteers for the local chapter. At first, the students were all over the place, setting unrealistic objectives. They were trying to create awareness in 40 percent of college students, acceptance in 20 percent and action in those same 20 percent. This meant that everyone who might want to volunteer actually would do so. Unlikely. It also means that if the objectives were to be met, there would be 10,000 new volunteers, an impossible number for the chapter to deal with.

Here's how we talked things out in class. First we worked backwards, focusing on just how many volunteers the organization realistically could use. The number: about 200. Then we considered how many college and university students there were in the region: about 50,000. Then we discussed some realistic expectations. How many of those 50,000 could the campaign reach? The 40 percent (20,000) seemed realistic, given the fact that students are reachable through a relatively narrow channel of communication vehicles such as campus media, social networking, and perhaps direct mail with fraternities and sororities.

Then came the questions about acceptance and action. How many of those 20,000 students who hear about the organization would think it was a good idea? The planners estimated perhaps one in 10, or 2,000 students; that is, 4 percent of the original population. And how many of that 2,000 would be likely to volunteer? Perhaps one in 10 again, or 200 student volunteers; 0.2 percent of the original total. Sounds like a small percentage, but that's just what the Alzheimer's association needed.

Adding some complexity to the process, the planners were aware that most of the current volunteers for the chapter were women and the organization needed some male volunteers. So a ratio of 70:30 women-to-men volunteers was factored in. Here are the resulting objectives:

- To create awareness of Alzheimer volunteer opportunities among college students, specifically 40 percent, or 20,000 of the 50,000 students in area colleges and universities within six months.
- To create a level of acceptance among college students, specifically generating interest among 4 percent of the student population, or 2,000 students within six months (of these, 70 percent or 1,400 women; 30 percent or 600 men).
- To generate action among college students, specifically to achieve a 0.4 percent action rate with 200 new volunteers (70 percent or 140 women; 30 percent or 60 men).

Writing Objectives

In writing public relations objectives, keep your language simple and brief. Avoid jargon. Use everyday language and strong action verbs. As part of the planning for a strategic communication campaign, objectives are not meant to be presented publicly, so don't worry if they begin to sound repetitive and formulaic.

The guidelines that follow can help you deal with each important element of a well-stated objective.

PUBLIC

Indicate the public to whom the objective is addressed.

WRITING PUBLIC RELATIONS OBJECTIVES

Public	Objective for	_____
Category	To have an effect on	☐ Awareness
		☐ Acceptance
		☐ Action
Direction	Specifically, to	☐ Create, Generate
		☐ Increase, Maximize
		☐ Maintain, Reinforce
		☐ Decrease, Minimize
Effect	(w/ awareness)	☐ Attention, Comprehension, Retention
	(w/ acceptance)	☐ Interest, Attitude, Intention
	(w/ action)	☐ Opinion, Behavior
Focus	About	_____
Performance Metric		_____
Time Period	_____	

CATEGORY

Indicate simply the category of the objective: awareness, acceptance, or action.

DIRECTION

Indicate the direction of movement you are seeking. Here are your choices: to _create_ or _generate_ something new that did not exist before, to _increase_ or _maximize_ a condition, to _maintain_ effects or _reinforce_ current conditions, or to _decrease_ or _minimize_ something. Notice that _eliminate_ is not an option because a public relations undertaking is seldom able to completely remove an unwanted effect; the best we can hope to do is minimize it. Another observation: Public relations and other strategic communication programs too often don't pay enough attention to maintaining current support. While generating new support is important, don't overlook those who currently help you and agree with you.

SPECIFIC EFFECT

Indicate the specific effect that you will address. If you are writing an awareness objective, the specific effect should deal with receiving the message, understanding it, and remembering. If you are focusing on the acceptance level, deal with generating interest and intention to act, reducing apathy, or fostering attitudes (usually positive attitudes, such as support for wearing a helmet while cycling; sometimes negative attitudes, such as a sentiment against drinking alcohol during pregnancy). For action objectives, focus on evoking a particular opinion or drawing out a desired action.

FOCUS

Indicate the focus of the specific effect you hope to achieve. Provide some detail about what you are seeking. However, don't move away from objectives by providing information about either strategy or tactics. That will come later in the planning process. Stick to articulating the impact you hope to make on your public. If you get into how to make the impact or what tools you will use to communicate, you've gone too far for this step.

EXAMPLES OF POORLY WRITTEN OBJECTIVES

Here are three examples of poorly worded objectives. Note how each can be improved.

Poorly Worded Objective 1

- To interest more people in recycling as soon as possible.

Critique: No public is indicated, merely a vague reference to "people." "Interest" is a nonspecific term. Recycling is a very broad concept. The focus is on communication activity rather than impact in the public. Measurement is nonexistent. The time frame is imprecise.

Restatement: To have an effect on the *action* of Allen County residents; specifically *to generate telephone inquiries* to the CLEAN UP help line (100 telephone calls during the first two months of the campaign; 400 telephone calls within six months).

Poorly Worded Objective 2

- To prepare a new brochure about recycling.

Critique: No public is indicated. The focus is on communication activity rather than impacting the public. Measurement and time frame are not included.

Restatement: To have an effect on the *awareness* of residents of the Oxford Apartments; specifically *to increase the understanding* of students about the benefits of recycling (45 percent during the fall semester). [Note that a brochure will be among the tactics to be outlined in Step 7; for now, just make a note to explore that tactic.]

Poorly Worded Objective 3

- To become more student focused.

Critique: This is a strategic choice more appropriate for the next step, but it doesn't indicate a desired outcome.

Restatement: To have an effect on the *acceptance* of students at St. Martin's College; specifically *to increase positive attitudes* toward the student-centeredness of the Career Counseling Center (50 percent increase within two years).

Phase Two

STEP
4

PERFORMANCE METRIC

Indicate the desired level of achievement in measurement terms. Raw numbers or percentages usually do this well. The number itself should reflect baseline research and/or desired outcomes. For example, a university library might calculate that 35 percent of students use the library facility in any two-week period. However, guidelines from the Association of College and Research Libraries might suggest that 50 percent is the desired usage pattern, including both in-person use and Internet connections. Therefore the campus library's public relations campaign might aim for a performance increase to 50 percent of the students. Stated other ways, the objective might specify a 30 percent increase over the present usage or an increase from the present 2,800 students to 4,000 out of a total student population of 8,000. Each variant aims for the same level of usage.

TIME PERIOD

Indicate the desired time frame, either within a single period or in multiple stages. Here again, you can be specific (a May 15 deadline) or relative (within six weeks, by the end of the fall semester).

What's Next?

This concludes Step 4 in the planning step dealing with strategy. With this step behind you, you should have a clear indication of what you hope to achieve through your plan. This includes the positioning you hope to nurture, as well as the goals and associated measurable objectives that the plan aims to achieve.

STEP
4

PLANNING EXAMPLE 4 **Establishing Goals and Objectives**

Here is the first part of strategic planning for Upstate College.

UPSTATE COLLEGE

Position

Upstate College wants to be known for its quality education and for its accessibility in terms of both cost and admission standards.

Goals

1. Re-create the college's image into that of a four-year institution (reputational goal).
2. Recruit more students (task goal).
3. Generate new donor support (task goal).

Objectives

Re: Goal 2 for High School Students in a Three-County Area [selected examples]

2.1. To have an effect on *awareness* of high school students; specifically *to increase their knowledge* that Upstate College is expanding into a four-year college (75 percent of students during their junior year).

2.2. To have an effect on *acceptance*; specifically *to generate interest* in attending a growing institution (25 percent of high school students during their junior and senior years).

2.3. To have an effect on *action*; specifically *to obtain inquiries* from an average of 15 percent of high school students in the college's primary three-county area during their junior or senior years.

2.4. To have an effect on *action*; specifically *to obtain applications* from an average of 5 percent of all high school graduates in the college's primary three-county area during their senior year.

[Note: You also will have objectives for each of your other key publics for every goal.]

Here is the first part of strategic planning for Tiny Tykes Toys.

TINY
TYKES
TOYS

Position

Tiny Tykes wants to be known as the company that cares about babies more than about its own profitability.

Goals

1. Regain customer confidence (reputational goal).
2. Recapture the company's previous sales rates (task goal).

Objectives

Re: Goals 1 and 2 for Parents [Selected examples]

- To have an effect on *awareness*; specifically *to create knowledge* among 75 percent of parent-customers about the redesign of the baby toy within six weeks.
- To have an effect on *awareness*; specifically *to create understanding* by 65 percent of the parents about the sacrifices and commitment that the company has made by recalling and redesigning the toys.
- To have an effect on *acceptance*; specifically *to regain trust* among 40 percent of these parents that the company has acted responsibly in redesigning the toy.
- To have an effect on *acceptance*; specifically *to create interest* among 30 percent of the parents in buying toys from the company within the next two years.
- To have an effect on *action*; specifically *to foster sales* to 25 percent of the parents from the company within the next two years.

[Note 1: You will have objectives for each of your other key publics for every goal.]

[Note 2: Each of these examples uses a different format for presenting the outline of goals and objectives. Use whatever style works best for your presentation.]

[Note 3: Numbering goals and objectives makes it easier to reference them within the planning team and when meeting with clients.]

Phase Two

STEP
4

☑ *Checklist 4* **Goals and Objectives**

Basic Questions

1. What position do you seek?
2. What are the goals?
3. What are the specific objectives (awareness, acceptance and action for each public)?

Expanded Questions

A. POSITION

1. What is a key public for this product/service/concept?
2. What position do you seek for your product/service/concept for this public?
3. Is this desired position appropriate? If no, reconsider the position.
4. What is your current position?
5. What change do you need to make to achieve the desired position?
6. What is the competition?
7. What is its position?

[Note: Replicate the above position questions for each public.]

B. GOALS

1. What are the organization's reputation goals on this issue?
2. What are the organization's relationship goals on this issue?
3. What are the organization's task goals on this issue?
4. Do any of these goals contradict another goal? If yes, which goal(s) will you eliminate?
5. What is the relative priority among the viable goals?
6. Does the organization have resources (time, personnel, money, etc.) to achieve these goals? If no, can resources be obtained? From where?
7. Does the organization have willingness to work toward these goals? If no, how can willingness be generated?
8. Are there any ethical problems with these goals? If yes, how can you modify the goals to eliminate the problems?

C. OBJECTIVES

1. Write at least one awareness objective for each key public, such as "To have an effect on awareness; specifically . . . "
2. Write at least one acceptance objective for each key public, such as "To have an effect on acceptance; specifically . . . "
3. Write at least one action objective for each key public, such as "To have an effect on action; specifically . . . "

4. Answer the following questions for each individual objective:

-   Is this objective linked to the organization's mission or vision statement?
-   Is this objective responsive to the issue/problem/opportunity/goal?
-   Is this objective focused on a particular public?
-   Is this objective clearly measurable?
-   Does this objective indicate a time frame?
-   Is this objective challenging to the organization?
-   Is this objective realistically attainable?

CONSENSUS CHECK

Does agreement exist within your organization and your planning team about the recommended positioning, goals and objectives?

☐ Yes. Proceed to Step 5, Formulating Action and Response Strategies.

☐ No. Consider the value and/or possibility of achieving consensus before proceeding.

Phase Two

STEP
4

STEP 5

Formulating Action and Response Strategies

Effective public relations and marketing communication involves deeds as well as words. Strong programs are built only on solid and consistent action. Ideally, actions and messages work hand in hand, complementing each other as the organization interacts with its publics. This step of the planning process will focus on decisions about action strategies for achieving objectives.

Strategic communication planners have many options for what their organization can do and say on any particular issue. The strategy underlying these actions can be either proactive or reactive. Here's an overview of each.

PROACTIVE STRATEGY

Sometimes an organization takes the initiative to engage its publics. Such a **proactive strategy** enables it to launch a communication program under the conditions and according to timelines that seem to best fit the organization's interests. There are two types of proactive strategies: action and communication. We'll look at each of these below.

Action strategies can be most effective because they are proactive. That is, they are implemented according to the planning of the organization, rather than by a need to respond to outside pressure and expectations from publics.

Key communication strategies also are initiated by the organization. There are several types of communication-focused strategy, including the generation of publicity, presentation of newsworthy information, and development of a transparent communication process.

REACTIVE STRATEGY

Conversely, a **reactive strategy** responds to influences and opportunities from an organization's environment. Such **response strategies** include pre-emptive action, offensive and defensive responses, diversion, commiseration, rectifying behavior, and **strategic inaction**. We'll look in depth at each of these later in this chapter.

TYPOLOGY OF PROACTIVE STRATEGIES

Proactive Strategy 1:
Action

Organization performance
Audience engagement
Special events
Alliances and coalitions
Sponsorships
Strategic philanthropy
Volunteerism
Activism

Proactive Strategy 2:
Communication

Publicity
Newsworthy information
Generating news
News peg
Transparent communication

Proactive Strategy 1: Action

The first category of proactive public relations strategies involves **action strategy**, tangible deeds undertaken by the organization in an effort to achieve its objectives. Let's look at the eight categories: organizational performance, audience engagement, special events, alliances and coalitions, sponsorships, strategic philanthropy, volunteerism, and sometimes activism.

Organizational Performance

The **performance** of the organization is what it does, as compared to what it says. This is the first and most important area to consider when weighing various strategic communication initiatives. This is where all strategic planning begins.

Ensure that the organization is working at its highest possible level of quality for its customers. One of the first questions in the formative research phase of this planning process (Step 2, Analyzing the Organization) was designed to identify the quality of the product or service associated with the issue being addressed. Public relations and marketing communication can't be expected to promote the good name of an organization that doesn't give good performance. Products or services must reflect a level of quality that meets the wants, interests, needs, and expectations of key publics.

What do customers want? Quality products. Value. Customer service. Reasonable prices. They also expect the organizations they choose to patronize to be responsible members of society.

Some companies have been unpleasantly surprised to find that customers won't buy products made by exploiting child laborers or cosmetics developed through animal testing. Some consumers avoid firms with poor records on safety, pollution, discrimination, treatment of employees, or international practices.

In his book *Building Your Company's Good Name*, Davis Young (1996) notes that a good reputation—an organization's most valuable asset—is built on performance, not on mere words.

Phase Two

STEP
5

One of the principles of effective public relations is **adaptation**, the willingness and ability of the organization to make changes necessary to create harmony between itself and its key publics. The box on Attributes of Strategic Communication in the Introduction of this book notes the importance of adaptation to new environments and changing needs of publics and markets.

Some organizations use strategic communication to convince their publics to conform to the offerings of the organization. This is the persuasive model of public relations. Another model of public relations based more on relationships aims to enhance the mutual rapport between the organization and its publics. This means that sometimes the organization will need to change.

If a university wants to promote registration for its summer program, for example, one of the first activities should be to research key publics (such as currently registered students, incoming freshmen, and people who applied to the school and were accepted but who did not register), identifying the courses they want and the schedules they prefer. In other words, the school would create the summer program around its key publics' needs, rather than building it around the convenience of the faculty and administrators.

Phase Two

STEP
5

CASE IN POINT Adapting for Renewable Energy

The international campaign to select a world headquarters for the International Renewable Energy Agency (IRENA) shows the importance of performance and adaptation.

The intergovernmental agency required its 130-plus members to agree on a location for the new headquarters. Countries such as Denmark, Germany, and Austria pushed their status as recognized leaders in renewable energy.

But a strong campaign managed by Edelman, the global public relations agency, on behalf of the United Arab Emirates helped shape a surprising outcome.

There was irony in the fact that UAE is one of the world's leading producers of oil, and IRENA is focused on renewable energy. Fossil fuel was seen as the enemy. For years though, UAE had been making a commitment to renewable energy. It built the city of Masdar near Abu Dhabi as the world's first carbon-neutral, zero-waste city with sustainable technology.

The IRENA@UAE campaign was a research-based plan built around a message strategy emphasizing sustainabile energy as an issue particularly facing developing countries.

Public relations showcased the Emirates' forward-looking energy policy and shored up its diplomatic role in the international community. It also linked the bid to scholarships in alternative energy and a $350 million loan program for sustainable energy projects in developing countries.

In 2009, IRENA overwhelmingly voted to establish its international headquarters in Masdar, a recognition that UAE's performance on clean energy had matched its words.

Six years later, the Renewable Energy Agency opened the doors to its new headquarters in Masdar. The building is one of the greenest office buildings in the world. Oriented toward wind flow, it has a solar power system and solar water heater, making it a model of energy, water, and carbon efficiency.

Similarly, if a dental office wants to attract a professional clientele, it might schedule office hours on weekends and evenings, perhaps on a couple of nights with appointments as late as 10 or 11 p.m. to accommodate busy executives. That's been done by some forward-looking practices.

Audience Engagement

Another important strategy initiative for the public relations planner is **audience engagement**. This involves using strong two-way communication tactics and engaging audiences and publics in your communication activities.

AUDIENCE INTEREST

One way to do this is to communicate about the audience's relevant interests rather than the needs of the message source or the sponsoring organization. The formal term for this is **salience** of the information—the degree to which an audience perceives information as applicable or useful. Use examples and applications that address a key question of your public: What's in it for me?

In a fundraising letter for cancer research, for example, tell your readers that they can help make a cure possible rather than merely citing the researchers' need for financial support. When possible, base your message on values shared by the organization and the public.

AUDIENCE PARTICIPATION

Audience participation can be built on activities that bring individual members of your publics into direct contact with the products and services of your organization. For example, police departments in many cities routinely use ride-along programs to give key citizens a firsthand look at their communities from inside a patrol car. Cosmetic companies give free samples, health clubs give low-cost trial memberships, and private schools have shadow programs for prospective students.

Several years ago the Union of American Hebrew Congregations (UAHC), the denominational leadership of Reform Judaism in the U.S., wanted to strengthen bonds with Reform Jews around the country. Invoking the principle of audience participation, UAHC invited its 800 member congregations to participate in a video project by sharing their success stories. More than 200 congregations responded and asked to be included in the documentary, gaining a sense of solidarity with the national association—virtually guaranteeing their use of the eventual video.

AUDIENCE FEEDBACK

Still another way to foster audience participation is by generating feedback. Create convenient ways your audience can respond to your message and engage in dialogue. Use techniques such as toll-free phone numbers, online surveys, question-and-answer sessions, interactive websites, and similar tools. Facebook, Twitter, and other embodiments of social media are great assets in generating such feedback, with opportunities for liking, retweeting, sharing, commenting, and online polling.

A company may look to research in determining whether to establish a consumer complaints hotline as a form of feedback. A complaints department can gauge customer satisfaction, minimize the loss of customers and perhaps identify ways to prevent problems.

> ### CASE IN POINT Bosque Builds Community Support
>
> Audience participation was at the heart of a campaign to restore the Bosque de Chapultepec in Mexico City, the hemisphere's oldest urban park, where 15 million visitors a year had endangered the park's 686 hectares (1,695 acres, nearly twice the size of New York City's Central Park).
>
> The public relations strategy centered on building a sense of public stewardship and a personal stake in the park among the city's residents and visitors, as well as creating strategic alliances with corporations.
>
> Specifics of this approach included encouraging visitors to minimize and perhaps reverse pollution by using sanitary facilities. The plan also relied heavily on volunteers and donors.
>
> The campaign developed several tactics including typical media relations activities such as news conferences and interviews. Tactics also included networking among environmentally involved groups, special events surrounded phased reopening after the park was closed for several months, and attention-getting activities such as concerts and cultural events by celebrities to attract local residents of various ages.

Several studies (Nyer, 2000; Kowalski and Erickson, 1997) suggest that soliciting complaints can actually help an organization reduce customer dissatisfaction. It seems that people feel better about the organization they complain against when they actually have an opportunity to voice those complaints. After venting, they also feel better about the product or service they had complained about, according to the studies.

TRIGGERING EVENT

You also can build into your program a **triggering event**. This is an activity that stimulates action among key publics. Examples of triggering events are speeches that conclude with an invitation for the audience to sign a petition, or an open house that ends with an opportunity to join.

Sometimes the triggering element is built into an event, such as Election Day as the triggering event for a political campaign. In themselves, awareness weeks don't cut it; they are too many and too mundane. But good planning can create interesting activities that can draw attention to the sponsoring organization.

Experienced public relations practitioners realize that sometimes triggering events may be unplanned, so they are quick to take advantage of opportunities that present themselves. The election of the first openly gay Episcopalian bishop in 2005 served as a triggering event, both positive and negative, for issues such as gay rights and the meaning of church unity.

Some tragic events, in their very wretchedness, can focus attention and generate quick action on particular issues. The 2015 massacre of nine people in a church in Charleston, S.C., by a white supremacist triggered an almost immediate movement across the South to remove the Confederate flag from state buildings, public monuments, and license plates. National companies such as Amazon, Walmart, Sears, and eBay removed products showing the symbol from their shelves. They agreed that, despite some Southerners' affection for the flag, it had become an irredeemable symbol of racism, slavery, and discrimination.

The death of a celebrity also can serve as a triggering event, focusing attention on the illness or lifestyle that caused the death. Such was the response to the deaths of Whitney Houston, Philip Seymour Hoffman, and Amy Winehouse calling attention to cocaine, heroin, and alcohol abuse, respectively, and to Robin Williams' suicide shedding light on depression. Each of these deaths caused spikes in hotline calls for help from people with these problems.

Sometimes a triggering event brings unwanted notoriety. The Spanish public was outraged in 2012 when it learned that, while the country struggled with an economic crisis including 23 percent unemployment, King Juan Carlos had taken a lavish elephant hunt to Botswana. The public learned of the expensive safari only when the king broke his hip and had to be flown back to Madrid for surgery. The outrage prompted the first-ever public apology in his 23 years as monarch.

But Juan Carlos also was president of the Spanish branch of the World Wildlife Fund. For years his support of bullfighting had been a thorn in the side of pro-animal activists. But the international embarrassment of this ill-timed safari renewed attention on some of his earlier transgressions of environmental principles, including a previous elephant kill in Africa and bear hunts in Russia and Romania. WWF/Spain quickly removed Juan Carlos from the honorary leadership post.

This was not the first time that big-game hunting made the headlines. The incident came only a month after Donald Trump's two sons were photographed hunting elephants, leopards, and other exotic animals in Zimbabwe. Soon after, photos surfaced of England's Princes William and Harry displaying their trophy kills in Spain and Argentina.

Such incidents only serve to heighten international opposition to big-game hunting parties for the rich and famous, triggering renewed attention on the broader issue of human sport and threatened animal habitats in Africa and elsewhere.

Special Event

A **special event** is another useful way to generate audience participation. A special event is a **staged activity** (sometimes called a **pseudo-event**), which is an activity that an organization develops or orchestrates to gain the attention and acceptance of key publics. Special events need to be legitimate, meaning they are designed primarily as a means of engaging publics and encouraging their interaction with your organization, with the potential for media attention being secondary.

The polar opposite of special event is the **publicity stunt**, which is merely a gimmick planned mainly to gain publicity, having little value beyond that. Avoid self-serving publicity stunts, but don't dismiss the news value of legitimate special events. An appropriate event can attract the attention of reporters and generate interest among your publics.

A special event sometimes can provide a great **photo op** (short for photo opportunity) that can attract the attention of visual media and offer opportunities to extend the organization's message to newspapers and magazines, television and online video, and photographic venues.

For example, the Almond Board of Australia has as its mission to promote the health benefits and good taste of almonds as a way to boost sales. In addition to the usual package of media interviews, the board developed a photo op that played on visual imagery. The board asked an up-and-coming designer to create a dress hand-sewn with 3,000 almonds. It then had a model parade through a pedestrian mall in the central business district of Sydney, giving away tins of fresh almonds to passersby. Photos of the dress were uploaded to Flickr, and

OPPORTUNITY BORN OF TRAGEDY

Suffering in silence may be a virtue, but suffering in public can make money. When public misfortune becomes a triggering event, it can make your cause hot.

When First Lady Betty Ford went public with her diagnosis and treatment for breast cancer in 1974, she broke a social taboo against discussing personal issues in the media. Her honesty and candor did more than put the disease on the public agenda; they provided a lesson for public relations practitioners: Move quickly when injury or disease captures the nation's attention.

Since then, attention often has surrounded celebrity. When *Saturday Night Live* star Gilda Radner was diagnosed with ovarian cancer, her treatment, remission, and subsequent death from the disease drew media attention that led to steadily increasing attention to the disease and the benefit of early detection.

When actor Michael J. Fox revealed that he suffered from Parkinson's disease, public interest sparked donations for the National Parkinson Foundation and later for his own foundation, which has raised more than $450 million for Parkinson's research.

Donations doubled for the American Paralysis Association after actor Christopher Reeve was paralyzed in a horse-riding accident; the association even changed its name to the Christopher Reeve Paralysis Association. Contributions to the Alzheimer's Association jumped after President Ronald Reagan was diagnosed with the disease.

Assisting the public relations efforts of some organizations, celebrities have helped turn the spotlight on illnesses and diseases afflicting themselves or their loved ones. Awareness of testicular cancer, for example, is the cause of comedian Tom Green, actor Richard Belzer, and athletes such as cyclist Lance Armstrong, hockey forward Phil Kessel, third baseman Mike Lowell, wide receiver Kevin Curtis, and skater Scott Hamilton, themselves survivors of the disease.

Other celebrities giving publicity to various maladies include actor Jimmy Smits for colon cancer, country singer Toby Keith for childhood cancers, talk show host Montel Williams for multiple sclerosis, basketball star Alonzo Mourning for anemia, basketball star Magic Johnson for HIV/AIDS, R&B singer T-Boz Watkins for sickle cell disease, and quarterback Doug Flutie for childhood autism.

Diabetes awareness is the cause supported by soul singer Gladys Knight and actors Halle Barry and Cuba Gooding Jr. Breast cancer awareness has strong support from entertainers such as Christina Applegate, Taylor Swift, Reese Witherspoon, Nicole Kidman, Wanda Sykes, and Kylie Minogue.

Social causes often attract celebrity representatives. Angelina Jolie has traveled the world as a celebrity ambassador with the UN High Commission for Refugees, along with her work for cancer awareness and many humanitarian programs. Various animal charities get support from many celebrities, including Ellen Degeneres, Ian Somerhalder, and Carrie Underwood. The Wounded Warrior Project earned support from celebrities including Joan Jett, Alec Baldwin, Matthew Modine, and Al Roker.

In 2014, Hugh Jackman, Ricky Gervaise, and William Shatner joined more than 771 million people posting crotch-grabbing photos for the #FeelingNuts social-media campaign against testicular cancer. See also checkyonutz.org to see how public relations students at Canisius College in Buffalo developed an awareness campaign for testicular cancer.

Like Michael J. Fox, some celebrities even have created their own foundations: Matt Damon founded Water.org to provide access to safe water and sanitation in developing areas of the world. Other foundations have been established by Lady Gaga (promoting gay acceptance and fighting bullying), Mark Walburg (youth programs), Leonardo DiCaprio (wildlife habitats), Sir Elton John (AIDS), Bono (disease in Africa), Oprah Winfrey (Boys and Girls Clubs), Sean Combs (programs for inner-city kids), Angelina Jolie and Brad Pitt (eradicating extreme poverty), and many more.

video was placed on YouTube. The board achieved its objectives of generating coverage in print and online trade and consumer publications, achieving record sales in the following three months.

To distinguish a legitimate special event from a publicity stunt ask yourself: Even if the news media don't report this activity, will it still be worthwhile? If you can answer "yes" to this question, then it's probably a real special event.

Another important requirement for effective special events is that they should be creative, with a spark of originality that sets them apart from the ordinary and the routine. Brainstorming with your colleagues sometimes can suggest an approach that would be distinctive enough so that the special event can become, literally, "the talk of the town."

There are many types of special events, which are outlined in the next section on tactics. For now, simply consider the wide range of possibilities:

- Artistic programs, such as recitals and art shows
- Competitions, such as sporting events and essay contests
- Community events, such as parades and festivals
- Holiday celebrations for civic, cultural, ethnic, religious, and other occasions
- Observances, such as anniversaries, birthdays, and special days or months
- Progress-Oriented activities, such as groundbreaking ceremonies, cornerstone placements, and grand openings

A later section in this chapter on activism deals with special events of a more polemic or confrontational nature.

Alliance and Coalition

You've heard the phrase "The whole is worth more than the sum of its parts." That's about **synergy**, when two or more organizations work together to produce an outcome that is greater than the input (and likely outcomes) of each group separately.

Phase Two

STEP
5

ETHICS: PUBLICITY STUNT

In a campaign titled "Holocaust on Your Plate," People for the Ethical Treatment of Animals compared the slaughtering of chickens to the murder of Jews by Nazis in World War II. Not unexpectedly, PETA drew hostile criticism and a lot of negative media attention to its cause of animal rights. While attention does not necessarily result in support, the action did seem to further PETA's publicity agenda.

In developing public relations strategies, give thought to the ethical considerations that underlie publicity stunts.

- Does the action have any intrinsic value, or is it mainly for show?
- Will it be offensive? To whom?
- If it is offensive, does this matter to your organization?
- Does the publicity stunt trivialize an otherwise serious topic?

When organizations work together in a common purpose, the combined energy offers a real opportunity for strategic communication initiatives. Such synergy comes in two forms.

- An **alliance** tends to be an informal, loosely structured, and perhaps small working relationship among organizations.
- A **coalition** is a similar relationship that is a bit more formal and structured than an alliance.

Alliances and coalitions seek to forge relationships—often new ones—with groups that share similar values and concerns. Using this strength-in-numbers approach, organizations try to compound their influence toward meeting objectives and to enhance their ability to break through barriers while trying to relate to their publics.

Some alliances involve people (such as customers or celebrities) rather than organizations alone. When Lee Jeans joined with the Entertainment Industry Foundation (Hollywood's leading charitable organization) to promote National Denim Day, the company called on people to put on their favorite jeans and donate $5 for breast cancer research. Lee also invited the participation of celebrities Zac Efron, Christina Applegate, Billy Ray Cyrus, Mariska Hargitay, Steve Carrell, Jessica Simpson, Lucy Liu, and others. Since 1996, the annual Denim Day has raised more than $91 million, making it one of the largest single-day fundraising events.

Inspired by a *Sports Illustrated* column, the Orkin pest control company teamed with the United Nations Foundation, NBA and WNBA charities foundations, and the community outreach program of Major League Soccer. The result was a "Nothing But Nets" program that has raised $35 million since 2006 to buy and distribute mosquito nets in 20 nations in sub-Saharan Africa, where malaria is a leading killer of children.

Sometimes organizations seek alliances with influential individuals, particularly with community leaders who are respected among the organization's publics. An organization trying to encourage African Americans to participate in a bone marrow screening, for instance, may look to respected leaders in the community or perhaps to influential organizations such as the National Association for the Advancement of Colored People or the Urban League, professional sports teams, black professional fraternities or sororities, or similar groups.

Organizations that recognize they have a poor reputation with their public sometimes seek alliances with organizations having a better standing with the public. For example, several years ago when the U.S. Immigration and Naturalization Service (INS) declared a legalization program for undocumented immigrants who met certain residency requirements, in several communities it turned to churches that had an existing credibility within the Hispanic community. The hope was that the immigrants' distrust of the INS would be overcome by their greater trust in the churches. The third-party endorsement the churches were able to provide the INS helped many people become legal residents.

At times, coalition building can lead to some unlikely bedfellows. In some communities, for example, coalitions advocating sexual responsibility or access to prenatal and postnatal care bring together pro-life and pro-choice activists who otherwise would have little in common.

Alliances sometimes are made with internal publics, such as when a company convenes a task force of its employees to consider workplace concerns. Other alliances focus on external publics. For example, a health-care system facing unprofitable duplication of services among several of its hospital sites might hold public hearings to discuss the problem and invite community input toward finding a solution, thus building an alliance with its publics.

ALLIANCES AND OPINION LEADERS

A particularly beneficial alliance can exist between an organization and opinion leaders. Having identified opinion leaders in Step 3, public relations planners can find themselves in a good place to develop a strategy for communicating with them.

One piece of advice from the field is to involve opinion leaders early. For example, 39 percent of pharmaceutical companies communicate with opinion leaders before they launch the public phase of their public relations tactics, according to a survey by Cutting Edge Information, a pharmaceutical research/planning firm in Durham, N.C.

Jason Richardson, president of Cutting Edge, explained the value of taking an early lead with opinion leaders: "One of the biggest mistakes pharmaceutical companies make is waiting to contact key opinion leaders—and not involving them enough. Opinion leader relationships are built on activities that begin years before a product reaches the market."

Richardson also reports that too few companies allot adequate funds to communicate with opinion leaders, whom he calls "thought leaders."

A campaign to reduce AIDS and other sexually transmitted diseases consciously drew on Everett Rogers's diffusion of innovation theory by targeting bartenders as opinion leaders with influence through the social network of bars.

The campaign also identified as opinion leaders people who were popular and well liked and who have frequent interaction with the key publics of the campaign. The campaign then enlisted the involvement of these opinion leaders, providing training on how to encourage behavioral changes to lower the risk of HIV infection. The campaign reported a 25–30 percent decrease in risky behaviors following the intervention of the opinion leaders.

Phase Two

STEP
5

Sponsorship

Another proactive step that organizations can take to gain visibility and respect among their key publics is through **sponsorship**. A sponsorship is a significant strategy for programs oriented toward community relations. It involves either providing a program directly, or providing financial, personnel, or other resources the program requires.

Make sure there is a logical link between the activity being sponsored and the purpose or mission of your organization. For example, a science museum might sponsor a trip to view a space shuttle launch; a university might host a summer boot camp for high school journalists; a bookstore might support a literacy program.

It's a good idea to establish levels or categories for potential sponsors so smaller businesses or individual funders will be able to participate, as well as larger and better-funded sponsors. An organization may seek a single program or "title" sponsor giving a major donation, as well as a dozen or more corporate patrons and individual sponsors giving lesser amounts.

Membership organizations such as zoos and museums likewise have varying levels for individual sponsors. Beyond the levels of individual and family memberships, zoos often create categories for more involved donors. Some zoos use clever names for various membership levels: Animal Kingdom Club, St. Louis Zoo; Curator's Club, Nashville; Koala Club, San Diego; Penguin Patron, Kansas City; Wildlife Champion, Louisville; Keeper's Club, Indianapolis.

Some sponsorships are based on existing marketing relationships. For example, Lexus sponsors polo championships because polo enthusiasts reflect the luxury car's customer base. So too with Budweiser's sponsorship of the Super Bowl and Snickers' arrangement as the official candy of Little League Baseball and U.S. Youth Soccer.

Other sponsorship programs are designed to appeal to new publics. These programs often have a clear marketing connection, paving the way for the company to obtain new customers.

Another type of sponsorship is the naming of buildings, stadiums, rooms, and other locations. Corporations name buildings, and universities ask donors to name art studios and science labs—all for a price, of course. More on this in the section on branding rights in the next step of this strategic planning process.

Sponsorships can stretch a company's promotion dollars much further than media advertising, at the same time creating more intensive relationships between the organization and its publics. For example, during the Gay Games IX in 2014, Cleveland hosted 20,000 athletes from 60 nations, pumping more than $51 million into the Cleveland economy.

Sponsors abounded, including the Cleveland Foundation as the presenting sponsor, the United Church of Christ as the first religious denomination to sponsor the games, and corporate

---

CASE IN POINT Greenpeace vs. Kleenex

Kleenex has engaged in corporate sponsorship beginning with the 2004 Olympic Games. Its series of "Kleenex Moments" focused on human emotions in various athletic events, which research showed often were watched by couples.

The campaign involved marketing, advertising, Internet, and media relations. The media outreach alone generated more than 1,700 news stories with a total audience of nearly 135 million readers and viewers.

In an example of the no-good-deed-goes-unpunished maxim, the environmental organization Greenpeace used the publicity generated by Kleenex to criticize its parent company, Kimberly-Clark, the world's largest manufacturer of tissue products. At the time, K-C was making 4 million tons of tissue products each year from old-growth forests in Canada.

Greenpeace leveraged the publicity associated with the 2006 Winter Olympics and sarcastically gave Kleenex a gold medal for "a new world record for fastest forest destruction."

After a five-year global campaign against K-C, Greenpeace joined the corporation in a joint news conference in 2009 to announce a truce: The company pledged to no longer use trees from the ancient forests, to use more recycled paper, and to strengthen its policy toward sustainable forest management. In return, Greenpeace would halt the boycott.

Ironically, Greenpeace itself was criticized by Marcal, a company that manufactures paper goods from only 100 percent recycled products. Marcal accused Greenpeace of lowering its standards to get the K-C agreement.

sponsors including the Cleveland Cavaliers, Cleveland Indians, Coca-Cola, Marriott, United Airlines, Wells Fargo, Key Bank, GE, Sherwin-Williams, and Labatt Blue.

Organizers, sponsors, and consumers alike have noted the value of such sponsorships, and many participants and fans in past games reported that they went out of their way to buy from the sponsors. Advertisers and sponsors called it **niche marketing**, an approach to marketing and public relations intended to shore up its relationship with consumers.

Yet such sponsorships are not without risk. Kraft Foods and Walmart, both sponsors of the 2006 Gay Games in Chicago, were heavily criticized by conservative consumers, spurred on by the well-funded American Family Association, which charged the corporations with promoting homosexuality. Both companies refrained from sponsoring the Cleveland games.

Ben & Jerry's ignored possible criticism (but prepared for it) when research showed that key customers supported the company's commitment to social justice. In 2009 when same-sex marriage became legal in its home state of Vermont, Ben & Jerry's partnered with the Freedom to Marry organization to activate consumers to support marriage equality. The company mobilized a social-media campaign and renamed its iconic "Chubby Hubby" ice cream as "Hubby Hubby" in its Vermont stores. The campaign received nationwide media coverage (86 percent of it rated positive or neutral), increasing sales in the process.

Strategic Philanthropy

Successful sponsor organizations find ways to attract continuing visibility and reputational benefits. This is the notion of **strategic philanthropy**, in which businesses fund or otherwise support community relations gestures with an eye toward enhancing their own business interests as well as the interests of their employees and customers.

Strategic philanthropy is more than charity. It is part of the wider approach to corporate social responsibility in which organizations realize that their success depends in part on the goodwill of the community and their perception as being a contributing member of society.

It's also part of a community relations program tailored to the strategic interests of the organization. For example, a newspaper or TV station might give scholarships for communication students, a pharmacy for medical students, a sports team for student athletes, and so on. Increasingly such corporate donors are asking what they get for their money.

Recipients of corporate charity would be wise to find ways to publicly recognize their donors and other supporters, not only as a matter of common courtesy but also as a way to foster an ongoing mutually beneficial relationship between the corporate donor and the recipient organization. For example, the recipient university of a corporate scholarship fund should ensure that the donor name is prominently recognized.

BOEING

The Boeing Corporation has an eye on its customers and other support bases as it uses strategic philanthropy to generate tangible benefits, create enduring value, reach target publics, and build sustainable long-term relationships. Its corporate beneficiaries include the Kennedy Center for the Performing Arts and sponsorship of the national anthem at all home games of the Chicago Bears (Chicago being its corporate headquarters), as well as signage at the Seattle Mariners baseball field and support for its Museum of Flight near its operations in Seattle. The company, which posts its philanthropic criteria at its website (boeing.com), reported charitable giving of $188 million in 2014 from the corporation, its employees, and its charitable trust.

PRINCIPLES OF STRATEGIC PHILANTHROPY

The guiding principle of strategic philanthropy is to get the biggest bang for the buck. This can be accomplished in three different ways.

Give More Bang for the Buck

This principle is one of basic economy: Provide something more valuable to others than it is costly to you. A dollar given that generates only a dollar's worth of benefit is not a good sponsorship investment. A more strategic sponsorship is a donation with more value to the recipient than cost to the giver.

For example, if a company that makes television sets wants to sponsor an educational program through the county library system, it could give $80,000 to the library for new books, earning a modest amount of visibility and appreciation. A better move, however, might be to donate $80,000 worth of television sets so that the library can expand its use of educational and cultural videos. This donation might have cost the company less than $25,000 to manufacture the TV sets, a high return on investment for the company that would be a continuing reminder to library patrons of the company's donation to the community's quality of life.

Give What You Already Own

A parallel principle of sponsorship also is one of economy: Give away something of value that you already own, thus costing you nothing.

This is the premise behind Operation Home Free, begun by Trailways Bus Lines and continued when Greyhound bought that company. The program formed an alliance with the International Association of Chiefs of Police and the National Runaway Switchboard to help runaway youths. Over the years it provided free bus rides to more than 10,000 runaways returning home.

The value? Tickets worth $120,000 in the first year alone.

The actual cost? Virtually nothing to Greyhound, since its buses already were running, usually with some empty seats.

The benefits? To runaways, a safe return home. To the police and runaway agencies, assistance in getting kids off the streets, into counseling, and back home. To Greyhound, a boost in its reputation among employees, customers, police, and other important publics. A real win–win–win situation!

Because of the success of the program and the growing need, Operation Home Free has been replicated by Greyhound Australia.

Maximize Your Investment

Another sponsorship principle is to make the most of what you donate, in terms of recognition. Consider giving several small gifts, each with the potential for significant publicity, instead of a single large one. While a large gift might yield one-time publicity, a series of well-timed and strategically placed smaller gifts might generate greater overall attention.

Additionally, while anonymous giving may be good for the soul, corporate philanthropy generally needs the public spotlight. Give items or support projects that can be labeled with your organization's name, out there for all to see.

CARIBOU COFFEE

Sometimes the link between a company and a nonprofit cause is less apparent. Caribou Coffee developed Amy's Blend to raise money to battle breast cancer. Some research suggests that drinking coffee can reduce the risk of getting breast cancer, but that wasn't the motivation for Caribou. Instead, it was a tribute to one of the company's original roastmasters who died from breast cancer. For 18 years, the company has donated 10 percent of its profits from Amy's Blend to cancer research. The effort has resulted in the largest donations in the company's history, $250,000 in recent years. In 2015, Caribou matched customer purchase by donating a cup of coffee to nurses and families in cancer centers around the country.

Corporate Social Responsibility

David Eisenstadt, partner with TCI/The Communications Group based in Toronto, points out that, in the past, some corporate giving was based on whim. The CEO's wife loved figure skating, so the company gave to a skating program. But such a gift didn't necessarily serve the corporate interest.

Eisenstadt counsels that such philanthropy, part of a program of **corporate social responsibility**, should be a business decision, not an emotional one. "Our strategy is kind of back-to-basics," he told a reporter from *Strategy*, a Canadian marketing magazine. "If women are the people who make the buying decisions for our clients' services, then we would be looking at charitable organizations that have a strong female connect. The objective is that everybody should win" (Minogue, 2003).

Nonprofit organizations seeking corporate contributions should do their homework before seeking a corporate gift, first determining how to add public relations value for a potential donor.

Before asking for funds, anticipate ways to acknowledge the gift, both immediately and in a continuing way. For example, tangible gifts might feature a sign or a plaque recognizing the donor. Other substantial gifts might result in using the corporate name for a program or facility. All gifts can be acknowledged in newsletters, at websites, in the organization's social media, and at events such as banquets and dedication ceremonies.

Often corporate social responsibility is generated by the organization itself. Here as well, the key is to support a cause that reflects the company's mission.

FOOD LION

The Food Lion grocery chain refocused its philanthropy on its main product—food—by launching Food Lion Feeds. The program matches customer purchases of its reusable shopping bags by donating meals to local food banks in more than 1,100 communities where the stores are located. Its goal is to provide 500 million meals to families in need by the end of 2020. The campaign was focused on a variety of employee relations projects, including employee-driven social media postings.

TOM'S SHOES

Each year, Tom's Shoes sponsors One Day Without Shoes to spread awareness that a simple pair of shoes can prevent infection and allow access to education for millions of children. The project generated attention on social media and through traditional media. Tom's invited customers to send Instagram photos of their bare feet, promising to donate a pair of shoes for each photo. Its one-day event in 2015 resulted in shoes for 296,243 children, earning the company a Shorty Award (short-form social media content) in the "social good" category.

DICK'S SPORTING GOODS

Because of cuts in school athletics budgets, 60 percent of children must pay to play interscholastic sports. Dick's Sporting Goods operates nearly 700 stores nationwide. So it was a logical connection that led the company's nonprofit foundation to launch its Sports Matters initiative.

The foundation set two goals: to increase awareness about both the underfunding of school sports and the benefits of playing sports, and to raise $2 million to support school sports programs.

Media relations efforts and advertising in national print, television, online, and social media highlighted the importance of saving youth sports. A TV documentary about two high school football teams forced to merge because of budget cuts aired on ESPN and ABC. In-store donations coupled with crowdfunding raised more than $4 million, which saved more than 180 youth sports programs. The program won a 2015 PRSA Silver Anvil award of excellence.

FEDEX

Some campaigns respond to data pointing toward the need for higher visibility and public awareness of its commitment to social responsibility.

Over the years, FedEx has transported eagles, sea lions, dolphins, and sea turtles. Flights dubbed the Panda Express have transported giant pandas to and from China, Washington, DC, Paris, Toronto, and other cities around the world.

Most such flights have been low-key, but a few have generated high visibility. Such was the return of 19 penguins to New Orleans in the aftermath of Hurricane Katrina from a temporary shelter in California. FedEx created a series of media moments for the "flight" of the flightless penguins: a police escort as they left Oakland; a ceremonial arrival in New Orleans featuring a jazz band and another police escort; and an event with a large crowd, including 250 "influentials," at the aquarium as the penguins returned home.

RACE FOR THE CURE

Increasingly, national causes are going local with a coordinated series of events, blending strategic philanthropy with alliances.

One example of this is "Race for the Cure" (komen.org), which has 1.6 million runners in 150 walks, races, and marathons around the U.S. and eight other countries. Since its founding more than 30 years ago, the organization has raised more than $2.5 billion for breast cancer awareness and research.

In addition to holding its own races throughout the country, the foundation works with affiliated activities. Condé Nast Publications' "Rally for the Cure" has raised $63 million. Other multimillion-dollar fundraising endeavors include "Bowl for the Cure" organized with the U.S. Bowling Congress; "Pink for the Cure" from the sale of pink-packaged cereal, soup, and cookie mix from General Mills; New Balance shoes' "Lace for the Cure"; Major League Baseball's Mother's Day event, "Going to Bat Against Breast Cancer"; and "On Deck for the Cure" sponsored by Holland America, Princess, Carnival, and other cruise lines.

CASE IN POINT **Rock the Vote**

Some sponsorship activities focus more on issues rather than on events. An example of this is the Rock the Vote campaign (rockthevote.org), which encourages young adults to register to vote. Using donated radio and television spots, as well as its own online and social media, RTV has registered 6 million voters aged 18–29 since it began in national elections of 2000.

The group cites research that 84 percent of young registered voters actually go to the polls during national elections, significantly higher than average.

The organization has built its success on alliances, including promotions cosponsored by malls, sporting events, and university campuses, as well as its interactive website and a toll-free 800 phone number promoted on television—particularly on MTV. It joined with Facebook to provide online registration for Facebook users.

Its online voter registration tool offers assistance in 14 languages—English and Spanish, as well as most Asian languages including Tagalog and Ilocano (Philippines), Thai, Urdu (Pakistan), and Bengali (Bangladesh and India).

Working with LL Cool J's Camp Cool Foundation, RTV formed the Hip Hop Coalition for Political Change, extending its message into the inner city. It also formed Radio Rocks the Vote, a partnership with urban, alternative, and Top 40 stations.

Such efforts have attracted more than three-dozen celebrity spokespersons, including Jake Gyllenhaal, Mylie Cyrus, will-i-am, Romeo, Kinky, Macy Gray, and Ricky Martin to participate in RTV public service ads.

Does all of this happen because MTV and the radio stations are civic-minded companies? They probably are. But there's also an element of self-service, as there is with every good sponsorship. The purpose behind Rock the Vote, founded in 1990 by recording industry folks concerned about free-speech issues, is to motivate a core of supporters who can use the political process to the advantage of the music industry.

Phase Two

STEP
5

Volunteerism

Some sponsorships have involved a strong component of **volunteerism**, which is a corporate policy of encouraging, facilitating, and rewarding employees in projects that contribute to a better quality of life in a community.

AT&T provides its employees worldwide with paid time off for volunteer work in community activities. In 2013, AT&T employees contributed 5.3 million volunteer hours, worth more than $118 million. AT&T has been cited by Forbes magazine as ranked among the most generous corporate foundations.

Altruism isn't the only motivation for community volunteer programs. AT&T believes the move gives it a better standing in the community and potentially higher profits.

Similarly, the MTV Network believes its generous policy on employee volunteerism helps attract and keep younger workers. The Points of Light Foundation (pointsoflight.org) offers similar examples of corporate volunteerism: a law firm that gives an hour a week for each employee to tutor a child in the community; a manufacturer that allows up to 40 hours a year for volunteer work; a utility that bases 20 percent of its incentive pay on community involvement.

Such perceived value is not just anecdotal or wishful thinking. A health-care system, for example, tracked the productivity of its workers relative to its policy of one and a half hours a week paid time for volunteering. The company found that people who volunteer work faster, get more accomplished on the job, are better organized, manage their time better, and are more enthusiastic about their job.

Other studies show that pro-volunteer policies increase employee morale, retention, productivity, and team building, while providing training for employees.

BENEFITS OF EMPLOYEE VOLUNTEER PROGRAMS

The Corporation for National and Community Service found that 26 percent of adult Americans (61 million people) volunteer 8.1 billion hours, worth $158 billion. It also found that 48 percent of companies include employee volunteerism as part of their overall business plan. The Bureau of Labor Statistics reports that most volunteer time goes to coaching, fundraising, tutoring, providing professional assistance, and distributing food.

Both Junior Achievement (ja.org) and Volunteer Match (volunteermatch.org) pulled together these and several other studies on employee volunteer programs. Here are some of their findings.

- *Benefits to Corporations*. Employee volunteer programs offer bottom-line benefits to the company, according to survey respondents. Specifically volunteer programs address public relation goals (83 percent), meet marketing and communication objectives (64 percent), develop employee skills (60 percent), recruit/retain employees (58 percent), further corporate strategic goals (nearly 80 percent), attract better employees (almost 90 percent), keep valued employees (nearly 80 percent), contribute to the bottom line financially (64 percent), and boost productivity (reported by 60 percent of the executives, 75 percent by employees).
- *Benefits to Employees*. Such programs offer specific employee benefits, including increasing competency by up to 17 percent, increasing job satisfaction (67 percent), improving leadership skills (75 percent), and improving morale (57 percent), all factors in increasing productivity.
- *Benefits to Customers*. Employee volunteer programs also improve customer satisfaction, thus increasing company profits.
- *Benefits to Communities*. Finally, such volunteer programs offer indirect community benefits by helping create "healthier" communities improving corporate public image (more than 90 percent each), and improving relations with the community and with local government (nearly 85 percent).

Activism

Another initiative that campaign planners can use is **activism**, a confrontational strategy focused mainly on persuasive communication drawing on the advocacy model of public relations. It's a strong strategy to be used only after careful consideration of the pros and cons. Done correctly, activism offers many opportunities for organizations to present their messages and enhance their relationship with key publics, particularly their members and sympathizers.

Activism generally deals with causes or movements, such as social issues (crime, capital punishment, or abortion, for example), environmental matters (pollution, suburban sprawl, nuclear waste), political concerns, and so on.

As to the various players on the field, a distinction should be made between **advocates**, who essentially are vocal proponents for causes, and **activists**, who are more inclined to act out their support for the cause. Look at the discussion on opponents in Step 3, Analyzing the Publics, for more background about advocates and other types of social activists.

Consider some of the tactics associated with the strategy of activism: strikes, pickets, sit-ins, petitions, boycotts, marches, vigils, rallies, and outright civil disobedience.

Activists often make effective use of the news media because their tactics involve physical protests and thus are highly visible. The nonviolent international Occupy movement, which opposed social and economic inequality, grew because it attracted the attention of both traditional and social media around the world. Sympathetic media coverage increased in the U.S. when a video went viral showing police using pepper spray against peaceful Occupy Oakland protestors.

Effective activism usually has an element of visual appeal. More than a publicity stunt, activist events involve newsworthy action done as much for the television viewers as for any other public. For example, when demonstrators have marched past the governor's mansion and capitol in various states to protest the death penalty, they often have dressed in mourning clothes and carried cardboard coffins and plastic tombstones. News photographers and television crews undoubtedly appreciated their visual creativity.

Sometimes activism involves **civil disobedience**, a nonviolent and nonlegal—but generally visual—undertaking, often in support of social causes such as civil rights, environmentalism, Native American sovereignty, and similar issues. Often such protests are loaded with symbolism from tactics such as marches, rallies, building takeovers, lobby sit-ins, and so on.

This kind of activism often transforms itself into theater, particularly when protestors are courting TV coverage. The term **street theater** (alternatively called **guerrilla theater**) refers to social and political protests that take the form of dramatizations in public places. When members of a political activist/environmental group in Madison, Wis., decided to protest a coal-burning power plant that they said threatened polar bears and other species, the protestors dressed as polar bears and staged a "die-in" at the plant's headquarters.

Amnesty International coordinates an annual International Day of Action protesting the lack of due process for the 779 prisoners held by the U.S. military at Guantanamo Bay, many for more than a decade, most without access to lawyers, all without trial. In 83 cities around the world, protestors dressed in orange jumpsuits and black hoods, courting media attention. They also delivered more than 300,000 petitions to the White House demanding the military prison be shut down.

The author's award for creative activist strategy goes to this well-orchestrated 1999 publicity stunt: Two dozen New York City community activists were protesting the mayor's decision to sell abandoned city-owned lots that neighborhood groups had turned into community gardens. The protesters staged a sit-in on the marble floor of City Hall, singing "We Shall Overcome" accompanied by kazoos. Protestors wearing bee outfits danced around others wearing flowered hats. Wait, there's more: Enter the New York Police Department in riot gear. As the protestors went limp, the police had to carry them, still dressed as bees, to a waiting police van. Now, that's entertainment!

Many protests are more serious. The Makah, an American Indian tribe in Washington State, is the only whaling tribe in the lower 48 states, with the right to maintain its 2,000-year-old whaling tradition enshrined in federal treaty. After the tribal whaling commission declared its intention to return to its traditional ways and hold a whale hunt, its first in 70 years, a successful hunt was televised by American and international media, including the ceremonial butchering of the captured whale.

The hunt attracted many demonstrators including whaling protestors, animal-rights activists, and anti-Indian groups, all of them courting (and receiving) media attention. It also sparked a spirited discussion of conflicting goods—on the one hand, the value of protecting endangered animals; on the other, respect for enduring cultural practices of a marginalized indigenous people.

Activists sometimes stretch ethical boundaries, entering an area that public relations practitioners should avoid. **Pie throwing** (or pieing) became a tactic-of-choice for some activists, who found they could gain media attention and thus a platform for their messages by pulling their relatively benign but purposefully humiliating stunts on famous people.

Targets of pieing-as-political-protest have included media executive Rupert Murdoch, pied in London during parliamentary hearings on phone hacking; Canadian oceans minister Gail Shea, pied by PETA to protest seal hunting; fashion designer Oscar de la Renta, pied because of his use of fur; the late Fred Phelps, pastor of the anti-gay Kansas church that pickets military funerals; Proctor & Gamble chairman John Pepper, over animal rights; Ralph Klein, premier of the Canadian province of Alberta, for opposing the Kyoto environmental accords; Dutch finance minister Gerrit Zalm, over the euro currency; Renato Ruggiero, director general of the World Trade Organization, over endangered sea turtles; the archbishop of Brussels because of the Catholic Church's stand on abortion; and Microsoft chairman Bill Gates, just because.

Usually the only consequence of pie throwing is media coverage. But three San Francisco activists who protested the mayor's policies on the homeless by throwing tofu-cream and pumpkin pies in his face were sentenced to six months in prison. In Europe, several anti-Euro protestors who used lemon meringue as their gastronomic weapon of choice received short jail terms. In Tucson, Arizona, two men calling themselves members of "Al Pieda" were arrested for assault and disorderly conduct after they pied conservative pundit Ann Coulter, but charges were reduced and fines suspended. Meanwhile, no charges were filed against students at Brown University who pied *New York Times* columnist Thomas Friedman because they sought to dramatize their opposition to the university sponsoring him as part of Earth Day events.

If you are planning an activist strategy, keep a clear eye on all your publics. Certainly the news media are important. So too are the targets of your activism, whom you are attempting to persuade toward some kind of action or response.

But perhaps even more important is your internal public—frequently volunteers, often with mixed motivations—who are being asked to give time and perhaps take risks on behalf

SYMBOLIC ACTION

Effective strategic communication activity should be more than mere words, and symbolic actions can be powerful tools that not only enhance the message but also actually can become the message itself.

History has many examples of powerful symbolic action: the Boston Tea Party, the driving of the Golden Spike that completed the transcontinental railroad, the raising of the American flag over Iwo Jima. Much of the video-born beheadings, burnings, bombings, and other atrocities of the Islamic State terrorists have been symbolic actions—though whether they are symbols of defiance, determination, or depravity is a decision that belongs to the person watching such videos.

Political and governmental leaders continue to engage in symbolic action because it often strikes a chord with voters. That's why you see political candidates serving sandwiches in soup kitchens and wearing hard hats at construction sites to show their concern for the poor and for working people, respectively.

Consider some of the classic and more recent examples of symbolic action that support a public relations purpose.

Because of their high visibility, popes have been particularly able to harness the power of symbolic action: Pope Paul VI's unexpected brotherly embrace of Greek Orthodox Patriarch Athenagoras after centuries of animosity between the Roman Catholic and Eastern Orthodox churches; John Paul II's habit of kissing the ground on his international trips as a sign of respect for the land and its people; Benedict XVI's meetings with Holocaust survivors and victims of sex abuse by priests.

The decade's best example of a master of symbolic action probably is Pope Francis. From the first moments when he selected his papal name, Francis' papacy has been bursting with symbolic actions: washing the feet of women and Muslims during his first Holy Thursday service; continuing to live in a dorm rather than the spacious papal apartment; meeting at the Vatican with a transgendered man; serving meals in a soup kitchen; carrying his own luggage while traveling; visiting a Pentecostal church and asking forgiveness for his church's past mistreatment; inviting Muslim refugee families to live in Vatican City; riding in his little Fiat in Washington, DC, surrounded by huge and heavily armored Secret Service SUVs; and praying in synagogues, mosques, and Buddhist temples.

All of these symbolic actions effectively emphasize his messages of service to the poor and marginalized, compassion, respect for individuals, and other values he has tried to highlight.

Phase Two

STEP
5

of the cause. Activist strategy must provide for the "feeding" of these troops with continuing motivation, ongoing communication, and when possible, the attainment of milestone victories that can shore up their dedication.

Proactive Strategy 2: Communication

While the previous proactive strategies focus on the action of the organization, another cluster of strategies deals more with communication. **Communication strategy** is a category that includes publicity, newsworthy information, generating news, news pegs, and transparent communication.

Publicity

Most organizations intuitively understand the value of **publicity**, which is the attention given by the news media to an organization, person, event, product, or idea.

CEOs, program directors, and other organizational leaders often put much faith in the premise that public attention is good. For this reason, they often press public relations specialists into holding news conferences, distributing news releases, and otherwise inviting the media to report on the activities and concerns of the organization.

What is the value of news reporting about your organization? Corporate executives sometimes believe there is a causal link between publicity and public support. It's not that easy, as we will see later in this section.

The underlying value of publicity is that it provides **third-party endorsement** for the organization's message. This refers to the extra credibility that comes with the endorsement of an outside and unbiased agent.

MEDIA CREDIBILITY AND POLITICAL LEANING

Some media are more believable than others and thus deserve particular attention from the public relations strategist. The difference often lies with the specific audience.

In general, readers give high credibility for specialized newspapers and magazines—in one category, those dealing with business, industry, and the professions; in another, those focused on a specific ethnic, political, religious, cultural, or lifestyle group.

Likewise, certain commentators or talk show hosts carry enormous influence among their steady listeners and readers. But the specifics vary with the sociopolitical self-identification of the audience.

In 2014, the Pew Research Center reported a range in credibility among news organizations by Internet-using U.S. adults. CNN earned 54 percent trust, ABC and NBC 50 percent, CBS 46 percent, Fox News 44 percent, PBS and BBC 38 percent, *New York Times* 34 percent, *USA Today* 33 percent, *Wall Street Journal* 31 percent.

But as in most cases, these generalities are misleading without looking at some of the specifics. The study found a wide disparity among people self-identifying as liberals or conservatives, with the former likely to trust a variety of news sources and the latter decrying the media as fake or biased.

Pew reported, for example, that 47 percent of news consumers who call themselves "consistent conservatives" say they trust Fox News, which held the trust of an additional 31 percent by people who say they are "mostly conservative." Other information sources ranking high among conservatives include DrudgeReport.com and Breitbart.com, and commentators Sean Hannity, Rush Limbaugh, and Glenn Beck. Conversely, these were among the most distrusted sources among liberals.

Meanwhile, liberals and political moderates spread their credibility among many information sources: all the major TV networks except Fox; newspapers led by *The Wall Street Journal*, *USA Today*, *The New York Times*, and *Washington Post*; online sources including Google News, Yahoo News, Slate, Politico, and the Huffington Post; and television sources including the *Daily Show* and the *Colbert Report*.

For additional details on the Pew report, see "Media and News" at journalism.org.

MEDIA CREDIBILITY

Particularly credible are media **gatekeepers**: reporters, editors, news directors, bloggers, and others who control access to the media. Audiences generally assume that the news they obtain from television, radio, and newspapers is more believable than information they obtain directly from the organization through advertising, websites, brochures, and the like.

That's because the information reported in the news media has passed the screen of the gatekeepers.

Audiences know that not everything gets on the air or in the paper, so intuitively they recognize that the professional journalists have made some choices as to what information is worth presenting as news. A reporter or an editor considered what the organization had to say and decided it was accurate enough to pass along to the audience.

An interesting study by Kevin Barnhurst and Diana Mutz observes that newspaper journalism is moving away from simply reporting events to providing news analysis. They note that in 1960, 90 percent of front-page election stories were about events; 32 years later, 80 percent of front-page stories were interpretive, what the researchers call "new long journalism."

Meanwhile, in broadcast reporting, the length of candidate sound bites decreased during the same time period as election coverage became more centered on journalist commentators. "To qualify as news these days, an event also must fit into a larger body of interpretations and themes," the researchers report (1997, p. 51). The study hasn't been updated, but in today's media environment the trend seems to be evolving even more toward subjective reporting.

The lesson for practitioners, then, is to build events and frame messages around the larger issues that blip on the media agenda screen.

Sometimes you will find that newsworthy activities are occurring within your organization. If so, your role becomes that of an in-house journalist reporting on the existing news events. More often, your role will be that of public relations counselor and strategist. Public relations people regularly create or orchestrate newsworthy events within their organizations to carry an important message to the key publics.

NEGATIVE PUBLICITY

There is a saying, "I don't care what they say about me, as long as they spell my name right" (for the record, it didn't originate with carnival showman P.T. Barnum, despite that recurring miscitation).

That approach is simplistic and naive, because public relations professionals know that all publicity cannot be treated the same way. Positive publicity obviously helps an organization, but negative publicity can have a devastating impact.

Negative publicity has hurt many companies. When the media reported that cyanide poison was discovered in Tylenol pain relief tablets, Johnson & Johnson stock dropped by $1 billion, 14 percent. During the Gulf of Mexico oil leak, BP stock fell 52 percent and cost the company an annual loss of $3.7 billion. Exxon stock dropped $3 billion after the *Exxon Valdez* oil spill. Motorola stock dropped $6 billion after reports linking cell phones and brain cancer. Those companies recovered financially.

But companies such as Quiznos subs, Sbarra pizza, Enron accounting firm, and Lehman Brothers financial services have gone bankrupt in the wake of negative publicity.

Ironically, negative publicity actually can help an organization. Traditionally, Boston was one of the first cities to book a play as it was leaving Broadway and beginning a nationwide

Phase Two

STEP
5

CASE IN POINT   Crystal Cathedral Ignores Media Relations

Robert Schuller was one of the best-regarded clergymen in North America, the father of "positive thinking." His Crystal Cathedral megachurch ministry was a model for effective media use, particularly his "Hour of Power" television program with an audience of 13 million.

Schuller built his ministry in Orange County, California. He went from a drive-in theater to an $18-million, 2,700-seat church (the largest glass building in the world) that was debt-free when it opened in 1980.

By 2009, Schuller's enterprise began to collapse, brought down by mismanagement aggravated by missed communication opportunities. This is a case study in ineffective media relations and miscues on crisis management.

Dwindling membership coincided with decreasing contributions. Schuller's son was installed as senior pastor, then quickly removed and replaced by his sister. Lucrative key leadership positions went to other family members, who often quarreled publicly.

The church went into bankruptcy. It cut back on broadcast time, laid off 140 staff including the choir, and cancelled income-producing Christmas and Easter pageants. It defaulted on $7.5 million owed to creditors, yet gave $1.7 million to 23 board members.

Through it all, the Schuller ministry misused the media in so many ways. This was studied in depth by Douglas J. Swanson (2012), published as "From 'Hour of Power' to 'Days of Demise'" in *Case Studies in Strategic Communication*.

The content-analysis study found that the Schuller ministry generally avoided the media throughout its financial crisis. Nearly half of 80 relevant news articles in the study had no direct quotes from ministry leaders. What comments there were came mainly through press statements rather than interaction with reporters.

The church said little to reassure members, failed to respond to criticism, blamed the economic recession without cutting expenses, closed down an opposition website, failed to rein in the extravant lifestyle of the Schuller family, and at the same time failed to counter media narratives of an entitled family.

Swanson observed: "If at any point during the crisis period, Robert H. Schuller had offered the media 'his side of the story' in depth and detail, it's hard to imagine that the media would not have given it extensive coverage."

Eventually a bankruptcy court reviewed several purchase offers and ordered the sale to the Catholic Church, which retrofitted Crystal Cathedral as Christ Cathedral of the Diocese of Orange.

What are the public relations implications of this case? Crises create the need for information. When the facts are not forthcoming, crises mushroom. Whether they wish it or not, organizations are held accountable by the media and, more importantly, by members and supporters. Observers see in Schuller's demise a predictable result of an organization failing to apply standard procedures for crisis management.

tour. Because of Boston's conservative social sensitivities, it sometimes banned plays or books as being too offensive. Producers noted with interest that the very banning of plays in Boston often assured their success in attracting audiences elsewhere, and some theatrical companies deliberately tried to get banned from Boston.

Negative publicity often has had a positive effect on generating interest, particularly among potential audiences. Seldom is this more true than with religiously motivated protests. Rudy Giuliani unwittingly generated valuable publicity and increased audiences for museums when he publicly criticized them while he was major of New York City: an exhibit with a photo of Christ depicted as a naked black woman; a display with a portrait of the Virgin Mary in African style made with elephant dung. Movies such as Martin Scorsese's *The Last Temptation of Christ* and Mel Gibson's *The Passion of the Christ* gained attention and audiences as various religious groups lined up in protest.

But these remain exceptions to the rule that bad publicity is bad for business.

Newsworthy Information

Presenting newsworthy information is a must for any organization that hopes to use the news media to carry its message and capture the interest of its publics. For the communication strategist, news is one of the strongest proactive strategies because something truly newsworthy is almost guaranteed to gain the attention of the news media and, through them, the organization's other publics. Even if you are presenting a message through personal or organizational channels, keep in mind that your audiences will be more drawn to a newsworthy message.

What is news? **News** is information that offers the audience a new idea or the latest development. From a journalistic perspective—which is the perspective every public relations practitioner needs to respect and adopt—news is information that involves action, adventure, change, conflict, consequence, contest, controversy, drama, effect, fame, importance, interest, personality, prominence, proximity, and dozens of other attributes often listed in journalism textbooks. That's a bulky list of attributes.

For our purposes, we can more simply define news as significant information relevant to the local area, presented with balance and objectivity and in a timely manner. The value of news is magnified by two more elements: unusualness and fame.

Let's simplify things even more with the initialism **SiLoBaTi + UnFa**. This is a convenient way to remember the main ingredients of news. It is made up of the first two letters of each of the elements: *si*gnificance, *lo*calness, *ba*lance, and *ti*meliness, plus *un*usualness and *fa*me.

- *Significance.* First, news is information of importance and significance. It has meaning to many people, even those beyond the organization. It is information of consequence and magnitude.
- *Local.* News also deals with information relevant to the local area, as defined by the coverage area of the news medium featuring the information.
- *Balance.* News is information with objectivity and balance. While the public relations practitioner uses information to promote the organization or client, it should not be presented merely in a promotional manner. Rather, it should be presented with an air of detachment and neutrality.

- *Timely*. The final key ingredient in news is that it is current and timely, being connected with contemporary issues, especially those high on public and media agendas.

These four key elements are basic to any information that is to be considered as new. In addition to these elements, newsworthiness is magnified by two other factors.

- *Unusualness*. News interest is enhanced when the information deals with unusual situations. This is what writers call human interest, that hard-to-define quality involving rarity, novelty, uniqueness, milestones, or slightly offbeat occurrences.
- *Fame*. News interest also is enhanced when the information involves fame. "Names make news" isn't idle chatter. Well-known or important people can add interest to a newsworthy situation. Sometimes their involvement can take an otherwise routine event and elevate it to the status of news.

For more about newsworthiness, see Smith (2017).

News judgment is relative. Public relations writers attempt to predict newsworthiness, but the decision to call something news is made only by the media gatekeepers, those people who control the flow of information in their various publications, newscasts, or talk shows. Examples of media gatekeepers are editors, columnists, news directors, producers, and webmasters.

As a public relations professional, part of your job is to analyze the relationship among three things to establish newsworthiness: (1) your organization's activities and messages, (2) the media agenda, and (3) the interests of a key public. The Venn diagram in Exhibit 5.1 shows this relationship through overlapping circles of interests.

- *Circle A* indicates information about the organization and issues important to it. This circle is of interest to the public relations practitioner because it is related to the organization's mission and strategic goals. Media gatekeepers are not interested in all the information within this circle.
- *Circle B* represents the interests of the news media. It is what the gatekeepers consider newsworthy. The media wish to report this information because they consider it of potential interest to their audiences. Such determinations will vary with different media.
- *Circle C* signifies the interests of the organization's key public. Whether positive or negative toward the organization, it is something that coincides with their wants, interests, and needs.

These three components exist independent of each other. For example, the organization has much information that the media do not consider newsworthy, much of which also doesn't interest each public. But sometimes the information in each circle may overlap, providing an environment for public relations to get into the action.

- *Area AB* depicts newsworthy information about the organization that the media might be interested in reporting. The media gatekeeper is focused on the people who read the online newspaper or its blogs, listen to the radio newscast, or view the television broadcast. Your job, as a public relations person, is to find out where Circle A overlaps

EXHIBIT 5.1 Model of Overlapping News Interests

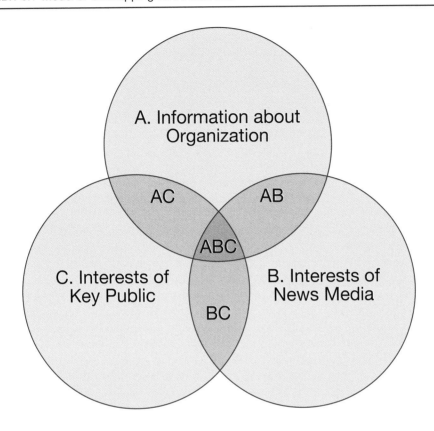

Phase Two

Circle B for a particular news venue, then call this to the attention of the media gatekeeper.

- *Area AC* shows what we can call **direct news**. This is information that, though news media may not care, nevertheless is of interest to the key public. Public relations writers dealing with such information may rework it to make it of more interest to the news media. Alternatively, they may take this information directly to the key public through organizational media, especially new technologies involving the Internet and social media.

- *Area BC* is of little interest to public relations writers, because it deals with news that doesn't involve the organization. The first inclination may simply be: Hands off. But practitioners might want to consider opportunities to insert their organizations into the news of the day.

- *Area ABC* represents **strategic news**, which is information involving your organization that is of interest to both news media and your key public. The ABC area represents information that is the primary focus of a media relations person. As news, it serves the interests of the media. As information with some benefit or consequence to your key public, it is likely to attract their attention when it is presented through the media.

Generating News

To attract the interest of news media, particularly of television reporters, news and publicity events must have a strong visual element. Stand-up commentators or talking heads don't make it on most television news reports, other than on occasional local-access cable programs that few people watch.

Audiences have become sophisticated, some might say spoiled. Regardless, they demand active, even entertaining, visual presentation of their news. Reporters do their best to comply with the expectations of their audiences. So unless you are able to present newsworthy information with a visual dimension, you are unlikely to find the news media receptive vehicles for your message.

The quest for a strong visual element to news is an opportunity for creative minds, as noted in the previous section on the strategy of activism. Even in nonconfrontational situations, events staged for their publicity value have their place—as long as they are vehicles for news and not simply hollow attention-getters.

At one university, a student theater group called Casting Hall wanted to attract attention and new members, so its members went "fishing" in the student union on a very snowy January day. Students in waders carried fishing poles, casting and reeling in new members. It was a visual pun, appropriate for both the name and the theatrical nature of the organization. The gimmick drew attention, generated publicity, raised some interest, and signed up several new members.

Alchemy doesn't work. It's not possible to turn lead into gold; neither is it possible to turn non-news into newsworthy information. Public relations practitioners shouldn't delude their bosses or clients, certainly not themselves, that facts without a news context are worth presenting to the media. Our credibility rests on the ability to determine what is news and what isn't.

But if a particular bit of information isn't newsworthy, we don't necessarily have to discard it. News media may not be able to use it right now, but there are two things we can do. One is to take the information directly to our publics, circumventing news media by using organization tools such as websites, Twitter, a brochure, Facebook, and other communication vehicles.

The second alternative is to proactively generate newsworthy activity for an organization. We might creatively and strategically develop an approach that will become newsworthy. There are many ways to generate news for an organization. Here's a Top 10 list of possibilities.

1. Give an award to draw attention to values and issues.
2. Hold a contest to involve others in your values and issues.
3. Select personnel to head a new program or begin a new project.
4. Comment on a local need or problem.
5. Conduct research and issue a report about a local need or problem.
6. Launch a campaign to accomplish something.
7. Give a speech to a significant audience and tell the media about it.
8. Involve a celebrity to visit and/or address your organization on a topic of concern to you.
9. Tie into an issue already high on the public or media agenda, or link your organization to the top news of the day.
10. Localize a general report.

For more on how to generate news, see Smith (2017).

NAMES MAKE NEWS

Public relations planners often try to involve celebrities who not only can attract media attention but who also might impact on key publics.

Studies show that 88 percent of Americans get most of their health information from television. Thus the National Cancer Institute works with Hollywood and with advocacy groups to promote TV storylines. It has tip sheets and other resources for writers and producers. The institute teamed with the Centers for Disease Control and Prevention and the Annenberg Norman Lear Center to recognize television's attention to health issues with the Sentinel Awards.

Documented results of the cooperation between Hollywood and advocacy groups have been surprising, showing some celebrity-based activities to effect major public response.

TV journalist Katie Couric became a national spokesperson for awareness about colorectal cancer after her husband died from the disease. Couric herself underwent a colonoscopy live on national television. The result? Testing for the disease increased 22 percent nationwide and held steady for almost a year. Media analysts dubbed this "The Couric Effect." Five years later, Couric broadcast her own mammogram to similarly influence women to undergo the life-saving exam for breast cancer.

Publicity about celebrities and their illnesses can cause others to pay closer attention to their own health. A study (Larson et al., 2005) showed that celebrity endorsements led to a 21 percent increase for mammograms, 31 percent for prostate exams, and 37 percent for colonoscopies.

Health statisticians documented increased interest in diagnostic exams when then-Vice President Dick Cheney received a pacemaker and when Colin Powell was treated for prostate cancer when he was secretary of state. Other researchers pointed to a storyline in the British TV series *Coronation Street* about a character's death from cervical cancer as the major cause of a 21 percent increase in testing for that disease.

Celebrities also are effective in focusing the attention of lawmakers on various social issues. The Alzheimer's Association said an appearance at a congressional caucus by its spokesperson, actor David Hyde Pierce, not only brought publicity for the cause but the increased participation attention among legislators. Similarly, when film star Julia Roberts went to Congress to speak about a rare neurological disorder, Rhett syndrome, influential lawmakers paid attention.

Other celebrities have given congressional testimony on issues in which they are involved, giving media attention that both they and lawmakers seek in furtherance of the cause. Recent celebrity-experts have included actress and United Nations ambassador on domestic violence Nicole Kidman; Seth Rogan about Alzheimer's disease, which afflicts his mother-in-law; Ben Affleck on economic issues in the Congo, where he has long been involved in humanitarian work; Nick Jonas on the diabetes he suffers; and Dennis Quaid on medical errors such as those that nearly killed his infant twins. With less-obvious credentials, Lindsay Lohan testified about jobs and Stephen Colbert spoke on immigration.

At first glance, some spokespersons seem unlikely. The Muppets have participated in congressional news conferences about public funding for television. Elmo (Mr. Monster, according to House transcripts) is the only non-human to address Congress, speaking in support of music education. Another spokesperson with dubious human credentials is Ian Somerhalder (*The Vampire Diaries*), who used not only his fame but also his credentials as an environmental philanthropist to speak on behalf of wildlife.

Phase Two

STEP 5

News Peg

The Venn diagram (Exhibit 5.1) showing overlapping news interests is a useful way to visualize the interconnectedness of information. Often strategic public relations practitioners find that topics associated with all three groups (media, publics, and the organization) result in a **news peg**—that is, an item that the media is already reporting on that also touches, in some way, on the organization.

For example, if the media are reporting on a national story involving an international crisis in Asia, a local Asian-based cultural organization may contact the media and offer an informed local perspective on events half a world away. Or if a high-profile celebrity goes public with a diagnosis of depression, a mental-health clinic might move quickly to offer media interviews on how to identify and deal with the illness.

Even negative information can provide a positive public relations springboard. For example, reports of a black youth shot by police in a distant city can provide an opportunity for comment on the more positive relationship between police and the local minority community. News about sex abuse in a public school across the state can be the spark for inviting the media to look at more-positive statistics of the local school district, and perhaps steps the district has taken to minimize such abuse locally.

Public relations practitioners are quick to identify overlaps with their organization's mission and what the media are covering. For example, Donald Trump's controversial statements on immigration, Muslims, and Hispanics helped the Ku Klux Klan recruit new members. A leader of the white supremicist group said Trump and the media coverage he attracted create topics that the KKK uses as conversation starters through which members can engage potential new members. Trump's comments also generated support for Democratic Party organizations and for various civil rights groups.

Here's another example: An advocacy group for the homeless may find that attempts to interest reporters in covering the issue aren't getting anywhere. The story has no legs, as they say. But if a vicious attack on a homeless man occurs in the community, the situation changes. The attack becomes the news peg that is likely to heighten media attention to the message of the advocacy group.

Here are several real-life examples of how organizations have attached themselves to a news peg.

DAWN DETERGENT

Dawn, a skin-friendly but high-powered household cleaner, is used by International Bird Rescue Research Center as its cleaning agent of choice for oil-covered birds. The center persuaded the U.S. Fish and Wildlife Service to recommend Dawn for cleaning birds caught in oil slicks. After the Exxon oil spill in 1989, Proctor and Gamble gave IBRRC hundreds of cases of Dawn for the clean-up effort. The company also gave thousands of bottles to that group and to the Marine Mammal Center for animal-rescue efforts in the Gulf oil spill of 2010. In 2015, Dawn was used to clean hundreds of sea birds in San Francisco Bay after a mysterious goop from an unknown oil spill killed at least 200 birds and threatened hundreds more. Proctor and Gamble frames the donations as part of wider corporate commitment to wildlife, which includes a blog, Facebook and Twitter, corporate advertising, and direct fundraising with consumers on wildlife issues.

SAVE THE CHILDREN

Immediately after the Sandy Hook school massacre, Save the Children posted on its website an article, "How to Help Children Cope with a Crisis." The article featured 10 suggestions for teachers, parents, and other caregivers on ways to talk with children about shocking news.

OAKLEY SUNGLASSES

Oakley makes high-performance sunglasses with a high level of protection against ultraviolent rays. In 2010, at the request of a Chilean insurance company, Oakley donated 35 pairs of its Radar-style glasses with special tints for the miners who had been trapped underground for 69 days. Oakley said the glasses would help the miners' eyes return to normal after so much time without sunlight. Each pair cost about $180, so the retail value was about $6,300. Front Row Analytics, a sponsorship evaluation company, estimated that the media exposure Oakley received when the miners emerged was worth $41 million.

SUPER BOWL

Minutes after the TV blackout in the 2013 Super Bowl, Tide detergent sent out this tweet: "We can't get your blackout, but we can get your stains out." Walgreens tweeted: "We do carry candles." And the Radiology Association of America posted on Facebook: "Well, at least radiologists can work in the dark."

RAY RICE

Some corporate tweets associated with news pegs backfire. During a news conference after release of a video of Ray Rice attacking his then-fiancée, someone with the Ravens social media team tweeted: "Janay Rice says she deeply regrets the role that she played the night of the incident." Critics retaliated with hundreds of blame-the-victim tweets. Later, DiGiorno Pizza took a hit for joining a tweeted discussion about victims of domestic violence: "#WhyIStayed. You had pizza."

KENNETH COLE

The clothing designer used the Syrian civil war as a news peg with its tweet: "'Boots on the ground' or not, let's not forget about sandals, pumps and loafers. #Footwear." The widely criticized tweet prompted a nonapologetic explanation from Cole, who said he courts controversy. "Billions of people read my inappropriate, self-promoting tweet," he said, boasting that "our stock went up that day, our e-commerce business was better, the business at every one of our stores improved, and I picked up 3,000 new followers on Twitter."

Transparent Communication

A relatively new concept is an important idea in developing a proactive public relations communication strategy. **Transparent communication** is the term given to the notion that open and observable activity by an organization helps publics understand the organization and support its actions.

Transparent communication simply means making your case. No secrets. It deals with the awareness objectives of increasing knowledge and understanding. Many communication efforts have failed because the publics are made aware of facts but not the reasons behind them.

Phase Two

STEP
5

CASE IN POINT Casket-Making Monks

Step 1 pointed out that a basic question for public relations practitioners is whether they can turn a problem into an opportunity. Often, publicity is a key to accomplishing this. Here's an example of how one problem was reshaped through publicity.

All Benedictine monasteries are expected to be self-supporting through manual labor. Some sell breads or work in stained glass. Others print books or operate farms. Some make wine or brew beer.

Monks at St. Joseph Abbey in southern Louisiana cut and sold timber. But when Hurricane Katrina devastated their lumbering options, they turned to a familiar craft. Ever since their abbey was founded in 1889, the monks had been building simple caskets for themselves. Now they began selling their handcrafted cypress caskets at prices less than funeral homes charge.

That's when the Louisiana Board of Embalmers and Funeral Directors stepped in. The board told the monks to stop selling caskets because, it ruled, only state-licensed funeral directors could do that. In response, the 37 monks of the abbey sued the board. After five years of attention-getting publicity, a federal court ruled in the abbey's favor, calling the board's ruling a transparent protectionist measure designed to limit competition. The board appealed to the Supreme Court, which—after another two years of media attention for the abbey—refused to hear the case, leaving the appeals court ruling in place. Thus the monks retained the right to sell their woodcrafts.

Abbot Justin Brown said all the media attention about the lawsuit brought more publicity than his monks could ever have imagined, spurring sales of caskets and cremation boxes. With "all this excellent publicity . . . we are selling more caskets than we had ever expected."

Lesson for public relations practitioners: Never underestimate the value of publicity, especially when it can turn adversity into advantage.

Too often, organizations exhibit a "just trust us" mentality by announcing plans without providing reasons why those plans are necessary, and today's publics aren't inclined to trust blindly. For example, within a four-month period in one midsized city, community opposition was strong in four different situations: a proposed relocation of the zoo; an announcement by a health management organization to drop coverage for half the hospitals in the area; plans by a public radio station to suspend operations; and the decision of a bridge authority to turn away millions of federal dollars for a high-profile "signature" bridge in favor of a less architecturally impressive bridge.

In each situation, the organization in question drew criticism because it had failed to provide plausible reasons for its plans. Publics had been left surprised, confused, and only partly informed. Facts had been given, but without any convincing rationale for the decisions and plans.

When Meg Whitman became CEO of Hewlett-Packard, she championed transparent communication. Among her first actions was to tear down a military-style fence surrounding the corporate headquarters. She also eliminated walled offices and moved executives into cubicles. "We now walk in the same door as the rest of our employees. This was symbolic of the kind of culture that we wanted to build," she wrote in her company blog. "And in organizations as large as ours, symbolism actually matters."

Studies on workplace trends report that organizations that engage in transparent communication both enhance employee satisfaction and productivity and contribute to faster resolution of problems.

When organizations engage in transparent communication, they provide the kind of communication that identifies a problem, gets people interested, airs various options, and otherwise creates a climate of understanding and involvement before plans are announced that affect the publics. If financial pressures are pushing your organization to curtail services, let your publics know about the financial problems and the various options before announcing a service cutback. Nobody likes bad surprises, especially when it is clear that the organization has been hiding information from key publics.

Transparent communication is particularly relevant to the stereotypically secretive world of finance. When he was chairman of the federal Securities and Exchange Commission (SEC), Harvey Pitt identified one of the top SEC goals as "to ensure that our financial markets are transparent and fair to all investors."

Helen Vollmer APR, president of Edelman Southwest, advises her clients that today's marketplace requires transparent communication between corporate leadership and stockholders. The company lists transparency second only to credibility as the most important ingredients of an IR program.

In the field of public health, researchers have found that transparent communication is often the best way in managing a public health crisis. If the public is at risk, treatment options limited, resources few, and opportunities for direct intervention scarce, open public communication may be the only practical tool.

In the early months of the 2003 SARS crisis, authorities were reluctant to acknowledge and communicate potential problems about a disease that eventually created more than 8,000 cases and 774 deaths. It was only after public health officials decided to engage the media and focus on public awareness and behavior modification that the disease was contained.

The value of transparent communication had been learned by 2013, when the Ebola virus ravaged Western Africa and threatened to spread elsewhere, including into the U.S. Health officials communicated early and often, combating misinformation and attempting to inform the public without causing needless panic.

The Ebola experience offers four key lessons in crisis communication, according to Peter Sandman and Jody Lanard, writing for the Center for Infectious Disease Research and Policy at the University of Minnesota. Their main advice: Treat the public like adults. Here are their specific caveats:

1. Don't over-reassure. While it's important to try to alleviate unnecessary fear and panic, it's also important to acknowledge the realistic potential for harm.
2. Acknowledge uncertainty. But try to be confident that medicine has the ability to meet the challenge.
3. Don't over-diagnose or over-plan for panic. The Ebola scare gave rise to some unwarranted quarantines. But for the most part, media reporting and community response was reasonable and based on scientific knowledge.
4. Tolerate early overreactions; don't ridicule the public's emotions. The researchers cite an "adjustment reaction" as a temporary overreaction to a scary potential,

Phase Two

STEP 5

CASE IN POINT   Sexual Abuse at Children's Hospital

Balancing transparency and confidentiality were uppermost in the mind of leaders of San Diego's Children's Hospital in 2006, when two employees were arrested on child-abuse charges in unrelated cases. Police notified the hospital that they were investigating a respiratory therapist working with comatose children. A few days later, the man was arrested for abusing at least nine victims under his care at the hospital. Police discovered more than 100,000 child pornography images on his home computer.

The hospital's crisis plan went into effect. Letters in English and Spanish were sent to 176 families of his former patients. Another 30,000 letters were sent to people associated with the hospital, including employees, families of patients, donors, and legislators. Hospital administrators met with the families of the therapist's patients.

Adopting a posture of openness and transparency, the hospital gave media interviews, held a news conference, and set up a special telephone inquiry line. The crisis plan called for speed and flexibility; it valued transparency of information while at the same time seeking patient confidentiality. Media and law enforcement generally agreed that the hospital was transparent in this approach to the public.

Then lightning struck a second time. Within five and a half weeks, police notified the hospital that another employee was being investigated on similar charges. The hospital suspended the nurse, who a few days later was arrested for molesting a child at the hospital and for possessing child pornography at his home.

The hospital held a second news conference, with assurances that these were isolated cases. Eventually both men pleaded guilty, the first receiving a 45-year sentence, the second a 14-year prison term.

Later that year, the hospital presented its case study to colleagues attending the Boston convention of the National Association of Children's Hospitals and Related Institutions. It pointed to jarring statistics: An estimated 3–5 percent of males are sexually interested in prepubescent children and even a greater number in adolescents. Thus, a hospital with 1,000 male employees might expect 50 who are potential child abusers.

Alarmingly, the presenters noted that organizations such as children's hospitals are magnets for people with perverse interests in children and may attract an even higher rate of potential abusers. Thus the need for a carefully prepared program to screen employees, minimize risk, and react responsibly when the crime occurs. The hospital director said outcomes of the crisis included an awareness of the need for vigilance about sex abuse and an appreciation of public relations' role in a crisis.

Children's Hospital offered several lessons to its colleagues: (1) Have a crisis plan that balances transparency with patient privacy; (2) involve the CEO; (3) frame the response agenda to emphasize quality improvement; (4) communicate with all patients; (5) expect leaks to the media; and (6) visibly cooperate with law enforcement.

As with other situations of crisis communication, the public relations potential in such circumstances allows the organization to show its true colors—undue concern for secrecy, or transparent commitment to its many publics and its long-term reputation within the community.

followed by moderation of overstated fears. Public health officials can latch onto this as a teachable moment.

Media Theory and Public Relations

The value of theory is that it helps predict how actions and events may impact various outcomes. Insight drawn from theory thus can help public relations practitioners do a better job in promoting their organizations and clients.

No single theory covers all situations. Because public relations spans several disciplines, it can draw from theories in various areas. Some of these theories focus particularly on the media, offering insight into how public relations can work with journalism and through various types of news media. Social psychology and the many theories associated with that discipline also can be useful in the practice of public relations.

Let's first look at theories related to news and journalism.

Theory and News Media

How powerful are news media? Can they make us care about an issue or act on it in a certain way just because they report it? Or are they simply information sources used at the discretion of their audiences?

Insight into the role of theory in the practice of public relations often begins applications to media presentations and news audiences. In particular, three theories are useful in discussing the role of news media: agenda setting, priming, and framing.

Put succinctly, through agenda setting, the media imply that a topic is important and should interest audiences. Through priming, the media set the standard for audiences to evaluate a topic. In framing, the media induce audiences to think about the topic according to a particular narrative.

AGENDA SETTING THEORY

Communication researchers and public relations practitioners believe there is a middle ground between powerful effects and minimal effects of the media. This is explained by the **agenda setting theory** associated with Maxwell McCombs and Donald Shaw (1972).

According to this theory, news media are not powerful enough to force audiences to react in a certain way. Neither are they so inconsequential as to be irrelevant. Rather, the media raise issues that both they and their audiences consider to be newsworthy. In simple terms, news media tell us what to think about, but they don't tell us what to think.

Through the issues they choose to cover, called the **media agenda**, news media can legitimize a story and raise it as a topic that the citizenry or media audiences are interested in, called the **public agenda**. Conversely, failure to report on issues marginalizes a topic as not being newsworthy. There is still a bit of a debate: Does an issue move into the public interest because the media report it? Or, do the media report an issue because they think it already is a matter of public interest? Probably a bit of both.

For the public relations strategist, the important lesson from this theory is to link organizational information with the current news: What is the news of the day and how does my organization fit into it? Sometimes the link is obvious. During a high-profile trial in which child abuse is an issue, a child-services agency easily can become a helpful information resource to reporters about the nature and extent of child abuse in the local community.

At other times the public relations person must be creative in finding the connections: a hospital linking to news about genocide in Darfur because one of its doctors recently returned from a stint as a medical volunteer in that part of Sudan, or a university offering to host students from China who were displaced by an earthquake there.

PRIMING THEORY

A related theoretical concept is **priming**, which explains how the media set the stage to provide the context for public discourse on a topic. The observation is that the amount of time and space that media devote to an issue make an audience receptive and perhaps alert the audience to particular themes. This, in turn, sets standards on how people and policies are evaluated.

Shanto Iyengar and Donald Kinder (1987) identified a priming process in which media attention to or avoidance of various issues creates a framework for relatively uninformed audiences, calling up past information and applying it to present situations. For example, voters may evaluate a political candidate according to themes resurrected from previous media reporting on topics such as taxation, abortion, immigration, and other topics selected by the media.

Priming often takes the form of media suggesting the standard or measurement reference for making decisions. Many political arguments are based on jobs as the litmus test for all arguments. For or against immigration reform? Focus on the number of jobs your position will create. Concerned about pollution related to fossil fuels? Discuss how jobs will be impacted because of your position. How are jobs impacted by a new education budget, airport security changes, environmental safeguards, or elimination of transfats in food? Realistically, that may not be the pivotal question, but some partisans use job impact as the basis for supporting or rejecting any position.

Sometimes reporters chase their own and each others' tails over politically induced questions by political players. Donald Trump asked: Was Ted Cruz eligible to seek the presidency even though he was born in Canada? Republicans posed the question: Should Hillary Clinton be charged with sending classified emails, even after the FBI said she had done nothing illegal? Critics questioned Donald Trumps' charitable record, based on his own estimate of giving about $20 million annually to charity from his total wealth of $10 billion—0.2 percent of his worth, equivalent to a $280 donation ($23 a month) for someone earning $40,000 with assets of $100,000 in savings and a partially paid house).

The American news media have been criticized in how they prime audiences for discussions of mass murder, especially aspects of race and ethnicity. After the 2015 shootings of nine black people at a church service in Charleston, S.C., media observers pointed out that reporting quickly turned to questions about the mental health of the shooter. That is a not-uncommon question raised about white killers but seldom a factor in media coverage of killers who are black or Muslim.

FRAMING THEORY

A related and perhaps more useful theory deals with **framing**. It focuses on the presentation of the story and organizes discourse about the topic.

Framing explains how the media provide a perspective or frame of reference that influences public discourse on a topic. How do the news media frame a story? Is there an inherent "good guy" in the story? Whose side of the story gets top billing? Which version becomes the standard against which other points of view are measured?

For example, when Donald Trump addressed immigration during the presidential primary, journalists framed the public discourse on his standards. All the other candidates immediately were measured against Trump's proposed policies. Should Muslim refugees be allowed into the U.S.? Only Christian refugees? What about Mexican immigrants? Should immigrants already here be monitored? Registered? Deported?

Framing theory was developed by Erving Goffman (1974) and applied to communication studies by Dietram Scheufele (1999).

Framing provides a rhetorical context for the text, involving the use of metaphor, storytelling, jargon, word choice, and other narrative elements. For example, a report on repeat drunk driving might be framed in various ways: criminal recidivism, police incompetence, judicial lenience, irresponsible personal choices, or the power of addiction. Significant research

---

CASE IN POINT   **Cherokee Citizenship and Framing Theory**

Consider three theories—agenda setting, priming, and framing—in light of news coverage of the 2007 citizenship vote by the Cherokee Nation.

In the vote, the tribal government sought to end a 100-year confusion caused when the federal government determined that, after the Civil War, certain ex-slaves (called Freedmen) should be considered members of the tribe because they were living in the Indian territory of what is now Oklahoma. The Cherokees finally were voting on whether to restrict tribal citizenship to only those people—whether ethnically Indian, black, or white—who actually have Cherokee blood lineage.

In terms of agenda setting, the Cherokee-Freedmen story failed to register on the national agenda. It received limited national and international coverage, mostly from media that had previously taken an editorial stand on the topic. But during the first two weeks of March 2007, other news was ranked higher on the media agenda: a scandal over conditions at an army hospital; the conviction of a presidential aide for outing a CIA agent; scandals over politically inspired firing of federal attorneys; killer tornadoes in several states; continuing death in the Iraq War; and genocide in Darfur.

Priming influenced the Cherokee-Freedman story through prior ongoing media coverage of civil rights. Reports of the denial of voting rights in particular may have prepared audiences to see the story in that light. Likewise, the storytelling was impacted by the historical context unknown to journalists and audiences alike.

The relevant issue to the Cherokee-Freedmen story in the context of framing theory deals with the manner in which media reporting placed various elements. Such elements include the diversity of the mixed-race Cherokee community and its convoluted history. Other issues were racism, tribal sovereignty, and federal government complicity in creating the problem in the first place, as well as nuances in the voting procedure and the precise language of the ballot question. Framing also entered into which news sources were quoted and which side received top billing.

(For a full report of the media analysis on the citizenship vote, The Cherokee-Freedmen Story: What the Media Saw, see the author's website: ron-smith.com.)

has been undertaken to examine the role that race, ethnicity, and social status play in how the media report news about both victims and perpetrators of crimes.

If agenda setting tells audiences what to think about, framing theory suggests that the media influence how the audience thinks about an issue.

Theory for Strategic Communication

In addition to the theories of agenda setting, priming, and framing, several other theories are useful for people involved in strategic communication and public relations. Here is an alphabetical overview of some such theories and models.

COGNITIVE DISSONANCE

Social psychologist Leon Festinger (1957) introduced the notion of **cognitive dissonance** to explain the psychological discomfort people feel upon realizing that they hold contradictory attitudes or beliefs. Festinger observed that people try to reduce the level of discomfort, usually by changing an attitude or belief. An important element of this theory is **selective exposure**, presented by Joseph Klapper (1960) to suggest that, because people try to avoid dissonance, they reject information they think might oppose their bias and replace it with information supporting an attitude. The related concept of **selective perception** explains how different people can see the same information and reach different conclusions by interpreting the data to fit their existing bias.

CONSISTENCY

Several related types of consistency theory are based on the consistency of information and how people process messages. **Balance theory** associated with psychologist Fritz Heider (1958) observes that unbalanced mental positions create tension and encourage an individual to restore balance. Theodore Newcomb (1953) extended this to groups, calling it **symmetry theory**. Charles Osgood and Percy Tannenbaum's **congruity theory** (1955) adds attitudinal measurement. Public relations practitioners learn from consistency theories that information can stimulate attitude change.

CULTIVATION

George Gerbner's **cultivation theory** (1976) suggests that the media shape peoples' conception of social reality. Large doses of media exposure over time can affect not only individuals but also society as a whole. Gerbner argued that television cultivates a middle-of-the-road political perspective, though more recent observers have found that, with the fragmentation of media and the 24/7 news cycle on politically oriented TV networks, the effect now is more divisive in society as TV viewers select media that reflect their existing worldview and bias. Gerbner also articulated the **mean world syndrome** as one of the key effects of cultivation theory, observing that heavy users of media tend to be more fearful, suspicious, and susceptible to conspiracy theories and social paranoia.

DIFFUSION OF INNOVATIONS

Everett Rogers studied how new ideas are spread throughout society, shedding light on the likelihood that innovations (both products and ideas) will be adopted. His **diffusion of**

innovations theory (2003) identified five categories of adopters (innovators, early adopters, early majority, late majority, and laggards). Public relations practitioners can gain insight from this model on who and how to address in messages about new concepts.

GATEKEEPING

The role of editors or news directors in in determining what the media report on centers on the notion of **gatekeeper**. Related to the agenda setting theory, **gatekeeping theory** was articulated by Kurt Lewin (1951), who observed that even though journalists try to be objective, they base reporting choices on personal or organizational biases about what they presume to be the interests of their audiences. Public relations practitioners have learned to provide information to the media that gatekeepers will judge to be of interest to their audiences.

INOCULATION

William McGuire and Demetri Papageorgis (1961) proposed the **inoculation theory** and put the focus on whether beliefs are challenged or not. They suggest that persuasive information can sway unchallenged beliefs and attitudes, while previously tested attitudes are more change resistant. The latter aspect is particularly useful as strategic communicators seek to create resistance to potentially opposing arguments.

MULTI-STEP FLOW OF COMMUNICATION

Paul Lazarsfeld originally presented a **two-step flow model** (1944), later with Elihu Katz expanded into a **multi-step flow model**. This theory focuses on decision making and the role information plays in it. Underlying this model is the observation that media present information to **opinion leaders**, who in turn interpret the information and extend it to others in their sphere of influence.

RHETORIC

Aristotle's classical **rhetorical theory** continues to offer insight into the practice of public relations. The threefold outline—ethos, logos, and pathos—remains useful as strategic communicators focus on the message source by selecting a spokesperson on the basis of credibility, charisma, and control or influence over the audience. It deals with the logical aspect of an argument that gathers and presents facts and sound reasoning. And it considers the emotional impact of messages and the nonverbal communication that expresses them.

SITUATION

James Grunig's **situational theory** (1966) identifies publics as being active or passive. It observes that some publics are active on all issues, while others are active on only single issues. The value of this insight to strategic communicators is that it helps them engage publics effectively, drawing on the interests of the publics themselves.

SLEEPER EFFECT

Carl Hovland and Walter Weiss (1951–52) identified a **sleeper effect**, noting that the persuasive impact of communication sometimes increases as time elapses. Information people initially receive from a low-credibility source may become increasingly credible as the source fades from memory.

Phase Two

STEP
5

SOCIAL JUDGMENT

The **social judgment theory** articulated by Muzafer Sherif and Carl Hovland (1961) observes that people accept or reject messages to the extent they perceive them to reflect their internal anchors (attitudes and beliefs) and impact their self concept. This theory is related to cognitive dissonance.

SPIRAL OF SILENCE

Trying to explain how public opinion gave social power to the Nazis, Elisabett Noelle-Neumann (1993) put forward the **spiral of silence theory**. She explained that people identify the majority opinion from information they get from the media. People holding minority opinions often silence themselves so as not to be seen as going against the prevailing attitudes. Advocates for what appears to be a minority opinion have learned that they sometimes can unsilence people by showing that others hold opinions that run counter to the presumed majority point of view. This seems to be the theoretical underpinning for understanding the unexpected outcome of two major electoral decisions in 2016: the vote in the United Kingdom to leave the European Union, and the election of Donald Trump and near-unanimous Republican political dominance in the United States. In both cases, poll respondents did not express their true voting intentions.

SYSTEMS

The interdisciplinary **systems theory** is rooted in technology and biology, but it sheds light on some aspects of social psychology, especially the concepts of feedback and mid-course adjustment. Strategic communicators find it useful to understand how organizations relate with their various publics. The associated concept of **linkages** is especially useful, helping to identify various categories of publics and their relationships with an organization.

USES AND GRATIFICATIONS

The **uses and gratifications theory** looks at why audiences use various media and what they get out of it. Associated with Jay Blumler and Denis McQuail (1968), this approach observes that audiences take a proactive role in the information-exchange process. It helps strategic communicators satisfy the interests of people who may be actively seeking information. It also helps practitioners identify the reason audiences seek information for entertainment, news or surveillance purposes, personal identity, or other reasons.

Reactive Public Relations Strategies

When accusations or other criticisms have been made, or when an organization has been visited by difficulties or tragedies, public relations strategists are thrown into a reactive mode. In responding to outside forces, organizations should develop objectives such as gaining public understanding, maintaining and restoring reputation, and rebuilding trust and support.

The field of crisis communication management is rife with examples of response strategies that work, and some that don't.

The classical term for self-defensive communication rhetoric is **apologia**, which is associated with the rhetorical discipline called **apologetics** (from the Greek "speaking in defense").

This type of persuasive communication is an explanation or formal defense against criticism. It seeks to present a compelling evidence-based case for an organization's opinions, positions or actions.

Don't confuse apologia with apology. The latter is an expression of fault and remorse. An apologia is much more than an apology and, indeed, may not have to deal with blame. Through an apologia, an organization explains its actions and positions with a clear eye toward convincing critics of its rightness.

Applying the concept of apologia to corporate crises, Keith Michael Hearit notes that an apologia offers an organization a strategic opportunity to manage its reputation in the wake of accusations of wrongdoing. Hearit suggests a threefold approach: persuasive accounts offering (1) an explanation, and if necessary a defense, (2) statements of regret, and (3) disassociation tactics to separate the organization from the problem (1994).

Another approach to public relations response strategy considers the **theory of accounts**. Michael Cody and Margaret McLaughlin (1985) articulated this theory to describe the role of communication in managing relationships in the wake of rebuke or criticism.

An account is the language—verbal or nonverbal—that a person or organization uses to explain the reason for taking a particular action. As a narrative, it is useful in crisis situations and conflict resolution.

Accounts can range from defensive to offensive, and Cody and McLaughlin observed that the harsher the criticism, the more a strong offensive account is warranted.

That is a lesson not learned by several politicians in recent American presidential campaigns. John Kerry lost the 2004 presidential campaign in part because he failed to take seriously vicious criticism that demeaned his military service as a war hero. Some analysts said John McCain lost the 2008 election by failing to take seriously criticisms that he was out of touch with hard economic realities, similar to their observation that Mitt Romney failed to take seriously criticisms in 2012 that he focused only on the super-rich. The lesson may have been learned, because the 2016 primary campaign found many candidates quick to deal head-on with criticisms by their opponents.

In *Accounts, Excuses, and Apologies*, William Benoit (1995) deals with both accounts and apologia, drawing on research from sociology, social psychology, and communication. He presents a theory of **image restoration**, based on the presumption that, in the face of criticism, both people and organizations seek to maintain or rebuild a positive reputation. Benoit's model includes options such as denial, evasion of responsibility, reduction of offensiveness, and corrective action.

Organizations can use a range of verbal and behavioral reactions in managing their response to opposition and their recovery from criticism. The following typology of public relations responses is based on a reflection of contemporary research and consulting practices, as well as the work of the above-mentioned researchers.

Reactive Strategy 1: Pre-emptive Action

One type of strategy involves a **pre-emptive strike**, which is taken before the opposition launches its first charge against an organization. Some bureaucrats avoid such an approach in the naive hope that criticism won't emerge or bad news won't surface. The reality is simple: When something bad happens, word gets out.

TYPOLOGY OF REACTIVE STRATEGIES

25 Responses for Crisis Communication

Reactive Strategy 1:
Pre-emptive Action
Prebuttal

Reactive Strategy 2:
Offensive Response
Attack
Embarrassment
Shock
Threat
Standing firm

Reactive Strategy 3:
Defensive Response
Denial
Excuse
Justification
Reversal

Reactive Strategy 4:
Diversion Response
Concession
Ingratiation

Disassociation
Relabeling

Reactive Strategy 5:
Vocal Commiseration
Concern
Condolence
Regret
Apology

Reactive Strategy 6:
Rectifying Behavior
Investigation
Corrective action
Restitution
Repentance

Reactive Strategy 7:
Deliberate Inaction
Strategic silence
Strategic ambiguity
Strategic inaction

Prebuttal

The strategy of an organization releasing bad news about itself is called a **prebuttal**. The term itself is a play on the word "rebuttal." A prebuttal is a pre-emptive strike when bad news is inevitable. It is akin to the rhetorical concept of prolepsis, a figure of speech in which speakers raise objections to their own arguments so they can refute the opposing viewpoint.

In today's era of viral messaging in a fast-paced sociopolitical environment, prebuttals are becoming commonplace attempts to deflate opposing arguments even before they are made.

Prebuttals are becoming increasingly common in the political arena. It was a prebuttal in 2015 when congressional Republican leaders vehemently criticized the presumed outcome of President Obama's negotiation with Iran over nuclear containment even before any agreement had been reached.

Similarly, it was a prebuttal when Congressional Democrats "responded" to the Republican congressional leader's speech on the economy the day before he actually gave the speech. Likewise, it was a prebuttal when National Security Advisor Susan Rice criticized Israeli Prime Minister Benjamin Netanyahu's speech before Congress the day before he delivered it.

The concept of prebuttal is based on the observation that the first one to tell the story sets the tone, against which all alternative versions must compete. It's a lesson you may have learned in elementary school, when your sister or brother beat you home with a story of how you got into trouble on the playground. Following that account, your own version may have been not only second place but somehow second best. The first telling of the story becomes normative, and other versions are considered in light of the first account.

The same thing holds true for organizations. When something bad is about to happen, organizations can do more than merely brace for the aftershock. "Carpe diem!" as the Romans said. "Seize the day!"

Consider this real-life situation: A hospital had to deal with a pending report that would list it as having one of the highest patient death rates in the state. Knowing that the report was

---

CASE IN POINT   Metabolife Prebuttal

Attacking journalists is risky, because they have the last word. But the diet-pill company Metabolife set what became a classic precedent for public relations practitioners—one that goes against conventional wisdom about crisis communication.

The company insisted on making its own videotape of a 70-minute interview with its CEO and chief medical officer in 1999. ABC's *20/20* had spent four months in research and interviews, pulling some negative information from its chief competitor. Metabolife worried that its popular but controversial herbal diet pill would be portrayed unfairly when the news magazine broadcast its report, so it devised a first-strike strategy.

Combining the strategies of prebuttal and attack, Metabolife went online with its own videotape of the interview 10 days before the ABC program was scheduled to air. This apparently was the first time any company had released a complete unedited news interview prior to the broadcast date, a tactic since emulated by other organizations hoping to soften the glare of a media spotlight.

Along with its own tape of ABC's interview, Metabolife posted a full transcript and additional medical information it previously had given to the news program. The company also purchased full-page ads in *The New York Times* and *New York Post*, gained news coverage in *The Wall Street Journal*, and ran radio commercials across the country to draw hits to the website—all prior to the story's broadcast and designed to drive traffic to its website. Metabolife also placed a short ad during the program, inviting viewers to visit its website.

The website received 1.1 million hits a day, and the company later claimed that its pre-emptive action caused the *20/20* story to be fairer than it otherwise would have been. ABC denied Metabolife's interpretation, calling the company's action "a not-so-subtle form of intimidation" that the broadcaster claimed had no effect on the report.

There's a lesson here for all public relations people involved in crisis situations. Most crisis communication experts suggest that an organizational interview or news conference should always include at least an audio recording, preferably a videotape, of the media encounter. Make sure the reporters are aware of the recording. The creation of your own copy is a reminder that everything is on the record, minimizing the chance of being misquoted and providing proof if you are.

Phase Two

STEP
5

only days away and that it was statistically accurate, the hospital told reporters about the forthcoming report and explained why the rate was high: This particular hospital accepted charity patients too poor to have regular health care, specialized in geriatrics, and was the only hospital in the area treating AIDS patients at a time in the not-too-distant past when the disease meant certain death. These were important reasons explaining the high death rate. After getting the facts from the hospital, local reporters gave the announcement minimal coverage and ignored the state report a few days later as old news.

When is a prebuttal warranted? When the public inevitably will hear the accusation and when the organization can offer strong evidence for its publics to disregard the bad news or excuse the organization.

But there are disadvantages to prebuttals. Consider a nonpolitical example, criticism by climate-change deniers in anticipation of Pope Francis' encyclical on the environment even before his letter was issued. Now consider two downsides to such prebuttals. One is that they generate more of an audience for the issue than it might otherwise have garnered. They also can suggest a grasping-at-straws approach in which critics are seen as whining in desperation even before they know the facts. Both of these outcomes were evident in the public discussion over the Pope's encyclical.

Reactive Strategy 2: Offensive Response

Public relations planners sometimes use offensive response strategies, so named not because they are rude or vulgar but rather from the sports or military strategy of mounting an aggressive initiative.

The five types of strategic offense—attack, embarrassment, shock, threat, and standing firm in response to criticism—are based on the premise that the organization is operating from a position of strength in the face of opposition. Here is an overview of each of these strategies.

Attack

An **attack** is an offensive response strategy claiming that an accusation of wrongdoing is an attempt to impugn the organization's reputation by an accuser who is negligent or malicious. Often the objective underlying this strategy is to encourage an opponent to retreat or at least refrain from future criticism. Use this approach only when evidence can clearly show that accusers have grossly overstated the organization's involvement in a problem.

Let's look at two examples of the attack strategy—one that backfired, one that was successful.

SCIENTOLOGY

Some organizations have successfully attacked the attacker. One such group is the Church of Scientology, which proclaims that it is "not a turn-the-other-cheek religion."

The church—though it is not legally recognized as such in some countries—has filed thousands of lawsuits against journalists, documentary producers, politicians, former church members, and others who have criticized it.

Scientology even has written guidelines on how to investigate and publicly attack its critics. The "fair game" policy has been used to justify what critics and some courts have labeled as illegal surveillance, intimidation, dirty tricks, harassment, libel, and fraud.

Some of the lawsuits are based on copyright infringement, others on libel and slander. The late L. Ron Hubbard, a science fiction writer who founded the church, wrote that such lawsuits are intended "to harass and discourage rather than win."

DOW CORNING

In this classic public relations blunder from the late 1990s, Dow Corning used the attack strategy to its own misfortune in handling a series of class-action lawsuits over its silicone breast implants. Faced with reports filled with unfavorable and inaccurate scientific information, the company's first response was to attack the investigators. It unsuccessfully tried to cover up the problem. It also failed to demonstrate concern for women who said they were harmed, and it didn't address consumers who thought the company had deceived them.

Most of the strategy was driven by lawyers rather than by public relations counsel. The result was a $7.3 million judgment against the company and class action lawsuits of more than $4 billion that put the corporation into Chapter 11 bankruptcy for nine years. All this despite the fact that no reputable scientific evidence showed that the implants caused disease or illness. In fact, the U.S. Institute of Medicine later found clear evidence that silicone breast implants do not cause breast cancer.

Embarrassment

A related offensive strategy deals with **embarrassment**, in which an organization tries to lessen an opponent's influence by using shame or humiliation.

This strategy was in play when the anti-abortion Center for Medical Progress secretly taped Planned Parenthood officials and actors posing as biotech representatives. The group released heavily edited videos purporting to show negotiations over how much money it might charge for tissue from aborted fetuses intended for medical research.

Critics said the organization was selling baby parts. Planned Parenthood responded that the only thing being negotiated was the cost of transporting the tissue to research centers. The activist group was successful in causing serious embarrassment to Planned Parenthood, embarrassment that threatened its funding in various cities and states around the country. (More on this case in a subsequent section on concession.)

The embarrassment tactic often plays a role in political communication. In her 2010 campaign to become a Nevada senator, Tea Party candidate Sue Lowden suggested that people barter for health care by paying doctors with chickens. Her opponents created a fake "Chickens for Checkups" website. The ridicule became so strong that the state of Nevada banned chicken costumes outside polling sites.

Shock

Sometimes, in an effort to make a point, embarrassment may take a turn toward alarm. In public relations and strategic communication, **shock** is the attempt to startle and agitate the mind or emotions, particularly through the use of surprise, fear, disgust, or some other strong and unexpected stimulus.

Psychologists and other social scientists agree that shock advertisements increase attention. However, so-called "shockvertisements" seldom offer a long-term positive strategy for any organization unwilling to be seen as out of step with mainstream values of decency and fair play. Many observers link this limited impact to the response of many consumers to avoid such messages or to ridicule them. Think of them as the advertising equivalent of Jerry Springer or Howard Stern.

In a more nuanced observation, researchers Darren Dahl, Kristina Frankenberger, and Rajesh Manchanda (2003) testing ads on AIDS/HIV prevention found that shocking ads are remembered longer than parallel ads based on fear or information. But more notably, such ads promote message-relevant behaviors. The researchers speculated that the long-term positive effect may be because the ads were carefully aimed at a target population (university students) less likely to be offended and also because the shocking images and language were directly related to the subject matter of the message.

Certain fashion and cosmetics corporations—notably Calvin Klein, Dolce & Cabbana, Sisley, and Benetton—have produced many shock ads over the years.

But the organization that is most consistent in this approach has been People for the Ethical Treatment of Animals (PETA), which has built a reputation for outrageous strategies in its animal-rights campaigns. PETA used shock strategy to force McDonald's to agree to more humane practices in chicken coops and slaughterhouses under its control. The advocacy group distributed "Son of Ron Unhappy Meal" boxes with a plastic cow in bloodstained hay, a plastic butchered pig, and a Ronald McDonald figure wearing a blood-spattered butcher's apron and wielding a meat cleaver. When parents complained that PETA was upsetting their children, the group rejoined that more parents expressed disgust with how McDonald's treated animals.

After McDonald's conceded the fight, PETA turned its attention to how Burger King raised and killed chickens, quickly gaining the compliance of that company as well.

Threat

Making a **threat** is another offensive strategy, involving the promise that harm will come to the accuser or the purveyor of bad news. The threatened harm may be in the form of a lawsuit for defamation, for example. Public relations practitioners have learned to use public threats only if the information cannot be disputed in another way. They've also learned to beware of the ethical concerns about misusing this strategy.

Standing Firm

Abraham Lincoln's biographers attribute an interesting quote to him: "Be sure you put your feet in the right place, then stand firm."

That's the idea underlying the offensive strategy of **standing firm**, otherwise known as a doubledown. Sometimes an organization simply needs to reiterate its action or position as a matter of principle, allowing whatever consequences to occur.

Critics blasted Starbucks for its supposed "war on Christmas" because in 2015 it featured a plain red cup with a green corporate logo rather than a traditional holiday scene. The company again stood firm and largely ignored the critics, though corporate ads featured Christmas songs and a "My First Christmas" baby bib.

Competitor Dunkin' Donuts, meanwhile, used a holiday cup with holly leaves and the word "joy," earning praise from the war-on-Christmas crowd.

Occasionally, the standing-firm strategy comes with a bit of attitude, a kind of communication smackdown.

CASE IN POINT   PETA's Faith-Based Shock Strategy

People for the Ethical Treatment of Animals has a strong anti-meat, pro-vegetarian, pro-animal rights message aimed at "total animal liberation." The organization tries to convert religious observers of all faiths to its way of thinking, often using a shock strategy with religious imagery designed to surprise and even outrage its audiences.

One PETA ad depicted the Shroud of Turin, which many believe to be a remnant from biblical times with an image of Jesus' face, with the caption "Make a lasting impression. Go vegetarian." Another suggests, despite recorded biblical evidence to the contrary, that Jesus was a vegetarian—the "Prince of Peas."

Some ads focus on the Virgin Mary. One billboard depicted her breastfeeding the Infant Jesus with the caption "If it was good enough for Jesus . . . Dump Dairy." Reminiscent of medieval art, the ad didn't create much chatter. But Catholic groups demanded removal of a subsequent billboard depicting the Virgin Mary cradling a chicken carcass à la Michelangelo's Pietà with the theologically perplexing caption "Go vegetarian. It's an Immaculate Conception."

PETA campaign director Bruce Friedrich describes himself as a devout Catholic who believes that cruelty to animals is against his faith. That's one reason why he wrote to the Pope asking him to tell Catholics to keep lamb off the traditional Easter menu in Italy. The Pope didn't respond, perhaps because previously during a papal visit to Chicago, PETA protestors dressed as a nun and a cow with a placard "Eating meat is a bad habit."

Activists in Jesus costumes have protested at barbecue restaurants in Texas, Alabama, Mississippi, and other Southern states, where people take seriously both their religion and their barbecues. The group held a boisterous rally outside a church in Louisville, Kentucky, where the president of KFC was worshipping on Christmas Eve. During Holy Week, PETA placed a 10-foot cow dressed as the Pope with a crucified cow on his cross outside Catholic cathedrals in several Eastern cities. In New York, the papal cowmobile was ticketed for an illegal turn on Fifth Avenue.

PETA spokespeople say such shock tactics are timed to generate the most publicity for their cause. For PETA, negative publicity is considered positive.

If nothing else, PETA is an equal-opportunity instrument of religious shock. Its "Holocaust on Your Plate" campaign said "Six million people died in concentration camps, but six billion broiler chickens will die this year in slaughterhouses." As the exhibit toured 70 U.S. cities, three Canadian provinces, and 15 foreign countries, the public outcry was what you'd expect: quick, loud, and widespread.

In another Holocaust campaign, PETA displayed photos of dead Jews in Nazi concentration camps interspersed with photos of slaughtered pigs at a livestock farm and a caption "to animals, all people are Nazis." Germany's high court banned the ad.

PETA also has taken aim on kosher practice, asking Jews to abandon their ancient dietary laws.

It placed billboards in Utah saying that Mormons misrepresent their scripture and urging them to heed PETA's call for vegetarianism. The group has challenged Muslims' interpretation that the Quran permits meat eating. It also has taken on Hindus in Nepal, decrying the ritual sacrifice of animals—from rats to water buffaloes—to the goddess Gadhimai.

To date, only Buddhists seem to have escaped PETA's faith-based shock strategy.

Phase Two

STEP
5

Such was the strategy behind a message from the Starbucks CEO to conservative Christian stockholders who condemned the company's support for marriage equality. CEO Howard Schulz told the National Organization for Marriage that the stance was not a business decision but rather was about supporting diversity, one of its corporate commitments. Nevertheless, he told the critics, it wasn't bad for business.

During a shareholders meeting, Schulz responded to critics: "If you feel, respectfully, that you can get a higher return than the 38 percent you got last year, it's a free country. You can sell your shares of Starbucks and buy shares in another company. Thank you very much."

Reactive Strategy 3: Defensive Response

Another strategic communication response involves defensive response strategies such as denial, excuse, justification, or reversal—all of which involve the organization reacting less aggressively to criticism.

Denial

Using the defensive strategy of **denial**, an organization tries not to accept blame. It may claim that the reputed problem doesn't exist or didn't occur. Or if it did, that it's not related to the organization. In the latter case, the claim generally is either one of **innocence** ("We didn't do it"), **mistaken identity** ("You have us confused with someone else"), or **blame shifting** ("So-and-so did it, not us").

A few years ago, a student at a public university was arrested for prostitution. She tried to justify her actions by claiming that she couldn't otherwise afford tuition because of a financial-aid error. The university was quick to say "That's absurd!" and shifted responsibility back to the student.

Be careful in shifting blame because the strategy can backfire if the organization is ultimately responsible. An executive who claims that an employee's inappropriate action was against company policy must be prepared for scrutiny of both the company's official policy and its way of doing business. It is best to use the strategy of denial only when the case can be publicly supported and when it can be proven that neither the organization nor anyone in its policy ranks was involved in the wrongdoing.

Excuse

A commonly used defensive strategy is **excuse**, in which an organization tries to minimize its responsibility for the harm or wrongdoing. Excuse can take several forms, including provocation, lack of control, accident, victimization, and mere association.

The organization may claim **provocation**, essentially saying that it had no choice. Here's an example from one city. The police department had just eliminated its popular mounted patrol. Amid initial criticism, the police department excused this decision by explaining that the police union had provoked the decision. The union had insisted that seniority, not horse-riding ability, be the key factor in selecting officers for the patrol, which the department argued made the mounted patrol inefficient and even dangerous. With this information reported by the local media, public criticism quickly shifted from the police department to the union.

A variation on the excuse theme is **lack of control**, in which the organization reports that its actions were forced upon it. Basically this is an out-of-our-hands defense. An example of this is the manager of a manufacturing plant who blames local employee layoffs on decisions made at national corporate offices.

Another excuse is **accident**, essentially a couldn't-be-helped defense. The organization suggests that factors beyond anyone's control led to a problem. An example of this is a mayor who excuses his city's slow progress in snow removal on unusually heavy snowfall during a two-week period, or a governor who similarly blames weather for shutting down large sections of the state's highways and stranding hundreds of motorists.

A related but even stronger excuse is **victimization**, in which the organization shows that it was the target of criminals or a casualty of Mother Nature. Pepsi played this card successfully amid claims that syringes were found in diet drink cans in 1993. The corporate excuse and Pepsi's victim role was so thoroughly accepted that consumers barely cut back on their consumption, then rebounded to give the company one of its best quarters to date in terms of sales. Pepsi's handling of the syringe hoax has become a classic case of effective public relations.

This same victimization card has been played by many governors and mayors in excusing higher taxes and/or fewer services because they had to redirect resources toward rebuilding after natural disasters such as hurricanes, earthquakes, wildfires, and floods.

A final type of excuse deals with mere **association**, in which the organization claims that it more or less inherited a problem. For example, a newly elected city administration might try to disassociate itself from a $2 million income shortfall by claiming that careless planning by the previous administration caused the financial loss. The tactic of associating a problem with the previous administration is one that's also been used in Washington and state capitals for years, not always successfully.

Justification

Another defensive strategy is **justification**, which admits the organization did the deed but did so for good reason (or at least, not for a bad reason). Like the excuse response, justification has several subcategories.

One type of justification is based on **good intention**, in which an organization attempts to soften the blow of bad results by claiming that it was trying to accomplish something positive. For example, a cab company may justify one of its drivers sideswiping a parked car by claiming the driver was trying to avoid hitting a pedestrian. This defense generally fails to cover what was a bad decision at the beginning. So if evidence were to show that the cab driver was speeding at the time of the accident, the good-intention justification wouldn't stand.

Another type of justification is **context**, in which the organization asks its publics to "look at it from our side." Robin Hood seen from the point of view of the sheriff of Nottingham looks much different than from the perspective of the Nottingham peasants. Likewise, investors and environmentalists each may have different views of a company that violated technicalities of clean-air regulations. And the body politic often incredulously wonders how the same facts can be interpreted so differently by Democrats and Republicans in the U.S., Tories and Grits in Canada, Labourites and Conservatives in the U.K., Libs and Laborites in Australia, and so on.

Phase Two

STEP 5

Idealism is a type of justification based on an appeal to ethical, moral, or spiritual values, such as leaders of a church protesting against the death penalty who explain that their actions, though perhaps unpopular with some church members, are nevertheless in line with—even commanded by—their religious principles.

Here again, a card played doesn't guarantee a hand won. For years, Catholic bishops have been opposing the death penalty, abortion, and most U.S. military entanglements; their Methodist counterparts support abstinence from alcohol, drugs, and tobacco; and Episcopalians are on record for increasing the minimum wage—all without necessarily winning the hearts and minds of the folks in their pews.

CASE IN POINT Dyngus Day's Strategic Reversal

Reversal sometimes can be accomplished with grace, even humor. That was the outcome when CNN commentator Anderson Cooper appeared to criticize the Dyngus Day celebration in Buffalo. "So stupid. Really, so stupid," he said on air, later apologizing and trying to say that his remark was directed at himself for launching into a giggle befitting a 13-year-old girl, so much that he had to walk off camera to regain his composure.

Admittedly, Dyngus Day has some humorous elements. It's a Polish American custom on the day after Easter, celebrating romance and frivolity after the solemn spirit of Lent. It's a day with deep historic, religious, and ethnic roots in Western New York, which has the third-largest Polish American community in the U.S.

Young women, usually dressed in traditional Polish clothing, sprinkle men with water. The men chase the women and tap them with pussy willow branches. Sometimes folks toss buckets of water at each other. Okay, you have to admit that Cooper had something to giggle about.

Polish Americans often have been the brunt of ethnic jokes and demeaning stereotypes, so it was not surprising that they would take offense at the criticism in a national forum, questioning Cooper's insensitivity in what they considered an ethnic slur. A Jewish senator said the TV host "shouldn't mock what he doesn't understand." Others flooded CNN with responses, including 500 comments, mostly negative, on Cooper's Facebook page. Some accused him of bigotry and drew parallels with unlikely ethnic criticism toward Kwanzaa or St. Patrick's Day.

Others saw humor in the entire incident and praised Cooper for apologizing on air the next day. It was that apology that sent organizers of the annual event into a reversal strategy.

They publicly accepted Cooper's apology and sent him some Polish sausage and pussy willows. They reprinted newspaper articles about the incident on their website (dyngusdaybuffalo.com). They also invited Cooper to Buffalo the following year to assume the title of Pussy Willow Prince and lead the world's largest Dyngus Day parade, something Cooper said he looked forward to but didn't act on.

Their website added: "Dziekuje [jen-KOO-yeh, thank you] Anderson Cooper for helping make Dyngus Day in Buffalo an international news story." The group reported 90,000 hits to its website in the two days following Cooper's initial story, and many more after his on-air apology.

A final type of justification involves **mitigation**. This admits to the problem but seeks to lessen blame because of impairment, illness, coercion, lack of training, and so on. However, if the mitigating factor is the responsibility of the organization, the attempt at justification probably will fail. Mitigation didn't offset the reported drunkenness of the *Exxon Valdez* captain that factored in the Alaskan oil spill. Nor did it satisfy critics blaming New York City Mayor Rudy Giuliani for his budget-cutting decisions prior to 9/11 that hampered rescue and recovery efforts, adding to the death toll for police and firefighters.

Reversal

The phrase "turning the tables" comes from table games such as chess or backgammon. Turn the table around, and you play from the opponent's previous position.

In public relations, this is an apt analogy for **strategic reversal**, in which the weakened party becomes the stronger one. In this David-and-Goliath strategy, an organization under criticism gains the upper hand. This is the point of the Dyngus Day case in the accompanying box.

Another version of strategic reversal involves the organization taking criticism and turning it into a positive. That is what the Texas Road House (TRH) restaurant chain did by turning potentially negative publicity to its advantage after Consumer Reports labeled it "the noisiest chain in America."

TRH launched a "Proud to Be Loud" public relations campaign, arguing that upbeat music, laughter, crowds, and line dancing by the staff "sure beats the heck out of wine sipping, or chirping crickets, and clinking silverware." The chain reported media coverage that would have cost $500,000 in advertising, improved employee morale, and new customers not upset by the noise.

Reactive Strategy 4: Diversionary Response

Several diversionary response strategies also are open to communication planners. They include concessions, ingratiation, disassociation, and relabeling. All of these are attempts to shift the gaze of the publics from the problem associated with the organization.

Concession

Using the diversionary strategy of **concession**, an organization tries to rebuild its relationship with its publics by giving the public something it wants. The focus here should be on a concession that is mutually valued by both the organization and its public.

For example, after objections to a car advertisement parodying Leonardo da Vinci's *The Last Supper* with the caption, "My friends, let us rejoice, because a new Golf is born," Volkswagen France and its advertising agency offered as a concession a major financial contribution to a religious charity whose work was supported by the protestors. Both the company and its offended public recognized the value of the donation by Volkswagen France. That is necessary for the concession strategy to be effective.

Perceived value was missing when Chevron responded to a mine explosion that killed a worker and disrupted a small town near Pittsburgh by offering people in the town coupons for free pizza.

Phase Two

STEP
5

Instead of providing gifts to involved publics, some concessions are aimed at generating favorable publicity for an organization under fire.

Crisis counselor James Lukaszewski revealed that he advised Exxon to charter aircraft to carry volunteers from major U.S. cities to Alaska so they could help clean up some of the 11 million gallons of oil spilled in Prince William Sound. Exxon rejected the idea on grounds that the airlift would cost too much—a few hundred thousand dollars. The company eventually spent $2.2 billion in clean-up costs, another $1 billion to settle state and federal lawsuits, and $300 million in lost wages to Alaskan fishermen, plus millions in legal fees fighting lawsuits that ordered punitive damages as high as $11.9 billion, much of it linked to Exxon's poor reputation.

Certainly an environmental airlift would not have eliminated all of Exxon's expenses. But in hindsight, it seems fair to conclude that an airlift would have helped the company's reputation, which in turn could have eased its legal battles as well as its strained relations with stockholders, consumers, government agencies, and the media.

Business Week magazine later commented, "Exxon could have emerged from the case with a far better image if it had taken a more conciliatory approach. . . . Instead, Exxon took a tough stand. And more than a decade later, the furious debates, and the bitterness, continue" (Commentary: It's Time to Put the *Valdez* Behind Us, 1999).

Now, almost three decades after the oil spill, the *Valdez* case still has negative residual effects, such as the continuing and costly legal disputes in Alabama and Maryland (as noted in Step 1).

Another example of concession involves the response of Planned Parenthood to the controversy (see Embarrassment earlier in this section) caused by an edited video that appeared to show the organization negotiating the cost of human tissue intended for medical research. The organization vigorously denied it was selling baby parts, and quickly announced that it would no longer charge research facilities for transportation costs. But that concession failed to remove fuel from the controversy, and Planned Parenthood faced criticism and legal consequences threatening its funding.

Ingratiation

Another diversionary strategy, though one of questionable ethical standing, is **ingratiation**. Essentially, the organization attempts to manage the negative situation by charming its publics or "tossing a bone," giving something of relatively little significance to the organization in an attempt to turn the spotlight away from the accusations and criticisms.

Concession differs from ingratiation in that the former involves something of real value to the public; ingratiation is more cosmetic. Examples of ingratiation are seen in the case of state lawmakers who vote against long-term tax reform for homeowners while offering a token and temporary tax reduction.

Disassociation

Another diversionary strategy is **disassociation**, which attempts to distance an organization from the wrongdoing associated with it. This can be effective when a mishap has occurred not because of organizational policy but because policy was not observed, especially when the organization has severed ties with the cause of the problem.

CASE IN POINT   Boycotting Nestlé

Public relations strategists should use concession only if adversaries will value the gift and if the organization will remain committed to that concession.

A five-decade boycott shows that this was not the case with the multinational Nestlé company, which began facing criticism of its marketing of infant formula in lesser-developed nations during the late 1970s. At issue was the company's marketing efforts discouraging breastfeeding that risked the health and lives of millions of babies. The risk was particularly acute in developing areas of the world, where baby formula was mixed with contaminated water.

After several court challenges spearheaded by Catholic nuns affiliated with the Interfaith Centre for Corporate Responsibility, the Infant Formula Action Coalition launched a U.S. boycott of Nestlé products in 1977. Nestlé also was criticized by the American Association of Pediatrics, as the boycott quickly spread to Canada, Australia, and several European countries.

Attempting to offer a concession to its critics, Nestlé established a code of ethics and agreed to implement international standards set by the World Health Organization. As a result, the boycott was suspended in 1984.

But Nestlé's concession strategy provided only a temporary diversion for critics, who quickly saw evidence that the company was not abiding by its own code of ethics. Subsequent opposition to Nestlé grew in the face of what critics viewed as insincerity and hypocrisy. In 1989 the boycott was relaunched.

After 50 years, the International Baby Food Action Network is still opposing the Swiss-based multinational. Critics call it one of the most hated companies in the world.

In 2014, the network successfully pressured Nestlé to drop its promotional claim that its milk substitute gives babies a "natural start." But the following year, a protest at the company shareholders' meeting claimed that Nestlé was still violating international marketing protocols.

The network points to a record of success. After nine years of boycott pressure, Nestlé agreed not to give complimentary milk formula to mothers of babies under six months. In 2011, the boycott was relaunched in the Asia-Pacific region. In 2012, the group's Baby Milk Action coalition sponsored a Nestlé-free week and urged supporters not to use Nestlé candy for Halloween.

Meanwhile, the International Nestlé Boycott Committee claims success in 70 countries that have adopted stronger laws monitoring marketing practices. The list of boycotters includes groups as diverse as the Catholic Sisters of Mercy and the Muslim Women's Association, European political parties, and lawmakers in several countries.

Many North American and European universities still ban campus sales of Nestlé products, which include Cheerios, DiGiorno pizza, Juicy Juice, and Häagen-Dazs. The company also manufactures brands such as Carnation, Stouffer's, and Lean Cuisine; Purina, Alpo, and Friskies pet foods, and more than 100 candy products.

Phase Two

STEP
5

The University of Oklahoma accomplished disassociation in 2015 when it quickly expelled two students who led a fraternity in using racist slurs and chanting about lynching and perpetually banning black men from joining the fraternity. Immediately after the chant was posted online, the national Sigma Alpha Epsilon fraternity closed the campus chapter, and within hours the university shut down a fraternity house and evicted its residents.

Carefully think through the implications of disassociation. Justin Timberlake found that his success in distancing himself from Janet Jackson and the Super Bowl halftime "nipple flash" controversy in 2004 also alienated many of his African American fans.

Trustees of Penn State University tried to disassociate their school from reports that an assistant football coach, since retired, had molested young boys in the locker room. They said the school had not handled the charges appropriately after a graduate student reported what he had seen to head football coach Joe Paterno. The trustees immediately fired the revered coach, along with the president and other senior university officials.

From a public relations standpoint, the trustees clearly had to act decisively and quickly. But in a clumsy attempt to disassociate itself from the scandal by shifting blame to Coach Paterno, the university alienated many supporters, including wealthy and previously generous donors.

Likewise, the National Collegiate Athletic Association (NCAA) also tried to quickly disassociate itself with the scandal, fined the university $60 million, stripped the coach of 111 football wins from during the tenure of his assistant coach, banned postseason play for four years, and disallowed football scholarships.

Three years later, after a public outcry and amid internal pressures, NCAA restored the wins and eliminated the post-season ban, sort of disassociating itself with its own previous disassociation.

Relabeling

Another diversionary strategy, **relabeling**, tries to distance the organization from criticism. It involves offering an agreeable name in replacement of a negative label that has been applied by others.

Some relabeling is innocuous. Prunes became dried plums and sales increased. Rapeseed sounded nasty, so it became Canola oil. Likewise, popularity increased when dolphinfish was renamed mahi-mahi, goosefish became monkfish, slimehead turned into orange roughy, and toothfish was relabeled as Chilean sea bass.

Some relabeling is downright silly, like the unsuccessful attempt to rename French fries "freedom fries" because of anti-French sentiment after the U.S. invaded Iraq. The fact that French fries originated in Belgium didn't seem to enter the discussion. The same folks tried to give us "freedom toast," but they overreached when they questioned the heredity and patriotism of French's mustard, which is based in New Jersey.

But some relabeling has more significant associations. The Al Qaeda organization in Yemen tried to become known as Ansar al Sharia because the original name has negative connotations.

Much relabeling involves corporate names. For decades, Philip Morris was synonymous with tobacco, but when tobacco became a magnet for social criticism and lawsuits, Philip Morris Companies changed its name to the Altria Group in an attempt to insulate the company from political pressure. The company also bought web domain names such as altriastinks.org and altriakills.com to prevent rogue sites from having easy dissemination of anti-Altria messages. The name change also allowed Altria subsidiary Kraft Foods to dissociate itself from the tainted tobacco label and, as one critic said, "to make itself invisible."

Similarly, trying to create a distance from its own record of fraud and bankruptcy, WorldCom changed its name to MCI, the name of its more respected subsidiary. Charging that WorldCom had hijacked the name, critics called for a boycott, and the name change failed to help the company's reputation improve.

After the ill-fated *Exxon Valdez* oil spill, the vessel was successively renamed the *Exxon Mediterranean*, *SeaRiver Mediterranean*, *S/R Mediterranean*, and finally simply *Mediterranean*. Regardless of the name, the tanker was not allowed in American waters. In 2005 the vessel was sold to a Hong Kong shipping company and renamed *Dong Fang Ocean*. In 2008 it was retrofitted as an ore carrier and renamed *Oriental Nicety*. In 2012 the ship was sold for scrap metal.

Blackwater, the private military company disgraced by its actions in Iraq, changed its name to Xe Services. Two years later it changed the name again, calling itself Academi, which its CEO admitted was intended to reflect a more boring image that wouldn't reflect the business's controversial mission as mercenary soldiers.

Other examples of rebranding reflect a more positive rationale to capitalize on a particular consumer strength. Thus, Matsushita Kotobuki Electronics Industries changed its name to that of its most recognized brand and became Panasonic Shikoku Electronics. Federated Department Stores changed its name to the Macy's Group in a bow to the drawing power of its most famous brand.

The strategy of relabeling can backfire if an organization's publics conclude that relabeling is deceptive or, worse, if it trivializes the problem. When MTV created a new phrase, "wardrobe malfunction," to explain Janet Jackson's exposed breast during the 2004 Super Bowl halftime show it produced, the Federal Communications Council was unamused. It fined CBS a record $550,000 for indecency.

Chrysler exemplifies the high cost of deception associated with relabeling. Charged with odometer fraud, the company said that corporate executives had merely driven new cars with disconnected odometers as part of a "quality test program," even though some had been in accidents. Chrysler was fined $7.6 million for selling the cars as new vehicles.

Public relations strategists also need to consider the ethical issues. Relabeling is only a short step away from **doublespeak**, which is deliberately misleading language that all principled practitioners avoid. Don't go too far in your effort to put on the best face.

Reactive Strategy 5: Vocal Commiseration

Another family of strategies deals with **vocal commiseration**, in which the organization expresses empathy and understanding about the misfortune suffered by its publics. These include concern, condolence, regret, and apology.

Concern

One type of vocal commiseration is **concern**, through which the organization expresses that it is not indifferent to a problem without admitting guilt. Generally this is only a temporary response, usually accompanied by a promised investigation.

Phase Two

STEP 5

That was the scenario in 2013 when the Department of Homeland Security (DHS) expressed "serious concerns" about reports of abuses by Border Patrol agents in Arizona. But it could not stop there. DHS went on to promise an investigation and to improve training for agents.

Similarly, many athletic coaches and team owners have needed to express concern about off-field problems caused by players, often troubles associated with domestic violence, sexual abuse, misuse of alcohol and other drugs, and similar illegal behavior. Usually their statements of concern are accompanied by promises to investigate and cooperate with law enforcement, sometimes by firing, fining, or applying other sanctions to the offending players.

During the Deepwater Horizon oil leak in the Gulf of Mexico in 2010, many observers initially were willing to give the benefit of the doubt to BP, Transocean, and Halliburton in trying to repair the damage. BP at first accepted responsibility and seemed to be fulfilling its promise to work hard to contain the spill and then clean it up. Public sentiment shifted when BP chief Tony Hayward minimized the disaster, then gushing thousands of barrels of oil a day into the sea, as "very, very modest," and when he subsequently complained, "There's no one who wants this over more than I do. I would like my life back."

Condolence

A more formal type of vocal commiseration is **condolence**, in which the organization expresses grief over someone's loss or misfortune, again without admitting guilt. The strategy works best when the organization is free of blame in the cause of the problem.

A good example of this strategy is the response of Tony Fernandes, the CEO of AirAsia, immediately after the airline's passenger jet crashed with 162 persons aboard in 2014. The disaster was later linked mainly to equipment failure and weather conditions.

Fernandes tweeted: "My heart bleeds for all the relatives of my crew and our passengers. Nothing is more important to us." He posted with several more tweets in the following days, including: "My heart is filled with sadness for all the families involved. On behalf of AirAsia my condolences."

That was the same sentiment that ValuJet president Lewis Jordan expressed after one of his airplanes went down in the Florida Everglades, killing 110 people—a crash later attributed to a shipper who had illegally mislabeled canisters of flammable oxygen.

"It's Mother's Day weekend—we know that," Jordan told reporters the day after the crash. "Words in the English language, at least the ones I know, are inadequate to express the amount of grief and sadness we feel." The company, which later merged into AirTran, put action behind its words, sponsoring a memorial service for 46 victims whose remains could not be identified.

Regret

Another vocal strategy, **regret**, involves admitting sorrow and remorse for a situation, a wish that an event had not happened. Like compassion, regret does not necessarily imply fault; in fact, statements of regret may specifically not admit to any wrongdoing. This is an important perspective that public relations advisors bring in crisis situations. By expressing regret, public hostility can be tempered and the number and intensity of lawsuits may be contained.

Regret without apology sometimes is not enough. Japan's Emperor Akihito learned that lesson on a visit to England. The emperor spoke of his "deep sorrow and pain" over suffering during World War II. But former prisoners of war booed the emperor, and one protestor burned a Japanese flag in his presence. A spokesman for the veterans said, "The emperor's speech does not alter the position one jot as far as any expression of an apology to the POWs is concerned."

BP found that its online statement of nonapologetic regret for the loss of life and environmental damage caused by the oil leak from the Deepwater Horizon failed to satisfy critics seeking a real apology. The company CEO's testimony before a congressional panel wasn't any better.

Regret sometimes extends to the actions of others. After Congress demanded a formal apology from Japan for sex slavery in occupied territories during World War II, Japan's prime minister said it was "regrettable." Not the wartime military action; the American resolution. The prime minister said Japan had previously apologized and made amends for its wartime transgressions, and did not plan to respond to the House resolution.

Congress also incurred the wrath of the Turkish government in 2007 when a House committee passed a similar nonbinding resolution labeling as "genocide" the Turkish massacre of Armenians during World War I. The irony is that Congress had at that time yet to apologize to its own people for black slavery in the American South or the country's genocide campaign against American Indians.

Apology

The vocal strategy focused most on the public's interests and least on the organization's concerns is **apology**. Issuing an apology involves publicly accepting full responsibility and asking forgiveness. Use this strategy when the organization is clearly at fault and when long-term rebuilding of relationships is more important than short-term stalling or legal posturing.

Make sure the apology is straightforward, such as the statement by Frank Lorenzo, chairman of Continental Airlines, who said in a full-page newspaper ad, "We grew so fast that we made mistakes."

The reluctance of the Japanese government to officially apologize for wartime military atrocities strained its relations with a number of countries. It was only in the final days of 2015 that Japan officially apologized for forcing Korean women into sex slavery for occupying Japanese soldiers during World War II. On a state visit to Seoul, Japan's prime minister expressed "sincere apologies and remorse to all the women who underwent immeasurable and painful experiences and suffered incurable physical and psychological wounds as comfort women." He pledged $8.3 million to help South Korea assist the surviving sex slaves. In response, South Korea's president said her country would consider the matter closed and would refrain from "accusing or criticizing" Japan on the issue.

Communication strategists can take a lesson from etiquette columnist Judith Martin (1999), who advised in one of her Miss Manners columns that apologizing is a way to diffuse angry responses. A good apology, she wrote, should include an acknowledgment of having done something wrong, a sense of remorse, an attempt to repair the injustice (if possible), and a promise not to commit the offense again. They also should be timely, something Twitter and other forms of social media make more possible.

Phase Two

STEP
5

In 2015, the Seattle Seahawks tweeted about their come-from-behind victory over the Green Bay Packers, "We shall overcome. #MLKDay." Immediately followers began reacting: "unbelievable," "disgusting," totally inappropriate," "mock the legacy of MLK on MLK day." An hour later, the team deleted the post and tweeted: "We apologize for poor judgment in a tweet sent earlier. We did not intend to compare football to the civil rights legacy of Dr. King."

Bad boy-rapper Kanye West reaped a load of criticism for his rant after musician Beck received the top-album award during the 2015 Grammy awards. West said Beck didn't deserve the award and should have given it to fellow nominee Beyonce. Amid a flood of criticism, West backpedaled his criticism, even saying that Beck's album, which he hadn't listened to previously, was "kind of good." West then issued a quick tweet to his 11 million followers: "I would like to publicly apologize to Beck, I'm sorry Beck."

Simultaneously, he tweeted a reconciliation statement about Bruno Mars, whose artistry he previously had criticized: "I also want to publicly apologize to Bruno Mars, I used to hate on him but I really respect what he does as an artist."

In a pattern adopted by other athletes, Michael Vick scored high points for accepting personal responsibility, apologizing to kids who look up to athletes, and expressing shame for misleading teammates about his involvement in illegal dog fighting. Later, after prison

---

CASE IN POINT   Red Cross, Social Media, and Beer

Sometimes a light touch can modulate a strategic apology. The American Red Cross diffused a minor social media crisis with humor after its social media specialist tweeted not just to close friends as she intended but to the organization's 270,000 Twitter followers.

The rogue tweet read: "Ryan found two more 4 bottle packs of Dogfish Head's Midas Touch beer . . . when we drink we do it right #gettingslizzerd."

After getting phone calls in the middle of the night, social media director Wendy Harmon took down the tweet and added a humorous corrective note for the Red Cross Twitter followers: "We've deleted the rogue tweet but rest assured the Red Cross is sober and we've confiscated the keys." Tweeter Gloria Huang also apologized from her private account, blaming her inability to use HootSuite correctly.

The subject of the original tweet, Dogfish Head beer, then came to the aid of the Red Cross and did itself a favor at the same time. The brewer tweeted to its 240,000 followers: "#craftbeer @dogfishbeer fans, donate 2 @redcross 2day. Tweet with #gettingslizzerd. Donate here . . . "

Then some pubs that sell the craft beer in 30 states began a beer-for-blood offer: "Show us you donated a pint @redcross today & we'll buy you a pint of @dogfishbeer #gettingslizzerd."

The incident was not as damaging as it might have been without the quick and lighthearted response. By taking quick action, the Red Cross recovered from the incident with its dignity intact—and above-average donations for the next few weeks.

"We are an organization that deals with life-changing disasters," explained a Red Cross executive, "and this wasn't one of them." It also helped that the 130-year-old service organization consistently ranks high in credibility and community recognition.

and bankruptcy, Vick rebuilt his football career with the Philadelphia Eagles, New York Jets, and Pittsburgh Steelers, regaining some of his earlier product endorsements.

Similarly, after beating up his girlfriend and being suspended by the National Football League (NFL), Ray Rice apologized "to the kids who looked up to me" and others, adding that "there is no excuse for domestic violence."

Likewise, Adrian Peterson of the Minnesota Vikings quickly apologized for injuring his son in what resulted in a child-abuse charge. Peterson explained that he had disciplined his son with a tree branch, the way his father had disciplined him as a boy. He also indicated that he had seen a psychologist to learn about more appropriate ways to discipline children. The NFL suspended him for the remainder of the season.

After the Rice and Peterson cases, the NFL engaged in its own damage control, not apologizing for its past lax enforcement of weak personal conduct policy but announcing tough new rules on player misconduct including assault and domestic violence. Major League Baseball and its players association followed the NFL with requirements for investigation, education, intervention, treatment, and punishment for similar offenses. The National Basketball League moved quickly to enforce its strong policy against domestic violence, though the National Hockey League faced continuing criticism over its own weak policy against off-ice domestic violence.

CONTEXT FOR APOLOGIES

It's important to locate a corporate apology in the right context. For crises that involve the loss of human life, that context must be taken very seriously. Here's some advice from The Perfect Apology—a collegial assortment of professors, business people, and consultants. The online resource (perfectapology.com) asks its clients to answer four basic questions:

1. What are you apologizing for?
2. Whom are you apologizing to?
3. How do you apologize?
4. When should you apologize?

It advises that apologies should not include excuses, and reminds clients that a sincere and unprompted apology fits into a company's overall customer relations program.

TIMELINESS OF APOLOGIES

Corporations also benefit from quick action on the apology front. When it became public that JetBlue—a year earlier—had violated its own privacy policy by giving private passenger data to Pentagon researchers attempting to profile high-risk passengers following the 9/11 terrorist attacks, the company issued a quick apology. Public relations observers noted that the quick response shortened the news cycle, reduced speculation, and allowed the story to become yesterday's news. JetBlue weathered the potential crisis well and remained popular and profitable.

Sometimes immediacy is important. When an ice storm grounded hundreds of JetBlue airplanes and stranded hundreds of thousands of travelers in 2007, company CEO David Neeleman again was quick to apologize: "We are sorry and embarrassed . . . Words cannot express how truly sorry we are for the anxiety, frustration, and inconvenience that you, your family, friends, and colleagues experienced."

Phase Two

STEP
5

> ## CASE IN POINT　Different Apologies from Mattel and China
>
> Sometimes an apology needs to be put into context so the public relations impact is not overlooked. That was the case as concern grew about the safety of Mattel toys made in China. A top Mattel official met with China's product-safety official to issue an apology to consumers.
>
> Mattel said it was sorry for the recall of millions of toys and that it would try to prevent future problems—at least, that's the version reported in Europe and North America.
>
> The Chinese version went more like this: "Mattel is sorry for having to recall Chinese-made toys due to the company's design flaws and for harming the reputation of Chinese manufacturing companies."
>
> It was, in fact, a design flaw that caused the recall of more than 17 million toys. Only two million of those were recalled specifically because the Chinese firms used lead paint, which is prohibited in the U.S.
>
> China had previously been stung with a series of recalls undermining confidence in its manufactured goods (pet food, toothpaste, packaged seafood, baby cribs). China needed the public apology, and it needed the explanation to be clear that the fault was with Mattel, which critics agreed deserved the bigger blame because of corporate policies to cut costs and speed up production.

No "if you were inconvenienced"; this was a flat-out "I'm sorry" from the top guy, for a problem caused by Mother Nature. Other airlines have had similar delays, but they didn't communicate with their passengers in such a forthright way.

CULTURAL ASPECTS OF STRATEGIC APOLOGIES

Like all strategies, apology must be considered in light of the particular public involved. Don't assume that how organizational managers or spokespersons want to frame an apology is the best way to do so. Consider culture and how the key public will respond to the apology.

Naomi Sugimoto (1997) reported in a study, for example, that the Japanese are three times more likely than Americans are to ask for forgiveness as part of an apology. The Japanese request also is much more explicit ("Please forgive me") than is the typical American one ("I hope you will understand").

Apologies often are associated with relationship goals and with the symmetrical model of public relations that focuses on the long-term association of an organization with its publics. Michael J. Cody and Margaret L. McLaughlin (1990) point out that apologies are more likely to occur when it is important to save face.

APOLOGIES AND LAWYERS

Strategic apologies sometimes are opposed by corporate lawyers, who sometimes consider such expressions will be used against the organization in a lawsuit. This concern is legitimate, but it fails to consider the opportunities an apology makes possible.

CASE IN POINT   Navy Apology in Intercultural Context

An apology can take on differing expectations depending on culture. In Japan, for example, a person who injures another is expected to apologize personally.

Such an apology was expected following a sea tragedy off Hawaii in 2001, when a U.S. submarine surfaced quickly and collided with a small Japanese high school training boat. Five fishermen and four Japanese students were killed. The sub had been showing off for some civilian visitors; the visitors may actually have been at the controls when the accident occurred. Japanese media reported that the Navy ship did not try to assist survivors after the accident.

After the accident, the U.S. submarine captain issued a statement through his lawyer expressing "sincere regret." But the Japanese rejected the statement.

President George W. Bush apologized on U.S. television, but the Japanese people remained unsatisfied. Public apologies from the secretaries of state and defense were similarly dismissed, as was a personal apology by the U.S. commander of the Pacific fleet to the families of the victims. Even a personal apology by the U.S. ambassador to both the prime minister and the emperor was found insufficient.

Instead, the Japanese expected to hear directly and personally from the one man responsible for the accident—the submarine captain, Commander Scott Waddle.

Three weeks later, Waddle hand wrote nine letters and asked that they be delivered to the families of the victims. The Navy's second-ranking admiral went to a small town in Japan to meet with the fathers of two of the dead students. Bowing deeply in a gesture of profound humility, he personally apologized and promised a full investigation. But that still wasn't the personal apology expected by the Japanese families.

Navy officials, apparently unfamiliar with the healing that a personal apology could bring, refused to allow Waddle to personally express his sorrow and contrition.

But a month after the accident—against his lawyers' advice—Waddle finally met with family members who had been brought to Hawaii to observe the Navy investigation. He bowed deeply and spoke through tear-filled eyes about his remorse. And finally, the families understood his sincerity and accepted his apology.

Nearly two years later, newly resigned from the Navy, Waddle traveled to Ehime prefecture in Japan to apologize personally to the victim's families and to survivors of the accident.

Said the mother of one of the teenage boys who died in the accident: "I am first and foremost the family member of a victim, and Mr. Waddle is first and foremost a victimizer. But when I saw Mr. Waddle as a person who was crying and apologizing, I thought he was apologizing from the heart."

The aftermath of the apology has brought a measure of reconciliation. Hawaii built a monument with an annual memorial service. Boys from Hawaii and Ehime play an annual memorial baseball tournament. The current relationship also includes a new sister-school program, mutual tree-planting ceremonies, and a summer internship in Ehime for University of Hawaii students.

Phase Two

STEP
5

Public relations counsel should be quick to point out an important alternative: An apology can prevent lawsuits, or at least limit damages sought by claimants or assessed by judges or juries. It also can be good business with stockholders.

Some legal observers view Volkswagen's offer of $1,000 gift cards to 480,000 customers as a hedge against lawsuits over its diesel emissions scandal. Half a billion dollars is a lot of money, but legal experts warned that lawsuits could cost the company much more.

Fiona Lee, Christopher Peterson, and Larissa Tiedens (2004) looked at annual stock prices for 14 companies over 21 years and concluded that stocks increased for companies that accepted responsibility for poor financial performances, compared with those that blamed external factors.

Ford and Bridgestone/Firestone faced massive lawsuits after their products were linked to 148 rollover deaths. In 2001, three Ford officials went to the hospital bedside of a Texas woman who was paralyzed in one of the accidents. There they apologized, videotaping their action for broadcast on national television. The bedside apology ended an out-of-court settlement with the paralyzed woman.

Kathy Fitzpatrick and Maureen Rubin (1995) pointed out that collaboration between public relations and legal counsel usually results in more favorable media coverage and thus a more positive public response, serving the organization's long-term interests if the situation ends up in court.

When Odwalla, a producer of juice products, faced a crisis because its apple juice contaminated by E. coli was linked to a child's death and the illness of several other consumers, the company initiated a voluntary recall, sent representatives to meet with the family of the young victim, and set up a web page to update its customers.

Odwalla relied on advice from both public relations and legal counsel. A case study by Kathleen Martinelli and William Briggs (1998) found that nearly 47 percent of the company's statements reflected traditional public relations responses: explaining its policy, investigating allegations, expressing concern for victims, taking steps to prevent a recurrence of the problem. Only 12 percent reflected the common legal response of denying guilt, minimizing responsibility, and shifting blame to the plaintiffs.

Odwalla eventually was fined $1.5 million—a relatively mild sum. Compare this to the 1993 Jack-in-the-Box fast-food crisis, in which four people died from E. coli. The company's first response was from a legal standpoint: no comment, followed by attempts to shift blame to its supplier. Jack-in-the-Box eventually paid $58.5 million in fines.

It is the lack of prompt apologies that have been cited as the reason for many lawsuits, such as a $400,000 claim against police in London, Ontario, by a man erroneously accused of drug trafficking. He explained that he sued the police mainly because they would not apologize.

Similarly, a Las Vegas man who sued a doctor for keeping him three hours in the waiting room said all he really wanted was an apology. After the trial, which ruled in the man's favor, the doctor retorted that the patient should be the one to apologize for dragging the doctor to court for two and a half days. Finally, six months after the waiting-room wait, the doctor wrote a letter of apology. He had to pay the patient $250 plus court costs and make a charitable contribution as well.

Defense attorneys often fear corporate apologies, but in personal-injury cases in particular, apologies can save the company money. Some attorneys point out that clients seeking an admission of corporate guilt often bring lawsuits, and a public apology can lessen the amount of money sought by an injured party or awarded by a sympathetic jury.

Easing the way for corporate apologies, Massachusetts passed a law that "statements, writings, or benevolent gestures expressing sympathy . . . relating to the pain, suffering or death of a person involved in an accident . . . shall be inadmissible as evidence of an admission of liability in a civil action." California, Texas, Florida, and Washington followed with similar laws.

Additionally, 37 states have laws preventing expressions of condolence or apology by doctors to patients or their families being used in court as evidence of wrongdoing. According to the Sorry Works Coalition (www.sorryworks.net), these "I'm sorry" laws are meant to promote communication between doctors and their patients and to assist doctors in lawsuits. Meanwhile, some states are considering medical apology laws that mitigate malpractice lawsuits when a doctor expresses regret over a patient's death or injury.

> **CASE IN POINT** **Air Midwest and Legal Aspects of a Public Apology**
>
> The editor of the Aviation Law Section's newsletter for the Association of Trial Lawyers of America reported that corporate contrition, not monetary compensation, is the most important factor for surviving family members after an airplane crash.
>
> The newsletter cited a groundbreaking lawsuit, *Shepherds v. Air Midwest*, that yielded what the headline proclaimed as "Another Level of Justice: The Public Apology."
>
> An Air Midwest crash in North Carolina had killed all 21 aboard. The victim's families initially faced a cadre of corporate lawyers who took the usual legal stance opposing any public apology or admission of responsibility.
>
> The airline attorneys and trial judge were surprised by the families' lawsuit. The families refused to even negotiate compensation until the company first agreed to give a public apology and promise to put safety first. Eventually the airline's legal team agreed to the families' term that any settlement must include a public apology. The outcome was an out-of-court financial settlement, along with a public memorial ceremony attended by families and company officials.
>
> At the service, company president Greg Stephens noted a rigorous investigation that had led to several improvements in airplane maintenance, operation, and general safety issues.
>
> "We have taken substantial measures to prevent similar accidents and incidents in the future, so that your losses will not have been suffered in vain," said Stephens, whose apology was clear: "We are truly sorry, and regret and apologize to everyone affected by this tragic event."
>
> The law firm that obtained the apology later was hired to represent families of victims of a Continental flight that crashed near Buffalo killing 50 persons aboard. The crash investigation eventually led to changes in airline safety, including crew training and pilot fatigue.

Phase Two

STEP
5

PSEUDO-APOLOGY

And then there is the **pseudo-apology**, sometimes called a **nonapology**. This is an insincere or half-hearted attempt that, like the previously discussed concept of regret, can be worse than no apology at all.

A nonapology might blame the victim of the offense: "I'm sorry that you took offense" or "I regret you overreacted to what I said." Or this gem from radio talker Rush Limbaugh: "I regret that you heard me say that."

Some such pseudo-apologies take advantage of passive voice: "Mistakes were made." That's like Adam and Eve telling God: "Apples were eaten."

Beware also similar false apologies that lament the effect but not the underlying transgression. Avoid pseudo-apologies such as those by any number of politicians who have felt compelled to apologize "for anything I may have done that offended you," often adding, "but it was only meant as a joke."

A similar nonapology uses the "if" format: "I'm sorry if you were offended." What's missing from this is an admission " . . . by my blatantly offensive words and deeds." That would make it a real apology instead of a sloppy pretense that suggests the victim was simply oversensitive.

Other nonapology formulas include "I'm sorry you didn't get the joke," "I'm sorry I hurt your feelings," "I'm sorry my comments were taken out of context," "I'm sorry; I was just trying to help," and almost any sentence that begins, "I'm sorry, but . . . ."

Colorado's Republican Congressman Doug Lamborn quickly realized he had spoken with insensitivity, many called it racism, when he called President Obama "a tar baby." He soon posted a note on his website with a presumptive element: Lamborn "today sent a personal letter to President Barack Obama apologizing for using a term some find insensitive . . . He regrets that he chose the phrase 'tar baby' rather than the word 'quagmire.' The Congressman is confident that the President will accept his heartfelt apology."

Lamborn's pseudo-apology blamed people who were offended without accepting responsibility for having offended them. It then quickly kicked the ball to the other end of the field, setting up a scenario in which the president would look petty if he didn't accept Lamborn's quasi-contrition. Wisely, the White House ignored both the statement and the congressman's letter.

Sometimes an apology is hurt because the speaker doesn't know when to stop. Before he was ousted as owner of the LA Clippers basketball team, Donald Sterling went on television in 2014 to apologize for his racist comments. He started out fine: "I made a terrible, terrible mistake . . . I'm here to apologize." But later in his interview he said of successful Jewish businessmen like himself, "they will help their people"; but some successful African Americans, "they don't want to help anybody." Shortly thereafter, the NBA forced him to sell the team.

Reactive Strategy 6: Rectifying Behavior

A positive response to opposition and criticism involves **rectifying behavior** strategies, in which the organization does something to repair the damage done to its publics. These include investigation, corrective action, restitution, and repentance.

Investigation

Using the rectifying behavior of **investigation**, the organization promises to examine the situation and then to act as the facts warrant. This is only a short-term strategy, a way of buying time. Eventually the organization will have to respond with more substance. Use the investigation strategy only when the facts are uncertain enough to warrant a delay in other strategic responses.

Corrective Action

A stronger rectifying behavior is **corrective action**, which involves taking steps to contain a problem, repair the damage and/or prevent its recurrence. This is a strategy that can serve the

---

CASE IN POINT   Volkswagen Emissions Scandal

Volkswagen used the investigation strategy when the scandal broke in 2015 that it had installed software that masked illegal levels of emissions on its diesel-fueled Audi, Porsche, and Volkswagen autos.

U.S. environmental authorities uncovered the scandal. About 11 million cars and SUVs were involved globally, 8.5 million of them eventually recalled.

VW's initial statement was a public apology and the promise of an investigation led by outside experts, an international team headed by a U.S. law firm. The probe was to root out those responsible for the scam to beat emission standards for auto exhaust.

Quickly following this was the resignation of CEO Martin Winterkorn. His successor, CEO Matthias Müller, oversaw the firing or resignation of dozens of top engineers and other company officials. Others were suspended from their jobs until they might be cleared by the investigation.

The new CEO called the company's investigation and response "a painful process, but for us it is the only alternative. For us, the only thing that counts is the truth."

A couple of weeks later, VW appointed a new chairman, Hans Dieter Poetsch, who affirmed the investigation. He vowed that it was "leaving no stone unturned."

Reuters noted that "It takes an awful long time to build up a reputation and not long to destroy it, and . . . the interesting issue for VW going forward will be how to limit the damage and not cause the kind of brand destruction that has impacted other companies in the past."

Like Toyota's Lexus and GM's Saturn several years earlier, VW was hoping to use the recall as an opportunity to shore up relations with its customers and to actually enhance its brand reputation. Initially, the scandal had little to no impact on sales.

The company hoped to paint this as a one-time breach in ethics by some rogue employees that, now exposed, would allow VW to reclaim its reputation as a respected green company. Some observers predicted the eventual cost to VW would be about $50 billion or more for the recalls, lost sales, and likely lawsuits (it actually was about $22 billion). After its stock dropped about 25 percent, some investors were repurchasing VW stock and predicting a successful turnaround in VW's corporate reputation.

Phase Two

STEP
5

mutual interests of both the organization and its public. Take corrective action if the organization is in a position to fix a problem, especially if it was in some way unprepared or negligent.

This was the case with Texaco when, as noted previously, company executives made racist statements. Texaco responded aggressively with rectifying action that included sensitivity training and a procedure to weed out discrimination within the company.

Corrective action generally is expected when the organization has been at fault. But the response is even more powerful and positive when an organization willingly accepts responsibility for fixing a problem it did not cause.

An example of this strategy is Johnson & Johnson's handling of the cyanide deaths associated with Tylenol. Though it was clear from the beginning that the company was not even negligently responsible for the product tampering, Johnson & Johnson nevertheless accepted the challenge to contain the damage and prevent any more.

Combining various public relations response strategies, the company conducted an investigation and expressed compassion. But its strongest efforts were in taking corrective actions. Johnson & Johnson recalled the product and then introduced a new triple-seal safety packaging that soon became the industry standard.

Restitution

Another rectifying behavior, **restitution**, serves the mutual interests of the organization and its publics. It involves making amends by compensating victims or restoring a situation to its earlier condition. Such a response may be forced upon an organization through the legal process, but some organizations have found it beneficial to offer restitution before it is required.

Repentance

The strongest type of rectifying behavior is **repentance**, which involves both a change of heart and a change in action. Repentance signals an organization's full atonement in the classic sense that it turns away from a former position and becomes an advocate for a new way of doing business. Many organizations, caught in a moral or legal embarrassment, promise repentance and a future of right doing, but few achieve such a turnaround.

Sometimes an organization may combine repentance with several other strategies. A turnaround, for example, may also involve investigation, justification, restitution, and concession, along with an apology.

Some companies learn to improve their public relations even during a crisis. After Barilla pasta's CEO said in 2014 that his company wouldn't "do ads with homosexuals because we like the traditional family," the company quickly apologized, appointed a new CEO, hired a chief diversity officer, and created a "diversity and inclusion board" of outside consultants.

A year later, human rights activists were citing Barilla as a company that had done a 180 on gay rights. The company had funded anti-bullying groups, featured lesbians at its website, and expanded its anti-discrimination policy to include gay and transgendered people. Such actions earned Barilla a perfect 100 rating from the Human Rights Campaign.

Phase Two

STEP
5

One organization that seems to have repented is Denny's restaurants. It's a story of transformation from an embodiment of corporate racism to a model of workplace diversity.

Denny's faced accusations and lawsuits for racial discrimination at several of its restaurants during the 1990s. One of the most notorious cases involved 21 members of the Secret Service in 1994. While 15 white agents were served quickly, a waitress and manager delayed serving six black agents for nearly an hour, allowing their food to get cold.

The ensuing publicity highlighted a series of lawsuits for similar acts of discrimination at other Denny's restaurants: Asian American students at Syracuse University refused service and beaten by customers; Muslim customers in Montana served pork after asking for a vegetarian menu; Hispanic customers in San Jose refused service; a blind woman refused service because she was accompanied by a service dog; men of Middle Eastern descent kicked out of a restaurant in South Florida.

Denny's eventually paid $54 million in legal settlements. The company's chief diversity officer later looked back on that "historic low point" in Denny's history as presenting "huge opportunities. We had no place to go but up."

Dramatically from a public relations perspective, the company seems to have embraced the concept of corporate repentance. It adopted an aggressive anti-discrimination policy that included hiring minority managers, training employees, and firing those who discriminated. Denny's increased minority franchise ownership from one to 109 over a span of five years. Currently 46 percent of Denny's 1,685 franchises are minority-owned. The company reports 44 percent of its management and 45 percent of its corporate directors as minorities and/or women. It purchases goods worth more than $100 million a year from minority vendors.

Denny's launched a $2 million anti-discrimination advertising series. It gives proceeds from some sales to the King Center in Atlanta. It has supported the National Civil Rights Museum and scholarships for Wilberforce University, a historically black college. The company has worked with the Hispanic Association on Corporate Responsibility and the National Association for the Advancement of Colored People. It gave more than $1.5 million to civil rights groups and the United Negro College Fund.

The result of this turnaround is that Denny's and its parent company ranked No. 1 in *Fortune* magazine's listing of best companies for minorities, two years running. It received similar awards from *Black Enterprise*, *Essence*, *Asian Enterprise*, and *Hispanic Business* magazines.

So successful is its commitment to diversity, some white nativist organizations now are calling for boycotts because Denny's has become too multicultural.

Denny's certainly isn't the only company with such problems, and with 1,600 franchises throughout the U.S. incidents are bound to occur. But every time an allegation of discrimination is reported, the news media repeats the litany of past complaints against the company, while commentators and customers weigh the sincerity of Denny's protestations that it has repented of such sins and adopted new policies and training programs to prevent their repetition.

Phase Two

STEP
5

Reactive Strategy 7: Deliberate Inaction

The final category of public relations responses involves deliberate inaction, the considered decision by an organization under siege to offer no substantive comment though perhaps to quietly take some action (strategic silence), to respond vaguely and indistinctly (strategic ambiguity), or to say and do nothing and let the problem blow over (strategic inaction).

Strategic Silence

Occasionally the decision to remain nonresponsive—that is, **strategic silence**—is an appropriate public relations response. The strategy involves patience and composure. By not responding to criticism, an organization may be able to shorten the life span of a crisis situation.

Strategic silence can work when publics accept that an organization is remaining silent not out of guilt or embarrassment but because it is motivated by higher intentions such as compassion for victims, respect for privacy or other noble considerations, or simply because it is working on the problem and refuses to get sidetracked into talking much about it.

This concept of strategic silence sometimes is called **purdah** (a reference to the veil or protective screen used in the practice of social isolation of women in some Islamic and Hindu societies).

Maintaining strategic silence doesn't necessarily mean doing nothing. After a political blogger criticized Dunkin' Donuts for featuring spokeswoman Rachael Ray in an Arab-looking scarf (because, you know, anything Arab-looking must be supporting terrorists), the company at first dismissed the criticism as anti-Muslim hysteria unworthy of response. But as the right-wing blogosphere increased heat, Dunkin' Donuts quietly withdrew the ad. Some things aren't worth a fight, especially if the fighting could empower the opposition. There's wisdom in what playwrite George Bernard Shaw said: "I learned long ago, never to wrestle with a pig. You get dirty, and besides, the pig likes it."

Similarly, when cancer-causing benzene was discovered in bottled water produced by Perrier, the upscale European company said nothing. Its chairman refused to hold a news conference or give interviews. Such silence, though frustrating for the media, prevented the company from appearing to be under siege. Meanwhile, Perrier pulled millions of bottles from store shelves and replaced them with water without the benzene. By correcting the problem quietly, Perrier fostered a successful survival of the short-lived crisis.

In some circumstances, the law requires organizations to maintain silence, at least on particulars. If so, this requirement should be explained by the organization as the reason for its silence. For example, the Family Educational Rights and Privacy Act (FERPA) prevents universities from providing details about students' academic records. Similarly, the Health Insurance Portability and Accountability Act (HIPAA) sets national standards to ensure the privacy of medical records and other personal health information.

When considering strategic silence, however, remember that the response is likely to be accepted only by those publics that already trust the integrity of the organization. Opponents will find plenty of ammunition in the lack of response.

Silence also risks allowing negative statements to stand unchallenged, which could hurt the organization in the long run. Additionally, a policy of strategic silence may be difficult to maintain if a strong opponent is able to insist on a public response. Remember that silence can imply indifference not only to an opponent but also to the issue itself. An issue might be

---

Pepsi + Stem Cells = Boycott

Stem cell research is a controversial ethical issue, particularly when it involves using and destroying human embryos, which often are the result of abortion. It became a lightning-rod issue after the Food and Drug Administration in 2009 expanded clinical trials by researchers seeking cures for genetic diseases and degenerative conditions.

The biotech company Senomyx adopted a let-it-ride nonresponse when it was accused of conducting research using tissue from a stem cell line obtained from an embryo aborted in the 1970s. The line is commonly used in research by pharmaceuticals, food and perfume industries, and medical research.

When it learned that Senomyx does research on flavor enhancers for food and beverage manufacturers, Florida-based Children of God for Life mounted a blog-based campaign against it. Senomyx simply ignored the criticism. Because it isn't a retail company, it was pretty much immune from a consumer boycott.

Frustrated, the protesters turned to a common strategy among activists, focusing attention on well-known clients. They called for boycotts against Senomyx "collaborators" including Kraft Foods, Pepsi, Campbell Soup, Nestlé, and other companies what used Senomyx for flavor research.

The boycott call received some media visibility, though the companies themselves seemed not to take it as a serious consumer threat. Nestlé asserted that the cell line is well established in scientific research. Campbell merely said it values the customers' trust. Pepsi affirmed its commitment to ethical product development, and a year later said it no longer needed to use that cell line research.

Through the year–long controversy, Senomyx steadfastly remained silent toward the protesters. The protest fizzled, and the biotech went on with its business of finding ways to enhance the taste and smell of foods.

Phase Two

STEP 5

of real interest to some of an organization's key publics. By dismissing it, the organization risks slighting anyone who feels the issue is worthy of response.

Strategic silence is not the same as saying "No comment." Such a statement invariably is interpreted as an acknowledgment of guilt, implying that the organization not only did something wrong but did it so ineptly or so blatantly that it can't think of any explanation that would be accepted by its publics. Avoid "no comment" responses and related disdainful statements such as "we won't dignify that accusation with a reply."

Strategic Ambiguity

Similar to the concept of strategic silence is **strategic ambiguity**, the refusal to be pinned down to a particular response. Often this involves the artful dodging of a question.

In an ideal world, ethical decisions would be simple and clear-cut. But the world isn't an ideal place, so be prepared to carefully discern among competing loyalties and differing values.

Politicians use strategic ambiguity frequently so they can avoid taking a public stand or tipping their hand about future potentials. U.S. diplomats, for example, have for decades been deliberately vague about what action might be taken if China moves to forcibly implement its claim that Taiwan is part of China and not an independent nation. Washington and Beijing exchange ambassadors, while the U.S. maintains unofficial relations with Taiwan. The State Department uses terms such as "acknowledging" rather than "recognizing" a single Chinese political entity, and diplomats "take note of" rather than "support" Beijing's claim to be the legitimate government for all of China.

When President George W. Bush strayed from the standard U.S. line and referred to Taiwan as a country, his aides corrected him without correcting him. They said he gave behind-the-scenes disclaimers that this was merely an informal designation and did not signal a shift in U.S. foreign policy. When President Donald Trump tweeted a similar faux pas, within days he affirmed his support for the one-China policy.

Corporate leaders use the device of strategic ambiguity to avoid negotiating in public and to maintain their options. Much of the literature of crisis communication suggests that companies can minimize fallout by avoiding quick responses to stakeholder demands.

When a Rolls-Royce engine failed, a Qantas Airlines jumbo jet had to make an emergency landing in Singapore. The airline gave no interviews, nor did it make any public comment for the media. Instead, it posted at its website an explanation of sorts for all to read, full of engineer-geek talk that the media found difficult to include in their reporting.

When Paula Deen used racist slurs, The Food Network (TFN) said it supports diversity and would monitor the situation. Then, without any formal announcement, TFN acknowledged that it would let her contract expire. Quiet monitoring, a minimalist statement, then silence. This approach requires companies to be patient and to resist the temptation to over-comment.

Clearly there is an ethical dimension to the concept of strategic ambiguity. At what point does ambiguity become obfuscation? Under what circumstances, if any, is it ethical to answer a direct question with a deliberately evasive response? In the hierarchy of organizational objectives, does transparency trump ambiguity? How long can credibility be maintained when underlings have to explain away the language of the boss?

Strategic Inaction

A final category of the deliberate inaction strategy is **strategic inaction**, making no statement and taking no overt action. Instead, the organization simply waits it out and allows the situation to fade.

Strategic inaction may be a useful strategy if the stakes are not too high. But be forewarned: Some problems do not fade away, especially those fanned by the opposition. By doing nothing, an organization risks allowing the problem to grow.

In considering this strategy, ask a few questions. Why would an organization choose not to act publicly, especially in a crisis situation? When would a public official or celebrity under siege think that doing nothing is a reasonable response to criticism?

After releasing his birth certificate, President Obama ignored the continuing criticism of "birthers," including several prominent politicians, bloggers, and pundits. In the same vein, he steadfastly ignored provocative accusations about his patriotism and his religious beliefs. Such inaction stems from the twin conclusions that supporters have already been satisfied with information they have been given and that critics will never be satisfied with any response.

Sometimes the decision for strategic inaction is based on a cost–benefit analysis. This was the case when the Caterpillar corporation was accused of assisting the Israeli government's occupation of the West Bank because it had sold bulldozers to Israel. Some pro-Palestinian critics called for a boycott to investing in the company. Caterpillar basically ignored the criticism, apparently concluding that the economic downside of any boycott would not be significant to its financial bottom line.

Some cases support the notion that strategic inaction can shorten the life span of crisis. Often this is linked to the consider-the-source principle. When criticism comes from only a small source, especially one with low credibility, it may be safe to minimize response to such critics.

Consider the let-it-ride response that most of the health-care establishment has taken on the anti-vaccination issue. All credible players in the field agree on the evident value of vaccination.

So while credibility-challenged critics have fumed against perceived horrors of vaccines, most people simply ignored them. Doctors persist in promoting vaccinations. Educators encourage the practice. Schools require proof of vaccination. The media report on the value

MAKING ETHICAL JUDGMENTS

In considering various proactive and reactive strategies, it's worth asking one of those sometimes-uncomfortable ethical questions, the kind that doesn't have an easy answer, the kind that may give rise to more questions than answers.

"To whom is moral duty owed?" ask Clifford Christians and his fellow authors of *Media Ethics* (2015).

In response to this question, they suggest that communication strategists—journalists and editors, public relations practitioners, and advertisers—clarify who will be influenced by our decisions and what obligations we have to them. Good advice. Here are five obligations or duties, along with some thoughts on relevant considerations.

- *Duty to Ourselves*. Be careful to distinguish between following your conscience and simply acting in your own careerist self-interest. One way to do this is to pause and reflect on the basis of your own moral values and on the consistency with which you apply them in your own decision making.
- *Duty to Our Clients*. Our clients, as well as our publics and audiences, deserve our best efforts, especially when they are paying the bills. But don't just blindly go where a client would send you without giving some thought to the client's motives and moral base and how these intersect with your own.
- *Duty to Our Companies or Bosses*. Strike a balance between company loyalty and stoogism. Stick to the recurring advice: Consider motivations and the impact that a company's policies and actions are likely to have.
- *Duty to Our Professional Colleagues*. Consider how your work is enhancing the prestige of your profession and the reputation of your fellow practitioners. Consider especially the commitments implied in the codes of ethics of the various professional organizations.
- *Duty to Society*. This is the ultimate ethical test: What does an action do for people? What does it do to them?

Phase Two

STEP
5

of vaccinations. Parents continue to seek safe vaccines to protect their children against serious disease.

Most of the publics could safely conclude that anti-vaccination criticism would have a short shelf life before its dissidents move on to some other conspiracy theory.

Social media should be considered in any corporate decision to employ strategic inaction. The ubiquity of social media has increased pressure on organizations and public individuals to respond to criticism. A few critics can hijack social media venues to give a public platform for their accusations, which may call for an organizational response. On the other hand, some online critics reveal themselves as so outrageous and ill spoken that they render themselves as noncredible sources.

Weighing Options

Look back over the list of reactive public relations strategies. So many possibilities. How can an organization choose among all the options?

Research may play a role, as public relations practitioners consider some likely options and then put them to the test, perhaps by using focus groups, case studies, and other forms of research. Experience also plays a role, as practitioners draw on their knowledge of what has worked (or not worked) for them in the past.

Consider the situation faced by Network Ten, one of the major networks in Australia known for some edgy programming. In 2012, the network commissioned a reality series called "The Shire," branded as Australia's version of the U.S. series "Jersey Shore" and the U.K. version "The Geordie Shore." Immediately the planned series captured popular attention.

A promo video was leaked, showing scenes about breast implants, domestic violence, and wannabe porn stars. This created what some residents of Sutherland Shire saw as a negative impression of the Sydney-area community where the show was set. The mayor had "a heated meeting" with the network executive. The Shire council tried to ban producers from filming on area parks and beaches. A member of parliament planned to meet with the network bosses.

Network Ten faced several options in reacting to the rogue (and by then, viral) promo video.

- *Strategic silence.* It simply could ignore the video, not draw more attention to it, and hope the controversy would die out.
- *Denial.* It could use a strategy of defensive response. The network's contention was that the promo video was nothing like its series. It might prove this by releasing an authorized video trailer of "The Shire," inviting audiences to see for themselves that the leaked version was a flawed comparison.
- *Reversal.* Network Ten could accept the leaked video as a compliment and light-heartedly play along with the interest it was generating.
- *Threat.* The network could use an offensive response strategy by threatening the bloggers with legal action if they did not take the video down.
- *Attack.* The network could actually make good on its threat and try to attack the messenger by forcing bloggers who posted the video to take it down.

Network Ten chose a combination of threat and attack. After threatening a blogger who had posted the video, the network filed a copyright claim. Not surprisingly, these steps created even more attention. The network eventually forced YouTube to temporarily remove the video—but not before it had attracted 30,000 viewers in the first two days. The video later returned to several different video-sharing sites, and the number of viewers jumped to six digits.

The strategy of offensive response—and the inept handling if the network really wished to minimize publicity—prompted media critics to suggest that Network Ten purposely "leaked" the video to evoke a controversy and draw attention to the planned series.

Regardless of its motivation, the strategy of attack was seen as an example of the **Streisand effect**, which refers to the unintended consequence of fueling publicity by trying to have something censored.

The Streisand effect is the backfiring of efforts to remove information, especially photos and videos disseminated over the Internet. The term stems from entertainer Barbra Streisand's 2003 attempt to ban photos of her home—just one of 12,000 photos of California coastal erosion—from being displayed at an environmental website. The entertainer's $50 million lawsuit, which eventually was dismissed, created additional publicity. Before the lawsuit was filed, only six people had viewed the photo (two of them Streisand's attorneys). But publicity about the lawsuit drove half a million visitors to view the website photos, creating a boon for the environmental group.

Other celebrities have had similar experiences. Tom Cruise unsuccessfully attempted in 2008 to force YouTube to remove a video interview of him talking about his Church of Scientology, only to boost its popularity among viewers.

In 2009, Glenn Beck tried to shut down a satirical website raising the question of whether he had raped and murdered a girl, a question that parodied Beck's own interview style posing outrageous assertions to guests on his TV commentary. Beck lost the legal battle, but not before driving viewers to the social media sites posting the video and even attracting coverage by mainstream news media.

Corporations also have experienced the Streisand effect, such as when McDonald's sued two activists for passing out disparaging fliers at one London restaurant in 1990. Instead of having only a few hundred patrons exposed to the criticism, McDonald's launched a lawsuit that endured for 15 years, including a libel trial that lasted two and a half years, cost millions in legal fees, and drew international media attention as the McLibel case before it was finally settled. McDonald's lost.

When Fox Television sued Al Franken in 2003 claiming copyright infringement over the title of his book *Lies and the Lying Liars Who Tell Them: A Fair and Balanced Look at the Right*, the book shot to No. 1 on Amazon's best-seller list.

What's Next?

This concludes Step 5. You now should have a firm handle on the strategic direction of your planning. Specifically you have made some major decisions on using both proactive and reactive approaches to your key publics.

Next you will turn to the message itself—who should carry it and how it will draw on logical and/or emotional arguments.

Phase Two

STEP
5

PLANNING EXAMPLE 5 **Formulating Action and Response Strategies**

Upstate College will develop the following strategies:

Proactive Strategy

1. Involve student public in celebrations and other special events focused on the academic expansion.
2. Enhance alliances with high schools based on new academic opportunities at the college.
3. Take advantage of the many newsworthy activities associated with the expansion.

Reactive Strategy

No responsive strategy is anticipated, because the expansion to a four-year program is unlikely to generate opposition or criticism.

Tiny Tykes will develop the following strategies:

Proactive Strategy

1. Place a high priority on research and development as they relate to high-quality standards for toy products.
2. Form alliances with customers and consumer advocates focused on the safety of children's toys.
3. Initiate news activities focused on toy safety.
4. Engage in transparent communication to allow employees and consumer advocates to observe the company's efforts to produce safe and high-quality toys.

Reactive Strategy

1. Make a concession to customers and consumer advocates by sponsoring university research on the role of play in child psychological and educational development.
2. If necessary, reiterate statement of regret issued prior to the toy recall.
3. Display corporate repentance by publicly relaunching the product with a recommitment to quality and excellence.

[Note: Numbering strategies makes it easier to reference them within the planning team and when meeting with clients.]

Phase Two

STEP
5

☑ Checklist 5 **Action and Response Strategies**

Basic Questions

1. What proactive strategies might you develop?
2. What reactive strategies might you develop?
3. How consistent are these strategies with past practices of your organization?

Expanded Questions

A. PROACTIVE STRATEGY

1. Is it appropriate to use any of the following approaches? If "yes," how?

Action
- Organizational performance
- Audience participation
- Alliances
- Sponsorships
- Activism

Communication
- Publicity
- Newsworthy information
- Transparent communication

2. Summarize the proactive strategy of your organization.

B. REACTIVE STRATEGY

1. Is it appropriate to use any of the following approaches? If "yes," how?

Pre-emptive Action
- Prebuttal

Offensive Response
- Attack
- Embarrassment
- Shock
- Threat
- Standing firm

Defensive Response
- Denial
- Excuse
- Justification
- Reversal

Phase Two

STEP
5

Diversionary Response

- Concession
- Ingratiation
- Disassociation
- Relabeling

Vocal Commiseration

- Concern
- Condolence
- Regret
- Apology

Rectifying Behavior

- Investigation
- Corrective action
- Restitution
- Repentance

Deliberate Inaction

- Strategic silence
- Strategic ambiguity
- Strategic inaction

2. Summarize the reactive strategy of your organization.

C. ACTION/RESPONSE CONSISTENCY

1. Is this action/response consistent with past verbal messages of this organization/ spokesperson? If "no," explain the inconsistency.
2. Is the action/response consistent with past actions of this organization/spokesperson? If "no," explain the inconsistency.
3. Is the action/response consistent with the mission of this source? If "no," explain the inconsistency.
4. Is the action/response consistent with image of this source? If "no," explain the inconsistency.
5. Is the action/response ethical? If "no," develop a different response.

CONSENSUS CHECK

Does agreement exist within your organization and your planning team about the recommended strategies included within this step of the planning process?

☐ Yes. Proceed to Step 6, Developing the Message Strategy.

☐ No. Consider the value and/or possibility of achieving consensus before proceeding.

STEP 6

Developing the Message Strategy

Having identified publics and established objectives for what you want to achieve, and having set into motion the way the organization is preparing to act to achieve those objectives, it is time to focus on how best to communicate. Since strategic communication calls for carefully planned interaction between the organization and its publics, this is an important step.

Remember what was said earlier about publics and audiences: Publics are groups of people in a relationship with your organization; audiences are people who receive messages through a specific medium.

At this stage of the planning process, we begin treating publics as the audiences with whom we are communicating and we consider the various elements of effective communication. Who should present the message? What appeals should be made in the message? How should the message be structured? What words should be used? What symbols? How might we create a buzz with our message?

An estimated 3,000 public relations and marketing messages bombard people each day. That's about three different messages every minute of every waking hour—most of them trying to sell something or gain support in some way. Amid all this noise, how can your organization's message stand out? It's not easy, but effective communication can help your message rise above the clamor.

Communication Process

Several different approaches to communication are used in public relations and related fields. Three particular models are worth attention: information, persuasion, and dialogue. These align loosely with the classic models of public relations outlined by James Grunig and Todd Hunt (see the Introduction to this book).

- The **information model** of communication plays out as press agentry and public information.
- The **persuasion model** is asymmetric, with a focus on advocacy and attempts to influence.

- The **dialogue model** of communication is a symmetric approach rooted in relationships.

Let's look more closely at each of these communication processes.

Information: Flow of Communication

The information model of communication focuses on the content and channels of communication. It involves a message sent by a source to a receiver, with ideas encoded and interpreted through symbols (words, images, and gestures) that are transmitted person to person or through some technical connection.

Harold Lasswell (1948) offered a simple verbal formula of communication: "Who says what to whom with what effect." Today we add "how" and perhaps even "why" to this formula.

Exhibit 6.1 provides a visual model of information-based communication. This model is based on the frequently cited work of Claude Shannon and Warren Weaver (1949) and Norbert Wiener (1954), echoed later by David Berlo (1960) and Wilbur Schramm (1971).

Shannon and Weaver, scientists with Bell Telephone Laboratories, developed a visual model of what they called the **mathematical theory of communication**. Their approach was linear, with virtually tangible data encoded and transmitted through a channel to a receiver. In essence, theirs was a model for monologue, with the source person or organization talking at an audience. In simplified terms, this is the press agentry model of public relations.

Wiener's **cybernetic model of communication** was more circular in design, involving feedback from the receiver to influence the sender. The model shown in Exhibit 6.1 is consistent with this, focused as it is on two-way communication. It involves talking *with* an audience (similar to the public information model).

Persuasion: Attempt to Influence

Another process of communication, the persuasion model, consciously attempts to influence people, using ethical means that enhance a democratic society. Persuasion is an inherent part of social interaction, something people everywhere do. Don't confuse persuasion with deception; the latter relies on miscommunication. Neither is persuasive communication involved with coercion, which relies on force rather than on communication. Nor is it **propaganda**, which is a debasement of persuasive communication because it is associated with half-truths and hidden agendas.

Ethical persuasion is particularly associated with advocacy, the asymmetric approach to strategic communication. An organization presents its point of view in an attempt to convince its publics to give their agreement and support.

The practice of persuasion is widespread and popular. In marketing, for example, most companies try to convince potential consumers to buy the company's products or services. In public relations, organizations try to convince publics to agree with this concept, support that candidate, or follow those procedures. In public health and safety campaigns, agencies try to persuade young people to stop smoking, motorists to start wearing seat belts, and middle-aged people to get more exercise. In international relations, governments try to convince counterparts in other countries to adopt democratic practices, and nongovernmental organizations try to influence governments to respect human rights or to eliminate gender-based, religious, tribal, or racial discrimination. All of these are examples of persuasive communication focused on the betterment of society.

Dialogue: Quest for Understanding

The dialogue model involves the deeply conscious interaction of two parties in communication. It involves a sincere and competent attempt at mutual understanding, paralleling the symmetrical model of public relations.

Dialogue is the kind of communication described by existentialist philosopher Martin Buber (1947), who saw communication as the basis of both an I–It connection with the world and a more meaningful I–Thou relationship with other people.

It is what Evelyn Sieberg (1976) called "confirming communication," which seeks to heal and strengthen relationships. "Confirmation," notes Sieberg, "like existential dialogue, is a mutual experience involving sharing at several levels—sharing of talking, sharing of self, sharing of respect, sharing of trust."

Dialogue involves four goals useful to public relations:

1. Nurturing an information exchange between individuals or groups.
2. Helping communication partners make responsible and mutually acceptable decisions.
3. Reviving the original vitality of a relationship.
4. Deepening a relationship that continues to unite communication partners ever more closely.

Dialogue also generates two management practices—consensus building and conflict resolution—that help parties consider issues in light of their mutual needs and arrive at solutions that enhance their relationships.

Consensus building is a process of identifying and then preventing or overcoming barriers between people and/or organizations.

Conflict resolution involves making peace and restoring harmony, often with communication as the primary tool.

Carl Botan (1997) has observed the relationship between dialogue and ethics. He notes that dialogic communication is characterized by a relationship in which both parties genuinely care about each other rather than merely seek to fulfill their own needs. This kind of relationship is embodied in the symmetrical model of public relations, in which organizations try to adapt and harmonize with their publics. It elevates publics to an equal footing with the organization itself, allowing either party in the interchange to take the initiative.

An example of dialogic communication would be an equal relationship between corporate management and either an external public such as an activist group or an internal public such as an employee union, in which either side could call meetings, propose agenda topics, conduct research, launch a communication program, and so on.

Botan also noted that advances in communication technology have made it easier for organizations to engage with their publics in a two-way dialogue. Advances in Internet-based technology are breaking down old hierarchical structures in communication.

In the practice of strategic communication, there is a role for each type of communication model: information, persuasion, and dialogue. Information approaches to communication often focus on the message sender and receiver, while persuasive communication deals with the

Phase Two

STEP
6

EXHIBIT 6.1 Information-Based Communication Model

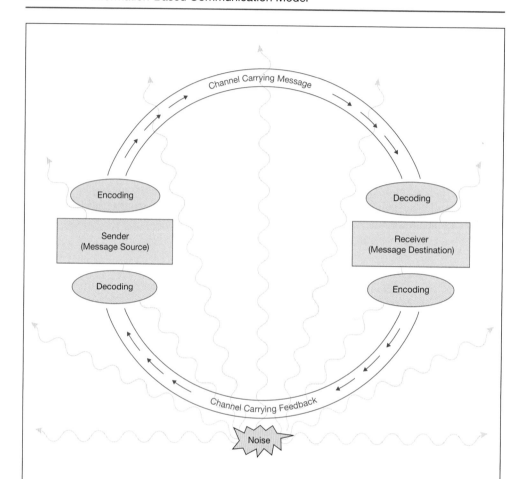

In this model of communication, a **sender** (which can be a person or an organization) **encodes** a **message** using verbal and/or nonverbal symbols. This message is carried through a particular **channel** (such as a speech, blog entry, phone call, photograph, and so on) to a **receiver**. This receiver interprets or **decodes** the message. This is one-way communication, depicted in the top half of this graphic visualization.

In a two-way communication situation, the receiver reacts and responds to the original message by encoding a **feedback** message that is sent back to the original sender. This might involve a question, a blog comment, an ongoing phone conversation, applause from an audience, and so on. This sending-feedback process is depicted through the full graphic.

A communication context potentially involves **noise**, which is any interference that limits the ability of the channel to carry a message faithfully from sender to receiver. Such interference can be in the encoding or decoding of the message or in the channels used to transmit the message.

content of the message. Dialogue, in turn, emphasizes the relationship between the parties in the communication process. Each of these elements is important to public relations, which necessarily deals with the actors in the communication process, the messages shared between them, and the relationship they share.

Rhetorical Tradition of Persuasive Communication

The use of communication to influence ideas and actions and to strengthen relationships is a basic element of human society. History has handed down to us some ancient examples of the art of effective communication. Much of it comes from the dawn of Western civilization in the lands encircling the Mediterranean Sea.

Two of the oldest-known pieces of literature, the *Iliad* and the *Odyssey*, both ascribed to the Greek poet Homer about 2,900 years ago, feature examples of effective persuasive speeches. Consider Odysseus's plea with the Cyclops about why the monster should not eat him, or Paris's entreaty for Helen to leave her husband and go off with him, or the acclaim given to Hector and Achilles for their speeches that stirred up their military troops.

Sun Tzu's *Art of War* (about 400 BCE), despite its title, focuses on the role of communication and persuasion in the process of managing conflict.

Even earlier pieces of literature, though difficult to date precisely—the Pentateuch of the Hebrew Bible, the epic of Gilgamesh—have passages with strong persuasive rhetoric, such as Moses' persuasive skills before the pharaoh and his verbal arguments with God.

The Egyptian philosopher and court official Ptah-Hotep advised the pharaohs to link their message to the interests of their audience.

The effective use of persuasive communication was a particular interest in classical Greece, with its focus on participatory democracy. In the fifth century BCE, Corax of Syracuse wrote a handbook on **rhetoric**, the art of using words effectively in speaking and writing for the purpose of influencing, persuading, or entertaining. Basically, rhetoric is persuasive communication. Corax noted the relationship between certainty and probability: While physical evidence can prove something true and thus beyond argument, **verbal evidence** can show only greater or lesser probabilities that something is true.

Later in Athens, Socrates and his student Plato criticized rhetoric as verbal maneuvering that could make right seem wrong and important appear unimportant. They called for a grounding in truth and taught some of the skills associated with ethical communication, such as logical organization of ideas. Plato outlined the differences between true and false rhetoric.

The first person known to have studied persuasive communication systematically was Plato's student Aristotle, who became the court educator to Alexander the Great. Twenty-five centuries ago, in his treatise called *Rhetoric*, Aristotle identified three central elements that today remain the cornerstones of persuasive communication: ethos, logos, and pathos. Following the don't-mess-with-success principle, *Strategic Planning for Public Relations* uses these elements as the framework for developing a strategic and effective public relations and marketing communication message. Each will be discussed in detail shortly.

From the Greek foundation, the study of communication passed over to classical Rome, where Marcus Tullius Cicero organized rhetoric into five principles (roughly argumentation, organization, style, delivery, and memorization). Marcus Fabius Quintillianus wrote on the education of communicators, advising that they were about more than simply persuasion; they also were in the business of informing, motivating, and inspiring.

Phase Two

STEP 6

During the Middle Ages, the Saxon theologian Alcuin, teacher and advisor to the emperor Charlemagne, reinterpreted Roman rhetoric and applied it to practical areas such as public policy, legal and judicial proceedings, and the placement of blame or praise.

Rhetoric also influenced the field of religion, and vice versa. Augustine Aureleus, a professor of rhetoric at Milan who returned to Roman Africa and became bishop of Hippo Regius (today's Annaba, Algeria), was one of the most influential figures in persuasive communication with his study, teaching, and personal examples dealing with preaching. Augustine was influential in developing the practice of **apologetics** (the systematic attempt to explain the reasonableness of religious faith and to refute opposing arguments) and **homiletics** (the study and application of effective communication for preaching).

After the fall of Western civilization, the teaching of Aristotle was virtually lost to European society. During the ninth century, Muslim scholars, Christian Arabs, and Arabic-speaking Jews kept alive the study of Aristotle in the Middle East. The Crusades introduced Arab scholarship to the West, such as the "science of eloquence" associated with Abd al Jurjani. Through Arab scholars, the West also rediscovered Aristotle.

During the thirteenth century, the Italian philosopher-monk Thomas Aquinas applied Aristotelian principles of ethos, logos, and pathos to the understanding and explanation of religious belief, and he wrote on topics such as truth, knowledge, and communication. Known as the Christian Aristotle, Aquinas is considered one of history's most influential theologians and philosophers.

During the Enlightenment period of the sixteenth century, Desiderius Erasmus of Rotterdam influenced a renewed interest in rhetoric with a more secular perspective. The seventeenth-century English poet John Milton wrote a textbook on rhetoric, and his contemporary, philosopher Thomas Hobbes, also wrote on rhetoric.

More contemporary figures from the past century in the evolution of our understanding of communication include American language theorist Kenneth Burke, who studied the nature and power of symbols in human interaction; language critic Richard Weaver, who dealt with the cultural role of persuasion; Belgian philosopher Chaim Perelman, who analyzed how communicators can gain "the adherence of minds"; and Canadian theologian and philosopher Bernard Lonergan. Canadian theorist Marshall McLuhan wrote his doctoral theses at Cambridge University on the history of rhetorical thought; he became the most widely publicized scholar of rhetoric in the twentieth century.

Most of the study of rhetoric has been done from a Western perspective, though increasingly attention is being given to Asian traditions. From a Buddhist perspective, the characteristics of speech are said to be that it is true, real, and useful. The Buddha's description of an effective preacher is a monk who abandons falsehood and is truthful, faithful, and trustworthy. Confucius recognized that sincerity and respectfulness are important elements of effective speaking.

The African, Asian, and Native American traditions, as well as the Semitic communication style of the Middle East, often have placed a lesser value on persuasion than in the Western world. Philosophers and linguists in these cultures more often emphasize storytelling, the graceful use of language, the development of consensus, even the communicative value of silence—all concepts with practical relevance for today's public relations practitioner.

This doesn't mean that persuasive communication is not a universal aspect of human society. Rather it points to the priority that Western culture has given to persuasion and the functionality of language, whereas some other cultures have focused more on building and maintaining relationships.

[For a more in-depth background on persuasion and public relations communication, see the author's website: ron-smith.com.]

Ethos: Message Source

Ethos is communication effectiveness based on the character of the speaker and on the common ground shared by speakers and audiences.

Years of research by social scientists have produced a snapshot of an effective message source. This is a person or an organization perceived by an audience as being credible, having charisma, and exercising some kind of control—what we might call the "three Cs" of an effective communicator. These are presented visually in Exhibit 6.2. Individually, each of these perceptions is a powerful tool for the practitioner. In combination, they create a compelling factor in effective communication.

It is important to note that each of these elements is based on the audience's perception of the speaker. Aristotle observed that reputation precedes the speaker, setting the stage for the audience to accept or reject the speaker's message. Even before the speaker presents a message, the audience makes a judgment based on the speaker's prestige and prominence, as well as their presumption that they may or may not agree with the speaker. Precisely because reputation has such a direct and predictable impact on their ability to influence their publics, organizations pay much attention to what people know and think about them.

EXHIBIT 6.2 Three Cs of Effective Communication

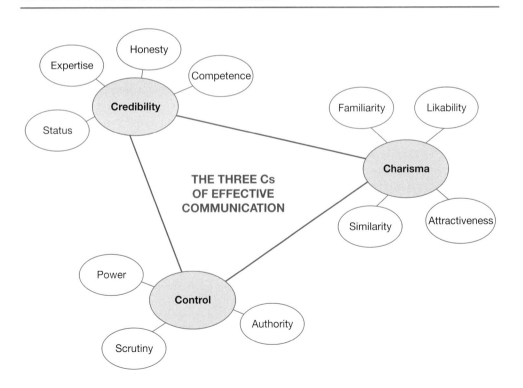

Phase Two

STEP
6

Credibility: Power to Inspire

The power to inspire belief—**credibility**—is tremendously important to persuasion. Though we might wish it were different, being a good speaker or writer is more effective than having good physical evidence. Sources perceived as being highly credible are believed on their own merits and whatever evidence they present has little added value. Even audiences that don't understand an issue often will accept a message when they think the source is believable.

Highly credible sources can appeal to fear and use intense or opinionated language that would be counterproductive coming from sources with lesser credibility. Presidential politics gives several examples of this. It was his high credibility that allowed President Ronald Reagan to call the Soviet Union "an evil empire" and be effective in such extreme speech. When President George W. Bush revived the phrase in reference to an "axis of evil" encompassing Iraq, Iran, and North Korea, his credibility was low and the phrase was criticized, belittled, and parodied as an "axis of weasels," "axis of feebles," and "asses of evil." Because of such criticism and his low personal credibility, Bush didn't use the phrase again in a public speech.

As part of the process of strategic planning, you can enhance source credibility by reinforcing the characteristics of ethos. A credible source is one with expertise, status, competence, and honesty.

Audiences need to see such qualities, whether real or merely projected. Remember that perception is the key. The source's expertise and honesty must be apparent to the audience. Some campaigns have faltered because the audience didn't realize the source was an expert or because the source didn't appear trustworthy.

EXPERTISE

The most important factor in making a message source effective is **expertise**, which means that the source knows what he or she is talking about.

The perception of expertise can be intensified by using a message source who has experience, knowledge, intelligence, occupational or professional background, or the wisdom that comes with age. Of course, this must be relevant to the topic being addressed—a physician may be very credible on the issue of health but not particularly so on a political topic. Entertainers and athletes who make political pronouncements, for example, may find that they are ignored, even ridiculed, when they leap beyond their base of competence.

Expertise and status can be borrowed from recognized experts by quoting them, though the impact of this is rather weak.

STATUS

Related to expertise is **status**, but this rests more with the audience's deference to the social position or prestige of a message source. As with expertise, perceived status is enhanced by the use of message sources whom the audience see as having prestige. Also similar to expertise, the status needs to be relevant to the topic for it to influence an audience.

COMPETENCE

Another related concept is **competence**, the ability to remain calm under pressure and to be clear and effective in presenting the message to others, especially those who may not share the same knowledge or loyalties.

EXPERTISE AND CREDIBILITY ON CLIMATE CHANGE

A Yale University survey of 2,030 American adults—Americans' Knowledge on Climate Change—probed the relative credibility of different types of news sources on an environmental issue, specifically climate change.

The researchers with the university's Project for Climate Change Communication (Leiserowitz, Smith, and Marlon, 2010) identified several information sources on climate change and asked respondents to rate the level of trust they had for each information source. Here are the credibility levels (strongly or somewhat trust) reported in the survey:

78%	National Oceanographic and Atmospheric Administration
74%	National Science Foundation
72%	Scientists
72%	Science TV programs on PBS and Discovery
72%	Natural history and science museums
67%	Zoos and aquariums
64%	University professors
62%	Schoolteachers
61%	Environmental Protection Agency
50%	TV weather forecasters
42%	Military leaders
35%	Mainstream news media

What's the lesson to be learned from this research? It deals with expertise. Recognized experts without apparent self-interest are the most credible message sources. The public may admire celebrities, but people are more likely to be persuaded by unbiased individuals and organizations that know what they are doing and saying.

Phase Two

STEP
6

Communication competence is a matter of perception. The audience perceives that the speaker is calm, clear, and able to communicate well (or not).

Perceived competence can be enhanced by two elements associated with effective presentations. One element combines physical stature and stage presence. This includes being tall, sitting or standing erect, maintaining eye contact, and having facial composure.

The second element that enhances competence is vocal quality. This involves enunciating clearly, initiating communication, speaking with conviction and authority, exuding energy and enthusiasm, and avoiding language fillers such as *um* and *uh*. Two kinds of skill builders—coaching for public speaking and training for media interviews—can help a speaker strategically develop vocal emphasis, convincing gestures, and other aspects of communication competence.

HONESTY

Finally, **honesty** means that the source is willing to provide full and accurate information and is operating without bias, thus worthy of trust.

Like the other characteristics of credibility, audience perception of honesty can be enhanced to help a source appear more trustworthy by emphasizing the objectivity, integrity, and neutrality with which the source approaches the subject. Message sources who advocate positions contrary to their personal interests or who take an unexpected position have a special credibility. For example, a physician who recommends herbal medicine will be particularly believable because the health-care establishment traditionally has ignored, even scorned, the medicinal value of herbs.

Honesty also is enhanced when the message source shows a consistency between past and present, and between words and deeds.

If you are presenting a position that differs from one taken by your organization in the past, signal the change and carefully explain not only the new posture but also the reason for the change. Try not to allow yourself to be labeled as inconsistent or as contradictory of past statements. In the current political and social climate, charges of flip-flopping on issues and changing positions are exploited by opponents as signs of weakness, lack of underlying values, and political pandering.

Certainly you may change your mind, but make sure you let your audience know the reason for such a change and see it as legitimate rather than merely pandering to the current whim.

Charisma: Power of Personal Charm

The magnetic appeal or personal charm that some message sources enjoy over an audience is called **charisma**, another important element of persuasion. Like credibility, charisma is a matter of perception, and it varies greatly from one person to another and from one public to another.

The so-called **halo effect** demonstrates that a source perceived as credible, charismatic, and/or in control can rely on this reputation. Think of the many situations in which a politician—you supply the name, from either side of the aisle—can do no wrong in the eyes of supporters but can do nothing right in the eyes of those who despise him or her. The same can be said about some athletes and entertainers who evoke passionate responses of either adoration or condemnation.

The halo effect is very useful for the communicator. But halos slip and stars fall, so be careful about where you shine your spotlight. Also, realize that while one person may have a halo effect on some members of an audience, the same person may have an opposite **horns effect** on other members of the audience who dislike the messenger. Both halos and horns often evoke unreasonable passion.

Charisma has several specific characteristics: familiarity, likability, similarity, and attractiveness.

FAMILIARITY

One important aspect of charisma is **familiarity**, the extent to which the audience already knows (or thinks it knows) the message source.

LIKABILITY

Charisma also involves **likability**, the extent to which the audience admires what it knows about the source or what it sees and hears when the source begins to communicate.

This generally means that the message source is neutral on divisive social and political issues and not associated with controversy or partisanship—unless the audience itself is partisan. The principle of likability may suggest that, for a general and mixed audience, you would avoid using a message source who is closely associated with a particular cultural, ethnic, or religious group because the audience may not like someone closely identified with alien characteristics.

SIMILARITY

Charisma also involves **similarity**, the extent to which the source resembles the audience (or the way in which audience members would like to see themselves). This may be a reflection of audience demographics in terms of age, gender, occupation, ethnicity, religion, culture, shared values, or sociopolitical perspectives.

Thus the principle of similarity offers a parallel guideline to that of familiarity. You might consider using a message source closely associated with a particular cultural, ethnic, political or religious group when the audience also is associated with that group. Similarity is particularly important when a communicator is seeking long-term persuasion, less so for short-term objectives. It also is a major factor in enhancing dialogic communication.

ATTRACTIVENESS

Finally, charisma is affected by the **attractiveness** of the source, which involves the source's physical looks, demeanor, poise, and presence. It also is impacted by both the clothing worn and the setting in which the source is presented. Note, however, that physical attractiveness and beauty are significantly less important than credibility and other aspects of charisma. Despite the Hollywood emphasis on sex appeal, beauty, and hunkiness, average-looking people can be highly effective message sources.

Indeed, speakers who are very good-looking, especially if they flaunt their looks, may have difficulty being perceived as much more than pretty faces and buff bodies.

Control: Power of Command

The third component of an effective message source is **control**, which is rooted in a message source's command over the audience and on perceived willingness to exercise that control.

POWER

One of the most important aspects of control is **power**, the raw and recognized ability to dominate and to reward or punish. Guilt appeals (which we will discuss later) often are associated with powerful message sources.

AUTHORITY

Control also may be based on a message source's **authority**, which is the right to rule over or direct the actions of another. Authority implies that the audience more or less willingly has granted the right of control and thus will give obedience. Authority often involves a legal or social prerogative. It also can involve moral leverage, such as by summoning the audience to its stated values or calling it to its accepted duty. Both guilt appeals and virtue appeals (which we will discuss later) may be associated with authority figures.

SCRUTINY

Finally, the persuasive element of control suggests **scrutiny**, the ability to examine. Someone who is able to investigate also is able to pronounce blame, proclaim innocence, and perhaps grant forgiveness. As with the previous characteristics of an effective source, control must be perceived by the receiver. Keep in mind that perceptions change.

Organizational Spokespeople

The elements of credibility, charisma, and control can be maximized as part of strategic planning, for example, by selecting an appropriate spokesperson who is likely to appeal to an organization's publics.

Celebrity Spokesperson

Celebrities often are used because they are charismatic and familiar. Entertainers and sports figures frequently are spokespersons for companies and nonprofit organizations as well as for social and political causes.

Celebrity endorsement doesn't automatically translate into money or votes, but it can garner media attention and public interest. It also encourages audiences to look at websites and to read brochures and letters they otherwise might ignore.

Celebrities are in great demand by charitable causes. Thus we find Nicole Kidman, and Reese Witherspoon promoting breast cancer awareness; Toby Keith creating attention for childhood cancers; Jimmy Smits for colon cancer; and Halle Barry and Cuba Gooding Jr. for diabetes awareness.

Jennifer Love Hewitt has good things to say on behalf of the Veteran's Administration and various veterans groups, while Kirstie Alley, Tom Cruise, and Isaac Hayes have pitched anti-drug messages.

Angelina Jolie is a goodwill ambassador for the U.N. High Commissioner for Refugees. She, Brad Pitt, George Clooney, Sean Penn, and Bono are well known for espousing various humanitarian causes, many inspired by international crises. Meanwhile, Colin Firth promotes use of fair-trade products from developing countries; Drew Barrymore lobbies for child feeding programs as a goodwill ambassador for the U.N. World Food Program; and Leonardo DiCaprio works on various environmental causes.

Sometimes a local incident gains celebrity interest. After a 14-year-old boy in Buffalo, N.Y., committed suicide, Lady Gaga and her Born This Way Foundation sparked new awareness for the cause of anti-gay bullying.

After newsman Mike Wallace went public with his struggle against depression, the Colorado Behavioral Healthcare Council felt he would be just the famous face to use in its public service campaign on suicide and depression prevention. Organizers of the New York City Alzheimer's Association credited the onstage hosting of Jean Smart at a fundraising dinner for a $400,000 increase in donations from the previous year.

Sometimes spokespersons actually are likable "spokes-characters," such as Morris the Cat for Nine Lives cat food, McGruff the Crime Dog, or Geico insurance's gecko. Other spokes-characters have included the Budweiser Clydesdales, Elsie the Cow for Borden's Milk, and Charlie the Tuna for StarKist. *Advertising Week*'s Walk of Fame on Madison Avenue in New York City honors advertising icons such as Juan Valdez (for Columbian Coffee), Colonel

Sanders (for KFC), the Aflac duck, Tony the Tiger (for Kellogg's Frosted Flakes), and the Pillsbury Doughboy.

Researchers Alan Miciak and William Shanklin (1994) report that advertisers look for five characteristics in spokespersons: being trustworthy, readily recognizable, affordable, at little risk for negative publicity, and appropriately matched to the audience.

Public relations and marketing people selecting celebrity spokespersons also look for a connection with their key publics. It's not accidental, for example, that Hurley Hayward is the spokesperson for Porsche. About 90 percent of Porsche's customers are men, and research showed that most of them are racing fans. Hayward is a multiple winner of the LeMans, Sebring, and Daytona races.

However, it's hard to see the logic behind using celebrities not connected with the product, for example, Kobe Bryant, who was hired to promote Turkish Airlines. The Los Angeles Laker had never been to Turkey but said he's heard it's a hot place to visit. Bryant's paid endorsement earned him some backlash from Armenian Americans angered over Turkey's historic refusal to acknowledge its role in the massacres against their grandparents 100 years ago that gave rise to the term "genocide."

Golf icon Tiger Woods was among the highest-rated celebrities, earning $105 million in endorsements, until that pesky scandal in 2009—car accident, extramarital affairs, call girls, public apology, messy divorce. He lost most of his endorsement contracts. But by 2014, Tiger was back in the endorsement game, with $55 million in contracts with Nike, Rolex, Upper Deck, and NetJet.

In 2015, sports marketing company Opendorse rated Woods at the second highest paid sports endorser with $50 million, following No. 1 Roger Federer with $58 million in endorsements. Other top-earning sports endorsers were LeBron James and Phil Mickerson at $44 million, Kevin Durant $35 million, Rory McIlroy $32 million, Novak Djokovik $31 million, Rafael Nadal $28 million, Christiano Ronaldo $27 million, Mohendra Singh Dhoni $27 million, Kobe Bryant $26 million, and as the highest-paid woman athlete Maria Sharapova $23 million.

Once again, research challenges common wisdom. As for celebrity political endorsement, a 2010 study from North Carolina State University suggests that they are not particularly useful. Political science professor Michael Cobb found that celebrity endorsements don't help political candidates. Young voters actually may be turned off toward the candidate because of such endorsements.

On the other hand, Anita Elberse and Jeroen Verleun (2012) published a report on the economic value of celebrity endorsements, concluding that "enlisting the help of celebrity endorsers pays off." Looking specifically at athlete endorsements for sports apparel companies, they reported that the endorsements generally increase sales and the value of stock. The sales increase is modest, about 4 percent, but that averages $10 million a year.

Company Spokesperson

In identifying organizational spokespersons, don't be confined to a single individual if more than one would better facilitate communication needs with various publics. Your organization must speak with a single voice, but effective communication may be accomplished with two or more speakers presenting coordinated and complementary messages. The important thing is to make sure that a single, consistent message is being presented in the name of an organization.

CELEBRITY ENDORSERS GONE WILD

Both business and nonprofit organizations have found that they need to exercise discretion in identifying celebrity spokespersons. Fame might draw attention. But celebrities aren't yours alone, and endorsements can bring unwanted attention.

Some organizations have been humiliated by celebrity spokespersons and endorsements have fallen off, at least temporarily. Soccer great David Beckham lost endorsements when the British tabloid press reported that he had cheated on his wife. After the issue died down, he emerged with a $10 million contract with Gillette, followed by a $161 million lifetime deal with Adidas. Beckham later was courted by Nike.

L.A. Laker Kobe Bryant lost endorsements because of his 2003 sexual assault charge, but he came back and is now among the highest-paid pitchmen in the sports world.

After a British newspaper published a photo in 2009 of Michael Phelps smoking a bong, the Olympic swim champ salvaged millions in endorsement deals (Speedo, Omega, Mazda, and Visa). He quickly apologized, attributing his transgression to youthful bad judgment, and promising it wouldn't happen again. But advertising analysts warned that this, following a DUI arrest four years earlier, was Strike 2—Phelps' last chance to maintain his endorsements worth about $12 million a year with companies including Visa, Hilton, Louis Vuitton, Under Armour, and Subway.

AirTran, Powerade, Coca-Cola, Rawlings, and Kraft Foods each dropped their advertising contracts with Atlanta Falcons quarterback Michael Vick in 2007 after he pled guilty to illegal dog fighting. Nike dumped his $2 million annual contract, Reebok dropped his replica jersey, and Upper Deck pulled his trading card. When Vick emerged from jail to be signed by the Philadelphia Eagles, he spoke out against dog fighting, and in 2011 he picked up endorsements by Unequal athletic gear and by Nike, apparently the first time a company had re-signed a pitchman it had previously dropped.

Endorsement problems are not limited to celebrity athletes. After a British tabloid published photos of Kate Moss snorting cocaine, the model lost her contracts with Chanel and Burberry. She kept contracts with Yves Saint Laurent and Gucci, which have edgier ads. Similarly, St. John fashions dropped Angelina Jolie because some customers were put off by her social activism.

Abercrombie and Fitch pre-empted embarrassment by offering to pay Mike "The Situation" Sorrentino of *Jersey Shore* to stop wearing its clothing. A&F said in a news release that, by wearing its clothing, Sorrentino was damaging its reputation. The JS personality then sued A&F for $4 million for using his name in what MTV called "a clever PR stunt."

Some examples of wayward celebrity spokespersons fall into the "What were they thinking?" category. The Beef Industry Council dropped Cybill Shepherd after she told a national magazine that one of her beauty secrets is avoiding red meats. And when Brylcreem sales dropped 25 percent after its celebrity hairdo guy David Beckham shaved his head, Beckham lost his $7.9 million contract.

Also, give careful thought about who from your organization might be selected as a spokesperson for a particular issue. Some companies used the CEO-as-spokesperson approach, which has worked well with corporate founders while they lived: popcorn king Orville Redenbacher, Wendy's Dave Thomas, Frank Perdue of chicken fame. Redenbacher was authentic, Thomas was likable, and Perdue—well, anybody who can successfully brag about dead chickens must have something going for himself.

But the CEO may not be the best person in every case. Here are three good reasons not to use the CEO as organizational spokesperson.

1. Don't overexpose the boss. Save her for the big issues.
2. The CEO may not know the level of detail necessary for a news conference or interview. Perhaps a project planner, department manager, or another hands-on person would be more knowledgeable and credible.
3. The CEO may not have the personality to exhibit in public or especially on camera the calm, credibility, charisma, or other characteristics of an effective spokesperson.

Some organizations buffer the CEO by appointing another spokesperson for negative news, saving the CEO for the more positive public and media encounters. In a news conference, the CEO could be put on the spot and expected to indicate what the organization's activity or response might be. Another organizational spokesperson might more easily deflect such forecasts and avoid inappropriate speculation.

Don't presume that the public relations director should automatically become the spokesperson. Especially in confrontational or other crisis situations, the director may be busy behind the scenes advising on strategy and message delivery. Also, the media often don't recognize the public relations director as a high-ranking organizational official; instead they see her as a mere mouthpiece for the people they really wish to interview.

The Public Relations Society of America found that public relations specialists rank low in terms of credibility as corporate spokespersons. Most organizations use their public relations directors not as spokespersons but as preliminary media contacts, conduits for factual information that doesn't require attribution, and sources for other media background information.

CASE IN POINT   PETA—When the Fur Flies

People for the Ethical Treatment of Animals faced its own ethical problem when supermodel Naomi Campbell, a PETA volunteer who had pledged not to wear natural fur, was reported to be modeling in Europe wearing fur. After unsuccessful attempts to reach her, PETA took a public tack: With much fanfare, it fired Ms. Campbell as a volunteer.

The firing was strategic, a twist to the news-making advice to involve a celebrity, link to a public issue, and appoint personnel as a way to highlight an issue. Instead, PETA publicly "unappointed" a volunteer—not coincidentally, a wayward one who also happened to be a big celebrity.

PETA spokesman Michael McGraw described the activist group's plan: Once it got the media's attention by firing Campbell, PETA would turn the focus back to the issue of the animal suffering perpetrated in the name of fashion.

"We were able to turn something quite negative into something quite positive," said McGraw, "because what it allowed us to do was get the message out that the fur industry hurts animals and kills them and tortures them."

Spokespeople and Ethics

Celebrity or not, speakers should strive to identify with their audiences. One way is to emphasize similar backgrounds, especially when such common ground may not be evident to the audience. For example, a university professor before a group of entering freshmen may recall her first months in college or an affluent politician may explain to a group of inner-city residents his experience of growing up amid poverty, albeit of a rural variety.

Another way for speakers to emphasize similarity is to avoid language that separates them from their audience. A white speaker cannot use the phrase "you people" before a black audience without emphasizing his differentness and insulting his listeners.

Be careful about uncommon words that people may misunderstand. An aide to the mayor of Washington, DC, was fired (later rehired) because he used the term "niggardly." Though

ETHICS AND CELEBRITY ENDORSEMENTS

There is an ethical consideration for nonprofit organizations over the use of celebrity endorsements.

Some charities simply cannot afford the price tag that comes with many celebrities—who don't necessarily donate their time. For some charities, fame is not worth the price. The American Diabetes Association (ADA), for example, chooses not to spend donated money on celebrity spokespersons. The ADA says it's not interested in redesigning its campaign to fit the publicity needs of celebrities and their agents.

Industry sources report that celebrity endorsers generally receive honorariums as high as $100,000. Not all celebrity spokespersons are paid. WebMD (webmd.com) reports that both the National Parkinson Foundation and the Alzheimer's Association indicate that their celebrity endorsers donate their time and even pick up their own travel expenses.

The Entertainment Industry Foundation, a clearinghouse for many entertainers who become involved with charity work, insists that its celebrity "ambassadors" work for free. Most of the expenses are picked up by sponsoring companies such as Revlon, *People* magazine, and Lee Jeans.

Pharmaceuticals sometimes offer to pick up the tab for celebrity endorsements of a medical charity. Such offers usually come with strings. Often the arrangement calls for the celebrity to endorse the company's product. Such an arrangement came to light when the late Lauren Bacall, who generally avoided TV talk shows, started showing up on the circuit talking about friends with macular degeneration and the drug that treated it. The *Today Show* discovered that her appearance was paid for by the Novartis drug company.

The Amgen company sponsored Rob Lowe to go on the talk-show circuit for its drug to treat a side effect of chemotherapy. Similarly Wyeth Laboratories paid Kathleen Turner and GlaxoSmithKline paid Kelsey Grammer to promote their drugs on talk shows without acknowledging that they were paid spokespeople.

Some observers question the criteria that some celebrities use in deciding whether to align themselves with charitable causes. Dr. Arthur Caplan, a medical ethicist at the University of Pennsylvania, noted that some celebrities gravitate toward illnesses they perceive as "mediafriendly—less stigmatizing and less embarrassing" and that "otherwise worthy diseases, some that impact far more people, go unrecognized simply because they have less sex appeal" (Bouchez, n.d., p. 2).

the word simply means "stingy," an unknowledgeable listener mistook the reference for a racial slur, and the issue went viral. Similarly, the University of Wisconsin killed a proposed speech code after a student ignited a campus controversy because she was offended when a professor used the same term in a literature class.

In both situations, the term "niggardly" was used correctly. But from a public relations perspective, it is usually best to avoid language that may not be properly understood, especially language that is not part of the shared experiences of both the speaker and the audience. After all, people who don't know any better may think "titillate," "jaculate," "bumfiddle," and "masticate" are nasty words.

PLANNING EXAMPLE 6A **Selecting Message Sources**

In its current efforts to expand enrollment and retention, financial contributions and community support, Upstate will use the following three spokespeople:

UPSTATE COLLEGE

Dr. Alexandra Jolin, president of Upstate College

Dr. Jolin will be perceived by most audiences as highly credible because of her position. She is a dynamic speaker who projects an enthusiasm and friendliness that most people appreciate. In addition, she holds various leadership positions not only with the college but within the local community and within the state's higher education establishment.

Michael McMillan, chair of the Upstate College Board of Trustees, Upstate alumnus and prominent business leader in Upstate City

Mr. McMillan will be perceived as a credible source, especially by residents of Upstate City. He has received media training and is articulate and competent in media and other public presentations. He is in a position of leadership.

Inez SantaElana, president of the UC Student Government

Because of her leadership position with the student government, Ms. SantaElana will be perceived as a credible source, especially with current and potential students. She also is a regional celebrity among area high school students who has developed much poise and confidence as a result of her athletic achievements, including state records in speed skating.

In its campaign to increase consumer confidence, Tiny Tykes will use the following two spokespeople:

TINY TYKES TOYS

Michael Beaucheforte, senior vice president for consumer affairs

Mr. Beaucheforte will be perceived as credible because of his expertise within the company and because he was hired specifically to address consumer issues. He is a persuasive speaker, with a friendliness that exudes trust and disarms skeptics. (Note that company president

Theodore Frankelberger should not be used as a spokesperson in media situations because he becomes very nervous when speaking in public. This nervousness is often perceived as insincerity and evasiveness.)

Mary Margaret O'Sullivan, Tiny Tykes Consumer Advisory Council member

Ms. O'Sullivan is a consumer whose child was stained by the defective toy. She now sits on the Consumer Advisory Council that helped relaunch the product. Because of her personal involvement, Ms. O'Sullivan will be perceived as a trustworthy and expert spokesperson. She is not an accomplished public speaker, but her uneasiness adds to her credibility and charisma.

 Checklist 6A **Message Sources**

Basic Questions

1. Identify several possible spokespersons who could present your message.
2. What is the level of credibility for each possible spokesperson?
3. What is the level of charisma for each?
4. What is the level of control for each?

Expanded Questions

Answer the following items for each possible message source. Then compare your responses to determine the sources best suited for this communication task. An effective message source will have mainly high and positive rankings in each item.

A. CREDIBILITY

1. How expert on this topic is the message source?
2. How well known are his/her credentials to the audience? If expertise is high, should the audience be reminded of this? If expertise is not known, can the audience be made informed of this?
3. Does the message source enunciate clearly?
4. Does the source speak with dynamism and authority?
5. Does the source speak calmly and reassuringly on this topic?
6. How trustworthy will the source be perceived?
7. Can the source speak truthfully and independently about the topic?
8. Does the source have any associations that compete with the organization?
9. Does the source have any associations that are inconsistent with the organization's image?
10. Is the source available to your organization?

B. CHARISMA

1. How similar is the source to the audience?
2. How familiar is the audience with the source?
3. How attractive is the source to the audience?
4. Can the source be presented in an attractive setting?

C. CONTROL

1. Does the source have any power or moral leverage with this audience?
2. Does the source have the willingness to use this power or leverage?
3. Does the source have the ability to investigate this audience?
4. Does the source have the authority to reward or punish this audience?

Logos: Appeal to Reason

Having selected the spokesperson for the campaign or project, the strategic planning next focuses on the content of the message. What will be said, and how will the message be framed? Will you appeal to the intellect or to the emotions—or to both? What facts and arguments will you offer? What examples might you suggest?

Let's first consider messages based on logic; then later, messages on sentiment.

Communication effectiveness based on the rational appeal of the message was known to the ancient Greeks as **logos**. The conscious attempt to root your persuasive appeals in logos— logic and reason—is an obvious place to start planning your strategic message. Distill your message and resist the temptation to bombard your audience with every bit of information available to you. Clarify and simplify.

The ancient art of rhetoric is kept current with an expanding research base (see Benjamin, 1997; Infante, Rancer and Avtgis, 2009; Larson, 2000; Ross, 1994). Following is a summary of recommendations and conclusions from many different research studies into effective communication and persuasion.

The primary idea in a speech, editorial, advertisement, television program, or any other communication vehicle is called a **proposition**, also known as a **claim**. Only one proposition should be presented at a time. More than this can confuse the audience and lessen the impact of the message. There are four kinds of propositions: factual, conjecture, value, and policy.

A **factual proposition** states that something exists, based on provable (usually physical) evidence. For example, environmental tests can offer proof of an increase in urban air pollution. Factual claims often link to communication objectives focused on awareness, which seek to increase attention or build greater understanding.

A **conjecture proposition** states that something probably exists, based on reasoned conclusion drawn from physical evidence. It asks audiences to agree with the conclusion. An example of this is a conclusion for or against the continuation of affirmative action regulations, in which the conclusion flows logically from the facts as they are presented. Conjecture propositions often relate to communication objectives dealing with acceptance, fostering supportive attitudes.

A **value proposition** identifies the virtue of something, such as the merits (or folly) of immigration reform, campus speech codes, or some other issue. Value claims also relate to objectives dealing with acceptance, which try to increase interest or build positive attitudes.

A **policy proposition** identifies a course of action and encourages its adoption, such as advocacy for changing the legal drinking age or for beginning a school dress code. Policy claims often reflect objectives associated with opinion and action.

Whatever the type of proposition, it should be supported with strong arguments and clear proof. The value of such proof varies from person to person and from group to group. To some, an intelligent argument with understandable data and logical conclusions may prove a point; to others, only the strongest and most consistent of physical data may be considered as proof.

Occasionally, facts may be disputed by other facts, such as one study that contradicts another. The existence of such conflicting evidence likely will weaken the argument for the proposition.

Even more difficult to deal with is the phenomenon—some say a growing one—in which some people disbelieve facts, doubt science, and dismiss evidence that runs counter to their bias and prejudices. Some less-educated or highly partisan people have adopted an anti-science stance that feeds their suspicion of science and education, resulting in an audience that essentially has made itself immune to facts and reasoning. Climate change is a current example of a topic that has some anti-science critics. There is little a communicator can do to create any convincing message when an audience will not permit itself to be open to evidence.

Similarly, some people may oppose a logical argument because they don't trust the data used to prove a point or the source of that data. Some critics, for example, are quick to disbelieve anything associated with government or with a particular political party. Again, public relations practitioners must concede that there is little they can do to dissuade such disbelief.

Verbal Evidence

About 2,500 years ago, Corax of Syracuse taught that disputes are settled easily when clear physical evidence shows inarguably the truth or falsity of a claim. That remains true today. Most of the time, however, we are not lucky enough to have such unchallenged hard evidence, so we have to rely on corroborative arguments. This verbal evidence can take several different forms, including analogies, comparisons, examples, statistics, and testimonials. Here's a brief look at each.

ANALOGY

As a type of persuasion technique, an **analogy** uses familiar situations and allusions to help an audience understand new ideas. Specifically, an analogy makes a comparison between two things that are essentially different but nevertheless strikingly alike in an important aspect. For example, cars double-parked on a congested city street can be analogous to the effect of cholesterol in clogging arteries. Analogies usually are presented through the grammatical forms of similes and metaphors.

COMPARISON

By highlighting the characteristics or values related to an issue, a **comparison** can liken it to something else the audience might understand. Positive comparisons are made to things the

Phase Two

STEP
6

audience already acknowledges and admires, negative comparisons to things the audience holds in low esteem. Any such comparison should be easy to understand, showing how one issue, product, or theme relates to another.

EXAMPLE

Another type of verbal evidence, **example**, provides conclusions drawn from related instances. Such an illustration can be effective, particularly if the case is recent, reliable, and relevant to the situation at hand. Be careful not to argue from far-fetched examples that are easy to dismiss as being not only irrelevant but also deceitful.

STATISTICS

The use of **statistics** can provide clear and hard-to-dispute facts in order to make the best case. For example, it is easy to argue the superiority of a particular automobile with statistics dealing with safety, cost, and other easily understood data. But be careful, because statistics can be misinterpreted and manipulated, and many people have learned through hard personal experience that comparative statistics are not always as neat and clean as they appear to be.

TESTIMONIAL AND ENDORSEMENT

Comment by witnesses or people who have used an organization's product or service is called a **testimonial**. Comment by people who espouse an idea an organization supports is called an **endorsement**. By these definitions, a testimonial may be an endorsement, though it is not uncommon for celebrities to endorse a product that they haven't personally tried or used.

Both testimonials and other types of endorsements can provide effective verbal evidence. Testimonials can take the form of letters, likes, online comments, or other statements of support from satisfied customers or engaged employees. Retweets sometimes become a type of endorsement as well.

Similarly, endorsements and recommendations from celebrities can be persuasive, especially if the endorsement is also a testimonial. This occurs when the celebrity is known to have used the product (such as Michael Jordan's endorsement to drinking Gatorade), participated in the service or program (Kirstie Alley for the Jenny Craig weight-loss program), or espoused the idea being presented (Whoopi Goldberg for abortion rights, Brooke Shields for pro-life issues).

Visual Supporting Evidence

Strong visual presentation can enhance the effectiveness of these writing techniques. Use photographs, charts, graphs, and diagrams as visual aids in presenting statistical and technical information. Also think about ways to include demonstrations and performances in your presentation. Consider, too, the role that computer-based presentations can make.

Errors of Logic

As you are preparing your rational message, avoid errors in logic. Some common errors result from unfounded presumptions.

For example, don't over-generalize the argument or leap to an **unwarranted conclusion**, which is a deduction that is not supported by evidence. Make sure your facts are indisputable

Phase Two

STEP
6

> ### CASE IN POINT Pope Francis and the Environment
>
> Politicians line up celebrity endorsements to translate fame into voter influence. Historians say the practice began in 1920 when Hollywood heavyweights Al Jolson, Lillian Russell, Douglas Fairbanks, and Mary Pickford threw their fame behind presidential candidate Warren G. Harding. He won, and candidates have courted celebrity endorsement ever since.
>
> Recent election cycles have continued the trend popularized by George W. Bush campaigns that drew heavily on celebrity religious endorsers. Republicans especially court such endorsements, which generally come from evangelical Christian clergy. Clergy are in the business of opinion leadership, but little research has been done to suggest whether endorsement by religious figures helps or hurts a political candidate.
>
> However, some studies suggest that endorsement by religious leaders can be persuasive in some areas of public policy.
>
> In spring 2015, various polls reported that between 25 and 29 percent of Americans viewed the environment as a moral issue. Then Pope Francis issued his encyclical letter and addressed Congress, identifying environmental care as a moral and ethical imperative.
>
> Follow-up polling showed that 61 percent of Americans, regardless of religion, supported his moral argument of caring for the earth's environment. Environmentalists called it "the Francis effect," noting that the Pope's call to action on environmental change had sparked discussion around the world, intensifying a pro-environment trend they had been tracking for several years.
>
> "A key principle of communication is that the messenger often matters more than the message itself," observed Anthony Leiserowitz of the Yale Project on Climate Change Communication. Thus the American public, which polls showed already found the Pope popular and trustworthy, was swayed and energized by his support for environmental action.
>
> "The Pope has succeeded in initiating a discussion on these issues that just hasn't been there before," said Leiserowitz.

and understood by your audience. Building on incorrect or uncertain data will create a case that is easy to refute.

Also, be careful not to make a **false assumption**, a conclusion that the audience may not accept. An example of a false assumption would be arguing that U.S. schools should adopt a Japanese school calendar on the untested presumption that the audience agrees that the intensity of Japanese education produces better graduates. A similar false assumption would be that the calendar and the associated number of days in school (average 180 in the U.S., and about 200 in Japan) is the primary reason for better-educated students in Japan.

Other errors in logic deal with ignoring the issue and instead attacking the person or reacting with an air of pity or disdain. Finally, remember that any appeal to authority or tradition will be effective only if the audience already respects and accepts that authority or tradition.

Statistics

The nineteenth-century British prime minister Benjamin Disraeli once wrote, "There are three kinds of lies: lies, damned lies, and statistics." That captures the feeling of many people, who in the face of the supposed statistical evidence have learned that statistics aren't always to be trusted. Inaccurate data usually can be spotted. The problem lies less with the statistics and more in their interpretation. Often it's a matter of arriving at a common definition of terms.

Take the simple concept of "average." In general terms, **average** refers to the usual or ordinary instance. But in dealing with statistics, average can be a real sticking point for understanding, because it can mean different things. Consider the following information about annual wages for 11 university students who share a dorm suite.

- Alan works in the dean's office and earns $10,000.
- Jere, Jamal and Monika work for the university police and earn $7,500 each.
- Maria and Tomiko work in the library and earn $5,000 each.
- Tim, Pat and Lori work in the department office and earn $4,000 each.
- Sylvia and Juan work with food service and earn $4,000 each.

What's their average salary? It could be $5,682 (if you calculate average as the **mean**, total wages divided by the number of wage earners). Or, the average is $5,000 (if you use the **median**, the middle number on the list; in this case, Tomiko). Or you can say the average is $4,000 (if you reference the **mode**, the most common number; that is, the number occurring most frequently). It all depends on how you define "average." All three of these definitions are legitimate. The point is, make sure you are clear in your terms and what they mean.

Often, the problem with statistics is how they are interpreted. Here's an example. Few things in society are more contested and controversial than the issue of abortion, and statistics seem only to muddy the waters. One side says most people support access to abortion services; the other side says most people oppose abortion. Both can't be right, can they? Well, yes, depending on how you interpret the nuance of the data. Consider the following survey results, all presumably accurate statistics.

- CNN Poll, 2015: 30 percent of Americans think abortion should be always legal, 13 percent legal in most cases, 37 percent legal in only a few circumstances, and 18 percent always illegal.
- Gallup Poll, 2015: 29 percent always legal, 13 percent legal in most cases, 36 percent illegal in most cases, and 19 percent always illegal.
- NBC/*Wall Street Journal* Poll, 2013: 26 percent always legal, 19 percent legal in most cases, 42 percent illegal in most cases, and 10 percent always illegal.
- Quinnipiac University Poll, 2014: 23 percent always legal, 33 legal in most cases, 24 percent illegal in most cases, and 12 percent always illegal.
- *Washington Post*/ABC Poll, 2013: 20 percent always legal, 35 percent legal in most cases, 26 percent illegal in most cases, and 15 percent illegal in all cases.
- A Marist poll for the Knights of Columbus, 2013: 11 percent always legal, 33 percent legal in most cases, 46 illegal in most cases, and 10 always illegal.
- CBS News Poll, 2015: 38 percent say abortion should be generally available, 34 percent available under stricter limits, and 25 percent not permitted.

Phase Two

STEP
6

So what do such statistics say? One interpretation is that because 10–25 percent would ban abortion, the remaining 75 percent or so support it, right? Well, that's not quite what the data reveal. Another interpretation is that if 13–38 percent would allow abortions for any reason, the remaining 62–87 percent must be against abortion. Again, it's not quite that simple. Obviously, numbers can be found to support the bias of a writer, but perhaps the most fair interpretation is that the data show a lot of centrist and nuanced opinions, not a clear-cut mandate on either side of this public policy discussion.

Here's another example of misleading statistics. Your campus provost's office tracks and reports on cases of plagiarism each year. The current report notes that 150 of the 200 incidents of plagiarism involved the Internet, 75 percent of the cases. This compares with 108 of 180 incidents during the previous year, 60 percent.

What can you say about this increase? You could report a 15-point rise in the percentage of Internet-assisted plagiarism cases. Or is it a 25 percent increase (the proportional difference from 60 to 75)? Or you might cite a 39 percent increase in the number of cases (180 compared to 150). All of the figures are mathematically accurate, but they leave significantly different impressions.

The key to using statistics that do not mislead is to interpret them fairly and honestly, and to be clear about what the numbers really mean—in this example, whether you are comparing total plagiarism cases or the annual percentage change.

Also, take care not to confuse cause with coincidence. There are about as many vegetarians in the U.S. as there are Lutherans (about 12.5 million people, 4 percent of the population). There are as many French speakers in the U.S. as Episcopalians (2.3 million, 0.8 percent). But these numbers, while accurate, are meaningless and irrelevant, and unethical if used to create a false context.

Pathos: Appeal to Sentiment

Human beings are not mere thinking machines. We see in Mr. Spock of the original *Star Trek* TV series examples of inappropriate responses that are so "logical" they are absurd. As humans, we rely heavily on our feelings, and effective communicators take this into consideration. An important part of the strategy of public relations and marketing communication is to link the message to an emotional appeal, either positive or negative.

Positive Emotional Appeal

Many persuasive appeals seek to generate responses based on a variety of positive emotions. Here is a brief look at positive appeals to love, virtue, humor, and sex.

LOVE APPEAL

A **love appeal** can feature a variety of approaches: bittersweet poignancy, family togetherness, nostalgia, pity, compassion, sensitivity, sympathy or any of the many other sides of love. Pleasant images lead consumers not only to remember the persuasive message but also to be more likely to act on the message. For years, Michelin has built a successful advertising campaign around warm images of cute babies sitting in tires, and the verbal cue "so much is riding on your tires." Maxwell House coffee and Hallmark greeting cards also have been successful with this "warm and fuzzy" approach. Fundraising appeals frequently evoke images of compassion and sympathy.

FACT VERSUS PERCEPTION IN THE CLERGY ABUSE SCANDAL

How accurately do statistics reflect the population under study? Accurate use of statistics is based on both what is included and what is left out. It's a matter of context. Ethical use of statistical data can put a situation into a clearer focus.

Consider the scandal of sexual abuse among Catholic priests and the media scrutiny using today's standards for decisions made 30 or more years ago when law enforcement and psychologists had far different ideas on how to treat abusers.

"A casual observer relying on the mass media would form the overwhelming impression of a Church institution awash in perversion, conspiracy, and criminality," notes Philip Jenkins (2003, p. 137). A Penn State University professor who is not Catholic, Jenkins has studied the church's abuse problem for 20 years.

Early media reports relied on claims by activist and victims' groups, which counted as many as 10 percent of priests as pedophiles, about 5,000 of the 53,000 American priests living at that time. A *Wall Street Journal*/NBC News poll reported that 64 percent of adults think priests "frequently" abused children.

More reliable statistics paint a different picture. Studies in some of the largest dioceses indicated that about 3 percent of priests had been accused, less than 2 percent with credible evidence. Many of the accusations involved adult women and men as well as adolescents—all, by definition, not pedophilia. A 2004 nationwide study by John Jay College of Criminal Justice found that 4 percent of priests had been accused during the previous 50 years.

Estimates by psychologists and law enforcement are that 3–5 percent of the entire male population in North America is linked to child or adolescent sexual abuse. The National Center for Missing and Exploited children said the problem among priests is no greater than among clergy in other denominations. Clergy of many religious groups—Episcopalian, Presbyterian, Eastern Orthodox, Mormon, Baptist, Hare Krishna, and Orthodox Jews, among others—had been similarly accused of child sexual abuse. Insurance companies say claims against priests are not proportionally different than for clergy in other churches. Baptist-affiliated Baylor University reported in 2009 its national study that found clergy abuse has occurred in all denominations.

Meanwhile, the abuse issue is present in secular organizations as well. The Boy Scouts reported dismissing more than 5,000 scoutmasters for alleged sexual abuse—more than 3 percent of all Scout volunteers. An educational activist group reported that up to 5 percent of teachers sexually abuse their students, with more than a third of them keeping their jobs. In Step 5 we noted estimates of 5 percent or more of health workers who are sexually attracted to children, even higher among those working in children's hospitals.

So the clergy abuse situation seems no different statistically than the rest of the population, perhaps lower than in some professions. While this fact doesn't minimize the tragedy of sexual abuse nor absolve organizational leaders for mishandling associated crimes, it does point out that statistics that are of doubtful reliability and/or out of context can mislead.

Phase Two

STEP
6

But message effectiveness remains important. For several years, Budweiser featured puppies in its Super Bowl commercials. Folks loved the little critters, so cute and cuddly. But "they have zero impact on beer sales," noted a Budweiser advertising exec. "Those ads I won't air again because they don't sell beer." However, the iconic Clydesdales will remain part of Budweiser's advertising strategy.

VIRTUE APPEAL

An appeal based on something good, a **virtue appeal**, can evoke any of the various values that society or individuals hold in esteem. These are qualities that most people treasure. Consider how natural disasters such as earthquakes and floods inspire volunteerism, blood donations, and financial contributions to relief agencies.

- Justice appeals deal with fairness, human or civil rights, and issues of right or wrong.
- Altruism appeals focus on generosity, charity, kindness, and unselfishness.
- Loyalty appeals focus on patriotism and fidelity.
- Bravery appeals evoke images of boldness, endurance, and courage.
- Piety appeals focus on religious faith, spirituality, and prayer.
- Discretion appeals relate to restraint, moderation, wisdom, and self-control.
- Improvement appeals focus on progress, social advancement, and making the world a better place.
- Esteem appeals focus on self-respect, pride, vanity, and self worth.
- Social acceptance appeals focus on the importance of peer support—the everybody's-doing-it theme.

HUMOR APPEAL

A **humor appeal** can be powerful because comedy and amusement are strong human instincts. Humor is useful in reinforcing existing attitudes and behaviors, but it generally is not very effective in changing them. Humor can make the speaker more liked by the audience, but seldom does it make the speaker more credible. However, the use of humor can reduce the speaker's likability when audiences perceive the humor as excessive or inappropriate.

Humor gets old fast, so its use in public relations and advertising limits the effectiveness of the otherwise valuable practice of repeating messages. Finally, if audiences evaluate the message from an entertainment perspective, they can fail to take it as a serious persuasive message.

With these cautions in mind, here are some guidelines on using humor in persuasive communication.

- The humor should complement a clear and consistent message about the organization or the product/service/concept. It should never be used as a substitute for an understandable message.
- The humor should be relevant to the issue and appropriate for the organization. For instance, it is unlikely that a funeral home could effectively use humor at its website.
- The humor should be tasteful. The *South Park* phenomenon aside, bathroom and bedroom humor generally are counterproductive for most audiences, as is disparaging humor directed against others, particularly groups of people. Self-deprecating humor can be effective in causing an audience to like a speaker.

- The humor should be funny. This is difficult to achieve, because what is humorous to one person may be droll, too cute, ludicrous, or simply unfunny to others. Make sure the humor does not insult people's intelligence by becoming absurd or pointless. Also, given the choice, prefer the lighthearted and amusing touch over an attempt to present uproarious farce.
- Humor is more effective with dull topics that need sparking up than with topics the audience already finds interesting. With interesting topics, humor can detract from the message.

SEX APPEAL

A **sex appeal** can range from nudity to double entendres to outright shock. These sexual messages can be effective in commanding attention, though audience demographics affect how that attention is received.

But the very pulling power of sex appeals has a built-in problem. Tests show that audiences often remember the sexual content of an advertisement but fail to associate it with the brand being promoted or the sponsor presenting the message. Likewise, what one demographic group may find appropriate and positive, another may judge unnecessary and negative. For example, women respond to sex appeals less than men do, and younger people are more positively influenced by sex appeals than older audiences.

An even bigger problem with sex-appeal messages is that, for all their high ability to gain attention, they are notoriously weak in leading receivers toward desired action.

One consistent finding from persuasion research is that sex appeal should not be used simply for shock value. It is far more effective when the sexual theme has a legitimate association with the product (such as lingerie, perfume, or condoms) or with the cause (such as birth control or responsible sexual behavior).

Sometimes humor and sex appeal comingle. When Phillips Norelco launched its Bodygroom "manscaping" shaver to men, the promotion went edgy. The result was one of the most successful product launches in company history. It also helped mainstream a previously taboo subject—body grooming to enhance a man's self-esteem and sexual appeal. Strategy for the body groomer included power words and slogans such as "Shave Your Kiwis" when the product was previewed at the Sundance Film Festival and The Optical Inch listener-interactive radio programming. Tactics included creation of a website called ShaveEverywhere. com, loaded with innuendo; leveraging a partnership with Howard Stern; focusing an extensive media-relations program toward magazines popular with the key public of young adult males; promoting a Shave the Brave manscape-for-charity competition between firefighters in Chicago and New York.

Negative Emotional Appeal

Some messages invoke responses based on negative emotions—fear and guilt being the most common. A third type of negative appeal, to hatred, has no ethical use for public relations and thus is not worth considering here.

FEAR APPEAL

Fear is one of the strongest human emotions, and a **fear appeal** is intended to arouse anxiety or worry among receivers. Examples are advertising that focuses on the fear of body odor

> ## CASE IN POINT **Budweiser on the Meaning of 'No'**
>
> Here's a case that falls into the what-were-they-thinking? category.
>
> "The perfect beer for removing 'no' from your vocabulary for the night." That's the label Anhauser-Bush thought was good for its Bud Light beer. Who would have expected any backlash from, say, women everywhere? Or any clear-thinking person who thinks rape jokes are never cool?
>
> A Reddit posting sparked a social media conversation that ended badly for A-B. Budweiser apologized—sort of—as it pulled the controversial label from its Up for Whatever campaign. "It's clear that this particular message missed the mark, and we regret it," said a statement posted on its website. "We would never condone disrespectful or irresponsible behavior." Of course not.
>
> Criticism was immediate. *Mother Jones* magazine called Bud Light "the official beer of rape culture." *Fortune* magazine speculated on the lack of sensitivity of the beer company that had only one woman on its board of directors.
>
> Anhauser-Bush laid the slogan on the doorstep of its ad agency, Energy BBDO, and said it was "regrettable" that the slogan passed its "extensive review process." BBDO had no public comment. By mid-summer 2015, three months after the crisis erupted, A-B took Bud Light's $350 million account to a new agency.
>
> Internet analytics showed that the Up for Whatever campaign had been the topic of about 60 percent of Anhauser-Busch's social media chatter. This label controversy turned much of this social conversation to rape and the relationship between alcohol and sexual assault, as well as many negative comments about the beer itself.
>
> Amid the controversy, A-H advertising executive Jorn Socquet announced a corporate turn-around in an interview with *Bloomberg Business* (2015). "Objectification of women is going away," he said. Advertising will become more gender friendly in an effort to sell more suds to women (who currently account for only about 25 percent of beer sales). So, no more scantily clad women frolicking in Budweiser ads?

and political messages centered on the alleged disasters that await the public if the opposing candidate or party is elected.

Politicians, particularly in recent years, have stepped up their use of fear appeals. The Wesleyan Media Project reported that 70 percent of ads for the 2012 U.S. presidential race were negative. That's more than 3 million ads costing about $2 billion—all to attack opponents. People who track such political ads say they are getting nastier and less hampered by facts.

Why the negative thrust? Electoral politics frequently uses fear appeals to scare voters away from opposing candidates or office holders. Politicians press for quick passage of security-based and financial-related legislation, often without time for thoughtful consideration of the potential impact. For all the talk that the electorate doesn't like negative ads or fear appeals, it's clear that such ads do, in fact, work. Why? For one thing, they are more memorable.

As to their effectiveness, the 2015 elections in England show that ads that made a political or policy point rather than a personal jab seemed to be more effective at the polls.

The key to using fear appeals effectively is to accompany them with a quick fix featuring an easy, reasonable, and immediate solution to the problem. Fear appeals to persuade audiences to obtain a one-time vaccination, for example, are more effective than those designed to persuade audiences to floss over a lifetime in the name of dental hygiene.

Beware of offering too much of a good thing. Moderate fear appeals can be effective, but too much fearful content can make people either avoid the message or take a defiant stance against it. Appeals that present harsh consequences may cause audiences to cope with their fear simply by refusing to consider the message or even by denying the underlying issue.

Another problem with fear appeals is that the balance point between effective and ineffective shifts according to varying demographic factors such as age, education, and gender. Younger adults, for example, have higher resistance to fear appeal than do older adults. Some research suggests that fear appeals likewise have only a limited effect on audience members with high self-esteem who feel immune to impending doom.

Fear appeals may increase levels of awareness without delivering the desired action. For example, strong fear appeals used in a seat-belt campaign may make drivers aware of the consequences of not wearing seat belts—perhaps even fostering an intention of wearing them—without actually changing the likelihood that they will, indeed, buckle up.

Here is a way to make fear appeals more effective: Include in the message a strong how-to approach. For example, don't just deal with the dangers associated with poor nutrition, give several clear and simple examples of how to prepare or order more nutritional meals.

Source and significance also play a role in the effective use of fear appeals. For example, fear appeals are more effective when they come from highly credible sources who are dissimilar to the audience. Often this credibility can be reinforced by symbols, such as clothing a doctor in a lab coat as she presents moderate fear-based information about disease prevention or using someone in a military uniform to speak about threats to national interests and preparation for war.

Fear appeals also can be effective when the issue is significant or important to the audience. In a study related to environmental threats—specifically, plutonium contamination from a nuclear weapons plant—Connie Roser and Margaret Thompson (1995) observed that fear appeals can motivate even latent publics to become active, especially to take action against the fear-producing organization.

Aaron Delwiche, a communication professor at Trinity University in San Antonio, Texas, supervises a propaganda website (propagandacritic.com) in which he identifies four elements of a successful fear appeal: (1) a threat, (2) a recommendation about how the audience should behave, (3) audience perception that the recommendation can effectively address the threat, and (4) perception that the audience can actually behave as recommended.

GUILT APPEAL

Appeals to a personal sense of guilt or shame comprise another negative message strategy, one that is the flip side of the virtue appeal. A **guilt appeal** is a common persuasive technique, particularly in the area of marketing communication and fundraising.

Consider the "Buy American" theme. Only a fine line separates a positive appeal to patriotism and national pride from a xenophobic message that tries to make people feel guilty about buying goods produced in another country. With a positive approach, the message focuses on the common economic good, shared values among citizens, and a healthy respect for the quality of American products. With a negative approach, the same appeal can elicit a sense of guilt for having bought foreign-made products. Since nobody wants to feel guilty, a typical reaction against guilt appeals is to justify our actions ("But foreign cars are better made") and to lament the alternative ("American cars just don't last as long").

Like fear appeals, the use of guilt strategy can be effective in moderation. In a fundraising message, for example, a guilt message might try to make readers feel a bit uneasy or apologetic in their relative comfort amid so much misery elsewhere. But try to move guilt appeals away from the negative emotion and toward a positive sentiment such as compassion and justice.

APPEALING TO HEARTS AND MINDS

Research tells us that it is tremendously important to provide messages that appeal to both the mind and the heart. Three areas of study—two from psychology, one from physiology—shed some light on the question of how we can best frame messages to our audiences.

Psychological Type. The concept of **psychological type** is based on the work of Carl Jung and the application of his theories by the mother–daughter team of Isabel Briggs Myers and her mother, Katharine Briggs (see Myers, 1998; Myers and Myers, 1995) and a host of their disciples. This approach observes that people have different natural preferences in how they gather information, make decisions and act on those decisions. Some people, labeled "thinkers" in Myers–Briggs terminology, tend to rely mainly on logic and data in making decisions. "Feelers," on the other hand, base their decisions more on sentiment and emotion. Seldom will your publics and audiences be so like-minded as to uniformly prefer one type of message appeal over the other. Thus, good strategy calls for the use of both types of messages.

But this may not be a natural response for many practitioners, because many of the artistic or creative disciplines—writing, journalism, design, advertising, and public relations—tend to attract people who themselves are feelers rather than thinkers. The disciplines more associated with management, such as research and marketing, attract a higher-than-average percentage of thinkers. In either case, it is undependable to rely simply on your personal preferences.

Temperament. The concept of **temperament** is an approach related to personality and natural disposition, associated with psychologist David Keirsey (1998). From him we learn of four specific temperaments—artisan, idealist, guardian, and rationalist—with different innate preferences regarding organization and creativity.

Left Brain/Right Brain Differences. The working of the human brain—and, in particular, the relationship between the two hemispheres of the brain—has been explored by Roger Sperry (1985) of the California Institute of Technology. He received a Nobel Prize in 1981 for his pioneering work. Evidence suggests that the left side of the brain is responsible for logical and analytical thought, while the right side controls creativity and imagination. Like psychological type and temperament, hemispheric brain studies suggest that most individuals use both functions but are stronger in one or the other.

These three fields have many common bonds. That's not surprising for the first two, because Keirsey's research is a conscious reworking of the psychological insights of Myers and Briggs. Sperry took a different path that led him through physiology, but he arrived at surprisingly similar patterns.

By comparing and blending this research, evidence suggests that some people are innately more deliberate or logical, while others are more spontaneous and imaginative.

If guilt appeals are to be effective, their messages must make people feel part of the solution. "Will you help? Or will you turn the page?" is the kind of modest guilt appeal that can be quite effective. Like the fear appeal, guilt appeals should feature solutions to the problem of conscience that they raise.

PLANNING EXAMPLE 6B **Determining Message Appeal**

Upstate College will combine rational and emotional message appeals in its message.

UPSTATE COLLEGE

Rational Appeal

Upstate College will present two types of appeals:

- A factual proposition based on advantages to students, including current and future academic programs, accreditation, financial aid, and alumni and community commitments for internships and mentoring.
- A value proposition asserting that this expansion is in the best interests of students and this region of the state.

These messages will include statistics, personal endorsements, and specific examples of hypothetical students in various academic and economic situations. They also will include visual elements such as photographs, charts, and graphs.

Emotional Appeal

UC will present appeals to positive emotions, particularly the virtues of self-improvement and the realization of personal potential. For fundraising purposes, it will appeal to the virtue of altruism and sharing with students who need an assist in obtaining a college education.

Tiny Tykes will present both rational and emotional message appeals.

Rational Appeal

Tiny Tykes will present several rational propositions:

- A factual proposition based on information about the product redesign.
- A value proposition stating a renewed commitment to consumer safety.
- A policy proposition asserting the rightness of continuing to use Tiny Tykes products, which have a long history of being responsive to customer concerns.

These messages will include physical evidence from outside testing agencies about the safety of Tiny Tykes products, a comparison with similar products by competitors, and testimony by consumers and consumer advocacy groups.

Phase Two

STEP 6

Emotional Appeal

Tiny Tykes will present two types of emotional appeals:

- Appeals to positive emotions, such as child development and family fun.
- Appeals to negative emotions such as a mild level of fear appeal about using toys not tested and approved by independent agencies.

Regardless of the type of emotional appeal being made, consider the ethical ramifications. Ask yourself: Is this appeal ethical? Is it the right way to communicate about this issue? Is it fair? Will the organization gain respect by using this approach?

 Checklist 6B **Message Appeal**

Basic Questions

1. What is the key message that forms the basis of this public relations or marketing communication program?
2. How does this message use a rational appeal?
3. How does this message use an emotional appeal?

Expanded Questions

1. Does your message include a rational appeal and/or an emotional appeal? (Note: Most persuasive messages provide both kinds of appeals.)

A. RATIONAL APPEAL

1. How does your message make a rational appeal?
2. Does the message feature a factual proposition, a value proposition or a policy proposition?
3. Which of the following provide arguments for your claims: physical evidence, analogy, audience interest, comparison, context, examples, statistics, testimony and endorsements, and/or visual presentation?

B. EMOTIONAL APPEAL

1. How does your message make an emotional appeal?
2. Does the message feature an appeal to positive emotions or negative emotions?
3. What is the emotion?

Love Appeal
- What kind of love?

Virtue Appeal
- What virtue?

Humor Appeal
- Will the use of humor make the source more persuasive?
- Is the humor relevant to the issue?
- Is the humor funny?
- Is the humor appropriate for the audience?
- Is the humor appropriate for the organization?
- Will the humor enhance the message?
- Will the humor help meet the objectives?

[Note: If you answer "yes" to these questions, the humorous message may be effective.]

Sex Appeal
- Will the use of sex appeal make the source more persuasive?
- Is the sex appeal relevant to the issue?
- Is the sex appeal appropriate for the audience?
- Is the sex appeal appropriate for the organization?
- Will the sex appeal help enhance the message?
- Will the sex appeal help meet the objectives?

[Note: If you answer "yes" to these questions, the sexual message may be effective.]

Fear Appeal
- Will the use of fear appeal make the source more persuasive?
- Is the fear appeal relevant to the issue?
- Is the fear appeal appropriate for the audience?
- Is the fear appeal appropriate for the organization?
- Does the message include a solution to overcome the fear?
- Will the fear appeal enhance the message?
- Will the fear appeal help meet the objectives?

[Note: If you answer "yes" to these questions, the fearful message may be effective.]

Guilt Appeal
- Will the use of guilt appeal make the source more persuasive?
- Is the guilt appeal relevant to the issue?
- Is the guilt appeal appropriate for the audience?
- Is the guilt appeal appropriate for the organization?
- Does the message include a solution to overcome the guilt?
- Will the guilt appeal enhance the message?
- Will the guilt appeal help meet the objectives?

[Note: If you answer "yes" to these questions, the guilt appeal may be effective.]

Phase Two

STEP
6

Verbal Communication

Both kinds of appeals—logical and emotional—can be communicated either verbally or nonverbally. Let's look first at verbal and then at nonverbal communication as they apply to public relations, marketing, and related disciplines.

Verbal communication occurs through written and spoken words. The media can include newspapers and magazines, websites and blogs, video and audio venues, billboards and Facebook.

The right words—and the right use of those words—can effectively present your organization's message to its publics. Several verbal factors combine to create an effective message, among them structure, clarity, salience, power words, product and program names, strong quotes, and both ethical and legal language. Here is a closer look at each of these.

Message Structure

The structure of the message has been the subject of much research. Several particular elements have been researched: giving one or both sides of an argument, the order of presentation, and the value of drawing conclusions or making recommendations. Should you present only your point of view or address the opposition's argument? The research suggests that it depends upon both the audience and the circumstances.

ONE-SIDED ARGUMENT

A one-sided argument presents the organization's or speaker's point of view but not opposing views. This kind of argument is useful in reinforcing opinions, because one-sided arguments don't confuse the audience with alternatives. But one-sided arguments are less effective in changing opinions.

Four conditions warrant the use of one-sided arguments: (1) the audience is friendly and already agrees with your position, (2) its members have low educational or knowledge levels, (3) your position will be the only one presented, or (4) the objective is immediate opinion change. Presenting only one side of an argument can cause a temporary attitudinal change, but this probably will be eliminated if the audience later hears a convincing argument from the other side.

TWO-SIDED ARGUMENT

On the other hand, some arguments present both pros and cons of an issue, though not necessarily objectively. They usually criticize the opposition's position.

Two-sided arguments are necessary with better-educated audiences, audiences that are undecided on an issue or initially opposed to the idea being presented, and more knowledgeable audiences that are aware that another side of the issue exists or that are likely to be exposed to other sides in the future. Such two-sided arguments can improve your ability to persuade these audiences because you will be perceived as being more honest and more respectful of the audience's intelligence.

If you present each side of the argument, you have a better chance of achieving a greater attitude change that will remain high when the audience hears the opposing argument from another source.

ORDER OF PRESENTATION

The **order of presentation** refers to the way the argument unfolds. Should you present arguments in order of least to most important, or vice versa? It generally doesn't seem to matter, as long as you are consistent. In developing your persuasive message, you may have reason to choose one form over the other. For example, do you think your audience will be more attentive at the beginning of the message? If so, then use your strongest arguments there.

The final word is also very important, and plenty of research points out that the last point made is the one best remembered. This is especially true with less-sophisticated audiences, as well as for audiences that are less knowledgeable or less personally involved in the issue.

Comic Paula Poundstone said it well in a stand-up routine referring to a political campaign that dealt with economic policy: "I don't know anything about the economy. I tend to agree with the last guy who spoke."

In two-sided arguments, it may be best to sandwich the information. That is, first present your side—the first argument often is perceived as the strongest. Then present and refute the opposing arguments. Finally restate your position, because of the power of the last word.

DRAWING CONCLUSIONS

Presenting the evidence and then explicitly telling the audience how to interpret it—**drawing conclusions**—has been the subject of much research. Most of the findings suggest that making a recommendation or drawing a conclusion usually is more effective than leaving it to the audience to draw its own conclusion.

However, some evidence suggests that when audience members—especially educated ones—draw their own conclusion, both the conclusion and the attitude on which it rests are more resistant to change than if the conclusion is presented by the source. Some studies have indicated that when the purpose of a message is to reduce criticism or opposition it may be better not to draw conclusions for the audience. The question is, can you risk not having the audience draw the "right" conclusion?

REITERATION

The final area to consider for effective message structure, **reiteration**, refers to internal repetition of the main ideas within a persuasive message. This is not the kind of redundancy that involves superfluous turns of phrase, such as "puppy dog," "armed gunman," or "small village."

Rather, reiteration means presenting the same message in different forms, with different words and different examples, each reinforcing the other.

For example, an effective fundraising email will ask for a donation frequently throughout the letter, each time making the request with different words and phrases, and perhaps based on varying types of appeals. Such internal repetition can make messages more memorable and over time, more acceptable. Reiteration often means using synonyms—different words with similar meanings—as a way of restating the main point.

Another technique is to develop parallel structure within sentences and paragraphs to make your information easier to recognize and remember. For example, use a "B" list: "Be alert. Be prepared. Be resourceful." Alliteration, using words that have the same beginning sounds, is another memory enhancer.

BARRIERS TO EFFECTIVE COMMUNICATION

Several factors can limit the effectiveness of communication. Each of these is a type of **noise** within the communication process. By knowing what they are, communication planners may be able to eliminate these noise types or at least minimize their impact. Here are some of the common barriers.

- **Physical noise** is caused by ineffective communication channels that do not transmit the message, or distracting sounds that interfere with the receiver's reception of the message.
- **Physiological noise** includes things such as being hungry or tired, having a headache or some other pain, or being otherwise distracted by your body. Poor hearing and poor eyesight are other physiological barriers to effective communication.
- **Psychological noise** results from emotional distractions by the receiver. These could include bias, anger, stress, or other negative emotions.
- **Semantic noise** is related to the use of a language in which the sender or receiver is not fluent. It also may involve jargon, use of words with multiple meanings, or other word choice that is not mutually understood by sender and receiver.
- **Demographic noise**, sometimes called **cultural noise**, involves differences between sender and receiver in terms of age, gender, ethnicity, social status, and the like.

So many potential barriers to effective communication! It's a wonder people and organizations are able to communicate at all. But the noise can be turned down and the barriers overcome. Senders who understand the potential communication pitfalls can find ways to avoid them; receivers can be particularly attentive to the message and engage in active listening to overcome communication noise.

Phase Two

STEP
6

Message Content

The content of the message contributes significantly to the effectiveness of the message strategy. Whether positive or negative, the importance of content cannot be overstressed.

CLARITY

A message first and foremost must be understood. **Clarity** is a quality of writing and speaking, a clearness of expression and thought that helps the audience easily understands your message.

To craft a message with clarity, use words precisely. Keep an eye on their exact and commonly understood meaning. Use simple language—"try" instead of "endeavor," "use" rather than "utilize," "say" instead of "articulate." Avoid jargon unless the language is shared by your listeners, readers, or viewers. Be aware of the difference between confusing word pairs: "imply" and "infer," "disinterested" and "uninterested," "allusion" and "illusion," "mute and "moot," and many more.

In all cases, use a vocabulary appropriate to your audience. Consider the differences in language fitting for teens, senior citizens, or business executives. Consider also the setting for your verbal message, such as the differences in language appropriate for boardrooms, locker rooms, and dining rooms.

In addition to clear writing, communication strategists should ensure that their messages use correct and simple English, avoid redundancies, generally use an active voice, and observe other guidelines for good writing. Consult a good textbook on public relations writing to brush up on your writing skills.

READABILITY

Part of the analysis of the key publics in Step 3 was to identify the likely educational attainment, which in turn can be used to ensure that messages are written at an appropriate level.

Most newspapers are written at about a ninth-grade reading level so everybody with that level of education or more—the majority of readers—should be able to understand the articles, columns, and editorials. They may not necessarily agree with the articles or even be interested in them, but they are able to understand the writing. If you are preparing a news release or guest editorial for such a publication, plan on writing for readers with a ninth-grade reading ability.

On the other hand, if you are writing a fundraising letter aimed at health-care professionals, it would be safe to presume that all your readers will have completed some level of higher education. Whatever you estimate to be the appropriate reading level, test your writing against that estimate.

Robert Gunning's **Fog Index** (also called the **Gunning Readability Formula**) measures the level of reading difficulty for any piece of writing, allowing writers to adjust their text to the skills of their audience. It is one of the easiest readability measures to use. Use a search engine to find an easy-to-use online Fog Index calculator. Some word-processing programs also can calculate grade-level **readability** measures.

Some other commonly used readability instruments include Rudolf Flesch's Readability Score, which is more complicated than the Fog Index while also measuring human interest; the associated Flesch–Kincaid readability grade level; Edward Fry's readability graph, which relies on a chart to calculate reading ease; the Dale–Chall formula, based on sentence length and the number of infrequently used words; the Cloze Procedure, which measures comprehension of spoken and visual messages; and Irving Fang's Easy Listening Formula, which provides a comparable way to calculate the comprehension of broadcast copy.

Many computer word-processing programs feature one or more of these readership aids in the program's tools section. For example, Microsoft Word counts an average of 17.6 words per sentence in this chapter and calculates a 12.0 grade-level readability score, based on the Flesch–Kincaid score. Anybody with a high-school education should be able to easily read this chapter. Thus the intended audience—college students and professionals out of college—should find this chapter easy to read.

SALIENCE

In advertising, planners focus on the **unique selling proposition** (USP), that special something that their product or service offers that is different from all the competition. USP is a kind of niche statement that positions the product for the intended market segment.

We also use the concept of USP in public relations planning. We call it **salience**, the ability to stand out from the crowd. Specifically, salient information is that which speaks directly to the intended public by letting people know just how a product, service, or idea will help them.

POWER WORDS

The use of strong language can play a significant role in communication effectiveness. **Power words**, also called **grabbers**, refer to terminology and definitions that are so influential that they often can determine public relations success for a movement or campaign.

Edward Bernays, the public relations pioneer who rooted the profession in social psychology, said he had achieved "semantic tyranny" with his name for the anniversary campaign to commemorate Thomas Edison's invention of the electric light. Light's Golden Jubilee was the title Bernays devised, linking three words that he believed guaranteed interest and support.

Bernays' advice to choose words carefully is particularly valid today, when media are overflowing with messages that compete for attention and interest. Descriptions such as "low-fat," "environment-friendly," and "Bible-believing," and labels such as "family values," "flip flopper," "job creators," and "tax-and-spend liberal" are terms that have been carefully orchestrated to present a particular emotional connotation.

Instead of referring to "political prisoners," Amnesty International uses the ennobling term "prisoners of conscience." The U.S. government holds "detainees" in military prisons who, by that definition, are not entitled to legal protections of prisoners of war under international law.

Meanwhile, the gunmen who rob, rape, kidnap, and mutilate villagers in sub-Saharan Africa and parts of the Middle East have been called "freedom fighters" or "holy warriors" by their supporters and "terrorists" by opponents. Southern border states deal with "illegal immigrants," the same people others call "undocumented workers." The latter term avoids the stigma of lawbreaking, which is precisely the issue for some people.

Sometimes the grabber is a full paragraph. Consider the following statement that could be used by any of the 560 or so American Indian nations to explain their historic relationship with their lands: "My people lived on this land when Moses was crossing the desert. We fished these rivers when Cleopatra was queen. We hunted these mountains before Hannibal crossed the Alps. This land is as much a part of me as the color of my eyes."

Rhetorical warfare is associated with some of society's most divisive issues. For example, "pro-choice" activists generally disavow the label "pro-abortion" foisted upon them by the other side (which calls itself "pro-life," and which in turn is called "anti-choice" by opponents). One side speaks of a "fetus," the other side of an "unborn baby"—a differentiation in terminology on which hinges the entire controversy.

Sometimes the issue of power words becomes ethically compromised. The advocacy group Media Matters obtained a memo by a Fox News vice president telling his staff how to frame the debate around health care. "Please use the term 'government-run health insurance' or, when brevity is a concern, 'government option' whenever possible," read the memo. It was based on input from a Republican political consultant opposed to what became the Affordable Care Act.

Consider the strategy of language, as well as your potential role in what U.S. News and World Report columnist John Leo calls "compassionate incoherence," a type of political correctness that jeopardizes understanding. (Check back to the previous chapter about "strategic ambiguity.") There was a strategy behind Justin Timberlake's statement dismissing Janet Jackson's nipple flash during the 2004 Super Bowl halftime show as merely a "wardrobe malfunction." With more serious consequences, such intentional misrepresentation also underlies terms such as "ethnic cleansing," "detainee," and other whitewashed phrases.

If rhetorical warfare is part of society's divisiveness, then rhetorical peacemaking can lead to more beneficial relationships when organizations and their publics engage in shared language, and the path of consensus building and conflict resolution is made smoother by sensitivity to the words used to communicate.

PRODUCT AND PROGRAM NAMES

What we call things can greatly affect how others perceive them.

A **product name** is a title, often developed through extensive research, strategically designed to associate a product with characteristics that are thought to be desirable in the mind of the key public. Product names receive much attention in commercial enterprises. The California Prune Board went to court for permission to market prunes under the name "dried plums" because consumers had a better response to the new term. Similarly, the Patagonian toothfish was remarketed as Chilean sea bass, rapeseed oil became Canola oil, and the sea delicacy whore's eggs was renamed sea urchin or uni. It took six years to complete the marketing transition in the 1980s when Datsun cars were rebranded as Nissan. But it took only one year for the BackRub search engine to change its name to Google.

We find luxury automobiles with names such as Gran Turismo, Genesis, and Continental; sports cars such as Mustang and Viper; and SUVs Explorer, Blazer, and Pathfinder. If you aren't convinced of the power of names, try thinking up a promotional campaign for the all-wheel-drive Chevrolet Petunia, the luxury Ford Cockroach, the hybrid Toyota Slug, or the sporty VW Aardvark.

A **program name** is the parallel of a product name for services of both nonprofit organizations and businesses. Businesses often use many resources to research names for their products; nonprofit organizations, on the other hand, generally conduct less research and use less of a strategic approach when naming their programs. Organizations sometimes attempt to devise memorable acronyms, though these often end up being somewhat less effective than hoped. In the same locality, the acronym CASA might stand for Central American Scientific Association, Clean Air Strategic Alliance, Council on Alcoholism and Substance Abuse, Christian Associates in South America, Catholic Appeal for Saint Anthony, Center for the Advancement of Saudi Arabia, and Coalition to Annex South Alexandria. A title like CASA might look nice on the letterhead, but it doesn't communicate much about an organization.

BRANDING RIGHTS

The naming game can be a lucrative and mutually beneficial endeavor. Branding rights, the legal right to name a place or activity, has led corporations to spend big bucks to put their names on buildings and events. Sport venues and tournaments serve as the primary stage for branding rights.

After 21 years as the FedEx Orange Bowl, the annual football tournament became the Discover Orange Bowl, named for its new corporate sponsor, Discover Financial, only to morph into the Capital One Orange Bowl. What once was best known as the Virginia Slims Legends Tour for Women's Tennis Association became – thanks to new sponsors – an event serially renamed the Avon, Chase, Sanex, Home Depot, Sony Ericcson, Bank of America, and BNP Paribas championships. In 2016, the tennis association called it simply WTA Finals.

Early branding examples for sports venues are the Boston baseball park named for Fenway Realty and the Chicago baseball field named for Wrigley chewing gum. Named

NAMING ETHICS

Some program names can be misleading, and public relations professionals are careful not to be associated with such deception.

Front organizations are set up to appear to operate independently, when in fact they are controlled by another organization that wants to remain anonymous in the relationship. Serious ethical issues arise from names of front organizations or programs that fail to reflect their partisan or sectarian sponsors.

The Cult Awareness Network, World Literacy Crusade, and Citizens Commission for Human Rights have been exposed as front organizations for the Church of Scientology. The Physicians Committee for Responsible Medicine, which advocates vegetarianism, has been accused of being a front group for People for the Ethical Treatment of Animals. Americans for Technology Leadership, which advocates for limited government regulation, is said to be a front organization funded by Microsoft.

Because they are trying to hide their true nature, many front groups adopt misleading names. The oil company-funded Global Climate Coalition opposes climate controls. The National Wetlands Coalition funded by utilities and industrial companies actually opposes government efforts to protect wetlands. The Greening Earth Society was created by coal companies to present a message that coal burning is good for the environment. Farmers for Clean Air and Water was founded to lobby Congress to exempt large agricultural corporations from environmental regulations.

Meanwhile, a number of organizations have sprung up, purportedly over the issue of casino gaming, that adopt innocuous-sounding names dealing with equity and fairness but act on a consistent anti-American Indian agenda.

Related to front organizations are **Astroturf organizations**, which pretend to be grassroots efforts when they are in fact established and funded by corporations—hence the name suggesting artificial grass. The grassroots-sounding Coalition for Responsible Healthcare Reform was created by Blue Cross to fight the very thing that its name suggests. FreedomWorks and Americans for Prosperity are two related organizations with conservative agendas created and funded by individuals with strong Republican ties and by groups such as Koch Industries, Verizon, Philip Morris, and AT&T.

Unfortunately for our profession, some Astroturf organizations have been created by public relations agencies to help their clients avoid the glare of publicity, a dubious approach for a profession that values honesty, openness, and transparency. One of the most notorious of these was Citizens for a Free Kuwait, created by the Hill & Knowlton agency to promote the 1991 war in the Persian Gulf. Working Families for Walmart is funded by—surprise!—Walmart; it also is directed by the corporation's public relations agency, Edelman. Another agency, Manning Selvage and Lee, created the Center for Medicine in the Public Interest that furthers the interests of its many pharmaceutical clients.

During the 2004 presidential campaign, an organization was created called Swift Boat Veterans for Truth. Self described as a nonpartisan group, it actually was closely aligned with the Republican party. The group launched a smear campaign against Democratic candidate John Kerry, who had commanded a swift boat during the Vietnam War. During the war, Kerry received major military honors: three Purple Hearts, a Silver Star, and a Bronze Star. Based on the group's widely publicized and soon discredited campaign against Kerry, a new political term "swift boating" arose to describe an unfair/unsubstantiated/untrue political assault that without evidence attacks a candidate's patriotism and credibility.

sponsors often are local businesses, such as Molson Amphitheatre in Toronto, Heinz Field in Pittsburgh, and Coors Field in Denver.

San Francisco's historic Candlestick Park became a pawn in the corporate naming game when it became 3COM Park and later Monster Park. In 2004, voters decided to return to the historic Candlestick name permanently. The stadium was demolished in 2015, to be replaced with a shopping mall.

In a non-sporting venue, Citizens Bank had naming rights for the Boston subway's State Street station. There's AT&T station of the Philadelphia subway, Target Center in Minneapolis, Emirates Stadium in London, and both Snapple and Best Buy theaters in New York. And when scientists auctioned off naming rights for a newly discovered species of monkey, the Golden Palace online casino paid $650,000 to name the GoldenPalace.com Monkey.

Even naming programs can become controversial. After John DuPont of the wealthy Philadelphia family was convicted of murdering an Olympic athlete and found to be mentally ill, Villanova University changed the name of its basketball arena, the DuPont Pavilion, to simply The Pavilion. Amid the financial scandal in 2002, the Houston Astros bought back the naming rights to Enron Field and rechristened it the following year as Minute Maid Field. In 2015, Princeton University students mounted a campaign to rename the Woodrow Wilson School of Public and International Affairs because the 28th president was a racist and segregationist.

STRONG QUOTES

The statements that people make, **quotes**, are an important aspect of verbal communication. Such quotes should be memorable and meaty. Public relations writers should use strong quotes in their news releases, news conference statements and interviews, as well as on other occasions for interacting with the media.

Here is an example of a really pithy quote. Oliver Stone directed a television special that promoted the theory that TWA Flight 800, which had exploded in the late 1990s killing all 230 passengers and crew, was downed by a missile. FBI investigators had specifically ruled out that possibility. Consider the passion in this response by James Kallstrom, who headed the FBI investigation: "The real facts are glossed over by the likes of Mr. Stone and others who spend their life bottom-feeding in those small, dark crevices of doubt and hypocrisy." Wow! That is so much better than a dreary bureaucratic statement such as "The FBI stands by its original report" or "We disagree with Mr. Stone's missile theory." This is a quote with attitude. It both sings and stings.

Ethical Language

Using ethical language is a must for every public relations practitioner. In considering the verbal formulation of your message, pay attention to the implication of language. Certainly you will want to use language with pizzazz. Power words can lead audiences to perceive an image instantly and to take on an immediate mood—"beautiful people," "cutting edge," "right wing," "workaholic." But be careful with the stereotypes on which power words are built and make sure that reality underlies these images.

Pretentious language involves words or phrases that imply more than is warranted. Avoid such language, because it can mislead readers. Examples of pretentious language are "experienced vehicles" for used cars and "follically impaired" for bald. Such words can have

LANGUAGE IN TRANSLATION

Sometimes public relations or marketing messages need to be translated in a language different from the original. That situation introduces opportunity for errors.

We easily recognize the many examples of silly mistranslations into English. In an Austrian hotel: "In case of fire, do your utmost to alarm the hotel porter." In a Norway cocktail lounge: "Ladies are requested not to have children in the bar." In an Italian medical office: "Specialist in women and other diseases." In a Paris hotel: "Please leave your values at the front desk." And in a Paris dress show: "Dresses for street walking."

Asia is the home of many mistranslations. In a Hong Kong supermarket: "For your convenience, we recommend courteous, efficient self-service." On a bubble-bath package in Japan: "While solution is not toxic, it will not make child edible." In a Tokyo hotel room: "If you want condition of warm air, please control yourself." And in a hotel in Malaysia: "You are invited to take advantage of the chambermaid."

Likewise, there have been many mistranslations (or near misses) from English into other languages. Here are a few branding headaches.

In China, KFC's "finger-lickin' good" becomes "Eat your fingers off." Yum!

In Taiwan, "Come alive with the Pepsi generation" was translated "Pepsi will bring your ancestors back from the dead."

Colgate introduced a toothpaste in France called Cue, also the name of a porn magazine. And McDonald's introduced its Big Mac to France as the "Gros Mex," which means "big pimp."

Ads in Mexico were supposed to say that Parker Pens "won't leak in your pocket and embarrass you." But in translation, the ad said the ballpoint pens "won't leak in your pocket and make you pregnant." Because, you know, that would be embarrassing.

Perdue Chicken's long-time slogan "It takes a tough man to make a tender chicken" showed up on billboards across Mexico as "It takes an aroused man to make a chicken affectionate."

Coors' "Turn it loose" tagline translated in Spain as "You will get diarrhea." Perhaps that's an example of truth in advertising.

And when Ford realized that its Pinto translated into Portugese as slang for a small penis, in Brazil the company instead marketed the Corcel, which means horse. Ford might have been overcompensating with that one.

a backlash if they are perceived as either silly or too crafty. Sometimes pretentious language raises confusing questions. For example, if pets are "companion animals," then should pet owners be called "human associates of companion animals"?

Doublespeak is outright dishonest language meant to obscure the real meaning behind the words. Don't use such language. Besides being unethical, it invites the obvious criticism that the organization is trying to hide the facts. An example of doublespeak is military terms such as calling civilian deaths "collateral damage" or genocide "ethnic cleansing." Likewise, references to employee layoffs as "downsizing," "rightsizing," "employee repositioning," "workforce readjustment" or "retirement for personnel reasons." Bureaucratic reports have called drunkenness a "nonsober condition" and suicide on a train track "pedestrian involvement."

Unfortunately, many examples of doublespeak are associated with governmental agencies and officials who, through such language, betray an appalling lack of commitment to transparency and honest communication necessary in a democratic society. For example, the Secret Service in the second Bush administration had local police set up "free speech zones" to keep protesters far removed from the visiting president or vice president—and from the television cameras. Business and other organizational leaders, too, have demonstrated far too much creativity in concocting language that clouds, rather than illuminates, and deceitful language that fails the transparency test.

The task for practitioners of strategic communication is to avoid dishonest language for themselves and to counsel their organizations and clients to avoid it as well. There are two reasons for this. One is the ethical consideration, because it's the right thing to do. The other is the practical benefit that honest and clear language provides the best means to communicate effectively and thus to generate understanding and continuing support.

LEGAL LANGUAGE

Strategic communicators also are familiar with laws affecting their choice of language, and they respect both the letter and the spirit of such laws.

Defamation is a legal condition to be avoided at all costs. Defamatory language meets a fivefold test: It (1) is false information; (2) is published or communicated to a third party; (3) identifies a person; and (4) holds that person up to public hatred, contempt, or ridicule, while (5) involving some measure of negligence and/or malice on the part of the communicator. Defamation is classified either as **libel**, which is written or broadcast defamation, or **slander**, which is spoken defamation.

A related area of problematic language is information that intrudes on someone's **privacy**, which is the legal right to be left alone.

These language indiscretions generally can be avoided if you pay attention to ethical principles, such as those found in the professional conduct codes of such organizations as the Public Relations Society of America and the Canadian Public Relations Society. Such codes call upon practitioners to adhere to high standards of accuracy, honesty, fairness, truth, and concern for the public interest.

Nonverbal Communication

Nonverbal communication occurs through actions and cues other than words that carry meaning. Images and ambience create the most powerful and enduring aspects of communication.

When the words say "I'm happy to be here" but the facial expression shows boredom or disdain, we tend to believe our eyes. Likewise, corporate spokespersons who use facial or other body language associated with hedging and lying limit their effectiveness in gaining audience trust. Some of the 24-hour news and talk TV networks have begun hiring "body language experts" to dissect nonverbal cues of politicians and other newsmakers.

Nonverbal communication provides individuals and groups with many options for presenting or enhancing their messages. Here are some of the uses of nonverbal communication:

- To create impressions beyond the verbal element of communication
- To repeat and reinforce what is said verbally

- To manage and regulate the interaction among participants in the communication exchange
- To express emotion beyond the verbal element
- To convey relational messages of affection, power, dominance, respect, and so on
- To promote honest communication by detecting deception or conveying suspicion
- To provide group or social leadership by sending messages of power and persuasion

Much communication occurs not through words but through visual messages. Nonverbal communication has several elements dealing with body language, eye contact, social space, touching, vocal cues, and the use of time as an element of communication. Let's look briefly at each.

Kinesics

Kinesics deals with body language, sometimes called **affective displays**. It may deal with the body as a whole or with specific parts, particularly the face, hands, and arms. Kinesics also deals with body posture and with eye and facial expressions such as arching the eyebrows or rolling the eyes. Sign language is not part of kinesics.

Kinesics varies culturally, with significant differences in using hand movements, frowning, and so on. Smiling, for example, is universally associated with happiness. But in some cultures, smiling also is used to mask sadness, and giggling sometimes hides embarrassment or nervousness.

This aspect of nonverbal communication includes emblems, which are physical gestures that support or reinforce what is said verbally. Some emblems are universal, such as the uplifted shoulders and upturned hands to indicate "I don't know."

Other emblems are culture-bound. Consider the emblem of the encircled thumb and forefinger. That gesture can be interpreted as worthless in France; money in Japan; OK in the U.S.; a curse in Arab cultures; and an obscenity in Germany, Brazil, and Australia.

Hinduism, Buddhism, and Christianity traditionally use specific hand gestures in art and in the practice of prayer and meditation. Images of the Buddha often show hand gestures, called mudras, to express a particular theme: compassion, patience, welcoming, divinity, and so on. Similarly, images and icons of Jesus and the saints, especially those within the Orthodox tradition, feature specific hand gestures for blessing, peace, prayer, and so on.

Meanwhile, obscene inferences are imbedded in any number of gestures. Depending on the culture, the raised middle finger, a thumbs up, the A-OK sign, raising the fist and slapping the biceps at the same time, and the "V" sign with the back of the hand all mean the same thing. Add mooning to the list of obscene gestures implying the greatest of insults.

Gestures also arise from social or political situations. The hands-up gesture became commonplace among protestors and civil rights advocates in 2014 after a white policeman in Ferguson, Mo., shot and killed black teenager Michael Brown. The gesture became a rallying cry across the country for people protesting excessive police force, especially in minority communities.

Other gestures with cultural overtones include crossing legs, kissing on the cheek, pointing, and slurping while eating.

Occulesics

Closely related to kinesics is **occulesics**. It deals with eye behavior as an element of communication, such as a fixed gaze versus dynamic eye movement.

Eye contact is the subject of much interpretation by the observer, and much of it varies culturally. In the West, for example, direct eye contact (looking into the eyes of the other person) is common about 40 percent of the time while talking with someone and 70 percent while listening.

In Japan, it is more common to look at the throat of the other person. In China and Indonesia, the practice is to lower the eyes because direct eye contact is considered bad manners, while in Hispanic culture direct eye contact may be interpreted as a form of challenge and disrespect. In Arab culture, it is common for both speakers and listeners to look directly into each other's eyes for long periods of time, indicating keen interest in the conversation.

Proxemics

The social use of space in a communication situation is called **proxemics**. One aspect of this is the closeness between people when they speak, and the significant rule that culture plays in this. Distance generally is described on a continuum from intimate space (zero–18 inches), personal space (18 inches–4 feet), social space (4–12 feet) and public space (beyond 12 feet).

This, too, is associated with culture. In Northern Europe and North America, personal space is greater than in Asian, Middle Eastern, Mediterranean, and Latin American settings. African culture is diverse, but personal space generally is less than in North America.

Proxemics also deals with the effective use of space in social settings, such as businesses and homes, and the arrangement of space to encourage or inhibit communication.

Haptics

Touching as an element of communication is the subject of **haptics**. This includes both the frequency and intensity of touching.

Like so many other aspects of nonverbal communication, haptics is very much a function of culture. Mediterranean, Middle Eastern, Southern Asian, and Latin American cultures use much social touching in conversation, including embraces and handholding. In many places it is not uncommon for people of the same gender to hold hands without any sexual connotation. These are known as high-touch or high-contact cultures.

Moderate-touch cultures are associated with North America and Northern Europe, where touching is used only occasionally, such as in handshakes and sporadic shoulder touching or back slapping. In low-contact cultures such as in Northern Asian cultures, meanwhile, social touching in public is rarely done at all.

Additionally, culture influences other aspects of touching, including whether men and women should shake hands.

Vocalics

The category of **vocalics** or **paralanguage** deals with vocal cues such as accent, loudness, tempo, pitch, cadence, rate of speech, and nasality and tone. Vocalics includes several subcategories:

- Vocal characterizers include laughing, crying, yawning, burping, and so on.
- Vocal qualifiers such as volume, pitch, rhythm and tempo are associated with cultural distinctions. For example, speaking loudly indicates sincerity in Arab culture, whereas in North America it often is interpreted as aggressive.
- Vocal segregates are sounds such as "mmmm," "uh-huh," "oooo," and so on. These also differ greatly among various cultures.
- Vocal rate deals with the speed at which people talk, another factor that offers various interpretations.

Chronemics

Chronemics deals with the use of time as an element of communication. It includes specifics such as punctuality, dominance or deference within a communication exchange, and the use of **monochronemics** (doing or talking about only one thing at a time) versus **polychronemics** (doing or talking about several things at a time).

The impact of chronemics can vary with social settings, such as the likelihood among Americans of arriving early for business meetings but being "fashionably late" for social activities.

In Latin and Arab cultures, business people often arrive at a time Westerners would consider "late," taking business meetings as occasions for hospitality and socializing.

Meanwhile, in the Native American community, people often talk about "Indian time," with the notion that things will happen when they happen. The Sioux language doesn't even have a word for "late," reflecting this very relaxed cultural attitude toward time.

Visual and Aural Communication

Two other elements of nonverbal communication are visual and aural. Various sights and sounds can greatly impact the quality of communication.

Most communication relies not only on words but also on other elements of sight and sound that carry messages: images, symbols, setting, mood, music, clothing, and so on. In fact, many experts note that such nonverbal communication accounts for the majority of shared meaning among people.

Here is an overview of some of the most common visual and aural aspects related to nonverbal communication.

Symbol

As visual representations of realities beyond themselves, **symbols** are among the most effective ways to communicate. Good symbols have a complex and rich psychological impact on people who see and use them.

Baby harp seals and pink breast-cancer ribbons have generated widespread public acceptance for the causes associated with them. Armbands associated with the Holocaust or classic news photos of 9/11 can evoke a powerful emotional response years after those events. Personal keepsakes from childhood, proms, weddings, and special vacations summon up emotions over a lifetime.

Some of the most enduring symbols are rooted in religion (such as the crescent, cross, Star of David, and Madonna figure) and country (monuments such as the Statue of Liberty and especially the flag).

A nation's flag is more than a piece of cloth. To many people it is the symbol of family, country, patriotism, duty, and honor. It is something many have been willing both to die for or kill for. As such, it has the power to inspire devotion and to invite disrespect, and much energy has been spent in nations around the world on the issue of the appropriate role the national flag plays in both patriotism and social protest.

In some countries, the national flag may symbolize less about reverence and patriotism and more about social cohesiveness and cultural exuberance.

Symbols also can become the source of controversy. When Marines posed with an American flag and twin lightning bolts reminiscent of the Nazi SS of World War II, the Corps quickly moved to apologize. Military officials said the Marines made a naive mistake, intending the symbols to stand for Sniper Scouts. The Corps used the incident as a teaching tool to explain to troops about the interpretation and acceptability of symbols.

Likewise, Proctor and Gamble quickly apologized for "any false connotations" after displaying a soccer jersey with large numerals "18," which some consumers interpreted as a neo-Nazi code. Far-right extremists in Germany have used the number as a symbol of Adolph Hitler (referencing the first and eighth letters of the alphabet). Similarly, companies sometimes skip numbers such as four, seven, 13, and 666 because for some people they have connotations with evil or bad luck.

Symbolic meaning is an aspect of culture and, as such, can sometimes change. An example of the controversial aspects of flags is the passion surrounding the Confederate flag. Though the civil war occurred 150 years ago, the Confederate flag didn't become an object for public display until 50 years ago, when several Southern states adopted it as a sign of their opposition to civil rights. After the 2015 massacre of nine people in a South Carolina church by a white supremacist, several states moved with lightning speed to retire the flag to museums, and many businesses around the nation eliminated the Confederate symbol from their merchandise.

This is much like the manner in which the Nazis in Germany had usurped the swastika. This bent-cross figure had been a nearly universal religious symbol sacred to Hinduism and Buddhism and used in early Christianity, Islam, and some Native American religions. But after Hitler adopted it as his flag emblem, the swastika came to be irrevocably associated with the Nazi regime and white supremacy. So despised is the symbol that it is illegal to display it in Germany, Hungary, Poland, Lithuania, and Brazil.

Logo

Corporate **logos** are special kinds of symbols that visually identify businesses, nonprofit organizations and other groups. Contemporary or traditional? Elegant or casual? Much attention goes into the development of a corporate logo, which needs to present the right image and send the proper message.

Consider the promotional value and enduring impact of the Nike "swoosh" or the Dodge star. For an organizational symbol to be effective, it must be both memorable and appropriate for the organization. It also must be unique to the organization, one reason that much legal energy is spent protecting registered trademarks.

Physical Artifact

Symbolic value is sometimes attached to physical artifacts, such as the gavel used by a presiding judge or the badge worn by a police officer.

Over the years, cigarettes have been variously presented as symbols of independence, youth, rebellion, ruggedness, and adventure. Automobiles are presented as symbolic mirrors of the people who drive them. And it was the symbolic power of the Pentagon and the World Trade Center as icons of America that led terrorists to target those buildings on 9/11.

When a Florida Christian preacher organized a Burn the Quran rally and when U.S. troops in Afghanistan burned the Islamic scriptures, several people died in waves of anti-American protests in the Middle East and Central Asia. All this was because of the symbolic value of the Quran, ironically a value recognized by both the desecration-intent preacher and troops as well as the reacting protestors.

Clothing

A particular type of physical artifact—clothing—often takes on symbolic proportions. This is why much attention often is paid to military uniforms, academic attire, religious vestments, ethnic apparel, or royal garb, where each design element often has a special meaning. When President George W. Bush wore a Navy flight suit on an aircraft carrier to proclaim the end of the war in Iraq, his choice of clothing got a strong reaction—both pro and con.

Small controversies sometimes arise over the symbolism of clothing, particularly for women, such as the appropriate dress for nurses, Catholic nuns, or Muslim women.

Attention also is given to less formal but nonetheless powerful symbols such as designer clothing or trendy brand-name eyeglasses. For persuasive purposes, a spokesperson might wear clothing related to a particular profession or occupation as a way of suggesting expertise.

People

Even people can function as symbols—especially royalty such as a king or queen, religious figures such as the Dalai Lama or the Pope, and other important and well-known characters. As symbols, they stand as more than human beings. They represent the dignity and prestige of the office they hold.

Media attention given to scandals involving princes, presidents, and prime ministers, however, has weakened the symbolic value of such figures.

Mascot

Another kind of symbol is the mascot. From Smokey Bear to the San Diego Chicken, Philly Phanatic to Herbie Husker of the University of Nebraska Cornhuskers, mascots embody much of the spirit of an organization.

Many companies and organizations also use promotional characters such as Ronald McDonald, the U.S. Postal Service eagle, the Aflac duck, and the Geico gecko.

The symbolic significance of such fictional personifications can change. Betty Crocker and Aunt Jemima have gotten younger and more professional looking each decade as their company's customers have changed. Sports teams are under increasing pressure to retire their Native American mascots, which many people find offensive and archaic.

Color

Colors also can be symbolic or emblematic—green for environmental issues, pink for breast cancer and for Owens-Corning fiberglass insulation, rainbow colors for gay rights, and so on.

The symbolic value of colors is socially defined. For example, the Western identification of black for funerals is not universally shared. In fact, in many parts of the world, white is the appropriate color associated with death and funerals. This is something that communicators in international or multicultural settings need to consider.

National colors—red in Canada; red, white, and blue in the U.S. and U.K.; green, white, and red in Italy, blue and white in Israel and Argentina, and so on—often become visual symbols of the countries themselves.

Music

Music has a special symbolic value. Songs such as "Auld Lang Syne," "God Bless America," and "Pomp and Circumstance" have special meanings related to New Year's Eve, patriotic holidays, and graduation respectively. The next time you go to the movies, pay attention to the power of the background music in setting the right mood for romance, happiness, impending doom, and so on.

Music also can stir negative passions. The singing of the national anthem at sporting events sometimes results in perceived disrespect by players or fans, or disapproval of the musical style or behavior of the singers themselves.

A controversy was sparked by the Ice Bowl on New Year's Day in 2008 with the Pittsburgh Penguins at the Buffalo Sabers, the highest-ranking game for the National Hockey League in 12 years. In Buffalo, because of its proximity to Ontario, it is standard to sing both the U.S. and Canadian anthems at all hockey games. Irish tenor/Saber's fan Ronan Tynan opened the game with "God Bless America" instead of the national anthem. Then the Saber's regular anthem singer sang the Canadian national anthem. For days, critics complained about the appropriateness of the musical selections.

Passions were stirred in 1999 when Japan's parliament approved a law making the traditional "Kimigayo" the official national anthem. The vote over the imperial hymn, Japan's unofficial anthem since before World War II, revived bitter memories and renewed the controversy over nationalism and war guilt. Much of the debate centered on schools, particularly on how children should be educated about the war and the role of national symbols such as the anthem and the flag in school ceremonies.

Consider also the role of music in presidential campaigns. The tradition goes back to the early days of the nation, but it has taken off in recent years as candidates issue official playlists of music associated with their campaigns. Barack Obama's 2012 playlist included 24 songs and artists.

Here's a brief list of recent electoral music: Donald Trump "We Are the Champions" (Queen), Hillary Clinton "Takin' Care of Business" (Bachman-Turner Overdrive), Obama "Yes We Can" (will.i.am), Mitt Romney "Born Free" (Kidd Rock), John McCain "Take a Chance on Me" (ABBA), Al Gore "You Ain't Seen Nothin' Yet" (Bachman-Turner Overdrive), and Bill Clinton "Don't Stop Thinking about Tomorrow" (Fleetwood Mac).

But campaign music is not without controversy, because licensing arrangements by the American Society of Composers, Authors and Publishers, popularly known as ASCAP, stipulates that using a song in a political campaign implies that the artist is endorsing the candidate and thus requires permission. During the 2016 campaign season, Axwell and Ingrosso told candidate Marco Rubio to stop using "Something New" because they didn't want to be associated with his campaign. The same was true for Neil Young and his song "Rockin' in the Free World" picked up by candidate Donald Trump, who had similar wave-offs from R.E.M. and Adele. Meanwhile, Scott Walker's campaign received this tweet: "Please don't use our music in any way. We literally hate you!!! Love, Dropkick Murphys."

Language

In some contexts, language itself can be symbolic. Consider the cultural symbolism of Hebrew, Latin, Arabic, Hindi, and other languages associated with religious traditions. Consider also the recurring English-as-official-language controversy that appeals to populist feelings within American politics, the political aspects of the resurgence of Gaelic languages in Scotland and Wales, and the French versus English debate in Quebec.

Consider also how some of the "in" language used by groups of teens, for example, has a symbolism for its users that is neither appreciated nor understood—nor meant to be—by outsiders.

PLANNING EXAMPLE 6C **Verbal and Nonverbal Communication**

Here is an outline of the verbal and nonverbal communication strategies for Upstate College.

Verbal Communication

- One point of view will be presented: expansion is beneficial for students, the community and the college.
- A conclusion will be drawn: students should consider Upstate College.
- Message clarity will be enhanced by a Fog Index level of tenth grade.
- Messages will include power words such as "benefit to community" and "quality education."
- Messages will avoid any exaggeration.
- Messages will rely on facts and documentation rather than empty claims.

Nonverbal Communication

- The college logo will be featured in messages.
- Upbeat music popular with teens and young adults will be featured in messages.
- The college mascot, salamander "Upstate Eddie," will be featured.

Here is an outline of the verbal and nonverbal communication strategies for Tiny Tykes Toys.

Verbal Communication
- Opposing points of view will be included in messages: Tiny Tykes is committed to toy safety; the company had a problem in the past but has learned from mistakes and now is recommitted to toy safety.
- A conclusion will be drawn: the company now makes high-quality, safe toys and deserves consumer support.
- Message clarity will be enhanced by a Fog Index level of ninth grade.
- Messages will include power words such as "commitment to excellence" and "baby safe."
- Messages will avoid any exaggeration.
- Messages will rely on facts and documentation rather than empty claims.

Nonverbal Communication
- Messages will be enhanced by happy music.
- Corporate spokespersons will be shown wearing research and professional clothing, reinforcing the message of research and high standards.
- Clinical settings will be used for presentations by corporate spokespersons, reinforcing the message of research and high standards.

 Checklist 6C **Verbal and Nonverbal Communication**

Basic Questions

1. How does your message use verbal communication?
2. How does your message use nonverbal communication?
3. How can either be made stronger?

Expanded Questions

A. VERBAL COMMUNICATION

Message Structure
1. Does your message present only one point of view or more than one (opposing) point of view? If more than one point of view is presented, is your message sandwiched (stating your argument, noting the opposing argument, and finally restating your argument and refuting the opposing argument)?
2. Does your message present a conclusion?
3. Does your message reiterate its main idea?

Phase Two

STEP
6

Clarity

1. Will your publics find your message clear, simple and understandable?
2. What is the education level of your target public?
3. How does this compare with the Fog Index for your written message?

Power Words

1. Have you used powerful language in your message?
2. Does your product/program have a descriptive and memorable name?
3. Does your product/program have a descriptive and memorable slogan?

Ethical Language

1. Does your message use pretentious or exaggerated language?
2. Does your message use dishonest or misleading language?
3. Does your message use defamatory language?
4. How could any of these verbal elements be made stronger?

B. NONVERBAL COMMUNICATION

1. Does the presentation of your message include a symbol, a logo, music, symbolic language, symbolic physical artifacts, symbolic clothing, symbolic people, a mascot, symbolic use of color and/or a symbolic setting?
2. How could any of these nonverbal elements be made stronger?

CONSENSUS CHECK

Does agreement exist within your organization and your planning team about the recommended strategies included within this step of the planning process?

☐ Yes. Proceed to the next section, Branding the Strategic Message, and then on to Step 7, Selecting Communication Tactics.

☐ No. Consider the value and/or possibility of achieving consensus before proceeding

Branding the Strategic Message

A concept drawn from marketing that should be part of strategic communication planning is **branding**, which is the creation of a clear and consistent message for an organization. If one traditional description of public relations is valid—that public relations is doing good and receiving credit for it—then it can be said that branding is seeing that truth well told.

A **brand** is the articulation of an organization's purpose, the way it is presented to customers, employees, and other publics. The value of a brand is its ability to convey a message and associate the corporate name with a favorable concept in the mind of the consumer or other public.

Branding is rooted in an organization's strategic communication plan, shaping a messaging strategy to express its purpose and character so that audiences will understand it and differentiate it from other organizations.

The goal of branding is to foster understanding and goodwill, and to encourage participation and support. Strong brands come from what people say about you, not on what you say about yourself. That's one of the differences between public relations and advertising.

Corporations have used the concept of branding for years. Because it evolved in the corporate world, economic competition sometimes has taken the form of warfare. A car dealership has "the greatest deals in town," this toothpaste cleans "better than all the rest." There are good guys and bad, heroes and villains, us and them.

It might be unseemly for a university to proclaim itself the best in the state, or for a hospital to slam the competition. But nonprofit organizations and other non-business entities can work with a competitive concept. The enemy probably won't be another organization, but it might easily be an intangible foe. Even wholesome organizations and uplifting causes have foes to address. In fact, branding can fit particularly well with nonprofit organizations, for which the creation of an emotional perception is a natural goal of a communication campaign.

Thus the American Heart Association may declare war on obesity, the Anti-Defamation League can see religious bigotry as the enemy, and People for the Ethical Treatment of Animals might demonize some values of the fashion industry.

Consider some of the ideas presented by the National Mentoring Center and the U.S. Department of Education as part of a marketing panel for a program seeking male mentors for inner-city children.

- "We're looking for a few good MENtors."
- "Mentor one child. Change two lives."
- "See a man. Become a man."
- "Been there? Done that? Pass it on. Become a mentor."

Language of Branding

Previously in this step of the strategic planning process, we focused on verbal communication, particularly on developing the content of strategic messages. Particularly with an eye on branding, we can look to both verbal and nonverbal communication approaches toward creating an image for a business of nonprofit organization.

A **slogan** is the succinct catchphrase in a communication program. This sometimes is called a **verbal logo**. Along with an organization's graphic logo, the tagline presents a concise-yet-comprehensive message that identifies the organization and seeks to position it in the mind of consumers and other publics.

Often the term **tagline**, once associated mainly with marketing, is used in reference to slogans used for public relations and other promotional purposes. Serving more or less as a battle cry, a tagline can be quite effective, especially during the awareness phase of a strategic communication campaign.

Corporate advertising has created many notable taglines: Nokia "Connecting People," Nike "Just do it," Allstate "You're in good hands," and Kay Jewelers "Every kiss begins with Kay." Nonprofit organizations also have branded themselves with memorable taglines: Greenpeace "Take action for the climate" and March of Dimes "Saving babies, together." State tourism slogans such as "Find Yourself Here" for California, "Virginia is for Lovers" and "I ❤ New York" have been effective because they are both clear and open to having various interpretations.

Many effective taglines are associated with social movements or organizations. They serve the purpose of what anthropologists call **symbolic consensus**, a rallying cry for supporters. Consider these taglines of longstanding use associated with social causes: National Rifle Association "Guns don't kill people; people kill people," U.S. Forest Service "Only you can prevent wild fires," and United Negro College Fund "A mind is a terrible thing to waste."

What began as a hashtag slogan, "Black Lives Matter," after Trayvon Martin was shot in Florida in 2013 morphed into a movement after a string of other racially linked killings of black men by law-enforcement personnel. The movement created chapters in cities in the U.S., Canada, and Ghana.

The Seneca Nation of Indians developed a strong verbal logo amid an ongoing public controversy over state attempts to levy taxes on Indian lands. The Western New York-based tribe has a treaty with the federal government that business conducted in its territory is immune from state taxes. Using the slogan "Break a treaty, break the law," the campaign forced four successive New York governors to back away from plans to push for taxation.

The entertainment media use taglines aimed at potential audiences. Thus the film *Alien* promoted its sci-fi horror genre ("In space, no one can hear you scream"), the movie sequel *Saw II* drew on earlier success with the slogan "Oh yes, there will be blood," and *Scary Movie 2* appealed to a teen audience with the tagline "More sex! More blood! Less taste!" Humor was the theme for the tagline for *The Simpsons Movie* ("See our family and feel better about yours") and *The 40-Year-Old Virgin* ("The longer you wait, the harder it gets").

ESPN achieved ratings increases for the sports network and several marketing awards after it opted for a serial tagline. Some of the print and TV spots were serious: "Without sports, how would we know what we're made of?" But most had a humorous twist: "Without sports, what would we do over the holidays?" "Without sports, would you know how to spell J-E-T-S?" "Without sports, weekends would be weekdays."

Closely related to a slogan or a tagline is a **service mark**, which is a word and phrase that marketing and public relations people develop to be closely associated with organizations. Essentially, these are taglines that have been registered, much as trademarks are, to protect a service rather than a product.

Examples of well-known service marks are the Army's "Be all you can be," Budweiser's "This Bud's for you," and Nike's "Just do it." Burger King is the only restaurant that can legally claim to be the "Home of the Whopper" and *The New York Times* is the only paper that can claim to have "All the news that's fit to print."

Nonprofits also use such branding successfully. The University of Texas at Austin uses the tagline "What starts here changes the world." Homeboy Industries, which helps gang-involved youth, proclaims, "Nothing stops a bullet like a job." The Sierra Club enjoins people to "Explore, enjoy, and protect the planet." Catholic Charities focuses on "Providing help. Creating hope." Camp Fire USA touts "Today's kids. Tomorrow's leaders." Meanwhile "Only kids. Only Phoenix Children's Hospital" is a tagline for the only hospital in Arizona focused on children.

Corporate lawyers are vigilant in monitoring the use of trademarks, which include more than product names and slogans. College and sports mascots, Disney and the Peanuts characters, and Barbie and Ken dolls are protected by trademarks.

Trademark law was front and center when a double amputee-cancer survivor fan of the Buffalo Bills created a website titled 12thManThunder. The title was a reference to stadium fans being called the 12th man on the football team. But "12th man" is copyrighted by Texas A&M University, which threatened a lawsuit over the website name. Two NFL teams (the Bills and the Seattle Seahawks) pay royalties for permission to use the term, but that doesn't extend to their fan groups. After hearing from A&M's lawyers, the fan changed the name of his website.

Lessons about Branding

Good branding is a twofer, and getting two for the price of one is usually a good thing. It can help an organization (1) by defining and differentiating you in the minds of publics, particularly customers, and (2) by providing a structure to convey a consistent message.

Consider some of the branding strategies associated with businesses. Volvo brands itself as the car for safety. Maytag presents a message of dependability. Starbucks takes premium coffee as a given and brands itself as for community-mindedness. Holiday Inn boasts about "Pleasing people the world over" and Timex highlights durability with its slogan "Takes a licking and keeps on ticking." DeBeers' advertising line appeals to the sentiment of couples who see their relationship as permanent: "A diamond is forever."

Here are 15 suggestions about taglines:

1. Don't mistake a tagline for a proverb or a maxim, and don't think it's merely a mission statement, though that may suggest key phrases that can be developed into a branding message.
2. Make the tagline memorable. Cadence, rhythm, and rhyme can enhance this.
3. Keep the tagline short and succinct. Some suggest that seven or eight words should be the maximum.
4. Look at the organizational goals and allow the tagline to energize them, as in the Salvation Army's "Doing the most good."
5. Use a branding tagline to highlight your unique situation and to distinguish you from competitors and colleagues alike, as in Altoids' "Curiously strong peppermints."
6. Focus on a benefit, as in the American Society for the Prevention of Cruelty to Animals' "We are their voice."
7. Focus on a potential, as in St. Jude's Children's Hospital's "Finding cures. Saving children."
8. Offer a challenge, as in "The few. The proud. The Marines" and "The Marines are looking for a few good men" (a slogan first used in a Navy recruiting ad in 1779).
9. Draw on a positive association with your product or service, as in Hershey Chocolates' website, "The sweetest site on the net."
10. Address the wants and needs of your audience, as in "Wheaties, the Breakfast of Champions."
11. Turn a disadvantage into an opportunity, as in No. 2 car rental company Avis's "We try harder."

BRAINSTORMING FOR BRANDING

How do people come up with ideas for branding messages? The process isn't magical. It doesn't require genius, and it isn't necessarily rooted in lightning-bolt inspiration. But there are ways to create creativity, or at least to create a process where creative ideas can ripen.

An easy-to-apply group creativity technique called **brainstorming** is a useful tool in this part of the strategic planning process. Brainstorming is associated with the effective creativity addressed in the introduction to this book.

The first step in brainstorming is **divergence**, in which the group surfaces a large number of ideas on how to solve a problem or answer a question. Here's how it can work. Assemble a small team of people to consider questions such as the following:

- What do we want people to remember about our organization? Example: Pepsi wants you to make "The choice of a new generation."
- What do we want them to do? Example: The Yellow Pages people distilled this question into "Let your fingers do the walking."
- What feeling do we want to evoke, or what attitude do we want to bring to mind? Example: United Cerebral Palsy suggests "Life without limits for people with disabilities."
- What is our niche, or how are we different or unique? Example: M&Ms candies set themselves apart from other candy with "Melts in your mouth, not in your hands."

Do you have any artifacts associated with your organization? These might be personal items such as clothing and grooming, or cultural elements such as music, art, and architecture. Disney draws on images of its theme parks with the slogan "The happiest place on earth." Here are a few rules for effective brainstorming:

- Write down every idea.
- Don't edit or censor yourself.
- Put criticism on hold, because nothing is too "far out" at this point.
- Work with your colleagues on the brainstorming team, tossing around ideas and building on each other's contributions.
- Get as many different ideas as possible on the table.
- Consider each one, and see how many variations you can come up with.

The next step in the brainstorming process is **convergence**. As you pare down the list, select those few that are worth further consideration. With all of the ideas on the table, consider each one. It's best to have each member of the team rank each idea individually. Then compare results and hold on to those that seem most useful to the group.

At this point, you might want to get the input from others beyond the brainstorming team. Take the top three or four ideas to a wider group, perhaps a formal focus group.

12. Look for the inspiration, as in United Negro College Fund's "A mind is a terrible thing to waste."
13. Go with a pun. The public radio station at Morehouse State College, a historically black college in Atlanta, turned the tables with a health program called "A Waist Is a Terrible Thing to Mind."
14. Focus on a characteristic or quality, as in Chevy trucks' "Like a rock."
15. Focus on an attitude, as in Nike's "Just do it."

Note that, from a legal perspective, taglines are service marks, which enjoy protection similar to trademarks.

What's Next?

This is the end of Step 6, in which you have developed the message for your key publics.

This step also concludes Phase Two, the Strategy phase of the planning process for public relations and marketing communication. Having completed the three steps in this phase, which have built on those of the Formative Research phase, you now should have a clear sense of direction for your program.

Before going any further, present your planning thus far to the decision makers, such as your client or boss. Gain the buy-in from the key decision makers in your organization. They need to agree with the direction you suggest, with the objectives and with the resulting strategy recommendations. If there is not agreement, this is the time to rework the strategy before forging ahead.

In the next phase of planning, you will turn your attention to preparing and implementing specific communication tools to carry the strategic message you have just devised.

Phase Two

STEP
6

PHASE THREE

TACTICS

If the strategy phase of the planning process provided the skeleton and muscles for your communication programming, then Phase Three is the flesh. This section deals specifically with **tactics**, which are the things people see. Tactics are the visible elements of a public relations or marketing communication plan.

In the introduction to *Strategic Planning for Public Relations*, you encountered the concept of **integrated communication**. This is the conscious blending of the instruments of both public relations and marketing communication. Integrated communication creates a comprehensive and cohesive program aimed at implementing the best possible mix of communication tools.

It is here in Phase Three that this integrated approach will become most visible, as you consider the various communication tools that can be used to achieve your objectives. The menu of tactics outlined in this phase features communication tools drawn from the full range of disciplines and specialties. These break down into four sections.

1. First are interpersonal communication opportunities that involve speeches and special events.
2. Then, you look to organizational media, including conventional tools such as newsletters and websites, as well as social media such as Twitter and Facebook. This is the category of owned media.
3. Next on the menu is a full plate of tactics involving the journalistic side of the news media, both traditional and newer digital types of media. This is called earned media.
4. Finally, you consider tactics associated with advertising and promotion, the category of paid media.

The activities in Phase Three will also lead you to select an effective mix of tactics, packaging your creative and strategic ideas into a comprehensive program. To accomplish this, you need to tap into your creative side. Your goal as you work through the two steps associated with Phase Three is to boost your plan well beyond the level of a mere laundry list of tactics. Instead, you attempt to create a compelling and resourceful action plan that can help your client organization achieve its goals and objectives.

You also will deal with the administrative details of budgeting and scheduling that are so important for the smooth implementation of your plan. This tactics phase calls for the twin skills of creativity and attention to detail. All aspects of implementation involve many components, and the person who can manage simultaneous tasks skillfully should find success in the field of strategic communication.

The need for micromanaging the various tasks might seem overwhelming at first. But by remaining focused on your plan, you will avoid unnecessary side trips that sap your time and drain your resources without advancing you toward your goal.

At the same time, effective tactics call for a measure of creativity and innovation. Together, these produce a certain spark that separates the ordinary from the unusual, replacing the commonplace with the memorable and exceptional.

STEP 7

Selecting Communication Tactics

A communication tactic is the visible element of a strategic plan. This is what people see and do: websites and news releases, tours and billboards, blogs and special events, and so much more. Tactics are also the elements of the plan that can carry a hefty price tag, so planning and coordination are particularly important.

The range of communication tactics is extensive, and it is continually growing because of technological advances. Step 7 offers you a convenient menu of the various tactics. These tactics should be considered in light of your goals and objectives, evaluated in relationship to each other, matched to the taste of the organization and the publics, and chosen with an eye toward time and budget constraints.

At a restaurant, you wouldn't order every item on the menu. Likewise, don't try every tactic you can think of. Instead, review this menu of public relations tactics carefully, then select a full plate of items appropriate to the situation you are addressing.

Before we review the menu, let's look at some of the conventional categories of communication tactics, along with a description of the distinctions this book uses.

Conventional Communication Tactics

Media and media tactics are often divided into categories based on distinguishing features. Here are several frequently used pairs that describe types of media. These are based on factors such as organizational control, organizational ties, audience size, audience type, audience interaction, media ownership, media production, and media orientation. Each categorization can be useful, but as we will see, these conventional communication categories have some limitations as well.

ORGANIZATIONAL CONTROL

One category of media is based on the organization's ability to control the content, timing, packaging, and audience access of its messages.

Controlled media allow the organization to determine various attributes of the message—most notably its content, but also its timing, presentation, packaging, tone, and distribution.

Examples of controlled media are newsletters, brochures, advertisements, corporate videos, blogs, and websites.

Conversely, **uncontrolled media** are those in which someone unrelated to the organization, such as a media gatekeeper, determines those message attributes. Examples of uncontrolled media tactics include news conferences and interviews.

ORGANIZATIONAL LINK

Another category of media describes the relationship of the media to the organization, specifically whether these media are internal to the organization or external to it.

Internal media exist within the organization and thus parallel the previous definition of controlled media, with the exception of advertising.

External media, which exist outside the organization, may be controlled (such as advertising media) or uncontrolled (such as news media). Specific examples include billboards, newspapers, and television news broadcasts.

AUDIENCE SIZE

Still another category is defined by the size and breadth of the intended audience.

Mass media are those that are accessible to most people. Thus they are media that enjoy vast audiences, such as television networks and the mainstream daily newspaper establishment.

On the other hand, **targeted media** have not only much narrower but also more homogeneous audiences. Examples of targeted media are special-interest publications (such as a magazine for people who live aboard sailboats), broadcast programs that appeal to a particular narrow audience (such as a program on retirement finances), and special-interest cable networks (such as the DIY Network or a religion channel).

AUDIENCE TYPE

Media also can be categorized by audience type, with differences between those media available to a wide audience and those that can be accessed primarily by a more narrow audience.

Popular media focus on information of interest to people in their personal lives, including fashion, grooming, relationships, hobbies, and self-help, as well as news and current events. These are the publications found online or at the supermarket or bookstore. Examples of popular media include *Maxim*, *USA Today*, and top-of-the-hour radio news broadcasts.

Trade media, on the other hand, generally are distributed via subscription and are read for professional or business purposes. They are a main focus for many public relations writers. Examples of trade media include *Auto Glass Journal* and *Wine Business Monthly*.

AUDIENCE INTERACTION

Some media can be described as one-way communication vehicles while others are two-way in nature.

One-way media allow an organization to send messages to an audience without the likelihood of significant feedback. Examples of one-way communication tactics are brochures, television commercials, speeches, and news releases.

On the other hand, **interactive media** have two-way capabilities. They allow organizations to talk with their audiences. Examples of two-way communication tactics are social media, blogs, question–answer sessions, teleconferences, and in-person news conferences.

MEDIA OWNERSHIP

Another categorization defined by the audience, mainly in terms of availability and access, is public versus nonpublic media.

Public media generally are accessible to everybody. Examples of public media are local newspapers and both commercial and public radio and television stations.

Nonpublic media are more restricted in their coverage and their availability. They often choose to limit access and circulation to audiences drawn from specific occupations, professions, or associations. Examples of nonpublic media are company newsletters, email newsgroups, and magazines and other trade publications that circulate mainly to members of a particular industry or profession.

MEDIA PRODUCTION

This categorization of media is based on the technical production methods of the medium.

Print media are those that involve the printed word, such as newsletters, newspapers, and magazines.

Electronic media are based on newer technologies. Examples of electronic media include television (both broadcast and cable) as well as radio.

Digital media involve the newest and emerging technologies. These are the computer-based media such as email, websites, and mobile media.

MEDIA ORIENTATION

A final category of media is based on their orientation vis-à-vis the organization.

Owned media are those that are in the possession of the organization; literally media they already own.

Earned media focuses on the new media, through which organizations need to earn coverage of their activities and issues.

Paid media include advertising and other promotional tactics for which an organization must pay.

For more information and a look at the pros and cons of each type of media orientation, review the box Owned, Earned, and Paid Media in the Introduction of this textbook.

Strategic Communication Tactics

Don't look for any single categorization style to suit every purpose. For one thing, there is a significant amount of overlap in the conventional category systems. For another, none of the classification systems is necessarily superior to the others.

Rather, use these various categories to analyze the pros and cons of each communication tool you might consider as you put together your tactical plan.

Strategic Planning for Public Relations looks at the various media and communication tactics in their complexity. In doing so, this book tries to avoid oversimplification, so you won't find media grouped according to any of the conventional categories described in the section above. This is not a rejection of the conventional approaches but rather an attempt to go beyond the inherent limitations of each.

A better way to categorize communication media and tactics is to consider their distinctiveness as they relate to the organization using them. Thus, this book presents a menu of communication tactics in four categories.

Phase Three

STEP
7

- **Interpersonal communication** offers face-to-face opportunities for personal involvement and interaction.
- **Organizational and social media** (owned media) are published or produced by the organization, which controls the message content as well as its timing, packaging, distribution, and audience access.
- **News media** (earned media) provide opportunities for the credible presentation of organizational messages to large audiences via journalistic organizations.
- **Advertising and promotional media** (paid media) are controlled media, either internal or external to the organization, that also can offer access to large audiences.

Together, these four categories offer hundreds of different communication tactics. Each can be used by organizations to communicate with their publics, though not every tool is appropriate for each issue. Remember to be selective in choosing your communication tools.

These four categories of communication tactics complement each other. In Exhibit 7.1, notice how they fit within a ying–yang pyramid pattern. This reflects the relationship between the size of the audience that each type of media can reach and the impact it can have on that audience. Interpersonal tactics may reach only a few people, but they have a stronger impact on their audiences than any other form of communication. The reverse is true of advertising and promotional media: They can reach great numbers of people, but with far less impact. Don't forget that impact often is the bottom line for a strategic communication program, whether it uses the persuasion or the dialogue model of communication.

With insight into the strengths and limitations of various kinds of media, communication planners try to create a tactical mix, using several types of communication activities to engage key publics in different ways that, when blended together, will effectively and efficiently achieve the organization's public relations or marketing objectives.

Technological advancements are offering ever more new tools for communicators. Blogs and social media are new additions to the communicator's toolbox. Satellite-based telecommunication tools make low-cost interactive conferencing a practical tactic, and land-based mobile media are expanding their scope and reach.

Interpersonal Communication Tactics

In the disciplines of public relations and marketing communication, both the academic experts who are proficient in concepts and theories, and the professional experts with applied training and practical experience agree on a crucial point: Interpersonal communication is the most persuasive and engaging of all the communication tactics.

Don't think this statement demeans other forms of communication. To the contrary, newspaper and television news reports can extend an organization's message to vast audiences. Direct mail can be a cost-effective way to reach great numbers of the key public. Advertising can present messages to large numbers of people with great precision.

In terms of influential communication, however, the effectiveness of other types of communication pales beside the vigor of direct, face-to-face, interpersonal communication.

Interpersonal communication channels can serve the needs of both businesses and nonprofit organizations, as well as entities such as politicians and entertainers. Advocates for many types of causes—from gay rights to responsible parenting, from the environment to religious liberty—have successfully used interpersonal communication tactics.

EXHIBIT 7.1 Audience Reach vis-à-vis Persuasive Impact

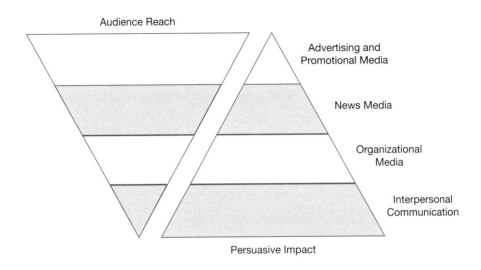

Thus, in your consideration of the various tools of communication, interpersonal methods should get your first attention.

Let's consider the strategy of using interpersonal tactics and then we'll look at the various types of face-to-face communication that can be used for public relations purposes: personal involvement, information exchange, and special events.

Strategy for Interpersonal Communication

Interpersonal communication tactics offer several strategic advantages to organizations. For one thing, they are controlled tactics through which the organization can oversee its message and the way that message is delivered. Remember, however, that audience response to the message can't be controlled.

For example, elected government officials can take their messages directly to their constituents through tactics such as town-hall meetings and blogs. But they cannot control how the audience may react to their message, the kind and intensity of questioning they may receive, even the hecklers and trash-talkers who may use the occasion to get their own message out in front of voters, news cameras, and other Twitter followers.

Like all public relations tactics, interpersonal ones can be misused if they are applied too generally. But with careful planning, they can be tailored for specific publics, both internal and external.

In terms of organizational resources, interpersonal tactics generally are relatively inexpensive. Costs associated with these tactics generally are only modest, though some types of special events can become quite expensive projects if the budget permits. Interpersonal tactics as a group claim more staff time to plan and implement than some of the other categories of tactics that we will consider.

Interpersonal tactics can work with either internal or external publics, but the organization should have some relationship with the publics for these tactics to be successful.

Interpersonal tactics have the potential to make a strong impact. They are particularly useful in achieving acceptance objectives, which is the most difficult category of objective to reach. Through interpersonal tactics, the organization can communicate with its publics in ways that can have a major effect not only on what they know but also especially on how they feel about that information. Thus interpersonal tactics are useful for both the persuasion and dialogue models of communication.

Similarly, interpersonal tactics generally involve **information-seeking publics**— people who have gone somewhat out of their way to interact with the organization. These

INTERPERSONAL COMMUNICATION TACTICS

Personal Involvement

- Organizational-site involvement (plant tour, open house, test drive, trial membership, free class, shadow program, ride along, sneak preview, premiere performance)
- Audience-site involvement (door-to-door canvassing, in-home demonstration)

Information Exchange

- Educational gathering (convention, council, convocation, synod, conclave, conference, seminar, symposium, colloquium, class, workshop, training session)
- Product exhibition (trade show)
- Meeting (annual stockholder meeting, lobbying exchange, public affairs meeting)
- Public demonstration (rally, march, picket, boycott)
- Speech (oration, talk, guest lecture, address, keynote speech, sermon, homily, panel, debate, forum, town meeting, speaker's bureau)

Special Events

- Civic event (fair, festival, carnival, circus, parade, flotilla)
- Sporting event (tournament, marathon, triathlon, outdoor spectator event, track meet, field days, rodeo, games, match, meet)
- Contest (science fair, spelling bee, beauty pageant, talent contest, dance-a-thon)
- Holiday event
- Progress-oriented event (launching, procession, motorcade, groundbreaking ceremony, cornerstone ceremony, dedication, ribbon-cutting, tour, grand opening)
- Historic commemoration (founders' days, anniversary, centennial, play, pageant, caravan)
- Social event (luncheon, banquet, roast, awards dinner, recognition lunch, party, dance, fashion show, tea)
- Artistic event (concert, concert tour, recital, play, film festival, art show, photo exhibit)
- Fundraising event (antique show, auction, haunted house, pony ride, murder mystery dinner theater, fashion show, house or garden tour, tasting party).
- Publicity event

people presumably are already interested in the issue, perhaps have some knowledge of the relevant facts and are at least open to (perhaps even leaning toward) the organization's message. They are the ones who attend town-hall meetings and speeches, who sign up for workshops, and who participate in special events.

The downside? Interpersonal tactics reach only a small number of people, compared to tactics in other categories. So if numbers are important, these tactics won't be heavy producers.

Like all the categories of tactics presented in this book, interpersonal ones should never be considered in isolation from those in other categories. These are the first ones to consider precisely because they can make such an impact (and because we have to start somewhere). But they are not necessarily the first ones that will be used in your general order of tactics.

Here are three different types of interpersonal communication tactics: personal involvement, information exchange, and special events.

Personal Involvement

Personal involvement is a powerful element of communication, whether for purposes of information, education, persuasion, or dialogue. When the organization actively involves its publics and creates an environment rooted in two-way communication, the mutual interests of both the organization and its publics are likely to be addressed. This category of tactics includes organizational-site involvement and audience-site involvement.

ORGANIZATIONAL-SITE INVOLVEMENT

A growing number of audience-involvement activities are bringing members of the audience to the organization, as more and more organizations realize the importance of public interaction. Welcome mats are replacing "Keep out" signs. Examples of this type of audience interaction include plant tours and open houses. For example, Hershey Foods sponsors Chocolate World, a free plant tour that feels like a theme park.

Such tactics offer for-profit and nonprofit organizations alike an opportunity to "show off" for the various publics of the organization: employees and volunteers, both current and prospective; current and would-be customers; investors, donors, and other funding sources; community or governmental supporters.

Some interpersonal tactics involve hands-on activities. Auto dealers, for example, give test drives. Fitness clubs, dance studios, karate dojos, and other activity centers offer trial memberships so potential members can experience the facility and its atmosphere. Educational activities such as martial-arts programs and cooking schools may offer a limited number of free classes to give potential recruits a sample of their offerings.

Private schools have shadow programs in which potential students are invited to spend a day accompanying a current student on the daily round of classes. Police, fire, and emergency crews offer ride-alongs so local residents can see firsthand how various situations are handled. Sneak previews and premiere performances of movies and plays also are effective in generating future audiences.

AUDIENCE-SITE INVOLVEMENT

Instead of inviting the public in, sometimes the organization goes to its publics, potentially a real convenience for the audience. For example, door-to-door canvassing offers an opportunity for organizations with a political, social, or religious cause to take their message or charitable

Phase Three

STEP
7

solicitation directly to people who might be interested. Petition drives seek to get signatures of voters and other constituents.

The downside of this, of course, is that people sometimes resent the knock on the door by an advocate with a message to share.

Meanwhile, some organizations offer in-home demonstrations to help potential customers to see how various products or services will work and personally evaluate their effectiveness. These demonstrations generally are scheduled ahead of time, usually at the initiative of the customer.

Information Exchange

Another significant category of interpersonal communication tactics, **information exchange**, centers on opportunities for organizations and their publics to meet face to face and thus to exchange information, ask questions and clarify understandings. This category includes educational gatherings, product exhibitions, meetings, public demonstrations, and speeches.

EDUCATIONAL GATHERING

Various types of meetings provide an opportunity for both commercial and nonprofit organizations to educate large numbers of information-seeking people.

Be aware that the following terms sometimes may be used somewhat interchangeably. But here is a definition of the difference among the various types of educational gatherings. Conventions are gatherings that generally involve the transaction of organizational business such as the election of officers; many conventions also have a component of education or professional development. Conferences are similar to conventions, though conferences transfer the focus away from organizational business and toward professional development and education. Councils are meetings with a policy-setting agenda. Convocations, synods, and conclaves are formal conventions, often with a religious or academic purpose.

Seminars are educational meetings, often ones that bring together peers who discuss issues among themselves. Symposiums also are educational meetings in which specialists deliver short papers, whereas colloquiums are educational meetings in which specialists deliver formal addresses and then conduct a public discussion of the topic. Workshops and training sessions have a more practical, applied focus, often with an interactive presentation style.

PRODUCT EXHIBITION

Companies often seek opportunities to display their products to sales people and potential customers. The special feature of these trade shows is that they bring together information-seeking publics—often people who attend trade shows specifically to find out about new products—as well as companies and their competitors. Because competitors are displaying their wares at the same show, each company is challenged to provide a bigger and better presentation than others with a similar product line. For this reason, trade shows generally feature elaborate displays and state-of-the-art interactive technology, often with colorful and attention-getting entertainment and refreshments.

Trade shows often are held as part of conferences and conventions that bring together potential customers. Indeed, one of the reasons people attend conferences is to view the latest products associated with their industry or profession.

MEETING

Various types of meetings provide an excellent opportunity for organizations to set up positive information interchanges with their publics. Some of these settings are formal occasions. For example, companies that issue stock are required to hold annual stockholder meetings.

While many such meetings are pretty dull, a growing number of companies are turning the required annual event into a sort of internal trade show with elaborate luncheons and colorful displays about the company's current and future products as well as its financial success. Some stockholder meetings feature top-notch entertainers.

Often meetings are businesslike occasions that involve only a limited number of participants. Lobbying exchanges and public affairs meetings, for example, may involve just one or two representatives of an organization and a few staff members to an elected official.

PUBLIC DEMONSTRATION

Some activities focus on advocacy or opposition. Rallies and other types of public demonstrations can bring together hundreds—even thousands—of people in support of a particular cause, often with speakers. Similarly, marches are public processions, often for the purpose of making a political or social statement. Consider, for example, the numerous rallies for social or political causes that are staged in Washington and in state capitals and other major cities.

Parades, meanwhile, often demonstrate civic pride such as with a victorious sports team, or community appreciation as with parades for returning military troops.

Other public gatherings may be confrontational or negative in nature. Demonstrations, with an element of protest, are opportunities for information exchange, often through speakers as well as by the distribution of printed literature.

Pickets are demonstrations against a particular organization. Often they involve an element of disruption, such as encouraging or trying to prevent people from doing business with the organization. Usually they include vocal and visual messages criticizing the organization.

Boycotts, meanwhile, are public protests, sometimes accompanied by picketing, in which customers refrain from using the products or services of the organization being opposed. Boycotts often are accompanied by public education endeavors.

All of these types of rallies and demonstrations also tend to generate news coverage, which we discuss later. Additionally, they can galvanize existing support.

SPEECH

Speeches are public discourses in which the speaker controls the presentation and intends to impact the awareness, acceptance, or action of an audience. As such, speeches are excellent vehicles for face-to-face communication, especially when question-and-answer sessions are part of the speech presentation.

Consider the different varieties of speeches. Orations are very formal and dignified presentations with a high and eloquent rhetorical style. Talks, on the other hand, are informal, off-the-cuff speeches, usually on a professional subject.

Lectures are carefully prepared speeches associated with classrooms and the presentation of academic information; guest lectures are often more practical educational presentations given by an expert in a particular area.

Phase Three

STEP
7

Addresses are formal speeches that require significant preparation, and keynote speeches are major addresses at conferences and other meetings. Two kinds of speeches are associated with the field of religion: sermons, which are moral exhortations based on religious teaching, and homilies, which are explanations of the practical application of a scriptural passage.

In some speech-like situations, the speaker gives up much of the control of the communication. Consider, for example, panels in which a moderator guides the discussion of several speakers. Panels often involve a short, formal opening statement followed by questions offered by the moderator or by other panelists. Debates are formal, adversarial speaking occasions in which one side (an individual or a team) argues with an opponent, often using a set of formal rules. Forums and town meetings are speeches with questions and generally lively discussion, usually on topics of civic or public interest.

A concept related to speech is the **speaker's bureau**, which is a program within an organization to promote the availability of knowledgeable and trained employees or volunteers to give presentations. These presentations usually are free for organizations within the community on topics related to the organization's interests.

For example, a fuel-gas company may make speakers available to community associations, tenants groups, and homeowners clubs, as well as to business and professional organizations that often have the ear of various opinion leaders. Topics for such a company might include energy saving, high-efficiency heating and cooling equipment, and energy tax matters.

Special Events

The most common category of interpersonal communication tactics is a **special event**, an activity created by an organization mainly to provide a venue to interact with members of its publics.

The list of special events is bounded only by the imagination of the planner. Some of the more common types of special events are civic events, sporting events, contests, holiday events, progress-oriented events, historic commemorations, social events, artistic events, fundraising events, and general publicity events.

CIVIC EVENT

Public activities can bring a community together in celebration and fun. One popular civic activity is a fair, which features food and entertainment. Parades on land and flotillas on water are other forms of popular civic celebration, as are themed events such as those associated with community history.

Another is a festival, which often has games and sometimes is organized around a theme such as ethnic heritage, flowers, or music. Some focus on food or drink, such as an Oktoberfest celebration or a soup fest; harvest events and wine festivals fit this category. Carnivals with an atmosphere of public merriment and circuses with performing animals can also be popular civic events.

Swearing-in ceremonies at which new citizens make an Oath of Allegiance often become community events, especially when they are moved from a courthouse and into a school assembly or outside during a Fourth of July celebration.

SPORTING EVENT

Many special events are created around a sports theme. Tournaments are often held for activities such as skiing, fishing, and golf that have several levels of difficulty and thus can attract a wide range of participants. Marathons are races of all sorts. Triathlons that typically combine running, cycling, and swimming are increasingly popular athletic events.

Also popular are outdoor spectator activities such as rodeos, lumberjack roundups, and Highland games.

Some athletic activities, such as track meets and field days, provide opportunities to turn sporting events into larger community activities. Many sporting events are designed both for participant interaction and as spectator activities.

The Olympics are perhaps the best example of sporting events that impact both public relations and public diplomacy. China used the 2008 Olympics and the 2010 Shanghai World Expo to promote "the Chinese brand." These extravagant events were designed to capture the world's attention and create a positive environment for Chinese culture and commerce, and Nielsen Media Research reported that 4.7 billion television viewers watched some part of the games.

Along with a platform for positive messaging to potentially massive audiences, events such as the Olympics also provide a stage for protests. China drew international criticism for expelling 100 Christian missionaries as it prepared to put a good face on the Olympics. It received environmental complaints for its inability to reduce air pollution in Beijing, causing health concerns for the athletes. And the 85,000-mile relay with the Olympic torch provided many opportunities for pro-Tibet protestors to shine an international spotlight on one of the negative aspects of Chinese policy.

CONTEST

Competitive engagements offer another type of special event, allowing participants to display their knowledge, skills, or other assets. By their nature, contests create winners, which leads to increased visibility because of the built-in news value.

Science fairs, spelling bees, and other types of academically oriented contests are popular, as are those that mimic various television quiz shows or reality shows. These and similar events such as beauty pageants, talent contests, and sing-offs can attract wide audiences of both participants and spectators.

Often grand openings and similar events feature purely fun contests—for pizza tossing, pie eating, dancing, and the like—in which every participant is a winner.

HOLIDAY EVENT

Some special events are based on popular and widespread observances. Many of these are civic celebrations, such as Memorial Day, Independence Day, and Thanksgiving. Some holiday activities are rooted within a particular cultural group: Kwanzaa and Juneteenth celebrations by African Americas, fiestas for Cinco de Mayo and Dia de los Reyes Magos in the Hispanic community, the Moon Festival in Asian and American Indian cultures, and Native American harvest festivals.

Various calendars lead the way for special new year's celebrations among Chinese, Muslim, Jewish, Ethiopian, Vietnamese, Hindu, and other ethnic groups.

Meanwhile, the LGBT community observes a number of commemorative occasions, including the Stonewall Riots anniversary, National Coming Out Day, and Pride Month.

Some of the most popular holidays have religious roots. Be careful not to give offense by trivializing an event that some of your publics consider sacred in nature, such as Hanukkah, Christmas, Eid al-Fitr, and Easter. Some other events are hybrids of popular religion and

Phase Three

STEP
7

cultural celebrations, such as St. Patrick's Day, observed by both the Irish and Irish-at-heart, or the pre-Lenten Mardi Gras and related Carnival festivities.

Holidays sometimes become occasions for social comment and action. For example, many American Indian protests around Columbus Day highlight the devastating cultural effects—both intended and unintended—of European contact. Some communities, especially those near Native communities, transform the observance into a Native American Heritage Day.

PROGRESS-ORIENTED EVENT

Several kinds of events celebrate the growth and development of an organization or community. Ships and boats traditionally are launched by smashing a champagne bottle on the ship's bow, or now by the more environmentally friendly pouring of champagne over the bow. Musical entertainment, fireworks, and other celebratory activities often mark progress-oriented events.

When a school or religious congregation moves into a new building nearby, the transition often is marked by a procession from the old building to the new. For example, students might carry symbols such as textbooks, globes, and other artifacts of school life to the new school site. Similarly, a motorcade might be arranged to inaugurate the opening of a new bridge.

A single project might lend itself to a series of progress-oriented special events. Consider, for example, the building of a new community center. You might schedule a groundbreaking ceremony for the turning of the first shovelful of dirt, a cornerstone ceremony when construction begins, and a dedication ceremony including a ribbon cutting to mark the completion of the center, and then follow these with tours and grand opening events.

HISTORIC COMMEMORATION

The history of an organization or community provides the background for another kind of special event. Towns observe founders' days; companies mark the anniversary of their incorporation. Sometimes historic events are observed by re-creating the sights and sounds of an earlier time, such as a centennial celebration that features costumes, buggies or antique cars, and music and food of the bygone era.

Some historic commemorations include plays, dramatic re-enactments of historical events, and pageants or historical plays with a certain amount of music and pomp. Additionally, caravans re-enact historic travels.

SOCIAL EVENT

Social events comprise a major type of special event. Luncheons and dinners are events sponsored by all kinds of organizations. These social events involve entertainment activities. Receptions with beverages and hors d'oeuvres or snacks are a similar kind of event.

Among the various special types of ceremonial meals are tributes that honor people or organizations, and banquets that offer more sumptuous menus and entertainment. Roasts use sarcastic humor to recognize a person's achievements and contributions.

Many social events are aimed at employees and volunteers, and their purpose is to thank or recognize members of an important public. The purpose of such awards dinners and recognition lunches is to enhance the camaraderie among people who work together, a potential boost to worker productivity. In other cases, luncheons and banquets often may have educational or fundraising objectives and involve a variety of publics. Other social events include fashion shows and teas.

Social events often occur at elegant or unusual locations, including cruise ships, museums, and private mansions. Budget limitations can be offset by an extra dash of creativity, and many social events have been successful because they have had an interesting theme, such as an imitation Caribbean getaway complete with appropriate music, food, and dancing, or historical themes related to the Old West, medieval knights, or the flapper era. Futuristic themes also can be popular.

Carefully think through the cultural sensibilities that may be associated with certain historical events, and be attentive to ethical considerations of social events. A party with the theme of the antebellum South may evoke images of fancy dress balls and sumptuous banquets amid lavish architecture, but that era also was associated with slavery—hardly a fitting theme for a fundraiser or recognition event for most publics.

ARTISTIC EVENT

Another area of special events deals with art and culture. Consider events such as concerts or concert tours, recitals, plays, film festivals, arts shows, photo exhibits, and related activities. Even these events are not without the potential for controversy, such as a museum opening for artworks that some people consider to be obscene, anti-religious, or in some other way offensive.

FUNDRAISING EVENT

Activities in which nonprofit organizations interact with their key publics, especially individual donors, for the purpose of generating support can be important public relations opportunities. Americans donated more than $359 billion to charitable organizations, according to the Giving USA report for 2015.Individuals gave about 72 percent of this, the remainder came through foundations (15 percent), bequests (8 percent), and corporations (5 percent).

Religious organizations received nearly a third of the total (32 percent) followed by education (15 percent), grant-giving independent and community foundations (12 percent), human-service organizations (12 percent), health agencies (9 percent), public-society benefit organizations such as United Way (8 percent), arts and cultural groups (5 percent), international affairs (4 percent), environment and animals (3 percent).

In addition, elections raise vast sums in contributions, which mushroomed after the Supreme Court's Citizens United ruling allowing unlimited and anonymous corporate funds. For presidential races, the estimates are $2.8 billion in 2008, $2.6 billion in 2012, and as much as $5 billion in 2016. The combined cost of congressional campaigns is even higher. Still, political fundraising accounts for only about 2 percent of all charitable and nonprofit giving.

The variety of fundraising events is limitless. Consider the following ideas: an antique show, an auction, a haunted house, pony rides, murder mystery dinner theater, fashion show, house or garden tour, or tasting party (Amos, 1995; Williams, 1994). All of these require careful planning and an eye for detail.

The ethics of both public relations and fundraising require honest and forthright disclosure of organizational information to donors and to the media.

PUBLICITY EVENT

Some activities simply fall into a category of general publicity activities. They include the staged activities noted in Step 5. Such events are limited only by the creativity of the planners, tempered by the ethical restraint of needing to offer legitimate news while posturing for the

CASE IN POINT **Ice Bucket Challenge**

The ice bucket challenge raises money, lots of it, for organizations dealing with ALS (amyotrophic lateral sclerosis, also known as Lou Gehrig's disease) and related diseases.

How did it begin? Chris Kennedy of Sarasota, Fla., was challenged by a friend to contribute to charity. So he doused himself with ice water and, in a YouTube video, challenged a relative in Pelham, N.Y., whose husband had been diagnosed with ALS to do the same and keep the challenge going. Jeanette Senerchia accepted the challenge, posting a similar video nominating more people. The challenge spread among friends in the small community.

Eventually the challenge reached two other men diagnosed with ALS, Pat Quinn in Yonkers and Pete Frates of Boston. They, in turn, challenged their friends and social media networks, creating alsicebucketchallenge.org.

The challenge went viral in the summer of 2014 with the simple premise: Once you are challenged, you have 24 hours to donate, videotape yourself being doused with ice water, or both.

Soon thousands of videos were showing athletes, celebrities, polilticians, and of course thousands of college students accepting the challenge and being doused with ice—having fun and doing good. Celebrity participants included actors Channing Tatum and Hugh Jackman, celebrities Oprah Winfrey and Martha Stewart, singers Taylor Swift and Mackelmore, politicians Chris Christie and Lisa Murkowski, athletes LeBron James and Steve Gleason.

ALS-related organizations are the primary recipient of contributions, which raised $100 million for the ALS Association, nine times what it usually raises, and $26 million for the ALS Society of Canada. A year later, the co-founders were reporting that the challenge had raised $220 million worldwide to various ALS and muscular dystrophy charities.

Additionally, some participants used the ice bucket challenge to solicit donations to other local and national charities.

media. Within such ethical bounds, there are many activities that could be developed to present the organization's message amid a creative and camera-friendly presentation that offers news to the media.

Here's an example of a successful and ethical publicity event that promoted a dog-food brand and raised money for animal charities. Snausages is a brand of doggie treats made by Del Monte Foods. Its future was threatened by competitors who were outspending the company in advertising, enough to cause some retailers to threaten to pull the product off their shelves. Snausages turned to public relations to pull out of its slump.

The Iditarod is a well-known dogsled race, with teams of huskies pulling drivers more than 1,000 miles across Alaska. Snausages turned the tables and garnered national and local publicity, including ESPN, with a "man sled" race in 2010.

Teams of men pulled canine mushers (dogs that had previously pulled in the Iditarod). An Associated Press photo of the event was the most emailed photo on Yahoo News for three days running. The brand mascot, Snocrates, refereed the race, ensuring the Snausages connection in photos and video footage. Donations went to animal charities of all the human participants in the race, upping the publicity factor.

The event created a 30 percent increase to traffic at the Snausages website, and increased customer demand ensured that the Del Monte brand kept its shelf status and distribution levels.

Another type of special event can be used as part of an advocacy campaign to attract attention to an issue. This was the strategy for the Nuns on the Bus information tour during the 2012 U.S. presidential campaign. The strategy involved plenty of visual appeal. A group of Catholic nuns traveled through eight states in a brightly painted bus. With backdrops of homeless shelters and soup kitchens along the way, as well as legislative offices, the nuns focused international media attention and much local awareness as they lobbied legislators and otherwise provided a platform to speak out on social justice in opposition to budget-cutting proposals in Congress that they said would unduly hurt the poor.

So successful was the advocacy tour that the nuns repeated it in 2013 for immigration reform, in 2014 for health-care reform, and in 2015 for voter registration.

Planning Special Events

The various types of **special events** and most of the other tactics noted in this section require a tremendous amount of careful planning.

Attention to detail is a must during the preparation stages. Organizations sometimes handle these details internally; other times, they hire events-management companies to help plan and execute the activities. Either way, consider some of the following practical questions that can arise around a special event:

- Is the event of legitimate interest to the identified key publics? If the intention is to attract media attention, is there a significant news element to warrant inviting journalists to report the event?
- Is the date appropriate for everyone? Does it conflict with holidays (particularly cultural or religious holidays that may not be familiar to the planners)? Does it conflict with other major happenings, such as sporting or social activities—not only local events but larger events such as the Kentucky Derby, the Super Bowl, an important soccer game, or the opening of the fishing season? Any such competition can limit attendance and diminish publicity about the event.
- What is the appropriate length of an event? If it is too long, participants will become bored or restless and may leave early. If it is too short, they may decide it's not worth attending in the first place.
- Is the theme appropriate? Will it offend anyone? Will anyone feel excluded?
- Is the site appropriate and accessible? Is climate a factor? If it is an outdoor event, is there an indoor location to serve as a backup in the event of bad weather? Does the location of a conference or meeting offer too many diversions that might tempt participants away from the conference itself?
- Are speakers and entertainers appropriate to the participants of the event?
- Is planning assistance available through a convention center or visitors' bureau in the host city of the meeting? If so, the agency may be able to involve local contacts.

All special events call for careful planning, staffing, and financing, and they need creative promotion. Use the planning process presented throughout this book to identify and analyze key publics, establish objectives, and develop a strategy for the special event or other type of interpersonal communication tactic. Also make sure to evaluate its effectiveness, showing in measurable terms how well the activity achieved its objectives.

PLANNING EXAMPLE 7A **Selecting Interpersonal Communication Tactics**

UPSTATE COLLEGE **Upstate College will develop interpersonal communication tactics to publicize its expanded program:**

Interpersonal Tactic 1: Open house for recruiting
- Key publics, hands-on, low cost, audience feedback

Interpersonal Tactic 2: Rededication ceremony
- Low cost, news value, reaffirming existing support

Interpersonal Tactic 3: Existing event
- Little additional cost, news value, power of ritualization

Interpersonal Tactic 4: Musical events
- Key student publics, moderate cost, serving acceptance objectives

Interpersonal Tactic 5: Festival
- Key student publics, high visibility, moderate cost

Interpersonal Tactic 6: Banquet
- Key publics (community leaders, donors), high cost, high impact

---

TINY TYKES TOYS

Tiny Tykes will develop the following interpersonal communication tactics for an employee-oriented public relations program:

Interpersonal Tactic 1: Customer satisfaction workshops
- Key external publics, high impact

Interpersonal Tactic 2: Work-group meeting
- Key internal public, interaction and feedback

Interpersonal Tactic 3: Product safety and quality session
- Key publics, direct benefit to employees and training management, indirect benefits to customers

Phase Three

STEP 7

Interpersonal Tactic 4: Motivational speech by CEO about safety and quality
- Key employee public, low cost, moderate impact

Interpersonal Tactic 5: Samples of reintroduced products
- Maintain credibility with employees (and family/friends of employees) as customers, moderate cost

---

 Checklist 7A **Interpersonal Communication Tactics**

Basic Questions

1. What interpersonal communication tactics will you use?
2. How will these tactics help the organization achieve its objectives?
3. What resources will these tactics require?

Expanded Questions

A. SELECTION OF TACTICS

From the following categories of interpersonal tactics, identify several that you would consider using.

Personal Involvement
- Organizational-site involvement (plant tour, open house, test drive, trial membership, free class, sample, shadow program, ride-along, premiere)
- Audience-site involvement
- Door-to-door canvassing, in-home demonstration, petition drive

Information Exchange
- Educational gathering (convention, council, convocation, synod, conclave, conference, seminar, symposium, colloquium, workshop, training session)
- Product exhibition
- Trade show
- Meeting (annual stockholder meeting, lobbying exchange, public affairs meeting)
- Demonstration (rally, march, demonstration, picket, boycott)
- Speech (question-and-answer session, oration, talk, lecture, guest lecture, address, keynote, sermon, homily, panel, debate, speaker's bureau, forum, town meeting)

Special event
- Civic event (fair, festival, carnival, circus, parade, theme event)
- Sporting event (tournament, marathon, triathlon, outdoor spectator event, meet, field day)

Phase Three

STEP
7

- Contest (science fair, spelling bee, beauty pageant, talent contest)
- Holiday event (civic, cultural, religious)
- Progress-oriented event (procession, motorcade, grand opening, groundbreaking, cornerstone, dedication, ribbon cutting)
- Historic event (founders' day, anniversary, centennial, play, pageant, caravan)
- Social event (luncheon, dinner, reception, tribute, banquet, roast, awards, recognition, fashion show, tea)
- Artistic event (concert, concert tour, recital, play, film festival, art show, photo exhibit)
- Fundraising event

B. STRATEGIC IMPLICATIONS

For each item identified, answer the following questions.

- Will this tactic help the organization to interact with the appropriate public?
- What level of impact will this tactic make on the key public?
- Will this tactic advance the organization toward its awareness objectives?
- Will this tactic advance the organization toward its acceptance objectives?
- Will this tactic advance the organization toward its action objectives?
- What is the main advantage to this tactic?
- What advantages does this tactic offer that other tactics do not?
- Are there any disadvantages to this tactic? If so, what are they?

C. IMPLEMENTATION ITEMS

For each item identified, answer the following questions.

1. How much will it cost to implement this tactic? Is the cost justified? Is the cost practical, based on the organization's resources?
2. How much staff time will it take to implement this tactic? Is the time practical, based on the organization's resources?
3. What level of skill, equipment, and expertise is needed to implement this tactic? Is the needed level available within the organization? Is it available from outside sources?

Owned Media: Organizational and Social Media Tactics

A host of communication vehicles are managed by each organization and are used at its discretion. These media generally are controlled, internal, nonpublic media that we can look at in five categories: publications, direct mail, electronic media, digital media, and social media. Let's consider the overall strategy and then look at each category of organizational media.

Strategy for Owned Media

When should you rely on owned media? That is, when should you select organizational media tactics? When your publics are too widespread or too large to interact with on a more personal level, but when you yet want to keep control of the content of your organization's message as well as its timing and distribution.

Conversely, when would you not use organizational media? When the audience is too small to warrant it, or so scattered that dissemination would be next to impossible. Or when you need the higher credibility that might be associated with other news tactics or the greater visibility that might be possible through advertising.

One of the benefits of organizational media tactics is that they provide a middle ground between high-impact, small-audience interpersonal tactics and lower-impact, large-audience news and advertising tactics. Organizational media can reasonably be addressed to both internal and external publics that fall in the midsized range. Because tactics in this category can be tailored to specific publics, they are more likely than news or advertising tactics to achieve success with acceptance and action objectives.

Another significant benefit of organizational media is that they are likely to be used by **information-seeking publics**, those who are actively searching for information on a particular topic. These are the info-on-demand people who will access a website, read a brochure, follow someone on Twitter, or subscribe to a blog.

Organizational media can be expensive to use, but because they can be targeted to specific publics and individuals, they usually are cost-effective. For example, the tactic of direct mail can involve high postage costs. But the impact of direct mail—if done properly—is higher than most other media, and thus the results should be greater.

Remember that organizational media are only one set of tools for public relations and marketing communication. Consider them carefully, but always with the intention of combining them with other kinds of communication tactics.

Publications

General publications include a variety of materials published and printed by an organization. Their distribution generally is handled by the organization as well. This category includes serial publications, stand-alone publications, reprints, progress reports, user kits, and research reports.

SERIAL PUBLICATION

Most organizations make heavy use of serial publications, which may be issued weekly, monthly, or quarterly. The most common serial publication is a **newsletter**, an organizational publication that combines the informative approach of newspapers and magazines with the relationship-building features of mail. It's hard to tell just how many organizational newsletters exist. Guesses put the figure at more than a million. This includes untold numbers of private publications and house organs, which are newsletters published by companies and organizations, with distribution to members, employees, and other groups of readers, even more when you factor in online versions.

Whatever the total, an estimated two-thirds of newsletters are internal publications directed toward employees, volunteers, alumni, members, customers, patients, and so on. The remaining third are external publications, a category that includes advocacy newsletters aimed at persuading readers, such as that published by a waste management company as part of a campaign to minimize opposition among local residents. They include special-interest newsletters dealing with a particular industry, profession, or pursuit (such as financial

OWNED MEDIA: ORGANIZATIONAL AND SOCIAL MEDIA TACTICS

General Publications

- Serial publication (newsletter, bulletin)
- Stand-alone publication (brochure, flier, booklet, folder, pamphlet, tract, circular, fact sheet, FAQ)
- Progress report (annual report, quarterly report)
- User kit
- Research report
- Miscellaneous print media

Direct Mail

- Memo
- Letter (appeal letter, marketing letter)
- Postcard
- Invitation
- Catalog (retail, full-line, specialty, business-to-business)

Electronic Media

- Audio media (telephone, dial-a-message, recorded information, voicemail, toll-free line, demo tape, demo CD, podcast)
- Video media (nonbroadcast video, videoconference, teleconference, videotape, slide show)
- Digital media (presentations software, email, listserv, Internet, newsgroup, websites, web home page, web-based television, web-based radio, touch-sensitive computer, cell phone)
- Electronic publishing

Social Media

- Blog
- Microblog (Twitter)
- Collaboration (Wiki)
- Social network (Facebook, LinkedIn, Google+)
- News aggregate (Reddit, DIGG)
- Media sharing (YouTube, Flickr, Vimeo, SlideShare)
- Customer review (TripAdvisor, Yelp, RateMyProfessor)

investments, stamp collecting, or white-water canoeing), or with a particular group of people (such as economists, breast-cancer survivors, or former nuns).

Another type of external newsletter is the subscription newsletter, which is often a high-cost publication providing insider information on a particular profession or industry; two such newsletters popular with public relations and marketing practitioners are *Media Relations Report* (ragan.com) and *Communication Briefings* (communicationbriefings.com).

Many public relations and marketing communication campaigns publish one or more newsletters as a convenient way to communicate with an organization's publics. If you plan to use the tactic of newsletters, having an appropriate mailing list is a must. When writing newsletters, follow the principles of newsworthiness and audience self-interest. Make sure the articles provide information of interest to the readers, and not just data that the organization wishes to present to the readers.

A **bulletin**, meanwhile, is a different kind of serial publication. Confusingly, some people use the two terms—newsletters and bulletins—interchangeably, though it is helpful to practitioners to distinguish between the two types of serial publications.

Typographically, bulletins often feature only headlines and short body text, with little or no graphic content. They generally include official organizational information and are most often circulated to internal audiences. Some examples of bulletins are listings of jobs or internships, notices of contracts or requests for proposals (called RFPs), or timely announcements by organizations such as churches or schools.

STAND-ALONE PUBLICATION

Another commonly used tactic in public relations is the stand-alone publication, which differs from a newsletter or bulletin in that it usually is issued only once rather than periodically (though stand-alone publications may occasionally be updated). This category of publications includes brochures, fliers, and fact sheets.

A **brochure** is a common stand-alone organizational publication, dealing with a particular topic or issue. Organizational brochures often focus on recruiting, product/service lines, membership services, organizational history, or some other aspect of a particular organization. Advocacy brochures attempt to educate or generate support on a particular issue important to the sponsoring organization. Additionally, some brochures are action-oriented publications with a definite sales pitch, though these are more likely to be associated with marketing efforts than with public relations activities.

A **flier** is similar to a brochure in that it is a stand-alone piece. Whereas a brochure is meant to be read in panels, a flier is meant to be read as a single unit as a kind of announcement.

Note that brochure and flier are commonly accepted terms for stand-alone organizational publications, but other names also may be used. Some names deal with the size of the publication. In addition to fliers, other terms for single-sheet publications include leaflets or folders. Alternative terms for brochures are pamphlets or booklets. Other name distinctions grow out of the purpose of the publication. Persuasive brochures called tracts deal with political or religious topics, and marketing-oriented stand-alone publications are often called circulars.

A **fact sheet** that presents information in bullet form is another common stand-alone piece, as is a **FAQ**, a presentation of frequently asked questions about a particular issue or organization.

Phase Three

REPRINT

Copies of published articles about an organization or an issue significant to it can be useful in meeting public relations objectives. Reprints are articles previously published in newspapers, magazines or newsletters. By issuing a reprint, the organization is able to extend the reach and impact of the original publication, particularly by giving it to the organization's publics, who may not have had access to the original article.

Fair-use provisions in copyright law allow an organization to circulate a limited number of copies of a published article for educational, research, or news purposes. Note that in 1991 a federal court ruled in the case of *Basic Books Inc. v. Kinko's Graphics Corp.* that it is illegal to photocopy published materials even for educational purposes except for brief passages. Informally, a passage of about 300 consecutive words is considered the maximum length that can be used without permission. This is not a fixed limit and may be less for shorter works.

Make sure to obtain permission from the original publisher before disseminating a reprinted article or photograph to a wide group for promotional purposes. This may involve a fee, and the permission granted is generally for one-time use only.

A similar tactic is to reprint speeches. This is done especially with formal presentations such as keynote addresses or testimony before state, provincial, or federal legislative bodies. These often are shared with key publics, such as boards of directors, major donors or stockholders, community and civic leaders, and other opinion leaders.

Related to reprints is the distribution of news releases to internal audiences. News releases will be discussed more in the section News Media Tactics later in this chapter. While releases are meant primarily for distribution to journalists, some public relations practitioners also selectively send them to key internal publics, such as senior executives, major donors, and stockholders.

PROGRESS REPORT

Several different types of progress reports focus on the continuing development of an organization, particularly its activity within a recent period of time.

The **annual report** is a special kind of progress report. The federal Securities and Exchange Commission (SEC) requires annual reports for American companies that issue stock. These can be simple statements with required information, such as the identification of corporate officials, the salaries and benefits of the top executives, financial statements, and the auditor's certification of accuracy. Often, however, they feature much more. Many annual reports are glossy, magazine-like publications designed not only to provide required information but also to affirm investors' loyalty to the company, attract new investors, and enhance the company's reputation with financial analysts and the financial media.

Some companies also produce **quarterly reports**, though these are not required by the SEC. Quarterly reports usually are not as elaborate as annual reports.

Though nonprofit organizations and private (non-stock issuing) companies are not required to issue annual reports, many do so voluntarily. These often provide financial and organizational information of interest to donors and other supporters. Businesses often find that annual and quarterly reports are convenient vehicles for attracting new customers by demonstrating the work they have previously done.

USER KIT

Another common print tactic, generically called a **user kit** or **consumer kit**, is associated with the people who use a product or service. These kits or manuals often include background and how-to information as well as implementation ideas. For example, teacher kits provide a variety of information and materials that can be used in the classroom. These often include sample lesson plans, suggestions for activities, posters, student handouts and even test items. To produce these, the public relations person will often team up with teachers so the information is most useful to the intended public.

RESEARCH REPORT

Sometimes, when organizations conduct or sponsor formal research on an issue related to their interests, they consider the information to be proprietary—that is, private and confidential. After all, they paid for the research and they may not want to share it with competitors.

Other times, however, they may choose to share the research findings. Many organizations are engaged in medical, social, or educational research, and their mission is to create knowledge and share it with others.

In issuing a research report, organizations have an ethical requirement to be clear as to their involvement in the research study. The report should include background information, a description of the research methods and how any samples were drawn, presentation and analysis of the research findings, and a discussion of the significance of the findings. Some reports also include recommendations based on the findings. The report may be distributed like other organizational media—to organizational managers, employees, stockholders or donors, regulators, and others.

The report also may be shared with the news media. It is never a good idea to conduct research simply so it can be used for publicity. That would be more like a publicity stunt, and it raises ethical questions about the appropriate use of research and thus about the organization's professionalism. But if the organization believes that a legitimate research report contains some newsworthy information, it may decide to publicize its findings. Often this involves providing reporters with the research report as well as a news release.

In the release, emphasize the validity and objectivity of the study while acknowledging the organization's involvement. Don't use the organization's name too many times in the release.

MISCELLANEOUS PRINT MEDIA

A whole range of other tactics offer several opportunities for the public relations planner. Consider the following tactics.

Posters are visual materials, often approximately 3x5 feet in size, which can be displayed prominently. Door posters may be smaller. Companies often use window displays to give visibility to their products or services; nonprofit organizations sometimes use commercial storefront space made available to them, often when there is a temporary vacancy in a store in a mall or on a downtown street.

Employees and customers alike can benefit from well-maintained bulletin boards, and suggestion boxes are excellent opportunities for organizations to solicit feedback and input from their publics. Other traditional tactics that still have value are pay stuffers or bill inserts, which are messages placed within pay envelops or bills, respectively. Door hangers that advocate a cause or promote a product or service also can be useful.

Business cards remain another effective tactic for organizations to keep their names before potential customers and associates.

Some miscellaneous tactics involve recognition programs. For example, certificates are used to acknowledge achievement or participation. Formal proclamations are issued by governmental and sometimes by organizational leaders to draw public attention to a particular cause or theme.

Direct Mail

Direct mail is a category of organizational print media that, though perhaps general in nature, can be addressed to individual recipients. Direct mail pieces can include memos, letters, postcards, invitations, and catalogs.

LETTER

In the category of direct mail, the most common vehicle is the business letter, which generally is a form letter addressed to individuals. Often these will carry the actual name of the reader, such as "Dear Mary Jones" or "Dear Ms. Jones." Sometimes for very large mailings the letters will be addressed more generically, such as "Dear Friend of the Environment" or "Dear Fellow Stamp Collector."

Appeal letters are direct-mail pieces sent to potential donors by nonprofit organizations engaged in fundraising campaigns. Marketing letters are direct-mail pieces sent by businesses for advertising purposes.

With both types of these direct-mail letters, response rates generally are very low, often less than 1 percent. But the response rate increases considerably when the letters are sent to people who in the past have made contributions or have done business with the sending organization. The best advice regarding direct mail, as with every other form of public relations or marketing communication, is to target the mail to each public and address the reader's self-interest.

Direct-mail packages generally contain more than a marketing or appeal letter. They often also include a brochure about the company or organization, a response device such as a donor card or order form, and a return device such as a payment envelope, usually with return-postage paid.

MEMO

A memorandum or **memo** is a brief written message addressed to an individual or to a group of people. Memos generally are internal messages; when issued externally, they usually are directed to persons known to the sender.

Memos begin with a format that clearly identifies the sender, recipient, date, and subject. In writing style, memos are informal, crisp, and usually action-oriented. Memos can be a good public relations vehicle for communicating with colleagues, media gatekeepers, or members of key publics, such as when you attach a memo to a reprint you are sending to a major benefactor or stockholder.

POSTCARD

Similar to letters, postcards generally are addressed to individuals, usually by name. Postcards, which include brief messages, are not placed in envelopes, and thus their content should never be of a personal or confidential nature.

Postcards often are used as announcements or reminders, and they often complement messages presented through news or advertising media. In some cases, postcards may replace other such tactics, especially when it is possible to obtain a mailing list of members of the key public. Organizations sometimes use postcards to drive traffic to their websites.

INVITATION

Organizations that sponsor events, whether public or private, often send formal, personalized invitations to prospective participants.

CATALOG

Catalogs are books or brochures aimed at consumer publics, generally with an inventory of items available for purchase, though nonprofit organizations can use the catalog approach to list available services or programs.

Several types of catalogs can be developed. Retail catalogs, with merchandise available in the sponsors' stores, seek to generate in-store consumer traffic. Full-line catalogs feature the entire range of items in a department store. Specialty or boutique catalogs feature products of very narrow consumer interest, such as a catalog of weaving supplies. Business-to-business catalogs contain information on products of specific interest to businesses.

In recent years, some companies have developed catalogs along the lines of lifestyle-oriented magazines, turning a traditional marketing tool into a public relations vehicle. For example, the Patagonia Company (patagonia.com) enhances its clothing catalog with pictures by award-winning outdoor photographers, commentaries on the environment, and field reports about outdoor activities around the world.

Abercrombie & Fitch (abercrombie.com) sparked calls for a boycott of the clothing store over what critics called racy photos and soft porn in its catalog. The company defended its quarterly publication as being not only a sales tool but also a magazine aimed at the young adult and college market.

Electronic Media

Technology has added new choices to the menu of tactics that can be used for public relations and marketing communication. Most of these electronic technologies in some way enhance the audio and/or visual aspects of communication. The technology that created radio and television has led to many opportunities for organizations. Specifically, this category includes audio media and video media, as well as electronic publishing.

AUDIO MEDIA

An expanding inventory of audio media is available to public relations planners. Telephone media involve new opportunities for information on demand, such as dial-a-message tactics that allow people to obtain information on topics such as weather or sports scores or to access self-help information and advice on a variety of categories. Dial-a-message services also offer prayers, jokes, and so on.

Technology makes it possible to disseminate recorded messages to thousands of phone users. Such automated calls can be used for telemarketing and for public education campaigns and other public service programs. They are most commonly associated with political candidates and partisan groups around election time. In that context, such **robocalls** (so named because the call comes from robots, automated telephone calls) are particularly controversial.

The benefits? They are inexpensive and fast—as many as a million calls within a half hour. The disadvantages? First, there is little evidence to suggest such calls are effective. Second, they often evoke a negative response, from mild annoyance to anger. Studies show that the more such calls are made during a political campaign, the less effective they are. Only 31 percent of recipients listen to robocalls, according to a 2010 report by the Pew Research Center for the People and the Press (people-press.org). This compares to 73 percent of people who listen to phone calls from a real person. But the reach to wide numbers of people offsets the high hang-up rate for robocalls.

The Federal Communications Commission (FCC) prohibits telemarketers from using robocalls to cell phones, but political groups and some other charitable nonprofit organizations are exempt from that exclusion. Additionally, the FCC allows informational calls such as a school district might make to parents to announce a delay in school opening. Thus such calls can play a role in an organization's public relations program and for emergency announcements.

Telephone media also can involve the use of recorded information or persuasive messages to help people wile away the time spent waiting on a telephone. Some organizations add a public relations dimension to their voicemail, such as a community college or car dealership whose president has recorded a brief welcome message as part of the routing of all incoming phone calls.

Organizations make frequent use of toll-free lines that give customers and other publics free telephone access to the organization; similar 900 lines, in which callers are charged for the phone call, can generate income for organizations. Some organizations also have found that demo tapes or demo CDs can be useful audio tools.

A **podcast** (a portmanteau for "iPod" and "broadcast") essentially is an Internet-based audio feed that allows users to listen to postings. These have many public relations uses. Consider the following examples: a destination guide by a hotel or travel agency, reviews by a restaurant or wine store, orientation information by a university, interview or speech by a political candidate, financial advice by an investment company, author interview by a publishing company, and actor interviews by a movie studio.

Many universities podcast guest lectures or interviews with faculty experts. Police departments, museums, churches, and advocacy groups use podcasts to present their messages to interested audiences. Many public relations agencies now include podcasts and other social media among the professional services they offer.

Sirius radio added a new dimension to audio tactics with its Town Hall series of interviews. The satellite radio network arranged exclusive interviews with high-profile guests, including entertainers such as Bruce Springsteen, Bono, Adele, Garth Brooks, and Eminem; musical groups Nirvana, KISS, and Coldplay; reporters Dana Bash and Jim Acosta; directors Oliver Stone, Ron Howard, and Michael Moore; athletes Mike Gronkowski and Tony Hawk; and other newsworthy individuals such as Cardinal Timothy Dolan and Education Secretary Arne Duncan. The studio interviews involve a host and moderator; in a unique twist, they also include several Sirius subscribers selected on the basis of pre-submitted questions for the interview guest.

VIDEO MEDIA

Various types of video media offer opportunities in nonbroadcast video that use television technology to produce programs that are then disseminated through organizational rather than public channels. For example, organizations may use **nonbroadcast video** in conjunction with a fundraising event, open house, or some other type of interpersonal tactic. Businesses use nonbroadcast video (also called **corporate video** and **internal video**) for training, employee information, product information for customers, stockholder meetings, and internal marketing.

A particular use of nonbroadcast video is as direct-mail video to promote products or causes. *Advertising Age* reported the effectiveness of direct-mail video (Kim, 1995). In one case, 94 percent of people viewed the video they received from a gubernatorial candidate in New Jersey. In another study, a direct-mail video that inaugurated a campaign to encourage landowners in the Connecticut River Tidelands region to develop long-term conservation plans was evaluated as being both educational and persuasive, with increases in six key indicators of environmental behavior (Tyson and Snyder, 1999).

Nonbroadcast video sometimes occurs live—as in **videoconferences**, also called **teleconferences**. Videoconferences use television technology to produce live informational or educational programs for remote audiences. These events are made interactive through the use of satellite or fiber-optic video transmission, sometimes with long-distance telephone connections to link the remote sites to the originating studio.

Increasingly, organizations are turning to the Internet to post their nonbroadcast video for presenting information to donors and stockholders as well as potential customers. Such video also can be useful for employee training. This **web video** or **streaming video** is a common feature on multipurpose cell phones that provide not only voice transmission but also text messaging, Internet access, and a range of video options.

Presentation software such as Microsoft PowerPoint, Apple Keynote, Corel Presentations, Prezi, and Google Slides provide a platform for informational or educational presentations. New technology enhances this tactic by making possible interactive multiple-slide presentations.

ELECTRONIC PUBLISHING

Another category of electronic media involves electronic publishing. Public relations departments can publish brochures and position papers, newsletters, even books and magazines, using their own in-house computers and printers rather than having to rely on outside printing companies.

Digital Media

This brings us to the growing field of computer-based **digital media**, which provides even newer strategic communication opportunities.

EMAIL

A mushrooming group of these tactics is associated with **email**. The benefits of instantaneous communication unbounded by distance are obvious to public relations and marketing practitioners. Organizations use email as the platform for preparing and disseminating newsletters, fundraising appeals, and news releases for notifying journalists, donors, and other key publics of new information posted as organizational blogs or websites.

Phase Three

STEP
7

ONLINE PUBLICATION

Just about any tactic identified previously in this section on print formats for organization media can be packaged and disseminated digitally. Brochures, annual reports, FAQs, consumer kits, and catalogs can serve an organization well when they are available online.

Some organizations, for example, have entirely replaced printed newsletters with online versions. One benefit of online newsletters is that they can be archived so readers can peruse past issues. Another benefit is that online newsletters can be evolutionary, with new daily or weekly postings as newsworthy information becomes available. Public relations practitioners often herald newsletters or updates with email alerts to potential readers. But be aware that inbox congestion is a growing concern; it's best to direct online newsletters only to those readers who have signed up to receive them.

Good practice, however, calls for modifying online publications to take advantage of the many opportunities for linking documents and allowing users to browse in an information-on-demand environment. The alternative to this is called **shovelware**, a poorly thought-out technique of merely dumping a printed publication into an online format without modifying it to maximize the potential of the online milieu.

Technology also is translating many elements of audio and video media into digital. Video is usually recorded digitally rather than onto videocassettes, and editing is now done digitally. Video footage is stored and transmitted using computer technology.

MOBILE DEVICE

Smart phones are another form of digital media increasingly being used for public relations and marketing purposes. These offer more than telephone service. They are cameras and video recorders. They link wirelessly with computers. They are used for texting, Internet browsing, music playback, games, radio reception, recording, video calling, and downloading for audio and video streaming. They also have calendars, clocks, and calculators among a rapidly expanding list of features and applications.

Meanwhile, other mobile devices, particularly electronic tablets, extend the portability of digital media. These wireless mobile computers have remote or on-screen virtual keyboards or digital pens to digitize handwriting. Many organizations create their own apps to help customers.

Thousands of apps, many created by companies for their own customers, have many positive implications for public relations: banking services, voting, ticket purchases, order tracking, maps, and scanner readers. Some specialized apps can write rudimentary news releases or pitch letters from information you submit.

Electronic publishing also has digital benefits to public relations practitioners. Some hardware and/or software can translate printed books into electronic formats. Some can actually translate from one language to another, or convert text into audio books.

WEBSITE

The Internet has made it possible for every organization and individual to have a **website**, a series of interconnected web pages, usually prepared and maintained as a collection of information by a person, group, or organization. Corporations and colleges, social advocates and political groups, cultural and arts organizations all use websites to communicate with people who are actively seeking their information.

The implication for public relations is enormous. For example, as the Makah people were planning to revive a dormant practice of hunting whales in the Pacific Northwest, the American Indian tribe used a website (makah.org) to provide a detailed question-and-answer page about its controversial plan. Animal rights protestors retaliated with a counterfeit rogue site (makah.com) that mocked the tribal site. The tribe has since obtained rights to the dot-com site.

President Barack Obama developed a tactic now emulated by most politicians when he established a website specifically to counter personal and political rumors and viral attacks. In response, Republicans set up a counter Obama fact-checking site.

Meanwhile several nonpartisan sites offer fact checking. Some of the leading sites are FactCheck.org by the Annenberg Center at the University of Pennsylvania, the Fact Checker blog at the *Washington Post* that awards Pinocchios for false statements, and PolitiFact.com associated with the Poynter Institute that uses a Truth-O-Meter that gives "Pants on Fire" ratings to outrageously false political claims.

Websites also give organizations access to online tactics associated with news media and promotional/advertising media. These will be discussed in subsequent sections of this chapter.

Additionally, touch-sensitive computers make it possible to apply an information-on-demand approach to several situations in which customers can use the computer to interact with the organization, both gaining and giving information.

Internet users distinguish between **Web 1.0**, which essentially was a one-way posting of commercial or promotional information by an organization, and **Web 2.0**, which involves using the Internet for interactivity, collaboration, and communication. Web 2.0 allows users to share postings and generate content for the website. Blogs, wikis, mashups, and other examples of social media are outgrowths of Web 2.0.

Social Media

The still-emerging phenomenon of social media provides various types of interactive media in which the audience is an active participant in the development and presentation of the messages.

Not only celebrities but also world leaders—kings, presidents, and prime ministers—are among the estimated 288 million Twitter users around the world. The Pope and the Dalai Lama, the Patriarch of Constantinople and the Archbishop of Canterbury, Pastor Rick Warren and Buddhist monk Thich Nhat Hanh all use Twitter.

After the White House, the most-followed Twitter accounts by government entities are those of NASA, Center for Disease Control and Prevention, Smithsonian Institution, State Department, and Agriculture Department. Other agencies with Twitter accounts include the Peace Corp, Bureau of Indian Affairs, FBI, National Park Service, and each military branch.

Social media can be useful during emergencies. Both FEMA and New York City used Twitter to present urgent information during Hurricane Irene. New Jersey used social media as part of the recovery effort after Hurricane Sandy. Philadelphia set up a network involving Facebook, LinkedIn, MySpace, Twitter, Blogspot, and YouTube to release emergency information. Twitter has been crucial for emergency communication during forest fires in Colorado and tornadoes in Oklahoma.

Anybody paying attention to world affairs knows that the grassroots revolutions in Egypt and Tunisia in 2011 were successful in large part because of social media. The terrorist organization ISIS has been very skilled in using Twitter, despite ongoing efforts to shut down ISIS-linked accounts. A Brookings Institution study released in 2015 estimated such sites at about 26,000.

How does all this use of social media impact public relations? Obviously, it enhances our toolbox with a powerful and wide-reaching new family of media. It also enhances credibility. The Nielsen Report found that only 55 percent of Americans trust advertising, but 78 percent trust recommendations on social media by other consumers.

With such widespread presence and popularity, it's not surprising that corporations and nonprofit organizations are finding social media useful. Politicians in particular have made social media a staple of their communication programs.

Politicians, as well as their supporters and opponents, use Twitter, Facebook, and other social media to announce, comment, criticize, berate, and otherwise communicate on every political topic imaginable. They try to turn their virtual friends into real, live voters. Using the technique of a **money bomb**, politicians have raised huge amounts of money during these one-day online events. Senator Rand Paul may have been the first to benefit from a successful money bomb when he raised more than $4 million in one day, followed a few weeks later by a second 24-hour blitz that raised more than $6 million.

The strategy of political candidates is not simply to use social media to issue pronouncements but rather to engage supporters, encourage them to share Facebook and tweets with others, register their likes, and retweet and reblog their messages.

BLOG

A type of social media, usually the work of a single author is the **blog** (a portmanteau for "web" and "log"). Some of these are the personal ramblings of individuals, though many reflect thoughtful opinions and information presented by recognized authorities in a subject.

Increasingly companies and nonprofit organizations use these open-to-all websites. Universities, advocacy groups, professional organizations, and similar institutions have set up some well-edited multi-author blogs.

Tumblr reports hosting 261 million public blogs in 2015, with 115 million at WordPress. Other popular blog-hosting sites include Blogger and SquareSpace.

Blogs feature postings of commentary, news, photos, and graphics, usually with links to other blogs or sites. Most are interactive, with users invited to react with additional questions, comments, and responses. Blogs generally focus on a particular topic, and the topics run the gamut: politics, travel, ethics, business, religion, environment, education, lifestyle, art, sports, and the like. They also commonly feature external links with social media used by an author or organization, such as a company Facebook site or an organization's YouTube page.

Adaptations of blogs include art blogs or photoblogs with their unique and obvious emphasis. Some specialty blogs even have their own names: **vlog** (a blog that contains primarily videos), **MP3 blog** (music), and **moblog** (written on a mobile device such as a cell phone).

Like blogs themselves, bloggers are a diverse group. Singers and athletes, senators and CEOs do blogging. Newspapers and television news stations have their own blogs in which reporters interact with audience members, and audience members with each other.

MICROBLOG

With limits of only a few characters, **microblog** sites provide users the opportunity to post on a wide range of topics.

WHO USES SOCIAL MEDIA?

From 89 percent of young adults to 54 percent of senior citizens, social media users are increasing in numbers. That's according to a 2014 report by the Pew Research Center.

According to the study, more than 1.15 billion users log into Facebook each month. The also-rans also have impressive stats: 359 million Google-Plus users, 215 million Twitter, 150 million Instagram, 20 million Pinterest, and 2 million Reddit.

Some politicians have as many Facebook friends and Twitter followers as athletes and rock stars. In 2015, President Obama (@BarackObama and @POTUS) had 85 million Twitter followers. Early in 2017, President Trump (@realDonaldTrump and @POTUS) had 42 million followers.

Another Twitter top spot for world leaders is Pope Francis (@Pontifex) with 23 million followers in nine languages. But with about 10,000 Spanish retweets and 7,500 English retweets, the Pope ranked the "most influential" social media user for three years in a row. The data is drawn from the 2015 Twiplomacy social media research study by the global public relations firm Burson-Marsteller. FYI, the Pope turns to his YouTube account or the Vatican's website when his message is longer than 140 characters. Or he uses his Instagram account (NewsVa).

The number of Twitter followers for popes and presidents pales in comparison to celebrities. Estimates are that Katy Perry has 96 million Twitter followers, Justin Bieber 92 million, Taylor Swift 83 million, Lady Gaga and Rihana 69 million each, Justin Timberlake 58 million, Ellen DeGeneris 66 million, Cristiano Ronaldo, Kim Kardashian, and Britney Spears 50 million each.

Every U.S. cabinet agency and all 50 state governors tweet. So too do 83 percent of Fortune 500 CEOs and 89 percent of American's top nonprofit executives, according to several recent studies.

Corporations likewise use social media. The Socialware company says 79 percent of Fortune 500 firms use corporate accounts for Twitter, YouTube, Facebook, or blogs to communicate with customers and other stakeholders. When it had to recall 2.3 million cars in 2010 because of faulty accelerator pedals, Toyota used social media to answer questions from customers.

Nonprofit organizations also make extensive use of social media. The Nonprofit Social Networking Report in 2015 found that 81 percent of nonprofit organizations use Facebook, 76 percent use Twitter, and 46 percent have YouTube accounts. A report by the University of Massachusetts ups that to 97 percent for all types of social media, concluding that nonprofits use Facebook, Twitter, LinkedIn, and YouTube even more than businesses do. Among the nonprofits, international associations lead the way, followed by environmental groups, with arts and cultural organizations coming in a close third.

The military and the government also use Facebook, Twitter, blogs, and other social media. The Navy has used a social media mix to commemorate the anniversary of the attack on Pearl Harbor. The Obama White House used social media to debunk myths about health-care reform and to orchestrate a worldwide audience to announce the killing of Osama bin Laden. FEMA gives disaster guidance on Twitter.

People in both Japan and the U.S. took to social media to commemorate the 70th anniversary of the atomic bombing of Hiroshima and Nagasaki.

Meanwhile, leading in Instagram accounts is Beyonce with 40 million followers, Kim Kardashian 39 million, Ariana Grande 38 million, Taylor Swift 37 million, Selena Gomez and Justin Bieber 37 million each, and Nicki Minaj 29 million. The average American teen has 150 followers, according to Statistica marketing research company's 2015 report.

Phase Three

STEP
7

Many microposts fall into the category of "What I'm thinking" or "What I'm Doing Now." As such, they often reflect a cult of personality based on the popularity of the microblogger. A study by Pear Analytics reported that 38 percent of Twitter posts are conversational, 4 percent news, 4 percent spam, 6 percent self promotion, and 40 percent "pointless babble."

The most common example of a microblog is Twitter, which claims about 350 million posts a day.

Twitter set the standard for Microblogging with its use of the hashtag, now common with other platforms including Google+, which allows its 550 million active users to organize around various thematic circles. Other platforms include Tumblr with 267 million blogs; Weibo, a China-based service; and Twister, a peer-to-peer service with no central point. This latter feature is important, because three nations—China, Iran, and North Korea—have managed to censor microblogging sites by blocking their central sites.

China, for example, is said to employ more than 2 million "Internet opinion analysts" to monitor microblog sites, deleting items with terms deemed "disharmonious"—social issues including drugs and pornography, and political themes including corruption, criticism of communism or of government policy, and mention of politicians out of favor with the government. The censorship takes various forms, including banning an account or an IP address, deleting posts, and hiding the post so nobody can view it.

Related to microblogs is texting, an example of Short Message Service (SMS) that includes text, video, and links.

COLLABORATION

As a collaborative community website, a **wiki** allows any user to edit the content of the website by adding material, modifying it, even deleting it if they wish. One of the most-used wikis is Wikipedia. Some companies and organizations use wikis as an active substitute for the more static Intranet that users cannot edit.

Some wikis draw on popular culture, such as those for TV series including *The Vampire Diaries*, *The Muppet Show*, *Walking Dead*, *My Little Pony*, and *Game of Thrones*, as well as *Call of Duty: Modern Warfare 2* and *Warframe* video games. There also are wikis for books such as *Harry Potter* and *Monster Girl* and sports wikis for baseball, basketball, ice hockey, football, curling, and wrestling.

One problem with wikis is online vandalism. Users can add false information, calling into question the credibility of all wiki information and fueling the criticism that wikis by nature favor consensus over credentials. This is the reason that many college professors, for example, ban material on Wikipedia from being cited in academic research papers.

What are the implications for public relations practitioners? For one thing, don't be surprised to see information about your company or organization at a wiki site. Realize that the rules of engagement on public relations use of social media are still evolving. Wikipedia, for example, allows anyone except public relations people to edit postings. Company policy specifically bans public relations practitioners from modifying entries on behalf of their organizations or clients. Instead, founder Jimmy Wales has said that public relations practitioners may merely post comments in the discussion section of the entry. Regardless of any such internal controls, the PRSA Code of Ethics calls for public relations practitioners to disclose any financial or other connections to subjects they write about.

SOCIAL NETWORKS

A variety of social forums are available online. In general, **social networking** refers to an online service aimed at building and reflecting a relationship among people who share common interests. More than half of adults in North America use at least one social network.

Posted information, responses, photos, and videos are common elements of social network sites such as Facebook (with more than 1.6 billion registered users), Twitter (1.2 million), Google+ (550 million), LinkedIn (400 million), Instagram (400 million), Snapchat (200 million), Flickr (112 million), and Pinterest and Vimeo (100 million each).

Many of these are discussion sites that provide virtual places for people to hold conversations on specific topics, which can range from genealogy to bodybuilding, erotic literature to personal finance.

Discussions generally are subdivided into threads or topics. Some allow for anonymous postings; other require users to register in order to post messages. Many are set up in question–answer format. Some have moderators who maintain standards of relevancy, eliminate spam, remove offensive posts, and so on.

Some social networking sites are specialized for particular audiences: ethnic-oriented sites such as BlackPlanet for African Americans and MiGente for the Hispanic community; religion-focused sites such as Muxlim for young Muslims and Xt3 for young Catholics; and nationally oriented sites such as LunarStorm for Swedish teens and Chirundu, which bills itself as "the place for homesick Africans." Other sites are focused around particular interests such as CafeMom for mothers, and Disaboom for people with disabilities, or around occupations, such as Labroots for scientists and TeachStreet for teachers.

Some business networks provide a point of interaction by people in a particular business or profession. Examples are Niznik, Fast Pitch, Young Entrepreneur, and Cofoundr.

Some forums operate like classified ads, offering users the ability to interact in order to buy and sell items. Craigslist is the largest such site. Other popular classified ad sites are Monster, eBay Classifieds, Geebo, Oodle, and ClassifiedsGiant.

Meanwhile, online gaming is the focus of some social forums, allowing users to interact. Some of these are card-playing sites, such as Bet Online and World Series of Poker.

Others such as Kongregate, Armor Games, Newgrounds, and the aptly named Addicting Games are homes to many different online games. These include shooter games, strategy games, multi-user virtual world games, and massively multiplayer online games (MMOGs) that may host thousands of players interacting at the same time.

Some reports indicate that the number of daily active online gamers worldwide is more than 150 billion.

Some corporations are using game-based training in their employee relations programs. Companies including Microsoft and Google use game-based principles that promote learning and help develop problem-solving skills.

NEWS AGGREGATE

Some social media sites exist primarily to provide news articles from various sources on topics of interest to readers. Many of these have a moderated top-news element, followed by news items in various categories selected by users. Thus users can tailor the site to focus on sports, business, entertainment, religion, politics, and/or many other areas of personal interest.

Yahoo News with 175 million daily visitors and Google News with 150 million are the largest independent news aggregating sites. Other sites are operated by various newsgathering

Phase Three

STEP
7

CROWDFUNDING AND VIRAL PHILANTHROPY

Nonprofit organizations use social media to increase membership and to raise funds, sometimes with spectacular success.

Crowdfunding is the name for the online process of raising money from a large number of donor/investors. An estimate by the research firm Massolution estimated that crowfunding raised more than $34 billion worldwide in 2015, and the growth has been doubling every year. Massolution is associated with crowdsourcing.org, a kind of portal for research, links, and other resources for online philanthropy.

Massolution has identified 1,250 active crowdfunding platforms around the world. Most crowdfunding activity is with start-up businesses seeking investors. Other top categories are social causes, film and performing arts, real estate, and music and recording arts.

Here are some specific examples. Kickstarter claims to have generated more than $1.5 billion for more than 200,000 creative projects such as music, films, food, fashion, and so on. MicroVentures, EquityNet, IndiGoGo, and SeedInvest connect investors with start-up companies. Razoo claims to support more than 100,000 fundraising websites that have generated $400,000 in contributions.

Some platforms focus on personal fundraising. GoFundMe says it has raised more than $1.3 billion online, focusing on life events such as accidents and illnesses. Other large personal and charitable fundraising entities include Crowdrise, Crowdfunder, Fundly, GiveForward, and DonorsChoose.

Online fundraising starts with a compelling cause. The global relief agency Oxfam had no advertising budget for its program to raise $35 million to address the famine in East Africa. So Oxfam turned to YouTube and Facebook. The agency parlayed the donation of a dress worn to the Academy Awards by Jennifer Aniston into a nine-day eBay auction that raised $50,000—enough to immunize 50,000 children in Africa.

More important for Oxfam's long-term visibility with a new and younger audience, the auction attracted 2,500 online observers for the final bidding.

The Oxfam project is one example of nonprofit organizations using social media to raise awareness of a social issue and to raise funds to address the problem. It's called **viral philanthropy**, an emerging aspect of fundraising in which many people are asked to give a little bit to the cause and encourage their friends to do likewise.

With little or no advertising budget, viral philanthropy turns its attention to social media such as bloggers and social networking media such as MySpace and Facebook, which have embraced the concept of charitable giving among participants. Facebook Causes, a site for Facebook members to create or promote a cause, claims to have raised more than $40 million for everything from educating girls in Africa and fighting anti-Semitism to opposing bullying and supporting arts in public schools.

The Aniston gift to Oxfam was part of a campaign by the Clothes Off Our Back celebrity auction program founded by husband-and-wife actors Bradley Whitford and Jane Kaczmarek. The foundation has raised more than $4 million in 10 years. Meanwhile, Keira Knightley gave the gown she wore in the movie *Atonement*. That dress was auctioned on eBay for the benefit of the Children's Charity of Southern California. From an opening bid of $1,000, bidding reached $46,000.

Other organizations have turned to social networking media to support humanitarian causes. Following the Asian tsunami in 2004, the Yarn Harlot, a blog about knitting, asked readers to give $1 each to Doctors Without Borders, an international medical aid agency. By 2016, the project, called Knitters Without Borders/Tricoteuses sans Frontières, had raised more than $4,102,600 and continues to foster donations for the international medical charity.

Meanwhile, People for the Ethical Treatment of Animals created a MySpace profile and recruited 120,000 new supporters interested in animal rights.

Collecting Facebook likes, posting Pinterest, and changing Twitter icons often becomes a social networking end in itself. There's even a name for it—slacktivism. It means drawing attention to a cause but doing nothing practical to address it.

In 2013 UNICEF Sweden created a social media campaign to challenge the perception that liking is a useful result. Its "Likes don't save lives" campaign featured four YouTube videos. In one video, for example, two celebrities tried to pay for food and a sweater with likes. In another, a 10-year-old boy responsible for caring for his younger brother notes that UNICEF soon might reach 200,000 likes, "then we should be alright."

Meanwhile, an online ad—"Like us on Facebook, and we will vaccinate zero children against polio"—went viral. The videos were viewed more than 750,000 times in 195 countries.

"We have nothing against likes, but vaccine costs money," continued the ad. The message was persuasive, with enough money raised to vaccinate more than 637,000 children. Advertising critics rated it as one of the most effective social ads of the year.

organizations, led by CNN with 95 million, *New York Times* 70 million, Fox News 65 million, and NBC 63 million. EbixMBA tracks users for various types of online sites, from video games to politics, business to movies, gossip to sports.

Some sites also allow users to post news items. DIGG, Reddit, and Newsvine are examples of this type of social news site. On many such sites, articles receiving user votes are upgraded to front-page placement.

MEDIA SHARING

Some social networking sites offer opportunities for users to share photos, videos, and slides. Some sites are free; others charge consumers to host and share photos and videos. Advertising supports some free sites.

YouTube began as a video sharing website in 2005, now claiming 800 million unique visitors each month. Flickr began in 2004 as a photograph-sharing site, now boasting more than 3.5 million new images uploaded every day. Vimeo created an awards competition to showcase creative video content. SlideShare, which offers its 70 million monthly visitors both public and private modes, has been named one of the Top 10 tools for education and e-learning.

Public relations practitioners have found use for such sharing sites. Companies post job openings and marketing materials, news clips, and product how-tos. Some postings using video news clips and clips from films have raised copyright concerns on the part of mainstream news and entertainment media.

The Associated Press and Reuters news agencies post videos to YouTube, and other businesses and organizations are using the various video media to strategically present their messages to younger audiences.

Phase Three

STEP
7

The growing availability of user-generated **viral video** is playing an increasing role in strategic communication efforts. The term refers to the widespread dissemination and popularity of a video clip, generally circulated via email or text messaging and posted on Internet blogs or other websites.

In addition to the appallingly cute—kids, kittens, puppies, and hamsters—some viral videos have a definite news value. Many were originally caught on cell phones: a judge beating his disabled daughter, provoked and unprovoked violence, politicians and police in their unguarded moments, and racist rants. They also include a range of hugs and acts of human kindness.

Viral video has played a notable role in marketing of bands and movies. Super Bowl ads often get similar attention, as do celebrity shenanigans.

CUSTOMER REVIEW

Studies show that up to 90 percent of customers say their buying decisions are influenced by online review. Most of these also are ready to give their opinions about the quality of products and service.

Some sites are general purpose, such as Angie's List, Epinions, Consumer Reports, FourSquare, and Amazon Customer Reviews. Others are industry-specific: TripAdvisor and Virtualtourist for the travel and hospitality; Yelp, Zagat, and Urban Spoon for restaurants; and CollegeProwler and RateMyProfessor for education.

CASE IN POINT Online for Japanese Cuisine

The tech-savvy Japanese restaurant Sato is a newcomer to the food scene in Buffalo, N.Y. In its first year and a half in a trendy neighborhood in the city, owners Satomi and Josh Smith used social media to generate buzz and gain customers.

With many food bloggers in Western New York and Southern Ontario, it was natural that the restaurateurs initiated contacts with these semi-professional foodies. They periodically provided information to online and print food critics—awards from local food competitions, new menu items, catering, a gallery of signature dishes, and of course menus.

Sato's interactive website (SatoBuffalo.com) features news updates: Josh becoming a certified sake sommelier, their debut in making their own ramen and soba noodles, the opening of a Sato Ramen noodle bar near one of the city's universities, a contract with a local craft beer brewery to create a yuzu IPA beer, their selection to provide sushi for the Buffalo Bills, and the opening of a new venue, Sato Brewpub.

The website reprints or links to articles in newspapers and magazines that have reviewed their menu or publicized the restaurant. The site features podcasts of interviews with a food-and-beverage interview series, as well as articles on sake and Japanese food that Josh had written for other blogs.

The restaurant is involved in a full range of social media: Facebook, Twitter, and Instagram. Customers are encouraged to comment on Yelp. The site links to various Japanese music, art, and cultural sites. Meanwhile, its Sato Blog allows readers to filter by recency or popularity and to share the site with others.

Strategists say there are several ways to generate reader interest in review sites. One is by befriending customers and engaging them on a human level. Another is by responding to both positive and negative comments, though not defensively with the latter. Addressing complaints, even minor ones, is a good way to increase positive customer reviews. As a matter of ethics, never directly solicit or offer incentives for positive reviews.

One danger with review sites is that customers are usually more inclined to criticize than to praise. If the food at a new restaurant is excellent and the service top-notch, but you find a hair in your salad, what are you likely to say on social media? Reviewers also often come from a limited perspective, so they complain that the spaghetti sauce isn't authentic when they simply mean that it's not the way their Nonna made it.

Managers have learned to be patient, allowing other customers to counter negative comments.

PLANNING EXAMPLE 7B **Selecting Organizational and Social Media Tactics**

Upstate College will develop the following tactics using organizational media to publicize its expanded program:

- Virtual college tour—key publics, high visual impact
- Online transfer brochure—key publics, high impact, low cost
- Letter to former applicants—targeted, low cost
- Poster—moderate cost, high visual impact
- Video—targeting key publics, high cost
- Website: home page—information-seeking publics, low cost, for potential transfer students, interactive

---

Tiny Tykes will develop the following tactics using organizational media for an employee-oriented public relations program:

- Newsletter articles in employee publication about safety, quality, and customer satisfaction—key public, low cost
- Memo about product reintroduction—key public, low cost
- Employee bulletin with updates on customer response to product reintroduction (pro and con)—key public, low cost
- Brochures about safety, quality, and customer satisfaction—moderate cost
- Letter to families of employees thanking them for supporting employees and company during difficult reintroduction period—key public, low cost
- Suggestion box soliciting employee input about safety and quality, with feedback via employee—key public, low cost
- Newsletter—low cost, interactive

Checklist 7B **Organizational and Social Media Tactics**

Basic Questions

1. What organizational media tactics will you use?
2. How will these tactics help the organization achieve its objectives?
3. What resources will these tactics require?

Expanded Questions

A. SELECTION OF TACTICS

From the following categories of organizational media tactics, identify several that you would consider using.

Publications
- Serial publications (newsletter, house organ, bulletin)
- Stand-alone publications (brochure, leaflet, folder, pamphlet, booklet, tract, circular)
- Reprints (internal news release)
- Progress reports (annual report, quarterly report)
- User kits, teacher kits
- Research reports
- Miscellaneous print media

Direct Mail
- Memos
- Letters (appeal letter, marketing letter, postcard, invitation, catalog)
- Postcards
- Invitations
- Catalogs

Electronic Media
- Audio (telephone, dial-a-message, recorded information, demo tape, demo CD, podcast)
- Video (nonbroadcast video, corporate video, internal video, video conference, tele-conference, slide show)
- Electronic publishing

Digital Media
- Mail
- Website
- Cell phone

Social Media

- Blog
- Microblog (Twitter)
- Collaboration (Wiki)
- Social network (Facebook, LinkedIn, Google+)
- Media sharing (YouTube, Flickr, Vimeo, Slideshare)
- Customer review

B. STRATEGIC IMPLICATIONS

For each item identified, answer the following questions.

1. Will this tactic help the organization to interact with the appropriate public?
2. What level of impact will this tactic make on the key public?
3. Will this tactic advance the organization toward its awareness objectives?
4. Will this tactic advance the organization toward its acceptance objectives?
5. Will this tactic advance the organization toward its action objectives?
6. What is the main advantage to this tactic?
7. What advantages does this tactic offer that other tactics do not?
8. Are there any disadvantages with this tactic? If so, what are they?

C. IMPLEMENTATION ITEMS

For each item identified, answer the following questions.

1. How much will it cost to implement this tactic? Is the cost justified? Is the cost practical, based on the organization's resources?
2. How much staff time will it take to implement this tactic? Is the time practical, based on the organization's resources?
3. What skill level, equipment, and expertise are needed to implement this tactic? Is the needed level available within the organization? Is it available from outside sources?

Earned Media: News Media Tactics

News media are communication vehicles that exist primarily to present newsworthy information to various audiences. There is much diversity among news media. Consider the possibilities:

- Print media, such as newspapers and magazines (both in traditional print style and/or in digital format)
- News blogs
- Broadcast media, including radio and television
- Interactive news tactics, including interviews and conferences

Phase Three

STEP
7

Though all of these media are focused on news, each provides a somewhat different opportunity for public relations and marketing communication.

Strategy for Earned Media

News media offer public relations and marketing practitioners several benefits not usually associated with tactics in the other categories. They reach large audiences, cost little, and enhance credibility, which are the primary benefits that earned media have over owned and paid media.

First, news media generally reach large audiences—certainly larger than most audiences associated with interpersonal communication tactics, and usually larger than those for organizational media. News media audiences may encompass most residents of a particular community, most members of a certain profession, or most people who are seriously interested in a given topic. Thus, news media tactics can further an organization's pursuit of awareness objectives.

Second, the publicity that can be generated through these media is free. Unlike the built-in cost of organizational media and the high fees associated with advertising, no price tag is associated with publicity. Obviously the organization will have overhead costs, such as staff or agency/contractor time in researching and writing materials such as news releases, as well as the cost associated with printing and distributing such releases or producing electronic versions. But these are internal administrative costs and incidental expenses.

News media are considered uncontrolled media, creating the environment for the third, and perhaps most important, benefit they offer: They can add credibility to an organization's message. They have the power of what's called **third-party endorsement**, meaning that someone outside the organization preparing the message—a reporter, editor, blogger, or news director—is attesting to the significance and validity of the information being presented.

This concept of third-party endorsement has given news media high marks as credible disseminators of messages.

Unlike a newsletter, website, or advertisement in which the organization can say pretty much anything it likes, news media demand a certain level of accuracy and neutrality. Audiences presume that journalists evaluate the accuracy of information presented and check the claims being made before the story is presented to readers, listeners, or viewers. This added credibility can go a long way toward achieving the acceptance objectives of the organization.

Another aspect of the strategy of communicating through news media involves providing journalists with information in formats that they can use. Review Step 5 and make sure that you are offering real news.

Package news from your organization or client in a manner that journalists prefer. That means, for example, using Associated Press style guidelines for writing news releases and fact sheets.

Another strategic concern is to understand how audiences use the news media and then to write accordingly. News media carry the organization's message to people who are not actively seeking it. Readers and viewers intend to catch up on the day's events when they sit down with the newspaper or log on to an Internet news source, but they aren't especially looking for information about a particular organization. They more or less stumble over it and, if it seems to suit their interests and needs, they will read the information and perhaps act on it.

The lesson for public relations: Provide enough background and context so that audiences learning about your organization for the first time will have enough information to act on if they are so inclined.

Media Use and Credibility

The interesting thing about new technology is that it isn't squeezing out the old. People still report getting information from all kinds of media.

A Pew Research Center study in 2011 reported that 81 percent of Americans get news from television, 55 percent from newspapers, 15 percent from the Internet, and 19 percent from radio. However, some generational shifts are taking place that may mean significant changes in the future. Most Americans younger than 30 get their news online. Less than a third of young Americans turn directly to newspapers as their main news source.

Nevertheless, Pew notes that 48 percent of online news originates with general-interest newspapers, where most working journalists reside. Another 20 percent originates with local television. Thus traditional newsgathering organizations are responsible for most of the news available online.

There often is talk that the news media are dying. Not true. But they are changing. Increasingly, Americans are turning to social media for news, both for convenience and because they can comment on news topics. Young people in particular are accessing the news media in ways that are different from their parents.

When the Knight Foundation surveyed high school students in 2011, it found that, in a typical day, 77 percent of teens get their news from television, 54 percent by reading an article online, 48 percent by watching news video online, and 42 percent by reading an article in a newspaper. Yet 88 percent of the high schoolers said newspapers are generally truthful, compared with 78 percent of television news, and 58 percent of websites. They found only 34 percent of social media truthful.

In 2015, Pew reported that Twitter was topping Facebook 59–31 percent as a preferred new source. Pew found that 68 percent of smart-phone users at least occasionally follow breaking news on their phones; 33 percent frequently do so.

A major criterion in how public relations practitioners create a media mix for their messages is the relative credibility among the media venues. Credibility is a significant point of comparison among various types of media and news sources.

The 2011 Pew study reported that 69 percent of respondents say they trust information from local news organizations, 59 percent from national news organizations, 51 percent from state government, 50 percent from the White House, 44 percent from federal agencies, 41 percent from business corporations, 37 percent from Congress, and 29 percent from candidates running for office.

In 2015, Pew reported that roughly half of online users trust television news networks: 54 percent CNN, 50 percent ABC and NBC, 46 percent CBS, and 44 percent Fox. Such studies reveal a deep partisan divide. Democrats and/or liberals generally rate all news media as more credible than do Republicans/conservatives, with Independents solidly in the middle.

But local TV news tops the list of all news media for credibility. It has a believability rating of 65 percent, according to a 2015 Quinnipiac University Poll. Quinnipiac reported that

ABC and CBS each earn the trust of 64 percent of adults, followed by NBC at 60 percent, Fox at 55 percent, CNN at 54 percent, and MSNBC at 52 percent.

Newspaper

Newspapers are publications that boast of up-to-date printed information—reports of what happened the previous day or even earlier on the same day of their distribution. They may be published daily or nondaily (usually weekly, some with more or less frequency).

A helpful tool for public relations practitioners is a **media directory**, which provides information on media outlets. Directories include names and contact information for editors and other media gatekeepers, publication information, advertising rates, and other useful information.

Circulation for some daily newspapers is high. The *Wall Street Journal*, *USA Today*, and the *New York Times* are the three largest U.S. newspapers, circulating more than 2.1 million, 1.8 million, and 1.6 million copies respectively in 2014. Internationally, the *Yomiuri Shimbun* in Tokyo circulates 13.5 million copies daily to a total reading audience of 26 million. Four of the world's five largest newspapers are published in Japan. The largest U.S. newspaper is placed 17th.

The number of newspapers in North America has been declining in recent decades as the cost of publishing, corporate mergers, and the pressures of competition have forced financially weaker publications out of business. Simultaneously, newspaper audiences are getting older, and younger information consumers are more likely to get their news online. Nevertheless, most opinion leaders—business people, educators, politicians, clergy, and others in positions of influence—are newspaper readers, and many "average citizens" make newspaper reading a part of their daily information-gathering habit.

The Newspaper Association of America's audience profile reports the following profile of U.S. newspaper readers for both print and online versions of daily newspapers: 49 percent male readers and 51 percent female; 71 percent age 35 or older and 32 percent age 55 or older; 89 percent white; 63 percent married; 51 percent income of $50,000 or more; 26 percent college graduate. This profile could affect the future practice of public relations, with low newspaper readership among growing demographic groups within the population, particularly youth and minorities.

Here is a look at several categories of newspapers.

GENERAL-INTEREST NEWSPAPER

A **general-interest newspaper** represents the most common type of newspapers, appealing to the diverse interests of a wide spectrum of readers. Most of these are local newspapers published for the residents of a particular town, city, or metropolitan area; some are national in scope.

General-interest newspapers cover topics such as current events, including crimes, accidents, births and deaths; political and business news; sports and entertainment reports; information about the arts and leisure pursuits such as cooking and gardening; announcements of upcoming meetings and activities; and specialized information relating to issues such as education and health. Most local newspapers also include opinion sections with editorials and letters from readers.

SPECIAL-INTEREST NEWSPAPER

Special-interest newspapers are devoted to markets such as the arts, business, sports, entertainment, or other specific sectors. Though the topic for each publication is narrow, information in such newspapers is intended for a wide audience. *The Hockey News* and *Indian Country Today* are examples of special-interest newspapers.

TRADE NEWSPAPER

A similar type of publication, a **trade newspaper**, focuses on a particular industry or profession. Unlike organizational newspapers that are published by a particular company or nonprofit organization, trade newspapers are usually published by professional organizations or trade associations that serve the needs of several different companies and nonprofit groups linked to a particular industry or profession.

Some trade newspapers are independently published, such as *Overdrive,* a biweekly newspaper for truckers. Industry associations publish for people working in a specific field, such as *Carolina Cattle Connection,* the official newspaper for members of the North and South Carolina Cattlemen's Associations.

SPECIAL-AUDIENCE NEWSPAPER

A **special-audience newspaper** is similar to a special-interest newspaper, but it is written for particular audiences, such as gay and lesbian readers, the military, African Americans, and Jewish or Hispanic readers. Information in these newspapers is often diverse, though the appeal is clearly linked to a specific audience.

Such publications are published for many ethnic, religious, national, cultural, occupational, or other such groups. Some such newspapers are printed in languages other than English.

ORGANIZATIONAL NEWSPAPER

An **organizational newspaper**, also called a **house organ**, is published by a political, ethnic, religious, educational, and other type of group. Information in them generally deals with those organizations and their members. *Public Relations Tactics*, published for members of the Public Relations Society of America (PRSA), is an example of an organizational newspaper.

Organizational newspapers sometimes overlap special-interest and special-audience papers. For example, the *Navajo Times*, the official newspaper of the Navajo Nation, is primarily read by Navajos (special audience) and by others who are particularly interested in Native Americans in general or the Navajo people in particular (special interest).

Magazine

A **magazine** is a publication with less frequency and less immediacy than a newspaper. Prepublication time may be several days, even several weeks, from when a story is written until the time that magazine is distributed to readers. Some magazines are local or regional and thus focused on a particular geographic area, but most are of more general interest and their content is softer news and more feature-based than most newspapers.

Like newspapers, magazines based in the U.S. and Canada are published in many different languages—about 50 in all. These include the three most common languages in North America—English, French, and Spanish—as well as several Native American or First Nations

(Native Canadian) languages, and also less-common languages such as Welsh, Urdu, Latin, and Icelandic.

Writer's Market, a comprehensive listing of magazines published in North America, lists thousands of **popular magazines** (also called **consumer magazines**), the kind found on newsstands and through subscription services. These are published in several different categories: general circulation, college, health, foreign language, ethnic, music, men's interest, women's interest, sports, and so on.

Additionally, there are an untold number of house organs produced within a particular company or organization. These usually focus on organizational issues and are intended for employees, volunteers, stockholders, donors, and other interested audiences. Examples of house organs are *Police Chief*, a monthly magazine published by the International Association of Chiefs of Police, and *Boys' Life*, the official magazine of Boy Scouts of America.

Sometimes the categories can overlap. Some magazines are published for special audiences, such as *Essence* for black women and *Seventeen* for teenage girls. Meanwhile, trade magazines are published by and/or for particular businesses, professions and industries. Some of these are published by organizations, such as the *Canadian Guernsey Journal* published by the Canadian Guernsey Association. Other magazines are independently published, such as *Sheep!* for sheep farmers.

Especially in the trade press, distinctions often blur among newspapers, magazines, and newsletters, both printed and online versions.

Consider the financial media, for example. It includes daily business-oriented newspapers such as the *Wall Street Journal*, weekly newspapers such as the *Business Journal of Central New York*, regional magazines such as *Colorado Business*, business sections in most metropolitan daily newspapers, business magazines such as *Forbes* and *Business Week*, consumer magazines such as *Money* and *Fortune*, financial newsletters such as the *Kiplinger Report*, company newsletters published by individual brokerage firms and investment companies, and financial columnists such as Jane Bryant Quinn and commentators such as Suze Ormond.

The actual number of magazines is impossible to calculate accurately, but it is vast. In just the area of religion, for example, the American Society of Magazine Editors lists 784 magazines focused on religion, many of them associated with a particular denomination, diocese, or religious order. *Religious Periodicals of the United States: Academic and Scholarly Journals* has estimated that there are more than 2,500 religious magazines.

A new addition to the publishing field is the *e-zine*, an email-based magazine. The trend toward e-zines began in the mid-1990s, when magazine publishers began placing editorial content, stories and photographs at their magazine websites. Now thousands of e-zines are published online.

Many online magazines also feature interactive opportunities for readers, much of this involving catalog sections of the magazines in which readers can order products from a variety of companies. Examples are WeirdMusic.net about creative indie music, and Syscoezine.com for cooking enthusiasts.

News Blog

Blogs are merging with more traditional forms of news media. Some bloggers consider themselves journalists, and a few have broken stories that later are taken up by mainstream

TRUSTED NEWS SOURCES

A report for the Public Relations Society of America by Harris Interactive (2005) focused in part on the trust level for various information sources by a cross-section of American civil society: adult consumers, corporate executives, and bipartisan congressional staffers. The study found that National Public Radio (NPR) and TV's Public Broadcasting Service (PBS) are the most trusted news sources, and advertising the least trusted.

Here's a synopsis of the findings. The three numbers indicate the positive percentage of adult consumers, corporate executives, and congressional staffers, respectively.

- Belief that most of the news is accurate and unbiased (43, 38, 33 percent)
- Reliance on independent news sources such as Internet chat rooms, blogs, or other alternative media (42, 21, 30)
- Trust levels regarding news via NPR or PBS (61, 75, 70)
- Trust levels regarding news in national newspapers (56, 78, 78)
- Trust levels regarding television and radio network news (53, 59, 62)
- Trust levels regarding advocacy organizations such as the National Rifle Association, the American Association of Retired Persons, and the American Civil Liberties Union (44, 18, 39)
- Trust levels regarding public relations sources (37, 29, 29)
- Trust levels regarding celebrity spokespersons (30, 8, 13)
- Trust levels regarding advertising sources (25, 24, 20)
- Public relations people presenting misleading information (85, 67, 85)
- Public relations people raising public awareness on important issues (71, 84, 84)

newspapers and television. Many journalists publish their own blogs to provide additional commentary and insight into the stories they are reporting.

Blogs also are gaining influence in the political arena. Political blogs such as the *Daily Kos*, *Politico*, *Huffington Post*, *Drudge Report*, and *Salon* are hugely influential in American politics. Such blogs sometimes beat the mainstream media in reporting news.

Bloggers also create third-party endorsement, those independent and influential voices that have the ear of an organization's publics. Because of their independence, they also have potential high credibility. That's why Walmart enlisted bloggers in its campaign to counter media-reported criticism of its efforts to open new stores against rising consumer opposition. That's also why companies such as Cingular Wireless, Microsoft, and General Electric have met with bloggers before going public with new products. Meanwhile, restaurants court food bloggers, athletes interact with sports bloggers, and so on.

The rules about blogging vis-à-vis public relations are still emerging. Blog readers expect to find only firsthand accounts posted online, and most bloggers resent blatant public relations use of their medium.

Standard public relations practice involves providing advice and assistance on getting the message out. A politician or business executive may hire a ghostwriter to help with an op-ed piece or magazine article, and consultants often draft speeches and public statements. But many people feel that **ghost blogging** in someone else's name crosses the ethical line. The key seems to be the extent to which the blog is presented as being personal rather than corporate, and the amount of involvement that the named author of the blog has in the piece. The ultimate test is whether readers feel betrayed if they find out that someone ghosted the blog.

In a similar situation, some bloggers have lost credibility for themselves by willingly publishing verbatim "plants" from government or corporate sources without identifying them as handouts.

Blogs generally are search-engine friendly, and with now more than 257 million blog accounts on Tumblr alone, it's not surprising that many organizations are eyeing the use of blogs to promote their products, services, and causes. Some organizations even have people assigned to the post of **blogger relations**.

Many people in public relations and marketing communications make it part of their daily research to monitor blogs dealing with topics of interest to their organizations or clients. Blogs can provide a look at the competition and an insight into the interests of customers, donors, fans, and other publics. As an advance glimpse into what could grow into widespread public opinion, they also provide an early warning system into potential problems with your own organization.

How should you pitch a story to bloggers? Remember that bloggers work for themselves (or, figuratively, for their audiences). They are busy professionals. Here are some tips on how to approach them with a story idea.

1. Read the blog. That's perhaps the most important piece of advice. Learn about the blog, be familiar with the kind of material it uses, and then try to fit your pitch around what you know the blog is interested in.
2. Provide information relevant to this particular blog. There is no place for generalities. Rework your information to fit the specific needs of the blog you are hoping to interest.
3. Don't overlook smaller bloggers who may not be best known on this subject but who may have links with top bloggers in your field.
4. Make it easy for the blogger to use your information. Provide a summary, written to the approximate length of most of the entries in this blog. Add a link to a longer online news release or other document if it's relevant. Remember what you learned about writing good news leads.
5. Keep the blogger's audience in mind. Make sure you tailor your information to serve the interest and address the benefit for this particular audience.

Radio

Whether in traditional or new configurations, radio is found virtually everywhere. Audiences are large, with most people listening to radio at some time during a typical week. Combination news, talk, and information stations have the most listeners, followed by stations with a country-music format, according to Arbitron ratings.

One of the benefits of radio is its mobility. This is a positive quality in that it can travel with people. It's also a negative one from a public relations standpoint, because people listen passively to radio while doing other things (such as driving, working, and reading).

BLOGGER RELATIONS

Steve Rubel of Edelman Public Relations recommends that public relations practitioners focus on how they can help bloggers rather than how bloggers can help the practitioners' clients or organizations. Rubel advocates a strategy of blending both traditional media and bloggers in an effort to extend the reach and impact of an organization's message.

Blogger relations is a new form of public relations focused on the key public of bloggers. Many bloggers see themselves involved in **citizen journalism**, a phenomenon also known as **participatory journalism** or **grassroots journalism**.

The principle at work here is that such bloggers self-identify as playing an active role in gathering, reporting, and commenting on news. A few news bloggers have a growing credibility with mainstream news media, in part because, as mavericks who are not constrained by some of the corporate or ethical boundaries of professional journalists, they have occasionally broken important news stories. But some bloggers are seen merely as digital hacks unrestrained by ethical or other journalistic standards.

Only a few bloggers do original news research. Most blogs play the role of an alert system, repeating news from more standard journalistic sources.

Nevertheless, bloggers are making their presence felt. It was bloggers who fueled the debunking of military documents that newscaster Dan Rather and CBS News used in questioning President George W. Bush's military service. In 2007, the Associated Press partnered with the Media Bloggers Association to carry blog-generated news reports in its coverage of I. Lewis "Scooter" Libby's trial for outing CIA agent Valerie Plame for political purposes on behalf of the White House.

Indeed, many people who turn on radios can hardly be called listeners. They use radio mainly to overcome silence. Because of this, research shows that audience recall of radio commercials is less than for television commercials. However, the relatively low cost of radio advertising allows for heavier repetition than many organizations generally can afford via television. Radio generally attracts individuals alone (unlike television, which often is watched by people in groups). So when radio audiences do really listen, they focus on what is being said.

Because radio formats are specific, audiences tend to be very different from one station to another. National Public Radio, for example, is popular with opinion leaders in many different environments. Classic rock stations find that two-thirds of listeners are between the ages of 18 and 34; they are particularly strong with young men under age 25. News and talk stations draw an audience heavy with men and women 35–54, with the total audience better educated than Americans in general.

Studies also report that stations focused on contemporary music attract women under 30 and teenagers. Country music stations, long a staple in radio broadcasting, are losing audiences, particularly in urban areas where ethnic populations prefer different styles of music.

Phase Three

STEP
7

What are the strategic implications of all this? Let's say you are operating a restaurant or a retail store. If you want to attract younger customers, pipe rock music over the sound system. On the other hand, if you want more senior citizens, use easy listening or nostalgic music. Country music listeners tend to be women aged 25–54, with lower incomes than women in the Top 40 audience.

Thus it is important to know your key publics before making decisions about particular stations.

Here is an overview of three types of radio services: terrestrial, online, and satellite.

TERRESTRIAL RADIO

The category of **terrestrial radio** includes both the AM and FM formats, with signals sent via transmitters. Generally AM is more oriented toward news, sports, or talk, whereas FM often includes more all-music formats. The stations may be commercial or public.

Experts count about 44,000 radio stations worldwide. The U.S. and Canada together have about 14,500 radio stations; about 5,100 are AM stations and 9,400 are FM stations. Most of these are commercial stations but about 1,260 are public, plus about 2,500 educational stations.

Many radio news opportunities exist at the local level, others through about 115 national networks. These include large networks such as ABC Radio or the UPI Radio Network, and smaller, specialized networks such as American Ag Radio Network with agricultural information and Kidwaves Radio Network with children's programming.

ONLINE RADIO

The new forms of radio are making inroads in the audiences. **Online radio** (sometimes called **Internet radio** or **streaming radio**) carries web-based stations as well as radio-like collections of music in categories tailored to the individual listener's interests such as Pandora and Google Music and talk shows dealing with topics such as sports, politics, and religion.

Internet radio is a meaningful competitor to traditional AM and FM stations. EMarketer estimated 67 percent of adult Americans using online radio in 2015.

SATELLITE RADIO

Another category, satellite radio (sometimes called **subscription radio** or **digital radio**), offers clear digital signals to audience members who subscribe to the service. The signal is transmitted via satellite, so it covers thousands of miles, compared to the limited listening area of terrestrial stations. Satellite radio has advantages of being free from U.S. Federal Communications Commission content restrictions and of being relatively devoid of commercials. It is growing, while struggling for a wider audience.

Satellite radio generally is a subscription-based service that, unlike terrestrial radio, is nonlocal. The largest satellite radio company in North America is Sirius XM, which operates Sirius as a commercial-free system and XM with commercials. The company uses geosynchronous satellites to obtain a footprint that covers most of Canada, the U.S., and the northern third of Mexico.

Satellite radio also includes many small networks, such as the Beethoven Satellite Network of classical music.

Television

Like radio, television may be commercial or public, with opportunities to reach audiences through both local stations and national or regional networks. Other television opportunities include cable programming, both through national networks and local production facilities.

When public relations is able to gain the attention of television reporters, organizations find themselves facing potentially vast audiences. Obviously, however, not every public relations activity is newsworthy, nor should it be. To help you determine what is or is not newsworthy, review the definition of news and the characteristics of newsworthiness in Phase Two, Strategy.

Several types of television services are common: terrestrial, cable, online, and satellite. Here is a look at each.

TERRESTRIAL TELEVISION

The most common type of broadcast television is **terrestrial television**, also called **over-the-air television**. It can be defined by what it is not. It does not transmit via cable or satellite, but rather by radio waves sent to and from antennas. Most local television stations provide an over-the-air signal, which can be accessed for free with home or built-in antennas or rabbit ears.

Nearly 2,300 television stations operate throughout North America. These stations generally broadcast news and sports, as well as entertainment programming. Some of this programming is locally produced, but most stations draw most of their programming from an affiliated network that is a content producer and distributor of television programming.

In the U.S., the largest commercial networks are ABC, NBC, CBS, Fox, and CW with PBS as the public network. Each of these reaches about 97 percent of U.S. households. In Canada, CBC, and CTV are nationwide English-language television networks, and Radio-Canada is the French-language public TV network.

More than 80 television networks operate in North America, including many specialized networks such as Inuit Television of Canada, Newfoundland Television, Univision, and Telemundo Spanish-language networks, home-focused networks such as DIY and HGTV, several state-based PBS affiliates such as the Pennsylvania Public Television Network, four major home-shopping networks, and nearly 30 religious networks.

CABLE TELEVISION

About 59 percent of U.S. households receive **cable television**, which is a system of providing TV programming via coaxial or fiber-optic cables. More than 325 cable television networks provide programming in the arts, entertainment, foreign, children's interests, sports, shopping, religion, music, and pay-per-view. Cable TV audiences tend to be middle-class, suburban residents with higher-than-average income who purchase cable programming through subscriptions and as pay-per-view options.

ComCast and TimeWarner are the two largest cable services in the U.S. Rogers Cable is the largest such company in Canada.

ONLINE TELEVISION

Since 2009 in the U.S. and 2011 in Canada, all television stations are required to offer a digital signal, which offers many on-demand options. Streaming media such as Netflix, Amazon

Prime, and Hulu offer original programming, much of it of award-winning quality (such as *House of Cards*, *Orange Is the New Black,* and *Transparent*). Many streaming services host archives of many TV series.

SATELLITE TELEVISION

Satellite television allows customers to view TV signals on television sets or on computers. Some programming is free, though most satellite television is subscription-based. Programming generally includes a range of networks similar to cable television.

Dish and AT&T DirectTV are the leading satellite TV services in the U.S. Bell and Shaw Direct are the largest such companies in Canada.

Public Relations and Earned Media

The relationship between a public relations practitioner and a journalist is symbiotic; that is, it is a relationship in which each side needs the other and benefits from the other.

- Public relations people need journalists and information programmers who can provide a vehicle to present the organization's messages.
- Reporters need public relations practitioners to help them identify newsworthy stories and report on them.

Most newspapers are private commercial enterprises. Three-quarters of their income derives from advertising and the rest from circulation. News and commentary are the products these companies are selling.

There are legal differences among the various media. As businesses protected by the First Amendment of the U.S. Constitution, American newspapers are not required to publish any particular material, including news releases and other information originating from public relations practitioners. Not even government agencies can command news coverage.

Television and radio stations generally are private businesses as well. While they must meet certain government regulations (because they have, in effect, a franchise to operate on a particular channel frequency), they nevertheless have much discretion over what news to cover. An exception to this private ownership, of course, is the system of public radio and television networks.

Media Information Needs

Editors and news directors usually are receptive to public relations information when they believe it will satisfy the interests of their readers. The term **information subsidy** describes news and editorial material provided to journalists by public relations.

An estimated one-half to two-thirds of the information in daily newspapers originates from public relations practitioners, either through vehicles initiated by practitioners, such as news releases, news conferences, and media alerts, or because practitioners have responded to journalists with interviews or background information.

The rate for radio and television news broadcasts is slightly lower, because these media proportionally give more coverage to accidents, crime, and other breaking news that does not originate within organizations. As rising corporate costs lead to news-gathering teams becoming

PUBLIC RELATIONS HELPS WRITE THE NEWS

The news media owe a lot to public relations. Estimates vary on how much information carried in the news media comes from public relations practitioners, but it's evident that most editors and reporters get a lot of their information from public relations sources.

A classic 1981 study in *Columbia Journalism Review* counted 45 percent of the 188 news stories in one edition of the *Wall Street Journal* as originating with public relations practitioners.

Another academic journal reported that 78 percent of journalists use news releases, at least to spark story ideas, more than half of the time (Curtain, 1999). In that survey, many journalists said their publications and stations have strict guidelines for using public relations materials, such as using only those from nonprofit organizations promoting social causes but not from businesses seeking economic gain.

The term for such assistance is **information subsidy**—information from public relations sources that increasingly short-staffed editors use to help underwrite the costs of gathering news. Newsrooms have been turning more frequently to low-cost public relations information subsidies. That can be good for public relations practitioners.

But there is a downside to the trend. If media lower their journalistic standards and lose credibility with their audiences, public relations people will find less value in news media coverage. Thus, despite easier entrée to news columns and broadcasts, media coverage would be worth less. Some observers fear this weakening in media credibility is already happening.

Something to think about!

smaller at many publications and broadcast stations, news-oriented public relations practitioners can be of increasing assistance to the remaining reporters, and thus more effective in service to their organizations.

The most common way for public relations practitioners to provide news people with information is to give it to them in writing. A survey by TEKGroup International found that 95 percent of working journalists prefer to receive news and story ideas via email, and 60 percent want to get news from public relations practitioners on their wireless devices. Additionally, 43 percent prefer to receive news via Twitter.

A Survey of Media in the Wired World by Middleberg and Ross (2001) reported that 75 percent of journalists use Facebook as a tool for reporting; 70 percent use blogs, 69 percent use Twitter and 69 percent use mobile technology to gather reportable information. It found that, overall, 95 percent of journalists believe that social media are a reliable tool for sourcing stories. Additionally, 96 percent of journalists say they sometimes quote bloggers and 39 percent maintain their own blog.

Additionally, many organizations service reporters through online newsrooms where reporters can download news releases, fact sheets, interview notes, photos, and many other resources for their reporting.

What's a public relations person to do with such information? For starters, use it to develop a media-friendly website and online newsroom. Make the information easy for journalists to find, generally as a well-placed link from the organization's home page. Include the kind of information a journalist might need: basic facts, history, downloadable photos, stats, and so

Phase Three

STEP
7

on. Include an easy-to-navigate link to a public relations staff person. Invite reporters to sign up for customized emails that will alert them to topics of interest. Make sure you keep the site updated frequently, perhaps daily.

Researchers looked at information subsidies during the coverage of the 2007 Virginia Tech shootings. Shelley Wigley and Maria Fontenot (2009) found that, in today's high-tech media environment, early crisis reports may use eyewitness accounts, often accessed through

---

EARNED MEDIA: NEWS MEDIA TACTICS

Direct News Subsidy

- News fact sheet
- Miscellaneous print (event listing and interview notes)
- News release
- Feature release
- Actuality or audio news release
- B-roll or video news release
- Social media release
- Transmedia news package
- Media kit
- Online newsroom

Indirect News Subsidy

- Media advisory
- Story idea memo
- Query letter

Opinion Subsidy

- Position statement
- Letter to the editor
- Guest editorial

Interactive Media Engagement

- News interview
- News conference
- Studio interview and satellite media tour
- Editorial conference

For detailed instruction on writing for these various formats, see Smith (2017). Now in its 5th edition, *Becoming a Public Relations Writer* has been adopted for courses at 138 colleges and universities and has been acquired by 557 academic universities throughout the world.

cell-phone video, texting, blogs, Facebook, and tweets. They call this new type of crisis media a non-official technology source.

They found that reporters used unofficial sources (students, experts, community organizations, and so on) three-to-one over official sources (websites and interviews with university officials and police). In the Virginia Tech coverage, technology sources provided information subsidies to the traditional print and broadcast media in the early reporting of the crisis, followed by more official sources as coverage continued. Perhaps this says something about the availability of public relations sources, or the information they have, early in a crisis.

Let's look at some of the ways in which public relations practitioners can provide the news media with newsworthy information and thus disseminate their messages to the vast media audiences. There are four general ways to present information through the news media: direct information subsidy, indirect information subsidy, opinion subsidy, and interactive news opportunities.

Direct News Subsidy

One of the most frequently used categories of news media tactics is **direct news subsidy**. This is information that is presented to the media more or less ready for use. These tactics include news fact sheets, event listings, interview notes, news releases, feature releases, actualities and audio news releases, video B-rolls and video news releases, social media releases, media kits, and online newsrooms. Many of these tactics can be presented online or in print. Here's a brief overview of each.

NEWS FACT SHEET

A brief, generally one-page, outline of information about a newsworthy event or activity is called a **news fact sheet**. These often are presented as bulleted items. The format makes it easy for reporters in both print and electronic media to use the information as they write their own stories. People other than reporters, such as speechwriters, tour guides, employees, and customers, also can use fact sheets.

Fact sheets are easy to prepare. Simply gather the relevant information and present it along the traditional journalistic lines of who, what, when, where, why, and how. It also may be useful to add sections on background, history, significance, and benefits. Additionally, it may be appropriate to include a brief direct quote.

MISCELLANEOUS PRINT

Another information format for print media is the **event listing**, also called a **community calendar**. These are simple notices that most newspapers and many magazines print about upcoming activities such as benefits, meetings, entertainment events, public lectures, and the like. Many publications offer online postings of community events.

Another useful tactic is **interview notes**, which are verbatim transcripts presented in a question-and-answer format, based on an interview that a public relations writer has done with an organizational news source. For example, a university news bureau might interview a geology professor about breakthrough work involving earthquake prediction, then provide the transcript of that interview for science writers. Interview notes allow reporters to build their stories as they see fit. Even if they decide to do their own interviews, the notes can save time and give them information to build on.

NEWS RELEASE

Most organizations find that the **news release** is a mainstay of media relations. A news release is a news story written by public relations practitioners and given to media gatekeepers for use in their news publications, programs, and online information sites.

Submit news releases to newspaper city editors or to editors or beat reporters of special interest such as sports, business, or entertainment sections. Special-interest magazines also may use news releases, especially for brief items. For broadcast media, submit news releases to news directors or assignment editors. Also, consider taking the time to rewrite print-oriented releases when you intend to send them to radio or television stations.

Once news releases were distributed through the mail or were hand delivered. The previously cited Survey of Media in the Wired World reported that emerging media are supplementing but not supplanting older forms of media. For example, 53 percent of journalists prefer receiving email news releases and 34 percent prefer to interview news contacts by phone. Many organizations post releases online where reporters can retrieve the information. Releases also can be disseminated through commercial public relations wire services like PR Newswire.

If you are considering preparing a news release, note that there are several different kinds. An **announcement release** deals with events, personnel, progress, bad news, programs, or products. A **response release** deals with new or updated information, comments, public interest tie-ins, and speeches. A **hometowner release** is sent to newspapers serving the permanent residential areas of employees, students, members of the military, and so on.

NEWS BRIEF

Whereas a news release involves a page or more of information, a **news brief** is likely to be only a two- or three-paragraph story that provides the basic information of the summary lead

---

DIE! PRESS RELEASE! DIE! DIE! DIE!

That's the provocative title of a 2006 article by journalist/blogger Tom Foremski, publisher of the *Silicon Valley Watcher* blog. He obviously isn't a fan of "press" releases, which he pronounces as nearly useless. He says they typically feature a "tremendous amount of top-spin," "pat-on-the-back phrases," and "meaningless quotes." Well, yeah! When you put it like that, who wouldn't find them useless? Or worse.

But that's not how news releases should be written. To be fair to Foremski, he's probably inundated with wanna-be releases that are full of top-spin, self-congratulatory writing, and say-nothing quotes. After all, he works in Silicon Valley, where companies are busy trying to out-hype each other. But such writing breaks all the rules of ethical and effective public relations, which values accurate and honest facts.

Foremski has offered several reasonable suggestions for improving information releases. He asks public relations writers to provide him with a brief news announcement devoid of spin and hype, information sections that are clearly labeled, a few quotes from the CEO, financial information in various formats, and links to relevant info both within the company and outside.

Note that these are part of the transmedia news package that has become a common tool for public relations writers.

as well as a clear indication of the benefit. Some public relations writers try to write each news release so the first couple of paragraphs can be pulled out to serve as a news brief. Written this way, the news-brief portion also can serve as part of an online menu of articles, linking to the longer version for readers seeking more in-depth information.

FEATURE RELEASE

In addition to releases that present solid news, some releases focus on some kind of background on the news. Known as a **feature release**, this public relations tactic has several categories: biographies, histories, backgrounders, question-and-answer pieces, and service (**how-to**) articles.

A **biography** provides the personal background on newsmakers and other people significant to an organization. This can be written in chronological style or as personality profiles.

A **history** provides a similar focus on the organization itself, usually providing a chronological narrative or an outline of the development of the organization since its founding. Histories generally deal not only with milestones but also with issues facing the organization.

A narrative article providing objective information on an issue is called a **backgrounder**. Such pieces usually deal with the cause of the problem or issue, a history of how the issue has progressed, current status, and perhaps projections of its direction and likely future. Backgrounders also provide information on the significance or impact of the issue. The key element for a backgrounder is that it should remain neutral—objective and free of opinion or unsupported speculation. All sides in an issue should be able to agree on the facts within a well-written backgrounder.

Other categories of feature articles are labeled according to the writing format used in the release. Some releases are presented as a **question-and-answer piece**. Others are written in the step-by-step format of a **service article**, which provides readers with an instructional approach to solving a problem.

ACTUALITY AND AUDIO NEWS RELEASE

When public relations writers want to quote someone in a news release going to print journalists, they include a sentence or phrase in quotation marks. When they want to provide radio reports with similar quoted material, they use an **actuality** (sometimes called a **sound bite**), because radio stations need to present quoted information in the voice of the news source. An actuality is a recording—usually digitized and accessible by computer. It involves a couple of highlight quotes from a speech or statement by an organizational spokesperson.

Whereas an actuality is an audio sound bite, an **audio news release** (ANR) is an edited story package that public relations writers offer to radio journalists. ANRs are news stories complete with announcer and sound bite. Most U.S. radio stations use audio news releases in some ways, particularly if the ANR has a local angle. The ANRs that get on the air are most commonly 60-second spots plugged into the morning drive-time reports. Nonprofit organizations, corporations and government agencies produce audio news releases. For example, the U.S. Department of Labor posts ANRs with other materials at its media website, dol.gov/dol/media/.

B-ROLL AND VIDEO NEWS RELEASE

Quoted statements and other visual information can be made available to television stations through a **B-roll**, which is a tape providing a series of unedited video shots and sound bites related to the news story. A written news release or other background material often accompany B-rolls to give television reporters an idea of what the story is all about.

A packaged video bite edited into a complete story package is the **video news release** (VNR). Public relations people give this to television journalists. VNRs usually run 30 to 90 seconds long with narration, interviews, and background video, even names titled at the bottom of the screen. B-rolls are sometimes used with VNRs to provide for easier editing of newsworthy material.

VNRs generally are one of two types. A timely release focuses on a current news event. An evergreen release, often taking a human-interest approach, has a longer potential time frame for use.

Some VNRs are rejected because news directors find them overly commercial or lacking in local news value.

Because of production costs, most video news releases are developed by organizations with widespread publics rather than for single-market use. VNRs and B-rolls may be distributed nationally or regionally. National distribution can cost from $25,000 to more than $100,000. Local or regional distribution, especially of B-rolls, can involve only a nominal expense for an organization that has its own video production setup or the assistance of a video production studio.

VNRs have sparked some controversy. The watchdog group Center for Media and Democracy, which is critical of most things public relations, calls VNRs "fake news."

Both the Public Relations Society of America and the Radio Television Digital News Association have ethical guidelines calling for TV stations to indicate the source of VNR material used in newscasts. Various reports say adults believe TV news sources should indicate the source of stories generated by companies, government, or other outside organizations.

However, public relations professionals would consider labeling VNRs fake news as semantic overreach. Critics blustered against video news releases years before what is now known as fake news: politically inspired, Internet-based lies, hoaxes, and deliberate misinformation masquerading as news and intending to deceive citizens and destabilize governments, businesses, and other organizations. Additionally, some politicians now label as fake any news that criticizes them or their policies, though in actuality it is real news that simply makes them uncomfortable.

The emergence of fake news is generally dated to the 2016 political campaigns in the U.S. and Europe. It is increasingly identified as an element of international cyberwarfare using a Soviet-style disinformation arsenal. The mushrooming of fake news has sparked governmental investigations, academic analysis, and transnational intrigue—all far more serious than public relations critics fearing a VNR bogeyman.

SOCIAL MEDIA RELEASE

The **social media release** (SMR) is intended for blogs, websites, and other online uses. It includes many elements not found in a standard news release: liberal use of subheads to help move the reader along; summary statement as in a news brief; and bulleted facts (similar to those in the news fact sheet). It also includes links to photos, MP3 files, and other audio clips; graphics; logos; various types of video; downloads of related information and background materials; links to other coverage of the topic; links to additional commentary and quotes from organizational news sources; and links to additional background information, finances, history, and products or services of the organization, as well as a link to a traditional news release. The social news release also generally includes a time-date stamp to indicate when the information was last updated.

TRANSMEDIA NEWS PACKAGE

The latest entry into the field of dissemination tools is the transmedia news package. It combines elements of traditional print and broadcast news releases with those of the social media release.

This all-inclusive information package thus serves the needs of newspapers and newsletters, radio and television news, blogs, mobile media, and other online venues. It also can be useful for employees, volunteers, shareholders, donors, customers, and regulators.

A 2009 study by the online distribution service RealWire reported that newspapers publish information based on both traditional releases and digital/social media add-ons twice as often as from traditional releases. Blogs use them four times as often as print-only releases. And because they are so rich in content, they are more likely to be identified by search engines.

MEDIA KIT

Most of the above-described direct news materials can be gathered together in a **media kit**. These are presented to the journalists who attend news conferences and often are delivered to invited reporters who fail to attend.

In tangible form, media kits generally include one or more news releases along with fact sheets, feature releases, photos, and other graphics. However, the transmedia news package is replacing the printed media kit.

ONLINE NEWSROOM

An online newsroom is a comprehensive set of pages within a website that provides a home for most of the items listed above. An online newsroom generally includes print and social media releases, fact sheets, a photo gallery, executive bios and organizational histories, audio and video material, and virtual tours. Many also post videos of speeches and interviews, videos of their own news conferences, reprints or links of media coverage, and videos of their own news conferences.

Indirect News Subsidy

In addition to the direct materials noted earlier, public relations practitioners also can use **indirect news subsidy** to communicate with reporters, editors, and news directors. These are messages that are not meant to be published but are intended to interest or inform media gatekeepers. Consider the following in your tactical program: media advisories, story idea memos, and query letters.

MEDIA ADVISORY

A brief note given to media gatekeepers is called a **media advisory** or **media alert**. These memos inform the gatekeepers of upcoming news opportunities. For example, a public relations practitioner might use a media advisory to announce a news conference, to invite photographers to a newsworthy event, or to inform editors and news directors about a newsworthy activity involving the organization to which they are invited.

Media advisories differ from news releases in that the advisory is not meant to be published but rather is intended as useful information for a journalist. Realize, however, that

Phase Three

STEP
7

WHAT JOURNALISTS WANT AT ONLINE NEWSROOMS

Online newsrooms are a staple of media relations. In researching stories, 95 percent of working journalists said they visit online newsrooms. That's from a comprehensive study by TEKGroup International, an Internet software company that develops social media online newsrooms.

TEK's 2015 Online Newsroom Survey reported that 93 percent of journalists visit corporate blogs in researching a news story; 89 percent visit the company Facebook page, 75 percent view the YouTube channel of a company or organization, and 51 percent would receive Twitter feeds if available.

Here are some other findings of the report about what journalists think about online newsrooms (the full report is available at tekgroup.com).

- 97 percent say organizations should have an online newsroom.
- 96 percent want both low- and high-resolution photos.
- 94 percent prefer to receive story ideas via email, and 92 percent prefer to receive company information via email.
- 93 percent said they should be able to access breaking news at online newsrooms.
- 92 percent want to be able to access product information.
- 89 percent want an events calendar.
- 88 percent want access to executive bios.
- 86 percent think online newsrooms should include news coverage from other outlets.
- 84 percent want financial information.
- 81 percent want video files, and 67 percent want audio files.
- 75 percent want mobile access.
- 61 percent think such newsrooms should be accessible to all users.

Phase Three

STEP 7

information in a media advisory is not off the record, and enterprising journalists may use the memo to craft a news report pre-empting the announced news conference or special event.

STORY IDEA MEMO

Another useful news- or feature-oriented tactic is the **story idea memo** or **tip sheet**. These are informal idea memos submitted to the gatekeepers of newspapers, magazines, and electronic and digital news media. The intention is to spark a reporter's interest in developing a feature article. The public relations practitioners suggest available interview subjects or topics for articles that can be developed by the publication's own writers.

QUERY LETTER

A letter written to editors or broadcasters proposing a story and inquiring about their interest in it is called a **query letter**. These are commonly used by freelance writers more than by public relations practitioners, and they often are directed to magazines or feature supplements to Sunday newspapers. However, some practitioners find it useful to query magazines and then prepare feature articles if an editor expresses interest. Additionally, some practitioners work with freelance writers who prepare stories on assignment for magazines.

Opinion Subsidy

Another category of tactics rooted in the news media involves several opportunities for using newspapers, magazines, and radio and television stations to present an organization's opinion rather than simply the factual information that is the focus of most of the preceding news tactics. Both in proactive situations in which the organization wishes to advocate for a particular position, or when it reactively seeks to explain or defend its position, an organization often realizes several benefits by producing this opinion material.

Consider the following vehicles through which organizations can present their formal opinions about various issues: position statements, letters to the editor, and guest editorials.

POSITION STATEMENT

Going a step beyond backgrounders (discussed earlier in the section Direct News Subsidy), a **position statement** adds an organization's official opinion on an issue.

Position statements can be used in several ways. They are materials for journalists preparing news stories or editorials. They serve as the basis for editorials in organizational publications, source material for speeches and organizational letters, and documents to be provided directly to employees, donors or stockholders, supporters, legislators, and other influential publics. Some position statements remain internal within an organization; others may be published in print or online.

Position statements vary in depth and intensity. A **position paper**, sometimes called a **white paper**, may be a detailed and lengthy discussion of a major issue of long-term significance.

A **position paragraph** is a much shorter statement, often providing an organization's comments on a local or short-lived issue.

A **contingency statement** or **standby statement** is a prepared comment written so an organization may express its voice in various potential situations. For example, a company nearing the resolution of a lawsuit may prepare several contingency statements to cover the possible outcomes: winning the case, losing it, being convicted of lesser charges, having the charge dismissed, and so on.

LETTER TO THE EDITOR

Opinion letters written to newspapers and magazines offer many opportunities for public relations practitioners to communicate through the news media even when the gatekeepers have overlooked the organization.

Public relations practitioners use letters to the editor as publicity vehicles to announce things that don't make it into the news columns. They also use letters to advocate a cause that likewise hasn't caught the attention of journalists. Occasionally letters can be used to correct errors, though most organizations find it better to ignore all but the most serious factual misstatements in published reports.

GUEST EDITORIAL

Some commentaries can go beyond the length and impact of letters to the editor. A **guest editorial** generally is placed opposite the editorial page of a newspaper, hence its alternative name, **op-ed piece**.

A guest editorial is a grander version of a letter to the editor. It is a signed essay that, because of its length and placement, has higher prestige and credibility than a letter. Usually

Phase Three

STEP
7

it's necessary to contact the publication before submitting an essay to be considered as a guest editorial.

In many cases, public relations people write guest editorials that carry the signature of an organizational executive, thereby giving the piece additional credibility because of a high-ranking message source.

Interactive Media Engagement

A final category of news activities includes those communication opportunities in which public relations practitioners and journalists interact with each other. These include news interviews, news conferences, studio interviews and satellite media tours, and editorial conferences.

NEWS INTERVIEW

Sessions in which journalists ask questions and public relations practitioners or organizational spokespersons respond are a mainstay of the interaction between an organization and the media.

A **news interview** usually is a one-on-one question-and-answer session. Public relations practitioners prepare for interviews by anticipating questions reporters may ask and gathering relevant information to answer the questions. They also help organizational spokespersons frame appropriate responses to reporters' questions. Often this coaching includes mock interviews prior to the actual encounter between the spokesperson and the reporters.

Most interviews are face-to-face encounters. Sometimes, however, when a reporter is seeking mainly factual information, especially from a news source the reporter has worked with in the past, the interview may take place over the telephone or via email. See Appendix E, Media Engagement, for tips on good interviewing.

NEWS CONFERENCE

Essentially a group interview, a **news conference** is a contrived media happening in which an organizational spokesperson makes a newsworthy statement. Generally this is followed by a question-and-answer session with reporters.

Journalists do not particularly like news conferences because the format puts them in the awkward position of doing their newsgathering—always a highly competitive endeavor—in the presence of their competitors. Only a few circumstances justify holding a news conference.

1. To announce news or give a response of major importance (in the eyes of the media, not simply the hopes of the organization), such as a new product or policy initiative, response to an attack, update in a crisis situation, or comment on a breaking news story.
2. To serve the media's interests when a prominent spokesperson or newsmaker is available for only a short period of time, such as the whirlwind visit or sandwiched-in interview of a celebrity, official, candidate, or some other newsworthy person.
3. To avoid accusations of playing favorites among reporters, such as by disseminating information to one medium ahead of another.

As an alternative to a news conference, consider making the announcement through a news release, or invite reporters to a coordinated series of interviews with an organizational spokesperson. Another option is to invite reporters to a participatory activity, such as a media preview of the opening of a new roller coaster by an amusement park or a tasting session for food bloggers prior to the opening of a new restaurant.

If you do judge it appropriate to invite reporters to a news conference, consider the following guidelines.

- Invite all media that may be interested, even those you don't like. Notify wire services, which may announce the news conference to their member media.
- In a major market with a variety of media outlets, schedule the news conference mid- to late morning, if possible. Because normal business is slow on weekends, also consider Sunday or early Monday news conferences. In a smaller market with few print reporters and television reporters from stations miles away, try to accommodate the schedule of the reporters. In either case, ask key reporters about convenient times and conflicting news events.

MEDIA RELATIONS PRACTICES

A national survey of more than 2,000 journalists reported some interesting findings. The Journalist Survey on Media Relations Practices conducted by Bulldog Reporter and TEKgroup International (2010) sought to establish benchmarks for journalists who use the Internet to research and report on the news. Here are some of the findings.

- *Internet research*. On the biggest change in journalistic practices, nearly 79 percent of journalists identified their ability to use the Internet to conduct their research 24 hours a day; 68 percent identified access to media contact info online; 46 percent access to electronic press kits online; 43 percent identified the ability to search corporate news archives online.
- *Corporate websites*. More than 85 percent of journalists visit a corporate website at least once a month; more than half do so at least weekly.
- *Obscured information*. Reporters complain that corporate websites often make it hard to find contact information for media relations representatives of the organization.
- *Blogs*. Nearly 70 percent say they follow at least one blog regularly; more than 28 percent say they visit a social media site at least weekly as part of their reporting.
- *Audio and video feeds*. Nearly half of reporters say they use audio or video material from corporate websites at least occasionally, but 51 percent said they never seek such information.
- *Understanding the media*. Half of reporters say public relations people don't understand the media.
- *Phone calls*. More than 48 percent say phone calls from public relations people are a waste of time.
- *Quick response*. More than 54 percent of journalists disagreed with the notion that public relations people do not respond quickly enough.
- *Truthfulness*. More than 52 percent disagreed with the notion that public relations practitioners don't tell the truth.
- *Preferences*. Nearly 78 percent said they prefer to receive news releases via email; less than 2 percent sought releases via postal mail.

Phase Three

STEP
7

> ## CASE IN POINT   Dublin Zoo
>
> Facing a decline in visitors amid a national economic recession that led to a decrease in government funding, Dublin Zoo faced an uncertain future. Taking a step toward enhancing its own survival, Ireland's largest zoo embarked on a public relations plan in 2010. The goal was to attract more visitors at full-price admissions.
>
> The campaign relied heavily on a strategy of media relations, as the zoo solicited (and gained) media support from many sectors.
>
> To that purpose, the campaign provided media training for key zookeepers and became more proactive in reaching out to journalists. It developed a series of media-friendly events, such as a mock "zoo election" to select the zoo's most popular inhabitants. (The winner was an orangutan named Sibu.)
>
> The zoo provided media access leading to coverage of the birth of several new arrivals: a hippo, giraffe, elephant, rhinoceros, bongo, gorilla, and a pair of pandas. It also created special events such as Orangutan Awareness Week with a strong television presence to present a message of conservation and endangered animals.
>
> On the responsive side of media relations, the campaign used the news media effectively in several high-profile animal incidents, including the high-profile theft of a penguin that was returned unharmed. It produced a behind-the-scenes TV series called "The Zoo" that attracted about 300,000 viewers.
>
> Moving beyond established news media, the campaign created new social media opportunities. It developed an interactive website and promoted the zoo among 15,000 Facebook fans and 2,200 Twitter followers. The zoo also organized a "blogger's walk" with exclusive early-morning access for 20 of Ireland's leading bloggers and photobloggers.
>
> The result of the campaign was the highest profile among established news media profile the zoo ever had, along with a social media presence with more than 15,000 supporters.
>
> The bottom line? Dublin Zoo recorded the highest paid attendance—963,053—in its 180-year history. The benefits continued, with the zoo attracting more than a million visitors the following year and raising enough money to open a new Gorilla Rainforest.
>
> The campaign received a top award from the Public Relations Consultants Association of Ireland, Public Relations Institute of Ireland, Chartered Institute of Public Relations in Northern Ireland, and All Ireland Marketing Awards.

STEP
7

- Hold the news conference in a meeting room rather than in an office. Or if possible, hold the conference at an appropriate on-site location relevant to the information. For example, if you are announcing a new public housing project, hold the news conference at the building site.

Most news conferences are open to all reporters. Generally the word goes out, often posted on media events listings, and interested news media will send reporters. Sometimes invitation-only news conferences are held, open only to journalists credentialed by a government or corporate press overseer. As an attempt to control the media or show favorites, these invitation-only events can damage an organization's overall media-relations program.

Remember that journalists seek diverse outcomes from news conferences. Television reporters need visuals, so try to find an alternative to talking heads with some creative graphics or locations. Newspaper reporters need facts and a lot of them; media kits and online newsrooms can provide many supplemental materials for them. Bloggers and other alternative journalists may be interested in only a narrow area; some organizations have scheduled separate news conferences for them.

STUDIO INTERVIEW AND SATELLITE MEDIA TOUR

A **studio interview** is a hybrid between the regular interview and the news conference. Like regular interviews, studio interviews involve a reporter/questioner and generally a single interviewee. Sometimes they are set up as a questioner moderating an interview panel. Like a news conference, they often are televised, so everything is presented in "real time" with all the spontaneity of a live interview (even if it is taped for later broadcast).

The growth in popularity of talk radio and, increasingly, talk television offer opportunities to public relations and marketing people promoting new ideas, products, books, and the like. At-home interviews generally include feature or personality profiles for celebrities and other newsmakers. They can be useful in helping to humanize organizational leaders.

A related development and hybrid interviewing style is the **satellite media tour** (SMT). This blends an in-studio interview and a news conference with a widely dispersed audience.

The unique feature of the SMT is that a news source is interviewed by reporters who are in different locations, connected via a special television signal or computer link transmitted through satellite technology from the interviewee's location to many reporters throughout the nation, even around the world. Usually these are individual one-on-one interviews, packaged in segments of five minutes or less. SMTs have a role both in political campaigning and in crisis communications.

EDITORIAL CONFERENCE

Public relations representatives sometimes meet in an **editorial conference**, a meeting with editors and editorial boards of newspapers to present them with background information on important issues. Generally such conferences are arranged on the invitation of the editors, though public relations people often try to solicit such invitations. Such conferences may generate news reports, feature stories, and editorial comment on the issue.

Phase Three

PLANNING EXAMPLE 7C **Selecting News Media Tactics**

STEP 7

Upstate College will develop the following news media tactics to publicize its expanded program:

UPSTATE COLLEGE

- *News release*—low cost, accessible, target to potential students, parents, donors and community leaders
- *Fact sheet for media*—low cost, directed toward media publics
- *Fact sheet for students*—low cost, directed toward potential students
- *Media alert*—low cost

- *Transmedia news package*—low cost, information-on-demand for key publics
- *Photo and caption of preparation for ceremony*—low cost, interests community about expanded program
- *Letter to the editor*—low cost, aimed at key publics (parents, donors, community leaders)
- *Editorial conference*—low cost, interactive with media, potential to generate support for recruitment and fundraising
- *News interview with reporters*—low cost, high visibility

 Tiny Tykes will develop the following news media tactics to publicize its dedication to consumer safety and demonstrate its improved crib toy:

- *Letters to the editor*—low cost, directed toward key publics
- *Story idea memo to reporters*—low cost, possibly high visibility
- *News release*—low cost, accessible, aimed at key publics
- *Video news release*—high cost, possibly high visibility
- *Social media release*—low cost, targeted for parents

☑ *Checklist 7C* **News Media Tactics**

Basic Questions

1. What news media tactics will you use?
2. How will these tactics help the organization achieve its objectives?
3. What resources will these tactics require?

Expanded Questions

A. SELECTION OF TACTICS

From the following categories of news media tactics, identify several that you would consider using.

Direct News Material
- News fact sheet
- Event listing
- Interview notes
- News release
- Feature release
- Actuality
- Audio news release

- Video B-roll
- Video news release
- Transmedia news package
- Media kit
- Online newsroom

Indirect News Material
- Media advisory
- Story idea memo
- Query letter

Opinion Material
- Position statement
- Letter to the editor
- Guest editorial/op-ed piece

Interactive News Opportunity
- News interview
- News conference
- Studio interview
- Satellite media tour
- Editorial conference

B. STRATEGIC IMPLICATIONS

For each item identified, answer the following questions.

1. Will this tactic help the organization to interact with the appropriate public?
2. What level of impact will this tactic make on the key public?
3. Will this tactic advance the organization toward its awareness objectives?
4. Will this tactic advance the organization toward its acceptance objectives?
5. Will this tactic advance the organization toward its action objectives?
6. What is the main advantage to this tactic?
7. What advantages does this tactic offer that other tactics do not?
8. Are there any disadvantages to this tactic?

C. IMPLEMENTATION ITEMS

For each item identified, answer the following questions.

1. How much will it cost to implement this tactic? Is the cost justified? Is the cost practical, based on the organization's resources?
2. How much staff time will it take to implement this tactic? Is the time practical, based on the organization's resources?
3. What skill level, equipment, and expertise are needed to implement this tactic? Is the needed level available within the organization? Is it available from outside sources?

Phase Three

STEP
7

Paid Media: Advertising and Promotional Tactics

The final category of **communication tactics** involves media associated with advertising and promotion. The list in this category includes four major sections: print advertising media, electronic advertising media, out-of-home advertising media, and promotional items.

Strategy for Paid Media

Most advertising is used for marketing purposes to sell a particular product or service or to position a particular brand in the minds of its customers. But as noted earlier, the tools and techniques of advertising can serve the public relations goals of an organization as well.

Advertising can combine the strengths of two other important categories of tactics: organizational media and news media. Like organizational media, advertising is a form of controlled media that provides another opportunity for the organization to oversee all the details of its messages: content, tone, presentation style, and timing. Advertising also can reach vast audiences, a characteristic shared with the news media.

At the same time, advertising has the combined weaknesses of these tactics. Like organizational media, advertising lacks the credibility of third-party endorsement found in the news media. Like the news media, advertising tends not to be able to address itself to information-seeking publics but instead can simply be available when people stumble upon the message, such as while they are reading a magazine or watching television.

Advertising is more of a public medium than a personal one. It is used most often with external publics, mainly because many forms of interpersonal and organizational medium are better suited for internal publics.

A major negative for advertising is the cost. It is the most expensive of all the categories of communication tactics discussed so far. A midsized daily newspaper, for example, might charge $285 **per column inch** (pci) for an ad, meaning that one full-page ad (pci cost times 157 column inches) could cost $44,745 (actually, with volume discount, a full page would be more like $25,000 or $30,000 for a paper with a $285 pci rate). National magazines may charge $150,000 per page. One 30-second spot on the local TV evening news might cost $7,000 in a midsized market. Compare this with the cost of other tactics, and it is easy to see why advertising often is used as a tactic of last resort.

At one time, advertising was thought of only as a mass medium, but increasingly it is able to target audiences. This is so largely because advertising can piggyback on more and better-targeted media, both print and electronic.

Print Advertising

Because it can reach both local and more widespread audiences, and because it is less expensive than broadcasting alternatives, print advertising is used by many organizations. There are various opportunities available in the category of print advertising: magazine advertising, newspaper advertising, directory advertising, and house ads.

MAGAZINE ADVERTISING

Ads in magazines tend to focus on national brands rather than local retail outlets and individual products, because of the diverse and widespread readership of most magazines and because of the high advertising cost.

PAID MEDIA: ADVERTISING AND PROMOTIONAL TACTICS

Print Advertising Media

- Magazine advertising (center spread, advertorial, breakout ad)
- Newspaper advertising (display ad, classified ad)
- Directory advertising
- House advertising

Electronic Media Advertising

- Television commercial (network placement, spot, infomercial)
- Cable TV advertising (cable crawl)
- Radio commercial (network radio, spot)
- Digital media advertising (interstitial ad, superstitial ad, virtual ad)

Out-of-Home Advertising

- Outdoor poster (billboard, paint, rotary paint, digital billboard, spectacular, extra, wallscape)
- Arena poster
- Signage
- Out-of-home video
- Transit advertising (bus sign, car card, station poster, diorama, shelter poster, mobile billboard)
- Aerial advertising (blimp, airplane tow, skywriting)
- Inflatable

Promotional Items

- Clothing
- Costume
- Office accessory
- Home accessory

Phase Three

Magazine advertising generally is sold on the basis of full or partial pages. Most advertising is placed as **run of book** (ROB), which means the ad can be placed anywhere within the magazine. Trade magazines sometimes place ads with an eye toward the articles that are on the same or facing pages.

Special placements usually entail extra costs, with the highest costs going to advertising on the inside or outside covers. There are extra charges for a **bleed ad**, which eliminates the white border and carries the advertising image to the edge of the page, and for a **center spread**, which features two facing pages. Some magazines also can feature an **advertising insert** such as a coupon or postcard. Occasionally magazines will publish an advertising section, sometimes called an **advertorial**, a series of consecutive pages dealing with a single theme or product/service line. The term is a portmanteau of "advertising" and "editorial."

Increasingly, advertisers can place a **breakout ad** in national publications for distribution to particular groups of readers. Breakout ads run only in specific geographic editions, those copies of a magazine that are distributed within a particular region, perhaps a metropolitan area or a single state.

Some magazines also offer demographic editions aimed at subscribers with particular interests or backgrounds. For example, *Sports Illustrated* has special advertising packages for editions that are distributed to golf enthusiasts, homeowners, residents of particular regions, and residents of high-income zip code areas. *Time* magazine has an advertising package that can be directed to high-income and/or managerial subscribers.

NEWSPAPER ADVERTISING

Newspaper ads offer several different opportunities for promoting goods, services, and ideas. The two different kinds of newspaper advertising are display ads and classified ads.

A **display ad** is a common newspaper advertisement located anywhere throughout the newspaper. Display ads generally feature illustrations, headlines, and copy blocks. Most are marketing-oriented ads by local retailers selling various products and promoting sales.

Some display ads, however, are placed for public relations purposes, such as to promote events, support political candidates, or present position statements on public issues. For example, a hospital that has come under public scrutiny because of accusations of sexual or racial discrimination may choose to address those charges in a full-page newspaper ad where it can control the entire message—its content, packaging, and timing. Likewise, a health maintenance organization (HMO) that feels reporters have not adequately explained its new coverage policy may use a full-page ad. The HMO may use such an ad even if it likes what reporters have written, simply as a way to increase awareness of its new policy.

Most newspaper advertising is purchased to run anywhere within the newspaper, called **run of press** (ROP), as compared to special placement on a particular page as in a specific section.

A **classified ad** is a brief, all-text message. In most newspapers, the three largest categories of classified ads deal with employment, real estate, and automotive sales, but they also are used to find roommates, sell used vacuum cleaners, find homes for puppies, and promote social causes. Classified ads may be used for some public relations purposes, such as to invite participants to job-training programs, college courses, and similar activities.

DIRECTORY ADVERTISING

Directory advertising uses the *Yellow Pages* and professional directories to place business promotional announcements. Some directories are focused on particular industries or professionals, such as the *Public Relations Tactics Green Book* published by the Public Relations Society of America with listings of service providers, and the PRSA *Blue Book* listing organizational members. Others are more geographic, such as directories published by telephone companies and by independent publishers who may target a particular area. Increasingly, directories are putting both their information listings and their advertising online.

HOUSE ADVERTISING

Some organizations place **house ads** or program advertising. These take the form of honorary or congratulatory announcements in the organization's name placed in programs and publications associated with special events or in publications such as school yearbooks and member directories. Opportunities for this type of advertising include a variety of programs for sporting events, banquets, anniversaries, graduations, and other occasions.

Electronic Media Advertising

Advertising on radio, television, and related media is a high-cost promotional expense that also can generate vast audiences. Consider the following possibilities: television commercials, cable television advertising, radio commercials, and computer media.

The broadcast day is divided into what the industry calls **dayparts**, which are blocks of time based on different audience patterns. Here are the common designations for dayparts for both television and radio.

DAYPARTS

Television Dayparts

Here are the standard time periods within a typical broadcast day for television stations. Times reflect Eastern Standard Time; there may be some variations with network programs in other time zones.

- Early morning—6 a.m. to 9 a.m.
- Daytime—9 a.m. to 4:30 p.m.
- Early fringe—4:30 p.m. to 7 p.m.
- Prime access—7 p.m. to 8 p.m.
- Prime time—8 p.m. to 11 p.m.
- Late news time—11 p.m. to 11:30 p.m.
- Late night—11:30 p.m. to 1 a.m.
- Overnight—1 a.m. to 6 a.m.
- Weekend morning—8 a.m. to 1 p.m.
- Weekend afternoon—1 p.m. to 7 p.m.
- Weekend overnight—7 p.m. to 8 a.m.

Radio Dayparts

Here are the standard time periods within a typical broadcast day for radio stations. Times are for Eastern Standard Time; there may be some variations with network programs spanning into other time zones.

- Morning drive time—6 a.m. to 10 a.m.
- Midday or daytime—10 a.m. to 3 p.m.
- Afternoon drive time—3 p.m. to 7 p.m.
- Evening—7 p.m. to midnight.
- Late night—midnight to 6 a.m.

Phase Three

STEP
7

TELEVISION COMMERCIAL

Commercial and public relations advertising messages are placed on television in one of two ways. **Network placement** puts the advertisement on all of the stations affiliated with the network. For some of the largest television networks in North America, that could mean hundreds of different local stations. Alternatively, organizations can use **spot advertising** to place messages on individual local stations.

Most television commercials are 30 seconds long, though stations are opening up shorter slots for 10-, 15-, and 20-second advertisements. Less-competitive time slots sometimes carry 60-second advertisements.

In addition to the regular commercial, many stations provide times of 30 minutes or more for an **infomercial**, a program-length advertisement that often is packaged as an interview, talk show, game show, or educational program, sometimes masking its true identity as paid advertisements. Certainly there is nothing wrong with combining promotion and entertainment, but an organization raises serious ethical questions if it hides behind artificial news or entertainment programs when in reality it is presenting a sales pitch.

When placing television advertising, consider the specific time of day the ad will run. Television programming is broken into **dayparts**, time periods that reflect different viewing patterns and thus have different costs associated with buying advertising and different opportunities for the public relations or marketing communications practitioner.

Local advertising tends to focus on specific stores or venues for purchasing products (for example, the Uptown Chevrolet dealership on North Main Street). National television advertising is associated with marketing of companies (the Chevrolet brand) or specific company products (Chevy Equinox crossover SUV).

Television advertising also provides some public relations opportunities. One such opportunity is associated with campaigns aimed at building awareness, acceptance, and supportive action toward an organization or an industry group (such as the Got Milk? campaign for the National Fluid Milk Processor Promotion Board). Additionally, public service advertising takes on even more public relations functions when it becomes an advocate, such as television spots encouraging the use of seat belts or the early detection of breast cancer, or discouraging drug abuse.

Nonprofit organizations sometimes find that limited budgets require them to be creative, but this also can produce some very effective campaigns. Additionally, many spots for nonprofit organizations are based on contributed services through the Advertising Council, a cooperative venture of the American Association of Advertising Agencies, the Association of National Advertisers, and various media.

The Ad Council estimates that its annual campaigns are worth $2 billion of donated media. It has produced many memorable campaigns, such as a series for the United Negro College Fund showcasing poet Maya Angelou, the McGruff the Crime Dog "Take a Bite Out of Crime" series for the National Crime Prevention Council, and the "Friends Don't Let Friends Drive Drunk" campaign for the U.S. Department of Transportation.

Another type of entertainment advertisement is the **stealth ad**, also called **product placement**. PQ Media, which tracks product placement on television, estimated that in 2014 the major U.S. networks featured product placements valued at more than $6 billion, with a growth trend to $11.4 billion in 2019.

Some stealth ads are placed directly online. Levi Strauss paid only a fraction of what it would have cost to advertise on national television to produce a web video of guys backflipping

---

CASE IN POINT **Navy Advertising**

Because of the appeal of many nonprofit causes, some high-profile organizations are able to attract top talent to take their messages to their publics.

That was the situation when the U.S. Navy fell 7,000 recruits short of its goal a few years ago. It turned to the BBDO advertising agency, which hired director Spike Lee to produce a series of recruiting commercials. Lee used a documentary style that focused on Navy SEALS, travel opportunities, sailors in a rock band, and related high-interest topics.

The Navy ended the subsequent years with more recruits than expected, while the Air Force, Army, and Marines fell short of their recruitment goals, despite an increase in marketing budgets for all branches of the armed forces.

---

in jeans. It became one of YouTube's most-viewed videos, 14 million viewers in the first few months, gaining coverage by mainstream media.

Stealth advertising is even making inroads into news reporting. Jim Upshaw, journalism professor at the University of Oregon, reported a study that found that 90 percent of 294 monitored newscasts had at least one example of stealth advertising in each newscast. The average was 2.5 instances.

The study also reveals some disturbing trends in the public relations–journalism relationships, including a bank executive in Washington, DC, who meets regularly with television producers to plan news coverage for his bank and a San Francisco news producer who has established a "**product integration** fee."

CABLE TELEVISION ADVERTISING

Cable networks offer much the same opportunities for advertising as do broadcast networks and local television stations. Additionally, cable television also offers the opportunity to feature **cable crawls**, messages that scroll out across the bottom of the TV screen, often on channels focused on weather, news, or television program listings.

In many areas, advertising contacts with cable companies are handled not by the individual cable system but by a cable broker that places advertising on a variety of cable systems.

RADIO COMMERCIAL

In placing commercials with radio stations, consider the audience you are aiming for and the time of day the spot will run. Media buyers and radio sales people can provide information on several aspects of a radio audience that you can use in comparing stations to make the proper placement choices.

Radio advertising spots generally run for 10, 30, or 60 seconds. Like television advertising placement, radio placement can be made through **network radio**, which includes about 115 national or regional networks providing advertising to perhaps several hundred network-affiliated stations. Or advertising can be **spot radio**, with placement on individual local radio stations. Radio commercials can be designated for a specific daypart, or they can be given to the station for use at any time, called **run of station** (ROS) placement.

BLENDING ADVERTISING AND PROGRAM CONTENT

Research indicates that 90 percent of households with digital recording capabilities use it to skip advertising. And unhappy advertisers are fighting back.

Some are pressuring programmers to disallow fast-forwarding over commercials or to insert a static ad or logo while a user engages the fast-forward button. Others are focusing on the programming itself with a pay-for-play approach.

The term **native advertising** refers to an ad placed within the context of its medium, matching the format of the medium itself. This may be a newspaper ad—sometimes called **sponsored news**—that looks like a news article, often with the term "paid advertising" in tiny type above the "headline." The previously noted advertorial is an example of this.

Forbes Magazine reported that advertisers spent $2.4 billion in 2014 on advertising designed to look like news articles. This despite a study by Contently, a marketing technology company, finding that 54 percent of readers feel deceived by native advertising and 43 percent said they lose trust in publishers that present native advertising from an untrusted brand. However, 77 percent said they often cannot interpret native ads as regular paid advertising. The study also found that consumers can more easily spot native or sponsored ads on Facebook than on publisher sites.

The 2016 Contently study, conducted with the Tow-Knight Center for Entrepreneurial Journalism, also reported that many journalistic sites rely on native advertising. A reported 90 percent of ad revenue in *The Daily Beast* comes from sponsored ads, 75 percent in *The Atlantic*, and 50 percent in *Slate* (Lazauskas, 2016).

In visual media it's called **product placement** or **branded entertainment**. It's a type of embedded marking in which a commercial product is woven into the storyline of films, television shows, songs, videogames, music videos, even comic books.

Movies have been using product placement for decades, featuring brand-specific products as part of the storyline. Among the best-known examples are the Reese's Pieces in the film *E.T. the Extra Terre*strial, Ray-Ban sunglasses in *Top Gun* and *Risky Business*, and FedEx and Wilson volleyballs in *Cast Away*. The James Bond *Skyfall* film had $45 million in product placement by Virgin Atlantic, Sony, Coke, Tom Ford, and others—one-third of the film's production cost. Heineken spent $75 million to promote the film as part of the deal.

On television, native advertising also takes the form of product use within the program: *American Idol* judges drinking from Coke cups, *CSI* characters drinking Pepsi and driving Fords, *Hawaii Five-O* characters driving Chevrolets and discussing the merits of Subway sandwiches—all because the companies paid to make it so. Likewise Sony, Verizon, Visa, and other advertisers paid $1 million an episode to be the featured company in *The Apprentice*. Such has been standard practice for decades by soap operas (the very name comes from both sponsorship by soap companies and product integration into the storyline).

In some instances, whole episodes revolve around a branded product, such as the iPad episode on *Modern Family* and the Kodak episode on *Mad Men*.

A newer technique with advertising potential is **digital insertion**. Using new technological advances, video editors are able to alter an image after it has been shot.

One of the first uses of digital insertion in television was a three-month partnership in 2012. England's Channel 4 TV teamed with PG Tips, a popular British brand of tea, to digitally map the tea logo onto blank mugs used by contestants on *Deal or No Deal*.

Why not just use the branded cups in the first place? For one thing, this technique allows the station to sell the logo placement later to another advertiser. It also allows films or TV programs with international distribution to be tailored for local audiences. That's what happened in the *Hannibal* TV series, in which a Bentley automobile was digitally altered to look like a Mitsubishi in Brazil, where the Japanese automaker was launching its new car. Ethical issues, anyone?

Many countries, including the United States and the United Kingdom, have restrictions on product placement. However, regulators are challenged to keep up with technological advances in videography and postproduction.

DIGITAL MEDIA AD

A new communication channel for electronic advertising is the rapidly expanding field of computer-based **digital media**. Internet websites offer a growing number of advertising and promotional opportunities.

For example, companies such as Volvo, Norelco, and Ford have created **web-only commercials**, video advertisements that are used only on the Internet. In 2006, Foster's beer dropped all television advertising in favor of web dissemination. Not only are such promotional strategies less expensive than television-based ads, but they also can appeal to younger audiences with an edgier message or presentation than might not be appropriate for broadcast television. Dunkin' Donuts, Audi, and Durex condoms have developed web-only ads targeted toward a younger demographic.

Much creativity goes into Internet promotion. For example, some beer sites on the Internet don't simply advertise beer. They also have games, music downloads, and contests so the sites can reinforce one of the perceived benefits of the beverage: fun and excitement. Likewise, websites for investment companies feature interactive financial and retirement planning with online calculators. Provide the asked-for data about your income, lifestyle, work plans, and financial obligations, and the program will tell you how much money to invest for the eventual savings you desire.

Several new forms of computer-based advertising have potential for public relations messages. Some websites feature **pop-ups** or **interstitial ads** that insinuate themselves onto the screen as a person is using the Internet. At other times while the user is waiting for a linked connection to load, pages called **superstitial ads** can appear to fill in the time.

Meanwhile, in a blend of computer and television technology, some companies are using **virtual ads** such as product billboards that appear in the background during a televised sporting event—except that the signs don't really exist on the field; they are digitally inserted for the TV audience. Thus they can be used in sequence to promote more than one sponsor during the program, or they can be tailored for viewers in different geographic areas.

Electronic catalogs are not merely electronic versions of printed catalogs. Instead they are interactive versions designed to engage the customers. For example, an online clothing catalog or a similar site for a furniture store can let users select among a range of styles, fabrics, and colors, and then see the result of this custom design.

LONG-FORM TV AND RADIO

Another emerging area of advertising focuses on **long-form television and radio**, generally defined as anything longer than two minutes.

Phase Three

STEP
7

One form is **sponsored news** or **sponsored public affairs programming**, in which organizations use their expertise to present objective and credible information to their publics. Strategically, this fits into their overall mix of media tactics, generally in support of information-based objectives.

One such example is *The Good Health Radio Hour*, a weekly 60-minute medical discussion program sponsored by Akron (Ohio) General Medical Center on local AM radio. Production costs are low and are handled through the hospital's public relations staff working with an outside production company. Guests are booked from the hospital staff and other local experts. The program has ranked seven out of 20 in its Saturday time slot. The sponsored radio program costs only one-third of what the hospital would spend on magazine advertising to pursue similar objectives. (For a full report, see James Armstrong's article in *Public Relations Tactics*, October 2007.)

PUSHING THE ENVELOPE TOO FAR

Imagine that you are a public relations director for a company or nonprofit organization, and you receive the following offer via fax and a follow-up phone call from a local television station.

> We plan to produce a series of news segments highlighting prominent businesses in the area, and we want you to be part of this series. Specifically we will produce three news segments in one week about your organization, along with several promotional spots. Remember that our newscast is the most credible programming for the image of your company. This will cost you $15,000.

That's the offer made a few years ago by WDSI Fox-61 television in Chattanooga, Tennessee. The offer surprised and shocked several area public relations practitioners, who criticized the TV station for "putting a price on its newscast." One called it "grossly unethical." Another said his organization wanted "to earn any good publicity we receive."

The TV station quickly backed away from its controversial offer, saying it had been considered but should not have been made. The offer was attributed to the naive but nevertheless good intentions of the advertising department.

Let's consider the ethical questions raised by this scenario.

- Is it ever appropriate for a television news team to offer (or appear to be offering) favorable news coverage for a price? For a public relations or marketing communication practitioner to accept such an offer?
- Is this offer substantively different from the practice of some television stations in which advertising sales people try to solicit ads from companies that, independent of the advertising department, are being featured in news stories?
- Is it substantively different from the common practice among newspapers of publishing topical advertising sections or progress editions in which stories and photos from the advertisers are prominently featured?
- Is it substantively different from the common practice within the trade press of linking advertisements with news or feature stories?

The prospect of long-form sponsored programs raises ethical concerns. One is that the sponsor of such programming be clearly identified. Another cause for anxiety is in the potential for further muddling the already blurred line between news and advertising. For decades, nonprofit concerns such as schools, hospitals, religious groups, and environmental organizations have provided television and radio programming in the format of news or public affairs. But when corporations get into the act, it raises some new issues.

Long-form advertising sometimes is presented as an **infomercial**, a portmanteau of "information" and "commercial." The term is properly reserved for advertisements that frequently push a product toward the audience. Infomercials usually are full of demonstrations and testimonials. They also often employ direct-response marketing techniques, such as inviting viewers or listeners to call 800 numbers, log into websites, or similarly interact with the company making the pitch for the product.

Anybody with insomnia or late-night viewing habits is likely to be familiar with infomercials for products such as the Bowflex home gym, TempurPedic mattress, Rosetta Stone language system, Billy Blanks Tae Bo workout program, Ginsu knives, and other assorted products "not available in stores." Some feature out-of-the-spotlight entertainers such as Cher pitching hair-care products, Chuck Norris for home gyms, and Suzanne Somers for thigh and ab tighteners.

Out-of-Home Advertising

Out-of-home advertising focuses on several different opportunities to take a persuasive message to a public that is on the move, making it possible to reach people subtly. Sometimes the advertising itself can become an attractive diversion. For example, people waiting for a bus, riding on the subway, or sitting in the stands at a sporting event often pay attention to outside advertising.

This kind of advertising offers several advantages over print and electronic advertising. Outdoor ads have 24/7 visibility to a wide variety of people. They offer repeat exposure to the advertising message. On the downside, out-of-home advertisements are expensive, and they are limited to short, simple messages.

Categories of out-of-home advertising include outdoor posters, arena posters, signage, out-of-home videos, transit advertising, aerial advertising, and inflatables.

OUTDOOR POSTER

In the realm of advertising media, **poster** is a generic name for several different kinds of outdoor stationary ad venues: billboards, paints, and spectaculars.

A **billboard** is a huge sign placed along highways, intended to be seen by motorists. Sheets of paper or vinyl are glued onto the billboards, usually for one-month periods. Some advertisers add **snipes** to their billboards. These are strips pasted over part of an existing billboard so its message can be updated without the poster being completely changed.

A **painted bulletin** or **paint** is another type of outdoor sign. These are larger than posters, usually 14 × 48 feet, and because they actually are painted signs they generally are more permanent than billboard posters. Most paints are sold on an annual basis. Permanent paints are displayed in a single location, most often along highways, where they advertise motels, restaurants, and tourist attractions. A **rotary paint** can be physically moved from one location to another.

Increasingly, public relations and marketing clients are turning to the **digital billboard** for both advertising and public service purposes. Images on digital billboards can change every few seconds, creating both visual appeal and opportunities for shared, part-time costs. Some states and communities are banning or heavily regulating digital billboards because of traffic safety concerns, such as motorists who glance too long at the changing and often distracting digital images. On the other hand, some communities use digital billboards to enhance the smooth flow of traffic or to engage motorists in looking for missing children.

The largest billboard in North America is a digital screen in Times Square, with its 24 million pixels covering an area eight stories high and nearly the length of a football field (25,000 square feet). Larger still is the billboard in Saudi Arabia's main international airport— 820 x 39 feet (32,000 square feet).

A **spectacular** is another type of outdoor poster involving some kind of extra elements, creatively called **extras**, to the basic flat rectangular surface of the poster. For example, some such billboards feature three-dimensional elements, such as one for an auto dealer with blinking "headlights" or another for a golf course featuring a giant 3-D golf ball.

On one spectacular, Mothers Against Drunk Drivers (MADD) hung the actual wreck of a car in which a family had been killed. Some spectaculars use computers to add a continuously changing message to billboards, such as a state lottery billboard with the amount of the current week's payout.

Another outdoor venue is the **wall mural** or **wallscape**, the painted exterior of a building leased for advertising purposes.

ARENA POSTER

Billboard-like advertisements placed on walls and fences of arenas such as sports stadiums and ballparks are called **arena posters**. Smaller posters are located inside arenas, often hanging in front of the various levels of seating. Some of these posters are computer generated, allowing for message crawls. In many sports venues, computer-generated posters are rotated every few minutes to provide a sequence of showing during a single public event.

SIGNAGE

Visible and appropriate signs can be important aspects in an organization's promotional program. **Signage** includes a variety of stationary outdoor signs, including signs enhanced by a variety of lighting techniques.

Some organizations try to make sure that their exterior signage is consistent with their architectural design. A Southwestern university with adobe-style buildings, for example, might want its signage to blend into that theme, as would a northeastern campus with Adirondack-style architecture or a campus with a classic neo-Greek design.

While most signage is considered permanent, some is meant to be temporary. Special signage is needed only a few days for a campus open house, yet attention to this tactic can go beyond the topical stick-in-the-ground signs such as those used to promote houses for sale or to solicit votes for the county sheriff. Temporary doesn't mean disposable, and some organizations invest in temporary signage that can be reused each year or for different events.

Another type of temporary signage is sidewalk chalk, which is often used in urban areas to promote events or to solicit support for political or social causes. Regular sidewalk chalk washes away with the first rain, but spray-on chalk lasts about three months, making it a more efficient medium for some signage.

Specially formulated turf paints used on athletic fields also can be useful in decorative landscaping for civic, cultural, and commercial buildings.

OUT-OF-HOME VIDEO

The category of **out-of-home video** is one of the newest additions to the inventory of advertising and promotional vehicles. Out-of-home video includes the giant video screens on which some sports arenas and concert halls present poster-like or full-video images. Another example of this tactic is the **video wall** that features an ever-moving series of computer-generated images.

Advertisements in movie theaters that precede the showing of feature films also fall into the category of out-of-home videos. Because of the variety in films, such advertising can be targeted to specific audience demographics.

TRANSIT ADVERTISING

Mobile ads placed on and inside of public commuter vehicles such as buses and trains are known collectively as **transit advertising**. The term also includes stationary ads located on bus shelters and at locations such as subway stations and airport terminals.

Bus signs are available in several common sizes for different areas of buses: streetside, curbside, front or back. Each can target different audiences, for example, curbside for pedestrians and streetside for motorists. **Car cards** are signs placed above the windows inside buses and trains. **Station posters** or **dioramas** often are small vertical panels located in subway, train, and bus stations, as well as in airport terminals. **Shelter posters** are located in bus shelters.

An advantage to transit advertising is that it can be very specific, focusing on local organizations and addressed to people who live in a particular neighborhood. In large cities, for example, shelter and subway signs may be in a language other than English that is used by a majority of the residents, or they may feature highly specific ethnic images or cultural symbols.

The category of transit advertising also includes **mobile billboards**, the painted sides of tractor-trailers or delivery trucks that increasingly are being rented out as advertising venues.

AERIAL ADVERTISING

Aerial advertising includes various vehicles: blimps with signs or computer-generated scroll messages, airplane tows featuring planes pulling banners over beaches and ballparks, and skywriting airplanes that trail smoke and write messages in the sky. These techniques can be particularly effective if much of your target audience is assembled in a single location. For example, a resort restaurant may use aerial advertising above a popular beach near its location.

INFLATABLE

Air-filled objects called **inflatables** are sometimes used as attention-getters. Inflatables range from giant outdoor balloons with a corporate logo to air-filled promotional items such as an ice-cream cone for the grand opening of a dairy bar. Some rooftop inflatables are 20 feet high or larger.

Promotional Items

Many organizations augment their advertising program with promotional items, giveaways for customers that the organization hopes will be a continuing reminder of its cause, product, or service.

Phase Three

STEP 7

Branded clothing includes designer labels such as Tommy Hilfiger or the Gap, which, because they are trendy, are particularly sought out by young people. Not all advertisers, however, are lucky enough to find that their logo is a popular status symbol. On the contrary, it is usually the advertiser that pays to place the logo on T-shirts, athletic and leisure clothing, and other garments. Uniforms for sports teams and individual athletes often carry the name and logo of the corporate sponsor. Companies increasingly are applying their name, with strong visual reminders, to everything from sports cars and golf tournaments to sports arenas and hospital waiting rooms.

Costumes are another type of promotional clothing, such as the flamboyant chicken suits that might be worn by promoters for the opening of a new fried-chicken restaurant.

Some organizations place promotional logos or messages on office accessories such as calendars, pens, and notepads. Others promote themselves through home accessories such as coffee mugs, refrigerator magnets, bottle openers, matches, napkins, and related goods.

Direct-mail gimmicks are another type of promotional item. Small or miniaturized samples of company products, for example, can be mailed to potential clients. Symbolic items also can be quite effective.

Be careful, however, about what you send through the mail. When one California law firm wanted to let potential clients know that it had the ammunition to fight their legal battles, it mailed out hundreds of fake hand grenades. The come-ons looked so real that some recipients evacuated buildings and called the bomb squads and postal inspectors.

In another what-were-they-thinking case, a dot-com company wanted to warn prospects not to be unprepared for computer viruses. Its message strategy: Don't shoot yourself in the foot. So the company mailed out empty bullet shells on a postcard without a return address—just to build suspense—asking, "Who's been shooting [your] readers?" Again, the police and FBI were called in.

What's Next?

This concludes the inventory of tactics that are available to public relations and marketing communication practitioners.

The next step will deal with developing these tactics into a cohesive and comprehensive package that can effectively and efficiently generate the outcomes identified in the previous Strategy phase.

Phase Three

STEP
7

PLANNING EXAMPLE 7D **Selecting Advertising and Promotional Tactics**

UPSTATE COLLEGE **Upstate College will develop the following advertising and promotional tactics to publicize its expanded program:**

- *Display ad in local newspaper*—moderate to high cost, focus on key publics
- *Display ad in campus newspapers at other colleges*—low cost, highlight directed toward transfer students

- *Cable TV crawl*—low cost, low impact
- *Radio commercial*—moderate to high cost, directed toward potential students
- *Promotional T-shirt*—moderate cost

(Note: No television advertising will be used because of the expense involved.)

Tiny Tykes will develop the following tactics for an employee-oriented public relations program:

- *T-shirts with safety logo*—low cost
- *Display ads in trade magazine* featuring employees with theme of customer safety moderate cost, directed toward industry leaders
- *Display ads in consumer magazines* featuring employees with theme of customer safety—high cost, directed toward parents
- *Sponsorship of public television series* about raising infants and toddlers—moderate to high cost, directed toward parents

 Checklist 7D **Advertising and Promotional Tactics**

Basic Questions

1. What advertising media and promotional tactics will you use?
2. How will these tactics help the organization achieve its objectives?
3. What resources will these tactics require?

Expanded Questions

A. SELECTION OF TACTICS

From the following categories of advertising and promotional tactics, identify several that you would consider using.

Print Advertising Media
- Magazine advertising, advertorial
- Newspaper advertising: display, classified, personal classified
- Directory advertising
- House ads
- Program advertising

Electronic Advertising Media
- Television: commercial, spot, infomercial
- Radio: commercial, network radio, spot radio

- Cable television: advertising, cable crawl
- Computer media: e-zine, electronic catalog

Out-of-Home Advertising

- Outdoor poster: billboard, paint, spectacular, wall mural
- Arena poster
- Signage
- Out-of-home video, video wall
- Transit advertising: bus sign, car card, station poster, diorama, shelter poster, mobile billboard
- Aerial advertising: blimp, airplane tows, skywriting, inflatable

Promotional Items

- Clothing, costume, office accessory, home accessory

B. STRATEGIC IMPLICATIONS

For each item identified, answer the following questions.

1. Will this tactic help the organization to interact with the appropriate public?
2. What level of impact will this tactic make on the key public?
3. Will this tactic advance the organization toward its awareness objectives?
4. Will this tactic advance the organization toward its acceptance objectives?
5. Will this tactic advance the organization toward its action objectives?
6. What is the main advantage to this tactic?
7. What advantages does this tactic offer that other tactics do not?
8. Are there any disadvantages to this tactic?

C. IMPLEMENTATION ITEMS

For each item identified, answer the following questions.

1. How much will it cost to implement this tactic? Is the cost justified? Is the cost practical, based on the organization's resources?
2. How much staff time will it take to implement this tactic? Is the time practical, based on the organization's resources?
3. What skill level, equipment, and expertise are needed to implement this tactic? Is the needed skill level available within the organization? Is it available from outside sources?

Phase Three

STEP
7

STEP 8

Implementing
the Strategic Plan

Now that you have put together a full plate of ways to present your message, turn your attention to implementing these tactics. In this step, you will consider two aspects of implementation: turning your inventory of tactics into a logical and cohesive program, and then dealing with the specifics of scheduling and budgeting.

Packaging Communication Tactics

The various communication tactics have been likened to items on a menu, so let's take the analogy a step further. Menu items can be grouped into categories: appetizer, salad, main course, dessert, beverage, and the like. When you order a meal, you'll probably cover the whole range of menu categories.

Additionally, when you review the restaurant menu, you often make your selections based on a particular culinary focus—Japanese, Tex-Mex, Southern, Italian, and so on. You don't order every item, and you don't order haphazardly.

It's unlikely you would start with tuna sashimi as an appetizer, add a dollop of cole slaw on a bed of lettuce, feature jalapeño chili relleno as main course, add sides of grits and ravioli, and end with a flaming cherries jubilee for dessert—served with ouzo and Pepsi Max. Just the thought is enough to make the stomach churn.

Rather, you'd probably develop a culinary theme. You would creatively package your choices to concoct a special dining experience appropriate to the occasion and suitable to your, needs, interests, and resources.

The same is true with strategic planning for communication. In Step 7, you considered items in each of the menu categories. You discarded some possibilities and sketched out ways to do others.

Now you need to package them into an effective set of tactics to help you achieve your objectives. This should be much more than a "to do" list. Consider how various tactics can be woven together. Group some around the themes associated with your strategic planning from Steps 5 and 6.

Remember: You don't need to be tied into a chronological implementation scheme just because you selected interpersonal items before those in the other categories. That was just to touch bases with each section in your toolbox. Let the natural relationship among tactics determine how they fit into your plan.

Consider what you learned in Phase Two, Strategy. For example, the diffusion of innovations theory tells us that information presented through the news media can pave the way for personal interaction between opinion leaders and the ultimate public. Also, think about the example of some companies mentioned in the Introduction of this book. There is precedence for implementing a publicity program before an advertising schedule, thus allowing for a smaller advertising budget with higher-than-usual results.

Thinking Creatively

What's the best way to present your plan? You decide. Look for the simplest and most logical way to present the tactics that grow out of your planning. Later on we'll look at some suggestions to help you get started. First let's consider the importance of creative thinking. As you decide how to package your tactics, try to leap ahead of the crowd with an innovative approach to the problem or opportunity you are dealing with.

For example, if you have a new organizational logo to unveil, consider making it a real unveiling. How about a ceremonial removal of a sequined cloth covering the logo? Or maybe you could have the logo painted large on the outside of the company's building, temporarily draped. One nonprofit organization introduced a new logo by involving five local political and media celebrities who each gave a short testimonial about the organization and then, one by one, placed together cut-out pieces of a giant jigsaw puzzle to create the new logo.

Consider another scenario. Your organization has an announcement to make—usually a routine matter. But you want it to stand out. One corporation engineered an interactive announcement in two cities at different ends of the state, with a teleconference hookup. The president of the corporation was in one city, a congressman who actively supported the organization in the other. The two together announced a significant multimillion-dollar project that the corporation was developing. Just in case the technology failed, the public relations planner had prepared a script and a videotape that could be used as a backup at each location.

An Indiana group used a symbolic protest as part of its announcement strategy. Hogs Opposed to Government Waste and Silly Highways (HOGWASH) sent Arnold the Pig to deliver a ham to the governor's press secretary, announcing its opposition to the extension of a highway in southern Indiana. The protesters said the road project was an example of pork-barrel politics, so it was only fitting for Arnold to be their multitalented spokespig, who also sang and danced for reporters.

Some organizations have specially designed vehicles used for promotion and other public relations objectives. For example, Rural/Metro Ambulance Service has a three-foot high talking, winking, lighted ambulance called Amby that paramedics take into classrooms during safety presentations. United Parcel Service has a miniature delivery truck that it uses in athletic arenas to deliver a coin for the ceremonial coin toss. Notice how each of these vehicles relates to the primary mission of the organization.

Some award-winning campaigns have found their success through creativity, such as the "man sled" race by Snausages (for details, see Step 7, Interpersonal Communication Tactics, Special Events).

"Organ donor" is a negative reference to motorcycle riders. But the nonprofit Lifeline of Ohio creatively embraced the term as a double entendre, changing it from an insult to a positive.

The "Live On, Ride On" campaign registered 3,000 new organ donors among motorcyclists in Central and Southeastern Ohio, with thousands more expected over the four-year cycle for renewing riders' licenses.

Likewise, AMResorts and its public relations agency got creative to combat health worries. The company's Mexican resort hotels were only half-full in 2009 because of fears of H1N1 swine flu. The company issued a "flu-free guarantee," promising that any guest who contracted swine flu at one of its resorts would get free return visits over each of the next three years. Bookings shot up 140 percent. Several other resort chains imitated the guarantee, and the Mexican government praised AMResorts for helping get Mexico's economy back to recovery.

Putting the Program Together

When the time comes to begin putting your public relations or marketing communication program together, first review the information gathered during the research phase of the program (Steps 1, 2, and 3). Reconsider the issue and review pertinent information about the organization, its environment, and perceptions about it. Next examine the various publics and your analysis of them.

Following this review, consider several different ways to package the tactics you have chosen. No particular format is best for every issue, so let common sense be your guide. Consider the most distinctive element of your program. Your purpose is to select the format

---

CASE IN POINT **Confused Insurance and Bubble Wrap**

A public relations agency in England trying to raise brand awareness of an insurance comparison company focused on three goals: driving traffic to the company website (confused.com), increasing visibility, and generating requests for insurance quotes.

Company statistics on insurance claims were researched to identify the most accident-prone street in the United Kingdom: Somerville Road in Worcester.

Then eight people worked 12 hours to bubble wrap the entire street. Nearly 1,500 square meters (1,800 square yards) of bubble wrap covered cars and trucks, houses, bicycles, dog houses, swing sets, trees and shrubs, even garden gnomes.

The light-hearted publicity event carried a serious message about the dangers of winter driving, raising it well above the level of a mere publicity stunt devoid of news value. Rather, it was a means of attracting media attention to a serious issue of public safety.

The public relations team contacted established news media, including major national newspapers, as well as emerging social media by posting photos on Twitter, Flickr, and Facebook. The combined buzz attracted more than 125 million viewers to blogs and articles, and the story was picked up by international news media in Australia and North America. The company's website saw a 20 percent increase in visitors on the first day of the publicity event, which passed its objective of generating an additional 4,000 requests for insurance quote.

In a final burst of publicity, the bubble wrap was donated to Oxfam, the international food-aid program, to package shipments to earthquake victims in Haiti.

that most readily allows you to present your analysis and recommendations to your colleagues, boss, or client.

Campaigns can package tactics by media category, public, goal, objective, and department. Look at each of these with an open mind. Perhaps you'll be able to devise a more effective way to package the tactical recommendations in your program.

PACKAGING BY MEDIA CATEGORY

Using this approach, you review the goals, objectives, and strategy associated with Steps 4, 5, and 6. Next, list each tactic according to the outline of media categories provided in the Step 7 inventory; that is, in order of interpersonal communication, organizational media, news media, and advertising media. With each tactic, indicate the relevant publics, and objectives.

This presentation by media type can guide you to draw tactics from each category, though the presentation can appear a bit disjointed because it may overlook a more logical grouping of tactics. Nevertheless, it may be a good starting point, at least an effective preliminary checklist, before using one of the following presentation formats. The presentation by tactics is followed by evaluation methods (Step 9), which will come a bit later in this book.

PACKAGING BY PUBLIC

The research phase moves to an outline of each key public and, for each, an overview of the relevant goals and objectives (Step 4). Then the strategy phase focuses on interacting and communicating with each public (Steps 5 and 6). This approach to packaging should include tactics associated with each strategy (Step 7) and evaluation methods (Step 9).

Use this format if the internal cohesion of your plan centers on the differences among several publics. For example, if you are planning a program that identifies three categories of publics—customers, employees, and community—you may decide that you can present your analysis and ideas best by focusing separately on each public.

PACKAGING BY GOAL

Using this approach, the plan begins with the common research phase and provides an overview of goals associated with the issue. It then identifies a series of initiatives based on each goal and focuses the rest of the plan serially on each initiative.

In your presentation of each initiative, identify relevant research and background information, key publics (Step 3), objectives (Step 4), strategy with key messages (Steps 5 and 6) tactics (Step 7), and evaluation methods (Step 9).

Use this format when goals are sufficiently distinct to allow you to treat each one independently. For example, a public relations and marketing communication program for a university might identify several goal-based initiatives. These might include enhancing the university's reputation among students in high school and community colleges; increasing support from the business and civic community; recruiting more students to professional development programs; and enhancing knowledge and pride among students, faculty, staff, and alumni. Campaign tactics could be associated with each of the four goals, a kind of sub-campaign for each component.

PACKAGING BY OBJECTIVE

Presentation by objective begins, like the previous approach, with the common research phase of Steps 1, 2, and 3. It then provides an overview of the goals and objectives from Step 4. Then it selects each objective as the focus for the remainder of the presentation, identifying key publics (Step 3), strategy with key messages (Steps 5 and 6), tactics (Step 7), and evaluation methods (Step 9) for each objective.

Use this approach when the objectives rather than the goals or publics are the most significant distinction within the plan. For example, a plan that has only a single goal might be presented according to the objectives associated with awareness, acceptance, and action.

PACKAGING BY DEPARTMENT

Similar to presentation by goals or objectives, presentation by department acknowledges that the distinctive segments of the strategic communication plan parallel existing organizational structures, such as departments, divisions, and programs within the organization.

Use this approach when the structure of the client's organization coincides with program areas in your strategic plan.

PLANNING EXAMPLE 8A **Packaging Communication Tactics**

The following initiative is packaged according to one of the four task goals identified in Planning Example 4: Establishing Goals and Objectives.

UPSTATE COLLEGE

Initiative on Transfer Students

(Transcribe research, goal, key public, objectives, and strategy information.)

- *Interpersonal Communication Tactics*: Upstate College will sponsor the "Celebration! UC" *weekend* (Friday evening, Saturday afternoon and evening, and Sunday afternoon), celebrating the expansion of UC to a four-year institution. Entertainment during this event will include a *picnic* with two *bands*, a formal *banquet* and strolling *entertainers* (students in the school's music department). The event will include a *rededication ceremony* with public officials, leaders of neighboring colleges and universities, and UC students, faculty, and alumni; a *fall festival* for current students and alumni; and *an open house* for prospective transfer students.
- *Organizational and Social Media Tactics*: Support materials for the festival will include a revision of the college *viewbook*, announcements posted at the college *Facebook* site, a new transfer *brochure* and a *poster*, as well as production of a *video*. A special page will be added to the UC *website* home page. Students who applied to UC within the last two years and were accepted but did not attend will be sent a letter, followed by a *tweet*, inviting them to the festival events, along with a *fact sheet* about Upstate College.
- *News Media Tactics*: More generally, the festival will be promoted with media fact sheets and *news releases*, a *photo* with caption, and a *cable TV crawl*. Students attending the event will be given an Upstate College *T-shirt* designed by UC art students. A *media advisory* will be sent to the news media, inviting them to cover the event, and *news interviews* will be offered with the UC president, provost, and student government president. Additionally, the media relations office will seek out an *editorial conference* with the local newspaper to elicit editorial support for the expansion. Failing that, a *letter to the editor* will be sent by a UC official noting the benefits of the program expansion for the community.

Phase Three

STEP
8

- *Advertising and Promotional Media Tactics*: The festival also will be promoted with a *newspaper advertisement* in campus newspapers at other colleges and with radio *commercials*. Additionally, a *display ad* in the local newspaper will be aimed at parents as well as community leaders, alumni, and donors.

(Note that each of the other goals would be developed in a similar manner.)

The following initiative is packaged according to the four key publics identified in Planning Example 3A: Identifying Publics.

Public Relations Program for Tiny Tykes Employees

(Transcribe research, goal, objectives, and strategy information.)

- *Internal Tactics*: The internal component of a training program for employees will include *workshops* on customer satisfaction as well as a *training session* on product safety and quality; *brochures* and *email notices* about safety and quality issues will be available. Several *work-group meetings* will be held, at least one involving a *motivational speech* by the CEO. Similar motivational themes will be presented in *newsletter articles* and in the online employee *bulletin*.
- *External Tactics*: The program will have an external component to provide employee support. Elements of this component will *include letters to families* of employees, *letters to the editors* of local newspapers about employee dedication to customer safety, and print *advertisements* in trade magazines and in the local newspaper. A *news release* will announce the new safety and quality initiatives, and a *story idea memo* will be given to reporters about employee dedication to customer safety.

(Note that each of the other publics would be developed in a similar manner.)

 Checklist 8A **Packaging Communication Tactics**

Basic Questions

1. What specific initiatives or sections make up this plan?
2. What tactics are associated with this plan?
3. What public and objective does each tactic serve?

Expanded Questions

A. SELECTING THE APPROACH

1. From the following categories, indicate which one offers the greatest likelihood of a package of program tactics that is cohesive and logical: by public, by goal, by objective, by department, or by tactic.
2. List specific initiatives or sections in your plan.

B. STRATEGIC IMPLICATIONS

1. Will this approach help the organization to interact with the appropriate public?
2. What is the main advantage to this approach?
3. What advantages does this approach offer that other approaches do not?
4. Are there any disadvantages to this approach?

Campaign Plan Book

The **campaign plan book**—or, more simply, "the book"—is the formal written presentation of your research findings and program recommendations for strategy, tactics, and evaluation. This report should be concise in writing, professional in style, and confident in tone. Here are some of the elements the plan book should include:

- *Title Page.* List a program name as well as the names of the client organization, consultant or team members, and date.
- *Executive Summary.* Prepare a one- or two-page synopsis of the plan written as an overview for busy executives and for readers who are not directly involved in the program.
- *Table of Contents.* Outline the major segments of the program.
- *Statement of Principles* (optional). Lay out the planner's approach to strategic communication campaigns (particularly whether it is rooted in public relations, marketing communication, or integrated communication). Include definitions of key concepts used in the book.
- *Situation Analysis.* Outline your research and analysis of the issue (Step 1), organization (Step 2), and publics (Step 3). Some program plans present the research data and summaries on paper of a different color from the rest of the report.
- *Strategic Recommendations.* Present your proposed goals and objectives, as well as your strategic plan for spokesperson, theme, key message, etc.
- *Tactical Program.* Present your tactical recommendations in whatever format you think works best (such as by public, goal, objective, program, or tactic) to show your plans and address the issue and implement the strategic recommendations.
- *Schedule.* Outline the time and calendar considerations for implementing the various tactics.
- *Budget.* Outline resources needed for the program. Include in this figure the cost of personnel time, money, and equipment, as well as any income to be generated or any donations that offset costs.
- *Evaluation Plan.* Provide information on the methods to be used to measure the program's effectiveness.
- *Consultant Credentials and Resources* (optional). Indicate the resources the consultant or agency can offer. This element of the plan is especially useful in competitive situations in which more than one consultant or agency prepares program recommendations.

Sometimes you may decide not to use a particular tactic, perhaps passing up even a particular category of communication tactics. For example, an employee relations project may not lend itself to involving the news media, or an investor relations project may not include advertising. It is appropriate to note the absence of a tactic and the reason behind your choice for not using it.

When you choose not to use what might seem to be an obvious tactic, it is particularly important to offer your reasoning in your plan. Especially if you are developing a proposal

---

EXAMPLE: TACTICS FOR OPEN HOUSE

Consider the following example outlining one tactic, an open house as part of a campaign proposal for a new dual-track program in landscape architecture and landscape design at a university in a mid-sized city. This tactic would be just one of several for the entire campaign.

Note that this example shows the internal linkage between a single tactic, previously identified publics, already determined objectives and strategy, administrative details such as budgeting, and subsequent evaluation methods.

- *Public*: Professional architects (specifically, approximately 145 practicing architects, landscape architects, landscape designers, and landscape contractors within a three-county area).
- *Objective*: To increase the understanding of this professional community about the new program (50 percent of the professional community prior to beginning the academic program).
- *Strategy*: Attract attention of the professional community and create a core of opinion leaders; give specific attention to leading architects and designers, particularly those who have received recognition, certification, or affiliation with processional associations related to landscaping.
- *Tactical Elements*

  1. Promotional materials including news release, email invitations, Facebook note, tweets, and outreach to appropriate blogs ($100).
  2. Information materials including an eight-minute video ($15,000 value; $1,000 cost in-house by broadcasting students).
  3. Information packet for visitors, with parallel information at website ($200).
  4. Logistical support including reserved space, parking arrangements, snacks, and beverages ($100).

- *Budget*: $14,500 value. Actual cost $1,500.
- *Evaluation Methods*: Attendance figures; follow-up minisurvey conducted as part of a telephone thank-you for attending.
- *Oversight*: Assistant Director of Community Relations.

In a complete proposal, each tactic would receive similar treatment. Even individual tactics might have multiple components. For example, the open house noted earlier might have additional publics, perhaps donors or potential students. Each of these would require its own statement of objectives and strategies, though the budget and evaluation methods may remain constant.

on competitive-bid basis, let the potential client know why you recommend against using what others might suggest.

Regardless of the way you package your tactics, it is important to show the internal logic within your planning program. Make it clear to your client or boss how the various elements work together for a common purpose.

A good way to show this internal harmony is to note for each tactic the specific public, goal, and objective to which it is linked. In this way, planners can make sure that the various tactics adequately serve each public. Likewise, planners can be certain that each goal and objective is played out through a variety of tactics.

Campaign Schedule

You already addressed one aspect of scheduling when you built into your objectives in Step 4 an indication of when you planned to achieve each. This provided the deadline upon which you will measure your effectiveness in reaching the objectives.

Now that Step 7 has generated an outline of tactics, you can establish specific time requirements. This involves two considerations: (1) the pattern and frequency of your communication tactics and (2) the actual timeline of tasks to be accomplished as the tactics are implemented.

Frequency of Tactics

As noted in Step 6, the average person is exposed to thousands of public relations and marketing messages each day, yet most of these messages fall on deaf ears. Clearly, mere exposure to a message is insufficient to move people to action. However, the frequency of exposure is an important factor in whether the message takes root in a person's consciousness.

Repetition increases awareness and leads to greater acceptance. Research has been done both on **message frequency** (the number and pattern of messages presented to a particular public in a given period of time) and on **message reach** (the number of different people who are exposed to a single message).

Most of this research has been focused either on advertising or on the learning process. However, it is possible to generalize a bit about applications for public relations. It is known, for example, that one exposure to a message has little or no effect unless the audience is unusually attentive. Minimally, three exposures are needed to even begin making an impact.

This concept has enjoyed general support within the advertising trade since it was articulated by ad manager and theoretician Herbert Krugman (1972). Subsequent researchers have noted that studies in laboratory settings confirmed Krugman's three-exposure formula. However, in natural settings in which consumers are distracted by competing messages, three presentations of the message may not be enough to generate three mindful exposures to the intended audience.

What do we learn from such research? Here are a few of the important lessons and observations for the public relations manager.

MULTIPLE PRESENTATIONS

Don't rely on just one presentation of your message to key publics. Don't think that even three exposures guarantee success. Find ways to repeat and reinforce your message, especially through various media. This will not only increase retention among your key publics but also add to the credibility of the message because it will have the third-party endorsement of several different media gatekeepers.

REPETITION OVER TIME

Another lesson gleaned from research is the value of repetition over a period of time. Most audiences remember a message they have seen daily for several days more than one presented several times in a single day. Too-frequent presentation of the message seems unnecessarily redundant and can lead to wear-out—which, by the way, comes faster with a humorous message than with a neutral or serious one.

AUDIENCE CONFUSION

A message presented may not be a message heard. There is no specific number for how many repetitions are best. Sometimes, even your best efforts won't gain complete success, especially with audiences who are not particularly interested in the issue. This is an unavoidable result of the information overload that all audiences encounter every day. They are aware of a message, but not particularly mindful of its content.

For example, for several years one of the most consistent television advertising campaigns featured a pink rabbit beating the drum for a battery company. Yet 40 percent of viewers in a national survey identified the wrong company as the sponsor of the ad, despite the company's best effort to promote its Energizer Bunny.

PATTERNS OF MESSAGE REPETITION

An insight drawn from advertising is that the pattern of communication can be of crucial importance for public relations and marketing communications. If you know that a one-time message is not likely to be effective, the questions are about when and how you should plan for repetition of the message. Consider four concepts: continuity, flighting, pulsing, and massing.

Continuity is an approach to scheduling that presents a message at a consistent level throughout a particular period of time. Use this approach if you need to maintain a consistent presence over a given period of time. But realize that it is expensive to use a continuous approach with enough intensity to generate an effective reach and frequency.

Flighting (also called **bursting**) refers to the presentation of messages in waves, with periods of intense communication interspersed with dark periods of communication inactivity. A variety of media can be used during the peak communication periods. This approach is useful when organizational activity falls into predictable and discrete periods.

Pulsing is a combination of the two approaches, with a continuous base augmented by intermittent bursts of communication activity.

Massing is the bunching of various presentations of a message into a short period of time.

These techniques are associated with advertising and most commonly involve different ways of timing a single advertising message. However, the concept of timing can be used to plan and schedule various complementary public relations and marketing communication tactics. These could involve not only advertising messages but also meetings and special events, posters and brochures, blogs and email, postings on the online newsroom, and so on.

KEY PUBLIC

Bruce Vanden Bergh and Helen Katz (1999) point out that most organizations with limited budgets must find a balance between reach and frequency. A basic guideline for advertising seems to hold true for other aspects of marketing communication and public relations: Focus on key publics. Rather than trying to reach a greater number of people, try instead to more frequently reach a targeted number of strategically important people.

Timeline of Tasks

At this point in your planning, you know three things about your tactics: (1) which ones will be used, (2) how they will be packaged, and (3) how often they will run.

Now turn your attention to carefully considering each significant task needed for these tactics. One of the easiest ways to schedule tasks is to work backward from the final tactic date. For example, if you want a brochure to be received in the readers' homes by May 15, work backward to develop the following hypothetical schedule:

May 12	Deliver to the post office.
May 11	Attach address labels.
May 10	Receive from printer.
May 5	Deliver to printer.
April 29	Finalize copy and design, and obtain approvals.
April 21	Complete draft, including copy, artwork, and layout.
April 14	Begin writing, develop artwork.
April 8	Assign writer and designer.
April 6	Obtain approval for objectives, determine budget.
April 2	Begin planning for brochure.

Total time required: 45 days.

This plan is your **timeline** or implementation schedule. Timelines are essential when you are dealing with a variety of tactics and managing different programs at the same time. Having a written plan makes it easier to train others and delegate responsibilities. Similarly, having a written timeline makes it easier to keep work records that may be needed for billing purposes.

A good way to manage the scheduling process is to chart out each of the tasks you have identified. You could use a large calendar or a timetable narrative with sections for time periods and bulleted task items to be accomplished during each time period.

However, flow charts are particularly helpful in tracking public relations tactics because they provide a visual representation of the tasks to be completed. Two commonly used types of flow charts at the Gantt chart and the PERT chart.

GANTT CHART

One frequently used type of flow chart is the **Gantt chart**. Engineer Henry Gantt developed this during World War I to track shipbuilding projects. The Gantt chart lists each tactic and the various associated tasks, then indicates the time needed for each task. Times can be indicated in days, weeks, or months, depending on the type of project.

Phase Three

STEP
8

The advantage of the Gantt chart is that it provides a map of the work that needs to be done. These charts can be kept on computer, written on paper charts, or displayed as wall charts. Several free templates for Gantt charts are available for download from online sites that can be found with a search engine. Some software or online sites allow for interactive Gantt charts so multiple users can work on comprehensive projects.

Exhibit 8.1 shows a Gantt chart for an activity for which implementation is just beginning. X indicates planned tasks. When these tasks are completed, replace the Xs with solid dashes.

Because the Gantt chart shows every task associated with the various tactics, planners can spread out activity according to a convenient schedule. For example, under normal conditions preparation of a brochure may take about six weeks. But the Gantt chart may show that several other important and time-consuming activities will be taking place within the same six-week period. Thus you may need to begin work on the brochure earlier.

PERT CHART

Another commonly used flow chart is the **PERT chart**, a process first developed for the Polaris missile system in the 1950s. PERT (Program Evaluation and Review Technique) charts generally include dates and assignment to particular individuals, though they lack the calendaring aspect of the Gantt chart. The PERT chart, shown in Exhibit 8.2, lists tasks within circles or boxes, with arrows indicating how one task flows into another.

An effective implementation schedule of public relations tactics generally includes more than dates. Include the name of the person or group responsible for the task. In addition to the deadline date, some charts indicate the latest date by which the tactic can be implemented and still remain useful.

EXHIBIT 8.1 Gantt Chart for Brochure

	April	May
	2 4 6 8 10 12 14 16 18 20 22 24 26 28 30	2 4 6 8 10 12 14
Brochure		
Planning (myself)	xxxxxxx	
Objectives (supervisor)	x	
Assign writer (myself)	x	
Writing (freelancer)	xxxxxxxxx	
Complete draft (freelancer)	x	
Final copy (myself)	xxxxxx	
To printer (myself)	x	
From printer (printer)	x	
Labels (staff)	x	
To Post Office (staff)	x	
Deliver (Post Office)	xxx	

Phase Three

STEP
8

EXHIBIT 8.2 PERT Chart

Campaign Budget

The development of resources needed to achieve objectives, the **budget**, is a topic that has been on the table since the beginning of this planning process.

In Step 1, you considered the importance of the issue and its potential impact on the bottom line of the organization. In Step 2, you analyzed the organization itself, with some consideration going to the level of resources available to address various aspects of public relations and marketing communications. These resources included personnel, equipment, time, and budgeted money.

Throughout the strategic development in Steps 4, 5, and 6, you were advised to be realistic in setting forth on a course of action appropriate to the organization. One measure of propriety is based on the organization's resources. At every turn in a planning process, you must be practical. Consider budget constraints and limitations—no organization is free of these—so your recommendations will be realistic, practical, and doable.

Budget Items

Remember that budgeting is about more than money. It deals with all the needed resources to implement a tactic. Thus budgets for public relations and marketing communications should consider five categories of items to be budgeted: personnel, material, media costs, equipment and facilities, and administrative costs.

PERSONNEL
Personnel items in a budget include the number of people with various skills and the amount of time needed to achieve the results expected of the tactic. This may include both organizational personnel and outside people, such as consultants, agency staff, subcontracted specialists, and freelance workers. Personnel costs may be associated with research, analysis, planning, writing, editing, design, photography, events management, and the like.

Personnel costs can be expressed either in terms of time (hours or days) needed to complete the task or in labor dollars. In some billing situations, public relations agencies present personnel items in the form of billable hours. Some agencies have a general and average hourly rate. Others make distinctions among strategic planning, research, account management, and administrative and support activities.

Remember to account for the time of salaried public relations staff within an organization. Increasingly, many corporations and nonprofit organizations have structured their public relations department to serve as in-house agencies. These often charge back the cost of their public relations activities on behalf of other departments, at least on paper. This chargeback allows the organization to more accurately see the role of public relations in its various programs and projects.

Phase Three

STEP
8

MATERIAL

Material items in a budget include the "things" associated with the tactics: paper for brochures, banners for an open house, media kits for a news conference, software for an online newsroom, uniforms for the company-sponsored softball team, and so on. Additionally, material items may be associated with research activities, such as the cost of questionnaires or materials for focus groups. This category also includes the time associated with activities such as developing websites and overseeing social networking sites.

Each of these tasks and items carries a price tag, and it is very important to know exactly the cost of each recommended tactic. If you simply guess or work from old figures, you may find that you cannot implement the tactic for the amount that has been budgeted. By budgeting for each item separately, you are able to make adjustments if, for example, you need to decrease the overall budget or channel more money toward a particular tactic.

Phase Three

STEP
8

FEE STRUCTURES FOR PUBLIC RELATIONS AGENCIES

Several different approaches to billing are common with public relations consultants and agencies, as well as with the growing number of public relations departments that are being reorganized using the in-house agency model.

Hourly or **per diem rates plus expenses** are based on the actual amount of time spent on a project, plus the amount of money spent on materials, production costs, and media purchases. Some agencies lower the hourly rate as the actual number of hours increases. Examples of hourly rates are $50 an hour for copyediting, $200 an hour for research analysis, or $250 an hour for account supervision. Some agencies charge a flat per diem (daily) rate.

Project fees or **fixed fees** are flat charges for various activities, such as $500 for a news release or $1,500 for preparing a brochure for printing.

Retainer fees are fixed monthly base charges paid in advance for a predetermined level of agency availability, often between $5,000 and $20,000 depending on the amount of work expected. The benefit to the agency is that a minimum income is guaranteed. The client benefit is that the retaining charge is calculated lower than regular hourly rates and gives the client access to a guaranteed minimum amount of public relations services.

Performance fees are a new and somewhat controversial way of charging a client. Under this system, the agency bills based on its success in achieving stated objectives, such as placement of news releases, generation of telephone calls or web hits, and so on. This is controversial because public relations practitioners deserve to be paid for their work, which cannot always be guaranteed to have the desired effect. For example, a practitioner can research, write, and distribute a news release, but he or she cannot guarantee that the new media will print it. If the client is charged only for releases that actually are published, the agency must be prepared to absorb the cost of work done on behalf of the client that does not generate the hoped-for use. Unconvinced that this is a sketchy practice? Would you expect your doctor to charge you only if and when you actually get better?

MEDIA COST

Money generally is needed for outside communication activities, particularly the purchase of time and space associated with advertising tactics. Budgets often identify commissionable media, which are advertising in newspapers and magazines; commercials on radio and television; or billboards and other such media.

When working with an advertising agency, you may find that a commission or agency fee of about 15 percent has been added as a surcharge to the cost of the final art, production charges for audio and video, and talent or model fees, as well as the cost of buying advertising time or space. Public relations agencies sometimes bill all out-of-pocket expenses (perhaps with the exception of travel expenses) at cost plus 15 percent. In the face of growing competition among agencies, however, commissions increasingly are being replaced with flat fees.

EQUIPMENT AND FACILITIES

This category includes the capital cost of equipment that must be purchased to implement a tactic. Examples of this would include computers, scanners, printers, or software needed to publish a newsletter or support a blog. Also included here are the capital costs of obtaining a needed facility, such as modifying a storage area into an in-house television studio.

Items in this category generally are one-time expenditures. Thus the cost might be calculated separately from the project for which the resources are purchased, under the notion that they may be used for other projects in the future. However, a forward-looking budget process would amortize such expenses over the expected life of the equipment or facility and would be prepared for the time when replacements will be needed.

ADMINISTRATIVE ITEMS

A budget should include the cost of telephone charges, delivery costs, photocopying, and other office activities, as well as associated travel costs. Some organizations assess a surcharge, often 15 percent, to offset the cost of overhead expenses such as rent, maintenance, utilities, taxes, and so on. Items such as software licenses and maintenance contracts also are included in this category.

Approaches to Budgeting

A recurring problem with budgeting is that public relations and marketing communication sometimes are seen not as strategic management but rather as the mere production and distribution of messages. Public relations may be thought to deal with hard-to-measure intangibles such as goodwill or visibility.

Because of this mindset, budgets sometimes are set according to a formula based on last year's budget, or worse, as an arbitrary percentage of the wider administration or marketing program of an organization.

If you have followed the guidelines in *Strategic Planning for Public Relations*, you should find that you can overcome these difficulties. You have learned to conduct public relations and marketing communication as a management activity, and you have learned to work with precise objectives that bring an element of measurement to concepts such as goodwill and support.

Still, the question often comes up: How much should an organization spend on public relations and marketing communications?

People asking this are often looking for a simple, accepted formula. But that doesn't exist. There is no simple answer to that question, because so much depends on variables: the nature of the issue being addressed, the objectives sought, the tactics employed, and so on.

Some nonprofit organizations can operate impressive and successful campaigns for only a few hundred dollars. On the other hand, national political campaigns raise millions for advertising and other promotional activities.

Some motion pictures spend more on promotions than for the production itself. *Titanic* cost about $200 million to produce and at least as much for marketing, a combo that earned $2.2 billion (more than two-thirds of that from international markets). *Star Wars: The Force Awakens* also had $200 million in production costs and probably more for marketing.

Every organization and every issue is different. Each requires careful attention and insightful management. Establishing an appropriate budget can be difficult. Often you will find that a client simply has no notion what the appropriate budget should be. Every organization wants to prevent unnecessary spending, but most also are willing to spend the necessary amount to get the job done.

Let's consider some of the many different ways to approach budgeting: competitive parity, same-as-before, percentage-of-sales, unit-of-sales, all-you-can-afford, cost–benefit analysis, what-if-not-funded, stage-of-life-cycle, zero-based, and objectives-based methods.

COMPETITIVE PARITY

The **competitive parity** approach bases an organization's budget for various activities on the level of similar activity by colleagues or competitors.

University A may base its budget for recruiting new students on the apparent budget of University B, its biggest competitor.

A drawback of this approach is that University A will have to guess what University B is spending, and much of that may not be apparent. Additionally, the two universities may have significantly different situations, such as the amount of informal recruiting being done by alumni, the visibility and reputation of the two institutions, and their financial resources.

SAME-AS-BEFORE BUDGETING

A budget developed on the **same-as-before** approach looks at how much the organization spent on a similar recent project and allows the same budget for this project. But such an approach presumes that two projects are sufficiently similar that one can serve as a benchmark for the other. It also presumes that the first project was successful and deserves to be imitated.

A related approach is **same-as-before-but-more** budgeting, which adds an inflationary increase to a same-as-before budget.

PERCENTAGE-OF-SALES BUDGETING

The **percentage-of-sales** approach to budgeting is drawn from the field of marketing, where some companies base their advertising budget on the previous year's profits. This approach may give a generous marketing budget following a good year but only a meager budget after a lean year—perhaps just the opposite of what is needed to overcome a sales slump.

In the university recruiting scenario above, the budget for public relations might be based on the amount of money obtained through tuition fees. For example, 2 percent of each tuition payment may be earmarked for the recruitment public relations program. However, because much public relations activity is difficult to quantify on a short-term basis, the percentage-of-sales method generally is a weak approach in this field.

UNIT-OF-SALES BUDGETING

Similar to percentage-of-sales budgeting, the **unit-of-sales** approach is based not on dollars but on prior outcomes.

In the university recruiting situation, the budget might be pegged to the number of people who register as full-time students. For example, for every student recruited, the university might earmark $100 for the public relations program. This approach has a similar drawback to the percentage-of-sales approach in that it pegs future budgets on past prosperity rather than current needs.

ALL-YOU-CAN-AFFORD BUDGETING

The **all-you-can-afford** approach to budgeting works better in good times than in bad. It provides for public relations funding when the organization's financial condition is sound, but limits funding during lean times. While this is not a good approach, in reality it is the way too many organizations approach public relations, as an optional luxury that can be dispensed with when money is tight. Actually, the hard times are when even more public relations activity may be needed.

COST–BENEFIT ANALYSIS

A less-arbitrary approach to budgeting is **cost–benefit analysis**. This approach identifies the cost of implementing a tactic, then compares that cost to the estimated value of the expected results. Ideally, the cost will be significantly less than the probable benefit.

For example, the cost of holding an open house for a day-care center for seniors with Alzheimer's disease might be $1,500, while the benefit of this tactic, if the projected registration goal is met, might be $10,000 from new donors to the program. Based on this formula, the open house would be considered a tactic worthy of being implemented.

WHAT-IF-NOT-FUNDED ANALYSIS

The consequence of inaction and its effect on its organization's mission is the concept underlying **what-if-not-funded analysis** (WINF). This approach to budgeting forces a planner to consider expected outcomes. It is tied to objectives that previously have been accepted by the organization.

For example, the what-if-not-funded scenario for the tactic of producing a video would have you indicate the expenses necessary to achieve the objective without the video. This might mean more workshops involving additional time from the CEO, or perhaps more brochures with fewer benefits than with the video. Implicitly or explicitly, the recommended tactic is compared with the alternatives. Some organizations pair this WINF scenario with a cost–benefit analysis to keep the advantages in view while comparing alternatives.

STAGE-OF-LIFE-CYCLE ANALYSIS

The **stage-of-life-cycle** approach to budgeting looks closely at the phase of development of the issue, knowing that start-up programs generally require more financial resources than maintenance programs.

Phase Three

STEP
8

Consider, for example, the needs of a university communication department in transition. Let's say the university is well known for its "academic" approach to communication, with a focus on research, theory, and critical analysis. Let's further presume that the university decides to extend itself into more applied communication areas such as public relations, advertising, and electronic journalism. Because of the change in emphasis, the financial resources needed to recruit students for the new program will be greater than what is simply needed to maintain applications to the current program focus.

ZERO-BASED BUDGETING

A technique known as **zero-based budgeting** is rooted in current needs rather than past expenditures. It is commonly used with ongoing organizational budgets, such as those associated with annual community relations or investor relations programs. However, the zero-based approach can work with one-time campaigns as well.

In this approach, various tactics are ranked according to their importance. The cumulative cost of each tactic is then calculated. The cut-off line of the predetermined budget indicates in effect when the client has run out of money and therefore must reject the remaining tactics.

This is not an effective method for public relations planning, because it allows a financial formula and a calculator to determine what tactics will be implemented and which ones will be passed over. It can, however, serve as a useful first look at tactical planning, but initial ranking needs to be re-evaluated with a cost–benefit analysis and a what-if-not-funded approach.

OBJECTIVE-BASED BUDGETING

A more enlightened approach is **objective-based budgeting**, a results-oriented approach that sees budgeting as the means to achieve agreed-upon outcomes.

By focusing on objectives, this approach deals with already identified needs and goals. It aligns with decisions already made by the organization or client earlier in the planning process, especially in Step 4.

The underlying premise of objective-based budgeting is that the organization will provide the resources necessary to achieve its objectives, which already have been approved by organizational decision makers. The consensus check that concludes Step 4 is perhaps the most important part of this approach to budgeting. It is at that point that agreement is reached on what must be accomplished. The subsequent tactics simply provide ways to achieve what already has been adopted as the objective.

Usually, this means that the organization will assign the needed resources to carry out tactics that are integral to reaching the set objectives. Occasionally, however, it means that the organization will scale back objectives to limit some of the tactics originally recommended.

Either way, objective-based budgeting puts the responsibility on the organization or client to establish objectives that it will support with appropriate tactics.

Even with the objective-based approach to budgeting, financial reality and common sense must rule. The wise strategic planner will develop tactics that are within the reach of the organization. The ability to create effective programs suitable to almost any budget is one of the real advantages of an integrated approach to public relations and marketing communication.

Be aware that this approach is sometimes called **performance-based budgeting** (PBB), though that term can be confusing. PBB does not draw on past performance but rather on the intended future results, which are more easily understood as objectives.

Basic Fixed Budget

In Step 8, you are developing the actual budget for your public relations program. The best way to do this is to list each of the tactics you recommended in Step 7, then indicate the various costs associated with each tactic.

For example, if you have recommended the creation of a brochure, indicate the various costs associated with this tactic. Include one-time costs such as copywriting, artwork, and design. Incorporate costs based on the number of brochures needed: paper, printing, folding, and mailing. Add in the value of personnel time, with hourly figures based on annual salaries of organizational employees or the hourly fees for outside consultants, agency personnel, or freelance workers.

Then total these various costs to obtain a full cost for the brochure tactic. Exhibit 8.3 shows how this budget item might look as a fixed amount (that is, for a specified number of brochures produced).

By breaking down each of the various costs associated with the tactic, you are able to more precisely predict the total cost associated with the program. Additionally, this breakdown allows you to adjust the total budget more easily. Say, for example, that all of your recommended tactics add up to $12,500, but your overall budget is supposed to be only $11,000. You need to shave $1,500 from your recommendations.

One way would be to find a tactic that costs $1,500 and eliminate it, but this probably would leave a hole in your plan. After all, the tactic was recommended to achieve a particular objective.

However, by knowing the cost of each aspect of every tactic, you can make minor revisions in several areas. Perhaps you could use spot color rather than four-color printing and save a few hundred dollars on the brochure, or perhaps mail fewer brochures and find an alternative distribution method that would cost less. By modifying enough tactics without eliminating any of them, you can keep your original plan intact and still meet the budget.

How closely should you stick with the overall budget that your boss or client originally indicated? That probably depends on the boss or client, and how you read the budget projection. If you think the budget was meant merely as a guideline, then going a bit over probably won't hurt. If you know the boss to be the type of manager who routinely cuts a percentage of every budget request, then you may be tempted to pad your budget request a bit, knowing that it will be cut back to the point where you really want it to be. But if you sense that the budget figure was firm, you should make sure your recommendations fall within the projected budget.

Variable Budget

When a budget doesn't seem to stretch quite far enough for your ideas, one solution is to offer the client a range of costs—low-end and high-end tactics, perhaps with a preferred or optimal level of funding.

Take another look at the basic budget for the brochure. The $3,100 total cost is based on two-color printing known as spot color (black ink and one accent color). But with a variable budget, you can present options to your client.

The final cost actually could range from a low of $2,475 by printing in one color only and not using the mail for distribution, to a high of $3,700 for four-color printing and mail distribution. Exhibit 8.4 presents such a variable budget.

EXHIBIT 8.3 Sample Fixed Budget for Brochure

$325	**Administrative Cost** Public relations director (in-house). (7 hours @ $33.65/hour, based on annual salary of $70,000)
$1,500	**Creative Development** $800 copywriting (8 hours @ $100/hour) $500 artwork (4 hours @ $150/hour) $200 design (4 hours @ $50/hour)
$775	**Production** @2,500 copies $125 paper $600 printing (two-color @ $0.24) $50 folding
$500	**Distribution** $500 mail distribution
$3,100	**TOTAL**

Still another way to stretch a budget is to provide a basic set of recommendations that fits within the projected budget, then offer an add-on list of optional tactics that the client may wish to fund because of the added expected benefit.

Budgets also have a way of inching upward. Perhaps a supplier charges a bit more than when you first called for an estimate. Or some of your expense items were based on a similar project six months ago, but those items now have increased in price. Most organizations are aware that budget creep can occur, and agencies or consultants often build into their contracts provisions for such changes. A common technique is to assure the client that, for any increase of more than 10 percent, the cost overrun will be submitted for the client's prior approval.

Once the budget has been approved, it should be used as a tool to help manage the implementation of the project. The budget can offer guidance in scheduling tasks, monitoring their progress, and assessing their results.

The budget should be treated as part of a living document. The strategic plan is not set in stone once it is approved. Rather, it must have the flexibility to respond to a changing environment and differing organizational needs.

Full-Cost Budgeting

In presenting the budget to your boss or client, include the full cost of all the tactics in the program, a **full-cost budget**. Some tactics may not have a specific price tag, but if they are

EXHIBIT 8.4 Sample Variable Budget for Brochure

$325	**Administrative Cost**
	Public relations director (in-house, 7 hours @ $33.65/hour, based on annual salary of $70,000)
$1,500	**Creative Development**
	$800 copywriting (8 hours @ $100/hour)
	$500 artwork (4 hours @ $150/hour)
	$200 design (4 hours @ $50/hour)
$550–$1,375	**Production** @2,500 copies
	$125 paper
	$275–$1,200 printing (one-color @ $0.15; two-color @ $0.24, four-color @ $0.48)
	$50 folding
$100–$500	**Distribution**
	$100 non-mail/bulk-mail distribution
	$0–$500 mail distribution

$2,475–$3,700 **TOTAL**

---

of value to the organization they should be noted, along with equivalent costs if the tactics were to be purchased.

Note the value of donated or contributed services. In particular, include the value of volunteer time as you calculate the full cost of the budget items. For example, a human service agency might get help from a college public relations class in developing a brochure for new clients. The students may not charge for their services, but the project budget should include a dollar estimate of what those services would cost if the agency had to hire professionals such as a freelance copywriter or a design firm.

Communication plans usually don't include many income items, but don't overlook implicit revenues. Corporate sponsorship may have a specific dollar value, which should be presented in the budget as an offset to expenses. It also is appropriate to include projected revenues if you have built a fundraising tactic into your program recommendations.

Likewise, it may be appropriate to include both the actual expense and real value of that expense item. For example, the full value of discounted consulting fees or free airtime for a public service advertisement can be listed to show the difference between the total value and the actual cost to the organization.

Phase Three

STEP
8

A word of caution: Don't be tempted to set a dollar value on publicity by calculating how much the same space would cost for advertising. This is discussed in more detail in Step 9; for now, let's just agree that publicity should not be confused with advertising.

By including all of this information, you are presenting a full view of the real value of the campaign, even though the organization's actual cost may be considerably less.

Exhibit 8.5 presents an example of a hypothetical budget for a brochure project for a nonprofit organization, a community dance troupe. Let's say that a friend of the artistic director for the troupe is a professional photographer whose daughter dances with the troupe. He is volunteering to take photos for the brochure and an accompanying website. Let's also say that a woman with a decade of public relations experience is relocating to this community and wants to network and become known as she sets up a freelance business. She has done similar work with artistic groups in other cities and is offering to cut her copywriting fees by 50 percent as she introduces herself to this community. Exhibit 8.5 shows how the budget for this project might look.

EXHIBIT 8.5 Sample Full-Cost Budget

Actual Cost	Total Value	
$0	$300	**Administrative cost** $0 cost; $300 value. Public relations director (in-house, 9 hours @ $33.65/hour, based on annual salary of $70,000)
$680	$1,760	**Creative Development** $0 cost; $600 value. Photography donated, based on 4 hours @ $150/hour. $480 cost; $960 value. Copywriting discounted, based on 8 hours @ $100/hour. $200 design (4 hours @ $50/hour)
$775	$775	**Production** @2,500 copies $125 paper $600 printing (two-color @ $0.24 per copy) $50 folding
$500	$500	**Distribution** $500 mail distribution
$1,955	$3,335	**TOTAL**

Optimal Success

It sometimes is important to ask the question: How much success is necessary? Or put another way: What level of achievement is needed simply to cover the cost of the program?

Calculate the **break-even point** (*BEP*) in three steps:

1. Identify the total project cost (*c*).
2. Determine the outcome value (*v*), the dollar value for each unit of the desired outcome, especially those associated with the action objectives.
3. Divide the total project cost by the value of the desired outcome.

Thus the formula is *BEP* = *c/v* (cost divided by value).

Let's say a private college will spend $160,000 of its recruiting budget this year to develop brochures and booklets, produce and distribute an informational video, and place paid radio commercials and billboards. Let's add $100,000 in salaries associated with this particular project. Add another $20,000 for expenses such as postage, travel, and phone calls. That's $280,000 for *c*, the total project cost.

Now let's presume that tuition at this private college is $35,000. Apply the formula: cost $280,000 (*c*) divided by outcome value $35,000 (*v*) equals 8 (*BEP*). That's the break-even point. Eight additional students must be recruited through these brochures, videos, and commercials before the communication program has paid for itself. (Note that this is an oversimplified example that doesn't take into account that the real cost of education is borne not only by tuition but also by donations, endowments, and sometimes state aid.)

Another useful budgetary calculation is the **per-capita cost**, the cost associated with the number of people needed to cover the cost. Calculate the per-capita cost (*PCC*) by dividing the total project cost (*c*) by the number of people (*p*) who perform the desired outcome. The formula is *PCC* = *v/p*.

Returning to the college scenario, divide the cost by the number of new recruits (let's say that's 1,800). Apply the formula: $280,000 divided by 1,800, which equals $156. This is how much the college is spending to recruit each new student through these new tactics of the brochures, videos, and commercials. In percentage terms, this is about 0.0056% of tuition income, or about half a penny for every dollar of the $35,000 tuition.

Break-even points and per-capita costs also can be calculated for other public relations objectives, as long as the objectives themselves have been stated in precise and measurable terms.

What's Next?

By completing this step, you have brought your campaign to the point of implementation. Practically, you can say you have completed your strategic planning.

But there is one more element, which is the evaluation that will take place after the plan has been implemented. Even though you won't do the evaluation until later, you plan for it now. That's the focus of Step 9.

Phase Three

PLANNING EXAMPLE 8B **Implementing the Strategic Plan**

The following schedule shows one of several events within the four initiatives of the plan to publicize Upstate College's expanding program. It shows the event and its component tactics, along with a cost, an assigned manager, and a start date for each tactic (as the number of weeks prior to the event).

Event: Rededication Ceremony

Tactic 1: Print and mail 1,000 invitations
Cost: $800   Manager: Publications Office   Begin Work: 12 weeks prior

Tactic 2: Print 500 programs
Cost: $0   Manager: Publications Office   Begin Work: 10 weeks prior

Tactic 3: Keynote speaker honorarium
Cost: $1,000   Manager: President's Office   Begin Work: 12 weeks prior

Tactic 4: Musicians
Cost: $800   Manager: Music Dept. Chair   Begin Work: 6 weeks prior

Tactic 5: Academic processional/ritual
Cost: $200   Manager: Provost   Begin Work: 6 weeks prior

Tactic 6: Video about UC expansion
Cost: $4,000   Manager: Video Task Force   Begin work: 20 weeks prior

Tactic 7: Viewing equipment
Cost $300   Manager: Facilities Office   Begin work: 4 weeks prior

Tactic 8: Plaque engraving
Cost: $400   Manager: Facilities Office   Begin work: 4 weeks prior

---

STEP 8

The following schedule shows one of the several events outlined for the employee publics of the strategic communication plan focusing on consumer confidence.

Tactic: Newsletter articles in employee publication about safety, quality, and customer satisfaction.

Implementation Schedule: With publication slated for the first Wednesday of each month, relevant articles will be written for each publication date, according to the following schedule.

Safety Issues
- *January*: Industry-wide safety standards and government safety regulations
- *April*: Product safety record of Tiny Tykes Toys for the last 15 years

- *July*: External—marketing consequences of product safety
- *October*: Internal—employee consequences of product safety

Quality Issues
- *February*: Industry-wide quality issues in the toy industry
- *May*: Quality comparison between Tiny Tykes Toys and major competitors
- *August*: Quality-control and quality-goal programs at Tiny Tykes Toys
- *November*: Involvement of employees in quality issues at Tiny Tykes Toys

Customer Satisfaction Issues
- *March*: Industry-wide importance of customer satisfaction to company's bottom line
- *June*: Importance of customer satisfaction to Tiny Tykes Toys' reputation
- *September*: Empowering employees to achieve customer satisfaction
- *December*: Employee training/motivation for customer satisfaction

Staffing: The communication director in the public relations office will notify appropriate interviewees two months prior to publication date. A communication specialist will arrange interviews three to four weeks prior to publication and will give the completed article to the communication director two weeks prior to publication date.

Budget: There is no significant operating cost to research or write articles. Staff time is already provided, but approximately five hours will be allocated for each article for preparation, research, interviewing, and writing.

 Checklist 8B **Implementing the Strategic Plan**

Basic Questions

1. What is the schedule for this project?
2. What is the budget for this project?
3. Who is responsible for this project?

Expanded Questions

A. SCHEDULING

1. What is the message repetition?
2. What is the message frequency?
3. What is the scheduling pattern (optional): continuous, flighting, pulsing, or massing?
4. What is the timeline for each tactic?
5. Who is the assigned manager for each tactic?

B. BUDGET

1. Identify the following budget line items:
   - Personnel
   - Materials
   - Media costs
   - Equipment and facilities
   - Miscellaneous expenses
2. What is the full-cost budget?
3. What administrative cost items are associated with this tactic?
4. What is the break-even point?
5. What is the per-capita cost?

CONSENSUS CHECK

Does agreement exist within your organization and your planning team about the selection and analysis of these key publics?

☐ Yes. Proceed to Step 9, Evaluating the Strategic Plan.

☐ No. Consider the value and/or possibility of achieving consensus before proceeding.

Phase Three

STEP
8

PHASE FOUR

EVALUATIVE RESEARCH

The strategic planning that began with research in Phase One comes full circle in this final phase of the process. Here you turn once again to research techniques, preparing to evaluate the effectiveness of your tactics in achieving your objectives.

Perform well in this phase and you may be able to soar above the competition, because public relations practitioners too often are weak in evaluative research. And they are the first to concede this fault. Professional workshops and conference presentations in evaluation and measurement always seem to draw large audiences.

Professionals and educators in the disciplines associated with strategic communication talk a lot about research. But interest doesn't guarantee implementation.

PRSA expects its Silver Anvil entries to specify how campaigns are evaluated. Implementation of program evaluation is becoming more common, but it is far from universal in practice. Even marketing executives—who are generally more comfortable with quantifiable evaluation criteria than are public relations executives—often put more attention on "doing marketing" than on proving that it works.

Surveys of public relations practitioners in all kinds of settings—agencies, corporations, and nonprofit organizations—indicate that, while they may talk about doing evaluative research, often their actions don't quite match their words.

Most practitioners, certainly most upper-level public relations managers and supervisors, say they recognize the importance of evaluative research. Yet in the same surveys and interviews, they admit that there are many times when they fail to act on that recognition, when they choose—for whatever reason—not to incorporate evaluation into the campaign design.

Much talk. Why not more action? Here are a half-dozen reasons (excuses, really) for the dearth of research in public relations programming.

1. It sometimes is difficult to know just what to evaluate and how to do so. Research is a specialty many practitioners have not mastered, perhaps not even studied.
2. Public relations measures may not be as precise as those used in areas such as finance, operations, and safety.

3. Another difficulty in measuring public relations is that everything is in motion, clouding the possibility of an accurate count. It's like going into a tropical-fish store and trying to count the number of neons in a tank.

4. Similarly, public relations campaigns and projects do not exist in a vacuum. Other forces are working on key publics at the same time an organization is mounting its public relations activities. It is difficult to isolate the influence of public relations.

5. Some public relations measures are negatives—to what extent something bad did *not* happen, or how many negative opinions were minimized.

6. Research takes time, money, and creative energy, three things public relations practitioners guard as precious commodities to be used in only the most important situations.

After all the explanations and excuses, it comes down to this: Evaluation is infrequent because public relations practitioners—or their bosses or clients—simply don't recognize its value and aren't willing to pay for it.

As you will discover in this final section of *Strategic Planning for Public Relations*, good evaluative research does not have to be costly or time-consuming. Nor is it beyond the means of an adequately prepared practitioner.

Properly built into the overall strategic plan, evaluative research can increase the effectiveness of public relations and marketing communication. Additionally, it can save time and money in future endeavors. These advantages should appeal to bosses and clients everywhere.

Finally, proper evaluation can enhance the prestige and role of public relations within an organization. That's an even bigger advantage—one that every practitioner surely can recognize.

It isn't the intention of this textbook to indict public relations professionals for not putting enough emphasis on evaluation. Rather, the purpose of this admittedly negative introduction to the final step is to lay the groundwork for students who wish to prepare themselves to be a step above their future competitors in the job market.

Employers value colleagues who know the importance of evaluation and who have the skills to do it cost-effectively. Employers hire such people entering the job market. Thus the logic here is that students who want to get hired should take advantage of this opportunity to learn about an aspect of public relations planning that employers both recognize as important and admit that they need help with.

Evaluating
the Strategic Plan

Program evaluation is the systematic measurement of the outcomes of a project, program, or campaign based on the extent to which stated objectives are achieved. As part of the strategic planning process, establishing appropriate and practical evaluation methods wraps up all the previous plans, ideas, and recommendations.

In this section, we will look at various aspects of evaluative research: what, when, and—most important—how to evaluate.

What to Evaluate

You've heard the phrase "starting off on the right foot." In precision marching, the most important step is the first one. This step—paradoxically always the left foot—sets up the pattern for the rest of the cadence.

The same is true in putting together an effective research program. Starting on the correct foot means setting out to answer the appropriate questions.

Katie Delahaye Paine, an authority on evaluation research, notes that "the future of public relations lies in the development of relationships, and the future of measurement lies in the accurate analysis of those relationships" (2011, p. 217).

The key to creating any program evaluation is to establish appropriate criteria for judging what is effective. This research plan considers several issues: the criteria that should be used to gauge success, timing of the evaluation, and specific ways to measure each of the levels of objectives (awareness, acceptance, and action). The plan may prescribe the various evaluation tools, and it also should indicate how the evaluation would be used.

Note that this planning happens before any tactics are implemented. Although the design of evaluative research focuses on the results of the program, the process is developed as part of the initial planning. It points to how evaluation will be conducted at the appropriate times.

Design Questions

As you design an effective program for evaluation research, ask yourself the following questions:

- On what criteria should the program be judged?
- What information is needed to make the assessment?
- What standards of accuracy and reliability are needed for this assessment?

Next, focus some attention on the source of the information needed.

- Who has this information?
- How can this information be obtained from them?

Finally, consider how the information will be used.

- Who will receive the final evaluation and what will be done with the information?
- How willing and able are decision makers to receive less-than-fully-positive evaluations?
- Besides decision makers, who else would have an interest in the evaluation?

Remember that research design is always a trade-off between the perfect and the practical. Strategic planners must make choices about the importance of the program, the accuracy and reliability of the information to be received, and the needed resources (time, personnel, financial, and so on).

Evaluation Criteria

Before you develop specific evaluation techniques, consider first the criteria on which you will judge something to be effective. These criteria are called **metrics**, the standards of measurement to assess the outcome of a program or project. Each metric needs to be appropriate for the objective it is measuring. In essence, a metric is the yardstick against which an objective is measured.

What metrics should you use? The appropriate standards vary with the objectives and the tactics, but here are a few general guidelines. Evaluation criteria should be (1) useful to the organization by being clearly linked with the established objectives; (2) realistic, feasible, and appropriate as to cost, time, and other resources; (3) ethical and socially responsible; (4) credible because supported by accurate data; and (5) presented in a timely manner.

Consider various criteria that might be evaluated in a public relations campaign. The best structure for this is to draw on the earlier-stated objectives. Here are some categories of appropriate evaluation metrics for each of the three types of objectives.

- *To evaluate awareness objectives*

    - Metric: Media coverage and calculation of media impressions
    - Metric: Post-campaign awareness survey

MEASURING ENGAGEMENT IN SOCIAL MEDIA

As public relations practitioners increasingly use social media as part of their media mix, the question eventually turns to matters of methodology and metrics: How can we evaluate the impact of social media? It isn't easy, but it is necessary to measure its effectiveness.

At the measurement blog at her website (painepublishing.com), Katie Delahaye Paine suggests that *engagement* is a synonym for *relationship*. That's something public relations practitioners are continually trying to nurture, though less often attempting to measure. How do you measure engagement? Track reader actions such as comments and shares.

Robert Scoble, blogging expert and self-identified tech evangelist, suggests asking these questions: To what extent does the reader become engaged in the piece? To what extent is dialogue taking place among readers who add comments? How often do you like, comment, and share other people's items?

Ian Lurie of Portent, an Internet marketing agency, cautions not to overvalue the number of followers. On his Conversation Marketing blog and in media interviews, he says it's more important to consider their degree of involvement with an organization's social media.

Meanwhile, Eric Peterson of Web Analytics Demystified (2007) defines engagement in terms of the degree and depth of visitor interaction with the site viewed against a defined set of goals for the social medium.

Here are several no-cost or low-cost steps that an organization can take to measure the effectiveness of its website and other social media.

- Use Google Analytics, WebTrends, or another visitor-tracking device.
- Track the number of followers on Twitter, Facebook friends, views on YouTube, and other measures of exposure and awareness objectives. Use metrics dealing with ease of navigating the site, breadth of content, tracking stats on visitors, and success in conveying key messages.
- Use these same venues to measure engagement and acceptance objectives, such as repeat visits, use of your Twitter hashtag, Facebook likes and shares, and the number and tone of comments on your various sites.
- Measure action objectives by capturing visitor names for response or follow-up by having visitors register for full access to the site, posting a poll or survey, connecting a blog and collecting names and email contact of those who leave comments.
- Use online tools that measure social media influence, such as Topsy, Kred, and Twtrland.
- Write a report, e-book, or other information source, make it available for free upon request, and then track the action.

- *To evaluate acceptance objectives*

  – Metric: Tabulation of requests for information
  – Metric: Post-campaign attitude/opinion survey
  – Metric: Tabulation of letters, emails, and phone calls expressing interest or support
  – Metric: Post-event audience evaluation

- *To evaluate action objectives*
  - Metric: Measures of results (ticket sales, attendance, memberships, donations, and so on)
  - Metric: Measures of improvement
  - Metric: Organizational or environmental change

Additionally, be prepared to identify and evaluate unplanned results of a campaign. Sometimes a campaign generates reaction beyond what was anticipated. This reaction may be positive or negative in the eyes of the organization, but it is worth considering unplanned results and unintended consequences, if for no other reason than they might be built into subsequent similar campaigns.

Notice that measures of message production and exposure are not included as significant. For example, what matters is not so much the number of hits but rather the number and content of comments by visitors to the site and the number of retrievable names so the organization can engage the visitor in two-way communication. With appropriate evaluation metrics in mind, the public relations strategist can turn to the task of developing evaluation measures that can rate the website on those criteria.

Notice, too, that all of the criteria should be developed before any implementation of the website, because the particular criteria you identify as necessary will determine some of what you do in putting the website together.

It is interesting to note that public relations practitioners generally value positive media stories more highly than CEOs value such publicity. It's not hard to understand this disparity. Public relations people operate in a world in which awareness generated through media is an intrinsic value. CEOs live in a show-me world where the value of results needs to be documented.

But the question is worth asking: Just what should we be measuring? Or more pointedly: Why should we continue to focus on awareness when our bosses and clients want to see how we influenced action? These are important questions that deserve consideration.

Ken Gofton (1999) has noted the difference between advertising and public relations measurement. He observes that advertising often focuses evaluative research on audience exposure. Public relations evaluation, on the other hand, goes beyond exposure metrics toward techniques such as profiling audiences, tracking attitude change, and assessing impact in terms of behavioral outcomes.

Walter Lindenmann, the acknowledged guru of public relations research, has observed that CEOs and organizational executives are increasingly more demanding of public relations practitioners. They expect practitioners to justify their existence, be accountable for their programs, and document their contributions to the bottom line.

A study of evaluation research for the Institute for Public Relations (Lindenmann, 2006) suggests that any credible evaluation program requires four major components: setting measurable goals and objectives, measuring outputs, measuring outtakes and outcomes, and measuring institutional outcomes.

When to Evaluate

There are three stages in the process of program evaluation related to timing: implementation reports, progress reports, and final evaluation. Each is different; each is important.

TWELVE TIPS FOR EVALUATIVE RESEARCH

Here are a dozen suggestions for an effective evaluative research program. Most of these tips are based on common-sense principles that you probably already know. But reminders are meant to be remembered, so review these tips as you prepare your evaluation program.

1. *Don't wait for the program's completion before you evaluate.* Evaluation begins with the planning process, before you actually *do* anything. Effective planning means you determine in advance what you will evaluate and how you will measure.
2. *Guesses aren't good enough.* Evaluation must rely on facts, not estimates. Hunches and gut feelings can point the way, but hard facts are needed to accurately assess impact.
3. *Friends may be telling you what they think you want to hear.* Get beyond the limitations of information volunteered by people who already look kindly on your organization. Be cautious of relying too heavily on information solicited from friends and other supporters in situations that don't encourage candor.
4. *Employees have a stake in the program's success.* Realize that they may be seeing what they want to see, for the programs they evaluate affect their own job security and economic future, as well as day-to-day social relationships on the job.
5. *Samples must reflect the population.* Formal evaluative research draws on a sample that represents the publics addressed in the public relations activity. This kind of research is more likely to generate information that is accurate.
6. *Hard work and cost aren't measures of effectiveness.* Be careful not to equate activity with achievement. Your campaign may have claimed many resources in time, energy, and budgets, but these are not the measure of program effectiveness.
7. *Creativity is not a gauge of effectiveness.* "Everybody thinks it's a neat idea" may indicate innovation, and a professional award may attest to your ingenuity. But neither is the mark of a successful program.
8. *Dissemination doesn't equal communication.* A mainstay principle of public relations is that distribution of a message does not guarantee that real communication is achieved. Every piece of unopened junk mail, every commercial zapped or TiVo'd, and every halftime show missed by spectators heading for the rest room are examples of failed communication.
9. *Knowledge doesn't always lead to acceptance.* Well-informed publics are supportive ones, says the common wisdom. Not necessarily. Knowledge is important on the road to support, but this road has off-ramps as well. Sometimes the more people know about an organization or its plans and policies, the less supportive they may be.
10. *Behavior is the ultimate metric.* Awareness and acceptance objectives are important, and many public relations activities seek to increase knowledge, generate favorable attitudes, or foster supportive opinions. But knowledge that doesn't lead to action is pretty weak, and attitudes or opinions that don't have an outcome in behavior are like books sitting unread on the shelf. Missed opportunities. Unrealized potential.
11. *Evaluation doesn't have to be expensive or time-consuming.* Like other aspects of strategic planning, evaluation research is linked to the organization's resources. Proper evaluation requires insight and creative thinking, not necessarily a lot of time or money.
12. *Evaluative research enables action.* It allows organizations to modify programs, analyze and justify the current program, or make decisions about similar future programs.

Phase Four

STEP
9

IMPLEMENTATION REPORT

The first potential point for evaluation is in tracking the implementation of each tactic, making sure that it is proceeding according to plan. This **implementation report** documents how the program tactics were carried out. In it, include a schedule of progress to date toward implementing each tactic, as well as any work remaining. Identify any gaps, defects, or potential delays that could hurt the plan. Note any difficulties encountered and how they were (or might be) resolved. Discuss the efficiency with which the tactics were set into motion.

Additionally, note the name of the person or group responsible for each tactic, as well as other personnel resources such as staff, freelancers, consultants, and so on. It might also be useful to include budgetary information, such as how much money has been spent or committed thus far.

PROGRESS REPORT

It is important to monitor progress at various key points as the tactics are being implemented. **Progress reports** are preliminary evaluations on which planners can make strategic modifications as they further implement the program. Such midcourse corrections can keep the project functioning at peak efficiency. In this way, the plan is used as a written guideline rather than a rigid rulebook.

Consider this analogy of an online travel app for a cross-country road trip. This mapping program receives hourly weather updates and daily progress reports on highway construction projects. It monitors traffic jams around congested urban areas and newspaper reports of tourism-related events.

Before you leave on the road trip, you map out a tentative plan, indicating your goal (travelling cross country) and your objectives (stopping at various points of interest along the way to the destination). A rigid use of your plan would be to follow the map with no deviation—after all, you've planned this trip for a long time and you shouldn't be distracted by unscheduled changes.

However, a more effective way to use the app would allow its mapping program to alert you to an interesting community festival only a few miles off the scheduled route or travel delays resulting from snow buildup on a mountain pass.

The mapping program demonstrates the value of feedback: You can use information gathered during the course of the project to update strategy, modify objectives, and adjust tactics.

This type of in-process evaluation is important for both public relations and marketing communication programs. After a pilot project and following each significant phase within a program, evaluate whether the program is unfolding as it was planned to do. Ask questions: Are the messages being disseminated as expected? Are they being understood? Are people responding as expected? If the answers turn out to be "no," there is still time to make adjustments before the rest of the program is implemented.

This kind of evaluation allows a public relations plan to be a living document that enhances the atmosphere of open communication. It allows the planning organization to be impacted by its environment and by its publics.

FINAL REPORT

The third type of evaluation report reviews the whole of the program. This **final report**, sometimes called a **summative report**, measures impact and outcome for the various tactics.

The final evaluation gauges how well the tactics achieved what they set out to achieve—namely, the various objectives.

Approaches to Research Design

The question of when to evaluate leads to a related aspect of **research design**: how to structure the evaluation in relation to the measurement standards. There are several possibilities, the most common being after-only studies and various approaches to before-and-after models.

AFTER-ONLY STUDY

The simplest research design is the **after-only study**, which is common in public relations precisely because of its simplicity. Implement a tactic, measure its impact, and presume that the tactic caused the impact. This approach can be appropriate for action objectives that measure audience response, such as attendance, contributions, purchases, and other easily measured reactions. For example, a political candidate running for office may need no preliminary baseline. She simply would be interested in the numbers of votes received in the election.

However, the after-only approach is not appropriate for every situation. Its weakness is its very simplicity, because this design presumes a cause-and-effect relationship that may not be accurate or complete. The after-only approach does not prove that the tactic caused the observed level of awareness or acceptance, only that the result occurred after the tactic. Perhaps the levels were there all along but simply not noticed.

BEFORE-AND-AFTER STUDY

Another format for evaluation research is the **before-and-after study**, also called a **pretest/post–test study**. This model involves an observation before any public relations programming is implemented. The initial observation provides a benchmark or baseline for comparing studies that will be conducted later.

For example, if the candidate noted above wanted to gauge the effectiveness of a new campaign message, she would need to measure her support before the message was presented and measure it again following the presentation. The difference would indicate the change—positive or negative—created by the new campaign message. In another example, a public transit system might compare ridership figures before and after a promotional campaign. Note that a before-and-after study is integrated into both the formative research and evaluative research phases of the planning process.

The simplest before-and-after study involves three stages: (1) observe and measure a public, (2) expose the public to a public relations tactic, and (3) measure the public again. Any change in the public's awareness, acceptance or action can likely be attributed to the tactic.

Public relations activities generally don't take place in a vacuum or in a pure environment. Be aware of extraneous factors. Not every change in your key public may appropriately be linked, cause-and-effect fashion, to your programming. One of the challenges for evaluative research is to sort out the effective public relations tactics from unrelated outside forces.

CONTROLLED BEFORE-AND-AFTER STUDY

A more sophisticated type of evaluative research takes into account those unrelated outside forces. Such a **controlled before-and-after study** involves two sample groups drawn from

Phase Four

the same key public. One sample is the group to receive the message; the other is a control group that does not receive the message.

This process has four elements: (1) observe and measure each group, (2) expose one group to a tactic, but do not expose the control group, (3) measure each group again, and (4) compare the results of each group.

The control group is likely to have remained unchanged, while any change noted in the exposed group presumably can be linked to exposure to the public relations tactic—the key difference between the two groups. For example, the transit system noted above might also compare before-and-after ridership figures with those of a transit system in a similar city in another state (the control group), where riders were not exposed to the promotional campaign.

Factors in Evaluation Design

Research design is always a trade-off. Strategic planners must make choices that consider the importance of the program, the accuracy and reliability of the information to be received, and the needed resources (time, personnel, financial, and the like). They also should look at the whole picture, focusing not on each tactic in isolation but on how the various tactics together have achieved their objectives.

Also be aware of extraneous factors that can mask your evaluation efforts. Not every change in a public's awareness, acceptance, or action may be caused by your public relations programming. Try to account for other activities and influences that the publics have been exposed to.

Let's return to the example of the transit system. If, a few days after the ridership campaign begins, an international political crisis sends oil prices up 30 percent, you probably would notice a lot more riders on the trains and buses. But you shouldn't attribute this to your public relations campaign. It's more likely that motorists are reacting to the higher cost of gasoline at the pumps, and your research report must note this.

A benefit of most evaluative research is that it is a form of **unobtrusive research**—the subjects in the study do not know they are being observed, at least not until after the fact, when their awareness of being observed can't affect what they have already done.

An exception to this is the before-and-after study. When conducting a before-and-after study, be aware of the **Hawthorne effect**, also called the **placebo effect**.

In the 1930s, researchers at Hawthorne Works, an electric power company near Chicago, were trying to find out how the intensity of lighting affected factory workers. The researchers increased the lighting, and productivity increased, then slowly settled back to the earlier level. Then they decreased the lighting and productivity increased again. At first, the researchers believed the changes were the result of teamwork among the employees. Similar studies manipulated other aspects of the work environment: pay incentives, shorter hours, longer hours, more breaks, fewer breaks. In each case, productivity increased for a short time.

In 1955, Henry Landsberger reanalyzed the older studies. He concluded that the boost in productivity was not caused by the amount of lighting but simply because the subjects knew they were being observed and knew that the company was concerned about worker productivity. Landsberger coined the term "Hawthorne effect," which since has been broadened to explain any impact, usually short-term, through which employees or volunteers are made to feel important or are aware that they are being observed.

CYBERNETICS AND PUBLIC RELATIONS

Norbert Wiener's **cybernetic model of communication** (1954) was introduced in Step 6, Developing the Message Strategy.

Cybernetics deals with the feedback mechanisms of goal-seeking systems, in which goals are established, action and **output** are monitored, and feedback mechanisms implement corrective action to keep the system on the target of its goal. Furnace thermostats, heat-seeking missiles, and cruise-control devices on cars are examples of cybernetics.

In public relations and marketing communication, examples of cybernetics include crisis planning and issues management that feature a radar-like early warning system for monitoring the environment in which the organization operates. An example is the developing approach to evaluative research being presented in this book.

Cybernetics in public relations operates most effectively in an open-systems approach. In this approach, public relations functions as the liaison between the organization and its publics, with responsibilities to each and to the mutual benefits of both.

Two-way communication between the organization and the environment keeps the organization moving toward its goal, with continuous adjustment through the feedback provided by the publics.

How to Evaluate

A question was posed at the beginning of Step 9: What information is needed in order to evaluate a program's effectiveness? Answer this question wisely, and you'll have a strong final phase to your strategic planning. Answer blindly, and you could end up measuring the wrong thing. Consider five levels of evaluation: judgmental assessments, communication outputs, awareness, acceptance, and action.

Judgmental Assessment

An evaluation made on hunches and experience is called a **judgmental assessment**. This type of informal feedback, sometimes called **seat-of-the-pants evaluation**, is not uncommon in public relations and marketing communication. It is the kind of research that everybody seems to do sometimes, because it comes naturally.

Judgmental assessment relies on anecdotal and subjective observations such as the following: "The boss liked it," "The client asked us to continue the project," "Everybody said this was a success," "The customers seem happy," and "Hey, we won an award for this project."

This approach is based on personal observation, which is both a strength and a limitation. Some judgmental evaluations, though informal, can be helpful to an organization. For example, assessment by outside experts, perhaps public relations colleagues in another organization, might offer an excellent analysis of the program.

Phase Four

STEP
9

So too with judgmental assessments based on a formal review of an organization's program by a panel of outside experts. An example is the on-site review teams fielded by the Accrediting Council on Education in Journalism and Mass Communications that assess various aspects of a college or university communication program seeking professional accreditation. Another example is an evaluation based on a program that received an award through a competition sponsored by a professional organization, such as the Silver Anvil sponsored by the Public Relations Society of America, the Gold Quill Award of the International Association of Business Communicators, and the ADDY awards given by the American Advertising Federation.

Additionally, senior practitioners often draw on their experience to make informal judgments about program effectiveness.

Such informal research is not without limitations, however. For one thing, informal assessments often are made by program managers, who are never disinterested and seldom impartial. For another, their personal observations are often imprecise and arbitrary, sometimes downright fickle. Granted, the anecdotes on which this feedback is based can provide much insight into the success or failure of a program, but because informal research and gut feelings don't involve representative samples and standard metrics they can't confirm the effectiveness of activities in public relations and marketing communication.

Another problem with judgmental assessment is that it often gives undue emphasis to apparent creativity and to the expenditure of energy and resources. Throughout this entire planning process you have put in a great deal of effort and energy. In doing so, you have articulated a strategy and produced a range of tactics. These, of course, are important, but they are not what you should be measuring. Rather, the evaluation phase should focus on your objectives at each of their three levels: awareness, acceptance, and action. Just like objectives, evaluation research should deal with the impact your program has made on your various publics.

Judgmental assessment also can lull you into taking for granted what you should be analyzing. Consider tax-free shopping weeks. Increasingly, state lawmakers are periodically waiving sales tax to encourage spending and help consumers save money. One popular time is the back-to-school shopping time in late August. It's oh-so-obvious that consumers win; they save money when buying clothing and school supplies. Politicians benefit from the

METHODS OF EVALUATIVE RESEARCH

Like formative research, evaluative research involves techniques that can be either quantitative or qualitative.

Quantitative research methods used frequently for evaluation include surveys, content analyses, cost-effectiveness studies, readership studies, head counts, and feedback tracking, as well as direct observation and monitoring of specific results.

Qualitative research techniques commonly used for evaluation include interviews, focus groups, and case studies.

Don't let the availability of so many different research methods hide the fact that direct observation of outcomes can be the simplest way to evaluate the effectiveness of public relations programs. For more information on research techniques, see Appendix A, Applied Research.

gratitude of their constituents. And merchants like it because buyers flock into their stores. On the surface, tax-free shopping weeks are both popular and successful.

Is popularity a valid standard? Evidence shows that consumers simply shift the timing of their purchases. Some stores that used to discount merchandise 15 or 20 percent no longer have sales because they know the consumers will flock in to save—what? 8.5 percent (the average state-and-local sales tax across the country)?

Meanwhile, states and local governments lose important tax revenues, threatening services or leading to increases in other kinds of taxes and fees to make up the difference. So customer satisfaction, if it is based on whim rather than fact, isn't a useful measure.

The lesson is this: Effective evaluation requires careful analysis. Don't rely only on the obvious—because what obviously seems true sometimes isn't. Let's look at a complementary approach to evaluation, this one based on the results of communication tactics.

Communication Outputs

Measuring communication products and their distribution is the focus of **outputs evaluation**, a method that concentrates on the development and presentation of a message. As an evaluation method it is not particularly effective.

Outputs may be necessary tasks to do, but they really are not effective measurement tools. Yet current researchers report that many practitioners still rely primarily on output measures (Rice and Atkin, 2002; Xavier et al., 2005). Various methods of measuring **communication outputs** include message production, message dissemination, message cost, publicity value, and advertising equivalency. Let's look at each.

MESSAGE PRODUCTION

Several techniques of evaluation research deal simply with whether the message is produced. For example, count the number of news releases written, brochures printed, or pages formatted for a website. Or note the creation of special message vehicles, such as a company float for the Fourth of July parade. Measurement of **message production** quantifies the work output of a public relations office, but not much more.

While it may be useful for a measure of individual job performance, don't be deluded into thinking that it is a measure of program effectiveness.

MESSAGE DISTRIBUTION

Another approach to awareness evaluation focuses not merely on the production of messages but also on **message distribution**. In this category, the evaluator focuses on media contacts and asks how many news releases were mailed, faxed, tweeted, posted on the blog, or uploaded to the website. Measuring message dissemination tells what an organization did to spread the message, but it doesn't measure the message's impact or its effectiveness.

MESSAGE COST

Another type of measurement deals with **message cost**. This approach analyzes how much money an organization spends to present its message. For paid media, such as brochures or advertisements, the organization simply divides the cost of the communication vehicle by the number of times the message has been reproduced. For example, if it costs $150 to produce 2,500 copies of a flier, then each piece costs 6 cents.

Phase Four

When dealing with electronic media, the common standard is **cost per thousand**, identified as **CPM** (from the Latin word *mille,* meaning "thousand"). For example, if a radio station with 75,000 listeners during a particular time period charges $150 for a 30-second commercial, it would cost $2 for each thousand listeners—a mere one-fifth of a penny per listener. Cost per thousand is an effective way to compare costs among various media, even print vehicles. Consider the following.

- A national magazine with a regional edition circulating 17,000 copies charges $9,000 for a full-page color ad; CPM = $529 (nearly 53 cents per local subscriber).
- A city newspaper with a circulation of 338,000 charges $22,000 for a full-page ad; CPM = $65 (about $6\frac{1}{2}$ cents per reader).
- A local radio station with an estimated 10,000 listeners charges $35 for a 30-second commercial; CPM = $3.50.
- A transit system of bus and light rail service in a metropolitan area charges $290 for each transit poster, with 40 needed to saturate coverage in what is called "100 showing" (100 percent of the audience, 3 million people likely to see the poster within a 30-day period). The cost for 40 posters is $11,600; CPM = $3.87.
- A cable advertising service charges $150 for a 30-second commercial on a cable network providing 25 channels to 520,000 subscriber households (average per-channel subscriber base of 20,800); CPM = $7.21 (less than a penny per subscriber).

When comparing media costs, remember that the elements you are comparing may not be similar. The impact of various media and the amount of repeat presentation for messages to have an impact must be considered, as well as how closely a particular media audience coincides with an organization's key public.

Consider this example of a newspaper ad and a direct-mail letter. A 50,000-circulation newspaper charges $5,500 for a half-page ad; CPM = $110. A printer charges $600 for 10,000 copies of a direct-mail letter; CPM = $60. Additionally, it will cost $1,900 to distribute the letters; now the CPM cost to the organization is $250 for the direct-mail letter.

Purely based on production and distribution costs, the newspaper ad is a better deal. But most newspaper readers skip over the ads because they are not particularly interested in the topic. Chances are you don't need to communicate with 50,000 newspaper readers because most of them are not even in the key public you identified in your planning. Meanwhile, people who receive letters are often more likely to read them, especially if the organization did a good job identifying its public and designed the letter to be of obvious interest to the readers. So the $2,500 letter could well be the more cost-effective way to communicate with members of the key publics. It costs less and, more important, results in more effective message delivery. On the other hand, if your public is widespread and difficult to reach individually, then the newspaper ad may be the better way to communicate with them.

PUBLICITY VALUE

The measurement committee of the Canadian Public Relations Society has developed a point system now used by most Canadian public relations agencies. Called **media relations rating points** (MRP), it is a standard for evaluating and reporting editorial media coverage for public relations initiatives. MRP is intended to help both practitioners and clients understand the relative value of various public relations tactics.

The principle is simple: The practice of public relations is enhanced by having a consistent and systematic way to calculate the relative value of various communication tactics.

While the principle is simple, the process of MRP is sophisticated. Using proprietary software, MRP yields a percentage point based on a calculation that includes the total number of articles or reports, reach or total impressions, budget, and tone. It also takes into account company/brand and product mentions, quotes by spokespersons, use of photos, call-to-action, key messages, and the length of the broadcast/print/online report.

ADVERTISING VALUE EQUIVALENCY

A common but highly inappropriate evaluation technique is related to the message cost. **Advertising value equivalency** (called AVE for short) purports to place a dollar value on publicity, confusing the distinction between earned and paid media.

The technique treats a nonadvertising item as if it were an ad. Specifically, AVE pretends to measure the supposed value of news coverage, equating the amount of publication space or broadcast time to the cost of purchasing that same amount as advertising.

For example, a news report about your organization may be published in a local newspaper, involving a space totaling 21 column inches including headline, story, and photo. How can you evaluate this report? Using the advertising equivalency method, you would look up the advertising cost for a 21-inch ad in that newspaper. At $165 per column inch, for example, that story would have cost $3,465 if it were an advertisement. So the publicity is said to be worth exactly $3,465.

That's a neat way to put a dollar figure on a news story, costing it out as if it were an ad. But that "as if" causes a big problem. A news story isn't an advertisement, so the dollar figure is meaningless. Why? Audiences know the difference between news and advertising, and they treat the two information vehicles differently. Generally news stories are far more credible than are advertisements. So how much extra should you add for credibility?

On the other hand, many news stories don't necessarily have only positive information about an organization. Maybe you should deduct some amount because the news report wasn't glowingly positive. But wait. People read news stories more than they do ads. Perhaps you should add value because of higher audience attention. Then again, what's the value of no negative coverage when the organization's public relations practitioners have been trying to keep a story out of the papers, or at least off the front page?

Back and forth it goes, and in the end any dollar value you give to the news story is simply a fiction—bad fiction at that. It is worse than worthless because it gives a false impression that a meaningful assessment has been made.

Despite the obvious misconception that underlies advertising equivalency, it's a myth that doesn't want to go away. Some public relations or marketing agencies even have devised formulas to impress their unsuspecting clients, taking AVE to the next absurd level. They apply a **multiplier**, calculating that if A represents the cost of advertising time or space in the media, and if publicity (P) is worth proportionately more than A, then the public relations value of the publicity would be A × P. For example, they calculate the value of publicity as being four times the cost of advertising. Or ten times. They can calculate it however they want. It's still just an arbitrary weighting scheme that is all smoke and mirrors.

The Institute for Public Relations points to two major shortcomings with advertising value equivalency:

Phase Four

OUTPUTS, OUTTAKES, AND OUTCOMES

Public relations evaluation includes some related concepts: output, outtake, and outcome. It is important to make a clear distinction among these terms.

James Bissland (1990) identifies a communication output as the work done in a public relations activity. He likens this work to the who-says-what-in-which-channel part of Harold Lasswell's classic verbal formula for communication. Walter K. Lindenmann (2006) has described outputs as short-term, immediate results of a public relations program.

An **output** is a "thing" produced by public relations practitioners: news release, tweet, blog post, special event, and so on. Outputs often involve numbers: How many speaking engagements? How many times was the organization mentioned on network news? How often is a company official quoted? How many people attend a special event? How many web pages are viewed? How many placements appear in the media?

As things that people see and hear, outcomes are relatively easy to measure. Often this is done by observing audience participation or by measuring program results.

An **outtake** is the concept that publics take away, such as their understanding of a news report or their emotional response to a speech. Outtakes might be considered short-term results. Often they are measured through benchmarking and monitoring of the social environment.

An **outcome** is far more important. Bissland calls outcomes "terminal goals," but often they are more like what this book calls objectives because they are measurable and time-specific. Examples of outcomes are the number of new recruits, the amount of money raised, or the passage of desired legislation.

Writing for the Institute for Public Relations Research, Lindenmann focused on the communication process.

[Outcomes] measure whether target audience groups actually received the messages directed at them, paid attention to them, understood the messages, and retained the messages in any shape or form. They also measure whether the communications materials and messages which were disseminated have resulted in any opinion, attitude, and/or behavior change on the part of those targeted audiences to whom the messages were directed.

(Lindenmann, 2006, p. 14)

Outcomes are always quantifiable, and measuring them often calls for sophisticated research techniques.

What do we learn from this glossary of evaluation terms? Measure outputs if you wish; they can provide useful assessment of what has been done and how you have used your resources. But don't stop there. Measure outtakes every time you engage your publics. Even more importantly, measure program outcomes specifically as they relate to your objectives.

- Editorial matter is not "free advertising."
- Dollar cost does not equal dollar value.

In short, public relations experts agree that the publicity is more valuable than advertising. They can point to numerous and consistent studies showing the higher credibility of publicity over advertising.

Why has AVE survived in the practice? It's simple, it looks good if you don't look too closely, and it appeals to an unwary client or a boss without savvy. But the overwhelming argument to shove AVE off the research palette is that it's a work of fiction. Advertising is not public relations, and advertising value equivalency simply isn't equivalent.

The Institute for Public Relations says "AVEs, random use of multipliers, and other silly metrics and practices diminish the integrity of the profession . . ." adding that AVEs are "rejected as a concept to value public relations."

Organizations have an obvious desire to track their return on their investment, so it's not unreasonable to look for a way to do this. The following sections outline several more valid alternatives that do have a place in the public relations game plan. The Barcelona Declaration, outlined later in this chapter on page 389, has more to say about advertising equivalency (spoiler alert: nothing good).

Evaluating Awareness Objectives

The methods associated with output evaluation focus on documenting communication activity. Perhaps that's a worthwhile exercise, but it doesn't give a solid basis for measuring effectiveness. So here we can make a shift in our approach to evaluation.

Step 8 introduced the concept of objectives-based budgeting. It is sometimes called performance-based budgeting, though we abandoned the latter term because it seems to focus on performance before any performance actually occurred. But here in Step 9, we can measure actual performance.

So rather than measure outputs, it's more important to demonstrate the value that communication tactics offer an organization, specifically their effectiveness in achieving awareness, attitude, and action objectives that already have been established.

The first level of public relations objectives—awareness—provides an important category of evaluation research.

Awareness evaluation focuses on the content of the message. It considers how many people were exposed to the message, how easy the message is to understand, and how much of the message is remembered. Some of the common measures for awareness evaluation include message exposure, message content, readability measures, and message recall.

MESSAGE EXPOSURE

Measurement of **message exposure**, which focuses on the number of people in key publics who were exposed to the message, is a bit more sophisticated than the previous evaluation methodologies. That's because these are objectives-based measures that look more closely at communication tactics, evaluating not only distribution but also audience attention.

For example, the evaluator may use metrics for media exposure that ask how many hits were registered at a website or the actual number of people in the audience who heard a speech or saw a performance. Instead of counting the number of news releases distributed, the evaluator

Phase Four

would ask how many newspaper stories or broadcast reports resulted from the release or, more important, how many people actually read those newspaper stories, heard the broadcast reports, or read the online posting of the news release.

This can be a difficult number to obtain. Some public relations offices track this on their own. Others may hire a **clipping service**, a company that tracks publications and/or broadcasts on a regional, national, or even international basis. A variety of services and software exists to track traffic at an organization's website, which might include an online newsroom where reporters can download releases and other visitors can read releases. The software can measure not only the number of visitors but where they came from, how long they stay at the site, what pages they visit, what they download, and so on.

Some measures of message exposure count actual audiences, such as the number of people who attend an open house or some other public relations event. Unfortunately, some other measures deal with inferred or potential audiences, weakening the value of this measure by linking it to mere estimates.

Some concepts associated with message exposure are drawn from advertising. Audiences could have been exposed to the message presented in various media, from interpersonal settings, to viewers of a television newscast, to motorists who pass by a billboard. Sometimes these calculations can be quite impressive, even seductive. Consider, for example, the 1.1 billion impressions counted by MasterCard for its sponsorship of the World Cup Soccer Championship through public relations tactics such as news conferences, news releases, interviews and bylined columns. Or the Epilepsy Foundation, which recorded 140 million impressions through a public service radio advertisement and a news release.

Other metrics for evaluating advertising and promotional messages include the length of time visitors spend at a website, use of coupons included in print advertising, and the use of dedicated phone lines to track orders.

Remember, however, that **media impressions** and other counts of message exposure may simply estimate audience size. Even if the count is an actual one, such measures indicate only how many people were exposed to a message, from which we can infer that they saw or heard it. But media impressions don't indicate whether the audiences actually understood, accepted, or acted on the message in any way. And they don't measure the extent to which the audience overlaps with key publics.

MESSAGE CONTENT

An important type of evaluation focuses on the content of the message. Was it positive or did it provide negative information? Erroneous data? Unwarranted conclusions? Outdated info? It is far more important to analyze the content of a message than merely to count the number of newspaper clippings.

Appendix D, Applied Research: Content Analysis, provides specific information on how to conduct a content analysis. For now, don't forget to include this method of research prominently in your evaluation program.

READABILITY

Another way to evaluate awareness deals with comprehension—how easy a message is to understand.

One of the first steps in developing a public relations plan is to identify and analyze the publics to be addressed and the level of language appropriate to them. You dealt with the concept of **readability**—the level of reading difficulty that a public can be expected to handle—back in Step 3 in analyzing key publics. This concept usually translates into the level of education achieved by members of the public. You also encountered the concept again in Step 6 about how to prepare a written message that can be readily understood by the key public.

Part of the analysis in Step 9 is to assess the reading level of the materials disseminated. Robert Gunning's **Fog Index**, which measures reading ease or difficulty, is one of the easiest readability measures to use. Review the directions in the discussion of verbal communication in Phase Two, Strategy on p. 233.

MESSAGE RECALL

Another technique drawn from advertising research is **message recall**. Day-after recall studies are commonplace in advertising. Using this method, participants in interviews, surveys, or

---

CASE IN POINT   What to Measure in a Milk Campaign

Knowing what to measure often is the key to effective evaluation research. The answer for what metrics to use generally can be found in the objectives. But sometimes the objectives themselves are in conflict, with one of them measuring positively and another barely moving the dial.

That was the case with the Got Milk? campaign by the National Fluid Milk Processor Promotion Board, which presumably sought—as a range of objectives—awareness, acceptance, and action.

The advertising series, which ran from 1993 to 2014, featured celebrity photographer Annie Leibovitz's popular photos of celebrities with milk mustaches. The ads were elegant in their simplicity. Visibility was high, and everybody seemed familiar with the campaign and the ads. The Promotion Board claimed a 90 percent awareness rate.

Acceptance also ran high. The Promotion Board's research showed that attitudes toward milk improved. The ads themselves earned praise from creative designers. They appealed to a diverse audience largely because of their use of many different celebrities and characters: Batman, David Beckham, Jackie Chan, Cirque du Soleil, Tony Hawk, Kermit the Frog, Marilyn Manson, Nelly, Conan O'Brien, Rihanna, Pete Sampras, Usher, Bart and Lisa Simpson—the list goes on and on.

There's just one problem: It cost $110 million a year, and there's no evidence that the campaign increased milk consumption beyond California, where it was modestly successful the first couple of years.

Overall milk sales dropped over the duration of the campaign. Oops! Milk usage continues on an overall downward spiral, as Americans consume only about half the amount of milk recommended by the government's dietary guidelines. There are reasons for this: Milk prices have increased, Americans are turning to breakfast bars and yogurt to start their day, and they have more beverage options.

It's impossible to know how milk consumption might have trended if the Got Milk? campaign had never been launched. But the question is posed: How effective is a campaign that generates high awareness, measurable acceptance, and even improved attitudes but doesn't effect action?

Phase Four

STEP
9

focus groups are exposed to a news story, television program, or the like. Then they are interviewed to determine what they remember from the message.

A staple of research drawn from advertising is the Starch Readership Reports. These indicate three levels of reader study: "noted" readers who remember having previously seen an advertisement, "associated" readers who can link the advertisement with a particular brand or advertiser, and "read most" readers who are able to describe most of the written material in the ad.

Consider this awareness objective: *to increase clients' understanding of changes in insurance policy coverage.* Possible evaluation metrics include noting exposure patterns, doing content analysis to gauge how consistent the messages are with the facts, and asking a focus group to discuss message recall.

Here's another awareness objective: *to increase awareness of a new consumer product being manufactured by a client.* Three ways to evaluate this might include (1) tracking dissemination of messages and noting the size of the potential audience, (2) analyzing the message content with attention to its accuracy and the use of the client's telephone number and/or website address, and (3) surveying customers in the company database regarding message recall.

Evaluating Acceptance Objectives

A major shortcoming of all the message-based evaluation techniques noted earlier is that they do not address the consequence of the public relations tactics. Instead, they simply gauge the existence of the tactics. At best, message-based evaluation techniques can deal with the level of awareness surrounding a public relations message. But as we see with the milk moustache campaign, awareness doesn't necessarily lead to success.

A more effective area of evaluation is based on levels of acceptance and action. Step 4 noted the importance of objectives focused on the desired impact on interest and attitudes (acceptance) and on opinion and behavior (action). Take steps now to evaluate how well each of those objectives has been achieved.

Two common approaches to measuring acceptance objectives are audience feedback and benchmark studies.

AUDIENCE FEEDBACK

Some evaluation measures count and analyze the voluntary reaction of the audience, such as the number of hits on a web page, the number of telephone calls and letters, or the number of requests for additional information. Or consider the frequency of liking, sharing, and retweeting on social media. Such **audience feedback**, an acceptance evaluation based on the voluntary reaction of an audience, can be an effective measure of the level of the audience's information and interest.

BENCHMARK STUDY

Another type of research is a **benchmark study** (also called **baseline study**), which provides a basis for comparing program outcomes against a standard. Actually, benchmark studies can be based on any of several different standards: the starting levels of interest or positive attitudes, outcomes of similar programs by other organizations, outcomes of the same program during

REAL-WORLD RESEARCH PRACTICES

Broadcast Mainland, a British public relations agency, reported on its 2010 study of how senior in-house public relations and marketing professionals evaluate their communication activities. Here are some highlights.

51%	Do not measure broadcast coverage.
50%	Measure social media coverage based on gut reaction.
50%	Are not satisfied with tools they use to measure social media.
40%	Expected to demonstrate value of public relations to senior executives.
48%	Use advertising equivalency to demonstrate such value.
34%	Realize that advertising equivalency is misleading.

The results reported in this study are disheartening. So few of practitioners realize that advertising equivalency is worthless. So many rely on gut feelings. So many don't know of objective evaluation tools, despite being held accountable by their bosses.

For students preparing to enter the field or young professionals already in it, studies such as this suggest a clear way to distinguish yourself. Develop a solid grasp of ways to properly evaluate media activities, and you will increase your career options.

a previous year or cycle, outcomes of industry or professional models, or the hypothetical outcomes of an "ideal" program.

Consider this acceptance objective: *to enhance favorable employee attitudes toward a client's company*. Here are four potential evaluation metrics: (1) compare retention figures from before and after the tactic was implemented, (2) record oral and written comments given to the human resource department of the company, (3) solicit anecdotal input from managers and supervisors, and (4) survey employees about their attitudes and try to learn what they have been telling family and friends about working for the company.

Here's another acceptance objective: *to increase employee affirmation of the company's need to change employee benefits*. Three possible evaluation techniques include (1) recording immediate anecdotal feedback after the announcement is made, (2) conducting a survey within two days of the announcement, and (3) after two weeks inviting employee feedback through response cards provided in pay envelopes.

Evaluating Action Objectives

The ultimate objectives for most public relations activities should focus on bottom-line issues for an organization, primarily the action sought from the key publics. In this evaluation phase of the planning process, careful consideration should be given to ways to measure these action objectives. Three approaches to action-focused evaluation research involve audience participation, direct observation, and relative media effectiveness.

Phase Four

STEP
9

AUDIENCE PARTICIPATION

Figures on the number of people who actively responded to the message generally are easy to obtain. Attendance figures are effective measures when attendance itself is the desired objective, as may be the case with concerts and exhibitions, athletic competitions, benefit fundraising events, and the like. Implicit in these attendance figures also is a measure of the effectiveness of publicity and promotion that preceded the events.

However, attendance figures can be misused if the presumption is made that attendance at some information-sharing session necessarily equates with some eventual action impact. For example, attendance at a political speech can't be used as a reliable indicator of either audience acceptance of the message or eventual support in the voting booth. People heard the speech and the message was presented, but desired action is not guaranteed. Therefore, be careful how attendance figures are interpreted and what value is placed on them.

Two events in 2016 brought attention to the role of polls as an indicator of likely audience participation. The Brexit vote set into motion the United Kingdom's exit from the European Union. The U.S. presidential election brought victory for Donald Trump and near-total Republican domination of American politics. Both events showed that polls can be poor vehicles for accurate predictions.

Consider the phenomenon of Donald Trump, who for months was the solid front-runner among Republican primary candidates. Doubters said the poll results were misleading because his base of support was large but weak and his messages were out of step with standards of decency and fairness. In the Brexit campaign, polls showed that the "remain" faction held a continuing lead prior to the vote.

Both events seriously undercounted the power of conservative voters seeking to change their country's direction and to protect their perceived self-interests. The reasons for these final votes are complex. But the consensus among research experts points to a combination of factors.

- Poll respondents not being truthful with pollsters, an example of the Spiral of Silence theory in action.
- The numbing effect of predictions of inevitability prior to the vote.
- Low turnout of young, urban, and/or minority voters, who largely would have supported the side that lost the election.
- Polling techniques that undercounted hard-to-reach voters.
- The presumption that late undecided voters would break for the status quo (for Clinton, for remaining in the EU), though instead they opted for change.
- The unexpected power of conservative messages appealing to base attitudes (in both instances, fear of immigrants, disparagement of minorities, and us-versus-them nationalistic protectivism) rather than appeals to higher human values.
- Fake news, a Soviet-style disinformation campaign disseminated via social media, that insinuated into the public discourse falsehoods masquerading as legitimate news, giving cover for prejudice, conspiracy theories, and political divisiveness.

DIRECT OBSERVATION OF RESULTS

Sometimes the simplest way to measure the effectiveness of action objectives is to look around. It's called **direct observation**.

Let's say the objective sought an outcome of enough voter support to win an election. If your candidate won, your objective was achieved. If you sought financial contributions of $2.2 million, count the total of donations and pledges; anything above the target amount means you were that much more successful than planned. Some other easy-to-quantify objectives deal with sales figures, academic scores, membership expectations, and capacity attendance for sporting and artistic events.

In some instances, the action objective deals with the general outcome rather than with any quantification. For example, passage (or defeat) of a particular piece of legislation may fully satisfy an action objective. Some evaluation research calls for strategic and creative thinking.

Individual behavior that may not be easily observable is more difficult to measure than the preceding examples.

Here is an example of how to deal with a difficult-to-evaluate action objective: *to increase the use of seat belts*. Surveying large numbers of people might be difficult. One possible way to evaluate this objective efficiently would be to place observers in highway tollbooths and have them record the number of drivers and driver-side passengers wearing seat belts as they pass through the booths.

Or consider this objective: *to have elementary, secondary, and college teachers become more active in lobbying state government for increased support of education*. An evaluation plan might include a tactic that encourages the sending of email letters to state officials, with instructions for sending a copy to your organization. A simple count of the number of copies received would yield data to evaluate this objective. To take it to a higher level of sophistication, an organization might work with several sympathetic state legislators and compare the number of email messages sent to their office with the number of copies the organization received.

HOW TO MEASURE PUBLICITY EFFECTS

Measuring the effects of media relations takes a bit of creativity, but it's not impossible. Consider the following possibilities.

1. *Set clear objectives* in advance and establish the criteria that will form the basis for success.
2. *Do a pretest* such as an awareness survey to identify the beginning point.
3. *Do a post-test* to measure changes in awareness in comparison with results of the pretest.
4. *Use a focus group* to probe the relationships among awareness, acceptance, and action.
5. *Track media placement* with clippings and logs. Evaluate these not only in terms of distribution, use, and other measures of audience exposure but also conduct some form of content analysis to evaluate the effectiveness of the message itself.
6. *Measure action* in some way, such as by noting changes in attendance, traffic, purchase, or other behaviors associated with the campaign.

Phase Four

From the difference, the organization could extrapolate the number of messages sent by teachers to all legislators.

Some of the benchmark techniques for evaluating acceptance objectives, noted earlier, can be equally useful for evaluating action objectives.

RELATIVE MEDIA EFFECTIVENESS

A final method of evaluating action objectives deals with the behavior generated by a particular medium compared to others. For example, did people vote for a candidate because of television coverage of a live debate or because of the candidate's Internet advertising? Often it is difficult to sort out the impact of a specific medium or tactic. But here's an example of how one organization managed to make the comparison.

In 2007, SeaWorld San Antonio introduced a new roller-coaster ride, Journey to Atlantis. The theme park invited members of the media to try out the new ride. The park's public relations–marketing team included social media in the mix. Twenty-two blogs and media forums were identified for their focus on roller coasters and invited to write about the new ride. Eventually 12 did so. The result was that SeaWorld San Antonio received 50 links from coaster-oriented websites. Media posted on YouTube, Flickr, and other social media sites generated hundreds of thousands of downloads, along with many positive comments.

Over two weekends two months later, a standard exit interview for SeaWorld visitors asked a typical question: Where did you hear about Journey to Atlantis? Forty-seven percent of respondents indicated social media as a source of their information. The research team looked at the various media used to promote the new ride (television commercial, newspaper ad, social media, radio spot, billboard, and so on) and concluded that the cost per impression for social media was 22 cents, compared with $1 for each television impression.

Data Analysis

Having gathered the data, it is now time to analyze it carefully. Match the observed and reported results with the expectations outlined in your statement of objectives.

If the program failed to meet its objectives, do some further analysis. Try to learn if the shortfall was because of a flawed strategy that undergirded the program or because the tactics were not implemented as effectively as they might have been. Consider also if there might be a flaw in the evaluation techniques used to gather the data.

If evaluation of the program is particularly important, ask an outside auditor to review the data. For some formal presentations of research findings, in order to enhance credibility, an organization may ask an outside expert or a panel of stakeholders to attest to the validity of the tools used in the evaluation research.

After the evaluation is completed and the information gathered and analyzed, make sure it is presented in a form that is understandable and accessible to decision makers within the organization. They usually are busy executives and managers with global but not necessarily specific understandings of the issue. They may not have a high level of insight or information about the program, so be careful not to obscure evaluation findings in the final report. Instead, be very clear, draw obvious conclusions, and highlight the most important data.

If the decision makers have been involved in establishing the objectives of the program, they probably will be disposed to using the evaluation findings. Another way to increase the likelihood that the evaluation will be used is to concentrate on elements that can be changed in subsequent programs.

There is much variety as to the format of evaluation reports. They may be presented separately or merged into a single report. The report itself can take the form of a formal document, an oral presentation, or a meeting agenda item. Whether written or verbal, evaluation reports should be carefully crafted to clearly link the expectations outlined in the objectives with the outcomes.

When writing a report, note how the outcomes were measured, discuss the degree to which they achieved the objectives, and note the significance of this achievement (or lack of it). Finally, make clear recommendations closely linked with the data. For reports of major significance, visual elements such as photographs, tables, and charts can enhance the understanding of readers and listeners.

Evaluation reports sometimes become the basis of a news release or even a news conference if the topic under review is one that is particularly newsworthy. For example, the final evaluation of public relations programs on popular and highly visible social issues such as campaigns to reduce drug abuse or bullying may warrant a news report.

Any evaluation report longer than five pages should be preceded by an **executive summary** that provides an overview of the findings and a simplified set of recommendations. An executive summary serves the needs of those decision makers—sometimes the most important ones—who may not have the time to digest the longer document.

Ultimate Evaluation: Value-Added Public Relations

Most evaluation of public relations and other strategic communication programs focus on objectives and tactics: What did we set out to achieve? What did we do? What did we accomplish by doing it? How effectively did this achieve what we set out to do?

Such questions are very important. But there is another equally important question to be answered: What did public relations do for the organization as a whole?

Once again, a reminder: The premise underlying *Strategic Planning for Public Relations* is that strategic communication is about more than mere tactics and activities.

Rather, it deals with the overall planned program of both proactive and reactive communication that enhances the relationship between an organization and its various publics, a relationship that needs to be linked to the bottom-line concerns of the organization. You might call it value-added public relations, the notion that public relations offers value and benefit to the organization as a whole.

Sometimes public relations practitioners are challenged to calculate the **return on investment** (ROI) for their client or boss as a way to justify the cost of public relations activities. ROI is the ratio of money gained or lost relative to the cost of a program or product. In some ways, this is an unfair expectation, because ROI is a financial metric measuring dollars spent vis-à-vis dollars saved or earned or offset by other revenue. Rather than return on investment, public relations practitioners prefer to deal in value that their activities add to an organization.

Based on qualitative interview research with both public relations practitioners and their CEOs, Linda Childers Hon (1997) has reported six such values that effective public relations bring to organizations or to the clients of a consultant or agency. Keep these in mind as you complete your evaluation and present it to your client or organization.

Phase Four

1. Effective public relations helps organizations *survive* by reversing negative opinions, promoting awareness of organizational benefits to the community, and effecting balanced media coverage.

2. Effective public relations helps organizations *make money* by generating publicity about products and services as well as the organization's plans and accomplishments; attracting new customers, volunteers, donors, and stockholders; and improving employee performance and productivity.

3. Effective public relations helps other organizational functions *make money* by creating an environment of understanding and goodwill, by influencing supportive legislation, and by enhancing fundraising efforts.

4. Effective public relations helps organizations *save money* by inducing favorable legislation, retaining members, and minimizing negative publicity during crisis incidents.

5. Effective public relations helps organizations *weaken opposition* by generating favorable public opinion and obtaining cooperation from governmental and other organizations.

6. Effective public relations helps organizations *save lives* through social goals such as advancing highway safety, medical care and research, and the like.

Public Relations Metrics

We noted earlier in this chapter that metrics are standards of measurement used to quantify performance outcomes and to measure the level to which objectives are met. Don Bartholomew of Ketchum Public Relations introduced a hierarchy for public relations metrics.

- **Exposure metric**: How publics have been exposed to a message
- **Engagement metric**: How publics interact with the organization and with each other vis-à-vis the message
- **Influence metric**: The degree to which message exposure and engagement impact on the publics' perceptions and attitudes
- **Action metric**: How the public acts on the message

Bartholomew's model applies to both traditional and emerging media, though he developed it mainly with social media in mind. (For more information, see Bartholomew's blog at MetricsMan.wordpress.com.)

Applied to social media, metrics for exposure might include the number of hits to a website, the number of unique visitors, search-engine ranking, and objective analysis of online comments or discussion. Engagement metrics could be repeat visitors, likes and recommendations, message recall measures, and RSS subscriptions. Examples of metrics for the influence category include measured change in awareness or attitudes, brand association, and purchase considerations. Action metrics might be store visits, event attendance, or the logical close-the-loop action such as purchases, votes, memberships, and so on.

Barcelona Declaration

Public relations practitioners from around the world met in Spain in 2010. Their mission was to articulate standards and common approaches for measuring and evaluating public relations.

The Barcelona Declaration of Measurement Principles emerging from these discussions includes seven principles that, over the years, have been adopted and broadly used.

The declaration was intended to begin an international conversation. That dialogue was continued in 2015 when the original working group of participants from 33 nations met with additional representatives from academia, government, and both the nonprofit and for-profit sectors.

The Barcelona Declaration 2.0 that emerged widened the scope beyond public relations to set standards for communications measurement overall. It reaffirmed the value of transparency and integration. Here are the seven principles.

1. *Goals and Objectives*. Goal setting and measurement are fundamental aspects of public relations and other communication programs. They should be quantitative and should address the intended effect.
2. *Outcomes over Outputs*. Rather than focusing on activities done by public relations practitioners (outputs), measurement should focus on results. It is more important to measure the effect on outcomes (including awareness, comprehension, attitude, and behavior) rather than outputs.
3. *Business Results*. Evaluation should measure business results from a consumer perspective, focusing on the quantity and quality of public relations activities on business metrics as they impact the organization's bottom line.
4. *Quality and Quantity*. Because measuring media placement and counting overall impressions are meaningless, measurement should focus on impressions on key publics and on the quality of media coverage, including its tone, the credibility of the medium, message delivery, inclusion of a third party, and prominence within the medium.
5. *Advertising Equivalency*. This approach measures the cost of media space and is rejected as a concept to place a value on public relations. Likewise, multipliers intended to present a formula for media cost as a factor of public relations value should not be applied. If a comparison must be made between earned versus paid media, validated metrics should be used.
6. *Social Media*. There is no single metric for measuring social media, which nevertheless can and should be measured against clearly defined goals and outcomes for the organization's use of social media. Measurement should focus on engagement, conservation, and community building rather than on coverage or vanity metrics such as likes.
7. *Transparent and Replicable*. Measurement methods should be both transparent and trustworthy. They should be repeatable, which requires accountability about methodology and analysis.

Many observers have called the Barcelona Declaration a game changer for public relations. They observe that the new 2015 principles are sounding a death knell to AVEs and multipliers that try to fix a dollar value on public relations by falsely comparing it to advertising.

Phase Four

CASE IN POINT Evaluation at Southwest Airlines

Southwest Airlines engaged in a series of evaluation tools as part of its media relations strategy, specifically its plan to link public relations with sales (Watson and Noble, 2007). Here's the company's five-point program.

1. Southwest conducted keyword research to learn how people search online. For example, research during one month revealed 1.3 million searches for "Southwest Airlines" but only 400,000 for "Southwest."
2. With this information, the company edited its news releases to include the full "Southwest Airlines" search term, making it more likely that online readers would find the company's postings.
3. Because research also showed that many online news readers do not scroll to the bottom of the release for links to additional information, Southwest imbedded links within its online news releases. Thus a release about a particular offer included a link to a web page where the visitor could purchase it and where the company could track it.
4. Southwest distributed its new releases through wire services that are "crawled" by Google, Yahoo, and AOL News, increasing the likelihood that online searchers would find the company information.
5. The airline evaluated three news releases to link publicity with sales. It found evidence that one release about a new route resulted in $80,000 in ticket sales, a Spanish-language online release led to $38,000 in sales, and the third release with a hyperlink in the first paragraph resulted in more than $1 million in ticket sales.

Additionally, the supporters report that organizational executives and CEOs adopted the original principles—and are expected to likewise embrace the 2.0 version—especially as they lead to more accountability for public relations and more integration with the organization's bottom line.

What's Next?

This ends the nine steps of strategic planning. In that sense, nothing is left to do. You've learned all the elements that go into an effective and efficient campaign for public relations or marketing communication.

In a very real sense, though, you've only just begun. Take the knowledge you've gained from this text and the practical experiences you have in working through the various activities you have encountered and run with them.

PLANNING EXAMPLE 9 **Evaluating the Strategic Plan**

Upstate College will evaluate its Initiative on Transfer Students according to the following five-part plan:

UPSTATE COLLEGE

1. Placement report tracking distribution and media use of news releases and other materials disseminated by its public relations department
2. Telephone survey among people who applied to UC two, three, and four years ago but did not attend; the purpose of this survey will be to assess awareness about the expansion and attitudes toward it
3. Focus group of new applicants to UC, discussing the source of their information about the expansion and their reasons for applying
4. Content analysis of newspaper articles, radio and television news reports, and newspaper letters to the editor and editorials, studying the positive/negative nature of the reports about UC's expansion
5. Brief survey as part of the application process, asking applicants the source of their information about the UC expansion

The evaluation report will be provided to the college president and provost, who prefer a well-documented and candid report. This report will become the basis for future recruitment and development activities.

(Note: you will develop similar evaluation plans for the other initiatives.)

———————————

Tiny Tykes Toys will evaluate the employee-oriented phase of its public relations program according to the following plan:

TINY
TYKES
TOYS

- *Before-and-After Survey*. Develop surveys of both employees and employees' family members, dealing with employee morale, job satisfaction, pride in company, and knowledge of recall, safety, and quality issues. The results of these surveys will be compared to ascertain any change in knowledge, attitudes, and behavior associated with the public relations program.
- *Employee-Initiated Feedback*. Review copies of comments and suggestions in the suggestion box, notes to company managers, letters to the editor of the company newsletter or other publications, and other print and/or email messages regarding the reintroduction program. These messages will be summarized and analyzed.
- *Analysis of Media Coverage*. Track placement, measure employee awareness of coverage, and do a simply content analysis on articles and news reports as to their positive or negative reflection of Tiny Tykes employees.

A written final evaluation will be presented to company managers and then will be shared with employees.

Phase Four

✓ Checklist 9 **Evaluation Plan**

Basic Questions

1. How will you measure awareness objectives?
2. How will you measure acceptance objectives?
3. How will you measure action objectives?

Expanded Questions

A. METHODOLOGY

1. How and when can this information be obtained: via after-only study or before-and-after study?
2. Which research methodologies would be most effective?

   - Judgmental assessment: personal experience or outside experts.
   - Interviews with key people. Which people?
   - Focus groups with representative publics. Which publics?
   - Survey of representative publics. Which publics? Control group?
   - Content analysis of representative artifacts. Which artifacts?
   - Readership study.
   - Media tracking.

B. EVALUATION CATEGORIES

1. Indicate how each of the methodologies below might be used to evaluate each individual tactic.
2. What standards of accuracy and reliability are needed for the evaluation?
3. Who can provide information for evaluation?

Evaluation of Outputs
- Message production
- Message dissemination
- Message cost analysis
- Advertising equivalency

Evaluation of Awareness Objectives
- Message exposure
- Message content analysis
- Readability measures
- Message recall

Evaluation of Acceptance Objectives
- Audience feedback
- Benchmark (baseline) study

Evaluation of Action Objectives
- Audience participation
- Direct observation of results

C. AUDIENCE

1. Who will receive the final evaluation?
2. How will it be used?
3. What level of candor do decision makers require?

D. EVALUATION SCHEDULE

1. Timeline for implementation report
2. Timeline for progress report
3. Timeline for final evaluation

E. EVALUATION PROGRAM CHECKLIST

For this evaluation program:

- Is it useful to the organization?
- Is it clearly linked to established objectives?
- Is it appropriate as to cost?
- Is it appropriate as to time?
- Is it appropriate as to other resources?
- Is it ethical and socially responsible?
- Is it credible, with accurate data?
- Is it doable?

APPENDIXES

APPENDIX A

Applied Research

As a student, you probably are already familiar with academic research from journals and textbooks. **Academic research** generates theory, explores new interests and focuses on universal knowledge. This is knowledge for its own sake. Academic research also is called **theoretical research**, **basic research**, and **pure research**.

In your professional life beyond the classroom, however, you are more likely to deal in **applied research** (sometimes called **market research** or **administrative research**). This type of research delves into the practical problems faced by an organization and guides effective resolution of those problems. Your bosses and clients will ask you to get information as quickly and inexpensively as possible to help solve their very real problems.

Your applied research may contribute to the theory base of your profession, but that is a side benefit. Its primary role is to deal with practical matters for your client. Sometimes applied research consciously draws on the theoretical outcomes of academic research to investigate practical issues.

This appendix provides an introduction to applied research, with a discussion of research ethics and an overview of the sampling process common to several research methodologies. It also will deal with secondary research and interviewing. Subsequent appendixes will highlight how-to guides to several techniques for doing applied research using focus groups, surveys, and content analysis.

Research Topics

Applied research is especially important when program planning brings together a specialist (you) working for an expert (your boss or client), because the research can help prevent problems by putting both the specialists and the experts more in touch with their publics.

Take, for example, the experience of a senior campaigns class in which university students developed a comprehensive public relations and advertising program for a new space exhibit at a science museum. The museum had a wealth of marketing research, but as part of the course assignment the four student teams tried out several different strategic concepts on a sampling of their target public: schoolchildren and their parents. This research paid off.

One team considered three different themes: a digitized close-up of a man in a spacesuit with the slogan "Put Your Face in Space"; a rocket being fired from its launch pad with the

ACADEMIC VERSUS APPLIES RESEARCH

Most of the studies published in the *Journal of Public Relations Research* deal with academic research, which by its nature is public and meant to be shared, challenged, and continuously developed.

Here are some topics from the last years: attribution theory and crisis communication, contingency theory of accommodation, ethics, the rhetorical-organizational approach to organizational identity, knowledge predictors, integrated symmetrical model of crisis communication, self-efficiency theory, blog-mediated crisis communication, image and symbolic leadership, news credibility, and situational theory. Several other journals also publish academic research focused on public relations.

Applied research more often remains unpublished because it is proprietary, meaning that it is conducted for and owned by a particular client, who generally doesn't want to share the research with competitors.

A review of the websites of several major public relations agencies indicates that they have conducted the following research topics for clients: media content analysis, survey of residents to identify a location for a chemical plant, monitoring legislation and conducting legislative research, corporate reputation, impact of public relations and advertising programs, Internet monitoring, audience surveys, audience analysis of sports organizations to increase fan and corporate support, content analysis of oppositional publications.

slogan "Blast Off! Explore the Infinite Possibilities"; and a close-up of a footprint on the moon with the slogan "Space. Touch it!"

When the students presented the three possible approaches to the museum CEO and his marketing and public relations directors, the clients were enthusiastic and unanimous. They really liked the footprint, because it so poignantly reflected the Apollo 11 lunar landing.

But the students cautioned, "Don't jump to conclusions. Our research supports the second option. We found that the children you want to attract like the action of the space launch much more. For them and their parents, the footprint from the first moon landing in 1969 is part of history, not something that excites their imagination."

Applied research prevented a false start with a misguided theme.

Do-It-Yourself Research

Many research experts offer a simple warning: Don't try this at home! They note that research methodologies can be incredibly complex, and many pitfalls exist for the novice who plunges headlong into research using inappropriate techniques that result in inaccurate data and unwarranted conclusions.

Clearly some issues are so critical and the needed research so important that you really should get professional research assistance. Nevertheless, the research techniques explained in these appendixes are not impossible for the do-it-yourselfer. The key is knowing when you should do it yourself and when to call in an expert. So the advice here is: Learn how to do it, then try to do it yourself. Even if you have to turn to a research specialist, these appendixes will help you manage the project.

Consider the following generalization: You might do your own research if your project meets all or most of the following criteria:

- Do you need objective data?
- Do you have the time, interest, patience, ability, and confidence to conduct your own study?
- Does your organization, boss, or client have enough confidence in you to respect and use your findings?
- Can you be objective in your study even though it involves your own organization?
- Are you comfortable with statistics and other data with a relatively wide margin of error?
- Are the decisions riding on the study relatively minor in terms of your organization's overall mission?
- Is your budget such that the choice is between doing your own research and doing none at all?

Research Ethics

Ethics deals with the rightness or wrongness of behavior, especially professional or organizational behavior (as compared with personal morality). Social science research involves several areas that can pose ethical risks and temptations.

The Principles of Disclosure of the National Council on Public Polls (ncpp.org) pledges the commitment of member organizations "to standards of disclosure designed to insure that consumers of survey results that enter the public domain have an adequate basis for judging the reliability and validity of the results reported."

Most colleges and universities have clearly defined policies related to research ethics. So do many companies and public relations counseling agencies. Specific standards may vary, but some common ground can be found in many ethical guidelines. Broadly speaking, the areas of common ground deal with the treatment of the people involved in the research study and the use of information.

Ethical Treatment of People

Below are eight guidelines for dealing ethically with people involved in research programs or projects. These principles apply to the kind of applied research that is common in public relations research practices.

DIGNITY

Respect the dignity of participants in every study. This is the umbrella that covers all the other principles. It is rooted in common sense and decent interaction with people. Most colleges and universities, as well as other research organizations, have formal requirements for research involving human subjects, so make sure your research is in compliance with these regulations. This is particularly important for public relations and marketing research with interaction through methodologies such as interviews, focus groups, and surveys. The principles do not apply to content analysis, because no active participants are involved in that kind of research.

PRIVACY

Respect the privacy of participants. Abide fully by any privacy commitments that are made. Note the difference between anonymity and confidentiality.

Anonymity means the participant's identity will not be known to anybody, including the researcher, and thus cannot be linked to a particular response.

Confidentiality means the researcher will not disclose the participant's identity nor allow it to be linked to a particular response.

Anonymity is difficult for most public relations research. Interviews and focus groups obviously can't be anonymous, and it is difficult to maintain anonymity for surveys that require more than one mailing. Confidentiality is the more likely protection for participants.

Remember that any privacy guarantees extend beyond the time of the research study. Questionnaires and notes should be stored in a nonpublic place and should be discarded when they are no longer needed.

VOLUNTEER PARTICIPATION

Seek only voluntary participation by respondents. Would-be participants in interviews, focus groups, and surveys should be told explicitly that they might choose not to participate. They must be allowed to decline at the beginning of the research activity or to end their participation at any point. The voluntariness of participation is less of an issue with mail or phone surveys, where respondents can easily ignore the questionnaire or hang up on the researcher.

CONSENT

Obtain informed consent. Participants should be told enough about the research project so they clearly know what they are being asked to do. When a person agrees to participate in an interview, survey, or focus group, informed consent can logically be presumed, and asking participants to sign consent statements could negate a guarantee of anonymity that might be part of the project.

Increasingly, however, researchers are asking participants in studies involving sensitive matters to sign a consent form. The confidentiality issue can be handled by having the consent form separate from any questionnaire that is part of the research tool. Consent forms are generally used for experiments, and they are becoming more common with other types of public relations or marketing research.

Informed consent extends to practical matters, such as telling respondents how much time will be expected for their participation.

PURPOSE

Disclose the purpose of the research to the participants. In some cases, the researcher does not want to indicate the full purpose of the study up front, because this might contaminate the results by causing the respondents to provide less-than-truthful information. Even if the respondents try to be truthful, knowing too much about the project could bias their responses. However, respondents or participants have the right to know at least the general purpose of the study. Participants usually can be told the purpose of the research when their role is ended.

RESEARCHER IDENTITY

Disclose the identity of the researcher. Active participants should know whom you are and that you are conducting research. This often can enhance the credibility of the study.

SPONSOR IDENTITY

Disclose the identity of the research sponsor. Would-be respondents and other participants have the right to know the name of the organization sponsoring and benefiting from the research. As with the item above about the purpose of the research, the identity of the research sponsor sometimes is withheld until the conclusion of the study, so participants can act and provide information without bias.

RESULTS

Inform participants of the research results. By debriefing participants, the researcher can explain the study and allow participants to see themselves in relation to the total sample. Especially if the researcher concealed information about the purpose or sponsor to ensure candid responses by participants, explaining to them afterward can make up for the deception.

ETHICAL USE OF RESEARCH DATA

Four ethical considerations are paramount related to the use of research data for public relations and marketing research of the kind considered in this book. Different ethical principles would apply to more experimental or laboratory-based social research.

Here are the four ethical considerations.

- *Develop a fair research process*. Draw samples with care so that they are likely to represent the target population. Don't yield to the temptation to obtain an easy or quick sample if good research calls for a more sophisticated sample. In reporting your research, explain the methodology you used in drawing the sample, and acknowledge any shortcoming in the sampling process.
- *Develop fair measurement tools*. Questions and response items should be designed to elicit honest responses, and research participants should not be tricked into giving information they don't believe in. Manipulation and coercion have no place in research.
- *Analyze and report data ethically*. Treat each piece of data with great respect; never fudge or falsify any data. Discard any data that is unclear, indecipherable, or otherwise contaminated. In analyzing the data, draw only those conclusions justified by the information obtained; never discount or misinterpret data in favor of your own bias or your client's wishes. Fully report the circumstances of the research project: geography and time frame, sampling techniques, and methodology. Include copies of questionnaires and other data-gathering tools.
- *Avoid using polling for propaganda*. Especially in the realm of political polling, it is not unknown that a candidate would commission polls with weak sampling and inappropriate wording of questionnaires just to get the results they want. Candidate A is running behind? Release a poll that show A neck-and-neck with the opposition, trying to increase the actual voter turnout. Want to sink Candidate B? Release a poll that puts her way behind your candidate, in hopes that B's supporters will not bother to vote for an obvious loser in the race. These are serious ethical breaches that no fair-minded researcher would be associated with.

Sampling

The purpose of research is to describe various characteristics (such as the level of information, existence of attitudes or opinions, or the extent of certain behaviors) of a **population**, which is a large group of subjects that are of interest to the researcher. For example, depending on the interests of the researcher, the residents of Kansas could be a population; so too Hispanic athletes at all Kansas high schools, or vegetarian restaurants in the Sunflower State.

The individual **element** of the population (also called the **unit of analysis**) usually is a person. However, elements could be organizations, products, media artifacts such as news reports or editorials, public relations artifacts such as news releases or brochures, or advertising artifacts such as television commercials or print ads. Each research activity also has a particular time period (usually defined in weeks, months, or years) and an extent (a geographic location such as a region, state, or neighborhood).

Sometimes we conduct a **census**, which is a comprehensive study that includes every member of the population in our study. An example of a census is a poll that a small business might conduct with every employee about an issue of companywide interest.

Other times, however, it is impractical to survey every member of a very large or scattered population. In such cases, a good alternative is **sampling**, the identification of a subset of the population of individuals (or objects) who reflect and represent the larger body. This subset is known as a **sample**. The value of sampling is that it saves time and money, allowing researchers to study a small group and then use those findings to make predictions for a much larger population, a process called **extrapolation**.

Depending on how a sample is pulled together, it may or may not be based on the concept of **probability**, which means that every element in the population has an equal chance of being selected for the sample. To help you understand sampling, consider the analogy of cooking stew. A cook mixes a variety of vegetables and herbs in a pot, then stirs—that's the key. Presumably, the stirring has mixed all the ingredients evenly. The cook then dips the ladle and takes a taste. No need to eat the entire pot to determine if more seasoning is needed; one spoon from a well-stirred pot provides a true sampling of the entire stew.

Over the years, the accuracy of polling has improved tremendously. Consider recent presidential polls. In 1936 the influential *Literary Digest* forecast that Alf Landon would beat Franklin Roosevelt 57 to 43 percent. Instead, Roosevelt easily won re-election with a landslide 61 percent of the vote. In 1948, the Roper Poll predicted that Thomas Dewey would beat Harry Truman by a 5-point margin in the presidential election. Instead, Truman won by 5 points.

By contrast, the National Council on Public Polls reported that national presidential polls in 2012 were off the actual vote by only 2.3 percent. That's the same percentage in the 2016 Trump–Clinton race, though the margin broke from the expectation that Clinton would win the electoral vote as well as the less-determinant popular vote.

The evolution of polling accuracy lies in the improved sampling techniques. *Literary Digest* polled 2 million people using a volunteer sampling frame including telephone listings (in 1936, phones were for the well-to-do) and country club memberships, favoring the wealthy and excluding the poor. The 1948 poll was a cluster sample of 20,000, weighted toward rural Republican voters rather than urban Democratic voters.

Now, sampling is down to an average size of about 1,000 respondents for the estimated 230 million voting-age Americans. These respondents are scientifically selected on age, income, ethnicity, location, occupation, religion, education, and many other factors that, taken

PROBABILITY AND NONPROBABILITY SAMPLING

Nonprobability sampling involves the selection of a sample in a manner through which each member of the population does not have an unequal chance statistically of being selected.

- Convenience sampling
- Volunteer sampling
- Purposive sampling
- Snowball sampling
- Quota sampling

Probability sampling involves the selection of a sample in a manner through which every member of the population has an equal chance statistically of being selected for the sample.
- Simple random sampling
- Systematic sampling
- Stratified sampling
- Cluster sampling

together, present an accurate picture of the American electorate. Over the years, progressively smaller but more representative samples have yielded greater accuracy.

Polling has become refined as it focuses on "likely voters," particularly for surveys that take place within a few days prior to an election. Surveys earlier in the election cycle often still rely on registered voters who are uncommitted at that stage and may be flirting with several candidates. The increasing incidence of Internet polling is hampered by greater likelihood of error than more traditional polling techniques.

Another area of concern for pollsters is the prevalence of cell phones, which generally are off the radar for telephone polls. Nine out of 10 adults in North America use cell phones, and nearly 4 in 10 households use cell phone only. This subpopulation tends to be younger, better educated, higher paid, and politically independent or politically liberal—all challenges for generating accurate samples.

Sampling can be largely divided into nonprobability and probability techniques. Let's look at each type.

Nonprobability Sampling Techniques

A variety of techniques are identified as nonprobability sampling because every person or artifact in the population does not have an equal chance of being selected for the study.

These nonprobability techniques offer both advantages and disadvantages. On the plus side, nonprobability samples can be chosen simply, quickly, and inexpensively. This technique allows subjects to be selected even if they cannot be identified ahead of time. On the minus side, because subjects are chosen with no great care as to their makeup, nonprobability sampling has limited credibility because it may not accurately represent the population.

Here are five types of nonprobability samples: convenience, volunteer, purposive, snowball, and quota.

CONVENIENCE SAMPLING

A frequently used technique is **convenience sampling**, which draws subjects because they are readily available to the researcher, such as people walking through a shopping mall, students enrolled in a particular university course, or participants in so-called (but not really) random street-corner interviews by reporters. This type of sampling is haphazard but not random. It generally is an unreliable indicator of a larger population, unless that population is, for example, shoppers at a particular mall or students in a particular class.

VOLUNTEER SAMPLING

Another sampling technique, **volunteer sampling**, uses subjects who ask to be included in the research study. One example of self-selected samples is magazines or websites that invite readers to respond to a printed questionnaire; another is talk show hosts who invite their radio listeners to phone in with comments. Social media polls fit this category.

The problem with volunteer sampling is that it sometimes is interpreted as being representative when it really isn't. What should we think about the situation in which the talk show's callers overwhelmingly support a political candidate who nevertheless is soundly defeated at the polls? We should remember that such programs attract people with certain preconceptions and biases. Thus the callers are not representative of all voters, perhaps not even of all the program's listeners. They merely are those listeners who felt strongly enough about the issue and took the time to express their opinion.

PURPOSIVE SAMPLING

A technique in which research subjects are chosen because they have certain demographic characteristics is called **purposive sampling** (also known as **judgment sampling**). For example, they may be people who were patients in a particular hospital, or they may be individuals who drive a particular brand of automobile. They are chosen on purpose for a study merely because they fit that single criterion. But remember that they are not representative of the entire population of hospital patients or motorists.

SNOWBALL SAMPLING

The technique of **snowball sampling** (also called **sociosampling**) begins with a small group of individuals with a certain characteristic who are asked to identify others to participate in the research. This technique often is used for populations where member lists do not exist and whose members are hard to identify, at least by outsiders. If, for example, you want to poll immigrants living in the U.S. illegally, you would have a difficult time. One way to do this is to gain the trust of a few such persons and ask them to put you in touch with others.

QUOTA SAMPLING

A technique that attempts to be more representative of the population is **quota sampling**. This involves the selection of subjects to fit a predetermined percentage. For example, if 40 percent of a company's employees have college degrees, a quota sample would ensure that college graduates make up 40 percent of the sample. Appropriate quota categories include age, gender, ethnicity, religion, occupation, geography, and other demographic factors. But like the purposive sampling, quota sampling is still haphazard because it is not representative of the entire population under study.

The disadvantage of nonprobability sampling is that it gives no reasonable certainty that findings will be representative of the larger population. To be useful, most sampling research must be applicable to the entire population rather than to only the relatively few people sampled.

Still, nonprobability sampling is not without its good side, and these techniques may have a legitimate role for public relations and marketing research. Consider using nonprobability sampling in the following situations:

- when the purpose of the study is to gain general, nonspecific insight into a particular group;
- when a high margin of error is not a major concern;
- when the budget does not allow for more costly probability sampling;
- when the schedule does not allow for more time-consuming probability sampling.

Avoid using a nonprobability sample when you want to be able to project the findings of your research onto a larger population.

Probability Sampling Techniques

The other category of sampling techniques is probability sampling. This approach follows the guidelines of mathematical probability, generally earning higher respect among researchers.

When the research study seeks to learn the attitudes, opinions, or behaviors of a large number of people, probability sampling ensures that every element within the population has an equal and known chance of being selected. Thus, some researchers refer to probability sampling technique known as an **EPSEM sampling** (equal probability of selection method). By using probability sampling, the researcher can legitimately calculate how accurately the sampled findings reflect the entire population.

Probability sampling requires that the researcher is able to identify every **sampling unit**, which is the individual element to be analyzed. Sampling units reflect the range noted earlier for population elements. For surveys, they usually are people in the various categories needed. But sampling units also may be organizations or products. In content analysis, the sampling unit would be media artifacts such as news releases, newspapers, magazines, advertisements, and so on.

The actual listing of sampling units is called the **sampling frame**. Often these are membership rosters or other comprehensive directories.

Some random samples have been based on telephone directories, though phone books generally are bad choices for general populations because they screen out people without landline phone service and those with unlisted numbers. This is an example of **sampling bias**, when the sampling technique itself introduces an element of weakness into the process.

Sampling bias also may be related to the timing of the data gathering. Consider, for example, a restaurant that has a busy professional lunch crowd, an early-bird dinner special that caters to college students and senior citizens, a formal and relatively upscale dinner crowd, and a trendy after-theater clientele. A study that draws its sample from only the early-bird group would yield significantly different results than one drawing from each of the four customer groups.

Following are four types of probability sampling: simple random, systematic, stratified, and cluster.

SIMPLE RANDOM SAMPLING

The basic type of probability sampling is **simple random sampling**. Think of a lottery-style drawing such as pulling names from a hat. Anybody who has ever played Bingo or a state lotto knows the pure randomness of such sampling.

Researchers often use a table of random numbers to select the subjects for their study. For example, if you are researching the behavior of 5,000 college students, you might work with a list from the registrar's office and assign every student a number, 0001 through 5000. Let's say you decide to have 250 respondents. Simply generate a list of random four-digit numbers, select the first 250 that match them up to the numbered names and interview the students.

The major advantage of **random sampling** is that it produces a sampling in which everyone in the population has an equal chance of being selected. This provides a generally unbiased group of respondents, which in turn is good for a research study seeking to project findings for the entire group. Random sampling is particularly good when a population is homogeneous, with no significant divisions within it.

However, simple random sampling has two major disadvantages. First, it requires a sampling frame, which may not be available for all target populations. Second, while random sampling gives every element within the population an equal chance of being selected, it does not necessarily produce a representative sampling if significant subsets exist within the population. For example, a sample of 250 students identified randomly out of a population of 5,000 could produce no students majoring in a foreign language. That could be a limitation if the study dealt with something like international exchange programs, language requirements for graduation, or student fees for language labs.

SYSTEMATIC SAMPLING

Another common technique is **systematic sampling** (also called **systematic interval sampling**). This involves the selection of subjects spaced at equal intervals, such as every twentieth name on a membership roster.

Let's stay with the example of the survey of college students. If you do the simple math and divide 5,000 by 250, then you would select every twentieth name from your sampling frame. To make the systematic sampling truly unbiased, use a systematic sampling with a random start. This involves a random selection of the starting number (in this case, a number from 1 to 20).

Don't use systematic sampling if a particular order or recurring pattern exists within the ranking. For example, if a listing of sororities always begins with the names of officers, then a systematic sampling of every fifteenth name with a starting number of 2 would result in a sampling top-heavy with sorority vice presidents—not very random after all.

Again, the inherent disadvantage of systematic sampling is that it doesn't account for specific groups within the population (such as the language issue noted above). The next technique can address this challenge.

STRATIFIED SAMPLING

A modification of random and systematic techniques is **stratified sampling**. This technique involves a ranking of elements on a list, such as four subset lists (freshmen, sophomores, juniors, and seniors) for your study of college students. Other relevant demographic categories for research might include age, gender, income, religion, media use, academic major, and product use—and in the case of the language issue, language proficiency, and international experience.

By stratifying a sampling frame by important characteristics, the researcher is able to ensure a greater likelihood that the sample will be representative of the population. One problem with stratified sampling is that the subsets may indicate more than they appear to. For example, subsets related to residency in different parts of a city may reflect not only geography but also different ethnic, occupational or socioeconomic patterns.

Stratified sampling may be **proportionate**, with research sizes based on their proportion in the population, such as a research project with a sample of 45 percent men and 55 percent women used for a college with a student population of the same gender proportions.

Or it may be **disproportionate** (also called **weighted sampling**) if particular attention is given to underrepresented members of a population. Using the college language scenario, if the student population is 4 percent international and foreign language majors also account for 3 percent of the student population, the researcher may want to have a sample of more than those percentages to provide a stronger representation among the respondents than might be expected with a random 3 or 4 percent. The researcher may weight the samples, perhaps replicating by five the responses of both groups.

CLUSTER SAMPLING

A technique known as **cluster sampling** (also called **multistage sampling**) is used when the researcher can't readily generate a sampling frame listing the entire population but can obtain listings of particular groups within the population.

For example, if your research population was all college and university students within your state, you would have a difficult time putting together a complete sampling frame listing every student in the state from which to draw a random, systematic, or stratified sample. But using the cluster sampling technique, you first would identify several schools (either randomly or through a stratified technique based on criteria such as size or location). Then you would select individual students (randomly, systematically, or through stratified techniques) using separate sampling frames, such as enrollment lists obtained from each school identified in the first stage.

Sampling Error and Size

In textbooks dedicated to research methodologies, you can find sophisticated information about research statistics. To simplify things here, let's consider a few key terms that deal with the inevitable limitations of sampling.

The **sampling error** (sometimes called the **margin of error**) is the extent to which the sample does not perfectly correspond with the target population. Sampling error is usually reported as a percentage. For example, a finding of 62 percent with a sampling error of 3 percent indicates that the finding actually could fall between 59 percent and 65 percent. The statistic used to describe sampling error is called the **standard error** (more correctly, the

Appendixes

standard error of the mean). Since sampling is an imperfect reflection of the population, researchers always expect some potential sampling error.

What is the ideal number of subjects for a research study? There is no single answer to this question, because so much depends upon what the researcher needs to accomplish. Focus groups use only a few people, generally 5 to 12 for each session. Surveys for pretest studies may use a sample of 15 to 30 subjects. Full surveys may need hundreds or even thousands.

Two concepts about sample size often are difficult for nonresearchers to grasp. First, a bigger sample doesn't necessarily mean better results. Second, the appropriate size of the sample is not based in any way on a percentage or fraction of the population. In general, samples of 200 to 400 are commonplace.

Roger Wimmer and Joseph Dominick (2013) note that researchers often use a sample of 100 subjects for each relevant demographic group likely to have distinctive characteristics (for example, 100 men and 100 women; or 100 each of undergraduates, graduate students, and alumni). Here are commonly used guidelines for samples with a 5 percent margin of error: 217 for a population or demographic breakout group of 500; 278 for 1,000; 322 for 2,000; 357 for 5,000; 370 for 10,000; 381 for 50,000, and 384 for an infinite number. Fewer could be used if you can tolerate a higher margin of error; more if you need a lower margin.

One thing is certain: More doesn't necessarily mean better. Very good research can be based on modest sample sizes. The idea underlying sampling is to use the smallest number of research subjects that can accurately predict characteristics of the population. A small appropriate sample is better than a larger haphazard one. Remember also that the smaller the sample size, the less expensive the study will be, the less time it will take, and the easier it will be to calculate, analyze, and report.

A common way of determining sample size is first to decide what margin of error you can tolerate in your sample. If the answer is zero, you are headed for a census of the entire population rather than a sampling. But think again, because research seldom requires perfect data. Even if your client or boss wants that, there probably isn't enough money in the budget to achieve it, unless the target population is very small.

Do a simple online search for "margin of error calculator" and you'll find several easy-to-use Internet sites for your research.

Secondary Research

One of the first steps in conducting research is to conduct **secondary research**. That is research conducted to find out what information already is available through existing sources. It is distinguished from **primary research**, which generates new data collected specifically for this investigation.

Why use existing information? Because it's there. And because it is less expensive to analyze existing data than if you gather new data. Secondary research helps refine the research topic, build files of previous findings, and keep current with new developments in the field. It also provides a launch point for your own additional research.

When using secondary information, evaluate it carefully. Consider the circumstances surrounding the data, such as when and how it was gathered, for what purpose, by what researcher and with what sample. Most especially, consider the objectivity and professionalism with which it was gathered. All these factors can affect the usefulness of the information to your situation.

Even if you have to purchase the data from a commercial information service, it still may be more cost-effective than mounting your own primary research activity. Remember also that even though you are interested in applied research for a particular client, you still can learn a lot from academic research. Because it is seeking insights into topics more than solutions to specific problems, academic research can provide valuable background information.

Secondary Information Sources

Secondary information is available in many different sources, including organizational files, trade and professional associations, public and academic libraries, government records, commercial information companies, and computer-assisted or online research sources.

ORGANIZATIONAL FILES

Information in the organizational files of your employer or client can provide a wealth of material for researchers and practitioners. Many public relations offices include files of news releases, brochures, annual reports, and internal documents, as well as information files about relevant issues. Some organizations also have extensive archives with historical data and artifacts.

TRADE AND PROFESSIONAL ASSOCIATIONS

Industry groups may offer much useful information for public relations and marketing researchers. For example, the Public Relations Society of America has extensive files about various aspects of public relations that it makes available to members. The *Encyclopedia of Associations* lists thousands of professional groups that can be very helpful in obtaining information about a specific industry.

LIBRARIES

Public and academic libraries provide an accessible source of information. Information also may be available in specialized libraries such as those operated by companies, museums, industries, hospitals, professional organizations, and so on. Materials available in libraries can be categorized as a one-step resource that provides information directly (such as encyclopedias and textbooks) or as a two-step resource that directs the researcher to information in other sources (such as indexes and directories).

GOVERNMENT RECORDS

Information gathered by governmental agencies is available both in public and academic libraries and directly from the agencies themselves. Vast amounts of information are generated by the U.S. Census Bureau, which actually produces 11 different censuses (population, governments, agriculture, housing, transportation, manufacturing, mineral industries, selected construction industries, selected service industries, retail trade, and wholesale trade). Other information is available from individual federal agencies dealing with commerce, education, labor, justice, and the like.

A useful guide to information available through the federal government is the monthly *American Statistics Index* compiled by the Congressional Information Service or the annual *Statistical Abstract of the United States*. Both publications are available in most libraries, and much information is available online.

Much information is available from state, county, and local governments. Additionally, individual foreign nations have information available to varying degrees, and the United Nations provides information about countries and about various global issues.

COMMERCIAL INFORMATION SERVICES

Commercial sources of information include polling firms such as the Gallup Organization, Harris Polls, and Zogby International. Other polling centers are associated with higher education, such as the National Opinion Research Center at the University of Chicago or the Quinnipiac University Polling Institute. Meanwhile, the Roper Center for Public Opinion Research at the University of Connecticut conducts no research of its own but instead serves as an archive (updated daily) for research from more than 125 research organizations.

Trade and professional associations also are sources of syndicated data. Media-ratings companies such as Arbitron and A. C. Nielsen have useful demographic data. Stanford Research Institute pioneered the VALS (values and lifestyles) system of **psychographics**, which combines demographic and lifestyle data.

Other companies have begun offering census-based marketing services using a technique called **geodemography**, which combines census and other demographic information with zip codes, census tracts, and other data to describe the characteristics of particular neighborhoods and the people who live in them. Geodemography has proved useful for marketing and fund-raising purposes. Sources of this information include PRIZM (Potential Rating Index Zip Markets), created by the Claritas Corporation, Strategic Mapping's ClusterPLUS, Equifax's MicroVision, and ACORN (A Classification of Residential Neighborhoods) by CACI.

ONLINE RESEARCH

Information searches conducted via computer are becoming increasingly common. Online sources can provide data direct from sources such as the Census Bureau or through commercial databases. Sources for online information can be identified through directories such as the *Directory of Online, Portable and Internet Databases* published by Gale Research. The Cambridge Information Group publishes *FINDEX: The Worldwide Directory of Market Research Reports, Studies, and Surveys*, and the British Overseas Trade Board prepares *Marketsearch: International Directory of Published Market Research*. Some online resources helpful to public relations and marketing practitioners include AMI (*Advertising and Marketing Intelligence*), LexisNexis, the *Foundation Directory*, the *National Newspapers Index*, the *Wilson Index* and the *Dow Jones News/Retrieval*, as well as *Psychological Abstracts* and *Sociological Abstracts*.

With its ability to connect you directly with the home pages of many businesses, nonprofit organizations, and other organizations, the Internet is a powerful research tool. However, there is also plenty of garbage and gossip online. In judging the quality of information you find on the Internet, ask the following questions:

- Is the source or sponsor of the information indicated?
- Is the information source respected?
- Is the information source knowledgeable about the subject?
- Is the information source free from bias on the subject?
- Is the information presented in an objective manner?
- Is the information documented and verifiable?

- Is the information current?
- Is the information consistent with information from other sources?
- Does the website present links to other sources of unbiased information?

If you can answer "yes" to the above questions, it is probably safe to assume that the information is trustworthy and accurate. However, let common sense prevail. Trust your instincts, which may suggest that some information may not be fully reliable. And remember

RESEARCH WEBSITES

Research Companies

- Claritas/PRIZM—segmentationsolutions.nielsen.com
- Gallup Organization—gallup.com
- Harris Poll—theharrispoll.com
- Nielsen (TV and radio)—nielsen.com
- Opinion Research Corporation—orcinternations.com
- Pew Research Center—people-press.org
- Public Agenda—publicagenda.org
- Rasmussen Reports—rasmussenreports.com
- Survey USA—surveyusa.com
- Zogby International—zogbyanalytics.com

Media-Related Polling Organizations

- ABC News Polling Unit—abcnews.go.com
- CBS News Poll (often paired with New York Times)—cbsnews.com
- FOX News Poll—foxnews.com
- NBC News Poll—msn.com
- New York Times Poll—nytimes.com
- Los Angeles Times Poll—latimes.com
- Washington Post—washingtonpost.com

University-Related Polling Organizations

- Marist College, Marist Institute for Public Polling—maristpoll.marist.edu
- Quinnipiac University, Polling Institute—qu.edu
- Princeton University, Survey Research Center—princeton.edu
- Rutgers University, Eagleton Poll—eagletonpoll.rutgers.edu
- University of Chicago, National Opinion Research Center—norc.org
- University of Connecticut, Roper Center for Public Opinion Research—ropercenter.uconn.edu
- University of Pennsylvania, Annenburg Public Policy Center—annenburg publicpolicycenter.org

always to attribute the source of information obtained from the Internet, just as you would any other information obtained from books, periodicals, or other sources.

Interview

Whatever you need to know, someone probably already knows it. As public relations and marketing research needs move beyond the information available through secondary research, interviews become a commonly used research tool. Researchers can obtain information by phone, email, Internet chat, or voice protocol such as Skype. In-person interviews generally are the best, however. They have the added benefit of allowing the interviewer to "read" the body language of the person providing the information.

All interviews have a common purpose: to obtain information from an expert. Some are general and open-ended, allowing the interview to unfold according to the interaction of the participants and as the information rolls out. Others are more focused and in-depth, with the interviewer sticking to a prepared list of questions. The latter approach is especially good for comparative studies when you ask each interviewee more or less the same set of questions.

Interview Questions

Interviews are a good way to get a lot of information quickly and easily. Good interviews require competence and cooperation by both parties. The quality of the information they yield can be limited by several factors, including poor rapport between the interviewer and the interviewee; an interviewer who does not understand the significance of the information; or an interviewee who is unable, unwilling or uncomfortable about providing information.

Still, when interviews are done professionally, they can be excellent research tools. Here are several suggestions for effective interviewing.

1. *Plan the interview.* Identify the topic of your research, noting specifically what information you need to obtain and where you might obtain it.
2. *Decide whom to interview.* Ask yourself who is likely to have the information you need. Perhaps people within your own or your client's organization would be good information sources. Librarians, government or industry officials, regulators, and professionals in the field may have the information you need. Consider reporters or other public relations practitioners familiar with your topic of interest. Witnesses to events can be particularly helpful.
3. *Build on what you already know.* Make notes on the information already available to you about the subject. If you cannot identify specific sources of information, try to identify knowledgeable people who could refer you to these information sources.
4. *Learn as much as you can beforehand.* Prior to the actual interview, study the topic by doing secondary research.
5. *Write out questions.* Before the interview, prepare a set of questions. Make sure they cover all the areas in which you need information. Be prepared to use these questions as a guide, but remain flexible to allow the discussion to move along its own natural course.
6. *Take good notes.* For lengthy interviews, consider recording the information, so you are freer to interact with the interviewee. Make certain the interviewee knows you are recording the conversation and has no objections.

7. *Build rapport.* At the beginning of the interview, try to create a bond with the interviewee. Show an interest in this person and the topic under discussion. Note what you might have in common with the interviewee. Explain the purpose of your interview and briefly summarize the background information you have already obtained.

8. *Build on existing information.* Instead of asking vaguely, "What do you think about the location for the zoo?" show that you have done your homework by saying, for example, "The planning commission is expected to recommend moving the zoo to the waterfront redevelopment area. What do you think of such a move?"

9. *If the interviewee closes a door, look for a window.* For example, if the head coach of a professional football team refuses to tell you why the contract has not been renewed for an assistant coach, ask what qualities the coach is looking for in a replacement. That might give you some insight into the firing.

10. *Distinguish between knowledge and opinion questions.* You will need some facts. You might ask for explanations: "What happened?" "How does this work?" "What do you know about X?" Ask for examples or anecdotes to clarify abstract points: "Can you give me an example of . . . ?" "Can you tell me about a specific case in which . . . ?" But go beyond the basics and probe for additional information by asking opinion questions that take you beyond the facts. "Why did this happen?" "How is this useful?"

11. *Consider attitudinal questions.* More than simple opinion items, affective or feeling questions seek to elicit how someone responds emotionally. "How does this make you feel?" may yield a different response than "What do you think about this?"

12. *Distinguish between experience-based and hypothetical questions.* It may be important to know both what an interview subject did in a certain situation and what he or she might do in a speculative setting.

13. *Don't rush into sensitive areas.* Tread gently if you wish to guide the interview into topics dealing with touchy areas, especially if they may be illegal, immoral or otherwise antisocial, or if they could impact negatively on the interviewee. Unless the interviewee clearly wishes to discuss such topics, build up to them gradually. When you have established a level of trust, such issues will be easier to discuss. One technique is to frame a question as a hypothetical: "If someone you trust asked about paying employees off the books, what would you tell her?"

14. *Don't argue with your interviewee.* Ask for clarification of anything you don't understand, and point it out if what you are hearing seems to run counter to other information you have.

15. *Remain neutral.* Your role as an interviewer is somewhat akin to that of a psychologist. Try to be nonjudgmental about the information you receive. If the interviewee says something offensive or outrageous, don't yell, "You did *what*?" or "Are you *insane*? I can't report that!" Refrain from commenting on what your interviewee says to you. Even positive feedback can be a problem. "That's good" or "I like what you are saying" could prompt the interviewee to try to please you or to focus on certain topics and avoid others.

16. *Nudge additional information.* Use probing or follow-up questions to elicit additional information from your subject. For example, use questions such as "Who else was involved?" "How did that come about?" and "What else was happening?" Use sentences such as "Tell me more about that" and "Give me an example."

17. *Ask for a response.* You often can get valuable information by noting that a third party said something and asking the interviewee to reply. "How do you respond to Senator Smith's criticism that you are wasting taxpayer dollars?"

18. *Invite additional information.* Conclude by asking the interviewee to provide any additional information that seems relevant to the topic. Ask if there is anything important that you didn't discuss. Review your notes and verify dates, spellings and other important details. Try to arrange a time when you can contact the interviewee to clear up any questions that may arise later.

Listening Skill

Good interviewing requires good listening skills. Consider the difference between merely hearing and actually listening.

Hearing is the physiological process of sound waves making the eardrums vibrate, which in turn stimulate nerve impulses to the brain. Hearing is the result of something that happens to us.

Listening, on the other hand, is something we *choose* to do. Listening is an interpersonal process in which you not only hear words but also interpret them, attempting to obtain essentially the same meaning in the words as the sender intended.

As the questioner during an interview, focus on what is being said. Avoid distractions, whether they are worries about your recording equipment or plans for your next question. Effective listening involves understanding the speaker. Try to achieve this, to the extent that one person can appreciate the background and experiences of another. As listening involves the interpretation of messages, try to obtain information with your senses beyond hearing. For example, listen with your eyes by observing the interviewee's body language and perhaps the surroundings.

Effective listening involves more than concentration. A person may pay close attention when someone speaks in a foreign language she has studied, though she still may not be able to understand the speaker very well.

Communicators talk about active listening or strategic listening, which goes beyond simply paying attention. Raymond Zeuschner (2002) identifies four steps for active listening.

1. Get physically and mentally prepared to listen.
2. Stay involved physically and mentally with the communication.
3. Keep an open mind while listening.
4. Review and evaluate the information after it has been received.

In addition to one-on-one interviews, researchers sometimes obtain information from an **intensive interview** (also called an **in-depth interview**). This involves a lengthy and detailed interview on a particular topic that can be conducted individually with several respondents. Intensive interviewers often present a set of carefully designed parallel questions for each respondent, so that information more easily can be compared or blended together.

Use this type of research technique when it is important both to give the research subject the opportunity to provide personal opinion and insight, and also to keep the subject on a narrow course. Another benefit of intensive interviews is that they reduce variation among different interviewers, since each is working from the same set of questions. Follow-up questions probe more deeply along the prearranged line of questioning.

APPENDIX B

Applied Research: Focus Group

A particular type of small-group discussion is a **focus group** (or less formally, a **group interview**), in which a researcher guides a conversation about an issue under study and, in doing so, enables group members to stimulate each other with their comments. The result is a more interactive and complete discussion than would be possible through individual interviews. These controlled group discussions usually are recorded so the researcher can later analyze them.

Focus groups generate ideas, comments, and anecdotes. These can help you gain insight into and understanding about an issue. Focus groups are good techniques for clients who want to know "why?" "how?" and "what if?" Specifically, they are used by public relations and marketing practitioners to test concepts, copy, and campaigns. They may be used to evaluate potential logo designs and advertisements or even program and product names.

Focus groups are inappropriate if you need statistical data. If your client wants to know "how much?" or "how many?" conduct a survey instead. Remember also that focus groups are not decision-making or problem-solving sessions; don't expect the group participants to resolve the issue you are researching.

In some cases, focus groups are the main research technique used. Other times, researchers use them to complement surveys, either as preliminary tools to gain a better understanding of the issue to be surveyed, or as follow-ups to shed light on the survey finding.

Focus groups have both pros and cons. They have the advantage of being quick, inexpensive, flexible, and very practical. On the other hand, they can become expensive and more complex if the client requires videotaping and a special viewing room with one-way mirrors. Such a video setup is particularly associated with marketing research, which has been criticized as being somewhat of a show for clients who, unseen behind their mirrors, believe that they are privy to consumer revelations. Still, it can be a useful tool in the right research situation.

Focus Group Process

Here's how to create an effective focus group. Assemble a small group of people who, as closely as possible, reflect your target population or a specific segment within the population.

The group typically consists of between 8 and 12 people, though some researchers find they get better interaction from groups as small as 5.

The **moderator** (sometimes called a **facilitator**) generally introduces the topic, explains a few ground rules, and then invites comments on the topic, often with an icebreaking question. For example, in a focus group with college-bound high school students, the moderator might begin by asking each participant his name, areas of academic interest and future career plans. After the introductions, the real research begins—gently, often wandering through the discussion topic. The session generally lasts 60 to 90 minutes.

Focus groups are meant to be flexible. The moderator has an agenda of topics and themes to present to the group, though not necessarily a specific list of questions. A good moderator

WHO'S WHO IN A FOCUS GROUP

The technique of a focus group involves a team of people to make it effective. Here is an overview of the various players on the field: research leader, moderator, assistant moderator, host, recorder and technician.

The **research leader** is the person who articulates the topic, conducts appropriate secondary research, selects the participants, and—most important—develops the discussion guide with its questions and agenda topics. After the session, the research leader prepares the formal written report.

The **moderator**, who often is also the research leader, is responsible for the flow of the discussion, especially keeping it on point. The moderator will use open-ended questions such as "What do you think about . . . ?" "Tell me more about . . . ." and "Let's now talk about . . . " The moderator encourages discussion by reserved participants and tempers the involvement of those who may be overly talkative or aggressive. The moderator must be emotionally detached from the issue under study; don't ask the public relations director to moderate a group about the effectiveness of the newsletter her own staff edits.

The **assistant moderator** or **host** greets and seats participants, offers refreshments if these are available, prepares nametags if this is appropriate and escorts any latecomers to their seats. The host is a liaison between the moderator and any viewers who might be present, sometimes delivering to the moderator questions that a viewer-client might wish to have discussed.

The **recorder** takes notes throughout the discussion, producing a log of the discussion and making it easier to obtain quotes from the transcript later on. Special sheets can be prepared for recording key words and phrases of participants; who said what; significant nonverbal activity such as body language, excitement, nods, and so on; and personal observations or insights. The recorder also prepares the typed transcript that the researcher will use in preparing a final report. In some situations, the recorder may be out of view, but in most focus group settings the participants easily ignore a recorder sitting off to the side. Two recorders may be used, perhaps alternating between discussion topics, or perhaps with one recording comments and the other noting nonverbals.

The **technician** is in charge of audio- or videotaping. This person should be as unobtrusive as possible.

It is possible to combine these roles. Many setups involve two people: a research leader/moderator and an assistant moderator/recorder/technician. For very simple situations, the research leader might handle all the roles.

is agile, allowing the discussion to flow gracefully through group interaction and keeping obvious control of the discussion to a minimum. In some focus sessions, the moderator will give a high degree of direction; in others, the moderator will manage the group with so much flexibility that it does not feel manipulated.

Consider the following real-life situation: A researcher conducted a pair of focus groups for post-master's degree students (all of them midcareer educational professionals), discussing the ideal learning environment as part of a study commissioned by a university vice president for renovating classrooms.

When the findings were shared with participants in a follow-up session, several said they were pleased to have felt unrestrained in their discussions. They confided that they had expected the focus groups merely to seek justification for foregone conclusions by the university. A few apologized for wandering away from the topic.

They were even more surprised when the researcher showed them a discussion outline, which included nearly every topic they had discussed. Instead of keeping a tight rein on their interaction, the moderator had allowed the discussion to meander through various aspects of the topic so gently that they felt they were involved more in a casual conversation than a research study. The research goals were accomplished without a feeling of manipulation or control. Mission accomplished.

Conducting a Focus Group

Various researchers may have slightly different approaches for preparing and conducting a focus group. Edmunds (2000), for example, identifies several variations on the standard focus group. These include a **telefocus group** conducted via a telephone conference call, a **minifocus group** with only five or six participants, a **triad** with only three participants, an **online focus group** facilitated with software such as Skype, and a **video focus group** conducted via teleconference.

Regardless of the variations, most researchers would find their personal techniques reflected in the following 12-step outline for conducting focus groups.

1. Identify the research topic.
2. Select the moderator.
3. Select the sample.
4. Determine the number of groups needed.
5. Select the participants.
6. Select the site.
7. Arrange to record the session.
8. Prepare the discussion guide.
9. Conduct the focus group.
10. Review and analyze the information obtained from the focus group.
11. Report the data.
12. Make recommendations based on the data analysis.

RESEARCH TOPIC

Do enough secondary research to gain a good understanding of the topic. Redefine or narrow the topic if you are not convinced the information generated by the focus group will have practical significance for your organization or client, or try a different research technique.

MODERATOR

Professional focus group moderators are available through marketing research firms and some public relations agencies, as well as through some colleges and universities. Look for someone who is unbiased about the issue under study, who has good communication skills (both listening and speaking), a strong ability to probe and analyze, a good memory and an engaging personality. The moderator must also be able to quickly learn new concepts.

Usually a professional moderator can handle almost any topic, but in some sensitive areas, consider carefully who should be selected as moderator. For example, female participants in a focus group dealing with reconstructive surgery following breast cancer are likely to be more comfortable with a moderator of their own gender, as might a group of men discussing products such as condoms or erectile dysfunction.

Should you facilitate your own focus group? It can save time and money, and you probably have more knowledge of the issue than an outside moderator. But the problem of bias, even an unconscious bias, can be difficult to overcome. Internal moderators may be tempted to explain and defend rather than merely elicit comments from participants. Meanwhile, participants may be less than candid with a focus group moderator who is professionally involved with the topic under discussion.

SAMPLE

Remember that the small size of focus groups makes a truly representative sample unlikely. A focus group studying attitudes toward a proposed new chain of coffee bars might include veteran coffee drinkers, young professionals, and retired persons. Some researchers find it useful to separate participants by age, gender, or other important characteristics, especially if such homogeneity would enhance interaction within the group. To obtain a group that is as unbiased as possible, avoid populating it with friends (your own or each other's), colleagues, or people associated with the client, such as donors, employees, customers, and so on.

NUMBER OF GROUPS

Determine how many focus groups you will need to obtain an adequate range of opinions. Because focus groups are so easily swayed by intragroup dynamics, it is wise to plan for at least a couple of groups; some researchers prefer as many as five similar groups for a true reading.

PARTICIPANTS

Identify the number of participants you will need. Perhaps add a few extra to compensate for the inevitable no-shows. Some researchers recruit 20 percent more than they actually need. When the research is done for commercial marketing purposes, it is customary to pay participants a participation fee. The rate varies, but currently $25 to $50 is common, with more for doctors, lawyers, and others with professional degrees.

SITE

Focus groups sometimes are held in special research labs equipped with video cameras, built-in microphones, and a viewing room behind a one-way mirror. A cost-effective alternative is a professionally furnished conference room with a circular or rectangular table and comfortable chairs. Focus groups also can be conducted in classrooms or in a living room or around a kitchen table. Make sure the site is conveniently accessible to your participants and that it is comfortable for them.

RECORDING

Decide whether audio-only is appropriate or whether you will need full videotaping. Though marketing-oriented focus groups often are videotaped, some researchers find the practice intrusive and instead prefer audiotaping.

The primary reason for taping focus groups is to generate a written transcript of the discussion, which means videotaping probably isn't necessary. Most focus group work done for public relations purposes can be accomplished with audiotaping. An omnidirectional zone-type microphone can be set inconspicuously in the middle of a conference table, and participants will scarcely notice a recorder on a side table. It is a good idea to make a back-up recording or at least to have a microcassette recorder available.

Videotaping allows a more careful review of body language and other nonverbal cues. It also allows researchers to edit the tape for presentations to clients, which can be more powerful than transcripts or quotes presented in a written report. On the negative side, video-taping can be intrusive for the dynamics of interaction among the focus group participants.

DISCUSSION GUIDE

It is possible to combine these roles. Many setups involve two people: a research leader/moderator and an assistant moderator/recorder/technician. For very simple situations, the research leader might handle all the roles. Prepare an outline of the questions that the moderator will use in leading the focus group. Organize any participant materials such as samples, brochures, photographs, advertising sketches, slides, and the like.

CONDUCTING THE FOCUS GROUP

Note the various distinct roles for the research team conducting the session. Make sure that the research process includes appropriate training for the moderator, assistant moderator, recorder and technician. If this will be the first time this team has conducted a focus group, the research leader should arrange for a mock run-through so that every person on the research team feels confident about how the session should unfold.

ANALYSIS

Immediately after the session, review the tape. If any parts of it were not recorded properly, write down everything you can remember. Even if the tape is complete, listen to it and review your notes. Add any additional observations or insights that you didn't have time to note during the session. Transcribe the tape.

Then begin to analyze the information obtained through the focus group. Unlike many other research methodologies, focus groups do not generate usable data in the form of numbers or percentages. There simply are not enough participants in a focus group to calculate percentages. Rather, focus groups provide comments that can be more meaningful than numbers and percentages.

The comment section of the focus group report includes both direct quotes and paraphrases drawn from the discussion, often divided into subtopics. Researchers usually highlight comments and themes that were echoed by several participants. For example, the research

EXHIBIT B.1 Sample Focus Group Discussion Guide

Client: Central University Enrollment Management Office
Purpose: To guide marketing decisions for university recruitment program
Participants 8–10 high school honor students (seniors)

1. **Introduction**
   a. Identify moderator and assistant moderator.
   b. Explain purpose of focus group.
   c. Note ground rules (confidentiality, candor, mutual respect, equal participation).

2. **Perceptions of Central University**
   a. What would your family/friends say if you decided to attend Central University?
   b. What do you know about Central University? How much?
   c. From what you do know, what does Central University do well?
   d. From what you do know, what does Central University not do well?

3. **College/University Selection**
   a. What are students looking for in a college/university? (Prompt re: location, cost, courses, reputation, jobs, parties.)
   b. What do your parents ask you to consider in choosing a college?
   c. What role do guidebooks and websites play in your college/university choice?

4. **Comparisons**
   a. What colleges/universities are you seriously considering attending? Why?
   b. How does Central University compare to these colleges/universities? (Prompt re: pros, cons.)
   c. In one sentence, what is your impression of Central University?

5. **Marketing Critique**
   a. Discuss samples of logos.
   b. Discuss samples of newspaper/magazine ads.
   c. Discuss samples of billboard ads.
   d. Discuss university website.
   e. Discuss messages.

report may separate comments that enjoyed general endorsement from those that were mentioned by only one or two persons.

FOCUS GROUP REPORT

The moderator generally prepares the report to the boss or client. It should include a statement of the purpose of the research, an overview of the selection process for participants, and a copy of the discussion guide.

The body of the report generally includes both selected comments made by the participants and perhaps recommendations gleaned by the researcher.

RECOMMENDATIONS

Some focus group reports conclude with specific recommendations that the researcher feels flow from the comments and observations. The decision about including recommendations is based on the expectations and needs of the client, as well as the agreed-upon role of the researcher.

APPENDIX C

Applied Research: Survey

One of the oldest and most common research techniques is the **survey**, which involves asking standard questions of many respondents and then comparing their responses.

Surveys, also known as **polls**, have many advantages. They are appropriate for description, analysis, and prediction—three major research needs. They are among the least expensive and quickest types of research. They can be applied to both large and small groups of people. They can be very accurate and their findings are easy to compare. On the downside, surveys are subject to both the bias and limitations of the researcher, particularly through inadequate samples or poorly worded questions.

Survey Administration

Surveys can be administered in a number of ways, each with certain built-in benefits and disadvantages.

TELEPHONE SURVEY

A **telephone survey** is quick to administer but limited to easy-to-understand questions. Three factors are making it increasingly difficult to conduct phone surveys: the duplicity of telemarketing posing as research; the prevalence of people with only mobile phones; and the ubiquity of caller ID, answering machines, and voicemail.

MAIL SURVEY

Another common type, a **mail survey** (also called a **self-administered survey**), is convenient for respondents. However, the response rate generally is lower than for more expensive telephone surveys.

INTERVIEW SURVEY

An **interview survey** is most expensive of all because it is time-consuming. It also is subject to interpersonal variables not found in most other types of surveys.

GROUP-ADMINISTERED SURVEY

Meanwhile, a **group-administered survey** is easy to execute, but there often is a concern about the appropriateness of the group. An example of this is a questionnaire administered to students as part of a university class.

ONLINE SURVEY

An **online survey** offers some benefits of mail surveys. But these often are focused on a volunteer sample, which may not be the most appropriate for the research needs.

Response Rate

Response rates vary considerably with surveys. Some research is reported on the basis of a response rate of 5 percent or less. Some surveys, especially those on controversial topics, have generated much publicity, despite having response rates of only 2 or 3 percent. Such low response rates raise serious doubts about findings.

Earl Babbie (2016) considers a response rate of 50 percent as adequate, 60 percent as good and 70 percent as very good. Many professional researchers also point out that a good sample is more important than a high response rate.

You'll have to decide what an acceptable rate is for your research, realizing that higher response rates generally are more reliable.

Some researchers use payments or other incentives to increase the response rate. Sometimes the payment is merely a token amount, perhaps a dollar, even a couple of pennies ("We want your two cents' worth"). Incentives may be pens, calendars, tickets or simple items associated with the sponsor. Some surveys offer a more elaborate gift through a raffle held among participants who return the questionnaires.

Better than incentives, however, is simply to develop a questionnaire that interests potential respondents and points to some organizational decisions on topics affecting them. For example, a university conducting a survey of student interests about summer classes doesn't need to entice respondents with money or trinkets. The topic itself should lead students who might take summer classes to share their opinion and thus perhaps affect the kinds of courses, times, locations, and other aspects of the summer term.

A stamped, self-addressed return envelope sometimes accompanies written questionnaires, making it easier for the respondent to return the questionnaire. Invitations linking to an online questionnaire are popular, particularly effective when targeted to an appropriate sample.

Much depends on how carefully you select the sample and how well you groom your chosen respondents. A general rule applies: The more involved the respondents are with the sponsoring organization or the more concerned they are with the issue, the higher the response rate. Some researchers have the head of the organization send a letter to respondents asking them to complete a questionnaire they will soon receive and noting the importance of the information to the organization.

Follow-up mailings can also greatly improve the response rate. The least expensive way is to send a reminder via email. It is more effective, however, to send another copy of the questionnaire, another reason to consider an online questionnaire.

If your client or boss is serious about wanting responses, the price of second or even third mailings is money well spent. Researchers generally follow a formula that a second mailing will generate half the percentage of response as the first mailing generated, and the third mailing

ONLINE SURVEY SITES

As online administration of surveys increases, so too does the number of survey software options—more than a hundred.

Some companies offer free or low-cost basic packages with limits on the number of questions and the number of surveys that may be conducted, graduating to monthly costs for more sophisticated and larger packages. Examples of these are eSurveysPro, PollDaddy, QuestionPro, Survey Methods, SurveyMonkey, SurveyQizmo, and Zoomerang.

Other companies specialize in more professional, and thus more expensive, products such as Grapevine, Moodle, Opinio, and Qualtrics.

half that of the second. Babbie (2015) recommends two or three follow-up mailings for the best response. He cites the experience of the Survey Research Office at the University of Hawaii, which found a consistent pattern of returns. It generally obtains a 40 percent response from its initial questionnaire mailing. A second mailing two weeks later brings in another 20 percent. A third mailing yields an additional 10 percent.

Another way to ensure adequate numbers of responses is to use a larger-than-desired sample, on the notion that not everyone in the selected sample will respond. Though this adds to the mailing cost, it may be a legitimate way to obtain responses, especially if it reduces the need for follow-up mailings.

Conducting a Survey

Here is a simple step-by-step formula for conducting a survey. The format is general, though steps 6 through 8 deal specifically with mail and online surveys; modify these for surveys administered over the phone or in person. Following these general steps, we'll talk more specifically about questionnaires with a more detailed look at each.

1. Identify the topic of your research.
2. Select a sample.
3. Write the questionnaire items.
4. Print the questionnaire.
5. Test the questionnaire and, if necessary, modify it.
6. Prepare a cover letter or introduction.
7. Administer the questionnaire.
8. Monitor returns and, if necessary, send follow-up mailings.
9. Report the data.
10. Analyze the data.
11. Make recommendations.
12. Write the comprehensive report.

RESEARCH TOPIC

Identify the topic of your research. Do enough secondary research to gain a good understanding of the topic. Redefine or narrow the topic if you are not convinced the information generated by the survey will have practical significance for your organization or client. If you cannot modify it, you may need to abandon the survey and use a different research technique.

SAMPLE

Select an appropriate sample for the survey. Make sure that the sample is appropriate for your organization in terms of reliability as well as time and cost.

QUESTIONNAIRE ITEMS

Write the items to be included in the questionnaire, which is the written document that presents questions or statements to respondents. Review the wording for each item. Keep the questionnaire as brief as possible. The more concise it is, the higher response rate you can expect.

PRODUCE THE QUESTIONNAIRE

Print the questionnaire or enter the questionnaire items in an online survey program. If the questionnaire is to be administered on paper, print it with the logo of the sponsoring organization on the first page. Visually, the questionnaire should be neat and user-friendly, with clear instructions, readable type, and easy response formats. For paper questionnaires, try not to split items over pages or columns.

TEST THE QUESTIONNAIRE

Administer the questionnaire to a small group of people reflecting the characteristics of your sample. Based on what you learn in this pretest pilot, you may need to modify the questionnaire.

COVER LETTER OR INTRODUCTION

For mail and email surveys, write a cover letter that introduces the survey to respondents. Identify the sponsoring organization, explain its purpose, note the level of confidentiality, and invite their participation. Include a telephone number where respondents can contact the research office with questions or simply to verify the legitimacy of the survey.

Some researchers prefer to use an advance letter in addition to the cover letter. This can be particularly useful when the questionnaires are going to people associated with the sponsoring organization, such as an advance letter from the director of a nonprofit organization announcing an upcoming questionnaire and encouraging participation.

For face-to-face administration of a survey, write a brief paragraph explaining the purpose of the survey and noting the amount of time needed from the potential respondent.

QUESTIONNAIRE ADMINISTRATION

For mail and online surveys, send the letter with the questionnaire or link. For mail surveys, always use first-class postage. Include a return envelope with first-class postage, or use envelopes with a postage-paid business reply imprint.

MONITOR RETURNS

For mail and email surveys, monitor the returns. Keep a daily count of the number of returns received. Be prepared to send a follow-up after about 10 days. If necessary and appropriate, send a second follow-up notice after another two weeks.

DATA REPORTING

The heart of the survey report is an item-by-item account of how the respondents replied. Report the findings for every item of the questionnaire. This reporting should include both raw numbers and percentages. Some surveys use advanced statistical analysis to report the data, though applied research for professional (non-academic) clients often rests more appropriately on easy-to-understand percentages.

TIMING AND WORDING AFFECT POLL RESULTS

The timing of polls and the way questions are worded can have a big impact on how people answer them. Here is an example related by Adam Clymer (2001), a columnist with the *New York Times*, who reflected on the fact that several conflicting surveys were being reported about supposed public support for federal funding of human embryonic stem cell research.

As the issue was heating up, an NBC News/*Wall Street Journal* poll said that 69 percent of Americans favored stem-cell research. A Gallup Poll for CNN and *USA Today* reported 54 percent in favor. A poll by ABC News and Beliefnet (a religious website) found 58 percent in favor. These three news-related polls had significant differences.

Meanwhile, two less-than-disinterested parties had reported even more disparate results. A poll by the Juvenile Diabetes Foundation, which favored stem cell research, said 70 percent of Americans favor the research. But the Conference of Catholic Bishops, which opposed the research on human embryos, reported a survey that said only 24 percent of Americans approve.

Clymer noted that some of the variations in the polling could be traced to how the questions were phrased. The NBC/*Journal* poll used the phrase "potentially viable human embryos," while the bishops' poll said "the live embryos would be destroyed in their first week of development." The bishop's poll also referred to "experiments," while the others alluded to the goals of the research.

Perhaps more important, the polls were so dissimilar because many respondents were unfamiliar with the topic. Each poll asked long and involved questions. Only the Gallup Poll allowed respondents to answer that they did not know enough about the issue to have an opinion, and 57 percent chose that response category.

Clymer (2001) quoted research experts that the polls were measuring "nonattitudes." One survey expert focused on the newness and complexity of the issue: "Americans are acquiescent so they'll give you an answer. [But] the mere fact that you've got to offer a lengthy summary implies that it's too early to sort it out."

The insightful columnist concluded with a warning for all of us: "Sometimes, the pollsters are measuring phantoms, and the politicians are calling on them for support."

DATA ANALYSIS

Equally important with data reporting is the analysis of this data. Sometimes these are two different sections of a research report. Often, however, researcher comments and observations are included within the item reporting, pointing to interesting correlations with other questions.

RECOMMENDATIONS

Usually the researcher includes a set of recommendations flowing logically from the findings.

WRITTEN REPORT

Survey results usually are reported with a degree of formality because they are serious research. Generally the written report will include a statement of the purpose of the research, an outline of the methods used to obtain and contact the sample, a copy of the questionnaire, a report on the number of responses received and a notation of any limitations or weaknesses in the survey.

Questionnaire

A **questionnaire** is the tool used for survey research. It is a written document that features a series of items such as questions or statements that call for a response.

Whether the questionnaire is delivered in person, over the telephone, in print, or online, the introductory statement sets the stage. This introduction should identify the researcher and the sponsoring organization, indicate the topic, explain why the respondent was selected, guarantee confidentiality, and note the approximate time required of the respondent.

Don't *ask* the respondent to participate, because this provides an opportunity for the respondent to decline. Instead provide the preliminary information and get right to the first question.

Data in questionnaires fits into several categories. The main content items generally follow the same hierarchy as do public relations objectives: awareness (knowledge, understanding, or retention of information), acceptance (interest or attitude), and action (opinion or behavior). Additionally, demographic items deal with the respondent's background or environment, which is useful information for analyzing the data gathered.

General Tips for Questionnaire

Asking the right questions in the right way is basic to conducting a good survey. Following are some general tips for questionnaire items, whether they are framed as statements or questions.

SHORT ITEMS

Using several short, specific items is better than using fewer items that are complex and confusing.

CLEAR AND SIMPLE LANGUAGE

Make sure the words and phrases are familiar to the respondents. Avoid jargon unless the respondents share the language. Avoid all but the most commonly used abbreviations.

SPECIFIC LANGUAGE

Avoid ambiguous words and phrases. For example, the seemingly simple question "Where do you live?" could actually generate a range of responses. Is the desired answer "United States"? Or perhaps "Cleveland," "23 Oriole Road," "In an apartment building" or "With my parents." Likewise, a question such as "What do you think about the mayor's tax proposal?" is unclear. One respondent may focus on the timing, another on the amount of money to be collected, still another on the method of collection or the eventual use of the money raised.

RELEVANT QUESTIONS

Don't let your curiosity run amok. Use only those items that are relevant to the research topic.

LOGICAL ORDER

Usually this means easy to difficult. Group items that deal with a similar topic together. Demographic items about the respondents should be kept together. Print and online surveys often place these items at the end, while telephone surveys may lead with these because they are easy for respondents to answer.

POSITIVE CONSTRUCTIONS

Arrange sentences to avoid negative phrasing. For example, ask "Do you participate in group exercise or fitness programs?" instead of the more negative "Do you avoid group exercise or fitness programs?" Especially avoid double negatives, such as the awkward "Do you disagree that lack of exercise is unhealthful?" (Presuming you have an opinion on the issue, try figuring out how to respond to that question.)

CLEAR MEANINGS

Every respondent must understand and interpret the questionnaire items exactly the same way. For example, "Have you ever considered having an affair?" begs the question of what "consider" means in this context. And what is an "affair"? Instead, try asking: "While you were married, did you ever engage in sexual activity with another person other than your spouse?"

DOUBLE-BARRELED ITEMS

Avoid items that include two different thoughts. Here's an example of such a double-barreled question: "Do you think Portland is a friendly and progressive community?" It's impossible for respondents to answer if they think Portland is friendly but not very progressive. The relationship between the two modifiers is unclear; they don't belong in the same question.

Writing Impartially

In general, researchers want questionnaires to be unbiased. Following are a few pointers in writing impartial questions.

NEUTRAL WORDING

Avoid leading items that indicate to the respondent what the researcher apparently sees as the "correct" answer. Example: "Do you agree with most Americans that more violent criminals should receive the death penalty?" Telling the respondent that most Americans agree with this statement is biasing the response.

SIGNALING BIAS

Make sure the wording doesn't suggest what you as the researcher might think is the appropriate response. Here's an example: "Do you prefer reading good literature or just popular novels?" *Good* literature? *Just* novels? No doubt about the preferred answer here.

LOADED LANGUAGE

Take care with socially or politically charged words. Kenneth Rasinski (1989) analyzed the wording in several national surveys. He found, for example, that 63 percent of respondents said too little money was being spent on "assistance to the poor," but only 23 percent said too little was being spent on "welfare." The difference is all in the wording.

VARYING MEANINGS

Realize that words have different meanings or open themselves to several connotations. This may be especially true with commonly used social and political terms. It's the old issue of connotation and denotation. Example: "Are you pro-abortion?" Respondents may consider themselves pro-choice but not pro-abortion, or they might be disinclined to answer such a complex question with a simple "yes" or "no." Whenever respondents feel a need to explain their interpretation of a questionnaire item, it is poorly worded.

PRESTIGE BIAS

Don't make associations with respected authorities or well-known figures. Example: "Do you agree with the mayor that property taxes are too high?" The same is true with disrespected figures. If the mayor has just been indicted for embezzlement and tax fraud, respondents may hedge on stating any agreement with a disgraced public official. Or they may be reluctant to agree with a leader of a rival political party (or disagree with one from their own party) in a highly partisan environment.

LEADING QUESTIONS

Use these only in special situations. Use them if you are dealing with a potentially embarrassing or controversial issue or if you feel a need to "give permission" to respondents to be truthful. For example: "Recently, several political leaders have admitted to adultery . . . "

Information Items

Items dealing with the respondent's level of information may offer a particular challenge to questionnaire writers.

KEY TERMS

Set the stage for respondents. If necessary, include a brief definition of key terms.

INTENDED RESPONDENTS

Make sure the topic is within their competence and comprehension. For example, don't ask a sample of people without a strong scientific background if fusion or fission is a better process for nuclear energy. Any response would be little more than an uninformed guess.

TESTING RESPONDENTS' KNOWLEDGE

Carefully explain when you are testing the knowledge of respondents. Example: "A main purpose of this survey is to find out how much residents know about the bridge proposal. The following six items present multiple-choice items about the proposal. Circle the answers you think are correct."

Opinion Items

Some special guidelines apply to questionnaire items that seek to elicit the respondent's opinion or attitude.

OPINION VERSUS FACT

Don't ask for opinions on questions that are matters of fact. For example, don't ask "Do boys get higher grades in mathematics than girls do?" because that question doesn't call for an opinion. You can easily research the facts on math grades. But a legitimate opinion question might be "Why do you think boys get higher grades in mathematics than girls do?" especially if your questionnaire is being answered by teachers, parents, psychologists, or others whose opinions might be relevant.

INFORMATION-BASED OPINION

Be careful about asking for an opinion related to information that the respondent may not have. For example, if a national magazine has just ranked Austin as one of the top 10 progressive cities in the U.S., don't ask, "Is Austin a progressive city?" Such wording is unclear if you are asking about the respondent's awareness of the ranking or simply a personal opinion. Instead ask, "Do you agree with a magazine ranking that Austin is progressive?"

SPECULATION

Avoid speculative or hypothetical questions. Example: "Would you prefer to move to a colony under the sea or in outer space?" An exception to this is if the item deals with a potential activity of the sponsoring organization. Example: "Given the opportunity, would you consider purchasing a vacuum cleaner that also served as an air purifier?"

SUBJECTIVE JUDGMENT

Avoid terms with interpretations that can vary from person to person. Example: "Is the current tax structure reasonable?" Various respondents may interpret the word "reasonable" differently. Instead ask more specifically, "Is the current tax structure affordable?" (Or "equitable" or whatever else you really want to know.)

Action Items

Items dealing with actions and behaviors, whether current or past, also can be particularly difficult for the questionnaire writer.

RELEVANT BEHAVIOR

If you want to know about what respondents do, ask questions that are relevant and useful. Example: "Do you ever shop at GreenGrocers?" Ever?

REASONABLY RESPONSIVE

Make sure the questions can realistically be answered. Avoid asking for highly detailed information. Example: "In the last six months, how many hours of television have you watched?" Who could know that? Instead, use a time frame easier for the respondent, such as, "On an average weekday, how many hours of television do you usually watch?" or, "On an average weekend, how many hours of television do you usually watch?" Then you do the math.

RELEVANT EXPERIENCE

Make sure the topic is within the respondent's relevant experience. Asking women about how frequently they practice self-examination techniques for testicular cancer is the sign of a poorly created questionnaire. Either limit the question to male respondents or replace it with a question dealing with the frequency of self-examination techniques in general, such as for two easily detectable cancers (breast cancer or testicular cancer). Most computer-based questionnaires can be set to hide contingency questions and use them only when they are relevant.

PRESUMPTIVE RESPONSE

Don't word the questions so that they presume a particular answer. This is especially important with sensitive issues. Example: "How often do you smoke marijuana?" This wording presumes that one smokes it at least sometimes. This might be better handled with a primary and a contingency question, "Do you smoke marijuana?" and then the contingency, "If yes, how often?"

INTRUSIVE ITEMS

Be careful with intrusive or potentially embarrassing questions, especially those that deal with legal, social, or moral transgressions. "Are you always truthful on your income tax returns?" may result in a less-than-truthful answer, in part because the respondent may be concerned about the confidentiality of the study, and in part because the respondent may simply be unwilling to confess a crime, even to himself.

Demographic Items

Asking for age, educational level, and other types of demographic information also requires careful attention by the questionnaire writer.

RANGE OF RESPONSES

Rather than ask a respondent's age or income, group such sensitive questions into ranges. Example: "Which of the following best describes your individual (not household) income last year? Less than $30,000; $30,001 to $80,000; more than $80,000."

TAILORED RESPONSES

Customize response categories to your target population. For example, fit educational levels to your research purpose, and consider asking for the highest grade or degree completed. Example: "How much education have you completed? Less than high school, high school, some college but no degree, associate's degree, bachelor's degree, graduate degree." If this was directed to academic professionals, the response choices might be "Bachelor's degree, academic master's degree, professional master's degree (MFA, MSW), academic doctorate (PhD, EdD), professional doctorate (JD, MD, DDS), postdoctoral study."

RACE AND ETHNICITY

Take care with items related to racial or ethnic background. When asking for such information, make sure all options are included. Also consider the wording of the question. The Census Bureau asks people to indicate the race they consider themselves to be, a subtle difference over the strictly matter-of-fact question, "What is your race?" Rather than a narrow black/white/other configuration, try to provide options for people to indicate their specific racial/ethnic identity. For example, though Arab and Hispanic are not racial categories, many members of those backgrounds choose "other" rather than "white." Similarly, people of Caribbean background often do not identify immediately with "black." Understand who may be asked to respond to the questionnaire and adjust the demographic options to reflect this. Also, because a growing number of people identify themselves as biracial or multiracial, consider allowing respondents to indicate more than one category, which will yield more information than a single "mixed" category.

RELIGION

For most surveys, demographic items dealing with religion would seem inappropriate. However, there are some research topics in which they might be particularly useful: practice of spirituality, politics involving the Middle East, or opinions on morality-related themes such as abortion, immigration, LGBT issues, even climate change. When dealing with this, carefully

OPEN-ENDED VERSUS CLOSED-ENDED ITEMS

Here are some guidelines for when to use open-ended questions and when closed-ended questions are more appropriate. Remember that both can be used within the same questionnaire.

Use closed-ended items if you:

- prefer that respondents use predetermined choice;
- want to make it easier for respondents by using predetermined choices;
- can anticipate the range of response choices;
- want to directly compare and correlate responses.

Use open-ended items if you:

- prefer that respondents answer in their own words;
- want to make it easier for respondents by answering in their own words;
- don't know the range of response choices;
- do not need to correlate responses from various respondents;
- are willing to consider dissimilar comments from respondents.

define the terms. Are you asking if respondents are members of a particular religious organization? If they were raised in a faith tradition? If they are practicing, active, and/or observant? If they have a cultural connection with a religious group. Some surveys try to shed more light on the issue by linking religious affiliation or practice with sociopolitical positions such as liberal, moderate, or conservative.

RESEARCH NEEDS

Tailor the demographic information to the research needs. For example, for surveys conducted near the northern U.S. border, demographic items might include the name of the specific province for someone who indicates a Canadian background. Likewise, in the Southwest, items might include the names of specific Central or Latin American countries or perhaps Mexican states, if that information is relevant to the researcher.

Types of Responses

Questionnaire design must give attention to the response categories for the various items. First of all, make the options visually simple and consistent. Use checkmarks, circles, boxes or other simple marks. One of the first considerations is the type of response categories. **Open-ended items** allow respondents to answer in their own words; **closed-ended items** provide for check-offs to predetermined response categories.

Researchers have devised several different types of items that can be used for responses in questionnaires. Some of the more common types are multiple-choice items, checklist items, forced-choice items and rating scales. A questionnaire may include more than one type of item, though it's generally a good idea to group similar items.

Multiple Choice

Questions or statements with a limited number of responses are called **multiple-choice items**. These allow respondents to choose from a predetermined set of choices. For example: "Indicate your favorite major television news network: ABC, CBS, CNN, FOX, MSNBC, NBC." Often multiple-choice items include an "other" category. Note that the responses are arranged alphabetically to eliminate bias.

Response categories for choice items must be both comprehensive and mutually exclusive.

- **Comprehensive**. A comprehensive set of responses ensures that each response category provides a full range of potential responses so there is an appropriate response category for every respondent.
- **Mutually Exclusive**. These ensure that there is only one possible response for each respondent.

For example, on a demographic question asking the income of respondents, the response categories might be "$20,000 or less," "$20,000 to $60,000," "$60,000 to $100,000," and "$100,000 or more." The categories are comprehensive, covering all the bases. But they are not mutually exclusive because they overlap—both the second and third choices are appropriate for someone earning $60,000 a year. A better way to write response categories might be "less than $20,000"; "$20,000 to $59,999"; "$60,000 to $99,999"; and "$100,000 or more."

Checklist

Sometimes it is more effective to allow respondents to indicate more than one response through a **checklist**. Example: "What kind of country music do you listen to most often? Check all that apply: bro country, classic country, new country, alternative country, bluegrass, Christian country, classic country, cowboy, cowpunk, country folk, country rock, country pop, gothabilly, hillbilly, honky-tonk, nugrass, outlaw country, progressive country, psychobilly, rockabilly, soul country, urban cowboy, western swing."

Forced Choice

Another type of response category is **forced-choice items** that feature two or more statements, with directions for respondents to select the one that most closely reflects their opinion. Example: "Of the following statements, select the one that comes closer to your own belief: Voting is a privilege and thus should be optional. Voting is a responsibility and thus should be required. Voting is a useless activity with no real consequences." In creating forced-choice items, try to make the statements different enough from each other so the respondent is actually indicating a useful preference.

Rating Scale

Some items have the advantage of focusing on the intensity of the respondent's feelings rather than eliciting a simple yes or no response. These are **rating scales**, in which respondents are asked to rate the degree of their feeling or certainty about an item. Some rating scales are bipolar instruments because they move in both directions from a neutral center point to either positive or negative points. Others are unipolar instruments that range from low to high points.

The popular **Likert scale** (pronounced LICK-ert) is a bipolar scale that asks the intensity of respondents' agreement to a statement along a range of negative and positive response categories, such as strongly disagree, disagree, agree, and strongly agree. The wording for the Likert scale can be modified, such as by asking approval, belief, interest, and so forth instead of agreement.

In some versions, the Likert scale includes a central or neutral option ("neither agree nor disagree"), and sometimes a "no opinion" or "neutral" item. For some issues, researchers use the neutral option; for others they would rather eliminate the midpoint and force the respondent to indicate a preference one way or the other.

When using rating scales, define response options carefully. Rating scales sometimes offer choices such as excellent, very good, average, fair, poor, and so on. A problem with such scales is that too many response categories can leave respondents confused about the differences among the categories—for example, between average and fair or between excellent and very good.

To avoid this ambiguity, some rating scales are presented numerically, as in the following example: "Indicate your preference for various flavors of ice cream (1 being dislike, 5 being like):

Vanilla 1–2–3–4–5
Chocolate 1–2–3–4–5
Strawberry 1–2–3–4–5" (and so on).

HOW AM I DOING?

The customer satisfaction survey is commonplace in helping managers understand how their customers feel about their products and services. Such surveys are used by manufacturers and retailers as well as by nonprofit organizations such as hospitals, colleges, cultural organizations, and service agencies. They also are commonly used to measure employee satisfaction.

With any survey, especially one that seeks to gauge the level of satisfaction by customers, readers, employees and other key publics, it is important to ask the right question. Most **customer satisfaction surveys** ask variations on "How am I doing?" Here are examples of some different scales that address this question. Note that some have mid-point or neutral responses, others force a response in one direction or another, and some begin with a zero point and move in only one direction.

- *Acceptability*: not at all acceptable, slightly acceptable, moderately acceptable, very acceptable, completely acceptable.
- *Appropriateness*: absolutely inappropriate, inappropriate, slightly inappropriate, slightly appropriate, appropriate, absolutely appropriate.
- *Awareness*: not at all aware, slightly aware, moderately aware, very aware, extremely aware.
- *Belief*: not at all what I believe, somewhat what I believe, moderately what I believe, very much what I believe, completely what I believe.
- *Expectation*: much less than expected, less than expected, as much as expected, more than expected, much more than expected.
- *Performance*: poor, fair, good, excellent, superior.
- *Requirement Frequency*: never meets requirements, rarely meets requirements, occasionally meets requirements, usually meets requirements, always meets requirements.
- *Requirement*: did not meet requirements, nearly met requirements, met requirements, exceeded requirements.
- *Satisfaction*: very dissatisfied, dissatisfied, neither satisfied nor dissatisfied, satisfied, very satisfied.

Professional researcher Howard Waddell observes that each of these scales share a weakness: they potentially point to problems but don't indicate to management how to act on these indications of customer satisfaction. Waddell, president of Decision Resource of Miami, suggests a better approach focusing on corrective action (1995).

An **improvement scale** presumes there generally is room for better performance, and it makes this the central point of the research. This scale can be used to guide management decisions about a variety of product and service factors. Using this approach, researchers ask customers to indicate how much improvement, if any, they feel is needed by the company. Only three response choices are offered: no improvement needed, some improvement needed, and considerable improvement needed.

This improvement scale offers several advantages over the other types noted above. It is unambiguous and thus simple for customers to understand. It evokes candor by not inviting charitable responses. And it fits all kinds of product and service attributes. Coupled with an opportunity for respondents to offer comments, it can elicit suggestions for improvement.

When rating scales are used numerically, it is logical to arrange them so that a low or negative response translates into low numbers. Example: "Rate the following on a scale of 1 to 5 (1 being low priority, 5 being high priority)." Reversing this, to rank low priority items with a five and high priority items with a one, would be confusing to respondents.

Rating scales can even be presented visually, such as with smiley face caricatures for children's surveys, ranging from very sad through very happy. Writing about questionnaires in a series of books on survey research, Arlene Fink (2002a) recommends five types of response options for rating scales (presented here in lowest-to-highest logical order).

- *Endorsement*: definitely false, probably false, don't know, probably true, definitely true.
- *Frequency*: never, almost never, sometimes, fairly often, very often, always.
- *Comparison*: much less than others, somewhat less than others, about the same as others, somewhat more than others, much more than others.
- *Influence*: no problem, very small problem, small problem, moderate problem, big problem.
- *Intensity*: none, very mild, mild, moderate, severe.

Note that the first four items are bipolar, with negative and positive ends of the scale. The last two examples are unipolar, moving from a zero point.

The **semantic differential scale** asks respondents to select a point on a continuum between two opposing positions. The scale generally uses opposing adjectives, usually with a five-point or seven-point scale. Example: "What are your perceptions about professional football? Interesting/uninteresting. Enjoyable/unenjoyable." This scale also can be presented numerically. For example:

Uninteresting	1	2	3	4	5	Interesting
Unenjoyable	1	2	3	4	5	Enjoyable
Uninteresting	1	2	3	4	5	Interesting
Unenjoyable	1	2	3	4	5	Enjoyable

APPENDIX D

Applied Research: Content Analysis

Some problems are inherent in focus groups and surveys. When you directly ask people their opinion, their response may not be genuine. It may be shaped by the fact that you asked in the first place, or it may be colored by their desire to give you what they think is an acceptable answer.

For example, ask an acquaintance if he likes you and the answer may be "Yes, of course." But is he saying that just because you asked, because he'd be embarrassed to answer "not really," or because he doesn't want to hurt your feelings?

Instead of asking outright, you could observe what he says and does without being asked. List all the significant interactions the two of you have had in the last several weeks—conversations, shared experiences, and so on. Then evaluate each activity as being either unfriendly or friendly (or perhaps more elaborately: very unfriendly, unfriendly, neutral, friendly, very friendly—essentially a 5-point rating scale).

If the friendly activities far outweigh the unfriendly ones, you can conclude that he likes you. If the negative interactions predominate, he doesn't act as though he likes you, no matter what he might say.

That's the idea behind the research methodology known as **content analysis**. It is the objective, systematic, and quantitative investigation of something that has been written down (or at least something that can be written down for research purposes). Content analysis implements the maxim that actions speak louder than words.

As a formal research methodology, content analysis has been used for years to study mass media. This research technique can be used to shed light on the messages of communication, assess the image of a group or organization, and make comparisons between media and reality.

Using Content Analysis

Researchers involved in public relations and marketing communication have found that content analysis can be useful in several different ways. Here are a couple of examples of how content analysis can be used to study various practical issues that could be important to your organization or client.

Let's say your client, an insurance agency, has a new policy covering sports cars. You want to reach your public—sports car drivers—on radio, using both public relations and advertising techniques. As you plan your campaign, you determine that you need to identify the most popular radio stations among people who drive sports cars. You could survey the drivers, but that might be unwieldy because obtaining a sampling frame would be difficult. You could ask the radio stations about audience demographics, but they probably don't know the kind of cars their listeners drive.

Instead, you might take a different tack. Ask mechanics at several maintenance and repair shops specializing in sports cars to keep a list of which stations the radios are tuned to when the cars are brought in. That's content analysis.

Here's another example. Perhaps you are researching consumer issues for your company, a garment manufacturer. Specifically, you want to know what people think about the new line of lightweight, high-insulating winter coats. You could conduct a survey or a focus group if you had the time. Instead, you might check the letters and phone calls received by the consumer affairs department and compare these with customer comments about other products. This, too, is an example of content analysis.

Using with Other Methodologies

Content analysis doesn't have to stand alone. It can be used to complement other types of research. Researchers in public relations and marketing communication sometimes compare the results of their content analysis with the information they are able to obtain from surveys or focus groups.

For instance, if you are evaluating the effectiveness of your internal newsletter as part of an overall program review of your employee relations program, you might begin with a content analysis of the last three years' issues to identify topics that have been covered. Then you could conduct a focus group or readership survey to find out what topics your employees want to read about. Finally, you might compare the results of the content analysis with the results of your questioning, and from that comparison create a more popular employee publication.

Let's look at one final example. Let's say you are a media relations manager for a large public utility. You know that many of your news releases have been ignored by the newspapers and broadcast media in your service area. At a "meet the editors" forum sponsored by the local PRSA chapter, you hear from editors and news directors that they prefer stories with a strong local flavor. You realize you should evaluate the content of your releases as they focus on information of apparent significance to each locality within your service area. So you decide to do a content analysis of your releases of the last two years.

Specifically, you evaluate four aspects of each release: the extent of the local significance of the issue or activity (1) as you know it to be, (2) as evident in the body of the release, (3) as identified in the lead sentence or paragraph, and (4) as specifically featured in the headline or title on the release. By combining the information you received from the media gatekeepers and your own analysis of local content, you can gain some helpful insight for both topics and effective writing techniques for your future releases.

Pros and Cons of Content Analysis

Content analysis has several advantages, including a low investment of time and money. It can be done by a person working alone with little equipment beyond a simple calculator or a computer with standard software. Content analysis is unobtrusive research done "after the fact," without any effect on the people or issues being studied. It also has the advantage of allowing you to look at the facts without being caught up by the heat of the moment, free of the passion and enthusiasm that often surrounds surveys or focus groups.

Content analysis also has the advantage of allowing you to go back in time to examine past messages. It can be used to compare an organization with industry norms or with wider trends. Finally, it helps the researcher separate the routine from the unusual.

Among the disadvantages of content analysis are its limitation to recorded (or recordable) information and its susceptibility to coder influence and bias. This is in part because content analysis deals with what researchers call **manifest content**, which is the obvious and apparent meanings and interpretations that, unfortunately, are not always equally obvious and apparent to everyone. Also, while content analysis can point to coincidences and concurrences, it doesn't establish cause-and-effect relationships.

Another aspect of content analysis—not necessarily a negative, but certainly a concern is the notion of **intercoder reliability**. This is the degree to which several coders agree on how to label the content being studied. The more consistency among various coders, the stronger the reliability of the study. Researchers foster high intercoder reliability by training coders to follow common rubrics when they are reviewing content in a media artifact.

Conducting a Content Analysis

Following is a step-by-step explanation of how to conduct a research study via content analysis.

1. Select an appropriate topic.
2. Identify the population, and select a sample.
3. Identify the units of analysis for the study.
4. Develop the mechanics for the study.
5. Report the data.
6. Analyze the data.
7. Make recommendations.

Let's look at each step in depth. The following explanations are framed around a running example of how a health-care company might use content analysis.

APPROPRIATE TOPIC

Begin by selecting a topic appropriate to this type of research. Content analysis has many applications for all the social sciences.

For academic research, it has been used in studies dealing with media content such as sex and violence. As a tool of applied research in public relations and marketing communication, content analysis can be used by planners who want to know what people are saying about their organizations, or how what they are saying coincides with the way they are acting.

Consider the following possibilities for public relations/marketing applications of content analysis:

- News coverage (topics, balance, frequency)
- Media artifacts (video news releases, radio actualities, blog posts, tweets, photographs)

- Organizational reputation among various media or particular public
- Letters to the editor (opinions, topics)
- Customer comments (emails, letters, telephone calls)
- Competitors (claims, offerings, positioning, advertising themes)
- Trends in graphic design or publishing techniques
- Effectiveness of various persuasive appeals
- Public issues affecting an organization
- Preferences of various media (story type, political bias, editorial coverage)

Topics appropriate for your organization are those that deal with the content of artifacts that have already been written (reports, releases, publications, scripts, etc.) or that can be put into writing for research purposes (conversations, speeches, etc.). The text may originate within your organization, or it may be rooted in the communication or activity of one of your significant publics. Ask yourself how accessible the texts will be for you. Also consider how the information will be useful to your organization, especially because content analysis can help you learn facts about the content but not reasons behind those facts.

POPULATION AND SAMPLE

Select an appropriate population to study. This may be people such as all your employees or just the employees with less than two years' experience on the job. Or the population may center on artifacts such as news releases, company publications, advertisements, and the like. After you identify the population, decide on a census or a representative sample.

UNIT OF ANALYSIS

Next, determine the appropriate unit of analysis for this research, that is, the specific media artifacts that you will review. Carefully define the terms related to what you want to study. For purposes of public relations and marketing communication, the unit of analysis may relate to various aspects of communication. Many research studies would involve several of the following approaches mixed together to provide a general view of the whole issue.

- Subject: sorted by themes and topics
- Communication element: headline, lead, news article, photo caption, letter to the editor, advertising illustration, and the like
- Incoming communication: sorted by various channels, such as newspapers, magazines, television, radio, direct mail, telephone calls, letters, coupons, and email
- Outgoing communication: sorted by various tactics such as newsletter, email, brochure, advertising spot, and web page
- Source of communication: sorted broadly by various publics or more narrowly by specific individuals or organizations or by subdivisions such as department, work site, and so on
- Destination: sorted broadly or narrowly; the same as for the source of communication (above)
- Results: sorted by outcome, effect, and consequence

Develop categories for coding your tallies of these units of analysis. These categories must meet the same two major criteria as response categories for surveys—that is, they need to be comprehensive (by including all the possible responses) and mutually exclusive (by not duplicating other possible responses).

Incoming telephone calls, for example, may be categorized as being positive, negative, neutral, or other. Too many responses in the "other" category indicate faulty categories.

Newspaper articles may be studied to count the number of references to your organization, by both name and implication, and then to assess these references as to how positive they are or how accurately they portray your organization and its products or services. It might also record the message source and the paragraph number in which the source was first identified.

MECHANICS OF STUDY

Develop the mechanics of the study; that is, the way in which you will implement it. This is a simple follow-up step to the previous one. Create a standardized coding form that allows you to record the numbers in each category. Usually this involves simple forms with space for tally marks (卌).

You may have other people work on this project with you. Using multiple coders is a good idea to minimize **coder bias**, which is the potential bias or differing judgments of individual coders doing content analysis. This will increase intercoder reliability.

With multiple coders comes the need to train these coders so they are applying consistent and uniform standards. Essentially this means writing out and explaining all your definitions so each coder approaches the item in the same way. Because some parts of the category selection may be subjective, there could be some differences here. For example, a positive reference to one person may be neutral to another. That's one of the shortcomings of content analysis. One way around this is to have three coders do each item and then record the majority response.

At this stage you also should pretest the coding instrument before actually doing the research. Go through a dozen or so items and see if the coding instrument works well. If not, go back and rethink your categories. When all of these tasks are completed, you are ready to actually measure the information and record it for later analysis.

DATA REPORTING

Indicate the data found through the content analysis. For every unit of analysis, report the findings as both raw numbers and the percentages. Keep the data reporting simple so you can more easily draw insight from it.

As you might guess, researchers have developed some sophisticated statistical techniques for use with content analysis. If you want intricate statistics, contact a professional researcher or refer to a statistics textbook. But you don't have to deal heavily with statistics. Many excellent content analyses rely on simple percentages.

DATA ANALYSIS

Once the data is reported, the researcher analyzes it. This analysis may generate formal reports to your client organization or employer, or it simply may remain as scribbling on your notepad for your own perusal and pondering.

The stage of data analysis calls for the researcher to use knowledge of the issue and the client organization as the basis for making informed and insightful observations. It calls for the ability to make connections among disjointed bits of data. As with the data reporting stage, analysis also calls for clear and simple presentation of data.

Note, for example, what was said above that percentages are more useful than raw numbers. You don't know much, for example, if you are told that 25 employees have made money-saving suggestions via the company suggestion box. Is that 25 out of 50 workers? Out of 5,000? But if you are told that those 25 employees represent one-third of the night shift, and that 75 percent of them work in the computer department, you have learned something interesting and potentially very useful about the quality of ideas originating with nighttime computer workers.

RECOMMENDATIONS

Many reports conclude with recommendations based on the findings and insights. Some researchers provide these at the request of the client. In other situations, clients may prefer to have the data, from which to draw their own conclusions and recommendations.

If you choose to prepare a formal report of the content analysis, include an explanation of the reason for your research, information about your sample and a copy of the coding form. Report the results in raw numbers, percentages, or—usually—both. Discuss generalities and insights that you glean from those findings.

EXHIBIT D.1 Example of Content Analysis

Here is an example of a content analysis plan for a hypothetical organization, MetroHealth, a large statewide health maintenance organization.

Appropriate Topic

You are public education manager for MetroHealth. One of your job responsibilities is to promote a series of patient workshops on topics such as weight loss, nutrition, exercise, and general fitness. You want to get an accurate picture of how the largest daily newspapers in the state deal with these issues. Your purpose for gaining this information is to arm yourself for an eventual public-education campaign that will look to the newspapers for support.

Before asking for this support, you decide that it will be helpful to know something about the newspapers' current and recent coverage of these topics.

Population and Sample

You identify the six largest newspapers in your state as the population for your study. Let's say you decide to limit your study to three areas: (1) news sections, including local, national, and international news, (2) relevant specialized sections such as lifestyle and science/health, and (3) online versions of the publication. Because it would be impractical to study every newspaper for every day over the last few years, you select a sample of publications.

This sample includes each of the six newspapers for the following varied schedule throughout the last 12 months; one daily edition each month according to this schedule: Monday, first week of January; Tuesday, second week of February; Wednesday, third week of March; Thursday, fourth week of April; Friday, first week of May; Saturday, second week of June; Monday, third week of July; Tuesday, fourth week of August; and so on. It also includes seven to nine Sunday editions, every sixth week following the beginning week, indicated by a throw of a dice.

Unit of Analysis

You will search each sampled newspaper, and count the number of articles and news briefs that deal with one of the topics of your interest (weight loss, nutrition, exercise, general fitness, and so on), as you have defined them. These numbers will be compared to the total number of articles and briefs in the publication. You then analyze each mention of these topics according to the following criteria.

- *Type of Article*: Code each published story as an article or a news brief. Define these terms clearly. For example, you might define the difference in terms of length—a brief is up to three paragraphs and an article is longer, or a brief is fewer than 150 words while an article is longer.
- *Attitude*: Each article related to fitness will be coded as "positive," "negative," "mixed/both positive and negative," or "neutral/neither positive nor neutral," depending on how its tone relates to MetroHealth's message of encouraging fitness.
- *Accuracy*: Each article will be coded as "very accurate," "moderately accurate," or "inaccurate," based on how well it presents information that is currently accepted by medical and fitness professionals. Or you might count the number of factual inaccuracies and unwarranted conclusions within the brief or article.
- *Prominence*: Each article will be rated for a "prominent position" (any location on Page One of a section, or top-of-page placement

on an inside page) or "nonprominent position" (placement elsewhere on a page).

- *Demographics*: Each article will be coded as to its evident appeal based on gender (men, women, or both) and age (young, middle, older readers, or all ages). This may be determined through criteria such as placement in a particular section (such as women's page, youth tab, etc.) or by the people shown in accompanying photographs or cited as examples within the article.

Mechanics of Study

You will work with a team of four coders. After training to ensure that coders are consistent in how they code the units of analysis, you will do a pilot test. This may lead you to rework the definitions for the coding.

Once you are confident that your coders are on track to generate consistent data, you will conduct the content analysis of each sample newspapers. You will have three coders review each unit of analysis and average their responses.

Data Reporting

Let's say that in coding your categories you arrive at the following results for three different newspapers, A, B, and C:

News Articles	Total Articles	Fitness Topic #	Fitness Topic %
Newspaper A	1,000	60	6
Newspaper B	940	54	5.7
Newspaper C	1,060	25	2.4

News Briefs	Total Briefs	Fitness Topic #	Fitness Topic %
Newspaper A	400	40	10
Newspaper B	640	50	7.8
Newspaper C	800	70	8.8

Articles and News Briefs	Positive %	Negative %
Newspaper A	80	20
Newspaper B	82	18
Newspaper C	53	47

Articles and News Briefs	Accurate %	Inaccurate %
Newspaper A	95	5
Newspaper B	88	12
Newspaper C	62	38

(Additional data would follow re: prominence and demographics.)

Data Analysis

The research shows that Newspapers A and B provide similar amounts of coverage to fitness-related information, both as news stories and as news briefs.

Newspaper C offers significantly less coverage to fitness information in the form of news articles, though it devotes slightly more space than the other newspapers do to fitness-related news briefs. Newspaper C also has a higher number of negative articles and briefs, as this relates to MetroHealth's conclusion about how the articles are likely to promote an appreciation for fitness. This newspaper also has a higher percentage of inaccurate articles and briefs, based on MetroHealth's understanding of up-to-date reliable information.

(Other findings would reflect additional data.)

Recommendations

Based on the data from this content analysis, we will consider the following recommendations.

1. *Review of Public Relations Materials*. Based on what was learned about Newspaper C, we will scrutinize our public relations procedures. This will include a review of news releases, website and social media postings, and other media materials to make sure that they clearly articulate the benefits for readers of the newspaper.

2. *Contact with Newspaper C*. We will contact the editorial staff of Newspaper C and arrange a meeting with editors of the various news, health, and lifestyle sections. The purpose of such a meeting will be to learn what the reporters and/or editors might find useful in any information emanating from your organization. At this meeting, we will noncritically present our findings that indicate the

newspaper's relative disinterest in fitness-related articles. Admitting that we are advocates for fitness information, we will point to surveys indicating a growing interest within the general population (and thus newspaper readers), offering possible ways in which MetroHealth could assist the newspaper in increasing its coverage of this topic. If we learn, for example, that the editors want a stronger local emphasis, we could highlight strong local angles to our general fitness information. Or if we learn that the newspaper would prefer to develop its own stories, we can offer MetroHealth experts as interview subjects.

3. *Contact with Newspapers A and B.* We also will contact Newspapers A and B and share our findings concerning their performance. This will be done to encourage their continued attention to fitness matters. For future research, we might conduct a similar study in one or two years to note any changes in the media trends.

APPENDIX E

Media Engagement

Media engagement deals with the various philosophical and practical ways an organization interacts with the news media.

A foundational concept for all effective engagements between an organization and the various news media is **transparency**, which involves proactive communication that presents an observable activity by an organization, which in turn helps publics understand the organization and support its actions.

Inexperienced people—whether organizational leaders or neophyte practitioners—who find themselves in a public relations situation sometimes are tempted to avoid engagements with the media. Or worse, they try to manipulate information that misleads the publics.

On the other hand, experienced professionals know that the best approach in all situations is communication that is as transparent as possible, respecting the occasional need to withhold certain information for reasons of confidentiality and legality. But such instances should be rare and of short duration.

Procedurally, media engagement sometimes is called **media training** or **interview training**. These are tools and instructional situations to help people develop skills in working with the media.

However, the term "engagement" suggests much more than merely practicing certain techniques. Media engagement involves a mindset through which an organization effectively and energetically interacts with the media as part of its overall efforts toward advancing its mission and promoting its bottom-line goals.

Effective media engagement is really about messaging. Some people talk about the elevator pitch, a brief (and usually rehearsed) explanation of the benefit of a product or the key element of a concept. Sometimes this can be as simple as asking a corporate CEO: "Tell me, Sir, what exactly does your company do?" The result often is either numbing detail or marketing hype, neither of which is very useful when interacting with reporters.

What follows in this appendix is an approach drawn from various actual media-interview training programs and crisis-communication consultations developed by the author, who has provided such training in both corporate and nonprofit settings. The principles themselves are straightforward and are drawn from standard approaches toward effective engagement with the media.

This appendix deals first with reputation and media relations and then with credibility.

The first aspect of effective media engagement calls for a focus on reputation. This is presented as a discussion-starter with the participation of both top- and mid-level management of organizations as well as their senior support staff. It is important, for example, not only to help a program director or corporate vice president be effective in communicating on behalf of the organization but for administrative assistance to help create an environment that gives priority to opportunities presented through the media.

This section seeks to provide insight into the role of the news media in molding the organization's reputation with various important constituent groups. Its aim is to help organizational leaders better understand both the benefits that a healthy relationship with the news media offers and the role these leaders can play in enhancing that relationship.

The second section is presented as a hands-on coaching of individuals likely to find themselves in front of cameras and microphones. It flows from three professional observations.

1. The media will report on an organization in good times and bad, with or without organizational involvement. The organization can impact such reporting positively or negatively.
2. By becoming more competent in communicating through the news media, spokespersons can extend the organization's message and foster public support for its mission.
3. Every interview offers the organization an opportunity to increase its credibility and enhance its reputation.

Some aspects of effective media engagement call for a **proactive strategy** with the organization taking the initiative to communicate with its publics, often through journalists. Other aspects may be a **reactive strategy** with the organization responding to inquiries by journalists on behalf of the organization's publics.

Reputation and Media Relations

The dictionary defines **reputation** as "honor, credit, recognition, or esteem given to a person or organization." Reputation lies at the heart of strategic communication. Effective engagement of news media requires a solid appreciation of the role that reputation plays in the life of an organization.

Structurally, this section presents a series of professional observations, followed by points for discussion. It should be used in a group setting, with a public relations professional guiding organizational executives through an active discussion of how reputation affects their organization and how they might impact that process.

DISCUSSION POINTS
- How important is your organization's reputation to your job?
- Is your job unaffected by your organization's reputation?

Reputation and Performance

Reputation involves perception. The reputation of an organization is the estimation by which it is commonly held, whether favorable or unfavorable. Reputation is based both on what people know about us and what they feel about us based on that knowledge.

Reputation should reflect performance. Ideally, what people think of the organization's performance will mirror its actual performance. More often, however, there is a distortion between our performance (what we do and how well we do it) and their perception (what people know and think about what we do).

Reputation as a Strategic Tool

A good reputation has practical value. In general, a positive reputation can give an organization a competitive advantage that others cannot easily match. What is your organization's reputation? Answer this carefully, based not on wishful thinking but on an honest assessment of how others perceive you.

A good reputation is an insurance policy. Especially in times of trouble, your organization's good reputation can maintain credibility and goodwill. These, in turn, give supporters reasons to continue their trust, defer criticism, balance the picture, and generally maintain their support.

> **DISCUSSION POINTS**
> • Does your organization have the ability to shape its reputation?
> • To what extent is this possible?

Reputation Management

Every organization can enhance its reputation. Reputation is manageable. It can be molded and developed by the way we actively and strategically interact with important groups of stakeholders. Reputation management involves research, strategic planning, deliberate implementation of that plan, and continual monitoring and evaluation.

Every organization can also jeopardize its reputation. Reputation will suffer if, through misjudgment or neglect, an organization fails to remain credible or responsive with important groups or if it does not communicate accurate and positive information.

> **DISCUSSION POINT**
> • What offices or entities within your organization should try to influence the organization's reputation?

Reputation and News Media

The news media help shape an organization's reputation. Newspapers, radio, and television offer opportunities for organizations to proactively present messages that strengthen their reputation and promote their mission. Social media networks provide even more personal platforms for organizations to communicate with their publics. The media also provide opportunities to respond to inquiries from journalists and bloggers, who can help present positive messages and minimize negative impressions.

> **DISCUSSION POINT**
> • How important do you think the news media are in developing your organization's reputation?

Organizations risk their good reputation by not responding to media inquiries. The media *will* report on your organization when they choose to. The issue is *to what extent* the organization will effectively and positively impact such reporting. If your voice is absent from the media, you give up the opportunity to talk with your publics, allowing others to interpret you to the community.

Reputation as a Participant Activity

DISCUSSION POINT
• How have recent events that have been reported in the news media affected your organization's reputation?

Your reputation is everybody's business. Public relations and similar offices may manage publicity and promotional activities that affect the organization's reputation. But ultimately, everyone associated with your organization can help or hurt its reputation. Consciously or not, an organization's reputation is impacted by everything said and done by management, employees, volunteers, even customers.

Your reputation is fragile. Like an old-growth forest ravaged by fire, a reputation can be destroyed in minutes. All associated with an organization must be continuously aware that what they do and say affects the reputation. Poor delivery of services and negative publicity easily lead to dissatisfied and angry consumers, the ultimate threat to reputation.

Headlines and Bottom Lines

DISCUSSION POINTS
Consider each of these headlines from three different perspectives.

1. As the parent of a high school student considering attending this university, how does the headline affect your thoughts about the university? What is the likelihood that you and your child will want to be associated with this institution?

2. As a student or faculty member here, how does the headline affect your pride in being associated with this university? Do you have any concerns about what others think of you and your colleagues?

3. As director of public relations for the university, what alternative headline would you have preferred in this situation? What could your institution have done to warrant your preferred headline?

News coverage can affect many different publics of an organization, often in unanticipated ways. This exercise uses the examples of a nonprofit organization (a university), but the principles can apply to any other nonprofit, as well as a corporation, membership organization, or government agency. Consider the impact of each of the following actual headlines.

•   "Low, Delayed Graduation Rates at Local University Cited in Report"
•   "Coed Nabbed for Prostitution; Blames Snafu in Financial-Aid Office"
•   "Local Student Charged with Arson, Attempted Murder for Firebombing Car of Fellow Student"
•   "Local University Drops in Rankings of Top Schools"
•   "Local Professor Accused of Anti-Gay Harassment"
•   "Dorm Fire Leaves 300 Homeless After Explosion by Student Cooking Drugs"
•   "Police Seek Cooperation in Nabbing Suspect in Dorm Break-ins"

Consider also the impact of some positive headlines from the same university and how students, parents, and faculty might view these.

•   "University Police Buy Christmas Presents for Kids in Apartment Dorm After Dad Steals Gifts in Bitter Custody Battle"
•   "PR Students Provide Real-World Assistance to 23 Community Organizations"
•   "University Sees Enrollment Skyrocket; Rents Dorm Space from Two Private Colleges"
•   "Department Earns Mass Comm Accreditation; First for Any Public University in State"
•   "University Reports Job Placement for Recent Grads Higher Than National Average"

Media Relations

Media relations is the subset of public relations and marketing communication dealing with an organization's ongoing involvement with news media for the purpose of enhancing its reputation and promoting its mission.

Media Relations . . . from the Media Side

Reporters want news. News is information that is timely, accurate and of significance to a particular audience. It may show subjects in a positive or negative light. In gathering news, reporters try to talk with many news sources: insiders, experts, and other people involved in the issue. They expect access to public institutions such as the university. They try to report all sides without taking sides.

> **DISCUSSION POINTS**
> • What does your organization expect from reporters?
> • What does your organization want from reporters?

Reporters are skeptical. They see it as their mission to probe beneath the surface, to not take things at face value and to seek out hidden agendas. They consider nothing to be none of their business. And if they catch someone doing something wrong and expose that, they see this as the rendering of public service.

Not all reporters are alike. Each medium of public communication has its own style of operating, and reporters have differing practices for interviewing:

- Newspaper reporters often work over the telephone. Their interviews may be either brief or in-depth. They may ask questions on side issues as well as the main topic, and they may quote extensively.
- Television reporters prefer to interview their news sources on camera. A reporter may talk with a news source on camera for five minutes or more and then use only one or two sentences during a newscast. Sometimes TV reporters do brief telephone interviews to get a sound bite.
- Television reporters are interested in photogenic situations that are colorful, active, and interesting.
- Bloggers or Internet journalists often are independent agents who value their autonomy and often are advocates of a particular social or partisan perspective.

Media Relations . . . from the Organization Side

Your organization wants fair treatment. As the subject of a news report, it wants, needs and deserves reporting that is fair and professional. This means expecting reporters to treat the organization with objectivity and neutrality. The organization also wants to be recognized as a contributing and respected member of its industry or profession and of its community.

> **DISCUSSION POINT**
> • How can your organization use the news media to its advantage?

Your organization benefits from a healthy relationship with the media. With fair and accurate reporting, your organization benefits by having a strong and respected voice in its industry or profession. Healthy media relations enable the organization to be recognized as a source of commentary about matters of interest to the community. It also gives the organization the opportunity to balance criticism. In short, healthy media relations can allow the organization to maximize good news and minimize bad news.

Appendixes

Media Relations . . . from Both Sides

DISCUSSION POINTS
• In what ways has your organization communicated with the media, both proactively and reactively?
• What sources of information have the media used in reporting on your organization?

Your organization communicates in two ways: proactively and reactively. Proactively, the organization provides story ideas and offers of interviews to reporters. It also disseminates news releases and tweets, and it presents speeches and news conferences. Reactively, the organization responds to reporters' questions and allegations.

Reporters have many news sources. In gathering information for their stories, reporters contact many different organizations and individuals. They check the validity of their information and question the motivations of their sources. Here are some of the ways they might obtain information:

- Official sources such as the public relations office and organizational spokespersons, through information vehicles such as news releases and interviews.
- Publications such as an employee newsletter, member magazine, mailings, and other semipublic publications, as well as information at your organization's website.
- Public records such as documents and statements involving regulatory agencies, as well as police and legal records.
- Unofficial sources such as employees, customers, and other persons willing to speak about (but not necessarily on behalf of) your organization. This includes people who may be misinformed or disgruntled.
- Buzz and the word on the street, rumor and scuttlebutt, hearsay and gossip.

Reputational Bumps and Bruises

Which puts the bigger dent in your organization's reputation? Consider the following:

- Inadequacy or arrogance
- Bad judgment or dishonesty
- Negative reports or poor performance
- Unpopular decisions or unexplained actions
- Being scrutinized or being found unresponsive

Points for Consideration

TRUE OR FALSE?

I shouldn't waste time talking with reporters who are already biased against my organization.

Consider this: If you want people to support you, first they have to understand you. Much of their impression about your organization comes through the media. Your time spent with reporters is not doing the reporter a favor; rather it is setting up a means of communication with your publics.

TRUE OR FALSE?

Reporters don't understand what I'm doing and they always get it wrong, so I should avoid them.

TWELVE PRINCIPLES OF EFFECTIVE MEDIA RELATIONS

1. A relationship is both inevitable and necessary between your organization and the media. The behavior of the organization will determine if this relationship is good or bad.
2. The organization should publicly speak with one voice in any situation, by designating and preparing a single spokesperson authorized to speak in the name of the organization.
3. The person closest to the situation should be the designated spokesperson, or at least should be in close communication with the spokesperson.
4. "No comment" is never an option. Every bona fide question should be answered.
5. The organization should look upon reporters as allies rather than as intruders or enemies.
6. The organization should consider itself accountable to its various publics: employees, volunteers, customers, donors, supporters, and the community. Further, it should view the news media as one of the vehicles available for communicating with these constituencies.
7. The organization should not expect to control the media's agenda or their assessment of what is newsworthy. But you can help add issues to that agenda.
8. Public relations professionals should always be "in the loop" in all newsworthy situations, especially those with negative potential.
9. Reporters should be accommodated with professional assistance such as parking permits and a functioning media room.
10. The organization should expect that it occasionally will "take a hit" in the media. The response should be to accept this, try to understand it and get over it as quickly as possible. Lingering hostility to reporters never serves the organization's interests.
11. Media skepticism and scrutiny can be more bearable when the organization interacts with reporters in a timely manner and with openness, accuracy, and candor.
12. Media coverage is considerably more credible than either advertising or the use of internal media such as brochures, publications, and websites. Effective use of the news media gives the organization a believable voice in the community.

Consider this: You can direct the tone of an interview. Invest whatever time it takes to educate reporters about what you are doing. Prepare for the interview, perhaps by providing a glossary and background sheet if necessary. Explain the significance of your actions and opinions.

TRUE OR FALSE?

If I don't talk to reporters, I won't get into trouble.

Consider this: If you don't talk to reporters, people won't know how honest, competent, and effective you are.

TRUE OR FALSE?

It's a real compliment to hear that our organization is one of the best-kept secrets in our area or within our industry or profession.

Consider this: Being called a best-kept secret is an insult to everyone associated with your organization. It means that neither you nor your colleagues are doing enough to share information about your organization's achievements and boast about its successes.

Credibility

Effective media engagement involves an applied set of skills and practices to help organizational spokespeople. This section offers tips and techniques on various aspects of interviewing, from the standpoint of the person being interviewed.

Interview Setting

There are at least 10 different ways that an organizational spokesperson or executive might be interviewed by the news media.

1. *In-person news interview.* This is the most common interview situation you are likely to face. A single reporter for print, radio, or television is interviewing you. The interview may take place in your office, in a studio, or in a remote location. Unless it is an ambush situation, you will have time to prepare for the news interview. Maintain eye contact and respond directly to the reporter. Ignore microphones and/or camera operators.

2. *Straight-to-the-camera interview.* A single television reporter who is doubling as the camera operator is interviewing you. Look directly at the camera, but visualize an individual member of your audience and speak to him.

3. *Telephone interview.* A reporter is interviewing you over the telephone. This is most commonly used by print and online reporters, who will either record your voice or simply take notes. It is used sometimes but infrequently by television reporters. Maintain a professional demeanor and posture even though you cannot be seen. Maintain a professional control of your voice. Handle this interview as carefully as you would a face-to-face encounter. Always presume you are being taped throughout the entire telephone interview.

4. *News conference interview.* News conferences have three parts: You present a brief statement or announcement; you then distribute prepared printed materials to a gathering of reporters from various media; this is followed by a question–answer session with these reporters. News conferences generally are videotaped; on rare occasions, they may be broadcast live.

5. *Panel interview or debate.* You are one of two or more interviewees being questioned by reporters from various media. Panels and debates often are held before an audience and many are broadcast live. They often involve questions from a panel of interviewers and/or from members of the audience. Before the interview, investigate the position of your co-panelists, and then frame your message with their positions in mind. Be prepared to fight nicely for a fair share of time to present your message. Avoid shouting matches, but do not hesitate to differentiate your position from that of others.

6. *Call-in radio interview.* This is a popular format for live radio. You are interviewed in a radio studio by a host, and at some point during the interview you will respond to phone-in callers. Listen carefully to questions and respond as personally as possible to each individual caller.

7. *Call-in television interview.* This is similar to the call-in format for live radio, except that you are being televised as you interact with the on-camera host and the phone-in callers. Thus your facial expressions and body language are important considerations.

8. *Videoconference interview.* This is a live format similar to a call-in interview, except that your audience can see you on a video monitor. Usually the audience gathers at remote sites, where they can telephone questions to you. As with a simple call-in interview, listen carefully to questions and respond in a personal tone.

9. *Email interview.* Sometimes distance prevents one of the above real-time interview formats, so reporters occasionally resort to providing a set of questions via email. This gives the news source time to carefully weigh the message, but make sure you don't become long-winded in responding to such questions.

10. *Video chat software.* Person-to-person interviews through software such as Skype can link organizational news sources with journalists. Such a format calls for the spokesperson to remain professional and to presume an on-camera presence for both questions and responses in their entirety.

If You Are Asked for an Interview

1. Make sure you understand the topic to be discussed.
2. Decide if you can do the interview. Do you have the basic information? Being available to reporters is more important than having every last detail on an issue, which would be more than you'd need anyhow. Being unavailable breeds suspicion among the organization's publics. It also ignores an opportunity to present your message, which will be accepted by somebody else, often a person with lesser qualifications to speak authoritatively.
3. Are you the appropriate person to speak on behalf of your organization? If not, try to suggest another news source. Don't put reporters off without good cause. But if you must decline the interview opportunity, tell them why.
4. Ask the reporter to identify the source of the information on which the interview will be based. If it is information with which you are unfamiliar, try to get a copy of the source material; usually the reporter will provide you with a copy or direct you to the source.
5. Ask about the nature, length, and eventual use of the interview. Find out if the interview will be taped or live.

Dress for Interview Success

Organizational spokespeople appearing on television need to dress appropriately. Generally this means wearing conservative professional attire that you would normally wear at work, avoiding fashion fads that might distract some viewers and detract from your effectiveness as a credible representative of your organization. Here are some reminders.

1. Keep the look simple. Avoid busy patterns such as narrow stripes, small checks, plaids, herringbone and other clothing with tight repeating patterns. These can cause video pictures to flutter.
2. Avoid large and flashy items of jewelry, especially necklaces, earrings, and tiepins. Avoid clothing with large, shiny buttons.
3. Seek moderation. Avoid extremes of black and white. Instead prefer medium and dark colors in place of black. Prefer light pastels in place of white. Ideal professional

and television-friendly attire is a conservatively cut suit of gray or navy, with a shirt or blouse of pale blue, pink, or beige, and a scarf or tie of a strong but not garish accent color.

4. Use medium colors. People with darker skin tones may use medium or light colors. If you have light or medium skin tones, prefer medium and dark colors. In any case, avoid strong or loud colors, especially bright reds, oranges, and purples except as accents (such as ties and scarves).

5. If the interview is to be conducted while you are seated, wear clothing that does not constrict your neck. Avoid clothing that bulks up around your chest and shoulders.

6. Just before the interview, make a final check for gaping buttons and mussed hair. Men should check for socks that are too short.

7. Don't worry about eyeglasses. If you normally wear glasses, wear them for the interview. To not wear them will probably make you uncomfortable, and you will look unnatural to others. Let camera operators and lighting people worry about eliminating any glare. Avoid wearing lenses that darken under bright lights.

8. Consider wearing distinctive professional clothing if you are to be interviewed in your work setting. A lab coat, for example, would be very appropriate for an on-site interview. Generally it is not a good idea to wear such clothing in a studio setting.

Interview Posture

Your posture will go a long way in helping you present a positive image during televised interviews. Here are a few reminders.

1. Sit with your back straight, knees together, both feet on the floor. Avoid twitching or moving your legs and feet.

2. Don't slouch into a comfortable position; on television, casual looks sloppy. Even in a print interview, your posture will spill over into your voice.

3. If you feel a need to reposition yourself, lean in toward the interviewer and/or camera. Never lean away.

4. Place your hands in your lap, on the arms of the chair, or on the table if you are seated at one.

5. Use your hands naturally, but avoid nervous movements. Don't drum your fingers.

6. Maintain eye contact with the interviewer.

Interview Planning

Here is a threefold approach to interview planning. In the first part, consider the following points of planning, which relate specifically to the organization.

1. *What*: State the issue clearly and concisely.
2. *Significance*: Note the importance of the issue and its potential impact on your organization.
3. *Who*: List individuals and groups involved.
4. *When*: Indicate any relevant time factors (future focus is preferred).
5. *Where*: Note any relevant locations or boundaries (try to focus on local situations).

6. *Communication history*: Consider the nature and extent of your previous communication on this issue.
7. *Credibility*: Consider how people perceive your organization's credibility on this issue.
8. *Organizational expectations*: Note what your organization wants from you regarding this situation.
9. *Motivation*: Summarize your motivation for being involved in this issue.

In the second part of your planning, consider the following points as they relate to the media audience and the organization's publics.

10. *Key publics*: List those groups most notably affected on this issue.
11. *Understanding the publics*: Note the wants, interests, needs, and expectations of the key publics you have identified.
12. *Benefits*: Summarize the benefits and advantages your organization offers each key public.
13. *Media interest*: Indicate why the media are (or could become) interested in this issue.
14. *Media expectations*: Note if the media want to or might interview you.
15. *Opponents*: List any groups or individuals who are likely to oppose you on this issue.
16. *Balance*: Indicate the nature and credibility of opposing perspectives.

Finally, conclude the planning by considering objectives and strategy.

17. *Awareness objectives*: Indicate the impact you hope to make about the publics' knowledge and understanding on this issue.
18. *Acceptance objectives*: Indicate the impact you hope to make about the publics' interest and attitudes on this issue.
19. *Action objectives*: Indicate the impact you hope to make about the publics' opinions and behavior around this issue.
20. *Tone of message*: Note appeals to authority, fear, or guilt, or appeals for confidence, responsibility, calm, caution, and the like.
21. *Visuals*: Try to incorporate visual elements and interesting locations into your interview.
22. *Power words*: Identify any particularly powerful and memorable words or phrases that you might incorporate into your message.

Preparing for an Interview

1. Never try to "play it by ear."
2. Know yourself. Rely on your own expertise.
3. Know your audience.
4. Know what you want to say.
5. Know what impact you hope to make.
6. Anticipate questions a reporter may ask.
7. Think of an anecdote or example that can enhance your key message.
8. Rehearse out loud.
9. Practice with a tape recorder.

10. Immediately before the interview, take a few moments to focus yourself.
11. Relax, but not too much. A little anxiety can give you an energetic edge.

Be-Attitudes for Interview Success

1. *Be accurate.* There is almost nothing worse than making an error of fact.
2. *Be honest.* The one thing worse than an error of fact is a deliberate error of fact. Remember that the long-term credibility of both you and your organization is at stake.
3. *Be brief.* Use short words and simple sentences. Think in terms of two or three sentences to present your message, or just enough time for a quick answer to a few questions. For most questions, you should be able to give one-sentence responses. Practice these.
4. *Be interesting.* Use colorful and pithy language. Give brief anecdotes and easy-to-understand analogies so your audience can grasp your message.
5. *Be enthusiastic.* Even be passionate. State your case and give your opinions with excitement. Show you care about the issue.
6. *Be clear.* Avoid technical or scientific language that you might use around your colleagues. Remember that your audience probably doesn't understand your professional jargon.
7. *Be positive.* Instead of dwelling on accusations, tell your side of the story.

Interview Attitude

1. *Remain confident.* You are the expert the reporter has sought out. You represent your client or organization in public.
2. *Remember your conviction.* Let your audience know that you believe in your message. If you appear to be unsure or unconvinced, you aren't likely to persuade others. Let your enthusiasm show on your face and in your speech.
3. *Try to be credible.* Persuasive message sources are those who are perceived as beingboth expert and sincere, in touch with their audiences, and friendly and/or worthy of respect.
4. *Display your motivation.* The impression you leave with the audience will linger far after it has forgotten your words.
5. *Speak clearly.* Speak distinctly in your normal voice. If you are a fast talker, try to slow down a bit.
6. *Smile naturally.* Don't overdo this, especially if smiling doesn't come naturally. There are fine lines distinguishing a smile, a smirk, and a pretentious display of teeth.
7. *Keep your cool.* Don't shout; don't swear; don't attack the questioner (even if you are asked a truly malicious question). Never show anger, no matter how angry you may feel.
8. *Don't be intimidated.* You are not on trial, nor are you obliged to "air dirty laundry" in public. In an interview, you have rights. One of them is the right to discontinue a line of questioning if the reporter persists in trying to draw you where you don't wish to go.
9. *Remember that an interview has mutual benefits.* It can help both you and the reporter. You are helping the reporter do a job; the reporter is helping you communicate with your audience toward achieving your strategic objectives.

Communicating during an Interview

1. *Note your common bond with the audience.* Show that you share their concerns and clearly explain the direct benefit for them.
2. *Propose convenient action* (if any) for the audience.
3. *Develop a sound bite*—a meaningful, succinct, and easy-to-recall message that you want your audiences to remember. Aim for 15–20 seconds.
4. *Stick to your key message.* Don't ramble, and don't allow yourself to be sidetracked. The more you talk, the more opportunity you give a reporter to use peripheral comments instead of central information. State the key message in different ways; keep coming back to the main topic.
5. *Don't comment if you can't.* "Off the record" is not an option. If you cannot answer a question publicly, don't try to answer at all. Don't put reporters in the awkward position of knowing information they cannot use.
6. *Give a reason for not commenting.* If for good reason you cannot comment, tell the reporter (and the audience) that reason. Don't say "No comment" if you mean "I don't know" or "I can't/won't talk about it now." Realize that most people interpret "No comment" as meaning that you have something to hide.
7. *Don't address the reporter by name.* Instead, speak to the audience. Imagine one individual (not the reporter) who is representative of your target public and address your comments to that person.
8. *Let the reporter worry about dead air.* Take a few seconds to think before you respond to the question. Rephrase the question while you're thinking of the best answer.
9. *Don't guess.* Say "I don't know" or "I'll find out for you." (But try not to appear ill prepared or uninformed.)
10. *Signal your message.* "The most important thing about this is . . . " or "Three things stand out here. One . . . Two . . . And finally . . . " But be crisp in your responses.
11. *Humanize statistics.* Say "two out of three people" rather than "65% of the population." Avoid using numbers as much as possible.
12. *Pay attention to body language and facial expressions.* Your nonverbal actions should complement your words.
13. *Don't be drawn into criticism.* Don't comment about what your opponent may do or say unless you strategically decide to do so.
14. *Don't volunteer information* unless it is something you really want to say.
15. *Have notes with you as you wish.* Glance at them if necessary, but don't read from them.

Problem Interviews

Most reporters you deal with will be professional. Expect this, and treat all reporters as professionals unless they prove otherwise. A professional, competent interviewer (1) has prepared and is familiar with the issue, (2) has a no-nonsense approach, and (3) is friendly without being overly familiar. Appreciate this, and be professional in return.

Occasionally you may get a dud. If you encounter problem interviews, consider the following responses.

- A *misinterpreter* draws an unwarranted conclusion.
  Your response: Refute the incorrect statement.

- A *paraphraser* puts words into your mouth.
  Your response: Restate your response slowly, word for word.

- A *mind reader* presumes to know your thoughts before you speak.
  Your response: Dispute the unwarranted insinuation and state your message clearly.

- An *unprepared reporter* did not adequately get ready for this interview.
  Your response: Suggest questions to support your message. This opportunity in disguise lets you give basic information. Keep things simple.

- A *bully* attacks with charges and allegations.
  Your response: Refute the charges as you are able, but do not repeat the accusations.

- A *machine-gunner* strafes you with nonstop questions.
  Your response: Pick the one you prefer to answer and ignore the others.

- An *interrupter* cuts you off before you have finished responding.
  Your response: Make sure you are being concise. If so, ignore the interruption and continue your previous response. Stick to your own agenda.

- An *extremist* frames the issue only in polarized terms.
  Your response: Point out the middle ground, and speak from that perspective.

- A *speculator* asks you why so-and-so said such-and-such.
  Your response: Avoid the temptation to guess. Don't try to explain the motives of another.

- A *false starter* frames questions on a false foundation.
  Your response: Clarify and restate the question. Then answer it.

- A *flatterer* puts you off guard with compliments.
  Your response: Repeat your main message. Don't be lulled into a false sense of security. A tough question may be lurking.

- A *trapper* tries to pit your personal opinion against organizational policy.
  Your response: Say what you can, but never speak "off the record." A news interview probably is not the best place for loyal dissent.

After an Interview

1. Review your performance. Note any misstatements and assess what you learned from the interview.
2. Take note of how the reporter handles the information, but don't second-guess the writing or reporting. You may have told the story differently, but that wasn't your role.
3. Put it behind you. You can't take back anything you said, and it's unlikely you can add anything useful to what you did say.
4. If you truly have been misquoted and your organization misrepresented in a way that will have long-term negative consequences, speak first with your media relations person. If there is consensus to seek redress, contact the reporter and, if necessary, the editor or news director. Ask for a follow-up interview; settle for a clarification (but don't expect most audiences to read it).

APPENDIX F

Crisis Communication

Effective media engagement reaches its advanced stage with concepts for organizational administrators who need to communicate in times of crisis. The objectives of this section on crisis communication are directed toward public relations managers and other organizational executives:

- To increase awareness and understanding of both the complexity of crises as well as the opportunities for successfully managing them
- To increase confidence that they can effectively manage crisis situations
- To enhance their crises management skills

Review Step 1 in the strategic planning process for additional information on **crisis management**.

This advanced stage of effective media engagement involves both strategy and technique, building on two assertions: (1) Crises are inevitable within any organization, and (2) it is within an organization's ability to influence the direction of media coverage and thus the consequences of a crisis. Indeed, organizations may be able to turn a crisis into an opportunity to enhance its credibility and its position vis-à-vis its many publics.

As noted in Step 1 of this book, a crisis is a turning point, the intersection of danger and opportunity.

It is important to understand that a crisis is not merely a problem for an organization. Problems are irritating annoyances commonplace in business and organizational life. Problems often focus on individuals and on interpersonal conflict. They can be serious—such as the need to fire an employee or to report low sales to stockholders—but they seldom rise to the level of a crisis, based on the following definition.

A crisis is a major, unfortunate, sudden, and unpredicted event. Every crisis has the following elements:

- Interference with and disruption of an organization's activity
- Likely negative impact on the organization's "bottom line" or mission
- Threat to the reputation and other assets of the organization
- Demand for quick reaction by the organization

- Likely escalation in intensity
- Occurrence in a public environment, so that even private businesses and nonprofit organizations cannot shield themselves from the expectation of being held accountable
- Invitation for outside scrutiny that can jeopardize the organization's reputation

If handled properly, a crisis presents the organization with an opportunity to create a positive impression on its key publics. A crisis shows what an organization is made of, by making visible under adverse situations its values, priorities, and commitments. A crisis brings out the best or the worst.

Types of Crises

The Institute for Crisis Management (ICM—crisisexperts.com) defines **crisis** as "a significant business disruption that stimulates extensive news media coverage. The resulting public scrutiny will affect the organization's normal operations and also could have a political, legal, financial, and governmental impact on its business."

Not surprisingly, not all crises are the same. Here are ten types of crises, four of them in the violent category, six nonviolent.

1. *Disaster (violent)*: A natural occurrence such as earthquake, flood, and the like with immediate damage. Example: A school is destroyed by fire.
2. *Disaster (nonviolent)*: A natural occurrence such as drought, epidemic, and the like with delayed damage. Example: Farm crops are destroyed by an early frost.
3. *Accident (violent)*: A mishap involving people or equipment, with immediate injury or death. Example: A company truck runs into and kills a pedestrian.
4. *Accident (nonviolent)*: A mishap involving people or equipment, with immediate damage. Example: A company truck hits and damages parked cars.
5. *Crime (violent)*: A personal action violating legal standards causing injury or death. Example: A pharmaceutical employee sabotages medicine with a poisonous substance.
6. *Crime (nonviolent)*: A personal action violating legal standards, with delayed damage. Example: A company executive steals money from an employee pension fund.
7. *Ethical/moral failing (nonviolent)*: A personal action violating ethical or moral standards (though not necessarily legal standards), with either immediate or delayed damage. Example: A public relations practitioner intentionally lies in a news release about a company product, with resulting media coverage of the lie.
8. *Mismanagement (nonviolent)*: Bad professional judgment impacting an organization's operations and procedures, with either immediate or delayed damage. Example: Financial planner loses hundreds of thousands of dollars for clients because of poor investments.
9. *Opposition (violent)*: Negative impact by external or internal forces, including product tampering, terrorism, and the like, with immediate damage. Example: Rioting at a political rally injures spectators.
10. *Opposition (nonviolent)*: Negative impact by external or internal forces, including competition, protests, recalls, lawsuits etc., with delayed damage. Example: A candidate is heckled at a political rally by supporters of the opposition candidate.

Some crises involve a combination of these types. For example, if it is found that the driver of the truck that hit a pedestrian was drunk at the time, the crisis is both a violent accident and a crime. If it becomes known that the driver's supervisor knew the driver had a drinking problem but did not report it, mismanagement also becomes an issue.

The Institute for Crisis Management reported in 2015 the following categories of organizational crises, noting that most crises are not the result of natural disaster or employee crime or error but instead are caused by management decisions, action, or inaction:

33%	Mismanagement
14%	White-collar crime
7%	Whistleblowers
6%	Casualty vehicle accidents
6%	Environmental damage
5%	Executive dismissal
4%	Consumer activism
4%	Cybercrimes
4%	Defects and recalls
4%	Discrimination
4%	Hostile takeover
4%	Labor disputes
5%	Other

It is interesting to note that—despite a year with many earthquakes, wildfires, floods, and other natural disasters—such acts of nature did not achieve a statistical significance in the ICM tally of the year's crises. Over the past 10 years, ICM concludes that management has been responsible for 52 percent of all organizational crises, employees for 29 percent, and other factors for the remaining 19 percent.

Sudden versus Smoldering Crises

Important in the various schemes of categorizing crises is the observation that few crises are unpredictable. They may be unpredicted, but it often is human error that caused a problem or early warning to be overlooked, mushrooming into a full crisis.

The Institute for Crisis Management distinguishes between a **sudden crisis** (a disruption of business that occurs without warning, with the likelihood of generating negative news coverage) and a **smoldering crisis** (a business problem not generally recognized that may generate negative news coverage if and when it goes public).

Sudden crises resulting from fires, floods, and other natural occurrences are unusual. Even some of these are somewhat predictable, such as a school or manufacturing company built in a flood zone or a high-rise office tower built in an area prone to earthquakes.

Most crises, however, are of the smoldering type. Smoldering crises often are associated with management error of some sort: safety checks improperly made, inadequate supervision of staff, deficient background checks on employees working with children or the infirm, unsatisfactory handling of consumer complaints, failure to apply laws dealing with discrimination or harassment—all management failings that could have been avoided.

SIX PRINCIPLES FOR CRISIS COMMUNICATION

Crises are inevitable within every organization. You can minimize their occurrence but you can't prevent them entirely. Rather, your aim should be to exercise control in the way you manage the crisis, impacting on whether the outcome is positive or negative. Here are several principles for crisis communication.

Principle of Existing Relationships

In crisis situations, communicate with employees, volunteers, stockholders, donors, and other constituent groups, as well as with colleagues. Minimally, keep these publics informed, because their continued support will be important in your rebuilding process following the crisis. Ideally, enlist their assistance during the crisis to communicate credibly and effectively.

Principle of Quick Response

Become accessible to your publics as quickly as possible. The one-hour rule applies here; within one hour of learning about a crisis, the organization should have its first message available to its publics, particularly the media, which generally are the most significant public in the early stages of a crisis.

Principle of Full Disclosure

Silence is not an acceptable response during a crisis. Without admitting fault, the organization should provide as much information as possible. The presumption should be that everything the organization knows should be made available, subject to specific justification for not releasing certain information.

Principle of One Voice

A single spokesperson should represent the organization. If multiple spokespersons are needed, each should be aware of what the others are saying, and all should work from the same set of facts and the same coordinated message.

Principle of Media-as-Ally

In crisis situations, organizations are best advised to treat the news media as allies that provide opportunities for the organization to communicate with its key publics and constituents. In situations in which the media are intrusive and/or hostile to the organization, this often is because the organization has not been forthcoming in providing legitimate information to the media and its other publics. A good existing program of media relations can minimize media hostility.

Principle of Recovery

The most pressing need in a crisis situation is for the organization to put the issue behind it and initiate a recovery program. Focus on repairing any damage to the organization's reputation and its relationship with important publics.

Appendixes

The 2015 report indicates that only 26 percent of the crises were sudden, 74 percent have smoldered before erupting because of lack of prediction and attention. In other words, three-quarters of all organizational crises could have been avoided if the organization had a good crisis plan and a priority of rooting our potential problems. Yet ICM notes that half of organizations worldwide do not have a functioning crisis plan.

Crisis Strategy

During a crisis, every organization has a range of strategic responses available to it. Here is an overview of eight strategic responses to crisis. These strategies exist on a continuum between full responsibility and full blame. Note that some of the strategies may be used in combination. For a fuller treatment of these strategic options, review Step 5 of the planning process outlined in this book.

1. *Attack.* The organization confronts the person or group who claims that a crisis exists or whom the organization accuses of causing the crisis, and threatens to use force or pressure against the person or group. Do not use this strategy to blame the messengers reporting the crisis. Use this strategy only when a strong case can be made that accusers have grossly overstated the organization's involvement in the crisis.
2. *Denial.* The organization states that no crisis exists and explains why there is no crisis. Or the organization denies that any culpability in a crisis might exist. Use this strategy only when the organization can present a strong case that it did not cause the crisis.
3. *Excuse.* The organization tries to minimize responsibility for the crisis such as by denying any intention to do harm or claiming that it had no control over events that led to the crisis. Use this strategy, perhaps in conjunction with compassion, when a strong case can be made that the organization did not intentionally cause any harm.
4. *Justification.* The organization tries to minimize the perceived damage associated with the crisis or claims that it had no control over events that led to the crisis. Use this strategy, perhaps in conjunction with compassion, when a strong case can be made that the organization is not to blame.
5. *Ingratiation.* The organization takes action to cause its publics to like and side with the organization. Use this strategy when the crisis has been a nonviolent one and when the organization has not been culpable in the crisis.
6. *Corrective action.* The organization takes steps to contain the crisis, repair the damage, and/or prevent a recurrence. Use this strategy if the organization was in any way unprepared or negligent in preventing the crisis in the first place.
7. *Compassion.* The organization expresses regret, remorse, and/or concern without admitting guilt. Use this strategy when injury, death, or serious damage has occurred to express the humanity of the organization.
8. *Apology.* The organization takes full responsibility, asks forgiveness, and makes compensation or restitution. Use this strategy when the organization is at fault and when long-term rebuilding of relationships is more important than short-term stalling.

An organization's choice among various crisis strategies depends on several interdependent factors, including the following.

- *Severity of the crisis.* The more serious the crisis, the less likely that excuses or denials will be accepted without strong and compelling evidence. Also, the more severe the crisis, the harsher the public verdict will be against the organization.
- *Culpability of the organization.* If the organization is fully or even partly responsible for the crisis, this inevitably will be revealed. Crisis managers must be aware of the role the organization played in the evolution of the crisis.
- *Preventability of the crisis.* Crisis managers must be aware of the extent to which the crisis could have been prevented. Culpability can be mitigated if the organization tried to prevent or minimize the crisis before it struck.
- *Organizational reputation.* As in every aspect of public relations, the reputation of the organization prior to the crisis will play a major role in how the organization manages the crisis and recovers from it. The goodwill of the public is invaluable to an organization.

Crisis Messaging

An organization's friends and supporters can tolerate error, but they will not tolerate lies or arrogance. Crisis communication must show that the organization values their support and that it will communicate honestly and respectfully. In addition to specific facts and attention to legal concerns, keep the following messages in mind:

1. Reassure publics about key points, including safety and security, as well as likelihood of recurrence.
2. Don't attempt to shift blame.
3. Show concern and compassion for injury, death, and other loss.
4. Stick to the facts.
5. Avoid speculation. In particular, don't speculate as to the cause or fault for the crisis, nor the financial or other costs involved. While the crisis is going on, it is too early to accurately assess either cause or consequences, and particularly when life and safety are at stake, it is unseemly to speculate about cost.
6. Be candid and honest.
7. "No comment" isn't an option. It implies guilt or cover-up.
8. If you can't comment, indicate why silence is necessary at this time and when you expect to have a comment.
9. Don't minimize the situation. Never characterize a real emergency as a minor incident, and don't point out that other situations may have been worse.
10. Balance the data content of your message with the symbolism and emotion it carries.
11. Try to prevent any unauthorized statements from organizational personnel.
12. Provide timely updates.
13. Communicate with all publics, not only with the media.
14. Try to time your communication program. Giving comment too early means you may not have adequate facts and could appear to be uninformed. Offering comment too late means that the media will release the facts first and you will appear to be hiding information.

FLOW OF INFORMATION DURING A CRISIS

Consider how each key public receives information during a crisis.

News media

- Public relations representative of the organization
- Organizational spokesperson or other official
- Police, fire, or other emergency scanners
- Unauthorized "leaks"
- Rumor
- Eyewitnesses or bystanders with knowledge
- Bystanders with hearsay information
- Outside "experts"
- Organizational and other websites

Employees, volunteers, clients, students, patients

- Direct knowledge
- Other employees, volunteers, clients, etc.
- News reports
- Organizational and other websites
- Email and text messaging
- Managers
- Rumor

Supporters, donors, stockholders

- News reports
- Email
- Letters
- Organizational and other websites
- Telephone contact
- Newsletters
- Rumor

Community residents, public officials

- News reports
- Organizational newsletters
- Organizational and other websites
- Rumor

Preparing for Crises

Because crises are an inevitable fact of life for every organization, preparedness is essential. Here are several aspects of preparing for crisis.

1. *Establish a crisis management team.* Provide training for its members, establish organizational policy for use during a crisis and conduct regular drills.
2. *Develop a crisis management plan.* Include a series of "to do" lists. Also include an outline of both the chain of command and the chair of communication. To implement these procedures, develop information materials such as telephone and email contact lists, media lists, fact sheets, and related information.
3. *Conduct regular crisis research.* Identify emerging issues with the potential for crisis. Investigate these issues and respond to them before they reach crisis stage. Even if they do emerge as crises, you will gain the support of your publics by showing that you tried to prevent or minimize them.
4. *Pay attention to rumors.* Listen to "the word on the street," which can serve as part of the early-warning system within the organization.
5. *Be prepared to communicate.* Create a plan for prompt communication with important publics and key constituents.
6. Try to avoid mistakes that lead to crises.

APPENDIX G

The PR 200 (What Every Public Relations Practitioner Should Know)

Here are 200 terms, concepts, how-tos, and cases that all public relations graduates and practitioners should be familiar with. Knowing these will help you converse professionally with colleagues and help you navigate job interview discussion topics. Ultimately, knowing these will make you a better public relations professional.

Strategic Communication

1. Dominant coalition
2. Integrated communication
3. Issues management versus risk management
4. Outputs versus outcomes
5. Public relations versus marketing
6. Role of advertising in public relations
7. Strategic communication
8. Technician versus manager

Publics

9. Active public
10. Advocate versus activist
11. Apathetic public
12. Aware public
13. Competitor versus opponent

14. Information-seeking public
15. Internal versus external publics
16. Key public
17. Latent public
18. Nonpublic
19. Opinion leader
20. Public versus audience
21. Secondary customer

Campaign Development and Implementation

22. Agency fee structure
23. Benefit statement
24. Campaign versus project
25. Categories of objectives: awareness/informational, acceptance/attitudinal, action/behavioral
26. Competitive parity
27. Continuity versus flighting versus pulsing
28. Controlled before-and-after study
29. Full-cost budget
30. Gantt chart versus PERT chart
31. Goal versus objective
32. Message frequency versus message reach
33. Objective-based budgeting
34. Obstacle versus opportunity
35. Performance fee
36. Plan book
37. Positioning
38. Retainer fee
39. Strategy versus tactic
40. Visibility versus reputation
41. Zero-based budgeting

Theories and Concepts of Public Relations

42. Agenda setting
43. Apologia
44. Balance theory
45. Cognitive dissonance
46. Cultivation theory
47. Diffusion of innovations
48. Face saving
49. Framing
50. Halo effect
51. Information model of communication
52. Maslow's Hierarchy of Needs

53. Multi-step flow of communication
54. Noise
55. Persuasion
56. Propaganda
57. Sleeper effect
58. Social judgment theory
59. Spiral of silence
60. Uses and gratifications

Public Relations Research

61. Academic versus applied research
62. Advertising value equivalency
63. Anonymity versus confidentiality
64. Benchmark
65. Best practices
66. Demographics versus psychographics
67. Environmental scanning
68. Evaluation metrics
69. Extrapolation
70. Formative versus evaluative research
71. Hawthorne effect
72. How to develop and conduct a focus group
73. How to develop and implement a survey
74. How to develop and implement content analysis
75. How to draw a sample for research
76. Judgmental assessment
77. Likert scale
78. Message recall
79. Primary versus secondary research
80. Proactive versus reactive strategies
81. Probability versus nonprobability sampling
82. Public relations audit
83. Questionnaire versus survey
84. Random versus systematic versus stratified sampling
85. Readability
86. Strategic research versus tactical research
87. SWOT analysis

Proactive Strategy for Public Relations

88. Adaptation
89. Gatekeeper
90. Media agenda versus public agenda
91. News
92. News peg

93. Newsworthiness
94. Organizational performance
95. Publicity
96. Special events
97. Sponsorship
98. Strategic philanthropy
99. Third-party endorsement
100. Transparent communication
101. Triggering event

Reactive Strategy for Public Relations

102. Apology versus pseudo-apology
103. Corrective action
104. Crisis
105. Disassociation
106. Investigation
107. Offensive versus defensive strategy
108. One-voice principle
109. Prebuttal
110. Regret versus apology
111. Relabeling
112. Repentance
113. Restitution
114. Strategic inaction
115. Strategic silence
116. Streisand effect
117. Sudden versus smoldering crisis

Elements of Message Strategy

118. Branding rights
119. Celebrity endorsement
120. Commercial speech
121. Credibility versus charisma versus control
122. Defamation versus slander
123. Dialogue
124. Doublespeak
125. Ethos versus logos versus pathos
126. Front organization
127. Positive versus negative emotional appeals
128. Proposition
129. Rhetoric
130. Salience
131. Slogan
132. Staged event versus publicity stunt

133. Stereotype
134. Symbol versus logo
135. Testimonial versus endorsement
136. Verbal evidence
137. Verbal versus nonverbal communication

Public Relations Tactics

138. Actuality versus audio news release
139. Advertising Council
140. Annual report
141. Billboard versus painted bulletin
142. Blog
143. Breakout ad
144. Cable versus broadcast versus satellite television
145. Citizen journalism
146. Daypart
147. Direct mail
148. Display versus classified ad
149. Grade newspaper
150. Information subsidy
151. Long-form television advertising
152. Media advisory
153. Media kit
154. Microwiki
155. News conference versus editorial conference
156. News release versus fact sheet
157. News versus feature
158. Newsletter
159. Nonbroadcast video
160. Online newsroom
161. Opinion subsidy
162. Out-of-home advertising
163. Podcast
164. Position statement versus backgrounder
165. Product placement
166. Run of book advertising
167. Serial versus stand-alone publication
168. Share sites
169. Social media
170. Social networking
171. Special event
172. Sponsored news
173. Spot radio advertising
174. Streaming video
175. Teleconference

176. Terrestrial versus satellite versus streaming radio
177. Transit versus aerial advertising
178. Video B-roll versus video news release
179. Wiki

Public Relations Cases

180. Air Asia & Malaysia Airlines disasters
181. Bridgestone Tire
182. Deepwater Horizon
183. Denny's Restaurant
184. Dove Campaign for Real Beauty
185. Dow Corning
186. Exxon Valdez
187. Got Milk!
188. Johnson & Johnson Tylenol
189. Ice Bucket Challenge
190. Penn State sex abuse scandal
191. Pepsi syringe hoax
192. PETA shock campaigns
193. Professional sports and player misconduct scandals
194. Toyota recall
195. Volkswagen emissions scandal
196. At least five cases and examples of effective public relations
197. At least five cases and examples of ineffective public relations
198. At least five cases and examples of effective research and evaluation
199. At least five examples of effective measurement of social media
200. At least five examples of outside-the-box strategies and tactics that are both creative and effective

Glossary

Number in parenthesis indicates the section in this textbook where the primary reference is located: 0 indicates Introduction, 1–9 indicate steps, letters indicate appendixes

academic research (A) type of research that generates theory, explores new interests and focuses on universal knowledge (also called theoretical research, basic research, and pure research)

acceptance objective (4) second level of objectives, the affective or feeling component, dealing with levels of interest or attitude (compare with awareness objective and action objective)

accident (5) (*see* excuse)

accounts (5) theory that identifies various communication responses to manage relationship in the wake of rebuke or criticism

action metric (9) measure of how a public acts on a message

action objective (4) third and final level of objectives, the conative or behavioral component, dealing with opinion (verbal action) or behavior (physical action)

action strategy (5) category of proactive public relations that involves organizational performance, audience participation, special events, alliances and coalitions, sponsorships, and strategic philanthropy

active public (3) stage of development in which a public recognizes that it shares an issue with an organization, perceives consequences as being relevant, and is organized to discuss or act

activism (5) confrontational proactive public relations strategy focused mainly on persuasive communication and the advocacy model of public relations

activist (2, 5) type of opponent, similar to an advocate, but seeking change rather than focusing on discussion

actuality (7) voice accompanying a news release and providing actual quotes or sound bites; may be cassette or digitized computer download

adaptation (5) willingness and ability of an organization to make changes necessary to create harmony between itself and key publics

administrative research (A) (*see* applied research)

advertising (0) persuasive communication through purchased media to promote a product, service, or idea on behalf of an identified organization or sponsor

advertising and promotional media (7) category of communication tactics using controlled and paid media

advertising value equivalency (9) type of outputs evaluation focusing on the relative costs that a particular public relations message would carry if instead it had been an advertising message (abbreviated AVE)

advertising inserts (7) magazine inserts such as coupons or postcards

advertisorial (7) type of print advertisement that features a series of consecutive pages dealing with a single theme or product/service line

advocate (2, 5) type of opponent that uses mainly vocal tactics against an organization because the advocate supports something else and because the organization appears to stand in the way of the advocate's goal

aerial advertising (7) category of advertising associated with airplanes, including blimps, skywriting, and airplane tows

affective component (4) emotional aspect of a public relations objective (*see* acceptance objective)

affective displays (6) (*see* kinesics)

after-only study (9) type of research design that reviews a situation after a communication project has been implemented (compare with before–after study)

agenda setting theory (5) theory that identifies the relationship between the media agenda and public agenda, observing that, by reporting an event or focusing on an issue, the media signal to audiences the importance of the event or issue

aggregate (3) non-homogeneous assortment of individuals with little in common (*see* audience)

all-you-can-afford budgeting (8) provides for public relations funding when the organization's financial condition is sound, but limits funding during lean times (compare with unit-of-sales budgeting and percentage-of-sales budgeting)

alliance (5) informal, loosely structured and often small working relationship among organizations (compare with coalition)

analogy (6) persuasion technique and type of verbal evidence using familiar situations and allusions to help an audience understand new ideas

announcement release (7) type of news release, generally dealing with events, personnel, progress, bad news, programs, or products (compare with response releases and hometowner releases)

annual report (7) category of organizational media; type of progress report required by the Securities and Exchange Commission of American companies that issue stock

anonymity (A) research term indicating that a respondent's identity project will not be known by anybody, including the researcher (compare with confidentiality)

ANR (7) (*see* audio news release)

anti (2) type of opponent that acts as a dissident on a global scale, being against seemingly everything associated with an organization

apathetic public (3) stage of development in which a public is aware of an issue involving an organization but is nevertheless unconcerned about this issue or its potential consequences

apologetics (5) systematic attempt to explain the reasonableness of religious faith and to refute opposing arguments (*see* homiletics)

apologia (5) formal defense that offers a compelling case for an organization's opinions, positions or actions

apology (5) vocal commiseration strategy in which an organization admits sorrow and accepts blame

applied research (A) type of research that deals with practical problems faced by organizations and guides effective resolution of such problems (also called market research or administrative research)

arena poster (7) billboard-like advertisements on walls and fences of sports arenas, entertainment centers or similar facilities

assistant moderator (B) person in focus group who greets participants and serves as liaison between moderator and client (also called host)

association (5) (*see* excuse)

Astroturf organization (6) group that pretends to be grassroots but actually is organized by a corporation with a vested interest in the issue

attack (5) offensive response strategy of claiming that an accusation of wrongdoing is an attempt to impugn the organization's reputation by an accuser who is negligent or malicious

attractiveness (6) aspect of persuasion that focuses on the message source's physical looks, demeanor, poise, and presence

audience (3) people who pay attention to a particular medium of communication (compare with aggregate)

audience engagement (5) using two-way communication tactics with audiences and publics

audience feedback (9) type of acceptance evaluation based on the voluntary reaction of an audience

audio news release (7) news release written and produced specifically for radio stations, presented as an edited story package (abbreviated ANR)

authority (6) aspect of persuasion that focuses on an audience's acceptance of a message source's right to rule over or direct its actions

AVE (9) (*see* advertising value equivalency)

average (6) term for usual or ordinary instance; statistically this can be a mean, median, or mode

aware public (3) stage of development in which a public recognizes that it shares an issue with an organization and perceives consequences as being relevant, but is not yet organized to discuss or act on the issue

awareness evaluation (9) research focusing on the content of a message. Evaluation includes message exposure, message content, readability measures, and message recall

awareness objective (4) first level of objectives, the cognitive or thinking component, dealing with levels of information, understanding, and retention (compare with acceptance objective and action objective)

B-roll (7) (*see* video B-roll)

backgrounder (7) narrative article providing objective information on an issue

balance theory (5) theory that identifies the tension caused by inconsistent information
baseline study (*see* benchmark)

baseline study (9) (*see* benchmark study)

basic research (A) (*see* academic research)

before-and-after study (9) type of research design that reviews a situation before a
communication project has been implemented, then investigates the situation after
the project is completed (also called pretest/post-test; compare with after-only
study)

benchmark (1) specific and measurable standard against which an organization can
compare its own products and services

benchmark study (1, 9) a specific and measurable standard, against which an organization
can compare its own products and services, with an eye toward improving these (also
called baseline study)

benefit statement (3) part of planning process that articulates a benefit or advantage that
a product or service offers a public

best practice (1) method of documenting and analyzing the behavior of an acknowledged
leader in the field; involves continuous and systematic research process of measuring
an organization and its products or services against the best practices of strong
competitors and recognized industry leaders, in order to improve the organization's
performance

billboard (7) stationary outdoor advertising sign with changeable messages

biography (7) type of feature release focusing on the background of a person

blame shifting (5) (*see* denial)

bleed ad (7) type of print advertisement that eliminates page borders and carries the image
to the edge of the paper

blog (7) short for web log—an open-to-all website—usually maintained by an individual

blogger relations (7) subcategory of media relations focusing on journalistic blogs

bottom line (3) term that identifies an organization's mission or fundamental goal

brainstorming (6) group-creativity technique consisting of two steps (*see* divergence and
convergence)

brand (6) articulation of an organization's purpose

branded clothing (7) promotional items such as T-shirts and designer labels

branding (6) creation of a clear and consistent message for an organization

break-even point (7) level of success required to offset the cost of the development and
implementation of a strategic plan; the point beyond which profit begins accruing

breakout ad (7) targeted approach to advertising in national publications, in which an
advertiser buys space for copies distributed in a narrow geographic area or to a
particular demographic group of subscribers

brochure (7) category of organizational media; stand-alone publication dealing with a particular topic or issue and used for recruiting, product/service lines, membership, and other purposes

budget (8) outline of financial and other resources within a strategic plan, including personnel, material, media costs, equipment and facilities, and administrative costs

bulletin (7) type of organizational publication featuring only headlines and short body text bursting (8) (*see* flighting)

bus sign (7) advertising located on buses, including street-side, curbside, front and back

cable crawl (7) message scrolled across the bottom of a TV screen, often associated with news/weather announcements, sports scores, election returns, and so on

cable television (7) system of TV programming via coaxial or fiber-optic cables

campaign (0) systematic set of public relations activities, each with a specific and finite purpose, sustained over a length of time and dealing with objectives associated with a particular issue (compare with project and program)

campaign plan book (8) formal written presentation of research findings and program recommendations for strategy, tactics, and evaluation

car card (7) advertising placed above windows inside trains and buses

casual research (1, A) gathering of information haphazardly and informally

census (A) research study involving every element within a population (compare with sample)

center spread (7) type of print advertisement that features two facing pages

channel (6) medium through which a message is communicated from sender to receiver

charisma (6) aspect of persuasion that focuses on the magnetic appeal or personal charm of a message source (associated with familiarity, likability, similarity, and attractiveness)

checklist (C) response type allowing respondents to indicate more than one response

chronemics (6) aspect of kinesics related to time aspects of communication such as punctuality

citizen journalism (7) (*see* participatory journalism)

civil disobedience (5) type of activism that involves nonviolent, nonlegal activities, generally with a strong visual component

claim (6) (*see* proposition)

clarity (6) aspect of verbal communication dealing with the ease with which a message can be understood

classified ad (7) type of advertisement common in newspapers featuring brief all-text messages

clipping service (9) company that tracks publications and/or broadcasts and provides evidence that a public relations message has been used

closed-ended item (C) format for survey questionnaire that provides for check-offs to predetermined response categories (compare with open-ended item)

cluster sampling (A) probability sampling technique that first subdivides a large and heterogeneous population, breaking into smaller sections before drawing the final sampling (also called multistage sampling)

coalition (5) formal, structured relationship among organizations (compare with alliance)

coder bias (D) potential bias or differing judgments of individual coders in content analysis

cognitive component (4) informational aspect of a public relations objective (*see* awareness objective)

cognitive dissonance theory (5) theory that explores the role of psychological discomfort rooted in information that contradicts beliefs, values, or attitudes

commercial speech (0) legal term denoting advertising messages

communication manager (0) organizational decision maker, either a tactical manager or a strategic manager

communication output (9) tactic implemented during a communication campaign, such as fact sheets distributed or news conferences held

communication strategy (5) part of an organization's inventory of proactive strategies focusing on publicity, newsworthy information, and transparent communication

communication tactic (7) menu of vehicle that an organization can use to present messages; four categories include interpersonal communication, organizational media, news media, and advertising and promotional media

communication technician (0) organizational specialist in public relations and marketing communication who performs tasks directed by others

community calendar (7) (*see* event listing)

comparison (6) persuasion technique and type of verbal evidence highlighting the characteristics or value related to an issue

competence (6) aspect of persuasion that focuses on the ability of a message source to remain calm under pressure and to be clear and dynamic in presenting the message

competitive parity (8) approach to budgeting based on the cost of similar activity by major competitors

competitor (2) public that is doing the same thing as an organization in the same area, thus competing head to head for the same resources

comprehensive (C) aspect of survey research in which all response choices provide a full range of potential responses

conative component (4) behavioral aspect of a public relations objective (*see* action objective)

concern (5) vocal commiseration strategy in which an organization expresses that it is not indifferent to a problem, without admitting guilt

concession (5) diversionary response strategy by which an organization tries to rebuild its relationship with its publics by giving the public something it wants

condolence (5) vocal commiseration strategy in which an organization expresses grief over someone's loss or misfortune, without admitting guilt

confidentiality (A) research term indicating that the identity of a participant in a research project, though known to the researcher, will not be disclosed or linked to a particular response (compare with anonymity)

conflict resolution (6) process of dialogue that involves making peace and restoring harmony, with communication as the primary tool

congruity theory (5) theory that adds the aspect of measuring attitudes to consistency theories

conjecture proposition (6) type of proposition stating that something probably exists, based on reasoned conclusion drawn from physical evidence

consensus building (6) process of dialogue that identifies and then prevents or overcomes barriers between people and/or organizations

consistency theory (6) family of theories dealing with the existence or lack of consistent information and the effect of this on message receivers

consumer kit (7) (*see* user kit)

consumer magazine (7) type of magazine commonly found at newsstands or obtained through subscriptions

content analysis (D) quantitative research technique based on the unobtrusive and after-the-fact analysis of a set of media artifacts such as a news cast, editorials, tweets, or articles on a particular topic

context (5) (*see* justification)

contingency statement (7) type of public relations writing in which an organization prepares written comment for various potential outcomes of a situation, releasing only that version appropriate to the outcome (also called standby statement)

continuity (8) approach to scheduling that presents a message at a consistent level throughout a time period

control (6) aspect of persuasion that focuses on a message source's command over an audience and on the perceived willingness to exercise that power

controlled before-and-after study (9) more sophisticated than before-and-after study as takes outside factors into consideration and involves two sample groups drawn from the same key public, one that receives the message, the other that does not

controlled media (7) media that allow the organization to determine various attributes (compare with uncontrolled media)

convenience sampling (A) nonprobability sampling technique that draws subjects because they are readily available to a researcher

convergence (6) part of brainstorming technique for creative problem solving in which a group pares down a list of possible solutions/questions

corporate video (7) (*see* nonbroadcast video)

corporate social responsibility (5) aspect of community relations and strategic philanthropy in which an organization contributes to the betterment of society

corrective action (5) rectifying behavior strategy in which an organization takes steps to contain a problem, repair the damage and/or prevent its recurrence

cost per thousand (9) standard measurement for expense of reaching media audiences, calculated not individually but rather as thousands (abbreviated CPM)

cost–benefit analysis (8) identifies the cost of implementing a tactic, then compares this cost to the estimated value of the expected results

costume (7) type of promotional clothing

CPM (9) (*see* cost per thousand)

creativity (0) ability to imagine new ideas

credibility (6, E) aspect of persuasion that focuses on the power to inspire belief, demonstrated through expertise, status, competence, and honesty

crisis (1, F) significant business disruption that stimulates extensive news media coverage, resulting in public scrutiny that affects an organization's normal operations

crisis management (1, F) process by which an organization plans for, deals with, and tries to overcome out-of-control issues

crowdfunding (7) online process of raising money from a large number of donors or investors

cultivation theory (5) premise that media shape peoples' conception of social reality

customer (3) type of public that receives the product or services of an organization, such as consumers, clients, patients, fans, parishioners, members, etc.

customer satisfaction survey (C) research to help managers understand how customers feel about products and services

cybernetic model of communication (6, 9) theory that identifies a model for two-way communication, moving from sender to receiver and returning via feedback

daypart (7) time period reflecting different audience demographics and usage patterns for television or radio, such as prime time and morning drive time

decode (6) process of interpreting verbal and/or nonverbal symbols in a received message to approximate the intention of the sender

decoding (6) process by a message receiver in interpreting the intended message of the sender

defamation (6) legal situation in which language (1) is false, (2) is published or communicated to a third party, (3) identifies a person, (4) holds that person up to public hatred, contempt or ridicule, and (5) involves some measure of negligence and/or malice on the part of the communicator

demographic noise (6) communication disruption caused by differences between message sender and receiver based on ethnicity, age, social status, and so on (*see* noise)

demographics (3) audience characteristics based on measurable physical criteria such as age, income, education, gender, geography, and so on (compare with psychographics)

denial (5) defensive response strategy in which an organization refuses to accept blame by claiming innocence or mistaken identity or by shifting blame

deontological ethics (1) approach to decision making rooted in a standard or moral code, suggesting that certain actions are good because the code says they are good (compare with teleological ethics and ethical relativism)

dialogue model (6) conceptual approach to communication that focuses on conscious interaction of two parties in communication for the purpose of mutual understanding

diffusion of innovations theory (3, 5) theory that identifies the role of opinion leaders as models in the process of mass adoption of new products or ideas

digital billboard (7) electronic advertising for advertising and public service purposes with continually changing images

digital insertion (7) production technique of altering an image after it has been shot

digital media (7) category of organizational media focusing on computer-based electronic media vehicles, such as email, websites, Intranets, etc.

digital radio (7) radio transmitted via satellite, therefore covering far larger areas than conventional terrestrial broadcasting (also called subscription radio)

diorama (7) (*see* station poster)

direct mail (7) category of organizational print media featuring written messages disseminated to individual recipients

direct news (5) information of interest to publics, often provided by an organization using direct media rather than news venues

direct news subsidy (7) category of news media including information presented to the media in ready-to-use format, such as news releases or feature releases

direct observation (9) type of action evaluation based on proof of audience activity, such as voting outcome, attendance, sales, and so on

disassociation (5) diversionary response strategy that attempts to distance an organization from wrongdoing associated with it

display ad (7) type of advertisement common in newspapers and magazines, featuring headlines, illustrations, and copy blocks

disproportionate sampling (A) approach to stratified sampling in which each demographic group is sized not according to its proportion in the population in order to compensate for its being a small proportion (also called weighted sampling)

dissident (2) type of opponent that combats an organization because of positions or actions taken by the organization

divergence (6) part of brainstorming technique for creative problem solving in which a group surfaces a large number of ideas on how to solve a problem or answer a question

dominant coalition (1) grouping of managers and executives who together wield power and make decisions within organizations

doublespeak (5, 6) words and phrases that are deliberately misleading and thus both dishonest and unethical attempts to obscure meaning, violating ethical standards (compare with pretentious language)

drawing conclusions (6) presenting the evidence and then explicitly telling the audience how to interpret it

drive-motive theory (3) (*see* hierarchy of needs)

earned media (0) placement through news media such as via interviews and news releases

editorial conference (7) formal meeting between news sources or organizational representatives with editors and editorial boards of newspapers in order to increase understanding between reporters and organizations and to elicit media support for the organization's agenda

electronic media (7) media delivered primarily through electronic vehicles (compare with print media)

element (A) (*see* unit of analysis)

email (7) type of organizational media using computers to transmit memos and letters

embarrassment (5) offensive response strategy of trying to lessen an opponent's influence by using shame or humiliation

enabler (3) type of public that serves as a regulator by setting the norms or standards for an organization, opinion leader, allies, or media

encode (6) process of using verbal and/or nonverbal symbols to carry a message

encoding (6) process by a message sender in creating a message that can be interpreted by a receiver with approximately the same meaning

endorsement (6) persuasion technique and type of verbal evidence using comments by people who espouse an organization's ideas

engagement metric (9) measure of how publics interact with an organization and each other vis-à-vis an organizational message

environmental scanning (1) process of seeking information in an organization's external environment to help managers chart the organization's future course of action

EPSEM sampling (A) equal probability of sampling methods (*see* probability sampling)

ethical base (2) foundation within organization for making and applying moral judgments

ethical relativism (1) approach to decision making suggesting that actions are ethical to the extent that they reflect particular social norms (compare with deontological ethics and teleological ethics)

ethos (6) principle identified with Aristotle that focuses on the communication effectiveness based on the character of a speaker and on the common ground shared by speakers and audiences

event listing (7) simple newspaper notice announcing upcoming events (also called community calendar)

example (6) persuasion technique and type of verbal evidence providing conclusions drawn from related instances

excuse (5) defensive response strategy in which an organization tries to minimize its responsibility for harm or wrongdoing by citing provocation, lack of control, victimization or mere association

executive summary (9) one- or two-page synopsis of a strategic plan or other report intended as an overview for executives and others who need general information but not details

existing relationships (1) strategic principle of crisis management that an organization should communicate with employees, volunteers, stockholders, community leaders, customers, and other groups to strengthen existing support

expertise (6) aspect of persuasion that focuses on the degree to which a message source knows what he or she is talking about (compare with competence)

exposure metric (9) measure of how publics have been exposed to a message

external impediment (2) social, political, or economic factor outside an organization that might limit the effectiveness of a public relations program (compare with internal impediment)

external media (7) media that exist outside of an organization (compare with internal media)

extra (7) name for additional feature within a spectacular billboard (*see* spectacular)

extrapolation (A) process of applying findings from a sample group to a larger population

face saving (3) strategy allowing opponents to resolve a situation while maintaining dignity and respect

facilitator (B) (*see* moderator)

fact sheet (7) category of organizational media that presents information in bullet form

factual proposition (6) type of proposition stating that something exists, based on provable evidence

false assumption (6) error in logic featuring a conclusion that an audience may not accept

familiarity (6) aspect of persuasion that focuses on the extent to which an audience already knows the message source

fanatic (3) type of zealot opponent without social stabilizers

FAQ (7) presentation of frequently asked questions about a particular issue or organization (*see also* fact sheet)

fear appeal (6) persuasion technique and type of negative appeal based on anxiety and worry

feature release (7) media release focusing on background info (categories include history, biography, backgrounder, Q&A, service article)

feedback (6) communication by a message receiver back to the sender

final report (9) (*see* summative report)

fixed fee (8) (*see* project fee)

flier (7) category of organizational media; stand-alone publication meant to be read as a single unit

flighting (8) approach to scheduling that presents a message in waves over a period of time (also called bursting)

focus group (B) qualitative research technique involving conversation among several participants, guided by a monitor and recorded for later analysis (also called group interview)

Fog Index (6, 9) formula to calculate the level of reading difficulty for any piece of writing (also called Gunning Readability Formula)

forced-choice item (C) response type allowing respondents to indicate only one response

formal opinion leader (3) opinion leader whose influence is based on structured authority role (compare with informal opinion leader)

formative research (1) first phase of strategic planning process, dealing with gathering and analyzing information about the public relations situation, the organization and its publics (also called situation analysis)

framing (5) manner in which the media provide a perspective or frame of reference that influences public discourse on a topic

free media (0) (*see* earned media)

front organization (6) group set up to appear to operate independently, but actually controlled by another organization that wants to remain anonymous in the relationship

full disclosure (1) strategic principle of crisis management that an organization should provide as much information as possible, without admitting fault or speculating about facts not yet known

full-cost budget (8) inclusion within budgets of the value of all items, not only those to be purchased but also those inherent within an organization and generated income

Gantt chart (8) common type of flow chart listing tactics and associated tasks, with indication of the time needed for each task

gatekeeper (5) media person (such as editor, producer, or webmaster) who controls the flow of information in publications, newscasts, and so on

gatekeeping theory (5) premise that journalistic interpretation of events is shaped by personal or organizational bias

general-interest newspaper (7) publication appealing to diverse interests of a wide spectrum of readers

geodemography (A) research technique combining elements of demographics and census data

ghost blogging (7) authoring a blog in someone else's name

goal (4) part of organizational strategy; statement rooted in organization's mission or vision, acknowledging an issue and sketching out how the organization hopes to see it settled

good intention (5) (*see* justification)

grabbers (6) (*see* power words)

grassroots journalism (7) (*see* participatory journalism)

group interview (B) (*see* focus group)

guerrilla theater (5) (*see* street theater)

guest editorial (7) enhanced letter to the editor, often commissioned by a publication (also called op-ed piece)

guilt appeal (6) persuasion technique and type of negative appeal based on shame

Gunning Readability Formula (6) (*see* Fog Index)

halo effect (6) phenomenon in which a message is likely to be believed mainly because the source is perceived as credible, charismatic, and/or in a position of control over an audience

haptics (6) aspect of kinesics related to the amount of touching between people in conversation

Hawthorne effect (9) (*see* placebo effect)

hearing (A) physical process of sound waves making the eardrums vibrate, stimulating nerve impulses in the brain (compare with listening)

hierarchy of needs (3) theory of human motivation that identifies structured levels of human needs, with one needing to be met before another becomes relevant

history (7) type of feature release focusing on the background or history of an organization

hometowner release (7) type of news release focusing on announcements about people and disseminated to their hometowns

homiletics (6) application of effective communication for preaching (*see* apologetics)

honesty (6) aspect of persuasion that focuses on the willingness and ability of a message source to provide full and accurate information, operating without bias

horns effect (6) opposite of halo effect

host (B) (*see* assistant moderator)

hourly rate plus expenses (8) fee structure for public relations agencies, charging actual time spent plus cost of materials, production, and media

house ad (7) type of advertisement placed in performance programs and other publications associated with special events, often focusing simply on corporate identity

house organ (7) (*see* organizational newspaper)

how-to piece (7) (*see* service article)

human motivation (3) (*see* hierarchy of needs)

humor appeal (6) persuasion technique and type of positive emotional appeal based on comedy and amusement

idealism (5) (*see* justification)

image restoration (5) theory based on the presumption that, in the face of criticism, both people and organizations seek to maintain or rebuild a positive reputation

implementation report (9) (research report documenting how program tactics are carried out

improvement scale (C) type of research to guide management decisions toward better performance

in-depth interview (A) (*see* intensive interview)

inactive public (3) (*see* latent public)

indirect news subsidy (7) category of news media including information presented for media guidance but not meant to be published or aired, such as media advisories and announcements of news conferences

inflatable (7) category of advertising using giant outdoor balloons or air-filled promotional items

influence metric (9) measure of the degree to which message exposure and engagement impact on the public's perceptions and attitudes

infomercial (7) program-length television advertisement often packaged as an interview, game show or educational program

informal opinion leader (3) opinion leader whose influence is based on force of personality and circumstance (compare with formal opinion leader)

information exchange (7) category of interpersonal communication tactics centering on opportunities for organizations and publics to meet face to face

information model (6) conceptual approach to communication that focuses on the content and channels of communication

information subsidy (7) information from public relations sources that editors use to help underwrite the cost of reporting news

information-seeking publics (7) people who have gone somewhat out of their way to interact with the organization

ingratiation (5) diversionary response strategy in which an organization tries to charm its publics or gives them something of little significance to the organization in an attempt to turn the spotlight away from criticism

innocence (5) (*see* denial)

innovation (0) ability to apply creative thinking

inoculation theory (5) theory that explores the role that persuasive information has on previously unchallenged beliefs and attitudes

integrated communication (0, 7) blending of communication functions within an organization designed to make all aspects of communication work together toward common goals, increasing impact at minimal cost; combination of the concepts and tools of both public relations and marketing communication

intensive interview (A) qualitative research technique involving lengthy, detailed, and systematic interview conducted with several respondents (also called in-depth interview)

interactive media (7) communication tactics that allow organizations to send a message to an audience and to generate feedback

intercession (3) process of using an influential go-between to link an organization and its public

intercessory public (3) transitional public that serves as a bridge between an organization and other publics

intercoder reliability (D) degree to which various coders in content analysis agree on their interpretation of a unit of analysis

internal impediment (2) obstacles within an organization that might limit the effectiveness of a public relations program (compare with external impediment)

internal media (7) media that exist within an organization (compare with external media)

internal video (7) (*see* nonbroadcast video)

Internet (7) vast computer network linking smaller computer networks worldwide

Internet radio (7) (*see* online radio)

interpersonal communication (7) category of communication tactics offering face-to-face opportunities for personal involvement and interaction

interstitial ad (7) computer advertising that insinuates itself on computer users without invitation (also called pop-up ad; compare with superstitial ad)

interview notes (7) verbatim transcripts presented in a question-and-answer format, based on an interview that a public relations writer has done with an organizational news source

interview survey (C) survey research administered through an in-person interview

interview training (E) (*see* media training)

investigation (5) rectifying behavior strategy in which an organization promises to examine a situation and then to act as the facts warrant

issue (1) situation that presents a matter of concern to an organization; trend, event, development, or matter in dispute that may affect an organization

issues management (1) process of monitoring and evaluating information by which an organization tries to anticipate emerging issues and respond to them before they get out of hand

judgment sampling (9) (*see* purposive sampling)

judgmental assessment (9) evaluation methodology based on hunches and personal experience

justification (5) defensive response strategy in which an organization admits doing wrong but claims it was for a good reason, citing good intention, context, idealism, or mitigation

key performance indicator (4) specific metric used in developing and evaluating objectives

key public (3) (*see* strategic public)

kinesics (6) body language

lack of control (5) (*see* excuse)

latent public (3) stage of development in which a public shares an issue with an organization but is not yet aware of this fact

libel (6) written or broadcast defamation

likability (6) aspect of persuasion that focuses on the extent to which an audience admires what it knows about a message source or what it sees and hears when the source begins to communicate

Likert scale (C) popular bipolar scale used in questionnaires to elicit response in categories such as "strongly agree," "agree," "disagree" and "strongly disagree"

limiter (3) type of public that reduces or undermines the success of an organization, including competitors, opponents, and hostile forces

linkage (3, 5) patterns of relationships that exist between an organization and its various publics

listening (A) interpersonal process in which a person not only hears words and other sounds but also interprets them, attempting to obtain essentially the same meaning as the sender intended (compare with hearing)

logo (6) type of nonverbal communication in which an image identifies an organization

logos (6) principle identified with Aristotle that focuses on communication effectiveness based on rational appeal of messages

long-form television and radio (7) advertising longer than two minutes

love appeal (6) persuasion technique and type of positive emotional appeal based on aspects of love, such as family, nostalgia, compassion, sympathy, etc.

magazine (7) category of news media; periodic publication featuring news, commentary, and feature information

mail survey (C) survey research administered through the mail; also called a self-administered survey

management by objectives (4) process by which organizations plan their activities based on prior objectives rather than present opportunities (abbreviated MBO)

manager (0) (*see* communication manager)

manifest content (D) obvious and apparent meanings and interpretations in content analysis methodology

margin of error (A) (*see* sampling error)

market (3) segment of a population including people with characteristics (age, income, lifestyle, and so on) that can help an organization achieve its consumer-oriented goals

market research (A) (*see* applied research)

marketing communication (0) management function that focuses on products and services that respond to the wants and needs of consumers, fostering an economic exchange between the organization and its consumers (compare with public relations)

mass media (7) media that are accessible to most people and thus enjoy vast audiences (compare with targeted media)

massing (8) bunching of various presentations of a message into a short period of time

mathematical theory of communication (6) theory that identifies a model for one-way communication, moving from sender to receiver

MBO (4) (*see* management by objective)

mean (6) type of statistical average calculated by dividing a total by the number of elements (compare with median and mode)

mean world syndrome (5) Gerbner's observation that heavy media users are more fearful of the world around them than are light-to-moderate media users

media advisory (7) type of indirect news material providing media gatekeepers with information about upcoming news opportunities (also called media alert)

media agenda (5) topics the media report on (compare with public agenda)

media alert (7) (*see* media advisory)

media directory (7) books and online resources providing information on media outlets, such as advertising rates, names of editors, and publication information

media engagement (E) philosophical and practical ways an organization interacts with news media

media impressions (9) potential total audience of people who could have been exposed to a message presented in a particular medium

media kit (7) collection of materials for reporters attending news conferences and other news-oriented events; includes news releases, biographies, photos, backgrounders, fact sheets, etc. (less accurately called press kit)

media relations rating points (9) Canadian standard for evaluating and reporting editorial media coverage

media training (E) type of preparation for organizational spokespersons who will interact with journalists and other publics (also called interview training)

media-as-ally (1) strategic principle of crisis management that an organization should treat news media as an ally offering an opportunity to communicate with the organization's publics

median (6) type of statistical average calculated from the middle number on a list (compare with mean and mode)

memo (7) category of organizational media; brief written message, usually internal to an organization

message (6) articulation of an idea in the mind of a sender that is communicated to a receiver

message cost (9) type of outputs evaluation focusing on the expense associated with the production of a particular message

message distribution (9) type of outputs evaluation focusing on the frequency and manner of message dissemination

message exposure (9) type of awareness evaluation based on the number of people in key purpose who were exposed to a message

message frequency (8) number and pattern of messages presented to a particular public in a given period of time (compare with message reach)

message production (9) type of outputs evaluation focusing on the number of messages written or produced

message reach (8) number of different people who are exposed to a single message (compare with message frequency)

message recall (9) type of awareness evaluation based on how frequently and accurately audiences remembered a previous advertising or public relations message

metrics (4, 9) standards of measurement to assess the outcome of a program or project

microblog (7) blog with limits of only a few characters, such as Twitter

minifocus group (A) focus group research with only five or six participants

missionary (2) self-righteous type of activist in support of a cause, often operating under the presumption of moral imperative

mistaken identity (5) (*see* denial)

mitigation (5) (*see* justification)

mobile billboard (7) painted side of tractor-trailer or delivery trucks, often leased for advertising purposes

moblog (7) blog written on a mobile device such as a smartphone

mode (6) type of statistical average calculated as the most frequently occurring number (compare with mean and median)

moderator (B) person who leads a focus group; also called facilitator

money bomb (7) 24-hour online fundraising campaign

monochronemics (6) aspect of kinesics related to doing or talking about one thing at a time

MP3 blog (7) type of music blog

MRP (9) (*see* media relations rating points)

multiple-choice items (A) questionnaire items with a limited number of responses

multiplier (9) dubious method of calculating the value of publicity as if it were advertising (*see also* advertising equivalency)

multistage sampling (A) (*see* cluster sampling)

multi-step flow model (5) development of Two-Step Model of Communication

mutually exclusive (C) aspect of survey research in which all response choices are not duplicative or overlapping

native advertising (7) advertising with the look and feel of its environment; for example, a newspaper ad that looks like a newspaper article

network placement (7) use of television advertising at the network level, with distribution through all stations affiliated with the network (compare with spot advertising)

network radio (7) same as network placement in reference to radio advertising

networking (3) (*see* intercession)

news (5) information that offers an audience a new idea or the latest development; information that involves action, adventure, change, conflict, consequence, contest, controversy, drama, effect, fame, importance, interest, personality, prominence, proximity (*see also* SiLoBaTi+UnFa)

news brief (7) type of news releases presenting two or three paragraphs of information

news conference (7) hybrid of speech and group interview used to announce important news to reporters

news fact sheet (7) bulleted presentation of newsworthy information (compare with news release)

news interviews (7) sessions in which journalists ask questions and public relations practitioners or organizational spokespersons respond

news media (7) category of communication tactics using journalistic media

news peg (5) topic that media are already reporting on that also touches on an organization

news release (7) news-type article written by a public relations practitioner and presented to a newspaper or other publication or media outlet; meant to be used either verbatim or as background information (compare with news fact sheet)

newsletter (7) category of organizational media; organizational publication combining the informative approach of newspapers with relationship-building features of mail

newspaper (7) category of news media; periodic publication featuring objective news and information; various types include general-interest, trade, special-interest, special-audience, and organizational newspapers

niche (2) aspect of an organization's internal environment focusing on the specialty or the unique function or role that makes the organization different from others

niche marketing (5) approach to marketing and public relations intended to shore up an organization's relationship with consumers

noise (6) concept identifying potential interferences with message communication; may be physical, psychological, semantic, or demographic

nonapology (5) an insincere or halfhearted apology

nonbroadcast video (7) category of organizational media using television technology for internal distribution (also called corporate video and internal video; compare with web video)

nonprobability sampling (A) a series of techniques for selecting samples of a population not based on the principle of probability (categories include convenience, volunteer, purposive, and snowball sampling)

nonpublic (3) group that does not share any issues with an organization

nonpublic media (7) media that are restricted in their coverage and their availability (compare with public media)

nonverbal communication (6) communication occurring through actions and cues other than words (compare with verbal communication)

objective (4) part of organizational strategy; statement emerging from an organization's goal, presented in clear and measurable terms, pointing toward particular levels of awareness, acceptance, or action (compare with goal)

objective-based budgeting (8) approach to budgeting based on established goals and objectives

obstacle (1) public relations situation limiting the organization in realizing its mission (compare with opportunity)

occulesics (6) aspect of kinesics related to eye contact

one voice (1) strategic principle of crisis management that a single, trained spokesperson or coordinated team of spokespersons should represent the organization by presenting a coordinated message

one-way media (7) communication tactics that allow organizations to send a message to an audience without feedback

online focus group (B) focus group research facilitated with software such as Skype

online radio (7) type of radio carrying web-based stations and radio-like music collections (also called Internet radio and streaming radio)

online survey (C) survey research administered over the Internet

op-ed piece (7) (*see* guest editorial)

open-ended item (C) format for survey questionnaire that allows respondents to answer in their own words (compare with closed-ended item)

opinion leader (3, 5) individual with a particular influence on an organization's publics (*see* formal opinion leader and informal opinion leader)

opponent (2) public that is against an organization

opportunity (1) public relations situation offering a potential advantage to the organization or its publics (compare with obstacle)

order of presentation (6) refers to how an argument unfolds; that is, the result of a strategic decision to offer certain bits of information before others

organizational media (7) category of communication tactics using media that are published or produced by organizations, which control the message content as well as its timing, packaging, and distribution

organizational newspaper (7) type of newspaper published by an organization or business (also called house organ)

out-of-home advertising (7) advertising venues designed to reach people in locations other than home or offices, including billboards, transit, and aerial advertising

out-of-home video (7) category of advertising featuring video in public locations such as sports arenas and concert halls

outtake (9) something a public takes away following a public relations engagement

outcome (9) accomplishment of objectives through a public relations engagement

output (9) work done in a public relations activity

outputs evaluation (9) evaluation methodology focusing on communication outputs

over-the-air television (7) (*see* terrestrial television)

owned media (0) media controlled by an organization, such as newsletters and websites

paid media (0) media placement purchased by an organization, such as advertising

paint (7) stationary outdoor advertising sign, also called painted bulletin, with relatively permanent message

paralanguage (6) (*see* vocalics)

participatory journalism (7) category of news reporting associated with bloggers (also called citizen journalism and grassroots journalism)

pathos (6) principle identified with Aristotle that focuses on communication effectiveness based on emotional appeal of messages

pci (7) (*see* per column inch)

per column inch (7) basic unit of measure for print advertising (abbreviated pci)

per-capita cost (8) association of budgetary expenses with the number of people needed to cover the cost

percentage-of-sales budgeting (8) drawn from the field of marketing, where some companies base their advertising budget on the previous year's profits

per diem rate (8) agency fees based on daily rate

performance (2, 5) aspect of an organization's internal environment focusing on the quality of the goods and services provided by the organization, as well as the viability of the causes and ideas it espouses

performance-based budgeting (8) approach to budgeting that draws on intended future results

performance fee (8) fee structure for public relations or advertising agency tying compensation to the achievement of stated objectives

personal involvement (7) action of an organization involving its publics and creating an environment rooted in two-way communication

persuasion model (6) conceptual approach to communication that focuses on ethical attempts to influence people

PERT chart (8) common type of flow chart using circles and arrows to visually display tasks associated with a strategic plan

photo op (5) publicity stunt with visual appeal, designed to attract media coverage in newspapers and magazines, television and online video and photographic venues

physical noise (6) communication disruption caused by use of inefficient communication channels

physiological noise (6) message interferences based on physical distractions by the receiver

pie throwing (5) protest tactic sometimes used by activists

placebo effect (9) research phenomenon in which change is noted but attributed not to the content of the campaign but rather to the mere fact that participants knew that a campaign was in progress and/or that they were being observed (also called Hawthorne effect)

podcasts (7) Internet-based audio feeds that allow users to listen to postings

policy proposition (6) type of proposition identifying a new course of action and encouraging its adoption

polls (C) (*see* survey)

polychronemics (6) aspect of kinesics related to doing or talking about more than one thing at a time

pop-up (7) (*see* interstitial ad)

popular magazine (7) (*see* consumer magazine)

popular media (7) media that focus on information of interest to people in their personal lives (compare with trade media)

population (A) research term indicating a large group of subjects that are of interest to a researcher

position paper (7) (*see* position statement)

position paragraph (7) shorter version of a position statement

position statement (4, 7) type of opinion material used by organizations to analyze issues and present formal opinions on issues of public policy (also called white paper; compare with position paragraph)

positioning (4) process of managing how an organization distinguishes itself with a unique meaning in the mind of its publics

poster (7) generic name for several kinds of outdoor stationary advertisements, including billboards, paints, and spectaculars

power (6) aspect of persuasion that focuses on the raw and recognized ability of a message source to dominate and to reward or punish

power words (6) aspect of verbal communication dealing with strong and evocative language (also called grabber)

prebuttal (5) term linked to the notion of pre-emptive strike when bad news is inevitable, referring to the practice of an organization announcing its own bad news

pre-emptive strike (5) defensive action taken before opponents launch a first charge against an organization

prepotency (3) ordered internal relationship among needs by which more basic needs must be addressed first (*see* hierarchy of needs)

pretentious language (6) words and phrases that imply more than is warranted, thus risking misleading audiences and raising ethical issues (compare with doublespeak)

pretest/post-test study (9) (*see* before–after study)

primary research (1, A) generation and analysis of new information to address a research question or problem (compare with secondary research)

priming (5) manner in which the media set the stage to provide a context for public discourse on a topic

print media (7) media delivered primarily through print vehicles (compare with electronic media)

privacy (6) legal right to be left alone

proactive strategy (5, E) approach to organizational strategy that enables an organization to launch a communication program under the conditions and according to the timeline that seems to best fit the organization's interests (compare with reactive strategy)

probability (A) the notion that every element in a population has an equal chance of being selected for a sample

probability sampling (A) series of techniques for selecting samples of a population based on the principle of probability; categories include simple random, systematic, stratified, and cluster sampling (also called EPSEM sampling)

producer (3) type of public that provides input to an organization, including employees, volunteers, suppliers, and financial backers

product integration (7) company pays for a commercial product to be woven into a TV or movie storyline (*see* branded entertainment)

product name (6) title strategically designed to associate a product with characteristics that are thought to be desirable in the mind of the key public (compare with program name)

product placement (7) (*see* stealth ad)

program (0) ongoing public relations activity dealing with several objectives associated with a goal; part of a continuing mission within the organization and focused on its relationship with a particular public (compare with project and campaign)

program name (6) parallel of a product name for services of both nonprofit organizations and businesses

progress report (9) research report monitoring program tactics at various key points during implementation period

project (0) single and usually short-lived public relations activity designed to meet an objective (compare with campaign and program)

project fee (8) fee structure for public relations or advertising agency featuring costs associated with specific tasks

propaganda (6) debasement of persuasive communication associated with half-truths and hidden agendas

proportionate sampling (A) approach to stratified sampling in which each demographic group is sized according to its proportion in the population

proposition (6) primary idea in a speech, editorial, advertisement, television program, or other communication vehicle; may be a factual proposition, conjecture proposition, value proposition, or policy proposition (also called claim)

provocation (5) (*see* excuse)

proxemics (6) aspect of kinesics related to closeness between people when they speak

pseudo-apology (5) insincere type of nonapology

pseudo-event (5) (*see* staged activity)

psychographics (A) audience characteristics based on lifestyle characteristics and interests (compare with demographics)

psychological noise (6) communication disruption caused by emotional distractions by the receiver

psychological type (6) concept observing that people have different natural preferences in gathering and processing information, making decisions and acting on those decisions (compare with temperament)

public (3) group of people that shares a common interest vis-à-vis an organization, recognizes its significance and sets out to do something about it

public agenda (5) topics the citizenry or media audiences are interested in (compare with media agenda)

public media (7) media that are generally accessible by everybody (compare with nonpublic media)

public relations (0) strategic communication process that builds mutually beneficial relationships between organizations and their publics; it is part of the management of an organization and includes research, planning, implementation and evaluation (compare with marketing communication and integrated communication)

public relations audit (2) analysis of the strengths and weaknesses of the public relations concerns of an organization or client

public relations situation (1) set of circumstances facing an organization, whether an opportunity or an obstacle

publicity (5) aspect of communication strategy that involves the attention given by the news media to an organization

publicity stunt (5) gimmick planned by an organization mainly to gain publicity, having little value beyond attention (compare with staged activity)

pulsing (8) approach to scheduling that combines continuity and flighting approaches, resulting in a continuous base of messages augmented with intermittent bursts of greater communication activity

purdah (5) (*see* strategic silence)

pure research (A) (*see* academic research)

purposive sampling (A) nonprobability sampling technique that includes subjects simply because they have a particular demographic characteristic (also called judgment sampling)

qualitative research (9) type of research based on informal methodologies not capable of generating number-based information and conclusions

quantitative research (9) type of research based on formal methodologies, generating number-based information and conclusions

quarterly report (7) category of organizational media published voluntarily to keep stockholders and others informed about an organization's progress

query letter (7) type of indirect news material inquiring whether editors or news directors would be interested in a particular article, particularly one contemplated by a freelance writer or producer

question-and-answer piece (7) type of feature release written in question-and-answer format (also called Q&A)

questionnaire (C) instrument of survey research that presents a series of questions/items and response choices

quick response (1) strategic principle of crisis management that an organization should be as accessible to its publics as possible, aiming to end the crisis as soon as possible

quota sampling (A) nonprobability sampling technique that begins with a selection of subjects based on demographic criteria, then continues with other nonprobability techniques

quotes (6) statements made by and attributed to individuals or organizations

random sampling (A) (*see* simple random sampling)

rating scale (C) response technique used in survey questionnaires calling for respondents to rate the degree of their feeling or certainty about an item

reactive strategy (5, E) approach to organizational strategy in which an organization responds to influences and opportunities from its environment (compare with proactive strategy)

readability (6) level of reading difficulty that can be calculated for any piece of writing, allowing the writer to tailor the writing to the abilities of the intended audience

receiver (6) recipient of a message

recorder (D) person in a focus group responsible for taking notes

rectifying behavior (5) strategy in which an organization repairs damage it inflicted

regret (5) vocal commiseration strategy in which an organization admits sorrow and remorse for a situation, without directly admitting fault

reiteration (6) internal repetition of main ideas within a persuasive message

relabeling (5) diversionary response strategy that tries to distance an organization from criticism by offering an agreeable name to replace a negative label applied by others

relationship management goal (4) type of goal focusing on how an organization connects with its publics

repentance (5) rectifying behavior in which an organization demonstrates a change of heart and change in action, signaling full atonement and becoming an advocate for a new way of thinking and acting

reputation (2, E) aspect of an organization's external environment dealing with how people evaluate the information they have about an organization

reputation management goal (4) type of goal dealing with an organization's identity and perception

reputation priorities (1) strategic principle of crisis management that an organization should set objectives to maintain and/or restore credibility, using a crisis as an opportunity to enhance its reputation

research (9) formal program of information gathering (*see* academic research and applied research)

research design (9) method of structuring evaluation in relation to measurement standards

research leader (D) person that articulates the topic, conducts secondary research, selects participants and develops discussion guide for focus group research

response release (7) type of news release that deals with new or updated information, comments, public interest tie-ins, and speeches

response strategies (5) category of reactive public relations

restitution (5) rectifying behavior strategy in which an organization makes amends by compensating victims or restoring a situation to its earlier condition

retainer fee (8) structure for public relations or advertising agency featuring fixed monthly rates paid in advance for a predetermined level of agency availability

return on investment (9) ratio of money gained or lost relative to the cost (abbreviated ROI)

rhetoric (6) art of using words effectively in speaking and writing for the purpose of influencing, persuading, or entertaining

rhetorical theory (5) Aristotle's premise that effective communication is rooted in ethos, logos, and pathos

risk management (1) process of identifying, controlling, and minimizing the impact of uncertain events on an organization

ROB (7) (*see* run of book)

robocall (7) automated telephone call from robots

ROI (9) (*see* return on investment)

ROP (7) (*see* run of press)

ROS (7) (*see* run of station)

rotary paint (7) type of outdoor advertising sign that can be moved from place to place

run of book (7) indication that an advertisement can be placed anywhere within a magazine, compared to special placement (abbreviated ROB)

run of press (7) indication that an advertisement can be placed anywhere within a newspaper, compared to special placement (abbreviated ROP)

run of station (7) indication that an advertisement can be placed anywhere within a daily cycle for radio advertising, compared with placement on a particular program (abbreviated ROS)

salience (5, 6) degree to which information is perceived as being applicable or useful to an audience

same-as-before budgeting (8) looking at how much an organization spent on a similar recent project and allowing the same budget for the new project

same-as-before-but-more budgeting (8) approach to budgeting that builds in an inflationary increase to a same-as-before budget

sample (A) subset of a population to be studied

sampling (A) research practice of first identifying a subset of a population that reflects and represents the larger body, then using this sample as the basis of study

sampling bias (A) element within the sampling process that leads to an incomplete or insufficient sample

sampling error (A) extent to which a research sample does not perfectly correspond with its population (also called margin of error)

sampling frame (A) actual listing of sampling units

sampling unit (A) conceptualization of individual element within a sample

satellite media tour (7) type of news interview featuring a news source at one location and reporters linked via satellite television from various locations (abbreviated SMT)

satellite television (7) system of providing TV signal on TV sets or computers

scrutiny (6) aspect of persuasion that focuses on the ability of a message source to examine or investigate an audience and thus to pronounce blame, proclaim innocence, or grant forgiveness

seat-of-the-pants evaluation (9) (*see* judgmental assessment)

secondary customer (3) subgroup of customer public that uses the services of the organization's primary customers, such as graduate schools or businesses that receive a college's graduates

secondary research (1, A) re-analyzing existing information obtained by previous researcher for a new and specific purpose (compare with primary research)

selective exposure (5) premise that people pay attention to information they expect to support their pre-existing bias

selective perception (5) premise that people perceive information based on their pre-existing bias

self-administered survey (C) (*see* mail survey)

semantic differential scale (C) type of rating scale asking respondents to select a point on a continuum between two opposing positions

sender (6) originator of a message

semantic noise (6) communication disruption caused by use of language not understood or appropriately interpreted by the receiver

service article (7) type of feature release providing step-by-step directions and practical information (also called how-to piece)

service mark (6) words or phrases developed to be closely associated with specific organizations and protected by law for the use of those organizations

sex appeal (6) persuasion technique and type of positive emotional appeal based on gender, nudity, and sexuality

shadow constituency (3) subgroup of customer public involving people who, though they do not have a direct link to the organization's products or services, can affect a public's perception of an organization

shelter poster (7) advertising panels located in or on bus shelters

shock (5) offensive response strategy of deliberately agitating the mind or emotions of publics through the use of surprise, disgust, or other strong and unexpected stimulus

shovelware (7) term for the posting of already published articles from newspapers and magazines in their original print version

signage (7) generic name for range of stationary outdoor signs promoting an organization and its facilities

SiLoBaTi+UnFa (5) acronym identifying the major elements of newsworthy information: significance, local, balance, timely, plus unusual and famous

similarity (6) aspect of persuasion that focuses on the extent to which a message source resembles the audience

simple random sampling (A) probability sampling technique exemplified by a lottery-type drawing

single-issue public (3) may be active on all of the issues important to an organization, active only on some popular issues or active on single and often controversial issues (*see* active public)

situation (1, 2) (*see* public relations situation)

situation analysis (1) (*see* formative research)

situational ethics (1) (*see* ethical relativism)

situational theory (5) classification of publics as either active or passive

slander (6) spoken defamation

sleeper effect (5) observation that persuasive communication may increase over time as people forget it came from a low-credibility source

slogan (6) catchphrase developed as part of a communication program or campaign (also called tagline or verbal logo)

smoldering crisis (E) disruption of business that is not generally recognized as potentially generating negative news coverage

SMR (7) (*see* social media release)

SMT (7) (*see* satellite media tour)

snipe (7) billboard overlay that can update existing poster messages without the need to change the poster completely

snowball sampling (A) nonprobability sampling technique that begins with a small group of individuals with certain demographic characteristics and continues with similar individuals they recommend (also called sociosampling)

social judgment theory (5) theory that observes that individuals accept or reject messages to the extent that they perceive the message as corresponding to their beliefs and attitudes

social media (7) type of owned media using interactive digital tools of communication

social media release (7) type of news release intended for online use (*see* blogs and websites)

social networking (7) online service aimed to building and reflecting a relationship among people who share common interests

sociosampling (A) (*see* snowball sampling)

sound bite (7) (*see* actuality)

speaker's bureau (7) organizational program to promote availability of knowledgeable and trained employees or volunteers to give presentations

special event (5, 7) category of interpersonal communication tactics centering on planned activities created by an organization for the purpose of interacting with its publics

special-audience newspaper (7) type of newspaper focusing on a particular audience

special-interest newspaper (7) type of newspaper focusing on a particular theme or market

spectacular (7) type of billboard featuring an element beyond the standard rectangular surface, sometimes 3-D add-ons or other feature

spiral of silence (5) theory that people may remain silent rather than challenge what they perceive as the majority opinion

sponsored news (7) organizations use their expertise to present objective and credible information to their publics

sponsorship (5) proactive strategy of offering or supporting programs oriented toward community relations

spot advertising (7) use of television advertising at the local level (compare with network placement)

spot radio (7) same as spot advertising in reference to radio

stage-of-life-cycle budgeting (8) examination of the phases of development, knowing that start-up programs generally require more financial resources than maintenance programs (compare with zero-based budgeting)

staged activity (5) activity developed or orchestrated by an organization to provide an opportunity to gain attention and acceptance of key publics (also called pseudo-event; compare with publicity stunt)

stakeholder (3) person or group that relates to an organization through its potential impact on the organization's mission and objectives

standard error of the mean (A) statistic used to describe sampling error

standby statement (7) (*see* contingency statement)

standing firm (5) strategy of doubling down after taking a position

station poster (7) advertising panels located in subway, train, and bus stations, and in airport terminals (also called diorama)

statistics (6) persuasion technique and type of verbal evidence providing clear and hard-to-dispute facts to make a case

status (6) aspect of persuasion that focuses on the social position or prestige of a message source

stealth ad (7) type of advertising now readily apparent to audiences (*see* product placement)

stereotype (3) oversimplified shortcut to describe groups of people, based on common and repeated perceptions of who people are, how they act, and what they think and value

story idea memo (7) type of indirect news material providing media gatekeepers with tips and ideas for feature articles (also called tip sheet)

strategic ambiguity (5) refusal to be pinned down to a particular response, often by artfully dodging a question

strategic communication (0) planned communication campaigns associated with public relations or marketing communication, undertaken by an organization, usually for information or persuasive purposes

strategic inaction (6) public relations response strategy of making no statement and taking no overt action, allowing a situation to fade

strategic manager (0) organizational manager who makes decisions concerned with management, trends, issues, policies, and corporate structure (compare with tactical manager)

strategic news (5) information involving an organization that is of interest to both the news media and the key public

strategic philanthropy (5) proactive strategy in which businesses fund or otherwise support community relations gestures with an eye toward employees and customers

strategic public (3) public with which an organization chooses to engage in communication and relationship (compare with target public)

strategic research (1) systematic gathering of information about issues and publics

strategic reversal (5) strategy through which a weakened organization becomes the stronger one

strategic silence (5) by not responding to criticism an organization may be able to shorten the life span of a crisis situation (also called purdah)

strategy (4, 5) organization's overall plan, determining what it wants to achieve and how it wants to achieve it, offering direction in both proactive and reactive organizational activity and messages: theme, source, content, and tone (compare with tactic)

stratified sampling (A) probability sampling technique that first ranks elements according to demographic factors, then draws elements from each factor using random or systematic sampling techniques

streaming radio (7) (*see* online radio)

streaming video (7) (*see* nonbroadcast video)

street theater (5) type of activism that focuses on dramatization in public places (also called guerrilla theater)

Streisand effect (5) unintended consequence of creating further publicity for negative information in an attempt to censor it

structure (2) the role public relations plays within the organization's administration

studio interview (7) hybrid of interview and news conference, featuring a media interviewer or host questioning one or more guests or spokespersons

subscription radio (7) (*see* digital radio)

sudden crisis (E) disruption of business that occurs without warning (compare with smoldering crisis)

summative report (9) research report at conclusion of strategic program, reviewing the impact and outcome of the complete program (also called final report)

superstitial ad (7) computer advertising that insinuates itself onto computer screens to fill in time between moves from one site to another (compare with interstitial ad)

supporter (2) public that currently or potentially can help an organization achieve its objectives

survey (C) quantitative research technique based on a standard series of questions and yielding statistical results and conclusions (also called poll; compare with questionnaire)

SWOT analysis (2) strategic planning tool analyzing an organization's strengths, weaknesses, opportunities, and threats

symbol (6) type of nonverbal communication in which visual representations point to realities beyond themselves

symbolic consensus (6) tagline that acts as a rallying cry for supporters

symmetry theory (5) theory that extends consistency theory to groups

synergy (5) two or more organizations working together to produce an outcome greater than the input of each group separately

systematic sampling (A) probability sampling technique involving the selection of subjects spaced at equal intervals (also called systematic interval sampling)

systems theory (5) approach to public relations focusing on linkages between organizations and publics

tactic (7) visible element of a strategic plan; a specific vehicle of communication

tactical manager (0) organizational manager who makes day-to-day decisions on practical and specific issues (compare with strategic manager)

tactical research (1) gathering of information to guide the production and dissemination of messages (compare with strategic research)

tagline (6) (*see* slogan)

target public (3) term sometimes used as synonymous with strategic public but carrying the connotation that the public is an object of action by an organization rather than a partner in a relationship (compare with strategic public)

targeted media (7) media that have narrow and homogeneous audiences (compare with mass media)

task management goal (4) type of goal concerned with getting certain things accomplished

technician (B) person in focus group responsible for audio- or videotaping

teleconference (7) (*see* videoconference)

telefocus group (A) focus group research conducted via telephone conference call

teleological ethics (1) approach to decision making focused on the impact that actions have on people, rooted in the notion that good results come from good actions (compare with deontological ethics and ethical relativism)

telephone survey (C) survey research administered over the telephone

temperament (6) concept observing that people have different approaches and predispositions (compare with psychological type)

terrestrial radio (7) AM and FM formats with signals sent via transmitters

terrestrial television (7) TV signal transmitted by radio waves (also called over-the-air television)

testimonial (6) persuasion technique and type of verbal evidence using comments by witnesses and by people who have used an organization's products or services

theoretical research (A) (*see* academic research)

theory of accounts (5) (*see* accounts)

theory of image restoration (5) (*see* image restoration)

third-party endorsement (5, 7) concept referring to the added credibility that comes with the endorsement of an outside and unbiased agent, such as a reporter or editor

threat (5) offensive response strategy involving the promise of harm toward an accuser

timeline (8) implementation schedule for strategic plan

tip sheet (7) (*see* story idea memo)

trade media (7) media that focus on information of interest to people in their professional lives (compare with popular media)

trade newspaper (7) category of newspapers with focus on a particular industry or profession

transit advertising (7) category of advertising on vehicles, including bus signs and mobile billboards

transparent communication (5, E) concept of proactive public relations strategy referring to open and observable activity by an organization that helps publics understand the organization and support its actions

triad (B) focus group with only three participants

triggering event (5) activity that generates action among key publics

two-step flow of communication theory (3) theory that identifies opinion leaders as a key link in the process of organizational communication with publics

uncontrolled media (7) media that limit or eliminate an organization's ability to determine various attributes (compare with controlled media)

unique selling proposition (6) niche statement about a produce, service, or organization that distinguishes it from competitors (abbreviated USP)

unit of analysis (A) individual element of a population being studied

unit-of-sales budgeting (8) based not on dollars but on prior outcomes

unobtrusive research (9) where the subjects in a study do not know they are being observed

unwarranted conclusion (6) error in logic based on a deduction not supported by evidence

user kit (7) organizational print material providing background and how-to information for consumers

uses and gratifications theory (5) analysis of communication based on why audiences use media and what they get out of it

USP (6) (*see* unique selling proposition)

value proposition (6) aspect of logical persuasive appeal arguing the virtue or merits of something

verbal communication (6) communication occurring through written and spoken words (compare with nonverbal communication)

verbal evidence (6) type of proof claim in a discussion or argument based not on physical evidence but rather on words and ideas

verbal logo (6) (*see* slogan)

victimization (5) (*see* excuse)

video B-roll (7) sound bites and raw, unedited footage provided to television stations to use in news reports

video focus group (B) focus group research conducted via teleconference

video news release (7) news release written and produced specifically for television stations, presented as an edited story package (abbreviated VNR)

video wall (7) out-of-home advertising venue with ever-moving series of computer-generated images

videoconference (7) television technology used to produce live informational or educational programs for remote audiences; also called teleconference

viral philanthropy (7) type of fundraising in which many people are asked to donate and encourage their friends to do likewise

viral video (7) widespread dissemination and popularity of a video clip

virtual ads (7) advertising that is digitally inserted for the TV audiences, such as product billboards that appear in the background during a televised sporting event

virtue appeal (6) persuasion technique and type of positive emotional appeal based on values that individuals and society hold in esteem

visibility (2) aspect of an organization's external environment focusing on the degree to which its publics know about the organization and the accuracy of that information

vlog (7) blog that primarily consists of video

VNR (7) (*see* video news release)

vocal activist (3) type of opinion leader who is linked with a particular issue and/or who acts as an advocate for a cause

vocal commiseration (5) response strategy of expressing concern, condolence, regret, or apology

vocalics (6) aspect of kinesics related to vocal cues such as accent, loudness, pitch, and so on; also called paralanguage

volunteer sampling (A) nonprobability sampling technique that draws subjects who willingly offer themselves to be part of a study

volunteerism (5) corporate policy of encouraging, facilitating, and rewarding employees in projects that contribute to community life

wall mural (7) type of outdoor advertising featuring the painted exterior of a building leased for advertising purposes (also called wallscape)

Web 1.0 (7) one-way use of Internet technology to post commercial or promotional information

Web 2.0 (7) interactive use of Internet technology to allow users to share postings and generate content for a website

web video (7) (*see* nonbroadcast video)

web-only commercials (7) video advertisements produced for and used only on the Internet

website (7) set of interconnected web pages, usually prepared and maintained as a collection of information by a person, group, or organization

weighted sampling (A) (*see* disproportionate sampling)

what-if-not-funded analysis (8) approach to budget that examines consequences of inaction and their effect on the organization's mission

white paper (7) (*see* position statement)

wiki (7) collaborative website where all users can edit and update content

word-of-mouth support (3) effective type of communication relying on opinion leaders

zealot (2) single-issue activist acting with missionary fervor

zero-based budgeting (8) approach to budgeting based on current needs rather than past expenditures

Glossary

Citations and Recommended Readings

Introduction

Austin, E. W. and Pinkleton, B. E. (2006). *Strategic public relations management: Planning and managing effective communication programs* (2nd ed.). Mahwah, NJ: Erlbaum.

Blakeman, R. (2007). *Integrated marketing communication: Creative strategy from idea to implementation*. Lanham, MD: Rowman & Littlefield.

Botan, C. H. (1997). Ethics in strategic communication campaigns: The case for a new approach to public relations. *Journal of Business Communication*, 34(2), 188–202.

Botan, C. H. and Soto, F. (1998). A semiotic approach to the internal functioning of publics: Implications for strategic communication and public relations. *Public Relations Review*, 24(1), 21–44.

Burnett, J. and Moriarty, S. (1998). *Introduction to marketing communications: An integrated approach*. Upper Saddle River, NJ: Prentice Hall.

Caywood, C. L. (1995). *International handbook of public relations and corporate communications*. Hillsdale, NJ: Erlbaum.

Caywood, C. L. (1997). *The handbook of strategic public relations and integrated communications*. New York: McGraw-Hill.

Clow, K. E. and Baack, D. E. (2006*). Integrated advertising, promotion and marketing communications* (3rd ed.). Upper Saddle River, NJ: Prentice Hall.

Crifasi, S. C. (2000, September). Everything's coming up Rosie. *Public Relations Tactics*, 7(9).

Cutlip, S. M., Center, A. H. and Broom, G. M. (2012). *Effective public relations* (11th ed.). Upper Saddle River, NJ: Prentice Hall.

Goldman, J. (1984). *Public relations in the marketing mix: Introducing vulnerability relations*. Lincolnwood, IL: NTC Business.

Gray, R. (1998, June 11). PR does the business. *Marketing*, 24–26.

Gronstedt, A. (2000). *The customer century: Lessons from world class companies in integrated marketing and communications*. New York: Routledge.

Grunig, J. E. (Ed.) (1992). *Excellence in public relations and communication management*. Hillsdale, NJ: Erlbaum.

Grunig, J. E. and Hunt, T. (1984). *Managing public relations*. New York: Holt, Rinehart, & Winston.

Harris, T. L. (2000). *Value added public relations: The secret weapon of integrated marketing*. Chicago, IL: NTC Business.

Harris, T. L. and Whalen, P. T. (2006). *The marketer's guide to public relations in the 21st century*. Mason, OH: Thomson/South-Western Educational.

Hendrix, J. and Hayes, D. C. (2012). *Public relations cases* (9th ed.). Belmont, CA: Wadsworth.

Hiebert, R. W. (2000, Fall). The customer century: Lessons from world class companies in integrated marketing and communications. *Public Relations Review*, 26(3), 381.

Holmes, P. (1998, September 28). With Bell's appointed, Y&R's commitment to integration now goes beyond lip service. *Inside PR*, 5(9), 2, 10.

Italian American stereotypes in US advertising (2003, Summer). Washington, DC: Order of Sons of Italy in America.

Kelly, K. S. (2001). Stewardship: The fifth step in the public relations process. In R. I. Heath and G. M. Vasquez (Eds.), *Handbook of public relations* (pp. 279–290). Thousand Oaks, CA: Sage.

Kendall, R. (1997). *Public relations campaign strategies: Planning for implementation* (2nd ed.). New York: Addison-Wesley.

Kitchen, P. J. and Schultz, D. E. (1999). A multi-country comparison of the drive for IMC. *Journal of Advertising Research*, 39(7), 21–38.

Kotler, P., Roberto, N. and Lee, N. (2002). *Social marketing: Improving the quality of life* (2nd ed.). Thousand Oaks, CA: Sage.

Ledingham, J. A. and Bruning, S. D. (2001). Community relations. In R. L. Heath (Ed.), *Handbook of Public Relations* (pp. 527–534). Thousand Oaks, CA: Sage.

Marston, J. E. (1963). *The nature of public relations*. New York: McGraw-Hill.

McElreath, M. (1997). *Managing systematic and ethical public relations campaigns* (2nd ed.). Madison, WI: Brown & Benchmark.

Nemec, R. (1999). PR or advertising: Who's on top? *Communication World*, 16(3), 25–28.

Newsom, D., VanSlyke Turk, J. and Kruckeberg, D. (2006). *This is PR: The realities of public relations* (9th ed.). Belmont, CA: Wadsworth.

Ostrowski, H. (1999). Moving the measurement needle. *Public Relations Strategist*, 5(2), 37–39.

Parkinson, M. and Ekachai, D. G. (2005). *International and intercultural public relations: A campaign case approach*. Boston: Allyn and Bacon.

PRSA (2006). State of the PR Profession Opinion Survey. www.prsa.org/SearchResults/view/2D0008/0/2006_State_of_the_PR_Profession_Opinion_Survey

PRSA (2011a). State of the Society. Retrieved August 27, 2012 from www.prsa.org/aboutprsa/stateofthesociety/documents/state_of_the_society_2012.pdf

PRSA (2011b) Business Leaders Survey. Retrieved August 27, 2012 from www.prsa.org/Intelligence/BusinessCase/MBAInitiative/PRSA%20Business%20Leaders%20Survey

Ries, A. and Ries, L. (2004). *The fall of advertising and the rise of PR*. New York: HarperCollins.

Ross, B. I. and Richards, J. I. (Eds.) (2008). *Where shall I go to study advertising and public relations? Advertising and public relations programs in the United States colleges and universities*. Lubbock, TX: Advertising Education Publications.

Scheufele, D. A. (1999) Framing as a theory of media effects. *Journal of Communication*, 49(4), 103–122.

Schultz, B., Caskey, P. and Esherick, C. (2009). *Media relations in sport* (3rd ed.). Morgantown, WV: Fitness Information Technology.

Schultz, D. E., Tannenbaum, S. I. and Lauterborn, R. F. (1993). *Integrated marketing communications: Pulling it together and making it work*. Lincolnwood, IL: NTC Business.

Seitel, F. P. (2006). *The practice of public relations* (10th ed.). Upper Saddle River, NJ: Prentice Hall.

Sirgy, M. J. (2004). *Integrated marketing communications: A systems approach*. Upper Saddle River, NJ: Pearson.

Readings

Wilson, L. (2000). *Strategic program planning for effective public relations campaigns* (3rd ed.). Dubuque, IA: Kendall-Hunt.

Zappala, J. and Carden, A. R. (2004). *Public relations worktext: A writing and planning resource.* Mahwah, NJ: Erlbaum.

Phase One

Aguilar, F. J. (1967). *Scanning the business environment.* New York: Macmillan.

Bakhsheshy, A. (2003). Chapter 5. Retrieved from home.business.utah.edu/mgtab/

Boe, A. R. (1979). Fitting the corporation to the future. *Public Relations Quarterly*, 24, 4–6.

Chang, M. (2010) The State of Asian American, Native Hawaiian and Pacific Islander Education in California. University of California, Asian American and Pacific Islander Policy Multicampus Research Program.

Chase, W. H. (1977). Public issue management: The new science. *Public Relations Journal*, 33(10), 25–26.

Cuddeford-Jones, M. (2002, March). Brand redemption and risk management: Morag Cuddeford-Jones asks if it is possible for brands to redeem themselves after a PR disaster. *Brand Strategy*, p. 10.

Dearing, J. W. and Rogers, E. M. (1996). *Communication concepts 6: Agenda-setting.* Thousand Oaks, CA: Sage.

Dewey, J. (1927). *The public and its problems.* Chicago, IL: Swallow.

Esman, M. J. (1972). The elements of institution building. In J. W. Eaton (Ed.), *Institution building and development* (pp. 78–90). Beverly Hills, CA: Sage.

Evan, W. H. (1976). *Interorganizational relations.* New York: Penguin.

Ewing, R. P. (1997). Issues management: Managing trends through the issues life cycle. In C. C. Caywood (Ed.), *The handbook of strategic public relations and integrated communications* (pp. 173–188). New York: McGraw-Hill.

Grunig, J. E. and Hunt, T. (1984). *Managing public relations.* New York: Holt, Rinehart & Winston.

Hart, R. (2006, April). Measuring success: How to "sell" a communications audit to internal audiences. *Public Relations Tactics*, 13(4).

Hedrick, T. E., Bickman, L. and Rog, D. J. (1993). *Applied social research methods; Vol. 32, Applied research design: A practical guide.* Newbury Park, CA: Sage.

Italian American stereotypes in U.S. advertising (2003, Summer). Washington, DC: Order of Sons of Italy in America.

Jackson, P. (Ed.) (1994). *Practical, actionable research for public relations purposes.* Exeter, NH: PR Publishing.

Jones, B. L. and Chase, W. H. (1979). Managing public policy issues. *Public Relations Review*, 5, 2–23.

Klein, P. (1999). Measure what matters. *Communication World*, 16(9), 32.

Lauzen, M. (1997). Understanding the relation between public relations and issues management. *Journal of Public Relations Research*, 9(1), 65–82.

Lazarsfeld, P. F., Berelson, B. and Gaudet, H. (1944). *The people's choice: How the voter makes up his mind in a presidential campaign.* New York: Columbia University Press.

Ledingham, J. A. and Bruning, S. D. (2000). *Public relations as relationship management: A relationship approach to the study and practice of public relations.* Mahwah NJ: Erlbaum.

Lippmann, W. (1922). *Public opinion.* New York: Macmillan.

Lukaszewski, J. E. (1997). Establishing individual and corporate crisis communication standards: The principles and protocols. *Public Relations Quarterly*, 42, 7–14.

Martin J. (2008, June 1). Miss Manners. Syndicated column. *Washington Post*.

Maslow, A. (1987). *Motivation and personality* (3rd ed.). Boston, MA: Addison-Wesley.

Matera, F. R. and Artigue, R. J. (2000). *Public relations campaign and techniques: Building bridges into the 21st century*. Boston: Allyn & Bacon.

Mau, R. R. and Dennis, L. B. (1994). Companies ignore shadow constituencies at their peril. *Public Relations Journal*, 50(5), 10–11.

Morton, L. P. (2002a). Targeting Native Americans. *Public Relations Quarterly*, 47(1), 37.

Morton, L. P. (2002b). Targeting Generation Y. *Public Relations Quarterly*, 47(2), 46.

Nisbet, M. C. and Kotcher, J. E. (2009, March). A two-step flow of influence? Opinion-leader campaigns on climate change. *Science Communication*, 30(3), 329–354.

Opinion leaders. New study outlines how to reach them. (1992, October 5). *PR Reporter*, 35(38), 1–3.

Packard, V. (1964). *The hidden persuaders*. New York: Pocket Books.

Rawlins, B. L. (2006). *Prioritizing stakeholders for public relations*. New York: Institute for Public Relations Research.

Regester, M. and Larkin, J. (2005). *Risk issues and crisis management* (3rd ed.). London: Kogan Page.

Rogers, E. (2003). *The diffusion of innovations* (5th ed.). New York: Free Press.

Salmon, R. and De Linares, Y. (1999). *Competitive intelligence: Scanning the global environment*. Bucharest, Romania: Economica.

Sandman, P. (2003). Stakeholders. Retrieved August 27, 2012 from psandman.com/col/stakeh.htm

Schwartz, P. and Gibb, B. (1999). *When good companies do bad things: Responsibility and risk in an age of globalization*. New York: Wiley.

Tsai, M., Veziroglu, A., Warren, S. and Que, Y. (2006) New energy opinion leaders' lifestyles and media usage. Proceedings of the International Conference on Emerging Nuclear Energy Systems.

Zaharna, R. S., Hammad, A. I. and Masri, J. (2009) Palestinian public relations: Inside and out, in K. Sriramesh and D. Vercic (Eds.), *The handbook of global public relations theory, research, and practice. Vol. 2* (pp. 220–242). London: Routledge.

Phase Two

Barlow, W. G. (1995). *Establishing public relations objectives and assessing public relations results*. Gainesville, FL: Institute for Public Relations Research.

Barnhurst, K. G. and Mutz, D. (1997). American journalism and the decline in event-centered reporting. *Journal of Communication*, 47(4), 27–53.

Benjamin, J. (1997). *Principles, elements, and types of persuasion*. Fort Worth, TX: Harcourt Brace.

Benoit, W. L. (1995). *Accounts, excuses, and apologies: A theory of image restoration strategies*. SUNY Series in Speech Communication. Albany, NY: State University of New York Press.

Berlo, D. (1960). *The process of communication: An introduction to theory and practice*. San Francisco, CA: Rinehart.

Blumler, J. and McQuail, D. (1968). *Television in politics: Its uses and influence*. Faber.

Botan, C. (1997). Ethics in strategic communication campaigns: The case for a new approach to public relations. *Journal of Business Communication*, 34(2), 188–202.

Bouchez, C. (n.d.) Hollywood takes action on health. Retrieved August 27, 2012 from http://men. webmd.com/features/hollywood-takes-action-on-health.

Buber, M. (1947). *Between man and man*. London: Routledge & Kegan Paul. Reprinted in F. W. Matson and A. Montagu (Eds.) (1967). *The human dialogue: Perspectives on communication*. New York: Free Press.

Christians, C. G., Fackler, M., Richardson, K. B. and Rotzoll, K. B. (2011). *Media ethics: Cases and moral reasoning* (9th ed.). New York: Longman.

Cody, M. J. and McLaughlin, M. L. (1985). Models for the sequential construction of accounting episodes: Situational and interactional constraints on message selection and evaluation. In R. L. Street and L. Capella (Eds.), *Sequence and pattern in communication behavior* (pp. 50–69). London: Edward Arnold.

Cody, M. J. and McLaughlin, M. L. (1990). Interpersonal accounting. In H. Giles and W. P. Robinson (Eds.), *Handbook of language and social psychology* (pp. 227–255). Chichester, England: Wiley.

Commentary: It's time to put the *Valdez* behind us (1999, March 29). *Business Week*.

Dahl, D. W., Frankenberger, K. D. and Manchanda R. V. (2003). Shocking ads! Reactions to shocking and nonshocking advertising content among university students. *Journal of Advertising Research*, 43(3), 268–280.

Delwiche, A. (n.d.) *Fear*. Retrieved August 27, 2012 from propagandacritic.com/articles/ct.sa.fear.html

Edelman Change and Employee Engagement, in partnership with PeopleMetrics. (2006). New frontiers in employee communications. Retrieved August 27, 2012 from http://www.edelman.com/practice/corporate/the-details/corporate-capabilities-employee-engagement/

Elberse, A. and Verleun, J. (2012, June). The economic value of celebrity endorsements. *Journal of Advertising Research*, 52(2), 149–165.

Fearn-Banks, K. (2007). *Crisis communications: A casebook approach* (3rd ed.). Mahwah, NJ: Erlbaum.

Festinger, L. (1957). *A theory of cognitive dissonance*. Stanford, CA: Stanford University Press.

Fitzpatrick, K. R. and Rubin, M. S. (1995). Public relations vs. legal strategies in organizational crisis decisions. *Public Relations Review*, 21(1), 21–33.

Gerbner, G. and Gross, L. (1976). Living with television: The violence profile. *Journal of Communication*, 26(76).

Goffman, E. (1974). *Frame analysis: An essay on the organization of experience*. London: Harper & Row.

Gottschalk, J. A. (Ed.) (1993). *Crisis response: Inside stories in managing image under siege*. Detroit, MI: Gale Research.

Grunig, J. (1966). The role of information in economic decision making. *Journalism Monographs*. Association for Education in Journalism.

Hammad, A.I. (2005). Theory and practice of public relations in the governmental organizations of Palestine: The fashioning of the national image in a non-sovereign state. (Unpublished dissertation, Aristotle University, Thessaloniki, Greece.)

Hearit, K. M. (1994). Apologies and public relations crises at Chrysler, Toshiba, and Volvo. *Public Relations Review*, 20(2), 113–125.

Heath, R. L. (1997). *Strategic issues management: Organizations and public policy challenges*. Thousand Oaks, CA: Sage.

Heider, F. (1946). Attitudes and cognitive organization. *Psychological Review*, 51, 358–374.

Heider, F. (1958). *The psychology of interpersonal relations*. New York: Wiley.

Hon, L. C. (1998). Demonstrating effectiveness in public relations: Goals, objectives, and evaluation. *Journal of Public Relations Research*, 10(2), 103–135.

Hovland, C. and Weiss, W. (1951–52, Winter). The influence of source credibility on communication effectiveness. *Public Opinion Quarterly*.

Readings

Infante, D., Rancer, A. and Avtgis, T. (2009). *Contemporary communication theory.* Dubuque, IA: Kendall-Hunt.

Infante, D. A., Rancer, A. S. and Womack, D. F. (2003). *Building communication theory* (4th ed.). Prospect Heights, IL: Waveland.

Iyengar, S. and Kinder, D. R. (1987). *News that Matters: Television and American opinion.* American Politics and Political Economy. Chicago, IL: University of Chicago Press.

Jackson, P. (Ed.) (1997). Items of importance to practitioners. *PR Reporter*, 40(46), 3.

Jenkins, P. (2003). *The new anti-Catholicism: The last acceptable prejudice.* New York: Oxford University Press.

Johnston, D. D. (1994). *The art and science of persuasion.* Boston: McGraw-Hill.

Juice-poisoning case brings guilty plea and a huge fine. (1998, July 24). *New York Times.*

Keirsey, D. (1998). *Please understand me II: Temperament, character, intelligence.* Del Mar, CA: Prometheus Nemesis.

Kelly, J. A., St. Lawrence, J. S., Diaz, Y. E., Stevenson, L. Y., Hauth, A. C., Brasfield, T. L., et al. (1991). HIV risk behavior reduction following intervention with key opinion leaders of a population: An experimental community-level analysis. *American Journal of Public Health*, 81, 168–171.

Kelly, J. A., St. Lawrence, J. S., Stevenson, L. Y., Hauth, A. C., Kalichman, S. C., Diaz, Y. E., et al. (1992). Community AIDS/HIV risk reduction: The effects of endorsement by popular people in three cities. *American Journal of Public Health*, 82, 1483–1489.

Klapper. J (1960). *The effects of mass communication.* Free Press.

Kotler, P., Roberto, N. and Lee, N. (2007). *Social marketing: Influencing behaviors for good* (3rd ed.). Thousand Oaks, CA: Sage.

Kowalski, R. M. and Erickson, J. R. (1997). Complaints and complaining: Functions, antecedents and consequences. *Psychological Bulletin*, 119(2), 179–196.

Larson, C. U. (2000). *Persuasion: Reception and responsibility* (9th ed.). Belmont, CA: Wadsworth.

Larson, R. J., Woloshin, S., Schwartz, L. M. and Welch, H. G. (2005, May 4). Celebrity endorsements of cancer screening. *Journal of the National Cancer Institute*, 97(9), 693–695.

Lasswell, H. D. (1948). The structure and function of communication in society. In L. Bryson (Ed.), *The communication of ideas* (p. 34). New York: Harper.

Lazarsfeld, P. F., Berelson, B. and Gaudet, H. (1968). *The people's choice: How the voter makes up his mind in a presidential campaign* (3rd ed.). Columbia University Press.

Lee, F., Peterson, C. and Tiedens, L. (2004). Mea culpa: Predicting stock prices from organizational attributions. *Personality and Social Psychology Bulletin*, 30(12), 1636–1649.

Leiserowitz, A., Smith, N. and Marlon, J. R. (2010). *Yale Project on Climate Change Communication: Americans' knowledge of climate change.* New Haven, CT: Yale University. Retrieved August 27, 2012 from http://environment.yale.edu/climate/files/ClimateChangeKnowledge2010.pdf.

Lewin, K. (1951). *Field theory of social science.* Ed. D. Cartwright. Harber Brothers.

Lipstein, B. (1985). An historical retrospective of copy research. *Journal of Advertising Research*, 24(6), 11–14.

The lives we touch. (1992). In J. A. Hendrix, *Public relations cases* (2nd ed.). Belmont, CA: Wadsworth.

Macdaid, G. P., McCaulley, M. H. and Kainz, R. I. (1986). *MBTI Atlas of Type Tables* (2 vols.). Gainesville, FL: Center for Applications in Psychological Type.

Marconi, J. (1996). *Image marketing: Using public perceptions to attain business objectives.* Lincolnwood, IL: NTC/Business.

Martin, J. (1999, May 10). Miss Manners. Syndicated column. *Washington Post.*

Readings

Martinelli, K. A. and Briggs, W. (1998, Winter). Integrating public relations and legal responses during a crisis: The case of Odwalla, Inc. *Public Relations Review*, 20, 443–460.

Martosko, D. (2005). *Holy cows: How PETA twists religion to push "animal rights."* Washington, DC: Center for Consumer Freedom.

McCombs, M. E. and Shaw, D. L. (1972). The agenda-setting function of mass media. *Public Opinion Quarterly*, 36, 176–187.

McGuire, W. J. and Papageorgis, D. (1961). The relative efficacy of various types of prior belief defense in producing immunity against persuasion. *Journal of Abnormal and Social Psychology*, 62, 327–337.

Miciak, A. R. and Shanklin, W. L. (1994). Choosing celebrity endorsers: The risks are real, but sports and entertainment spokespersons still burnish corporate images and sell brands. *Advertising Management*, 3(3), 51.

Minogue, S. (2003, June 30). How can you get the most marketing value out of CSR? *Strategy*, 18.

Myers, I. B. (1998). *Introduction to type* (6th ed.). Palo Alto, CA: Consulting Psychologists Press.

Myers, I. B. and Myers, P. B. (1995). *Gifts differing: Understanding personality type* (2nd ed.). Palo Alto, CA: Consulting Psychologists Press.

Nager, N. R. and Allen, T. H. (1984). *Public relations management by objectives*. Lanham, MD: University Press of America.

Newcomb, T. M. (1953). An approach to the study of communicative acts. *Psychological Review*, 60, 393–404.

Noelle-Neumann, E. (1993). *The spiral of silence: Public opinion, our social skin* (2nd ed.). Chicago, IL: University of Chicago Press.

Nyer, P. U. (1999). Cathartic complaining as a means of reducing consumer dissatisfaction. *Journal of Consumer Satisfaction, Dissatisfaction and Complaining Behavior*, 12, 15–25.

Nyer, P. U. (2000). An investigation into whether complaining can cause increased consumer satisfaction. *Journal of Consumer Marketing*, 17(1), 9–19.

Osgood, C. E. and Tannenbaum, P. H. (1955). The principle of congruity in the prediction of attitude change. *Psychological Review*, 62, 42–55.

Pfau, M. and Parrott, R. (2001). *Persuasive communication campaigns*. Boston, MA: Pearson. Pharma Opinion Leaders. (2003, November 11). *PR Newswire*.

Rank, H. (1976). Teaching about public persuasion. In D. Dieterich (Ed.), *Teaching and doublespeak* (pp. 3–19). Urbana, IL: NCTE.

Ray, M. (1973). Marketing communication and the hierarchy of effects. In P. Clarke (Ed.), *New models for communication research* (pp. 147–176). Newbury Park, CA: Sage.

Ries, A. and Trout, J. (2001). *Positioning: The battle for your mind*. New York: McGraw-Hill.

Rogers, E. (2003). *The diffusion of innovations* (5th ed.). New York: Free Press.

Roser, C. and Thompson, M. (1995). Fear appeals and the formation of active publics. *Journal of Communication*, 45(1), 103–119.

Ross, R. S. (1994). *Understanding persuasion* (4th ed.). Englewood Cliffs, NJ: Prentice Hall.

Scheufele, D. (1999). Framing as a theory of media effects. *Journal of Communication*, 49(1), 103–122.

Schramm, W. (1971). The nature of communication between humans. In W. Schramm and D. F. Roberts (Eds.), *The process and effects of mass communication*. Urbana, IL: University of Illinois Press.

Schreiber, A. L. (1994). *Lifestyle and event marketing: Building the new customer partnership*. New York: McGraw-Hill.

Seideman, T. (1997, May/June). Nonprofit prophets. *Reputation Management*, 46–53.

Shannon, C. E. and Weaver, W. (1949). *The mathematical theory of communication*. Urbana, IL: University of Illinois Press.

Sherif, M. and Hovland, C. I. (1961). *Social judgment*. New Haven, CT: Yale University Press.

Sieberg, E. (1976). Confirming and disconfirming organizational communication. In J. L. Owen, P. A. Page and G. I. Zimmerman (Eds.), *Communication in organizations*. St. Paul, MN: West.

Simons, H. W., Morreale, J. and Gronbeck, B. (2001). *Persuasion in society*. Thousand Oaks, CA: Sage.

Smith, R. D. (1993). Psychological type and public relations: Theory, research, and applications. *Journal of Public Relations Research*, 5(3), 177–199.

Smith, R. D. (2017). *Becoming a public relations writer: Strategic writing for emerging and established media* (5th ed.). New York: Routledge.

Sperry, R. W. (1985). Consciousness, personal identity and the divided brain. In D. F. Benson and E. Zaidel (Eds.), *The dual brain: Hemispheric specialization in humans*. UCLA Forum in Medical Sciences, No. 26. New York: Guilford Press.

Stewart, C. J., Smith, C. A. and Denton, R. E. (2001). *Persuasion and social movements* (4th ed.). Prospect Heights, IL: Waveland.

Sugimoto, N. (1997). A Japan–U.S. comparison of apology styles. *Communication Research*, 24(4), 349–370.

Swann, P. (2010). *Cases in public relations management*. New York: Routledge.

Swanson, D. (2012). From "hour of power" to "days of demise": Media portrayals of crisis and fractured social order within Robert H, Schuller's Crystal Cathedral ministry. In *Case Studies in Strategic Communication*, 1, 127–153.

Wiener, N. (1954). *The human use of human beings: Cybernetics and society* (2nd ed.). Boston, MA: Houghton Mifflin.

Wild, C. (1993). *Corporate volunteer programs: Benefits to businesses. Report 1029*. New York: Conference Board.

Young, D. (1996). *Building your company's good name: How to create and protect the reputation your organization wants and deserves*. New York: American Management Association.

Zaharia, R. S., Hammad, A. I. and Masri, J. (2009) Palestinian public relations: Inside and out. In K. Sriramesh and D. Vercic (Eds.), *The global public relations handbook: Theory, research, and practice*. New York: Routledge.

Phase Three

Amos, J. S. (1995). *Fundraising ideas: Over 225 money making events for community groups, with a resource directory*. Jefferson, NC: McFarland.

Armstrong, J. J. (2007, October). Don't touch that dial! Using long-form TV and radio programs to send health messages. *Public Relations Tactics*, 14(10), 15.

Brogan, K. S. (Ed.) (2007). *2008 writer's market*. Cincinnati, OH: Writer's Digest Books.

Brown, M. S. (Ed.) (2008). *Giving USA, 2008* (53rd ed.). Glenview, IL: Giving USA Foundation.

Bulldog Reporter and TEKgroup International (2010, October). *2007 Journalist survey on media relations practices*. Pompano Beach, FL: Bulldog Reporter/TEKgroup International.

Cameron, G. T. (1994). Does publicity outperform advertising? An experimental test of the third-party endorsement. *Journal of Public Relations Research*, 6(3), 185–207.

Corder L., Deasy, M. and Thompson, J. (1999a, Spring). PR is to experience what marketing is to expectations. *Public Relations Quarterly*, 44(1), 23–26.

Corder L., Deasy, M. and Thompson, J. (1999b, May). Answering the age-old marketing question: What have you done for me lately? *Public Relations Tactics*, 12.

Curtain, P. A. (1999). Reevaluating public relations information subsidies: Market-driven journalism and agenda-building theory and practice. *Journal of Public Relations Research*, 11(1), 53–90.

Edelman Change and Employee Engagement, in partnership with PeopleMetrics (2006). New frontiers in employee communications. Retrieved from http://www.edelman.com/practice/corporate/the-details/corporate-capabilities-employee-engagement/

Foremski, T. (2006). Die! Press Release! Die! Die! Die! *Silicon Valley Watcher* [blog] February 27, 2008.

Gale Research (2005). *Newsletters in print* (19th ed.). Detroit, MI: Gale.

Giving USA Foundation (2011). *Giving USA 2011: The annual report on philanthropy for the year 2010*. Chicago, IL: The Giving Institute.

Glass, S. A. (2001). *Approaching fundraising: Suggestions and insights for fundraising; No. 28, Summer 2000: New directions for philanthropic fundraising, sponsored by the Center on Philanthropy at Indiana University*. San Francisco, CA: Jossey-Bass.

Harris Interactive (2005, November). *Executive, congressional and consumer attitudes toward media, marketing and the public relations profession*. Rochester, NY: Harris Interactive.

Harris Poll (2001, May 18). *Presenting: The class of 2001: Millennium's first college grads are "connected, career-minded and confident"—way!* Rochester, NY: Harris Interactive.

Hunt-Lowrance, K. (Ed.) (2007). *Gale directory of publications and broadcast media* (142nd ed.). Detroit, MI: Gale Research.

Kim, J. B. (1995). The cassette is in the mail. *Advertising Age*, 68, 51.

Krugman, H. E. (1972). Why three exposures may be enough. *Journal of Advertising Research*, 12, 11–28.

Lang, K. and Lang, G. E. (1983). *The battle for public opinion: The president, the press, and the polls during Watergate*. New York: Columbia University Press.

Lazauskas, J. (2016). Fixing native advertising: What consumers want from brands, publishers, and the FTC. *The Content Strategist* [blog], December 2016, contently.com/strategist.

Lippy, C. H. (Ed.) (1986). *Religious periodicals of the United States: Academic and scholarly journals*. New York: Greenwood.

Maddux, D. (Ed.) (2008). *International yearbook 2008* (88th ed.). New York: Editor & Publisher.

McManus, J. (1994). *Market-driven journalism: Let the citizen beware?* Thousand Oaks, CA: Sage.

Middleberg, D. and Ross, S. S. (2001). *The Middleberg/Ross survey of media in the wired world, 2000*. New York: Middleberg Euro.

Moriarty, S., Mitchell, N. and Wells, W. D. (2007). *Advertising: Principles and practices* (8th ed.). Upper Saddle River, NJ: Prentice Hall.

Newport, F. and Saad, L. (1998). A matter of trust: News sources Americans prefer. *American Journalism Review*, 20(6), 30–33.

Pew Research Center for the People and the Press (2008, January 11). *Social networking and online videos take off; Internet's broader role in campaign 2008: A survey conducted in association with the Pew Internet and American Life Project*. Washington, DC: Pew Research Center for the People and the Press.

Piirto, R. (1994). Why radio thrives. *American Demographics*, 16(5), 40ff.

Project for Excellence in Journalism. (2011). State of the news media 2011. Retrieved August 27, 2012 from www.stateofthemedia.org/2011

Realwire. (2009). Social media news releases achieve double the editorial coverage, says RealWire study. July 23, 2009. Post at Blogit.realwire.com.

Rules of engagement: Six tips for pitching the blogosphere—and finding the right blog for your client (2005, April). *Ragan's Media Relations Report*.

Smith, R. D. (2017). *Becoming a public relations writer: Strategic writing for emerging and established media* (5th ed.). New York: Routledge.

Stenson, P. (1993). How (and why) corporate communicators use video. *Communication World*, 10(10), 14–15.

Survey shows radio use patterns. (1996). *PR News*, 52(15).

Tyson, C. B. and Snyder, L. B. (1999). The impact of direct mail video. *Public Relations Quarterly*, 44(1), 28–32.

University of Oregon (2007). "Stealth advertising" sliding under radar into TV newscasts. *Science Daily*, July 12, 2007.

Vanden Bergh, B. G. and Katz, H. E. (1999). *Advertising principles: Choice, challenge, change*. Lincolnwood, IL: NTC Business.

West Glen Communications. (2002, April). West Glen Communications releases new PSA survey. New York: West Glen Communications.

Wigley, S. and Fontenot, M. (2009). Where media turn during crises: A look at information subsidies and the Virginia Tech shootings. *Electronic News*, 3(2), 94–108.

Wilcox, D. L., Cameron, G. T. and Reber, B. H. (2014). *Public relations: Strategies and tactics* (11th ed.). Boston, MA: Allyn & Bacon.

Williams. W. (1994). *User friendly fund raising: A step-by-step guide to profitable special events*. Alexander, NC: WorldComm.

Phase Four

Bissland, J. H. (1990). Accountability gap: Evaluation practices show improvement. *Public Relations Review*, 16(2), 25–35.

Broom, G. and Dozier, D. (1990). *Using research in public relations: Applications to program management*. Englewood Cliffs, NJ: Prentice Hall.

Corder, L., Deasy, M. and Thompson, J. (1999, May). Answering the age-old marketing question: What have you done for me lately? *Public Relations Tactics*, 12.

Delahaye Paine, K. (2011). *Measure what matters: Online tools for understanding customers, social media, engagement, and key relationships*. New York: Wiley.

Dozier, D. M. (1984). Program evaluation and the roles of practitioners. *Public Relations Review*, 10(2), 13–21.

Edelman Public Relations, Opinion Research Corporation and Northwestern University. (1997, August 25). Planning, goals and measurement (Corporate Communications Benchmark 1997, Section III). Cited in Written PR plans now common—but many not integrated. *PR Reporter*, 3–4.

Evaluation research on the rise, study finds. (1994). In P. Jackson (Ed.), *Practical, actionable research for public relations purposes*. Exeter, NH: PR Publishing.

Fischer, R. (1995). Control construct design in evaluating campaigns. *Public Relations Review*, 21(1), 45–58.

Gofton, K. (1999, April 12). The measure of PR: Measurement and evaluation of public relations campaigns. *Campaign*, S13(1).

Hon, L. C. (1997). What have you done for me lately? Exploring effectiveness in public relations. *Journal of Public Relations Research*, 9(1), 1–30.

Hon, L. C. (1998). Demonstrating effectiveness in public relations: Goals, objectives, and evaluation. *Journal of Public Relations Research*, 10(2), 103–135.

Lindenmann, W. K. (2006). Public relations research for planning and evaluation. Retrieved August 27, 2012 from www.instituteforpr.org/topics/pr-research-for-planning-and-evaluation/

Peterson, E. (2007). How to measure visitor engagement-redux. Retrieved August 27, 2012 from http://analyticsdemystified.com/general/how-to-measure-visitor-engagement-redux

Rice, R. and Atkin, C. (2002). Communication campaigns: Theory, design, implementation, and evaluation, in J. Bryant and D. Zillmann (Eds.), *Media effects: Advances in theory and research* (pp. 427–452). Hillsdale, NJ: Lawrence Erlbaum.

Rossi, P. H., Lipsey, M. W. and Freeman, H. E. (2003). *Evaluation: A systematic approach* (7th ed.). Newbury Park, CA: Sage.

Scoble, R. (2006). New audience metric needed: Engagement. Retrieved August 27, 2012 from scobleizer.com/new-audience-metric-needed-engagement

Tellis, G. J. and Ambler, T. (1998). *The Sage handbook of advertising*. Reading MA: Addison-Wesley.

Watson, T. and Noble, P. (2007). *Evaluating public relations: A best practice guide to public relations planning, research and evaluation*. Philadelphia, PA: Kogan Page.

Weiner, M. (1995, March). Put client "values" ahead of newsclips when measuring PR. *PR Services*, 48.

Wiener, N. (1954). *The human use of human beings: Cybernetics and society* (2nd ed.). Boston, MA: Houghton Mifflin.

Xavier, R., Johnston, K., Petel, A., Watson, T., Simmons, P. (2005, September). Using evaluative techniques and performance claims to demonstrate public relations impact: An Australian perspective. *Public Relations Review*, 31(3), 417–424.

Appendixes

Ayles, C. B. and Bosworth, C. C. (2002, Summer). Campaign excellence: A survey of Silver Anvil award winners compares current PR practice with planning, campaign theory. *Public Relations Strategist*.

Babbie, E. (2016). *The practice of social research* (14th ed.). Belmont, CA: Wadsworth.

Clymer, A. (2001, July 22). The nation: Wrong number; the unbearable lightness of public opinion polls. *New York Times*.

Edmunds, H. (2000). *The focus group research handbook*. Lincolnwood, IL: NTC Business.

Fink, A. (2002a). *The survey kit: 2. How to ask survey questions*. (2nd ed.). Thousand Oaks, CA: Sage.

Fink, A. (2002b). *The survey kit: 6. How to sample in surveys*. (2nd ed.). Thousand Oaks, CA: Sage.

Fletcher, A. D. and Bowers, T. A. (1991). *Fundamentals of advertising research* (4th ed.). Belmont, CA: Wadsworth.

Haskins, J. and Kendrick, A. (1993). *Successful advertising research methods*. Lincolnwood, IL: NTC Business.

Lindenmann, W. K. (1977). Opinion research: How it works, how to use it. *Public Relations Journal*, 1, 13.

Mangione, T. W. (1995). *Mail surveys: Improving the quality*. Applied Social Research Methods Series No. 40. Thousand Oaks, CA: Sage.

Merton, R. K. (1987). The focused interview and focus groups: Continuities and discontinuities. *Public Opinion Quarterly*, 51, 550–566.

Morgan, D. L. (1997). *Focus groups as qualitative research* (2nd ed.). Qualitative Research Methods Series Vol. 16. Thousand Oaks, CA: Sage.

Rasinski, K. A. (1989). The effect of question wording on public support for government spending. *Public Opinion Quarterly*, 53, 388–396.

Rubenstein, S. M. (1995). *Surveying public opinion*. Belmont, CA: Wadsworth.

Seitel, F. P. (2006). *The practice of public relations* (10th ed.). Upper Saddle River, NJ: Prentice Hall.

Singletary, M. (1994). *Mass communication research*. White Plains, NY: Longman.

Waddell, H. (1995). Getting a straight answer: CSM scales all ask the wrong question: "How am I doing?" *Marketing Research*, 7(3), 5–8.

Wimmer, R. G. and Dominick, J. R. (2013). *Mass media research: An introduction* (10th ed.). Belmont, CA: Wadsworth.

Yin, R. K. (2008). *Case study research: Design and methods* (4th ed.). Applied Social Research Methods Series No. 5. Thousand Oaks, CA: Sage.

Zeuschner, R. (2002). *Communicating today: The essentials*. Boston, MA: Allyn & Bacon.

Readings

Index